Very few philosophers can boast, not only of Paul Livingston's breadth, but of the charity with which he takes stock of our present philosophical "situation." In showing how this situation "counts as one," he does not merely sum it up; rather, he produces within it what *should* be seen as a major philosophical "event."

Prof. Andrew Cutrofello
Department of Philosophy
Loyola University, Chicago

The Politics of Logic

Routledge Studies in Contemporary Philosophy

1 **Email and Ethics**
Style and Ethical Relations
in Computer-Mediated
Communication
Emma Rooksby

2 **Causation and Laws of Nature**
Max Kistler

3 **Internalism and Epistemology**
The Architecture of Reason
*Timothy McGrew and Lydia
McGrew*

4 **Einstein, Relativity and
Absolute Simultaneity**
*Edited by William Lane Craig
and Quentin Smith*

5 **Epistemology Modalized**
Kelly Becker

6 **Truth and Speech Acts**
Studies in the Philosophy of
Language
Dirk Greimann & Geo Siegwart

7 **A Sense of the World**
Essays on Fiction, Narrative, and
Knowledge
*Edited by John Gibson, Wolfgang
Huemer, and Luca Pocci*

8 **A Pragmatist Philosophy of
Democracy**
Robert B. Talisse

9 **Aesthetics and Material Beauty**
Aesthetics Naturalized
Jennifer A. McMahon

10 **Aesthetic Experience**
*Edited by Richard Shusterman
and Adele Tomlin*

11 **Real Essentialism**
David S. Oderberg

12 **Practical Identity and
Narrative Agency**
*Edited by Catriona Mackenzie
and Kim Atkins*

13 **Metaphysics and the
Representational Fallacy**
Heather Dyke

14 **Narrative Identity and
Moral Identity**
A Practical Perspective
Kim Atkins

15 **Intergenerational Justice**
Rights and Responsibilities in an
Intergenerational Polity
Janna Thompson

16 **Hillel Steiner and the
Anatomy of Justice**
Themes and Challenges
*Edited by Stephen de Wijze,
Matthew H. Kramer, and Ian Carter*

17 **Philosophy of Personal Identity
and Multiple Personality**
Logi Gunnarsson

18 **The Force of Argument**
Essays in Honor of Timothy Smiley
*Edited by Jonathan Lear and
Alex Oliver*

19 **Autonomy and Liberalism**
Ben Colburn

20 **Habermas and Literary Rationality**
David L. Colclasure

21 **Rawls, Citizenship, and Education**
M. Victoria Costa

22 **Objectivity and the Language-Dependence of Thought**
A Transcendental Defence of Universal Lingualism
Christian Barth

23 **Habermas and Rawls**
Disputing the Political
Edited by James Gordon Finlayson and Fabian Freyenhagen

24 **Philosophical Delusion and Its Therapy**
Outline of a Philosophical Revolution
Eugen Fischer

25 **Epistemology and the Regress Problem**
Scott F. Aikin

26 **Civil Society in Liberal Democracy**
Mark Jensen

27 **The Politics of Logic**
Badiou, Wittgenstein, and the Consequences of Formalism
Paul M. Livingston

The Politics of Logic

Badiou, Wittgenstein, and the
Consequences of Formalism

Paul M. Livingston

Routledge
Taylor & Francis Group

NEW YORK   LONDON

First published 2012
by Routledge
711 Third Avenue, New York, NY 10017

Simultaneously published in the UK
by Routledge
2 Park Square, Milton Park, Abingdon, Oxon OX14 4RN

*Routledge is an imprint of the Taylor & Francis Group,
an informa business*

First issued in paperback 2014

The right of Paul Livingston to be identified as author of this work
has been asserted by him in accordance with sections 77 and 78 of the
Copyright, Designs and Patents Act 1988.

Typeset in Sabon by IBT Global.

Library of Congress Cataloging-in-Publication Data
Livingston, Paul M., 1976–
   The politics of logic : Badiou, Wittgenstein, and the consequences of
formalism / Paul M. Livingston.
      p. cm. — (Routledge studies in contemporary philosophy ; 27)
   Includes bibliographical references (p.) and index.
   1. Political science—Philosophy. 2. Badiou, Alain. 3. Wittgenstein,
Ludwig, 1889–1951. I. Title.
   JA71.L595 2011
   320.01—dc22
                                                  2011006207

ISBN13: 978-0-415-89191-2 (hbk)
ISBN13: 978-1-138-01676-7 (pbk)

Contents

Methodological Preface   xi

Acknowledgments   xv

PART I
Introductory

1   Introduction: An Inquiry into Forms of Life   3

PART II
Paradoxico-Criticism

2   Origins of Paradoxico-Criticism: Structuralism and
    Analytic Philosophy   65

3   Deleuze, Plato, and the Paradox of Sense   95

4   Derrida and Formalism: Formalizing the Undecidable   113

5   Wittgenstein and Parmenides   131

6   Wittgenstein and Turing   148

PART III
Badiou and the Stakes of Formalism

7   Formalism and Force: The Many Worlds of Badiou   187

8   Badiou versus Paradoxico-Criticism   208

9   Paradoxico-Critique of Badiou   238

10   The Politics of Logic: Critical and Practical Consequences   281

      Notes   317
      Bibliography   363
      Index   373

καὶ οἱ μὲν παλαιοί, κρείττονες ἡμῶν καὶ ἐγγυτέρω θεῶν οἰκοῦντες, ταύτην φήμην παρέδοσαν, ὡς ἐξ ἑνὸς μὲν καὶ πολλῶν ὄντων τῶν ἀεὶ λεγομένων εἶναι, πέρας δὲ καὶ ἀπειρίαν ἐν αὑτοῖς σύμφυτον ἐχόντων· δεῖν οὖν ἡμᾶς τούτων οὕτω διακεκοσμημένων ἀεὶ μίαν ἰδέαν περὶ παντὸς ἑκάστοτε θεμένους ζητεῖν—εὑρήσειν γὰρ ἐνοῦσαν . . .

"And the people of old, superior to us and living in closer proximity to the gods, have bequeathed to us this tale, that whatever is said to be consists of one and many, having in its nature limit and unlimitedness. Since this is the structure of things, we have to assume that there is in each case always one form for every one of them, and we must search for it, as we will indeed find it . . ."

(Plato, *Philebus*, 16c–d)

τοῦ λόγου δ' ἐόντος ξυνοῦ ζώουσιν οἱ πολλοὶ ὡς ἰδίαν ἔχοντες φρόνησιν.

"But although the Logos is common the many live as though they had a private understanding."

(Heraclitus, fragment 2)

Methodological Preface

The aim of this book is to interrogate formal structures and results to determine their bearing on today's leading questions of social, linguistic, and political life. Because of the great scope and generality of this bearing, and its application across areas of contemporary thought that are often kept rigorously separate, this involves me in a project whose commitments may be heterodox in several ways. For one, the aim of interpreting formal-logical and metalogical results as bearing *fundamentally* on the structure of "intersubjective" language and collective life has suggested a traversal of the problems of political and social organization that is both a *retrieval* and a displaced *repetition* of the twentieth-century linguistic turn, nowadays so often and triumphantly dismissed. This means that here, as elsewhere, I have attempted to understand the implications of the twentieth-century philosophical recourse to language, its constitution and pursuit as a determinate object of investigation.[1] But since the nature of language is not self-evident, I have nevertheless aimed never to *assume* a substantial being of language, or a specific determination of its forms, until and unless such determinations are clearly motivated by the formalisms themselves.

It may be helpful to state more generally some of the (primarily negative) principles that determine the method of this book with respect to the analysis of language and reflection on its forms.

1) To begin with, I have not assumed any simple *outside* to language. For whether it is understood as the place of mute presentation to a simple aesthetic seeing beyond words, or the transcendental domain of an exemplary presence, the assumption of such an outside prejudices the problem of the *limits* of language, with which the present inquiry is much concerned. I have thus attempted never to foreclose this problem by allowing the formal analysis to submit to constraint from beyond by means of any simply assumed exterior. This is also, I believe, the key to purging contemporary critical thought of the remaining elements of theology or, equally, what has been called "onto-theology," both of which characteristically operate by positing a privileged being beyond language as its external constraint and ultimate delimitation.

2) I have not assumed, or made any substantial use of, the often presupposed distinction between *the natural* and *the artificial* as it bears, or is thought to bear, on language or languages. Thus, I make no use of the assumption of an irreducibly "historical" or "traditional" character of what are sometimes called "natural" languages. Nor do I assume any intrinsic gap in signifying power or referential scope between these and the so-called "artificial" symbolisms and calculi of "formal" logic. For, as I shall argue, the question of the "natural" or "artificial" status of *any* language is very much at stake, and still undecided, in an inquiry which, beginning with Plato, poses originally the problem of the origin of names and the force of laws, and which is here taken up anew on formal grounds. The presupposition of any ready distinction between the "natural" and the "artificial" (or "conventional" or "technical") character of language or languages can, I believe, only portend the avoidance or foreclosure of this profound and original problematic.

3) Although I thus attempt to understand better the structure and limits of the powers of language partially in the light of formal results, I have aimed to respect the commitments of "ordinary" language that pervade its practice and so structure its everyday life. In particular, against a lengthy twentieth-century tradition of the uncritical application of "technical" methods of logical analysis, I do not assume that the adumbration of purely formal results can suffice to motivate the revision or reformation of ordinary language or the commitments inherent therein. For instance, I have held to the assumption that the English terms "all" and "every," in their application beyond particulars and clearly bounded situations, do not simply represent some contingent and accidental feature of language or its powers, but rather remain essential to it, and indeed to anything we can legitimately call "language" at all. They are thus *not to be eliminated* as the result of a formal investigation which demonstrates the logical infelicities to which their use is likely to lead; rather, they are fitting objects of investigation for a critical reflection on language, its powers, and its limits. Only by respecting the commitments of ordinary language in this way, I believe, is it possible to turn the dramatic power of formalisms to a penetrating critical investigation of the stakes and structure of "our" language, as we speak it every day, and as it shapes and determines the forms of collective life.

4) I have not assumed the usefulness of any substantial distinction (thematic or methodological) between the "traditions" of "analytic" and "continental" philosophy, which are both (as I have argued elsewhere) heir to the linguistic turn of the twentieth century and equally privileged sites of the development of its most important results. The continued assumption of an analytic/continental distinction today shelters methodological prejudices on both sides which tend to debar

access to the unified formal problematic pursued here. On the continental side, a pious religiosity of hermeneutic practice protects the irreducible singularity of the "text" from the radical implications of its formally constitutive factors. Meanwhile, on the analytic side, an ascendant empiricist "naturalism" increasingly precludes thematic access to the profound historical results of rationalist thinking about logic and metalogic that once defined the greatest achievements of this tradition itself, and remain some of the most important accomplishments of twentieth-century thought.

The result of ignoring the analytic/continental "split," I hope, is a kind of "as-if" history of a significant strand of twentieth-century thought that presents its development as if such a "split" had never taken place, or at any rate had never become institutionally recognized and validated. It is my hope that philosophers of the twenty-first century will look to this kind of recounting as the basis for their own inheritance of what can once again be treated as a unified field of investigation, and thus can carry forward in a less divisive spirit the ongoing search for solutions to the problems formulated therein.

Acknowledgments

Over the roughly four years during which I have worked on this book, many people have contributed in different ways. First of all, I would like to thank John Bova, to whom I owe the greatest single impetus and stimulus to the project. Though he is still a graduate student at the time of this writing, through his work and in ongoing discussions, John has suggested or inspired several of the key ideas about formalism and its implications developed here, including the "metalogical duality" of which I make prominent theoretical use. Second, I would like to thank my friend and colleague Adrian Johnston. In spring 2009, Prof. Johnston generously allowed me to participate in a graduate-level seminar on Badiou at UNM, one of the first seminars on Badiou ever to be taught in an American philosophy department. The insights gained there, and in further conversations with Adrian, proved invaluable in determining the specific critical direction of this work.

I also owe special thanks to several readers who read and provided detailed comments on all or part of the manuscript. Tim Schoettle has read and provided insightful comments for several chapters. Adriel Trott, Luke Fraser, and Raoni Padui have also read and provided helpful comments on individual chapters or pieces of the book. I would like to thank Jack Woods for his detailed and helpful commentary on a shortened version of Chapter 6 at a meeting of the North American Wittgenstein Society in San Francisco in April, 2010. At a late stage of the project, Joe Spencer read the whole manuscript and provided *many* very detailed and helpful comments, as well as proofreading, for each chapter; special thanks are owed to him. Finally, I would very much like to thank Andrew Cutrofello and one anonymous reviewer for Routledge press for agreeing to review the manuscript and produce extremely detailed and helpful commentaries.

Many others have contributed to the book indirectly through seminars and conversations involving the figures and topics treated here. In this regard, I would especially like to thank my friend Walter Brogan, who allowed me to sit in on a seminar on "Postmodern Communities," taught at Villanova University in spring 2008, in which many of the topics and figures treated here were discussed. I would also like to thank Bill Martin, who participated in two sessions at the annual conference of the Society for Phenomenology and Existential Philosophy, in October 2009 and October 2010, where some of the material included here was originally presented. Others with whom I have discussed some of this material and who have contributed to the ideas and issues discussed here include: Brian Axel, Peg Birmingham, Jeffrey Gower, Martin Hägglund, Reuben Hersh, Michael Kim, Wayne Martin, Dalia Nassar, Michael Olson, Friederieke Rese, Gabriel Rockhill, Iain Thomson, and Samuel Wheeler. My apologies to anyone whom I have left out.

Some of the work that has gone into this book was completed while I was an Alexander von Humboldt Foundation faculty fellow at the University of Freiburg, Germany, in 2007 and again during my renewal of the fellowship in summer 2009. Once again, I would like to thank the von Humboldt Foundation and my faculty host in Freiburg, Prof. Dr. Günter Figal, for their continued and generous support.

Some portions of this work have previously appeared, or will soon appear, in other publications and formats. A small portion of Chapter 1 will appear in a forthcoming issue of *Cosmos and History* under the title "Badiou and the Consequences of Formalism," and a larger portion appeared as "Agamben, Badiou, and Russell" in *Continental Philosophy Review* 42:3 (2009), pp. 297–325. A portion of Chapter 2 appeared as "The Breath of Sense: Language, Structure, and the Paradox of Origin" in *Konturen* vol. 2 (2010), and online at: http://konturen.uoregon.edu/vol2_Livingston.html. Most of Chapter 4 appeared as "Derrida and Formal Logic: Formalising the Undecidable" in *Derrida Today* 3:2 (2010), pp. 221–39. Much of Chapter 6 appeared in *Linguistic and Philosophical Investigations* 9 (2010), pp. 215–47. Finally, Chapters 1 and 7 draw material from two previously published reviews of Badiou's work; first, a long review of *Being and Event*, which appeared in *Inquiry* 51:2 (2008), pp. 217–38, and second, a shorter review of *Logics of Worlds*, which appeared in the *Notre Dame Philosophical Reviews* for 10/8/09 (online at http://ndpr.nd.edu/review.cfm?id=17765). I would like to thank the editors of these publications for giving their permission for me to reuse this material here.

Finally, as always, I would like to thank my wife, Elizabeth, for her constant love and support during the completion of this project.

Part I

Introductory

1 Introduction
An Inquiry into Forms of Life

I begin with a formulation of Wittgenstein's, as enigmatic today as it was when written more than fifty years ago, which nevertheless captures the central problem on which a post-"analytic" philosophical reflection on language and a critical theory of politics in the "continental" mode are today converging:

> What has to be accepted, the given, is—so one could say—forms of life.[1]

In the *Philosophical Investigations*, Wittgenstein uses the term *Lebensform* (or *Lebensformen*) only a handful of times. But in these few cases, Wittgenstein employs the term in a positively assertoric voice that is rare within a text dedicated almost wholly to criticizing what we may otherwise take to be the "givens" of our language and everyday world. Contemporary interpretations oscillate between two ways of understanding Wittgenstein's elliptical invocation of forms of life as "the given." One line of interpretation understands it as indicating a conventionalist anthropologism of practices or cultures. This is a doctrine of the communal determination of meaning by means of shared practical conventions and norms "implicit in practice." Another takes it to suggest a biologism of adaptive forms, a "naturalist" reduction of language and meaning to broadly natural-scientific facts.[2] I shall argue, however, that Wittgenstein here gestures toward a different problematic altogether, one that actually tends to undermine the very terms in which this decision between culturalist and naturalist readings is normally couched.

Indeed, as I shall argue, the problem posed by Wittgenstein's invocation of forms of life is not located simply either in the question of the nature of lives *or* of their forms, but rather in what lies between these two terms: in what it is for a form to be a form *of* life, what it means that something like form or forms shape a (human) life at all. This relationship crosscuts the distinction between "culturalist" and "naturalist" conceptions of forms, or of the lives they shape. This problematic is thus not one of criteriology or genealogy; it cannot be resolved by a taxonomy of empirically determined ways of life, whether sociologically or biologically defined. Nor is it, however, the old Platonic problem of the transcendent *being* of forms, which is sometimes answered today by a naturalism of forms that is simply the inverted image of the dominant conventionalism of lives.[3] Rather, it is the problem of understanding the meaning of the connective "of" in *forms of life*: in what way does form *inform* a life, and what is it for a life to be lived in some determinative relation, obscure or clear, vague or explicit, to forms or to a form?[4] What is implicated in this question is the obscure link between form and matter, the ideal and the real, the universal and the particular, or the transcendent and the immanent. This is the place of what Plato called "participation." Contemporary thought has traced it as the place of the diagonal, the paradoxical, and the *chora*, but also the (history-making or supra-historical) "event," and the fragile possibility of a radically clarified life to come.

The aim of this work is thus to consider the relationship between *forms* or *form* and collective *life*, under the condition of an age determined by the technicization of *information* made possible by the logico-syntactical *formalization* of language. As I shall argue, this requires an investigation into the *consequences of formalism* in two senses. First, it requires a consideration of the ways that collective life can be theoretically reflected in formal-symbolic theoretical structures and the extent to which such structures can illuminate the lived forms of community and social/political association. Second, however, it is necessary to consider the effects of the material and technological *realization* of some of these very same formal structures *on* the actual organization of contemporary politics. This includes, for instance, the actual communicational and computational technologies that today increasingly determine social, political, and economic institutions and modes of action around the globe.

There are, of course, many available definitions of "forms" and "formalism." Here, though, I follow the suggestion of Georg Cantor in the inaugural definition of mathematical set theory, one of the most important developments of formalism in our time. As early as 1883, Cantor defined the notion of a set [*Menge*] in terms that already demonstrate his grasp of its profound philosophical significance:

> By a 'manifold' or 'set' I understand in general any many [*Viele*] which can be thought of as one [*Eines*], that is, every totality of definite elements which can be united to a whole through a law. By this I believe I have defined something related to the Platonic *eidos* or *idea*.[5]

Cantor here recognizes the relevance of his new concept of the set to the ancient problem that most vexed Plato in accounting for the Idea as the One that unites the Many of its participants. This is the problem of the One and the Many itself, which divided Parmenides from Heraclitus and was already avidly pursued by the Pythagoreans.[6]

If the Platonic *eidos* thus captures the original philosophical thought of the unity of the Many as One, the comprehensive set theory that Cantor founded, as I shall argue, transfigures this ancient problem in two further and interrelated ways. First, as Cantor and Frege already grasped, we may consider the relationship of a set to its elements as capturing the relationship between a *universal* and the *individuals* that fall under it. Thus, the definition of a set can be understood as formally identical to the definition of a *concept*, or a *general term*. According to this attitude, we behold, in the structure of sets and of the otherwise undefined relation ∈, the actual underlying formal structure of the relationship that holds between an *object* and a *predicate* or *property* that is asserted to hold of it.[7] This is nothing other than the relationship of the universal to the particular, the same relationship that Plato obscurely designated as "participation." By studying what is embodied in the fundamental consequences of set theory's axiomatic capture of the relationship between One and Many, we come to understand the possibility, range, limits, and structure of this relationship in a formally clarified light.

Second, Cantor's discovery provides resources for addressing one of the most ancient problems of *political* philosophy: namely, the question of the relationship of the One of the *state, social whole*, or *community* to the Many of its members and constituents. Since we may consider the relationship of a set to its elements to formalize this relationship, we may also thus take the generality of the set to manifest the "common" structure of any community, however this structure may be further defined or articulated. Accordingly, the formal structures of sets will also illuminate the basis of claims to unity, wholeness, or sovereign power that bind political communities together as wholes, as well as the disruptive aspects of non-inclusion that can lead to their sundering or transformation.[8] Over the course of the investigations of this book, I will therefore be interpreting formal results of set theory, and closely related results of computation theory, to discern their implications for the nature and structure of political life. Some of these connections will be direct, founded in what are arguably *homologies* of structure that result from the very inherent logic of the One and the Many as it finds application in the consideration of social unity and community. Others are less direct and more analogical in character. Even in these more analogical cases, however, I shall attempt to demonstrate, each time, the significant and illuminative bearing of the mathematical theory of multiplicity and unity, in connection with the metalogical theory of proof and truth, on the most important and central questions of the organization of collective life. The most important point of this bearing, I shall argue, is the application of these theories to the very idea of the (unified) meaning of a sign across the infinity of its possible iterations and the varied and multiple circumstances of its legitimate use.[9] Since this idea of the unity of meaning underlies the coherence of every intelligible form of collective *praxis*, the formal theories here find, through their relevance to language and meaning, a direct bearing on the question of the underlying structure of political life.

As I shall argue, set theory and the other developments of contemporary formalism uniformly arise from a transformative experience of what Greek thought already grasped as *logos*. Today, we *might* translate *logos* as "language." This translation misses the plurivocity of the original Greek term, which is ambiguous, for instance, between "language," "word," "meaning," and "account." And as is well known, the Greek experience of *logos* is the historical basis for all that develops afterwards as "reason" and "rationality," as well as for what we today understand, using the techniques of formal logic, as norms for the meaningfulness of language or the integrity of thought. Here, at any rate, I shall attempt to preserve the profound continuity that runs between Socrates' search for the *logoi* of the various phenomena with which he was concerned and today's critical inquiry, developed in part by means of formal, symbolic logic, into the constitutive structure of language as such. In the following inquiry, the "linguistic turn" taken in the twentieth century by both the "analytic" and the "continental" traditions (though in different ways) thus has a certain methodological priority. The aim is not, however, to theorize the structure and possibilities of an everyday human life by means of an external description of the empirical phenomena of language or its use, but rather to discern the basis of these phenomena themselves in the broader and more enigmatic phenomenon of the *logos*.

According to a long-standing philosophical tradition originating with Aristotle, the possession of *logos* defines the distinctive form of a human life. Although Wittgenstein does not simply concur with this tradition, he understands "language" (*Sprache*) as the name for an unparalleled site of problems, whose place is also that of the everyday, or an ordinary life. His analysis of these problems considers the pictures we are prone to offer ourselves of an individual or collective life, critically reflecting on the temptations that lead us to these pictures, their (limited) satisfactions, and their (manifold) frustrations. This consideration is "political" in the broad sense that it investigates the ways that we live our lives in relation to our own (individual or collective) self-conceptions of them. And although the direct political implications of Wittgenstein's arguments in the *Investigations* and other "central" texts are not always immediately obvious, it is nonetheless evident that he intended such analyses as the "private language argument" and the "rule-following considerations" to support a far-ranging critical reflection on the ordinary ways of life of the culture in which he found himself. This includes his critical engagement with the leading organizational structures and self-rationalizations of a twentieth-century industrial culture dedicated to (false or misleading, as Wittgenstein would suggest) guiding ideals of novelty and "progress" achieved through technical and organizational means.[10]

   In the twentieth century, the material and historical "rationalization" of social life (for instance, in the widespread development and standardization of technologies and practices of communication, information exchange, and commodification) is in fact closely linked with developments arising from critical *reflection* on language and its formal structure or structures. Accordingly, both the concrete historical and the abstract critical consequences of formalism must be treated together if we wish to produce an analysis adequate to the most important social and political phenomena of our time.[11] Many existing analyses take into account the effects on social life of technology, progressive rationalization, and "instrumental reasoning." But it is a substantial failing of many of these existing analyses that they do not consider, in any detail, the *internal* implications of the specific abstract and formal-logical structures that, on their own accounts, increasingly dominate social and political life. It is typical for these analyses, continuing in various styles the classical legacy of Kantian critique, to complain of the growing dominance of technical, instrumental, or calculative reason, while maintaining the possibility of a distinct, non-formal or "lived" modality of reason still accessible to critical thought and practice.[12] But if, as seems likely, the twentieth-century development of formal reflection on language and logic problematizes the very terms in which theorists have attempted to describe such an alternative modality of "lived" reason and reasoning, it may be that critical thought about technology and society must now continue explicitly in a formal mode, if it is to continue at all.

   This immediately produces a new question, which nevertheless may be seen, retrospectively, as having been one of the most significant questions of a wide variety of philosophical projects ("analytic" as well as "continental") in the twentieth century. This is the question of the *formalization of formalism* itself, of the reflection of formal-symbolic structures *within* themselves, and thus of the possibility of these structures coming to comprehend and articulate their own internal constitution and limits. Within the analytic tradition, this question is posed and pursued within the ill-defined field sometimes called "metalogic." Its results are recognized as profound, but their larger significance has, so far at least, been difficult to place. In particular, despite the largely negative significance usually ascribed to them, the transformative results of Russell, Gödel, and Tarski have fundamentally articulated what we can expect from a critical reflection on the nature of language and our human access to it. On the "continental" side, as well, such transformative critical meta-reflection has resulted from the massive mid-century project of structuralism, especially as "post-structuralist" philosophers have subjected it to internal critique on its own terms.

   One of my chief goals in the present work is thus to argue that these two strands of reflection on language—metalogical analysis on the "analytic" side, and post-structuralism in a deconstructive mode on the "continental"—can be allied, and thus can both be useful sources of *critical* reflection on the *political* implications of formalism as such. Their combination can yield, in particular, a formally clarified understanding of the constitution and structure of political communities, as well as of their possibilities of alteration and internal dynamics of change.

At *Politics* 1253a7–18, just after defining the human being in terms of its possession of the power of speech, or *logos*, Aristotle suggests an essential link between this definition of the human and the very possibility of politics:

> Now, that man is more of a political animal than bees or any other gregarious animals is evident. Nature, as we often say, makes nothing in vain, and man is the only animal who has the gift of speech. And whereas mere voice is but an indication of pleasure and pain, and therefore found in other animals . . . the power of speech is intended to set forth the expedient and inexpedient, and therefore likewise the just and the unjust. And it is a characteristic of man that he alone has any sense of good and evil, of just and unjust, and the like, and the association of living beings who have this sense makes a family and a state.

If the original "political" definition of the human animal correlates strictly, as is formulated here, with the claim of *logos* upon an otherwise animal life, then a contemporary critical reflection on the "meaning" of this life necessarily speaks the language of logic as fluently as it does that of politics.[13] And if, as Agamben has argued, today's global politics produce totalizing regimes of "biopower" that simultaneously construct and then capture the "bare life" of the simply living within the formal structures of institutions and economies, then the possibility of this capture is evidently thinkable only as a matter of the "logical form" of practices, institutions, and laws.[14] This critical reflection on formalism is not, then, a matter of applying an external "logic" (or logics) to the "political"—hence, not a "logic *of* politics"—but rather a matter of comprehending the very structure of logic itself in its inherently "political" dimension—hence, a kind of "politics *of* logic."

The ultimate question for this inquiry is not, then, how a community is structured out of a plurality of antecedently individual or self-sufficient lives, subsequently united by contract, convention, or common need.[15] Rather, its goal is the development of a "politics of logic" that ventures to comprehend *logos* itself—what Heraclitus long ago determined as the "common"—as *immediately* the necessary form of any common linguistic life, *prior to* the self-sufficient life of distinct individuals capable of agreeing on matters of fact or opinion.[16]

It is in this sense that Wittgenstein declares, in a cautious formulation that nevertheless suffices to indicate his radical break with all politics based on the norms of consensus, deliberation, and contract:

> It is what human beings say that is true and false; it is in language that they agree. That is not agreement of opinions, but in form of life.[17]

Here, the distinction between agreement *of* individual opinions and agreement *in* form of life, between agreement *on* claims, true or false, and agreement *in* language, marks the essential difference between the unity of contract (explicit or implicit) among individuals and the uncertain *formal* "attunement" that first defines the structure of a distinctively human life at all.[18] It is this attunement that, according to Wittgenstein, first *grounds* the very possibility of *any* subsequent agreement or disagreement on the level of opinions, facts, or norms. But just what kind of ground is this, recalcitrant to description but nevertheless demonstrated in the formal structures that evince what is presupposed as "given" in any explicit accounting for a linguistic human life? It is to this question that the current work is addressed.

BADIOU AND FORMALISM

In a 2007 interview, Alain Badiou offered an exemplary description of the deepest underlying commitments of his profound, systematic, and long-standing reflection on formalism:

> I believe that if all creative thought is in reality the invention of a new mode of formalization, then that thought is the invention of a form. Thus if every creative thought is the invention of a new form, then it will also bring new possibilities of asking, in the end, 'what is a form?' . . . Like Plato, who first thought this, thinking is the thinking of forms, something that he called ideas but they are also the forms. It is the same word, *idea*. It is different from Aristotle's thought where thinking is the thinking of substance. His paradigm is the animal. For Plato, it's mathematics. Mathematics holds something of the secret of thinking . . . This is the first point. I think I hold a fidelity to this idea, but, at the same time, the heart of the most radical experience is politics. Politics itself, in a sense, is also a thinking through forms. It is not the thought of arrangements or the thought of contracts or the good life. No. It is a thinking of form.[19]

Badiou's far-ranging investigation of the formalisms of mathematics yields a systematic conception of politics that is at once radical in its metaphysical depth and staggering in the scope of its contemporary implications. In *Being and Event* (1988), Badiou develops a dramatic interpretation of the implications of mathematical set theory for contemporary thought about the very structure of being and the most fundamental possibilities of political change and transformation. More recently, in the 2006 sequel *Logics of Worlds*, Badiou has supplemented this investigation with a detailed analysis, grounded this time on mathematical category theory, of the relationship between being as it is in itself (and is treated by "ontology") and *appearances* or *phenomena*, the subject of "phenomenology." Together, the two books thus comprise a highly sophisticated manifestation (probably the most highly developed to this date) of what I am here calling the "politics of logic." One main purpose of this book is thus to examine Badiou's system, both in its formal and its political registers. But while this demands some exegesis of Badiou's complex work, my aim here is not simply exegetical but also evaluative and critical.[20] In particular, as I shall show, Badiou's *application* of the mathematical formalisms to the diverse questions of social and political life repeatedly involves fundamental gestures of projection, whereby formal and mathematical structures bear the weight of the theorization of such diverse political and ontological concepts as those of presentation, representation, the subject, the state, and the very possibility of political change. Most important to the argument of *Being and Event* is a highly suggestive application of one of the most technically formidable and complex innovations of set theory, the method of "forcing" discovered by P. J. Cohen in 1963. Badiou uses the formal results of this method to support his theory of the "event," or the possibility of a radical and transformative break with the organizing logic of any specific political or social order.

In the following, I consider these projective gestures critically, evaluating their standing with respect to other possible ways of understanding the formalisms in question and their bearing on social and political life. My point is emphatically *not* that the formalisms themselves do not bear *anything like* the kind of significance that Badiou attributes to them. In fact, one of the most innovative and promising features of Badiou's thought is his ability to draw specific and determinate ontological and political results from the formal structures developed in logic, set theory, and mathematics. However, his specific ways of interpreting formalisms nevertheless involve, at several points, fundamental *choices* which he often leaves unmarked. This leads Badiou repeatedly to reject positions and orientations of thought with which he might otherwise be much more sympathetic, and which we ought to consider in the course of an investigation of the consequences of formalism for political life.

One of the most significant issues in dispute between Badiou and much of contemporary critical thought, in fact, is the legacy of the twentieth-century linguistic turn. When he discusses it, Badiou recurrently dismisses the linguistic turn and its legacy, often reducing it to a postmodern "sophism" that substitutes mere rhetoric and verbal manipulations for philosophy's venerable investigation into the nature of "the things themselves."[21] This rejection is presented as a consequence of the formalisms, but as an interpretation of them it is, as I shall show, highly prejudicial. In fact, it puts Badiou in the problematic position of having substantively to reject the massive contributions of twentieth-century thought in the linguistic mode—from continental structuralism to the analytic tradition itself—to the very kind of formal reflection he would like to carry out. We can reverse this prejudice, I shall argue, by reconsidering the formal underpinnings of these contributions and the interpretive decisions they permit. More specifically, Badiou's official decision *against* the linguistic turn and the wide gamut of critical thinkers who draw on it results directly from his own decision *for* what he calls the "generic" orientation in thought. This is a radical and productive orientation which Badiou opposes to both the essentially authoritarian and conservative orientation of traditional metaphysics and to the "constructivist" or nominalist orientation that restricts being to the fixed law of an existing language.

Badiou presents his decision in this respect as the necessary implication of a more fundamental rejection of any orienting "One-All" of thought, any assumption of the total adequacy of language to a universe complete and consistent in itself. However, as I shall show here, this presentation is misleading. For Badiou's own "generic" orientation does not so much result from a unilateral rejection of the "One-All" of traditional metaphysics as from a decision against *one aspect* of this "One-All," which is, in fact, simultaneously a decision *for* another aspect of it. In particular, Badiou rejects the possibility of describing the totality, the "All" of the set of all sets or the universe of all that exists. At the same time, however, he leaves intact and wholly unchallenged the other crucial formal aspect of the traditional "One-All," namely, that of *consistency*, or the demand that whatever may be said must be said without contradiction.

Indeed, there is in fact another possible orientation here that is wholly coherent with the formal results and entirely missed by Badiou. Moreover, it plausibly captures a wide range of contemporary critical thought, especially that which arises from the legacy of the linguistic turn. I call this other orientation of thought, distinct from Badiou's, the *paradoxico-critical* orientation. In the following, I develop the paradoxico-critical orientation by considering representative figures from diverse schools and traditions: Jacques Lacan, Giorgio Agamben, Jacques Derrida, Gilles Deleuze, and Ludwig Wittgenstein. Following this, I juxtapose each of these thinkers to Badiou's own ("generic") orientation on a series of interrelated points. All of the paradoxico-critical thinkers stand, in diverse ways and according to differing historical connections, in the legacy of the linguistic turn. Moreover, and crucially for their relevance here, all draw on highly specified *formal* reasoning to document the critical and productive consequences of a consideration of the structure and boundaries of language. As I shall demonstrate, their shared formal orientation results directly, along with all of its critical consequences, from their taking the alternative decision to the one that Badiou takes and leaves unmarked. Instead of making a decision for the One of consistency and sacrificing the All of totality, they jointly choose the All of totality and sacrifice the One of consistency. This leads to a rigorous and transformative articulation of the constitutive status of paradox and antinomy for the very structures of political life.

PLATO AND WITTGENSTEIN: FORCE OF NAMES AND LAWS

Almost 2,400 years ago, intervening in the debate of origins about *phusis* vs. *nomos* that framed, in the Sophists and Pre-Socratics, the deepest problems of self-understanding that a dawning culture of rationality could address to itself, Plato has Socrates interrupt a dialogue between Cratylus and Hermogenes over the "correctness of names" (*orthotes onomatos*). At issue is whether names have a certain kind of correctness by nature (*phusei*) or whether their relation to their objects is fixed entirely by the "convention and agreement" (*syntheke kai homologia*) (384c) of their users. To Cratylus' naturalism, Hermogenes opposes the "conventionalist" position that "whatever anyone decides to call a particular thing is its name" (385a). However, as Socrates, entering the debate, quickly points out, on the level of statements (*logoi*) at least, there is a difference between telling the truth and speaking a falsehood. He who makes a true statement must employ true names; but if we wish thus to succeed in naming, we must name things "in the natural way for them to be named" (387d). Indeed, a name is given by giving the *rules* for its use (388d). But who is it that sets these rules, and by what right?

As so often in Plato, it is a question of *techne*. A thing is named correctly if it is named "with the natural tool" for naming it; a name is thus "a sort of tool" (*organon*) (388a) and, like a drill or a shuttle, it will be successful only if well made. The success of the tool thus implies the existence of the craftsman (*demiourgon*), one who is skilled both in making the name (*onoma*) and setting the law (*hō nomos*). By way of this decisive ambiguity between names and the law, Socrates calls this craftsman the *nomothetēs*:

> *Socrates:* Can you at least tell me this? Who or what provides us with the names we use?
>
> *Hermogenes:* I don't know that either.
>
> *Socrates:* Don't you think that the law (*hō nomos*) provides us with them?
>
> *Hermogenes:* Very likely.
>
> *Socrates:* So, when a teacher uses a name, he's using the product of a law-giver (*nomothetēs*).
>
> *Hermogenes:* I believe he is.
>
> *Socrates:* Do you think that every man is a law-giver or only the one who possesses the craft (*technēn*)?
>
> *Hermogenes:* Only the one who possesses the craft.
>
> *Socrates:* It follows that it isn't every man who can give names, Hermogenes, but only a name-maker, and he, it seems, is a law-giver—the kind of craftsman most rarely found among human beings. (388e–389a).

Like the craftsman of a tool, the *nomothetēs* must, in order to establish the meaning of a name, possess knowledge that guides him toward the correct way of crafting the name out of the sounds and syllables available to him. However, there remains a paradox (cf. 438b–c). How is the *nomothetēs* himself to know the "correct name" for something before it has been fixed *as* the correct name by his very law-giving gesture of original naming? The paradox is the original paradox of meaning; it already vitiates any account that, like the theory of Cratylus, accords meaning purely to nature or, like that of Hermogenes, to the arbitrary decision of the individual speaker. However, Socrates does not hesitate to resolve it by means of a portentous appeal to a kind of knowledge that *precedes* the technical/instrumental knowledge of the craftsman himself. If, in the course of the craftsman's synthetic activity, for instance, the carpenter's activity of fabricating the shuttle, the instrument were to break, the craftsman would then look toward something that is common to all actual instances of the type:

> *Socrates:* Suppose the shuttle breaks while he's making it. Will he make another looking to the broken one? Or will he look to the very form to which he looked in making the one that broke?
> *Hermogenes:* In my view, he will look to the form.
> *Socrates:* Then it would be absolutely right to call that what a shuttle itself is. (389a–b)[22]

Thus the craftsmen, whether of shuttles or of words, necessarily looks to a knowledge of the *form* (*eidos*) of what he is making, what is common to all appropriately made instances of the type, and what we may indeed understand, in virtue of this appropriateness to the task, as being "the thing itself."[23] In this way, the *nomothetēs* too, the *demiourgen* of names and laws, envisions the form of language itself; under its guidance, he is able to enact his original thesis. This knowledge of "the thing itself" is more important than the particular material of which the artifact is made, in each case:

> So mustn't a law-giver also know how to embody in sounds and syllables the name naturally suited to each thing? And if he is to be an authentic giver of names, mustn't he, in making and giving each name, look to what a name itself is? And if different law-givers do not make each name out of the same syllables, we mustn't forget that different blacksmiths, who are making the same tool for the same type of work, don't all make it out of the same iron. But as long as they give it the same form—even if that form is embodied in different iron—the tool will be correct, whether it is made in Greece or abroad. (389d–e).

But how, then, is the successful lawgiver to gain knowledge of this form, which is never given simply in any individual instance? Again, Socrates does not hesitate to offer an answer. Knowledge of the form is to be found in that everyday *usage* (*ethos*) that embodies the role of the instrument in the life it facilitates. Just as the successful maker of lyres must himself be "supervised" by those who play lyres, so the work of the *nomothetēs* is itself to be supervised by one who knows the "correctness of names" in the actual *praxis* of their everyday life:

> *Socrates:* And who can best supervise the work of a rule-setter, whether here or abroad, and judge its products? Isn't it whoever will use them?
> *Hermogenes:* Yes.
> *Socrates:* And isn't that the person who knows how to ask questions?
> *Hermogenes:* Certainly.
> *Socrates:* And he also knows how to answer them?
> *Hermogenes:* Yes.
> *Socrates:* And what would you call someone who knows how to ask and answer questions? Wouldn't you call him a dialectician?
> *Hermogenes:* Yes, I would. (390c)

Plato thus finds an unprecedented answer to the problem of the original knowledge of names—the correspondence between words and things—in the everydayness of their use. The dialectician or philosopher, in his reflexive inquiry into the *logos* of names and laws, also possesses the skill to evince from the everyday *praxis* of language the obscure secret of their force.

Much later, this response to the problem of meaning and laws, to the authority of rules and the scope of meanings, is essentially *repeated* in another problematically dialectical text dedicated to the examination of language's relation to life and to the specificity of what may be called linguistic "use" or "usage." For Wittgenstein, it is again a question of laws and their force. At *Philosophical Investigations*, section 217, Wittgenstein poses in a radical form the critical question of the *force* of rules. This is the question of how we should understand the "capacity" of linguistic or grammatical rules to "determine" meaning in everyday life. As for Plato, the question links the problem of the origin of words with that of the *authority* of rules, the problem of what actually determines usage *de facto* with what assures its right to do so *de jure*. The *Investigations'* inquiry into this twofold question passes through a profound consideration of what it is to learn a rule, and what it is successfully to follow one, but at the root of this question, as well, is that of the original *institution* of laws and standards. Wittgenstein's demystification of the picture of rules as "rails laid to infinity" interrogates the claim of the rule to a superlative force grounded in the possibility of its "abstraction" from any (finite) number of its instances. The inquiry also passes through Wittgenstein's diagnosis—by way of an example that bears comparison to Plato's own invocation of the craftsman's necessary knowledge of the *organon* he creates—of the tendency, rooted deeply in ordinary language, to "sublimate" (cf. *PI* 38) the action of the machine and the law of its operation:

> 193. The machine as a symbol of its mode of action: the machine—I might say at first—seems already to have in itself its mode of action. What does that mean? In that we know the machine, everything else, namely the movement that it will exhibit, seems already to be completely determined.
>
> We talk as if these parts could only move in this way, as if they could not do anything else. How is this—do we, then, forget the possibility of their bending, breaking off, melting, and so on? Yes; in many cases we don't think of that at all . . .
>
> 194. When does one think: the machine has its possible movements in itself already, in some mysterious way? Well, when one philosophizes. And what leads us to think this? The kinds of way in which we talk about machines. . . .

Radically posing the question of what it is that leads us to think of language as such a logical machine, whose possibilities are determined in advance by the "rules of use," Wittgenstein identifies a far-ranging paradox of rules and their symbols. As he puts it in *PI* 201: "No course of action could be determined by a rule, because every course of action can be made out to accord with the rule." No symbolic expression of a rule is sufficient, by itself, to determine the infinite number of instances of its application. There remains, therefore, an essential gap in practice between *any* such symbolic expression (and thereby *any* explanation by means of language) and the understanding manifest in everyday life.[24]

Insofar as there is a conclusion to be drawn here, it is that no rule can determine its *own* application; that is, there is no symbolic expression that by itself determines how it *itself* is to be applied to any new case. This is what suggests the specification of another rule to determine the application of the first (cf. *PI* 86, 139–41); as if "every interpretation hangs in the air" (*PI* 198), waiting for further support. But this response cannot succeed, on pain of an infinite regress. It is thus clear that the attempt to understand the application of rules as wholly determined by their symbolic expressions also cannot succeed, and that it must therefore be supplemented by the dimension or aspect of understanding that Wittgenstein calls "mastery of a technique."[25] To be master of a technique—to know *how* to apply a rule—is then to possess a competence or capability whose extension *cannot* be fully explicated in finite, symbolic terms; yet it is the competence ascribed to any normal adult speaker who can use a general term at all.[26] The question of what is involved in this competence is the question of the *infinite* dimension of knowledge of language, or of the possibility of knowing and understanding the use of any term that *can*, in principle, be extended to an infinite number of cases. This infinite applicability is, again, formally modeled in the comprehension of a set of particulars within an (as it may be, infinite) set; it is the relationship of the general to the particular that Plato understood as "participation." There can be, it seems, no account of the *force* of a rule in governing its particular instances—or of the relationship between a general linguistic term and the particulars it characterizes—that does not account for the origin and entry of this infinite dimension of applicability into the "finitude" of a human life.

How, then, *is* it possible to follow a rule?[27] For Wittgenstein as for Plato (quite to the contrary of the usual interpretation of the former as a radical "anti-Platonist"), the answer is to be found, again, in the *givenness of form*. Like the "logical form" that precedes and anticipates it in Wittgenstein's own writing, a "form of life" is evidently not to be described or specified by any theoretical account. Nevertheless, the "givenness" of forms of life is closely connected with the "solution" that Wittgenstein offers, in the *Investigations*, to his own radically posed problem of rule-following:

> There is a way of grasping a rule which is *not* an *interpretation*, but which is shown in what we call 'obeying the rule' and 'going against it' from case to case of application. (*PI* 201; translation slightly altered).

Showable but not sayable, evident but not describable, forms of life are given, outside the assurance of any structure, in the immanence and heterogeneity of actual cases and the widely varied circumstances of an everyday life. As I shall attempt to show here, we may take this usage to evince what amounts to an inherent "ethos" of the ordinary, in a sense that has nothing to do with convention or conventionalism.[28]

So far, commentary on the "rule following considerations" of the *Philosophical Investigations* has massively emphasized the *social* aspect of Wittgenstein's apparent "solution" to the paradox in the remarks following paragraph 201. Thus, it is standardly supposed that Wittgenstein's main point here is to replace an "individualistic" theory of mind or understanding with an inherently *social* one, according to which rule-following is only possible within the context and constraints of an intersubjective community. The "private language argument" that follows is then often supposed to amount simply to the application of this communitarian moral to the question of what determines the correctness of any individual use of language, and the two skeins of argument are together supposed to support the thesis that only a community's norms or conventions can ultimately determine correct usage.

Though this replacement of an individual with a collective account of correctness is indeed *part* of Wittgenstein's point here, the commentary that reads Wittgenstein as a social communitarian has mostly ignored another, equally important dimension of it: namely, the equally significant emphasis Wittgenstein places on what we may call the *iterative* dimension of linguistic usage. As we will see in more detail in Chapter 6, it was crucially important to Wittgenstein that the use of language is always the realization of a capacity that is capable of supporting an indefinite *repetition* of linguistic symbols and justified uses. Thus, a rule is as such something that could not only be followed once; every rule is capable, as such, of interpretation or application in an *indefinite* and indeed properly *infinite* number of cases. This iterative dimension is always essential to Wittgenstein's invocation of "practices," "techniques," "usages," and the like, and plays a similarly essential role in his positive consideration of the very possibility of following a rule.

Wittgenstein's questions and statements around *PI* 201 emphasize this iterative dimension easily as much as the social dimension: "Is what we call 'following a rule' something that it would be possible for only *one* person, *only* once *in a lifetime*, to do?"; "It is not possible that there should have been *only one occasion* on which only one person followed a rule." (*PI* 199) (emphasis added). "As things are, I can, for example, invent a game that is never played by anyone. But would the following be possible too: mankind has never played any games; once, though, someone invented a game—which, however, was never played?" (*PI* 204). These formulations have the effect of emphasizing that any account of language usage as ultimately depending on participation in a *practice* or mastery of a *technique* will demand, in addition to whatever may be said on behalf of the essentially *social* dimension of usage, an account of the possibility of indefinite iteration that characterizes any rule (and hence any practice or technique), as such. Accordingly, it is not simply sufficient to replace the individualist "image" or interpretation, supposed to be present in an individual's mind and wholly responsible for her behavior, with a socially defined standard, rule, or norm, articulated by the conventions or the conventional patterns of education or enforcement within a community. For however these conventions or patterns are stated, the statement would itself seem to be in need of a further interpretation; and here, as a question of the regulative *force* of (what are supposed to be) conventions or conventional agreements, the underlying problem between rules and their interpretation again repeats itself. The problem of rule-following is not, then, to be answered simply by the invocation of communal standards or intersubjective conventions within an already existing community. There is a deeper question here, one that concerns the very *possibility* of forming a community at all. It is the question of the *basis* of the infinite iterability that constitutes a rule, practice, or law as such. Such iterability is the precondition of all possibility of the *application* of a rule or law, and thus of the possibility of any regular political structure as well.

To "agree" in a "form of life" is thus not to agree in opinions or beliefs; it is not to be party to an originally founding convention or a consensus founded on the "communicative" capacities of individuals. Wittgenstein says it is, rather, to "agree in language." And:

> To understanding through language belongs not only an agreement in definitions, but (as strange as this may sound) an agreement in judgments. This seems to abolish [or sublate] logic, but does not do so. It is one thing to describe methods of measurement, and another to find and express results of measurement. But what we call "measuring" is also determined by a certain constancy in the results of measurement.[29]

Wittgenstein's reference here to "agreement in judgments" does not indicate consensual agreement, but rather agreement in the *basis* of judgments—in what might be called, by way of a figure that, though itself foundational for all discourses of "normativity," remains metaphorical—the "agreed-upon standards" of judgment and decision. Such standards—if such there be—set the "measure" for a shared life, determine the basis for judgments of rectitude, and thereby "constitute" the community through "shared" agreement on its bounds. Yet rather than attempting to specify such standards or to argue (in conservative fashion) for their necessity, Wittgenstein proceeds directly to pose a deep paradox concerning them. Since the consideration of rules shows that the symbolic representation of these procedures cannot by itself determine the mutual attunement of form of life, it may seem that pointing to their limitations implies that logic must be left behind, transcended, sublated, or "abolished."[30] But as Wittgenstein hastens to point out, "it does not do so." For beyond or behind the signs of formal logic, and as I shall attempt to show here, there is another kind of formal relevance of *logos* to life, one not wholly determined on the level of given "rules of use" but shown in the everyday life of language as it problematically reflects itself.

The remnants of the tradition of (what is still called) "continental" philosophy are today converging, in multiple respects, on precisely this *logico-political problem of the nomothesis*, to which both Plato's and Wittgenstein's invocations of lived forms offer responses. This is the problem of the original positing of names; at the same time, it is the problem of the original force of law. Through what is by now a classic deconstructive gesture, the question of the *arche* of structure arises in a radical fashion as soon as structural analyses venture to consider their own conditions of possibility—as soon, that is, as the conditions for the possibility of a structuralist picture of language are thematized under the condition of just such a structure.[31] However, this problem of nomothesis is also the problem of the original *force of law*: the problem of the authority of whatever or whoever is entitled to pronounce or speak the law into force by original declaration or prohibition, and thus to pass judgment (in the name of the law thus enunciated) on the particular case. Here, the structuralist conception of language as a rule-bound structure of signs is just one figure of the original *force* of law over life. The sovereign law of structure is the capacity of language to bind the instances of a life into the regularities of ordered sense.

Today, a large (and growing) literature testifies to the constitutive instability of this sovereign position, both in its political and juridical forms.[32] Here, between what was once distinguished as "constituting" and "constituted" power, is the site of a double bind, an original paradox of the nomothesis that is suddenly discernible as the hitherto unthought basis of all instances of instituted sovereignty. The paradox is that the act of instituting the legal order cannot be legal, within that order itself. Thus the original institution and continuing force of law depends essentially on a founding gesture that is both illegal and *exceptional* with respect to the order that it founds. This paradox was perhaps first stated explicitly, amidst the breakdown of constitutional democracy in the Weimar Republic, by the German legal philosopher Carl Schmitt. In *Political Theology*, Schmitt argued for the "necessity" of an exceptional sovereign who, standing simultaneously both inside and outside the political order he institutes, grounds the original possibility of this order itself. Subsequently, political authority may be delegated to a constitution or a democratic or parliamentarian body; but the original essence of the political is, according to Schmitt, captured in the necessary and exceptional position of the sovereign whose "pure decision" first constitutes the legal order:

> The exception is that which cannot be subsumed; it defies general codification, but it simultaneously reveals a specifically juristic element—the decision in absolute purity. The exception appears in its absolute form when a situation in which legal prescriptions can be valid must first be brought about. Every general norm demands a normal, everyday frame of life to which it can be factually applied and which is subjected to its regulations. The norm requires a homogenous medium. This effective normal situation is not a mere 'superficial presupposition' that a jurist can ignore; that situation belongs precisely to its immanent validity. There exists no norm that is applicable to chaos. For a legal order to make sense, a normal situation must exist, and he is sovereign who definitely decides whether this normal situation actually exists.[33]

As theorists have emphasized, this exceptional position of the sovereign remains in the background of the normally functioning *polis*, even when it is obscured by mystifying figures or conceptions of the unity of the political community or its source. Contemporary regimes tend to expand this exceptional position to a more general "state of exception" which extends the claim of sovereign power indefinitely by citing the existence of an exceptional or "emergency" situation in order to reinstate and promulgate the original indistinction between fact and law.[34]

With this analysis, the long-standing "critique of metaphysics" takes on a new political dimension and an altered topological structure. In its deconstructive modality, critical interrogation of the structure of the sovereign exception operates to expose the inherent contradictions at the center of any constituted political order, and thus to expose its normative claims to immanent reflexive critique. Among these claims is the sovereign's claim to *totality*: that is, the claim of a constituted political order to normalize and decide upon the legality of each of the diverse and heterogeneous events and facts that are treated as falling within its scope. However, the claim of any particular form of sovereign power to constitute a political order, and thus support it in its totality, is not here criticized from a transcendent position "outside" the limits of that order itself. Rather, the original basis of sovereign power is recognized immanently as the *inconsistent* position at the paradoxical threshold of the constituted order and what it excludes.

Thus, the paradoxical topology of the sovereign position constitutes an original double bind between force and law.[35] This topology can in fact be understood quite generally not only as the basis for specific empirically described political orders but for the normative forces of reason and measure themselves.[36] It is determined, as we shall see, in a precise way by formally tractable results that arise from the profound twentieth-century logical and metalogical inquiry into totalities and their structure.

FREGE/CANTOR/RUSSELL: PARADOX AND THE UNIVERSE

When, in 1879, Gottlob Frege (then an obscure mathematician) published his *Begriffsschrift* or "concept-writing," he could scarcely have been aware of having founded a wide-ranging revolution of philosophical thought and *praxis*. His first goal was simply to place mathematical inference on a firm ground, formalizing inference by means of a logical system that "leaves nothing to intuition" and thereby submits mathematical reason to the rigors of pure, abstract thought. But the originally narrow program of logicism would lead in short order to the revolution of thought that, in originating the "analytic tradition," would transform the methods of philosophy and our understanding of the nature of language in fundamental ways. For the attempt to complete the logicist program soon led to a set of far-ranging paradoxes that also structurally articulate the limits of the possibility of formalization itself. Despite their decisive role in shaping (and limiting) the prospects of reductive analytic projects in the twentieth century, these paradoxes are even now often treated as mere curiosities or, at best, as applicable only to specific and narrowly defined problems of computation or formalization. However, I shall argue that the unprecedented *metalogical* insight whereby the formal or syntactic structure of language is itself made an object of systematic investigation, and the paradoxes to which this inevitably leads, remain deeply relevant to how we should think today about finitude, language, politics, and truth. More specifically, close attention to the consequences of formalism that make it possible for a formal system problematically to reflect "itself" (to encode, that is, its own formal structure and syntax, and thereby to "express" its own syntactic properties) can yield a new articulation of critical thought in its ongoing attempt to reflect upon the capabilities and limits of our understanding of the world.

As we have seen, Cantor's project, like Frege's, draws on a dramatic and unrelenting assumption of the formalizability of language and concepts. In particular, Cantor's theory of sets presupposes that the *unity* of the concept can be theorized as a *totality*: that it is possible, in other words, to theorize anything grouped together by a word or concept as a unified *one*. This has immediate consequences for the nature and structure of mathematics, which touch in a profound way on ancient philosophical problems as well. In particular, one of the most conceptually profound implications of his definition of the set as a "many which can be thought of as one" is Cantor's theorization of the *infinite* series of natural numbers (1, 2, 3, . . .) as comprising a single "completed" set. With this single, bold, theoretical step, Cantor reverses thousands of years of theory about the infinite, stemming originally from Aristotle, which had held that such infinities as the series of natural numbers could only be "potential" infinities, never existing as actually completed wholes.[37] Moreover, by demonstrating that it is indeed possible to think of infinite sets as completed, formally well-defined wholes, Cantor provides the basis for the "mathematical" concept of the infinite to be forever disjoined from the traditional religious or mystical concept which treats the infinite as an unthinkable transcendence, completely beyond the powers of human thought or cognition.

Cantor's innovation thus articulates in a fundamental way the possibility for philosophical thought to conceive of the infinite, and thus of its relationship of the infinite to a (finite) human life. It relies in detail on the technique of *diagonalization*, which plays a fundamental role in the generation of virtually all of the paradoxes and paradoxical structures I discuss here. The best way to understand diagonalization, in general, is to think of a (generally infinite) number of elements of a system, the totality of which exhausts the system as a whole, or comprises the totality of elements with a certain property within it. For instance, we might take the (infinite) set of natural numbers, or the (infinite) totality of sentences that are assertible within a given language. Diagonalization, then, operates on this totality as a whole to produce another element which is both: i) *formally* a member of the totality in question (that is, it bears the right formal properties to be a member of the totality) and, at the same time ii) *demonstrably* not the same as *any* of the (infinite number of) elements that already comprise the totality.[38] By means of diagonalization, Cantor, in particular, showed the strict excess of the size of the *power set* of any set—that is, the set of all possible sets recombining its elements—over the original set itself. By means of this operation, the vast Cantorian hierarchy of "transfinite" sets, each an infinity strictly larger than the last, is born.

Yet as soon as this step is accomplished, new questions arise. For instance, if Cantor's theory indeed allows us to consider totalities such as the set of all natural numbers as unified, completed wholes, does this formal tractability indeed extend to the thinkability of *all* that has traditionally been thought under the heading of the "infinite"? Can we, for instance, understand the infinite totality of the universe itself, or indeed the transcendence of the divine, in terms of infinite completed sets? Is there any limitation to the size of successive infinities formed by means of the power set operation, or does the hierarchy itself extend without any boundary? And what, then, should we say about the existence and size of the *whole* infinite hierarchy of infinite sets?

Here, the original intuition of unity *suggested* by Cantor's definition of a set, if drawn out rigorously, suggests a profound and radical transformation or replacement of the traditional theological categories of the *total* and the *absolute* on rigorous set-theoretical grounds. Nevertheless, Cantor's own thought about these questions remained motivated, in large part, by more traditional considerations. Interestingly, in fact, it was the thought of a divine, infinite transcendence that led Cantor both to the theorization of certain infinite sets as existing totalities, and to the claim that others *cannot* exist (or, at any rate, be treated mathematically). In particular, the idea of an infinite divinity led Cantor to believe both that the well-defined infinite sets of the naturals, or of the reals, *can* exist as wholes (in that God can indeed group them all together as unified sets, even if finite agents cannot) and, on the other hand, that the whole infinite hierarchy of infinite sets forms an "unincreasable" ultimate totality that cannot be treated mathematically at all, what Cantor (following tradition) called the *Absolute*.[39]

In fact, subsequent developments in set theory itself would appear to bear out Cantor's intuition of the absolute inaccessibility of the set of all sets, or of the totality of what exists. In particular, the subsequent development of a series of far-reaching set-theoretical paradoxes appeared to show that it is indeed *impossible to conceive* of such a totality, or of certain other closely related multiplicities, without encountering deep and fundamental contradictions. The first of these paradoxes was the one already discovered in 1897 by Cesare Burali-Forti. Burali-Forti's paradox concerns the size of the set of all orderable or "ordinal" numbers. Since this set itself can be considered as being an ordinal number, the question arises as to *its* size or magnitude; as Burali-Forti demonstrated, in fact, such a number must be, rigorously, both smaller than and bigger than itself. And just four years later, in 1901, the young Bertrand Russell, following out the consequences of the earlier results by Cantor and Burali-Forti, discovered the paradox of set membership that bears his name. Its consequences have resonated throughout the twentieth century's attempts to employ formal methods to clarify the underlying structures of logic and language.

In its most general form, Russell's paradox concerns the possibility of constructing sets or groupings of any individual objects or entities whatsoever. But since the operation of grouping or collecting individuals under universal concepts or general names can also be taken to be the fundamental operation of linguistic reference, it is clear from the outset that the paradox has important consequences for thinking about language and representation as well. In its historical context, Russell's formulation of the paradox bore specifically against Frege's logicist attempt to place mathematics on a rigorous basis by positing a small set of logical and set-theoretical axioms from which all mathematical truths could be derived. One of the most important and seemingly natural of these axioms was Frege's "universal comprehension principle" or "Basic Law V." The principle holds that, for *any* property nameable in language, there is a set consisting of *all* and *only* the things that have that property. For instance, if basic law V is true, the predicate "red" should ensure the existence of a set containing all and only red things; the predicate "heavier than 20 kg." should ensure the existence of a set containing all and only things heavier than 20 kg., and so on. As things stand, moreover, there is no bar to sets containing themselves. For instance, the property of *being a set containing more than five elements* is a perfectly well-defined one, and so according to Frege's principle, the set of *all* sets that contain more than five elements ought to exist. But since it has more than five elements, the set so defined is clearly a member of itself.

In this case and others like it, self-membership poses no special problem. But as Russell would demonstrate, the general possibility of self-membership actually implies a deep problem for the coherence of the natural-seeming universal comprehension principle. For (and here is the paradox) if the comprehension principle held, it would be possible to define a set (what is sometimes called the "Russell set") consisting of all and only sets that are *not* members of themselves. Now we may ask whether *this* set is a member of itself. If it is a member of itself, then it is not, and if it is not a member of itself, then it is. The assumption of a universal comprehension principle, in other words, leads immediately to a contradiction apparently fatal to the coherence of the axiomatic system that includes it.

Russell's demonstration of the paradox, which left Frege "thunderstruck," led him also to abandon the universal comprehension principle and to reconsider the most basic assumptions of his axiomatic system.[40] He would subsequently work on the reformulation of the foundations of set theory, given Russell's demonstration, for much of the rest of his life; it is not clear, indeed, that he ever recovered from the shock of Russell's remarkable discovery.

In a 1908 paper wherein Russell publicized the paradox and offered a detailed attempt to resolve it, he points out its close kinship to a variety of other formal and informal paradoxes, including the classical "liar" paradox of Epimenides, the paradox of the Cretan who says that all remarks made by Cretans are lies.[41] The paradox of the Cretan shares with Russell's the common feature that Russell calls *self-reference*:

In all the above contradictions (which are merely selections from an indefinite number) there is a common characteristic, which we may describe as self-reference or reflexiveness. The remark of Epimenides must include itself in its own scope . . . In each contradiction something is said about *all* cases of some kind, and from what is said a new case seems to be generated, which both is and is not of the same kind as the cases of which *all* were concerned in what was said.[42]

Each of the paradoxes he discusses results, as Russell suggests, from the attempt to say something about a *totality* (whether of propositions, sets, numbers, or whatever) and then to generate, by virtue of the definition of this totality itself, a case which, being a case, appears to fit within the totality, and yet also appears not to. Thus the remark of the Cretan, for instance, attempts to assert the falsehood of *all* propositions uttered by Cretans; since the scope of what it refers to includes itself, the paradox results.[43] Similarly, in Russell's own paradox, the apparent possibility of grouping together *all* sets with a certain property (namely, not being self-membered) leads directly to contradiction.

Putting things this way, indeed, it is clear that the paradox in its general form affects the coherence of several other kinds of totality that we might otherwise suppose to be more or less unproblematic. The totality of the *thinkable*, for instance, if it exists, presumably also has thinkable boundaries. But then we can define an element of this totality, namely, the thought of the boundaries themselves, that is both *inside* and *outside* the totality, and contradiction results. Even more fatefully for the projects of linguistic philosophy in the twentieth century, we may take *language* itself to comprise the totality of propositions or formulable sentences. But then there will clearly be meaningful propositions referring to *this* totality itself. Such propositions include, for instance, any describing the general character or detailed structure of language as a whole. But if there are such propositions, containing terms definable only by reference to the totality in which they take part, then Russell-style paradox immediately results. By way of a fundamental operation of self-reference that is both pervasive and probably ineliminable on the level of ordinary practice, language's naming of itself thus invokes a radical paradox of non-closure at the limits of its nominating power.[44]

As later developments of formalization and formal thought would spectacularly demonstrate, the underlying issue here is quite general, and appears to arise whenever any *totality* (or whole) is thought or invoked by means of something which is an element of that very totality. Thirty years later, two results deeply related to Russell's paradox would confirm the fundamental impossibility of a formalization of reason and language that achieves totality in its referential scope while avoiding paradox in its implications. These were the two infamous "incompleteness" theorems of Gödel.[45] By means, again, of diagonalization, Gödel demonstrated the possibility within any sufficiently complex formal system (for instance, the system of Russell and Whitehead's *Principia Mathematica*) of a sentence which "asserts" its "own" unprovability. The sentence is a "fixed point" produced directly by the diagonalizing technique of representing the system's regular structure of proof within itself. Given the existence of such a sentence, it is possible immediately to show that it is "undecidable"—that is, neither it nor its negation is provable—within the system itself. For, given that the sentence captures the logic of proof characteristic of the system as a whole, it is effectively able to "assert" that it, itself, is not provable. The sentence, then, cannot be proven, assuming that the system itself is consistent; for if it could be proven, a contradiction would immediately result. But neither can its negation; for a proof of the negation, i.e., that the sentence *can* be proven, amounts to a proof of the sentence itself, again resulting in a contradiction. Thus, by virtue of the existence of the formally undecidable sentence, the system is either *inconsistent* (in that it proves both a sentence and its negation, and so proves a contradiction) or it is *incomplete*, in that there is a truth—the truth of the Gödel sentence itself—that it cannot prove. Taking his theorem to demonstrate the latter, Gödel understood it to show a fundamental *incompleteness* of formal systems as such, an inability of any formal system ultimately to capture all of the truths of mathematics accessible to our own mathematical understanding.[46]

Though their implications differ in details, Russell's paradox and Gödel's theorems have often been compared, since their overall structures are remarkably similar. In particular, in both cases, a problematic element (the Russell set or the Gödel sentence) is produced by combining *totality* and *reflexivity*. The problematic element, in both cases, reflexively captures the total structure of the *whole* system (the universe of sets, or the formal system under consideration), of which it is a part, at a fixed, local point *within* that very system. Moreover, the historical upshot of both results was again quite similar. Whereas Russell's paradox was taken to spell the doom of Frege's own attempt to theorize the powers of language completely and consistently, Gödel's results, in an even more spectacular fashion, appeared to demonstrate the impossibility of any formalization of mathematical reasoning that combines both completeness (in its ability to capture *all* of the truths of mathematics) and logical consistency. In the first half of the twentieth century, in fact, both results were often taken together as demonstrating the fundamental untenability of the earlier formal projects of *logicism*, which had sought to reduce mathematical truths and objects to truths and laws of pure logic, and *formalism*, which had sought to reduce mathematical reasoning and inference to purely mechanical procedures.

However, further discoveries would confirm the rigorous applicability of these results to questions of meaning and truth, extending beyond the scope of these specific projects in the foundations of mathematics. In 1933, Alfred Tarski appealed to a result formally similar to Gödel's to argue that no formal language can specify the logic of its own truth-predicate.[47] That is, if we stipulate that the behavior of the predicate "true" for a language must be such that, for any proposition P, it is possible to assert:

"P" is true if and only if P,

then it is demonstrably impossible for the language to capture the logic of this predicate without inconsistency. The underlying reason for this is again the possibility of linguistic self-reference, as it figures in the classical "liar" paradox of Epimenides:

This sentence is false.

Given the possibility of such sentences—indeed, given the possibility of linguistic self-reference at all—it is readily possible to create sentences that "assert" their own falsehood, and so are apparently (given Tarski's schema) true if false and false if true. Therefore it is impossible, Tarski's result suggested, for any language *itself* to give a complete and illuminating description of what is involved in its own invocation of truth.

Formalists and mathematicians took the presence of each of these antinomies and contradictions (or indeed of any paradox at all) to be *intolerable* in the context of formal theories. Such theories, they typically supposed, must consist in rigorous, unified rules for rational thought admitting of no possible contradiction.[48] Thus, almost as soon as Russell discovered his paradox, he set to work trying to resolve it on formal grounds; indeed, he presents one influential attempt to do so in the 1908 paper. As we have seen, each of the paradoxes that Russell discusses depends on the formation of certain totalities which threaten to include themselves, thus leading to contradiction. If we wish to avoid paradox, therefore, this suggests that we must adopt some principle *prohibiting* the formation of the relevant totalities, or establishing that they in fact do not or cannot exist. In fact, because the paradox seems to demand that we abandon the universal comprehension principle according to which each linguistically well-formed predicate determines a set, it also suggests, according to Russell, that we must recognize certain terms—those which, if sets corresponding to them existed, would lead to paradox—as not actually capable of determining sets. He calls these "non-predicative" terms.

The problem now will be to find a principle for distinguishing predicative from non-predicative expressions. Such a principle should provide a motivated basis for thinking that the sets which would be picked out by the non-predicative expressions indeed do not exist, while the sets picked out by predicative ones are left unscathed by a more restricted version of Frege's basic law V. Russell, indeed, immediately suggests such a principle, what he calls the "vicious-circle principle":

This leads us to the rule: 'Whatever involves *all* of a collection must not be one of the collection'; or, conversely: 'If, provided a certain collection had a total, it would have members only definable in terms of that total, then the said collection has no total'.[49]

The principle, if successful, will bar paradox by preventing the formation of the totalities that lead to it. No set will be able to be a member of itself, and no proposition will be able to make reference to the totality of propositions of which it is a member; therefore no Russell-style paradox will arise. Nevertheless, there is, as Russell notices, good reason to doubt whether any such principle is even *itself* formulable without contradiction. The problem is that the very statement of the principle itself involves referring to self-membered totalities—such as the totality of propositions or properties—which are declared by the principle itself to be impossible to refer to.[50] The attempt explicitly to exclude the totalities whose formation would lead to paradox thus immediately leads to formulations which are themselves self-undermining in mentioning the totalities whose existence is denied.

In fact, as Russell himself notes, even if this problem can be overcome, the prohibition of the formation of totalities that include members defined in terms of themselves will inevitably lead to problems with the formulation of principles and descriptions that otherwise seem quite natural. For instance, as Russell notes, we will no longer be able to state *general logical laws*, such as the law of the excluded middle, holding that all propositions are either true or false. For the law says of *all* propositions that each one is either true or false; it thus makes reference to the totality of propositions, and such reference is explicitly to be prohibited.[51] Similarly, since we may take "language" to refer to the totality of *all* propositions, it will no longer be possible to refer to language in a general sense, or to trace its overall principles or rules as a whole.[52]

Nevertheless, Russell now turns to a more specific solution which, though also based conceptually on the vicious-circle principle itself, attempts to avoid the problems of the first attempt by means of a stricter formal regimentation. The underlying idea is to introduce rules that *effectively* prohibit the formation of any set containing either itself or any element definable solely in terms of itself, and thereby to block on axiomatic grounds the vicious circle that seems to result from self-membership.[53] This yields Russell's famous "theory of types," which aims to preclude self-membership by demanding that the universe of sets be inherently *stratified* into logical types or levels. According to the type theory, it is possible for a set to be a member of another, but *only* if the containing set is of a higher "type" or "level" than the one contained. At the bottom of the hierarchy of levels is a basic "founding" or "elementary" level consisting of simple objects or individuals that no longer have any elements; at this level no further decomposition of sets into their elements is possible.[54]

In this way it is prohibited for a set to be a member of itself; similarly, it is possible for linguistic terms to make reference to *other* linguistic terms, but in no case is it possible for a linguistic term or expression to make reference to itself, and the paradox is blocked. This general type of solution, in fact, underlies virtually *all* of the subsequent historical developments of set theory after Russell's work. For instance, a distinct but similarly motivated regulative attempt to prevent Russell's paradox is due to Zermelo and Fraenkel, and is preserved in the axiomatic system of the now-standard "ZFC" set theory.[55] In this theory, two distinct axioms work together effectively to prohibit the specific "impredicative" sets that Russell identifies as problematic. First, the axiom of "regularity" or "foundation" requires, of every actually existing set, that its decomposition yield a most "basic" element that cannot be further decomposed into other elements of that set or of its other elements. In this way, self-membership is again prohibited by requiring that each set be ultimately decomposable into some compositionally simplest element.[56] Second, the ZFC system includes an "axiom of separation," or *limited* comprehension; this is Zermelo's replacement for Frege's unlimited comprehension principle. Rather than holding, like Frege's principle, that a set exists corresponding to any predicate whatsoever, the axiom of separation holds that, *given* any existing set, it is possible to form the *subset* containing only the elements bearing any specific property. In this way the formation of the "universal" set containing all sets is apparently precluded, since it cannot be formed by means of separation from any existing set, unless it *already* exists.[57]

More generally, the intuition behind both Russell's type theory and the standard axioms themselves is captured by what has been called the standard "iterative conception" of sets.[58] On this conception, the universe of sets is inherently stratified into a hierarchical series of levels. It is possible for a set to be formed only from sets that are compositionally simpler, and at the simplest level there are only elements (either a number of so-called "ur-elements" or, in some versions, only the empty set itself) that are intrinsically simple and have no further set elements. It is thus, once more, possible to decompose any set into its compositionally simple elements, and at no point is it possible to form the total set of all sets, or, indeed, any self-membered set.

Thus, on all of the standard interpretations, Russell's paradox demands a conception of the universe of sets as *founded* on a basic level and rigorously ordered by increasing degrees of intrinsic complexity. This is a thoroughly *hierarchical* picture of the progression of totalities, regimented and ordered into a strict succession of levels of complexity or successive formation without any definite end or closure. Interestingly, the structurally similar results of Gödel and Tarski, though not applicable directly to set theory itself, have also usually been interpreted along analogous lines. In particular, almost as soon as they were derived, these "incompleteness" results were taken to demonstrate the need to supplement the internal, syntactic description of any language with a dimension of *external* meaning or reference, outside the capacity of the system under consideration *itself* to capture or model. In particular, given Tarski's own interpretation of his result as showing that it is impossible for a language to formulate its *own* concept of truth, it now appears necessary to consider the whole discussion of truth as taking place, not in the language itself under consideration, but rather in a *metalanguage* that can completely survey it. [59] Similarly, Gödel's result, which demonstrates the incapability of any sufficiently complex formal system consistently to represent its own logic of proof, was taken to demonstrate the existence of a metalanguage or -system which is capable of representing the proof logic of the original system, as well as the Gödel sentence for that language itself. Of course, the new system then generates its own, new Gödel sentence, calling for yet a third, stronger language to capture it, and so forth. In both cases, the price of the attempt to preserve both consistency and descriptive completeness is thus the iterated requirement to ascend an unlimited hierarchy of metalanguages, each of which can capture the logical structure of the one below it, but fails in attempting consistently to display its own.

This requirement of an irreducible and unlimited hierarchy of levels is structurally homologous to Russell's own type theory, which allows sets only to have members at a lower level or type than themselves, and indeed to the interpretation underlying all of the standard axiomatizations of set theory. Following Graham Priest, we can call this kind of solution (either in set theory or formal semantics)—which relativizes claims about language, truth, and reference to indexed types or levels—*parameterization*. As we have seen, type theory exploits this mechanism to prohibit self-membered sets, as does the more general "iterative conception" of sets itself. However, the price of this solution is again that it is apparently impossible to talk about the totality of all sets, or formulate in *any* terms the logic of a language that is *complete* in the sense that it can refer descriptively to anything that exists.

Parameterization, in all of its different versions, preserves consistency in the face of paradox and the threat of contradiction. But how successful is it as a strategy for actually *addressing* the underlying issues raised in all of these cases by the combination of totality and reflexivity? To begin with, even in the context of the axiomatic systems for which they were originally formulated, the restrictive devices of Russell and Zermelo/Fraenkel raise deep internal questions of motivation. As Hallett (1986) has argued, the attempt to avoid formal paradox has led virtually all of those who attempted the formal axiomatization of set theory to impose what amounts to various "limitation-of-size" principles. When faced with Russell's paradox and related paradoxes, each such axiomatization attempts to prohibit sets that are "too large" to exist, the "impredicative" sets, including the set of all sets, that would otherwise lead to contradictions. [60] Insofar as they explain the basis for such limitative devices at all, Russell, Zermelo, and other axiomatizers of set theory appeal to a *constructivist* picture: one, in particular, that holds that for a "new set" to be "formed" or "conceived" it is first necessary for its elements to be (already) "conceivable" or "available," either as simple elements or as constructed at an "earlier" stage.

This conception, as we have seen, effectively prohibits the problematic "impredicative" sets, and thus precludes the paradoxes and contradictions to which they would lead. However, as Hallett emphasizes, there is little reason to suppose that the picture's conception of the iterative operational *construction* of sets from others has any independent motivation whatsoever, beyond simply the desire to avoid paradox at whatever cost.[61] How are we to understand the metaphor of "construction" here? What kind of activity are we to suppose is involved in the successive "construction" of sets at various levels, or in their elements being "available" at "earlier" ones? The problem here (though this is *a* problem) is not *only* that the extension of constructivist intuitions to answer the question of the "formation" of infinite sets demands reference to an ideal *agent* capable of completing infinitely extended processes. Even worse, as Hallett points out, the motivation of the various "limitation-of-size" principles, even given the assumption of such an ideal agent, always involves an effective predetermination of which sorts of totalities are indeed "too big" to exist, and this requires reasoning about the very totalities whose existence is thereby being denied.[62] This is essentially the same problem that Russell had already anticipated, in acknowledging that the attempt to prohibit the "impredicative" sets risks undermining itself in its own statement. As Hallett emphasizes, *even when* the prohibition is imposed on the level of axioms rather than stated outright, this problem of self-undermining recurs as a problem of the *motivation* of the axioms themselves, which appear in many cases to have been historically based on constructivist pictures that are in themselves quite unmotivated. There is thus little reason to suppose that the use of limitation-of-size principles to attempt to prohibit totalities (including, as it may be, self-including ones) that we have not previously "constructed" or "made available" can be successful.

Here we face once again the profound question of the very possibility of the unity of the many as one, the question of the fundamental possibility of the formation of unities or totalities of any kind. As Russell's paradox and the related formal structures confirm, there is indeed a deep problem involved in the existence of such totalities as may naturally be thought to include themselves. This problem threatens the non-contradictory coherence of language itself, and the attempt of formalists from Russell to Tarski was accordingly simply to ban or foreclose the very possibility of such self-including or self-referring wholes.

However, the attempt to *prohibit* self-reference which yields all of these devices is also quite at odds with the actual commitments of ordinary speech and discourse. For instance, it is evident that expressions and propositions of ordinary language *can* refer to language itself; any systematic consideration of linguistic meaning or significance, after all, requires some such reference. Moreover, even beyond the possibility explicitly to *name* or *theorize* language as such, the problematic possibility of linguistic self-reference is, as Russell's analysis itself suggested, already inscribed in everyday speech by its ordinary and scarcely avoidable recourse to *deixis*—that is, to indexical pronouns such as "this," "I," "here," and "now." The real implications of the phenomena of totality and self-reference, as they figure in our everyday discourse and commitments, appear to be quite varied and profound. Without developing these implications exhaustively, I list four interrelated domains in which these phenomena are quite evident, and the attempt to foreclose them by means of parameterization, or limitation-of-size principles, accordingly quite implausible:

1) **Language.** Suppose I wish to speak about the very language I am using, e.g., English. For instance, I may wish to criticize the grammar of someone's utterance, or adduce general logical principles governing correct usage in English. I discuss the structure of the language overall, making reference to its constitutive principles using terms and expressions that are also in English. Supposing this reference is successful, it is precisely a situation in which an element or elements (those terms and expressions) succeed in making reference to the whole of which they are only elements. If Russell's type theory or any parameterizing solution were generally applicable, it would imply that such reference is impossible.

2) **Truth.** Very plausibly, what it is for an assertoric sentence to be true is for what it asserts actually to be the case. Thus, if I assert that "the cat is on the mat," then, barring ambiguity and failures of reference, what I have said is true *just in case* the cat is indeed on the mat. This is the intuition that is expressed in Tarski's "convention T," which holds that a legitimate truth predicate (Tr) may be characterized by the structure

   "X" is Tr *iff* X

   for all assertoric sentences of the language. It is very plausible that the predicate "true" in English fits this schema. However, if that is indeed the case, then it is another instance of a whole system (the logic of truth in English) being represented by one element within it, namely, the predicate "true" itself, and as we have seen, this leads necessarily to inconsistency.

3) **History.** It is plausible that our *representations* of historical events play a role in the constitution of these events themselves. For instance, the American Declaration of Independence plays a decisive role in the constitution of America as an independent state. Without any such declaration, the various activities and events of revolutionaries would not constitute the event of the independence of the U.S. itself. Thus,

here again, the total event of the independence of the U.S. from Britain is represented by one element within it.

4) **Sovereign Power.** As we have seen above, sovereignty, or the consistent rule of many by one, depends on an original paradox whereby the one must be both inside and outside the total order over which it rules. Since it derives its power from the whole, it cannot be simply outside it and so must be an element. But since it is able to rule over the whole, it must figure the entirety of its structure within itself.

5) **The Nomothesis.** In order for a new law legitimately to be instituted within a constituted political order, it is typically necessary for a leader or political body (such as a congress) to institute it. For the institution to be legitimate, this body must itself be legal and have (legally) the power to institute laws. Its power thus figures the entirety of the legal order, although it is just a single element within the scope of this order.

In each of these cases, both the Russellian gesture of prohibiting internal reference to the totality, and the Tarskian device of appealing to meta-languages, are strikingly implausible. We can hardly prohibit talk of language, or truth, or origins, or legality, while still preserving the structure of English (or any natural language). Nor is parameterization an option here, since there is no obvious metalanguage available in which to talk about the behavior of an ordinary language, such as English itself. Appreciation of this point leads to the suggestion that the problem of total self-reference that each phenomenon poses may not be well solved by the kind of parameterization that has been adopted in the context of formal languages, but that this problem may evince a fundamental set of paradoxes at the very boundaries of language and thought as such.

More specifically, all of these paradoxical situations are instances of what Graham Priest, in a far-ranging work, has formalized and treated as *limit-paradoxes* necessarily arising at the boundaries of thought.[63] Priest documents the arising and implications of such paradoxes in a wide range of philosophical projects involving accounts of limits, from Aristotle to Derrida. As Priest argues, it is possible to generate a formal limit paradox, or contradiction, *whenever* two formalizable operations are possible. The first operation is *closure*, which formalizes the conditions necessary for an element to be a member of a given totality (for instance, the totality of the sayable, knowable, or thinkable), thus essentially drawing the boundary of the totality in question. The second operation is *transcendence*.[64] *Transcendence* is any operation that, given a totality of a certain sort, can generate an element of a certain kind that is *outside* this totality. Its general paradigm is, again, diagonalization. Whenever an element satisfies both *closure* and *transcendence*, it is possible to generate a contradiction: the element both *is* (by *closure*) and *is not* (by *transcendence*) an element of the given totality. According to

Priest, this kind of contradiction at the limits of thought and language is just the formal version of paradoxes that have long concerned philosophers, and which result from any attempt to comprehend the boundary of any totality of thought or action to which the act of comprehension itself belongs. Since any such attempt necessarily, according to Priest, evinces the contradiction of an element that is both within and without the closure of the totality concerned, it is accordingly necessary to recognize at the very boundaries of thought and language an inherent structural form of contradiction, the paradoxical topology which we may, following Priest, term the *in-closure*.[65]

In each of these cases, it is admittedly *possible* to use parameterization to avoid paradox. Thus, for instance, it is possible to escape the paradoxes of truth arising from discussion within English of the English predicate "true" by affirming that it is possible to talk about this predicate only in a metalanguage that is not itself English; or we may affirm that it is only possible to name a historical event as such *after* it has taken place, and thus that the naming can take place only after the event has already determinately concluded. Or we may affirm that the legal power of the sovereign body in framing laws and conventions itself traces to a source that is not part of the legal order and cannot itself be legitimated by laws, a supra-legal source of mystical authority. But it is also clear in each case that parameterization is inadequate to the phenomena under consideration. We *do* talk about truth-in-English in English; and the representation of historical events *does* play a role in constituting them as such. Similarly, the appeal to a mystical authority is *itself* an event that plays a role in constituting this very authority. More generally, the devices of limitation and parameterization threaten to imply that we cannot use (our own) language to talk about (our own) language at all, which is clearly false.

We improve the situation by reconsidering what is involved in the underlying paradoxes themselves. As Priest has convincingly argued in an earlier treatment, despite their usual interpretation, these paradoxes are not in fact *intrinsically* such as to demand a solution in terms of parameterization.[66] In each case, the solution of parameterization implies that the original language we have used must be incomplete or inadequate to the phenomena: that there are important phenomena it cannot capture, including, for instance, the behavior of its own truth-predicate and indeed its own systematic logic.[67] However, the paradoxes by themselves do not necessarily *demonstrate* the incompleteness of any language, but rather face us with a choice, in the case of each actual language, *between* incompleteness and inconsistency.[68] Given the existence of in-closure paradoxes, we cannot preserve the completeness of the language, *on pain of inconsistency*; but we may indeed choose to shoulder the pain, or at least examine more clearly the underlying reasons for the forced choice itself.

In facing up to the paradoxes of self-reference, formal thought thus defines a fundamental choice: either consistency with incompleteness (and hence the prohibition of total self-reference, and the egress into an open iterative hierarchy of metalanguages) or completeness with inconsistency (and hence reference to paradoxical totalities). On the level of *formal* languages and systems, taken simply as neutral objects of description, either of these choices is evidently a possibility; we can save the consistency of our systems by ascending up the hierarchy of metalanguages or, as Priest suggests, we can model inconsistency within self-contained formal languages by means of what he calls a *dialetheic* logic, one that tolerates contradictions in certain cases. [69] However, if the paradoxes indeed have bearing on the *natural* languages that we speak every day, the *first* choice is, with respect to them, effectively blocked. [70] There is no distinct metalanguage to which we can retreat to render the underlying logic of English consistent; nor can we plausibly ban discussion of such phenomena as language, truth, and the law from the scope of these phenomena themselves. This general problem is, moreover, a feature of any natural language as such, for all natural languages are equipped with devices of self-reference that make reference to their own totalities possible (and problematic). Nor is the problem solved by using a *second* natural language—for instance, Chinese—to talk about the meaning of claims involving terms such as "truth" and "language" in English. For the problematic propositions in English (such as "Language as such is symbolic" or "Truth is Beauty") are best construed as formulating claims that are translatable into either language, and so would quickly lead to a repetition of the same problem. [71]

What, then, *is* the bearing of the somewhat aporetic results of the attempt to conjoin completeness and consistency on questions about the nature and structure of reason, thought, and language? There is a received and established attitude toward these paradoxes and aporias according to which, as demonstrations of the specific limits of the possibility of formalization themselves, they quite simply show the "impossibility" of formalizing the relevant structures of human thought and action. In the case of, for instance, Gödel's theorems, the demonstration of a fundamental "incompleteness" of any possible formal system is sometimes thought to show that *human* reason or mathematical thought is simply *incapable* of being formalized or treated formally at all. Certainly, it is true historically that Gödel's results played a major role in undermining the (reductive and foundationalist) program of "formalism" (as conceived, for instance, by Hilbert) which sought to produce a single formal system capable of accurately capturing *all* mathematical truths. However, although the argument for an irreducible specificity of human reason *vis-à-vis* formal systems has been made, it remains quite controversial, and highly questionable, whether it is actually *entailed* by the formal results themselves. [72] (We shall return to this question later, in Chapter 6.) At any rate, the aim here is not simply to decide upon the plausibility of such interpretations, but rather to reexamine the actual consequences of the formalisms for thinking about language, concepts, and community. These consequences can by no means be ascertained, it appears, if the formal results are taken to establish the existence of features or properties of human reasoning (or of the domain of mathematics in itself) that make it simply immune from, or exterior to, forms and the possibility of formalization.[73]

From this perspective, there is thus reason to think that the range of the bearing of Gödel's results upon interrelated questions of truth, meaning, and consistency extends much more broadly than their development simply in the context of formal systems like *Principia Mathematica* at first suggests. This is so not only because "natural" languages such as English bear within themselves exactly the resources of self-reference, reflexivity, and total expressive power that Gödel's theorems turn on in the case of "formal" languages but additionally because there is a further point of direct application to the very question of the structure of a language (*any* language) itself. This is the consideration that, if any symbolic language is to be learned and employed, it must consist of a *finite* corpus of symbols; but these must be capable of *infinite* iteration and application. There are classical arguments (e.g., by Davidson) holding that these considerations about learning and use *alone* establish that a ("natural") language must be, essentially, a finitely axiomatized or axiomatizable system.[74] But whether we accept these arguments or not, it is sufficient in order to see the relevance of the consideration of the structure of formal systems here to consider simply that there is essentially no alternative, if we are going to consider the *structure of a language* at all, to considering its structural principles and rules to be finitely expressible. Otherwise, we have (quite simply) no sense of what we are talking about in discussing its constitutive rules, regularities, and norms. Things are very much the same, as I shall argue, with respect to critical consideration of the structure and limits of communities. Here, as well, consideration of the problem of the force and authority of rules, laws, and norms itself demands an essentially formal reflection on the relationship of a finitely stateable rule to the infinite iterability of its consequences.[75]

Moreover, given the apparent forced choice between consistency and completeness, it is possible to specify the unified implication of the "formal" results in these domains quite precisely. In particular, given this forced choice, if parameterization and the decision for incompleteness (rather than inconsistency) are not an open option in the case of natural languages, then we are effectively forced to choose for *inconsistencies at the limits* of any system of thought or writing that can indeed represent itself. We are thus seemingly forced to the position that there are certain inherent contradictions, or inconsistencies, *involved in our very practice* of speaking (meaningful) language itself, contradictions not to be avoided as long as we *speak* or *think* about the totalities in which our very acts of speaking and thinking take part. Such contradictions are a problem for any (practical, philosophical, or political) project of enclosing these totalities within the assurance of a complete and consistent system. By the same token, though, they may also provide *opportunities* for the critical thought that challenges any such project.

Since Kant, critique has been understood largely as the practice of *tracing the closure of totalities*. This conception originates in the Kantian project of "limiting" knowledge to the boundaries of the experienceable and thus checking its claims to exceed those bounds, and continues in the various developments of the "critique of metaphysics" today. In its classical form, the critical project takes the shape of a consideration of the intrinsic limits of knowledge, which according to Kant may not exceed the fixed boundaries of intuitive givenness and the formal limitation of the categories. However, even in Kant there are already strong anticipations of the problem for critical thought that Wittgenstein makes explicit in his preface to the *Tractatus*:

> . . . in order to draw a limit to thinking we should have to be able to think both sides of this limit (we should therefore have to think what cannot be thought).[76]

The attempt to think the boundaries of thought, the closure of the totality of the thinkable, thus apparently demands of the critic an impossible perspective—a perspective that his very critical enterprise would tend to demonstrate to be impossible. But if the limit of a totality can only be reflected *within* that totality itself, then the critical position from which it can be traced can only be found along the diagonal that inscribes the law of the totality in some of the local, immanent moments subsumed to it. The price of this solution, however, is paradox: for as soon as the closure of the system can be reflected within the system itself, it is possible to generate out of this closure an *in-closure*. Such a point, like the Gödel sentence or the Russell set, belongs to the totality precisely in asserting of itself that it does not belong to the totality; with respect to it, there is therefore no *consistent* intra-systematic answer to the question of its belonging to the totality of the system. However, as we have seen, an extra-systematic answer is simultaneously ruled out by the original problem of perspective. For the solutions of parameterization or the invocation of metalanguages simply reinscribe the original problem of perspective once more. If, in each case, the critical tracing of the limit of a language, n, will only be possible in another language, n_1, then of course the constitutive principles of the language n_1, and hence the basis for the original tracing, will only be comprehensible by means of a third language, n_2. And then the possibility of *this* comprehensibility will only be comprehensible by means of a fourth language, n_3, and . . .

Thus, the phenomenon of undecidability immediately gives rise to the paradoxical structure of in-closure. From the point of its locality, the systematic possibility of decision—the systematic law of the totality of the system—is thinkable only, paradoxically, as *im*possibility; more generally, the closure of the boundaries of any system is thinkable only as its paradoxical in-closure. These terms—the "undecidable," the "conditions for possibility" as "conditions for impossibility," and the radicality of a critical practice that traces the closure of metaphysics as its paradoxical in-closure—are today familiar, most of all, from Derrida's long-standing project of deconstruction. From his first writings on Husserl and Saussure until the end of his career, Derrida sought to develop a writing that articulates the boundaries of the systems of metaphysics by tracing their paradoxical limits. However, the implications of this deconstructive method for the general questions involved in understanding the structure of language and the inherent limits of its conception as a rule-based structure are very close, as well, to those of the radical paradox of rule-following in Wittgenstein's *Philosophical Investigations*.[77] Here, as it is for Derrida, the question of what is involved in the practice of a language is very much the question of the possibility and force of rules, as these define the relationship between the (finite) sign and its (infinite) possibilities and contexts of use. In this precise sense, both Derrida's deconstruction and Wittgenstein's "therapeutic" practice of reflection on the often misleading terms in which language presents itself to itself can both operate as preeminent modalities of the critical reflection that considers what is involved in our relationship to the inconsistent totality of language as a whole. To fix terms, we may call this mode of criticism, in distinction to the older (Kantian) *criteriological* mode that seeks to draw and define a fixed boundary to language from a stable, transcendent position outside of it, the *paradoxico-critical* mode.[78]

AGAMBEN: LINGUISTIC BEING, STATE OF EXCEPTION, AND THE COMING COMMUNITY

We have seen, then, that the logical and metalogical results of Russell, Gödel, and Tarski, if taken as bearing on the fundamental issues of totality and reflexivity, suggest the existence of fundamental and structurally inherent *in-closure* contradictions at the limits of thought and language. What consequences do these rigorously developed formal results have for the critical theory of social structures and communities?

In a far-ranging 1990 analysis, Giorgio Agamben treats the worldly existence of language, as it is revealed through the endurance of the paradoxes of self-reference, as the potential site of a "community" of singulars that would no longer be definable either in terms of a commonly shared *identity* or the subsumption of individuals under the universality of a *concept*.[79] The underlying basis of this "coming community" is the possibility of grasping and appropriating the paradoxes of linguistic meaning:

> The fortune of set theory in modern logic is born of the fact that the definition of the set is simply the definition of linguistic meaning. The

comprehension of singular distinct objects *m* in a whole *M* is nothing but the name. Hence the inextricable paradoxes of classes, which no 'beastly theory of types' can pretend to solve. The paradoxes, in effect, define the place of linguistic being. Linguistic being is a class that both belongs and does not belong to itself, and the class of all classes that do not belong to themselves is language. Linguistic being (being-called) is a set (the tree) that is at the same time a singularity (*the* tree, *a* tree, *this* tree); and the mediation of meaning, expressed by the symbol ∈, cannot in any way fill the gap in which only the article succeeds in moving about freely.[80]

What Agamben here calls "linguistic being" is the capacity of any object or phenomenon to be named, its entry into the totality of language itself. If this totality of language cannot, on pain of paradox, be named, and yet its naming cannot be prohibited by any mandate or stipulation on the level of the sayable, then reference to this capacity will recurrently define the place of a fundamental gap or aporia between the general name and the individual things it names. In the case of any particular thing, if we should attempt to describe its "linguistic being" or its capability of being-named, we will then find, as a result of Russell's paradox, that this capacity is itself unnamable. The very condition for the nameability of any thing is its liability to be grouped with similar others under a universal concept, but this liability is, by dint of the paradox itself, without a general name. The paradox thus reveals, behind the possibility of any belonging of individuals to a universal set in terms of which they can be named, the paradoxical nonbelonging of the name itself.

It is in terms of this nonbelonging that Agamben describes the "whatever being" or *quodlibet ens* that, while neither object nor concept, defines the being of a singularity as simply the *being-such* (*quale*) of any thing:

> *Whatever* does not . . . mean only . . . "subtracted from the authority of language, without any possible denomination, indiscernible"; it means more exactly that which, holding itself in simple homonymy, in pure being-called, is precisely and only for this reason unnamable: the being-in-language of the non-linguistic.[81]

Defined by the nonbelonging of the name to the totality it names, "whatever being" is not, according to Agamben, either universal or particular; instead, it characterizes any singularity in a way that "reclaims" it *from* belonging to any class or set in order that it can simply be such as it is. In thus escaping the "antinomy of the universal and the particular," its place is, according to Agamben, akin to that of the paradigm or *example* in relation to the category it exemplifies.[82] The example used to illustrate or demonstrate a general category stands, in paradoxical fashion, for the entirety of that category despite being itself nothing more than an indifferent element among others. Thus being neither simply inside nor outside the category it exemplifies, but rather bearing witness to this category through its indifferent membership, the example demonstrates, according to Agamben, the "empty space" of a purely linguistic kind of being in which singulars are not defined by any property other than their pure being-called, their pure entry into language.

The communication of singularities without identity in the empty space of the example is therefore, according to Agamben, the unfolding of a "linguistic life" that is both "undefinable" and "unforgettable"; subtracted from any identity or belonging to particular classes or sets, its exemplars appropriate to themselves the identifying power of language itself.[83] In this appropriation they define, according to Agamben, the potentiality of the "community to come," a community of beings without discernible identity or representable common properties. Irrelevant to the state and so incommensurable with its logic, the possibility of this community will define the political or post-political struggles of the future for a redeemed human life that is simply its own linguistic being.[84]

The implications of Russell's paradox and the associated issues of self-reference therefore allow Agamben to characterize the twentieth century's philosophical recourse to *language* as involving the discovery or revelation of something like a universal presupposition to all discourse whose problematic existence nevertheless marks the limit or threshold of the concept of identity as it has traditionally organized political and philosophical thought.[85] With this revelation, the singularity of every being's being-such, marked obscurely in the "as such" that, according to an established phenomenological discourse, defines the structure of *apophansis* or demonstration, comes to light as an explicit determination of the "being" of every being.[86] The basis of this revelation is simply the disclosure of language itself as that which, as Agamben puts it in a series of texts, has no name of its own.[87] The consequent anonymity of linguistic being defines the nameless presupposition of the name, the bare belonging of singulars as such that preconditions every possible naming of them. The anonymous place of this precondition, which never defines a real predicate of beings, can then be seen, Agamben suggests, as that of what a traditional philosophical discourse recognizes as transcendence, or as the hitherto obscure basis for Plato's identification of the *idea* as the anonymous power that defines each singular thing, not as individual thing under the unity of the concept, but indeed as "the thing itself."[88]

As Agamben clarifies in the 1979 text *Language and Death*, the empty place of language is marked incessantly, in language's everyday *praxis*, by the presence of those indexical and demonstrative expressions that Jakobson, drawing on Benveniste's earlier analyses, termed "shifters."[89] According to Jakobson, these pronouns (such as "this," "I," "here," and "now") have no proper meaning of their own, since their meaning shifts or alters on each new occasion of use. Rather, their significance in each case depends on the concrete context of their utterance, on the actual linguistic performance or instance of concrete discourse in which they figure. It is in this sense, according to Agamben, that the constant occurrence of shifters in ordinary discourse bears witness, within that discourse, to the problematic taking place of language itself.[90] The linguistic reflection that reveals this dimension as that of linguistic being, or of the actual taking-place of concrete discourse, then also reveals the place of this precondition as that of the very paradox of self-reference that Russell first demonstrated. Like the example, deixis bears witness to the paradoxical status of what is constantly presupposed in the everyday production of any kind of meaningful speech whatsoever: the passage from abstract *langue* to concrete *parole* in the ever-renewed practice, use, or "application" of language in concrete instances of discourse.

In taking up the radical consequences of the problematic appearance of "linguistic being" in the world, Agamben can thus cite the demonstrative structures of deixis and the example as paradoxical markers of what underlies and founds the possibility of naming itself. In summoning a representative that is fully individual and yet stands for the whole universal class, the structure of the example is that of a kind of "exclusive inclusion," a demonstration of the general structure of inclusion within what is normal that nevertheless operates by excluding the exemplary, in the very moment of demonstration, from the normal case. Its exact inverse is then what Agamben calls the "exception." Thus, Agamben says in *Homo Sacer*, whereas the example operates as an "exclusive inclusion," the structure of the exception is exactly opposite: it is an "inclusive exclusion" which operates covertly to include and integrate what is ostensibly excluded.[91] Thus, while both exemplarity and exceptionality depend on a crossing of the traits of belonging and nonbelonging, and thereby demonstrate the paradox at the basis of the operation of grouping or the property of belonging itself, they do so in inverse fashion, evincing the power involved in grouping or naming from opposite directions. In the crossing that they both thus involve between the universal and the particular, both help to demonstrate the normally obscure but inherent structure of the "operation" of set grouping itself. Like the paradoxes of linguistic self-reference, they bear witness to a constitutive power of the name in presenting things, a power that ordinarily hides itself in the order of things presented. This power is the power of language, or of the ordinary constitution of the common that groups distinct individuals under general names and subsumes individual cases under concepts.

Agamben sees in this power of grouping whose basic ambiguities are shown by the opposed figures of the exception and the example, indeed, not only the basic operation of linguistic naming but the underlying basis of the *force of law* itself. For the originary power of language to subsume individuals under general concepts, beyond making possible the linguistic naming of anything at all, also underlies the *application* of laws, rules, or norms (which are general in their scope) to the particular cases of fact or action that fall under them. Here, as Agamben emphasizes, the operation of force depends not simply on any general logical or conceptual function that itself could be specified in abstract terms, but rather on the actual activity of a speaking subject in passing from the abstract rule to the particular case.[92] The application of law, referred by Kant to a faculty of judgment capable of mediating between the general and the particular, thus depends in each case on the same structure of subsumption that defines linguistic being as such. In both cases, the movement from the general to the particular depends on the appropriation of a power of grouping that allows the passage from the abstract structure of *langue*, the system of rules constituting and governing language as such, to the concrete reality of actual speech (or *parole*) and decision. The reflection that demonstrates the paradoxical foundations of this operation by marking its place, then, also points out the problematic practical basis of the specifically constituted power that underlies the force of the law in each particular case.[93]

In *Homo Sacer* and the more recent *State of Exception*, Agamben develops the connection first drawn by Carl Schmitt between sovereignty and exceptionality. As we have seen, according to Schmitt, the sovereign power defines the space of the political by its power of *deciding on the exceptional case*.[94] The ordinary application of law depends on the constitution of an order of normality in which the law is conceived as applicable. But for this order to be founded, it is first necessary, according to Schmitt, for a sovereign power to constitute itself as sovereign by deciding on what counts as normal and what counts as exceptional. This implies, as well, that it remains a permanent and structurally necessary prerogative of the sovereign to decide when facts or circumstances demand the *suspension* of the entire normal juridical order. It is, indeed, the sovereign's power to decide when an exceptional case of facts or "emergency" circumstances justifies the suspension of the entire order of law that marks the sovereign's original and founding position as simultaneously both *inside* and *outside* the order of law which it founds.

A typical example of this suspension of the ordinary rule of law—which, once performed, tends to become irreversible—can be found in Hitler's 1933 suspension of the articles of the Weimar Constitution protecting personal liberties, which essentially created the Nazi state.[95] But in the politics of the twentieth century, the total or partial suspension of the rule of law in favor of the state of exception is not, Agamben suggests, limited to those states identifiable as "totalitarian," but has become "one of the essential practices" of a wide variety of states, including those that describe themselves as democratic.[96] Contemporary politics, Agamben suggests, indeed tends to make the "state of exception" increasingly ubiquitous and thereby constitutes the space of the political as a growing zone of indeterminacy or ambiguity between "public law and political fact." Within this zone, the application of law to the determination and control of life becomes both pervasive and radically indeterminate, leading to the contemporary situation of "global civil war" in which state powers struggle both to produce and to control the "bare life" of the living being as such.[97]

The paradoxical structure of sovereignty, upon which is founded its power to determine the distinction between the normal and the exceptional, law and fact, is thus in fact formally identical to the Russell paradox. The sovereign, on Schmitt's analysis, is that which must be able to decide, in each possible case of fact or action, on the normalcy or exceptionality of the particular case. But in reserving to itself the power to declare a state of exception, and thus to suspend the entirety of this order, the sovereign demonstrates its exceptional position with respect to the entirety of ordinary distinction between normalcy and exceptionality itself. The very power to choose is neither normal nor exceptional; like the Russell set, it both includes and does not include itself.[98] It follows that the very power that decides between the normal and the exceptional, and hence applies the law to determinate cases, rests on a foundation of paradox even in its most ordinary operation.

The seeming prohibition of this paradox, within a specific, constituted legal order, makes it possible for law to function without its paradoxical foundations coming to light. Correspondent to the gesture of Russell and Zermelo, the stipulative or axiomatic sovereign interdiction of the paradox makes it possible for the ordinary operation of decision or grouping to appear to function routinely without the fundamental instability that actually underlies the normal order appearing as such. At the same time, the actual ineliminability of the underlying paradox is nevertheless shown in the arbitrariness and lack of motivation of the interdiction itself. Under the condition of an actual exercise of the power that the sovereign always reserves to itself (that is, an actual declaration of the state of emergency or exception), the paradoxical structure underlying sovereign power again comes to light explicitly and comes to determine the field of politics as a growing zone of indistinction between law and fact.

BADIOU: THE EVENT OF THE NEW

Since at least the *Theory of the Subject* of 1982 (comprising seminars held from 1975 to 1979), Alain Badiou has attempted in an unparalleled way to think the ontological and political implications of formalism. One of the most significant outcomes of Badiou's thought is his application of formal methods to what has also become an obsession of contemporary continental philosophy, the problem of theorizing the "event," or the transformative eruption of the essentially unforeseeable *new* into a given, determined situation.[99] According to a problematic already developed and pursued by

Heidegger, such genuine novelty demands, as well, a fundamental break with all that can be said with the language of the metaphysical tradition, including all that is expressed or expressible by the "ontological" language that comprises everything that can be said *of* what *is*. For Badiou, in order to develop such a theorization of novelty as such, it is thus necessary first to model the "ontological" regime of being, insofar at least as it can be described, in order thereby to develop a rigorous schematism of what occurs or takes place beyond this regime. This schematism will then be the schematism of the event itself, what is completely unpredictable in terms of the ontological order of being, but nevertheless can suddenly intervene within it to produce dramatic and radical structural novelty and change.

In *Being and Event* (1988), perhaps the most central axiom of Badiou's project is the identification of *ontology* itself with mathematical set theory. The axioms or principles of set theory that found mathematics will, according to Badiou, amount to a formal theory of whatever simply is. This identification proves essential not only to his description of the form and limits of a "fundamental ontology" of being, but to defining the possibility of the event as that which, although *heterogeneous* to being, nevertheless can occasionally intervene *within* it to bring about radical change. In particular, Badiou takes the axiom system of ZF set theory to present the very structure of presentation itself, what we may think of as the minimal structural conditions for anything to be presented as *being* or *existing* at all (since every being is a *presented* being). In this precise sense, according to Badiou, the axioms and structures of set theory present being itself, and thus serve formally to delimit the range of ontology, with which the event structurally breaks.

In the more recent *Logics of Worlds*, Badiou continues this analysis with a formal consideration, based this time on category theory, of the primarily linguistic establishment and transformation of the boundaries and structure of particular situations of appearance, or what he calls "worlds."[100] Here again, the possibility of any fundamental transformation in the structure of a particular, constituted situation depends on a formally characterized breach of the laws of ontology, a kind of "retroaction" by means of which an ontologically errant set-theoretical structure allows what was formerly utterly invisible suddenly to appear and wreak dramatic substantive as well as structural changes. In both of Badiou's major works, the interpretation of structures that have been considered "foundational" for mathematics thus operates as a kind of formalization of the limits of formalism themselves, which in turn yields radical and highly innovative interpretations of what is involved in thinking both the structuring of situations as such and the possibilities of their change or transformation.

One of the most far-ranging of these innovative consequences of the interpretation of formalism, as Badiou points out, is that it renders the *infinite* mathematically (and hence, according to Badiou, *ontologically*) thinkable. In particular, Cantor's theory of multiple infinite sets, which is at the very foundation of contemporary set theory in all of its versions, yields a well-defined mathematical calculus which allows the "size" or cardinality of various infinite sets to be considered and compared. This symbolism has, as Badiou emphasizes, profound consequences for the ancient philosophical problem of the one and the many, and hence for any systematic consideration (mathematical, ontological, or political) of what is involved in the formation and grouping of elements into a larger whole. [101]

In the first pages of *Being and Event*, Badiou describes set grouping or unification as the result of a fundamental operation of "counting as one" which forms an indifferent multiplicity into a structured one that can indeed be "counted" or presented as such.[102] The outcome of this operation is the formation of anything that can indeed be understood as a presented whole with any structure whatsoever; all investigation of the effects of structuration and formation on any existing situation can therefore proceed from an investigation of the possibilities and properties of this fundamental "count-as-one." Following Cantor's own terminology, Badiou calls the successful result of this operation—an actually existing set, be it finite or infinite—a "consistent multiplicity"; before the count-as-one, there are only "inconsistent multiplicities" which precede any formation into ones, and so indeed cannot be thought or conceived mathematically (or ontologically) at all.[103] The distinction between consistent and inconsistent multiplicities, so described, is to be regulated, Badiou holds, by an axiom system that implicitly defines which sets can exist (and hence also which multiplicities *cannot* be grouped as sets at all).[104]

This appeal to the axiomatic structure of set theory and the consequent need to avoid the formation as sets of any of the "too-large" inconsistent multiplicities forms the backdrop to the first and most general of the axiomatic "decisions" that comprise Badiou's own systematic ontology. This is the decision of the "non-being of the one" from which, as Badiou says, his "entire discourse" originates.[105] According to this decision, "the one *is not*"; fundamentally, there are only multiples and multiplicities (i.e., sets). These multiples can indeed, in general, be grouped into ones by the action of structure, or the "count as one"; what cannot exist, however, is the "One-All" or universe that would result from the grouping together of *everything* that is.

Badiou presents this axiomatic decision against the One-All as a fundamental rejection of the legacy of Parmenides and, indeed, of the entire ontological tradition he founded.[106] But although his rejection of the One-All is, like other significant decisions, axiomatic, Badiou does not hesitate to give a justification for it in terms of set theory. This justification turns on Russell's paradox and the related paradoxes, which led Russell and subsequent logicians to seek devices to prevent the possibility of forming certain problematic sets, such as the set of all sets, or indeed any set that is a member of itself.

As we have seen, the Russellian "theory of types" is one such device, as are the axioms of foundation and separation enshrined in the now-standard axiom system of Zermelo-Fraenkel set theory. For the purposes of ontology, Badiou follows the tradition of logicians in both prohibitions, holding that since the existence of a contradiction would "[annihilate] the logical consistency of the language,"[107] the problematic sets cannot be formed, or in other words that the problematic multiplicities, including the multiplicity of all multiplicities, do not exist as Ones. The universe described by language is thus, according to Badiou, essentially and fundamentally *incomplete*. This result provides formal grounds for the basic decision "against the One-All," which, Badiou holds, must be maintained by any systematic, axiomatic theory of being itself. Thus:

> Inconsistent or 'excessive' multiplicities are nothing more than what set theory ontology designates, prior to its deductive structure, as pure non-being.
>
> That it be in the place of this non-being that Cantor pinpoints the absolute, or God, allows us to isolate the decision in which 'ontologies' of Presence, non-mathematical 'ontologies', ground themselves: the decision to declare that beyond the multiple, even in the metaphor of its inconsistent grandeur, the one is.
>
> What set theory enacts, on the contrary, under the effect of the paradoxes—in which it registers its particular non-being as obstacle (which, by that token, is *the* non-being)—is that the one is not. (p. 42)

Since the "count-as-one" is thus itself the precondition for the existence of any entity as such, it is impossible further to theorize its operation or preconditions; however, once we are presented with various multiplicities as existing unities, we may consider the possibility of further operations of counting and regrouping. In particular, a set is formed out of a number of elements, but these elements may again be regrouped as subsets—or, as Badiou says, "parts"—of the initial set. Thus, for instance, the set containing Alain, Bertrand, and Cantor has three elements, but it has eight subsets; the set containing only Alain and Cantor is one of these, as is the set containing only Bertrand, and the empty set is a subset of every set. If we now gather together these eight subsets into a new unity, we obtain what is called the *power set* of the initial one. If the initial set, for instance, is *a*, then the power set *p(a)* is the set of all its subsets.

As Cantor demonstrated with the theorem that bears his name, the size of the power set (the number of elements it has) is always greater than the size of the initial set itself. Since the power set re-gathers all the possible groupings of elements present in the first set, it may thus be considered to re-count, in a faithful but nevertheless productive way, the elements counted as one in the initial grouping. This re-counting Badiou terms "representation," and identifies the distinction between the initial set and its re-counting in the power set with the distinction between *presentation* and *representation* quite generally. If the initial set is what Badiou calls a "situation," then its power set is termed the "state" of this situation; it contains whatever, presented in the initial situation, can again be regrouped and re-presented as a one in representation.[108] This distinction gives Badiou a rich and promising set of terms in which to discuss the difference between nature and history, the break with the natural order that comes with the first representational recounting of its terms, and the originary violence of the state that this recounting first makes possible.

Badiou's model for *nature*, plausibly enough, is the series of natural numbers: 0,1,2,3 . . . He follows the canonical technique for defining these numbers in terms of sets; on this technique, 0 is identified with the empty set, 1 is the set containing only the empty set, 2 is the set containing 0 and 1 (thus defined), and so forth. Using this technique, each natural number can in fact be defined as the set containing all of its predecessors. It follows that the natural numbers, within the hierarchy they themselves define, are what Badiou terms "normal."[109] That is, restricting ourselves to the natural numbers, if any natural number is *presented* in a situation, it is also *represented* in the state of that situation.[110] The number 5, for instance, contains as elements the numbers 0,1,2,3, and 4; each one of these (take, for instance, 3) contains only elements (0,1, and 2) that are also independently presented in the original situation; the state of the situation, regrouping these again, will re-present the original element (3) they comprise. In this case, in the gulf between presentation and representation, nothing essentially new emerges; representation simply reorders what was already presented without bringing anything new to light. That all of a situation's terms be normal in this sense is, for Badiou, the mark of its being a "natural" situation; in such situations, the very conditions requisite to eventual change are absent, since representation can only reorder possibilities that were already fully present at the level of the initial situation.

Quite different is the case of what Badiou terms "historical" situations. In these situations, an element may contain further elements that are not already presented independently elsewhere in the situation. Badiou calls such an element, which contains others not independently presented, a "singular" term; a singular term, while *presented* in the initial situation, will not be *represented* by the situation's state. Or the state may bring forth, through its regrouping, elements that were nowhere presented in the original situation; Badiou calls these "excrescences."[111] The possibility of excrescences is particularly significant, since it will be through these that the event works its consequences on the situation in which it intervenes.

The political register of the "state" metaphor is deliberate, and provides the basis for one of the most interesting political suggestions of the book.

It is that representative politics, even in its most democratic forms, works fundamentally not by representing the individuals who comprise a state but at one essential remove from them, by representing them only *qua* the subgroupings or constituencies in which they may be considered to participate.[112] Thus the state, as necessary as we may see its existence to be, is according to Badiou always essentially *excessive* with respect to the individuals whose interests it claims to address; its excess is that of representation over presentation, of the names and concepts that define groups and constituencies over the members of those groups themselves. It follows that any real intervention in a constituted political order is as much an intervention on names as it is on their bearers. Genuine political change, in other words, does not result simply (or even much at all) from the "collective" action of individuals, but rather from the formation of fundamentally new groupings and political identities. Thus, any possibility of genuine change depends on developing the latent possibilities of the names and concepts that are already circulating in order to undermine the logic of the existing situation. Such a self-nominating, in which the nominal intervention on what *will have happened* itself plays the most decisive role in determining what *has* happened, is what Badiou will term an "event"; with its doctrine, he will attempt to show how this paradoxical nominalization can be conceived as breaking not only with the constituted political order but indeed with all ontology, and thus as summoning forth "from the void" of ontological presentation the possibility of genuine novelty.

As we have seen in the last section, within the universe of ontology as identified by Badiou with ZF set theory, both Russell's paradox and the phenomena of self-membership or self-reference that lead to it are barred by fundamental axioms. The axioms of foundation and separation that most directly block, within ontology, the Russell paradox from arising do so by demanding that, in order for a set to be formed, there must already be some other existing being or beings from which it can be composed. They thus express, according to Badiou, the necessity that, in order for any determinate thing to be presented, there must already be something else; their role in the fundamental axiomatics of set theory demonstrates that ontology cannot establish, but must simply presuppose behind the description of whatever is, a more fundamental "there is . . ." of being itself.[113] The simplest such element demanded by the axioms of set theory is the so-called *empty set*, the set containing nothing; its existence and uniqueness are assured by another fundamental axiom. The empty set, in containing nothing, is the compositionally simplest element that assures that there is something in existence already, before anything else can be named or constructed.

In this sense, Badiou suggests, the empty set, what we may take to be the "name of the void," sutures or ties the universe of set theory to the basic assumption of being, thus constituting the order of ontology. The introduction of this name depends, however, on a fundamental act of *self-reference* or *auto-nomination*:

Naturally, because the void is indiscernible as a term (because it is not-one), its inaugural appearance is a pure act of nomination. This name cannot be specific; it cannot place the void under anything that would subsume it—this would be to reestablish the one. The name cannot indicate that the void is this or that. The act of nomination, being a-specific, consumes itself, indicating nothing other than the unpresentable as such. In ontology, however, the unpresentable occurs within a presentative forcing which disposes it as the nothing from which everything proceeds. The consequence is that the name of the void is a pure *proper name*, which indicates itself, which does not bestow any index of difference within what it refers to, and which auto-declares itself in the form of the multiple, despite there being *nothing* which is numbered by it.

Ontology commences, ineluctably, once the legislative Ideas of the multiple are unfolded, by the pure utterance of the arbitrariness of a proper name. This name, this sign, indexed to the void, is, in a sense that will always remain enigmatic, the proper name of being.[114]

Within the universe of what is, the empty set preserves a kind of mute reminder of what founds existence, the bare auto-nomination that introduces a first element from which everything else can be built. The axioms that block Russell's paradox by prohibiting self-reference within ontology thus nevertheless necessarily introduce a non-specific element that can only have come to exist through a paradoxical self-nomination. This element, summoning forth existence from the void, preserves in ontology the mark of what precedes or exceeds it, the "nothing" that cannot be presented as such in any of its multiples.

In this way the power of auto-nomination to call forth existent sets, though explicitly prohibited within ontology by its fundamental axioms, nevertheless proves essential in grounding its most basic presupposition, the presupposition of a "there is . . ." of being prior to any determinate set or property. Beyond this, according to Badiou, the name's power of self-reference, prohibited within ontology, will indeed prove to be the most essential single characteristic that marks the self-reflexive structure of the *event* which, beyond being, nevertheless occasionally intervenes within it. For the schema that portrays the infinite potentiality of the event breaks with the axiom of foundation by *explicitly asserting* that the event is a member of itself. This self-membership will simultaneously make the event indiscernible to ontology and assure the role of a paradoxical self-nomination in calling it forth from what must *appear to ontology* to be the void.[115] For the event is not simply constituted out of already existing elements, but rather, in recounting these already existing elements, calls itself into existence through its own power of auto-nomination.

To demonstrate how this works, Badiou develops the example of the French Revolution. The name "The French Revolution" encloses or refers to a vast variety of the individual "gestures, things, and words" that occurred in France between 1789 and 1794. But its ability to determine these various and multiple facts and circumstances as counting as one in the unity of an event depends, as well, on the moment at which the revolution names itself, and so calls itself into existence *as* the event it will have been:

> When, for example, Saint-Just declares in 1794 that 'the Revolution is frozen', he is certainly designating infinite signs of lassitude and general constraint, but he adds to them that one-mark that is the Revolution itself, as this signifier of the event which, being qualifiable (the Revolution is 'frozen'), proves that it is itself a term of the event that it is. Of the French Revolution as event it must be said that it both presents the infinite multiple of the series of facts situated between 1789 and 1794 and, moreover, that it presents itself as an immanent resume and one-mark of its own multiple . . . The event is thus clearly the multiple which both presents its entire site, and, by means of the pure signifier of itself immanent to its own multiple, manages to present the presentation itself, that is, the one of the infinite multiple that it is.[116]

The event's occurrence will therefore depend on its grouping together or re-counting as one both various elements of the situation in which it intervenes (Badiou calls the set of these elements the event's *site*) and, by a fundamental operation of auto-nomination, it itself. According to Badiou's schema, given any evental site X, the *event* for that site can therefore be defined thus:

$$e_x = \{x \in X, e_x\}^{117}$$

The event is the set composed of, on the one hand, all the elements of its site, and on the other, itself. The self-inclusion of the event allows it to summon forth a novelty previously indiscernible to the situation, to designate itself and so to call itself into existence as what will have taken place, its own appearance in the historical situation its occurrence will have transformed.

The self-inclusion or self-reference of the event also proves essential to answering the question Badiou next takes up, namely, whether the event will already have been *presented* as a term in the situation in which it intervenes. The question is a decisive one; because of the event's logic of self-inclusion, the answer to it will determine the happening of the event itself, whether it will have taken place within the situation or whether it will remain forever exterior to what is. But also because of this logic of self-inclusion, nothing on the level of the existent situation can, by itself, decide this essential question. For any element presented in the already existing situation to be the event, it would have to be clear that it includes itself. But this is just what cannot be clear on the level of the situation. It is possible only, as Badiou argues, to trace the consequences of the two divergent hypotheses, that the event will, or will not, have taken place in the situation.[118] If the event *does* take place, then it will be singular in the situation. For it presents the elements of its site, and these elements are not individually presented in the situation itself. The event, if it will have taken place, is therefore nevertheless not represented; it is indiscernible to the state and its representative re-counting. Re-counting or representation can never verify its having taken place; nothing representable on the level of the situation will be able to demonstrate it as being the event that it is. Nevertheless, on the assumption that it does take place, its having taken place will allow it to add itself to its site, "mobilizing" the elements of this site in a way that is essentially indiscernible to representation. It remains, however, perfectly consistent to maintain the opposite hypothesis: that the event has not taken place, that it has not been presented in the situation. If this is the case, then the event presents nothing that is also presented in the situation (not even itself); so from the perspective of the situation, it presents only the void. On this hypothesis, *nothing* will after all have taken place; if the signifier or name of the event nevertheless succeeds in being spoken, in adding itself to the situation, *nothing* will be named by it.[119]

In either case, whether we assume the event to have taken place or not, the question of whether it will have taken place cannot be settled in any regular way from the perspective of the situation alone. It follows, according to Badiou, that "only an interpretative intervention can declare that an event is presented in a situation."[120] Such an intervention will amount to a decision on what is, from the perspective of the situation, undecidable; it will itself force the taking place of the event that it itself calls into existence. It operates by drawing from the eventential site an *anonymous* or *indifferent* "name" or signifier, which is then declared to be the name of the event itself. Such an operation of decision or interpretative intervention will thereby summon the event into existence from what seems to be, from the perspective of the situation, only the void; it amounts to "the arrival in being of non-being, the arrival amidst the visible of the invisible."[121] Having thus been introduced, the event's existence will also elicit various consequences, now (because of the event) presented in the situation itself. Badiou terms the operation of tracing out these consequences, or recognizing them within the situation, *fidelity*. Finally, in a radical inversion of traditional substantialist or transcendental theories, the *operator* of fidelity, what traces or discerns the infinite consequences of the event within the situation, is termed the *subject*.

As Badiou recognizes, the biggest possible threat to the doctrine of the event, thus defined, will be posed by the claim that the event's paradoxical self-nomination is indeed impossible. A systematic basis for this objection can indeed be found in the orientation of thought that Badiou, generalizing the program of Brouwer and Heyting, calls *constructivism*.[122] The essential intuition of constructivism is that what can be said to exist at all is controlled and determined by what is *nameable* in a well-defined language:

> What the constructivist vision of being and presentation hunts out is the 'indeterminate', the unnameable part, the conceptless link . . . What has to be understood here is that for this orientation in thought, a grouping of presented multiples which is indiscernible in terms of an immanent relation *does not exist*. From this point of view, the state legislates on existence. What it loses on the side of excess it gains on the side of the 'right over being'. This gain is all the more appreciable given that nominalism, here invested in the measure of the state, is irrefutable. From the Greek sophists to the Anglo-Saxon logical empiricists (even to Foucault), this is what has invariably made out of it the critical—or anti-philosophical—philosophy par excellence . . . Furthermore, within the constructivist vision of being, and this is a crucial point, *there is no place for an event to take place.*[123]

For the constructivist, the universe of existents is limited to that which can already be named among what already exists. The power of the event's faithful operator to discern the indiscernible, to pick out the anonymous part of the situation that will be named as the event, and so called into existence, is thereby explicitly precluded. The constructivist orientation can, moreover, be schematized precisely; it allows for the construction of a universe of sets which, though infinite, are restricted to the condition that each existing set must be constructible out of already existing ones by means of the predicates already defined in a language. In the spirit of Russell's theory of types, the constructivist orientation therefore prohibits Russell's paradox by prohibiting the construction of any self-membered set. If its claims about being and language are correct, there will never have been any event, since no set will have the event's almost paradoxical structure of self-membership. It is therefore essential to the success of Badiou's argument for the possibility of the event that he demonstrate, on formal grounds, the possibility of an alternative to constructivism. This is accomplished, in the final chapters of the book, by his complex appeal to Cohen's technically sophisticated set-theoretical methodology of forcing.

FOUR ORIENTATIONS OF THOUGHT

On its face, Badiou's attempt to articulate symbolically the advent of novelty which occurs, for him, beyond the limits of "what can be said of being qua being" threatens to put Badiou—like others who have attempted to trace the "closure" of the "language of metaphysics"—in a somewhat paradoxical and even self-undermining position. This is the dilemma (familiar to readers of the early Wittgenstein) of the philosopher who would speak of what is by his own lights unspeakable, who would attempt by means of symbolic language to trace the very boundaries of the sayable in order to indicate what lies beyond. One sort of solution to this dilemma (which is, of course, not without its own problems) lies in the Wittgensteinian attempt to discern, beyond the ordinary signifying function of language in saying, an ineffable "showing" capable of operating where language exceeds its own bounds and thus falls into nonsense. Badiou, however, solves the problem in a very different way, one that suggests a radically different understanding of the significance of formalization itself. For faced with the dilemma of the demonstration of the unsayable, which cannot, on pain of contradiction, amount to a significative use of language, Badiou foundationally and completely disjoins the formalisms of mathematics from language itself. Thus he attempts a formalization both of all that is sayable of being *and* of what lies beyond this regime by means of the abstract (and, for Badiou, wholly non-linguistic) schematisms of mathematical set theory. For according to Badiou, where language cannot speak, the formalisms of mathematics, definable purely by their abstract transmissibility, beyond the constraints of any particular language, can nevertheless display the structure of the sayable, as well as the structure of the event which necessarily lies beyond it.[124]

Badiou is indeed right to hold that the paradoxes establish a fundamental result, transformative for all systematic consideration of the one and the many, in challenging the attempt of traditional metaphysics to think an unproblematically unified totality, the traditional "One-All" of the universe of all that exists. However, with respect to the formalisms themselves, there is an important alternative here which Badiou does not so much as acknowledge. For as we have already seen, it is not at all the case that the Russell paradox simply *forces* the decision *against* a One-All, or a set of all sets. For we may, by means of various alternative devices, *affirm* the existence of the total set while nevertheless acknowledging the Russell paradox. One way to do this is to permit axioms allowing the existence of self-membered sets, including the total or "universal" set, while still prohibiting the problematic Russell set itself.[125] Alternatively, we may tolerate the existence of the Russell set and the other contradictory sets by *allowing the existence of certain contradictions*—contradictions that characteristically arise in the course of thinking, or talking, about the limits of a totality in which the act of thinking or talking *itself* is a member.[126] Something directly analogous holds as well with respect to Gödel's (first) incompleteness theorem. As we have already seen, although the theorem is usually called the "incompleteness" theorem, it in fact faces us with a decision *between* incompleteness and inconsistency. Affirming the consistency of the formal system in which it is formulated (for instance, *Principia Mathematica*), we may take it that the result shows that this system is *incomplete*. But we may also just as well take it to show that the system is *inconsistent*, i.e., that there is some proposition, A, such that it proves *both* A and its negation.

More generally, then, we might put the situation as follows. It is not in fact the case that the implications of the Russell paradox or any of the related semantic paradoxes immediately force us to reject, as Badiou claims, the "One-All." The effect of the paradox is rather to *split* the One-All into two interpretive hypotheses and force a decision between them. *Either* we may reject the "All" of totality while *preserving* the "One" of consistency—this is Badiou's solution—or, alternatively, we may preserve the All of totality while *sacrificing*, at least in certain cases, the One of consistency. From a metalogical perspective, in view of the reflexive paradoxes and antinomies, there is, in other words, a rigorous duality or dichotomy, what we may call the *metalogical duality* between consistency (with incompleteness) and completeness (with inconsistency).[127] The first alternative is Badiou's; but the second, as I shall demonstrate, essentially defines the possibility of a *different* theoretical/critical orientation, one which certainly shares with Badiou's "generic" orientation his essential rejection of both constructivism and traditional metaphysics, but is nevertheless capable of underlying very different critical positions and results.

In a suggestive chapter from his 1998 book *Briefings on Existence*, Badiou describes what he sees as three possible "orientations in thought."[128] In each of the orientations, as Badiou notes, what is at stake is the relationship of thinking to being itself, the relationship famously named by Parmenides in the assertion that "The Same is there both for thinking and for being" or that "being and thinking are the same."[129] Each "orientation," then, regulates this relationship, or this possibility of thought to comprehend the infinite totality of being, by authorizing in different ways the inscription or assertion of existence.[130]

Since each orientation thus preconditions the thinkability of being as a whole, we may indeed take them to amount to a series of positional total relations to the infinite totality of what is, or what is sayable of it. And then we may see in philosophy a privileged domain of reflection on what is involved in these different ways of being oriented toward being itself, of "setting up" or "laying out" what it means to be.

So, what are the possible orientations in thinking, understood as possible relations to the totality of being as such, or as sayable? Badiou distinguishes among three, two of which we have already encountered. The first is what Badiou calls the "transcendent" orientation:

> The . . . transcendent orientation works as a norm for existence by allowing what we shall coin a 'super-existence.' This point has at its disposal a kind of hierarchical sealing off from its own end, as it were, that is, of the universe of everything that exists. This time around, let us say every existence is furrowed in a totality that assigns it to a place.[131]

What Badiou terms the transcendent orientation, thus, sets up the totality of beings by reference to a privileged being, a "super-existence" that assures the place of everything else, while at the same time obscuring its own moment of institution or the grounds of its own authority. Thus, the totality is conceived as the determined order of an exact placement of beings, while it is covertly regulated by an exemplary Being, conceived as superlative, transcendent to the order of things, and ineffable in its terms. Here, in a gesture typical of philosophy from Plato up to Nietzsche, the being of norms is assumed in the figure of a privileged, sovereign Being, while the basis of their authority is not further examined. Here as well, infinity is thinkable only in terms of such a sovereign Being, as the transcendence or ineffability of a singular Absolute wholly beyond the finitude of human life and existence, whose excess is simultaneously cloaked with obscurity. Without further ado, we may appropriate Heidegger's term (and indeed his whole description of it) for this orientation: thus, we term it the "onto-theological" orientation.[132]

The second orientation is also one we have already discussed. It is the one that is implicit in traditional nominalism, as well as in some forms of critical thought since Kant, but reaches its full methodological expression only with the twentieth-century linguistic turn. This is the orientation that relates to the totality of what is sayable about Being by means of an explicit tracing of the structure and boundaries of language; Badiou terms it "constructivist":

> [The constructivist orientation] sets forth the norm of existence by means of explicit constructions. It ends up subordinating existential judgment to finite and controllable linguistic protocols. Let us say any kind of existence is underpinned by an algorithm allowing a case that it is the matter of to be effectively reached.[133]

Here, with the "constructivist" (or, as we have termed it, "criteriological") orientation, the totality of existence is regulated by the discernable protocols of a meaningful language, comprehensible in themselves and capable of distinguishing between the sayable and the non-sayable. Thus, reflection on the (presumably determinate) structure of language yields a kind of critical enterprise that involves the drawing of a regulative line between sense and nonsense, or between the sayable and what cannot (within the determinate norms definitive of a language) be said. In some of its most exemplary forms, this is the project of a kind of limitative *policing* of the sayable; the verificationism of Carnap and Ayer is a prime example. Here, the totality of the sayable is itself understood as comprehended by the determinate syntactical rules for the use of the language in question, and thus as not only a *bounded* but a *finite* whole, outside of which it is possible for the theorist or the inventor of languages unproblematically to stand.

The "political" correlate of this orientation is thus the conventionalism that sees the totality of *a* language as wholly perspicuous from outside its determinate bounds, but forecloses or ignores the question of the possibility of *language*, or meaning, *as such*. Since it is always possible to stand outside a determinate language and specify its principles, it is always possible to exceed a determinate, bounded language with another one. Thus, the criteriological (constructivist) orientation can grasp infinity only as the *potentially* infinite openness of a successive hierarchy of types, or metalanguages, each one of which can grasp all of those beneath it, but at the cost of its own possible capture by a still higher language. This is the orientation at the root of *parameterization*, which attempts to resolve paradox by way of the inscription of a rigorous and unending hierarchy of types or languages.

Finally, Badiou poses as the third possibility the "generic" orientation that determines his own project in *Being and Event* and elsewhere. This orientation differs from the other two, at least, in insisting upon the relevance of actual and multiple infinities to our understanding of being as such. Arising in this way from the event of Cantor's discovery of multiple infinities, it takes into account (where the other two do not) the implications of the *self*-representation of the infinite totality, formally figured by diagonalization:

> The third orientation posits existence as having no norms, save for discursive consistency. It lends privilege to indefinite zones, multiples subtracted from any predicative gathering of thoughts, points of excess and subtractive donations. Say all existence is caught in a wandering that works diagonally against the diverse assemblages expected to surprise it.[134]

Thus, applying no norm *other than formal consistency*, the *generic* orientation relentlessly pursues, along the diagonal, the existence of all that which escapes constructivism's limitative doctrine of thought. Indeed, it is one of the most impressive accomplishments of Badiou's *Being and Event* rigorously to formalize both the constructivist and the generic orientations in terms of set theory. Badiou thereby shows how the apparatus of set theory leaves open the possibility, beyond anything constructivism can allow, of the "generic set" which, though real, is completely indiscernible within ontology, and hence also the possibility of the extension of any determinate situation by means of a generic "forcing" of the indiscernible which realizes, at its infinite limit, a new truth. This is the *coup de force* involved in Badiou's appeal to Cohen, which he takes to authorize the doctrine of the event that shows the inherent limitation of any constructivist theory and which ensures, for Badiou, that there can indeed be a schematism of the advent of the radically new, beyond what any existing language can possibly figure.[135]

Badiou's generic orientation is thus one that takes account of the paradoxical possibility of self-reference, indeed passing through such self-reference to generate the doctrine of multiple infinities and draw out the transformative consequences of Cohen's technique of forcing. In so doing, though, Badiou takes the generic orientation to refute *any* critical appeal to the structure or nature of language (which he assimilates uniformly to the constructivist orientation). Does it in fact do so, though? Or is there, in fact, *another* possible method by which thought, figuring the radical paradoxes of self-belonging and totality that find expression in diagonalization, Russell's paradox, and Gödel's theorem, can relate to the totality of what can be said, or of what is?

In fact there is another orientation, one that is fully cognizant of these paradoxes and yet does not refuse the relevance of internal linguistic reflection in the way that Badiou's generic orientation does. We have already met it: it is the *paradoxico-critical orientation* that operates by tracing the destabilizing implications of the paradoxes of self-reference at the boundaries of the thinkable, or sayable. That this orientation is indeed fundamentally different from Badiou's, despite its common passage through the paradoxes of self-reference, is already suggested by the very different relation it bears to the analysis of the structure of language. That is, whereas Badiou's generic orientation (officially at least) positions itself beyond or before all reflection on language and its structure, the paradoxico-critical orientation depends crucially, as we have seen, on the possibility of language self-referentially to figure itself by displaying its own structure (even if this figuring will necessarily be paradoxical).[136]

With this in mind, we can now specify the most basic distinction between Badiou's generic orientation and the paradoxico-critical one. It is this: given the paradoxes that force a choice, whereas Badiou's generic orientation decides *for* consistency and against completeness, the paradoxico-critical orientation is based on the decision *for* completeness and against consistency. Thus, whereas Badiou's generic orientation maintains the methodological aim of consistency at all cost, up to the point of denying the existence of a whole or totality at all, the paradoxico-critical mode typically works by *affirming* the existence of a totality (of all that can be said, or of the world, or of Being) and tracing the contradictions and antinomies that thereby arise at its boundaries and at its reflexive center. It does *not* necessarily seek a resolution of these contradictions, but indeed finds them to be necessary to the structuration of the relevant totalities that it considers. Thus, by contrast to Badiou's decision against the One, paradoxico-criticism can be considered to be committed to the relentless *affirmation* of the One, regardless of its being constitutively rent by the paradoxes of in-closure at its boundaries. It is in this fashion that it performs its critical work, tracing and documenting the complex topology of in-closure *without* attempting to resolve it into a univocally consistent doctrine of being.

By arranging the four orientations, we obtain the following schema, which displays some interesting symmetries and relations.

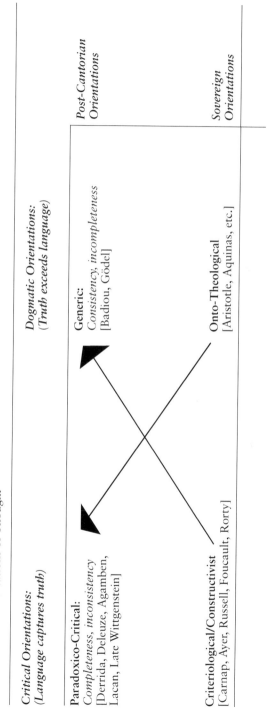

Table 1.1 Four Orientations of Thought

Critical Orientations:
(Language captures truth)

Dogmatic Orientations:
(Truth exceeds language)

Post-Cantorian
Orientations

Sovereign
Orientations

Generic:
Consistency; incompleteness
[Badiou, Gödel]

Onto-Theological
[Aristotle, Aquinas, etc.]

Paradoxico-Critical:
Completeness, inconsistency
[Derrida, Deleuze, Agamben,
Lacan, Late Wittgenstein]

Criteriological/Constructivist
[Carnap, Ayer, Russell, Foucault, Rorty]

We can also give brief definitions of the four orientations, differentiated according to their attitudes toward the totality of language, the thinkable, or being:

Paradoxico-critical: Any position that, recognizing reflexivity and its paradoxes, nevertheless draws out the consequences of the being of the totality, and sees the effects of these paradoxes always as operative within the One of this totality.

Generic: Any position that, recognizing reflexivity and its paradoxes, denies the being of the totality and sees these paradoxes as traversing an irreducible Many.

Criteriological/Constructivist: Any position that attempts to delimit the totality consistently from a stable point *outside* of it.

Onto-Theological: Any position that sees the totality as complete and consistent in itself, though beyond the grasp of finite cognition, which is located simply *within* the totality.

On the one hand, the paradoxico-critical orientation is clearly distinct, as we have seen, from the criteriological orientation that seeks to delimit being by means of an investigation of the fixed structure of a language. Rather than promote such a limitative doctrine, it takes account of the paradoxes of self-inclusion (which make it impossible to preserve both consistency and completeness simultaneously) in order to trace the fundamentally paradoxical structure of limits and limitation, up to the paradoxes involved in the fact that language appears in the world at all. A closely related distinction concerns the question of a metalanguage, for instance, a language *distinct* from English in which it would be possible to describe the structures of truth and meaning exhibited by the English language itself. As we have seen, the criteriological orientation of Russell and Carnap, which begins by attempting to specify the bounds of a single language by means of a description of its rules, invokes not only one but indeed a whole hierarchy of distinct metalanguages, each one necessary in order to describe the constituent structure of the one underneath. Paradoxico-criticism, by contrast, refuses to countenance any such metalanguage, affirming (though it may indeed lead to paradoxes) that a natural language such as English bears within itself all the resources (problematic though they may be) for talking about its own constituent structures.

On the other hand, the paradoxico-critical orientation is also distinct, as we have just seen, from the generic orientation. In particular, these differ fundamentally in how they consider the status of totality: whereas the generic orientation saves consistency by denying completeness, the paradoxico-critical orientation *affirms* an inconsistent totality, documenting the inconsistencies that inherently arise when language ventures (by a necessity of its own structure that can hardly be denied) to speak the whole as One. Here, the point of paradoxico-criticism is, though, not simply to insist upon this One but also to show how the most rigorous One essentially *becomes* many as soon as it passes through the "unifying" function of language, thus producing the gulf between the sign and its reference.[137] This radical gulf, present and unforeclosable beneath every ordinary use of language, is figured by the paradoxes of self-inclusion and self-reference that occur at the point of the manifestation of language itself, the point of a necessary indistinction between signifier and signified, where the very logic of language is manifest syntactically.

The two orientations at the top of the diagram both thus have it in common that they result from *differing* reactions to the paradoxes of total self-inclusion already implicit in Cantor's original definition of the set; in this respect they are distinct from the two orientations at the bottom, which must both, thus, be considered to be *pre-Cantorian* in maintaining the possibility of jointly preserving consistency and completeness. We may call these bottom two orientations, equally committed to the thought and praxis of a *total* social whole untroubled by any fundamental inconsistency, the *sovereign* orientations.[138] We can also distinguish categorically between the two orientations on the left and the two on the right. In particular, both "left" orientations share a *critical* motivation grounded in reflection on the structure of *language*. For both of these orientations, it is necessary, in understanding the possibility of speaking being at all, first to pass through (and do we ever emerge?) a deep reflection on language and its formal structure; it is in this way that they both figure the relationship of formalism to what is. For the two orientations on the right-hand side, Badiou's generic orientation as well as the traditional onto-theological one, by contrast, the structure of language ultimately determines neither what *is* nor what can *appear*; whatever is consequent upon the structure of language *per se* is itself secondary to the existence of beings and truths which may transcend or escape it. Of course, Badiou's generic orientation is not thereby equivalent, either, to the onto-theological doctrine of transcendence; whereas the (pre-Cantorian) orientation of onto-theology lodges truth in the privilege of a singular, obscure, and transcendent super-Being, Badiou's generic orientation sees truth only in the infinite procession of generic multiplicities, without end or higher synthesis.

Thus we may group the two orientations on the left as *critical* doctrines of language; whereas those on the right are *dogmatic* doctrines of truth. (I do not mean this term to be pejorative, here, but simply to indicate the point of their common *insistence*: that there must be some truth beyond language, whereas the orientations on the left are linked in refusing to consider truth outside its possibility for linguistic expression, however this possibility may manifest itself.)

Finally, there are also revealing connections along the diagonals. The diagonal from constructivism to the generic represents the common norm of *consistency*. This is as much a norm for (for example) Carnap's constructivism as it is for Badiou's relentless pursuit of mathematical structures; it is marked both in the absolute privilege of logical rules and the assumption that language, in order to discern a realm of Being, must maintain its consistency at all points. From onto-theology to paradox-ico-criticism, on the other hand, we may draw the line of *totality* (or completeness); for both orientations involve the assertion of an actually existent whole. This is evident, for instance, in the very direct way that paradoxico-criticism interrogates the position of the sovereign Being that assures the order of the totality within onto-theology; for in order to interrogate the force and authority of such a sovereign, it is necessary first to acknowledge and then to interrogate its actual relationship to the whole (of which it is, invariably, also an element). Just as profoundly, the diagonal line of consistency that links constructivism to the generic orientation denies or forecloses the existence of the totality by asserting the non-all, whether in the form of constructivism's infinite open hierarchy of metalanguages or the generic orientation's infinite procession toward the multiplicity of truths. The point of crossing of the two lines is, once again, the paradox of self-inclusion (in its Cantorian, Russellian, Gödelian, or Tarskian forms), which makes it impossible to preserve consistency and completeness simultaneously.

POLITICS OF LOGIC: FIRST LOOK

I have argued for the necessity of a pursuit of formal reflection that is simultaneously both political and logical, operating as a consideration on the lived consequences of formalism, and hence on the reflexive possibilities and limits of the formalization of formalism as such. If this kind of reflection is indeed pursued further, several consequences could result.

The first of these would be, as we have seen, a new kind of broadly critical thought about political structures. This kind of thought is already evident, in fact, in Agamben and Badiou, and we can recognize it retrospectively as already determinative in the thought of Wittgenstein and Derrida. It is a thinking of the possible forms of political life that passes through a profound reflection on formal structures, their application, and their limits. The aim of this kind of thought is not (as it is sometimes today argued) to "ontologize" politics but rather simply to demonstrate the implications of general phenomena such as inclusion, representation, organization, and the desires for consistency and totality, as these are thought and modeled formally, for the questions of political life.

At the same time, though, the new political thinking of logic also offers to comprehend and interrogate in a much closer way than has hitherto been possible the more complex and diffuse structures of power that operate through the formalization of life in today's "late capitalist" and post-industrial cultures, as these structures expand their claims of power and totality around the globe. As has been noted, the primary manifestations of the strategies and claims of power in the age of so-called "globalization" are no longer, for the most part, single "totalitarian" or onto-theological figures of the One, but rather (much more in constructivist fashion) the more diffuse and plural flows and networks of information and capital, as they are interlinked with networks of corporate, technical, and military power. Because these networks depend on the innovations of computational and communicational technology that are themselves the outcome of the radical experience of logic that has transformed the twentieth century, the politics of logic as I have described it is well suited to understand the basis of their power and the foundation of their effectiveness.

As I have argued, the *essential* innovation of a thinking of politics that inherits the formal innovations of the twentieth century, and thus marks it off from the political-philosophical orientations that have hitherto existed, is its consideration of the paradoxes of self-inclusion and self-reference, whereby the systematic law of the totality is reflected and figured at a specific, fixed point within it. By acknowledging the necessity of these paradoxes and tracing their implications, it seems, it may be possible for a futural thinking of community to transcend the very terms in which the twentieth-century debate over the foundation and potentialities of community has so far been conducted. For to affirm the radical paradox of nomothesis is to acknowledge the untenability of *either* a naturalist *or* a conventionalist account of the origin and institution of language and norms. It is thus to begin to discern a radical alternative to the debate between the (typically leftist or constructivist) politics of contingent historical conventions, on one hand, and the (typically rightist or onto-theological) politics of an assumed "human nature" or a divine dispensation, on the other. Indeed, as I have argued, if the originary structure of logic can be grasped as the locus of a politics of *formal* agreement or attunement that (as Wittgenstein suggests) *precedes* the possibility of any empirical (whether sociological or biological) agreement or disagreement on conventions or norms, then it becomes possible to overcome on this basis the whole debate about the fixedness or relativity of norms, regularities, or principles. That is, if, as I have suggested, the politics of logic can articulate and trace the pervasive orientations of contemporary thought as founded only upon their own suppression of the paradoxical position of reflexivity that is actually constitutive for anything like a political order as such, then it can just as thoroughly overcome, through its traversal of the paradoxes, the political versions of the two pre-Cantorian orientations. These two are, respectively, onto-theology and conventionalism; and if the romance of the political thought of the twentieth century (beginning with Nietzsche and continuing through Foucault and Rorty) has been the constructivist replacement of onto-theological positions by means of the adumbration of contingencies, the "liberatory" demonstration of the "actual" historical foundations of the presumptive institutions of force previously cloaked with the mystifying aura of authority, it is therefore possible to begin to anticipate that twenty-first-century political thought is today moving toward a discussion of quite different problems and structures.

Part II
Paradoxico-Criticism

2 Origins of Paradoxico-Criticism
Structuralism and Analytic Philosophy

As I have argued, the consequences of formalism today face critical thought with distinctive challenges as well as new opportunities. Indeed, it is the conjoint legacy of the parallel development of broadly *formal* methods and results in both the "analytic" and "continental" traditions of twentieth-century philosophy that probably alone makes possible something like a unified reception of both. In the following chapters, I describe and exhibit, by means of a series of examples, a shared "paradoxico-critical" orientation that can indeed, as I argue, capture the most important elements of the contemporary legacy of the twentieth-century critical approaches of continental and analytic philosophy alike. The distinguishing characteristics of this orientation, in both its continental and analytic forms, are: i) an elaboration of paradoxes or antinomies concerning the limits of language and involved in the syntactic or symbolic manifestation of the structure of language as such and ii) the critical use of such paradoxes to contest and destabilize assumptions about the consistency or coherence of this structure, or what is thought to authorize, originate, or maintain it, either on a theoretical or a political/practical level. In both its analytic and continental versions, the paradoxico-critical orientation, along with the formal paradoxes that define it, originates historically with internal problems encountered in the course of attempts to theorize language as a *structure* of signs or symbols. As I have argued elsewhere, both the analytic tradition in its methodological specificity and the structuralist tradition originating from Saussure owe their specific foundation to such attempts.[1] In this chapter, I shall briefly narrate the remarkably *parallel* development of paradoxico-criticism from earlier structuralist projects in both (the analytic and the continental "structuralist") traditions.

In their initial formulation, such structuralisms typically take the critical form of the *criteriological* orientation I have discussed in the introduction. Seeking to adumbrate structural principles and rules underlying the possibility of sense, they attempt a *juridical* regulation of language based on an examination of what are seen as its original founding principles. The spontaneous political philosophy of this orientation is *conventionalism*. For here, the original connection between signs and their meanings,

although liberated from any assumption of resemblance or direct representation, is instead seen as a matter of the arbitrary, conventional institution
of rules constitutive of the language as a whole. However, the criteriological attempt to delimit language by means of an elucidation of its structure
leads, almost inevitably, to a series of formal paradoxes that destabilize the
boundary-drawing project as well as its spontaneous conventionalism, as
soon as language is itself conceived as a *total* object of (linguistic) description. This demonstration, I shall argue, fundamentally influences the development of both the analytic and the continental traditions in the twentieth
century. More specifically, it leads, in both cases, to the breakdown of the
criteriological project, and can further lead to the replacement of this project with the paradoxico-critical orientation I describe here.

STRUCTURALISM

Saussure

The structuralist project of twentieth-century continental thought in philosophy, anthropology, psychology, linguistics, and the variety of related
fields once termed the "human sciences" begins with Ferdinand de Saussure's elaboration of a structuralist picture of language, most notably in
the *Course in General Linguistics* (1906–11).[2] The most radical and historically transformative aspect of Saussure's conception is his treatment
of *language as a whole* as a system or structure of *signs*, and of linguistic
meaning as a systematic effect of this structure.

The basic "unit" of language is, for Saussure, the sign. Such signs include
not only words in the narrow sense, but indeed any perceptible item that
also accomplishes signification, or has a meaning at all. Saussure thus recognizes two dimensions or aspects to every sign: a sensible or perceptible
aspect by virtue of which it signifies, and a non-sensible and imperceptible
dimension of what is signified. The sign is thus, for Saussure, the unity of
two elements, what he calls the "sound-image" or *signifier* and the "concept" or *signified*. Although the first, the signifier, is "sensory," Saussure
does not conceive it directly as a material object. Instead, it is a "psychological imprint" on our senses, for instance, the image or impression made
by the sound of a word. The "concept" or "signified" is, by contrast, the
idea or thought signified; it has no sensory component but is simply a "psychological" object of thought.

The sign requires both elements, in coordination, to be the sign that it
is. However—and decisively for the entire structuralist picture—Saussure
holds that the connection between a particular signifier and its particular signified is always *arbitrary*. One and the same signified, for instance,
the concept *tree*, can be signified by any of the various diverse signifiers:
"tree"; "Baum"; "arbor"; etc. This is enough, Saussure argues, to show that

there is, in general, no *natural* link between signifiers and their signifieds. Instead, the connections are, Saussure suggests, fixed in the case of each language by convention. Thus:

> The arbitrary nature of the sign explains . . . why the social fact alone can create a linguistic system. The community is necessary if values that owe their existence solely to usage and general acceptance are to be set up; by himself the individual is incapable of fixing a single value.[3]

Although Saussure does not give any detailed picture or account of the *institution* of language as such, he considers the arbitrariness of the linkage between signifier and signified itself to demonstrate the essentially social and conventional character of the entire system of language. "Every means of expression used in society," he says, "is based, in principle, on collective behavior or—what amounts to the same thing—on convention."[4]

In speech (*parole*), signifiers become manifest, over time, in sequence. We can thus, according to Saussure, think of the actuality of speech as a *dual* series of signs, in which the chain of auditory signifiers runs along in parallel with the chain of signifieds. The two parallel chains are, according to Saussure, like two sides of a sheet of paper, or two parallel streams. These are at first like "two parallel, shapeless masses" but they are given articulation by being broken up into discrete "thought-sounds" or signs.

This leads Saussure to the most novel suggestion of the entire structuralist picture. It is that language as a whole is a system of *pure differences*, without positive terms. In particular, since the connection between the particular signifier and the particular signified is itself completely arbitrary, each term of each of the two parallel chains or series (the series of signifiers and the series of signifieds) must be defined wholly in terms of the other elements of its own series. Accordingly, each element (whether signifier or signified) has its "value" only in relation to all of the others, and has its specific place in the entire system only by virtue of the system of its differences with these others. The properties of signification are thus defined wholly by the *differences between* significant elements, rather than by the intrinsic properties of the elements themselves. Indeed, as Saussure says:

> Everything that has been said up to this point boils down to this: in language there are only differences. Even more important: a difference generally implies positive terms between which the difference is set up, but in language there are only differences without positive terms.[5]

Like the "conventional value" of money, which does not reside in the intrinsic properties of the material token (for instance, a coin) but rather in the shifting system of exchange that fixes it, the "value" or meaning of any linguistic element (including, Saussure says, not only spoken words and phonemes but written words and letters as well) is determined only by its differential relations to all of the other elements of the system in which it is a part.

Lévi-Strauss

Saussure's conception of language would soon provide the systematic vocabulary and much of the inspiration for the vast structuralist movement, which by the 1950s extended from linguistics proper to anthropology, psychoanalysis, philosophy, literary interpretation, and the theory of history. One of the most influential representatives of the movement was the anthropologist Claude Lévi-Strauss, who used the Saussurian picture of language to understand the systematic structure of kinship relations, systems of gift exchange, and the role of taboos in determining and regulating social behavior. For Lévi-Strauss, all of these systems were regulated by structural "codes" definable in terms of comprehensive systems of difference and completely separable from the volitional action of any individual subject. Thus, as Saussure had already suggested, the systematic study of social relationships becomes equivalent to the study of the abstract, differential relations exhibited among signifiers as they are used in a community. Indeed, as Lévi-Strauss wrote in the *Introduction to the Work of Marcel Mauss* in 1950, the work of structuralism in its tracing of the autonomous effects of language is:

> ... not a matter of translating an extrinsic given into symbols, but of reducing to their nature as a symbolic system things which never fall outside that system except to fall straight into incommunicability. Like language, the social *is* an autonomous reality (the same one, moreover); symbols are more real than what they symbolize, the signifier precedes and determines the signified.[6]

As in Saussure's original picture, the total phenomena of language and social life are, here, comprehensible only in terms of the differential structure and action of the two series of the signifiers and signifieds. However, as Lévi-Strauss emphasizes, the absence of any natural or fixed relation between the two series means that there is a deep and structurally significant disharmony or *mismatch* between them as well. Rather than being determined (as in pre-structuralist pictures) by their signified concepts, the meaning or value of signifiers depends on the systematic effect of their entire structure in its totality.

This leads to a "precedence" of the signifier over the signified and to the essential possibility of a determinative structural "excess" of signification over the signified. In particular, as Lévi-Strauss emphasizes, the very possibility of human knowledge depends on the preexistence of a *total* system of possible signification, which must be presupposed as a kind of latent dimension of total structure prior to the specific discovery of elements in the domain of the signified. It is as if, Lévi-Strauss says, human knowledge depended on the pre-givenness of an "immense domain and the detailed plan of that domain, along with a notion of the reciprocal relationship of domain and plan" but nevertheless were constrained to spend millennia "learning which specific symbols of the plan represented the different aspects of the domain."[7] This pre-given structure is nothing other than the total structure of language itself, which is also the underlying structure of the social whole. In that this structure must be pre-given prior to any individual or any specific discovery, it is true that in a certain sense "the universe signified long before people began to know what it signified"; in particular, the universe, conceived as the totality of the knowable, has always already constituted a structural whole that is "closed and complementary to itself" as is shown in the total structure of language itself, requiring only subsequent human processes of "correcting and recutting of patterns, regrouping, defining relationships of belonging and discovering new resources . . ." in order to become known in detail.[8]

This preexistence of the total structure of language—its being given to each speaker or social actor in advance of whatever he or she may use it to signify—thus suggests that *signification* as such defines, in effect, a kind of paradoxical dimension of latency at the basis of *all* uses of language, as well as the social whole itself. Thus, Lévi-Strauss holds that:

> . . . still constantly in our own societies (and no doubt for a long time to come), a fundamental situation perseveres which arises out of the human condition: namely, that man has from the start had at his disposition a signifier-totality which he is at a loss to know how to allocate to a signified, given as such, but no less unknown for being given. There is always a non-equivalence or 'inadequation' between the two, a nonfit and overspill which divine understanding alone can soak up; this generates a signifier-surfeit relative to the signifieds to which it can be fitted. So, in man's effort to understand the world, he always disposes of a surplus of signification (which he shares out among things in accordance with the laws of symbolic thinking which it is the task of ethnologists and linguists to study).[9]

The effects of this structural excess (which in one sense is at the basis of all possibility of human knowledge) show up in detail, according to Lévi-Strauss, at specific points in the structure of any particular, culturally specific language.

In particular, through his anthropological work Lévi-Strauss followed Marcel Mauss and others in recognizing the common occurrence, across a wide range of communities, of certain enigmatic signifiers, which are seemingly invested with great importance in the ritual life of the society, but whose specific reference or meaning is mysterious and variable. One of the best examples is the signifier *mana* and its related terms, used across a wide range of cultures and apparently capable of signifying a magical object or substance, a person without a specific name, a mysterious animal, or many other things.[10] Lévi-Strauss suggests that we can gain an understanding of the real functioning of *mana* and structurally similar terms like *wakan*, *orenda*, and *manitou* only if we see them as reflecting the problematic relationship between signification and the signified itself in its constitutive disequilibrium. Thus, such terms—what Lévi-Strauss called *floating signifiers*—are in fact nothing other than expressions of a kind of "semantic function" which "allows symbolic thinking to operate" despite the contradictions inherent in the very possibility of signification as such. They do so, more specifically, by marking a kind of "zero symbolic value"; by failing to signify anything specific, floating signifiers function as a kind of supplementary intra-systematic manifestation of the permanent excess of signification that allows symbolic language to be possible to begin with.[11] Their "sole function" is thus "to fill a gap between the signifier and the signified, or, more exactly, to signal the fact that in such a circumstance, on such an occasion, or in such a one of their manifestations, a relationship of non-equivalence becomes established between signifier and signified . . ."[12]

In this way, the floating signifier is the very signifier of the possibility of signification itself. Possessing, itself, no specific referential value, it stands, within the system, for the disequilibrium and excess of signifiers over the signified that makes knowledge and discourse possible, figuring the totality of the system of signifiers at a specific, local point within it. For Lévi-Strauss, this conception of the character of the floating signifier and its capacity to manifest the entirety of the symbolic order is deeply linked, moreover, to the structure of the social whole, which must itself be grasped as a *totality* if it is to be understood at all. This totality correlates strictly to the total system of signification, and in understanding it we inevitably reckon with structures and forms of meaning that we ourselves deeply *share*. In particular, in investigating the linked structural preconditions of language and social life, the anthropologist must consider "forms of activity which are both at once *ours* and *other*: which are the condition of all the forms of mental life of all men at all times."[13] In discerning these structures, the anthropologist must therefore grasp the social whole, as a totality, both "from outside, like a thing," but simultaneously, and in the same conceptual process, nevertheless as a "thing which comprises within itself the subjective understanding (conscious or unconscious) that we would have of it, if, being inexorably human, we were living in the fact as indigenous people instead of observing it as ethnographers."[14] This twofold operation, Lévi-Strauss argues, is the comprehension of a "whole which, to be valid, has to be presented in a systematic and coordinated way."[15] This systematic whole of signification or the total social fact, as it is shown in the reflexive moment by which we consider ourselves to be elements within it, is thus the basis for any possible anthropological understanding of individual or collective action and behavior.

In this way, the system of signification, for Lévi-Strauss, always precedes the substantial being of the subject. The action of the individual human subject is discerned as a determined outcome of the structural network of signs in their articulation of differences and in their constitutive and paradoxical excess over the signified meanings.

Benveniste

Elsewhere in the burgeoning structuralist movement, this systematic consideration of the totality of signification gave rise to a structurally transformed conception of the nature and role of the *speaking subject* itself. Drawing on Jakobson's earlier theory of personal and other deictic pronouns as "shifters" (capable of shifting, or changing, their meanings from context to context of utterance), the structuralist linguist Emile Benveniste drew out the radical consequences of structuralism for subjectivity in a series of articles written in the late 1950s and early 60s. According to Benveniste, the personal pronouns "I" and "you" have a linguistic function that is categorically different from that of objective terms whose reference is fixed; rather than referring to any fixed object or referent, an utterance of "I" refers to the individual who is uttering it in the present instance of discourse.[16] As such, these and other demonstrative pronouns, as well as other indicators of tense and place, bear a special and unique relationship to the fact of discourse itself, as it occurs in each particular case of their production or utterance. In particular, Benveniste suggests, the existence of demonstrative indicators allows language to solve the problem of "intersubjective communication" by making possible the capacity of each individual to express her "subjectivity" and thus to take up her own unique place in the intersubjectivity of communicative practice.[17] As such, these terms function as initially "empty" signifiers which are "filled" with a determinate reference on each occasion of their successful use. In being used, they accomplish a kind of "conversion" of language (the abstract, synchronic total system of signifiers) into the (concrete, diachronic) reality of discourse as it unfolds.[18]

As Benveniste notes, this has radical consequences for the nature of subjectivity itself in its relationship to the total fact of language. Thus, the existence of the personal pronouns and other deictic indicators show that "Language is so organized that it permits each speaker to *appropriate* to himself an entire language by designating himself as I."[19] That is, it is in the use of such a self-designation that a speaker identifies—and so constitutes—himself not simply as an indifferent individual but also *as* a speaker, one who is capable of identifying himself as a *subject* and participating in the possibilities of discourse that the language as such affords.[20] It is with such ongoing appropriation that the very possibility of communication and dialogue, which always depends on the possibility of an exchange of positions between the "I" and the "you," is first structurally attained. This suggests not only that "Language is possible only because each speaker sets himself up as a *subject* by referring to himself as *I* in his discourse" but also, even more radically, that "It is in and through language that man constitutes himself as a *subject*, because language alone establishes the concept of 'ego' in reality, in *its* reality which is that of the being."[21] It is, in other words, only through the linguistic existence of the otherwise "empty" deictic signifiers that it is possible for a subject to exist. In each case of the use of such a signifier, the empty place established by it is filled in by the subject's self-constituting action of appropriating to himself the *whole* of the structure of signifiers—the whole language—of which it is an element.

In "Analytical Philosophy and Language," Benveniste draws out the consequences of this structuralist conception of the basis of subjectivity in the assumption of the total function of discourse—the subject's self-constituting appropriation of the entire linguistic order—for the theory of speech acts, as classically treated (for instance) by J. L. Austin. As Austin had pointed out in his groundbreaking analysis, speech acts or performatives (such as declarations, avowals, promises, commandments, etc.) are not directly descriptive, but are rather ways of "doing things" with words that bear importantly different conditions of success than those of descriptive utterances. For Benveniste, this specificity traces again to the formal structure of deixis, which is involved in each case of a performative utterance. Like the issuance of deictic signifiers itself, the utterance of a performative is tied to its situation and circumstances of utterance. This constitutive link is what allows a performative utterance to function as an "individual and historical" act, and constrains anyone who repeats it to first turn it into a constative, or descriptive, utterance.[22] This special capacity of speech acts to amount to individual, datable actions or events traces, like the specificity of deictic pronouns itself, to their quality of being "self-referential." That is, a performative utterance has the quality "of referring to a reality that it itself constitutes by the fact that it is actually uttered in the conditions that make it an act." [23] It is this self-referential quality of the performative utterance that both ensures its constitutive tie to the circumstances and context of utterance and ensures that it is capable of functioning, in those specific circumstances, as an action or event. In so functioning, the performative utterance draws on and is conditioned by the subject's self-constituting relationship to the whole of the structural order of language in which she takes part.

Lacan

Lévi-Strauss and Benveniste thus both insist upon a dimension of total structure that is present in language as such and prior to any individual action or occurrence. Moreover, this dimension both conditions and accounts for the psychologically or empirically determined substance of subjectivity itself. These implications of the total existence of the symbolic order, or of the total structure of signification in its conditioning of what is otherwise grasped as "individual" psychological phenomena, would become the basis of the radical transformation and development of Freud's psychoanalytic theory in the work of his greatest disciple and rebellious heir, Jacques Lacan.

From beginning to end, Lacan's project is determined by the proposition that the Freudian unconscious is "structured like a language" and thus can be read and interpreted in the terms provided by Saussure's structuralist picture and its subsequent refinements. This conception led Lacan, early in his career, notoriously to distinguish among the three "registers" or "orders" of psychoanalytic interpretation: the Real, the Imaginary, and the Symbolic. Whereas the Real is the domain of actual, occurring processes and events, conceived as external to language and independent of it (and hence, as Lacan would often suggest, "impossible" to conceive for humans whose entire psychic life is determined by language and its structure), the Imaginary is a domain of images and representations, whereby the ego or the self constructs its characteristic aspirations and demands.[24] However, *both* are to be rigidly distinguished from the order of the Symbolic, which owes nothing either to the reality of signified events *or* to resemblance and representation. Instead, the Symbolic order of language is a wholly autonomous domain of structure; our necessarily traumatic introduction into it defines our very status as speaking subjects as well as the possibility of any form of relationship to a larger social whole.

In his second seminar in 1954–55 on Poe's *The Purloined Letter* (partially reprinted in *Écrits*), Lacan already insists upon the essential autonomy of the symbolic order and its systematic effects in determining psychical reality as a whole. Central to these effects, once again, is the specific action of the signifier in relation to the total structure of signification that yields its value. Here, Lacan conceives this action as a kind of "insistence" of the signifier in the unfolding of the signifying chain, whereby the signifier has effects, and organizes psychological phenomena, in a way that owes nothing to its capacity to stand for a real object of signification, or represent it by means of resemblance.[25] This conception organizes Lacan's reading of Poe's story, which plays massively on the homology between the "letter" whose displacement and absence underlies the story's arc and the "letter" as the signifier, or the pure instance of signification as such. In particular, Lacan says:

> . . . the signifier is a unique unit of being which, by its very nature, is the symbol of but an absence. This is why we cannot say of the purloined letter that, like other objects, it must be or not be somewhere but rather that, unlike them, it will be and will not be where it is wherever it goes.[26]

Lacking, as Saussure already emphasized, any essential relationship to a positive being, and being constituted as such only by its role in a system of differences, the signifier can ultimately be conceived, in its specific effect, only as the symbol of an absence, or as the possibility of a continual displacement in its repetition along the signifying chain. Such repetition, Lacan suggests here, is the underlying structure of what Freud grasped as the "repetition automatism" or the compulsion to repeat found characteristically in cases of neurosis and conceived by Freud as essentially linked to the fundamental inclination toward destruction and negation that he called the "death drive." In fact, for Lacan, the specific basis of *all* of the psychological effects that determine the life of the subject (including "foreclosure, repression, and negation itself")[27] are to be found in the specific action of the signifier in its relation to the total order of the symbolic. This suggests (as it already had for Lévi-Strauss and Benveniste) that the "symbolic order . . . is constitutive for the subject"[28] and that this constitution is to be understood in terms of the systematic effects of *syntax* by means of which the signifier is repeated, displaced, and differentiated from other signifiers in the structure of the symbolic order as a whole. Accordingly, "the program traced out for us is . . . to figure out how a formal language determines the subject."[29] Already for Lacan in 1954–55, this implies a systematic pursuit of formalism and its implications, tied constitutively to the autonomous order of the symbolic, which is, he says, not to be understood in terms of "the signifier's 'conventional' nature, as it is incorrectly put, but rather its priority over the signified." [30]

In 1957, Lacan again emphasized the specific effect of the signifier and its role in producing the constitutive phenomena of subjectivity in "The Instance of the Letter in the Unconscious, or Reason Since Freud."[31] The word (*instance*) that is here translated as "instance" is in fact difficult to translate univocally, meaning not only "instance" in the sense of "event" or "occurrence," but also "agency" (Freud used *Instanzen* to refer to the three "agencies" of the ego, id, and superego) or even "authority."[32] In any case, Lacan here defines the letter as "the material medium [*support*] that concrete discourse borrows from language."[33] It is this medium that, once again, preconditions the very structure of the subject as such; thus: ". . . the subject, while he may appear to be the slave of language, is still more the slave of a discourse in the universal movement of which his place is already inscribed at his birth, if only in the form of his proper name."[34] Lacan emphasizes that this "universal movement" of discourse precedes and conditions any reference to the "experience of the community," which is actually of little use in the psychoanalytic explanation; for the very structures of community themselves depend on and result from "an ordering of exchanges which, even if unconscious, is inconceivable apart from the permutations authorized by language."[35] Indeed, this precedence, Lacan says, has as a probable result a "giving way" of the ethnographer's traditional duality between nature and culture.

At the root of all of these implications is the structure of language as the system of signifiers, as originally described by Saussure. For Lacan, the most important outcome of Saussure's original definition of the sign is that it is impossible to signify the barrier between signifier and signified, or to presume any relationship of correspondence or representation between them. This leads to the possibility of a systematic study of the structure of signifiers as such, and to their effect in engendering and transforming the signified. Such a study, Lacan says, "goes well beyond the debate over the arbitrariness of the sign"[36] and depends on the fundamental insight that "no signification can be sustained except by reference to another signification."[37] This means that every language represents, as such, a totality of signifiers whose capability in principle to cover the entire field of the signified cannot be disputed.[38] Due to the lack of any ready-made connection between the chain of signifiers and that of the signifieds, however, it is necessary to inquire into the systematic structure of this totality of signifiers; here we find "the locus whence language questions us about its very nature."[39] Specifically, Lacan says, we must here accept "the notion of an incessant sliding of the signified under the signifier," which Saussure had already suggested with his picture of the two parallel streams, and the specific place of the subject as that of a kind of captivation point (*point de capiton*) within this sliding.[40] Moreover, the specific structure of the signifying chain, when conceived as making possible *intersubjective* language, also displays the place of the subject in relation to others and to the overarching structure of language itself:

> What this structure of the signifying chain discloses is the possibility I have—precisely as I share its language [*langue*] with other subjects, that is, insofar as this language [*langue*] exists—to use it to signify *something altogether different* from what it says. This is a function of speech that is more worthy of being pointed out than that of disguising the subject's thought (which is usually indefinable)—namely, the function of indicating the place of this subject in the search for truth.[41]

The problem of determining the structure of the subject and the work of psychoanalysis then become, as Lacan says, the problem of determining how the place one occupies as "subject of the signifier" is related to the place one occupies as "subject of the signified." This is not, Lacan says, the problem of knowing whether my speech about myself corresponds to my true nature, but rather that of knowing "whether, when I speak of myself, I am the same as the self of whom I speak."[42] It is, in other words, the problem of the *reference* of the "I" in relation to the entirety of the symbolic order in which it subsists, the same problem to which Benveniste responded with his account of deictic indicators as accomplishing the "appropriation" of the whole structure of language itself. For Lacan, however, the question of the meaning and reference of "I" is not simply one of the functioning of certain privileged signifiers, but indeed of the entire position and privilege of what traditional thought discerns as the subject, here conceived as radically "ex-centric" in its movement along the chain of signifiers, which is also the movement of desire. Both the possibility of desire and the unconscious field are to be understood, again, only in terms of the structural potential of the signifier for repetition and displacement. This structural potential of the signifier as such defines both the possibility of any memory, and the very life of the human subject in its characteristic traumas, its desire, its past, and its future.[43]

Already in the 1950s, then, Lacan insisted upon the structure of the signifier in its relation to the systematic whole of language as essential both to the actual practice of psychoanalysis and to the very constitution of the subject as such. This already implies a precisely determined formalism, both to characterize the structure of the subject and to provide schemas for the analysis of its linguistic place and displacement. However, to see more clearly the implications of this formalism, which would yield Lacan's famous "mathemes" and his groundbreaking schematization of the four types of discourse, it is helpful to turn to one of Lacan's last texts, that of his twentieth seminar ("Encore") in 1972–73.[44] Here, Lacan continues to emphasize the determination of the subject by the signifying chain; as in Lacan's first structuralist texts, "The subject is nothing other than what slides in a chain of signifiers, whether he knows which signifier he is the effect of or not."[45] In this text, however, Lacan's consideration of the role of the signifier and the implications of formalism, in connection with the problematic of the sexual relationship which would form a One of two (and which, as Lacan consistently insisted, "does not exist"), leads to a philosophically penetrating and radical consideration of the ancient problem of the One and the Many. This yields Lacan's emphatic motto, which runs as a *leitmotif* through the seminar, that "there's such a thing as (the) One"; and it is to the demonstration of the implications of this problematic motto that he devotes a host of formalisms, as well as the resources of set theory and mathematics.[46]

As in the earlier texts, the subject is, here, nothing other than an effect of the structure of signification as such, and it can accordingly itself be presented only through a formalism that exhibits this determination. In particular, here and in other texts Lacan symbolizes with the small "a" the "object" or "thing" of desire, what the subject incessantly pursues along the signifying chain. He uses the capital "A," short for "Autre" (or "Other"), for the "place" of the indifferent Other in the subject's discourse, or exchange of signs; as such, the "A" stands also for the general field of the production of signs, the symbolic as such.[47] This means, according to Lacan, that what it designates (in the first instance at least) is simply a "place" or a "locus," the place from which the claim of the Other (which is the same as that of signification as such) is heard and experienced. As the designation, in the structure of the subject's own discourse, of an Other place as such, it is essentially *empty*. Lacan compares it to the symbolization with which the set theory of the Bourbaki group designates the place of the variable, which is an empty square. Here, in the structural necessity of such a single, "empty" signifier that figures the problematic relationship of the subject to the total system of signifiers, we may certainly recognize, in another incarnation, Lévi-Strauss's "floating signifier," as well as (as we have seen) the necessary structural basis for the deictic indicators in which Benveniste locates any possibility of subjectivity.

In particular, in identifying the structure of subjective desire as that of an incessant "slide" along the chain of signifiers, Lacan also identifies the subject's relationship to satisfaction as the point of a general structural impasse, which is shown in the emptiness or "barring" of this structural place of the Other itself:

> Thus, I wasn't making a strict use of the letter when I said that the locus of the Other was symbolized by the letter A. On the contrary, I marked it by redoubling it with the S that means signifier here, signifier of A insofar as the latter is barred: S(A̶). I thereby add a dimension to A's locus, showing that qua locus it does not hold up, that there is a fault, hole, or loss therein. Object *a* comes to function with respect to that loss. That is something which is quite essential to the function of language.[48]

That is, because of its status as the empty signifier of the locus of the Other as such, which can never correspond to a plenitude of realized satisfaction (or *jouissance*), the barred A can symbolize the structurally necessary place of the subject's pursuit in the chain of signifiers which determines him, and the signifier S(A̶) can stand, within the symbolic order, for the structurally necessary absence, lack, or failure which motivates the subject in this pursuit.[49]

Indeed, Lacan's constant designation of the subject as such as "$," the "barred" subject, expresses something similar, in that it stands for the subject's essential relationship to the totality of the symbolic order, from which it is nevertheless "barred" in that it essentially lacks full or complete knowledge of this totality of possible signification. However, it is not at all the case, for Lacan, that the subject of desire is simply without any relation to the "One" of the totality of signification. Rather, the specific relationship of the subject to this totality, for Lacan, is specifiable precisely as the relation to a "not-all" or "not-whole" that is precisely equivalent to the necessary inscription—in any envisaged totality of desire as such, or of knowledge—of a structurally unknowable Other.[50] Lacan suggests that the problematic structure of this "not-whole," by which the subject is essentially related to the totality of signification from which it is nevertheless essentially barred, also already implies a transformed logic and an essential link of the subject to the infinite.[51]

For Lacan, in fact, the whole problem of the One (which is, of course, in many ways coextensive with philosophy as such) is a consequence of the specific structure of signification in its problematic relationship (or, rather, non-relationship) to the signified. Thus, "we know of no other basis by which the One may have been introduced into the world if not by the signifier as such, that is, the signifier insofar as we learn to separate it from its meaning effects."[52] More specifically, it is the problematic phenomenon of signification [*signifiance*] as such, in its necessarily *serial* structure, that introduces the problematic of the One and the Many and to which it is necessary for psychoanalytic theory ultimately to turn, finally transfiguring Saussure's initial conception of the signifier/signified connection as "arbitrary" into something quite different:

> Don't forget that, at the outset, the relationship between signifier and signified was incorrectly qualified as arbitrary. That is how Saussure expressed himself, probably in spite of his better judgment—he certainly believed otherwise, that is, something far closer to the text of the *Cratylus*, as is seen by what he had in his desk drawers, namely, his anagrams. Now what passes for arbitrary is the fact that meaning effects seem not to bear any relation to what causes them.
>
> But if they seem to bear no relation to what causes them, that is because we expect what causes them to bear a certain relation to the real. I'm talking about the serious real. The serious—one must of course make an effort to notice it, one must have come to my seminars now and then—can only be the serial. That can only be obtained after a very long period of extraction, extraction from language of something that is caught up in it, and about which we have, even at the point at which I have arrived in my exposé, only a faint idea—even regarding this indeterminate "a" (*un*), this lure that we don't know how to make function in relation to the signifier so that it collectivizes the signifier. In truth, we will see that we must turn things around, and instead of investigating a signifier (*un signifiant*), we must investigate the signifier "One" (*Un*)—but we haven't reached that point yet.[53]

Thus, what is at stake, ultimately, in the necessary serial structure of signification and in its problematic relationship to the Real of the signified is nothing other than the status of the One, or of what is involved in the possibility of unitary reference that is indeed presupposed in the use of any signifier as such. If it is indeed the case, as Lacan insists, that "the signifier is posited only insofar as it has no relation to the signified,"[54] then Saussure's radical discovery of its structure bears witness not as much to the sign's "arbitrariness" as to its capacity to bring about, by virtue of its own serial structure, a radically different relationship to the Real than is presupposed in any classical theory of representation or resemblance.[55]

In fact, it is "scientific discourse" that most clearly exhibits these consequences, most completely in the symbolization of mathematics, where any hint of a representational relationship to the signified (indeed, of any relationship at all!) is radically absent. This demands an analytic practice, and theory, which has as its fundamental goal the production of a mathematical symbolization in which the symbols bring forth pure structures capable of being "integrally transmitted" without any historical or cultural admixture.[56] Although these structures are mathematical, and hence independent of any particular language, they are also, Lacan suggests, the pure structures of signification as such, wherein the pure effects of the structure of the signifier on the constitution of the subject and the problem of the One itself can be seen and measured most directly. In particular, the formalization of set theory accomplishes, according to Lacan, a radical transformation in what can be thought (or said) concerning the One and its possibility:

> Set theory bursts onto the scene by positing the following: let us speak of things as One that are strictly unrelated to each other. Let us put together objects of thought, as they are called, objects of the world, each of which counts as one. Let us assemble these absolutely heterogeneous things, and let us grant ourselves the right to designate the resulting assemblage by a letter. That is how set theory expresses itself at the outset . . .[57]

By looking at the "meaningless" formalizations of mathematics as such, and especially at the formalization of set theory, we are in a position to approach the One of any unification whatsoever as a One composed, as Lacan emphasizes, of completely heterogeneous elements. In this respect, set theory accomplishes a liberation from the "intuitive, fusional, amorous way" in which the One was always formerly approached, and hence to a radically transformed understanding of the unity of significative meaning, or the signifying accomplishment of the signifier or the letter itself.

It is thus in the pure signifiers of mathematics that we will ultimately locate the structure of signification as such and discern its role in allowing any possible access to the Real:

> This [i.e., in formalism] is where the real distinguishes itself. The real can only be inscribed on the basis of an impasse of formalization. That is why I thought I could provide a model of it using mathematical formalization, inasmuch as it is the most advanced elaboration we have by which to produce signifierness. The mathematical formalization of signifierness runs counter to meaning—I almost said *"a contre-sens."* In our times, philosophers of mathematics say 'it means nothing' concerning mathematics, even when they are mathematicians themselves, like Russell.[58]

It is, in other words, in the formal schematizations of mathematics, which are without meaning, that it is alone possible to locate the Real as it manifests itself in signs; this manifestation is to be found, moreover, at the structurally necessary point of the *impasse* of formalization, where the "non-whole" of the entire structural order is itself signified by the mathemes of the subject.

Because of their "meaningless" status—their clear lack of any specific relationship to a signified, and their universal transmissibility—the formalisms of mathematics are especially well suited to display this structure, and indeed to manifest, *within* the Symbolic order of signifiers, the very being of the Real itself. However, as Lacan repeatedly emphasizes, this does *not* mean that the mathemes are capable of breaking with the structure of signification as such; indeed, it is precisely *as* pure signifiers that they maintain an essential and constitutive relationship to this structure. This is, indeed, precisely what qualifies them to manifest the problematic (non)relationship between the Real and the Symbolic at all, which they do, as we have seen, by formalizing signification in the very *impasse* of its attempt to speak consistently of the whole in which it takes place. Accordingly, Lacan emphasizes that the mathematical formalisms, though ideally transmissible, nevertheless "are not transmitted without the help of language"[59] and that their writing "constitutes a medium [*support*] that goes beyond speech, without going beyond language's actual effects" (p. 93).[60] Indeed, for Lacan the essentially linguistic and symbolic character of the pure signifier, even the pure signifier of mathematics which is without any relation to a specific signified, is *essential* to their ability to manifest the structure of the subject and its relationship to the Real itself. For as Lacan recognizes, "no formalization of language is transmissible without the use of language itself" (pp. 119–108). Accordingly, as he emphasizes at the end of the seminar, it is decisively *impossible* to postulate a metalanguage which would formalize language (or the symbolic) as a whole from an outside point: if there is a formalization of the Symbolic as such, it will necessarily take place within that very structure and bear the constitutive paradoxes and impasses of total self-reference that this implies. Indeed, Lacan suggests in a series of provocative formulations, it is *by* exhibiting these very impasses and paradoxes that the formalization of the Symbolic accomplishes the specific demonstration of the subject's relationship to being:

> This is one of the essential things I said last time—analysis can be distinguished from everything that was produced by discourse prior to analysis by the fact that it enunciates the following, which is the very backbone of my teaching—I speak without knowing it. I speak with my body and I do so unbeknownst to myself. Thus I always say more than I know (*plus que je n'en sais*).
>
> This is where I arrive at the meaning of the word "subject" in analytic discourse. What speaks without knowing it makes me "I", subject of the verb. That doesn't suffice to bring me into being. That has nothing to do with what I am forced to put in being (*mettre dans l'etre*)—enough knowledge for it to hold up, but not one drop more . . .
>
> There is some relationship of being that cannot be known. It is that relationship whose structure I investigate in my teaching, insofar as that knowledge—which, as I just said, is impossible—is prohibited (*interdit*) thereby. This is where I play on an equivocation—that impossible

knowledge is censored or forbidden, but it isn't if you write "inter-dit" appropriately—it is said between the words, between the lines. We have to expose the kind of real to which it grants us access.[61]

It is thus the radical and structurally necessary impasse of formalization, shown in the constitutive structure of the subject as the structurally neces-sary interdiction of a metalanguage, that bears essential witness to that problematic relation of the subject to the Real of being that exceeds any possible knowledge of forms and the objects in which they "participate." The source of this relation, and its revelation to the analytic discourse which first discerns the radical heterogeneity of the order of the Symbolic from those of the Real and the Imaginary alike, is the necessary formal impasse of the One of the total symbolic order in its attempt to symbolize itself. It is thus that psychoanalysis depends, for the very truth of which it is capable, on a relentless pursuit of the possibility of the One, up to the formal impasse that necessarily interrupts it at the point of totality. Thus:

> We must begin with the fact that this "There's such a thing as One" [*Y a d'l'Un*] is to be understood in the sense that there's One all alone (*il y a de l'Un tout seul*) . . . In analysis, we deal with nothing but that, and analysis doesn't operate by any other pathway.[62]

Thus Lacan designates under the heading of the discourse of analysis the specificity of a paradoxical knowledge that, beyond any assurance that would link the real of being to the sayable of the symbolic, functions simply by relentlessly documenting what is shown by the essential and structural impasse of symbolization in its necessarily interdicted attempt to signify the One of its own totality.

Miller

In 1968, Jacques-Alain Miller published in the journal *Cahiers pour l'Analyse* an article entitled "Action of the Structure" and intended to clarify the basis for the "discourse theory" then being pursued by several students of Lacan.[63] In the article, Miller pursues the development of a "logic of the signifier" which will clarify the specific relationship of linguis-tic structure as such to subjectivity. The attempt to think the place of the subject inherently involves, he argues, a *reflexive redoubling* that allows an otherwise synchronic structure of language to take on the diachronic movement and active organization of life. If, in particular, we must begin with a distinction between the "actual" dimension of structuration as it conditions its elements and the "virtual" position from which it can be understood, then the introduction of a reflexive element collapses this dis-tinction and inaugurates a constitutive "absence" that makes the action of structure as such possible:

If we now suppose an element that turns back on reality and perceives it, reflects upon it and signifies it, an element capable of redoubling reality on its own account, a general distortion follows which affects the whole structural economy and recomposes it following new laws. As soon as this element is introduced:
—Its actuality becomes experience
—the virtuality of the structure becomes an absence
—this absence is produced in the real order of the structure: the action of the structure comes to be supported by a lack.
The structurer, to disappear (*pour n'y être pas*), governs the real. Here we grab hold of the driving strife: the introduction of the reflexive element is enough to institute the dimension of the structured qua lived, as taking effect only of itself. . . .[64]

Thus, for Miller, it is the reflexive element itself—which we may identify with the subject, or anything which reflects the totality of structure into itself—that comes to "support" the total effects of structure, and any action of which it is capable, by "disappearing" or manifesting itself as a generative absence or lack. This reflexive element, Miller suggests, also locates "the utopic point of the structure . . . or its point at infinity"; in other words, as for Lacan, it is the precise location at which all the structural effects of desire, oriented toward a progressive movement, can operate. Thus, at this precise point, "a self-reflexive object, thus a self-reproducing object, takes for its correlate an impossible construction, or an infinite activity."[65]

As Miller argues through an interesting analysis of Frege's conception of number and the role of the signifier "0," the mark of such a lack also stands at the origin of the *iteration* that characterizes structure as such, underlying the very possibility of repetition that is essential to all signification.[66] In particular, by being "counted as one" even though nothing corresponds to it, the "0" is capable of engendering the whole series of its successors, each of which then amounts to a "counting" of its immediate predecessor. According to Miller, this is structurally exactly similar to what Lacan understands as the "relation of the subject to the field of the Other," in which the constitutive lack that is the subject is nevertheless marked, in its very "excluded" status, as an originary element capable of generating a trail of subsequent signifiers which amounts to its discourse.[67]

All of this is a necessary outcome of the very possibility of the reflexive moment whereby the total logic of the system is figured within itself by a single paradoxical element. This reflexive redoubling implies, as well, a transformed *topology* of structure in which "outside" and "inside" are no longer clearly distinguishable, but interpenetrate at the point of the figuration of the structure within itself. This altered topology is more closely described by Miller in the 1966 article "Suture." Here, Miller again considers the specific "relation of the subject to the chain of its discourse"; which takes, in particular, the form of a "general relation of lack to the structure."[68] This figuring of the subject within the chain of signifiers as the lack that manifests the whole is what Miller terms "suture," noting that it is "constantly present" in Lacan's system even if it is not named there explicitly. The structurally necessary place of this suture implies, according to Miller, that the entire field of signification can no longer be represented as a "closed surface." It is, instead, a complex surface on which "not being situated on the inside does not relegate you to the outside" for "at a certain point, excluded from a two-dimensional topology, the two surfaces join up and the periphery or outer edge crosses over the circumscription."[69]

This is, in other words, the topology of the Möbius strip, on which inside and outside interpenetrate one another and the position of the subject (as "inside" or "outside" the system) becomes systematically undecidable. In an article from 1975, Miller describes it in just these terms.[70] We may easily recognize this topology as, precisely, that of *in-closure* (see Chapter 1). By means of a consideration of the constitutive place of the reflexive element, which is neither inside nor outside, it complicates and renders undecidable the distinction between "inside" and "outside" which was formerly the basis for all operations of critical or systematic totalization. Indeed, its structural basis, as was already clear in Lacan, is the *inconsistent totality* that results, necessarily, from the structural failure of thought (given the reflexive element) to gather all of its elements into a complete, consistent whole. Thus:

> Each signifier has for its correlate a set (n-1), and there are as many of these sets as there are signifiers—without ever reaching the whole set, n. This totality is unclosed, perforated, open, it doesn't hold together, it is a unity (space, law, function) of dispersion. A proverb: structure isn't everything [*la structure n'est pas un tout*].[71]

And, accordingly:

> The categories of more-than/less-than, of the inconsistent totality, of the antinomic element give rise, if you will, to those of anticipation, of deferral [*l'apres-coup*], of the lightning flash of the instant.[72]

In this way, by insisting upon the paradoxical implications of the antinomic element that represents the total logic of the structure and the inconsistent totality of in-closure that it generates, Miller identifies the One of structure as constitutively rent by lack and inadequacy to itself. This inadequacy characterizes, necessarily, any relation of the subject to language, and hence any possibility of the intersubjective relation of subjects (which must, of course, be understood as the specific possibility of communication). This means, according to Miller, that the intersubjective relation between one subject and another can no longer be thought in terms of a "simple reciprocity" or a "reversible" relation of one to another; even the most simple relation of one human, speaking subject to another is already, also, a relation of each to the constitutively rent, inconsistent totality of language as a whole.

That the attempt to remedy this inadequacy, on the level of political thought, by filling the lack with an imaginary principle of self-consistent wholeness must always be unsatisfactory is the basis for the specific political implications of this altered conception of intersubjectivity, which Miller does not hesitate to draw:

> No relation between a subject and another subject, or between a subject and an object can fill up (*combler*) the lack, except in the imaginary formation that sutures it together, only to be found again on the inside. The contestation of reciprocity in the psychologies of intersubjectivity must come in corollary to the refutation of every politics of liberalism or humanism. These, it could be said, stem from reciprocity, and are perpetually in search of the object that will come and fill the stomach of human hunger, satisfy what they conceive of as human "dissatisfaction" (Locke's uneasiness) and thus assure the transparence of all inter-human relations. Knowing that it's not after a "having" that man has, but rather, after his "being" or, without the metaphor, that the imaginary determines a structure which includes and comports a subject, a politics of happiness, i.e. an adaptive politics (*politique d l'ajustement*) must be considered the surest means to reinforce the inadequacy that goes from subject to the structure.[73]

ANALYTIC PHILOSOPHY

Carnap

The tradition of analytic philosophy in the twentieth century, like the tradition of continental structuralism, begins with a formative conception of language as a total structure of signs. This conception is already present in Frege's original theory of language and meaning; early on it yields the methodology and project of "logical analysis" practiced by Russell, Wittgenstein, Moore, Carnap, Schlick, and others.[74] Already in its first instances, this conception of language and the modality of analysis that it inspires implied, as in the structuralist tradition itself, a decisive break with any conception of language as primarily mimetic, representational, or founded in natural relations of resemblance or similarity. This led to distinctive critical consequences, including prominently the linguistically grounded rejection of psychologism in Frege and Wittgenstein and, in the project of the Vienna Circle, the attempt to replace all traditional metaphysics with the "logic of science."

At first, these projects took the *criteriological* form of attempts to delimit the scope of meaningful language by means of an abstract, logical as well as empiricist delimitation of the possibility of significant meaning. The methodology of this limitative project was the verificationism of the Vienna Circle, which held the scope of possible meaning to extend no further than that of empirically verifiable or logically (formally) meaningful propositions, themselves empty of empirical content. At the basis of this *criteriological* project, however, was a programmatic *constructivism* whose essence is well expressed by Russell's motto: "Wherever possible . . . entities should be replaced by logical constructions." Carnap used this motto as the epigraph for his first masterpiece, *Der Logische Aufbau der Welt* (or *The Logical Structure of the World*) in 1928. Its aim, in accordance with the motto, was to replace the entities assumed to exist in the various empirical sciences with constructions grounded in a total, unified logical structure, ultimately reducible to the most basic of relations. Such an analysis would amount, Carnap suggested, to a kind of differential and structural "construction of the world" and lead to a unified, logically grounded science and to a repudiation of all forms of metaphysics that extend beyond it.

The initial project of logical empiricism was thus strongly criteriological and constructivist; it is not surprising, therefore, that it was strongly *conventionalist* as well. Given the development, chiefly through Frege's innovative logic, of an autonomous field of logical relations that owe nothing to natural relationships of resemblance or similarity, but nevertheless could be seen as governing the possibilities within a language as a whole for the meaningful use of its signs, it was natural to construe these relations as fixed by linguistic *rules of use* and of the source of these rules as ultimately residing in the conventions of a community.

In particular, according to the picture which Carnap propounded beginning in *Logical Syntax of Language* of 1934, any language is specified by a description of the formal *rules* for forming sequences of signs (Carnap called these the "formation" rules) together with the rules for deriving sign sequences from one another (which Carnap called "transformation" rules).[75] Both sets of rules are said to be "formal" in the specific respect that they can be specified without antecedent reference to the *meaning* of the terms involved.[76] A language (whether "natural" or "artificial") can be formally treated, then, as nothing other than a total *calculus* of conventionally instituted rules:

> By a calculus is understood a system of conventions or rules of the following kind. These rules are concerned with elements—the so-called **symbols**—about the nature and relations of which nothing more is assumed than that they are distributed in various classes. Any finite series of these symbols is called an **expression** of the calculus in question.
>
> The rules of the calculus determine, in the first place, the conditions under which an expression can be said to belong to a certain category of expressions; and, in the second place, under what conditions the transformation of one or more expressions into another or others may

be allowed. Thus the system of a language, when only the formal structure in the sense described above is considered, is a calculus.[77]

The formal consideration of language as a calculus led Carnap to a "principle of tolerance" with respect to the creation and investigation of sign
systems. According to this principle:

> . . . we have in every respect complete liberty with regard to the forms
> of language; . . . both the forms of construction and the rules of trans-
> formation (the latter are usually designated as "postulates" and "rules
> of inference") may be chosen quite arbitrarily.[78]

This completely free choice of rules and postulates, according to Carnap,
determines "what meaning is to be assigned to the fundamental logical
symbols."[79] This conception of the grounding of formal meaning provides
the philosopher with two kinds of analytic work. First, it makes possible
philosophical analysis of *actual* "natural" languages in order to determine
their overall structure and the actual underlying meaning of their terms.
Second, and just as significantly, it enables the philosopher or creative logician to propose and propound wholly *new* or "artificial" languages or language frameworks, simply by *laying down by stipulation* the formation
and transformation rules determining the use of their terms. On this position, as Carnap put it, there is no single "right" or "true" logic of language;
the solution to logical questions is, rather, to be determined by means of
the specification of rules for the formation and intercombination of sign
sequences, rules which can in principle, Carnap supposed, *always* be conventionally stipulated without recourse to any sense of the already existing
meanings of the terms in question.

Indeed, the conception of *all* languages (natural as well as artificial) as
essentially consisting in freely instituted calculi or structures of rules was
crucial to Carnap's conventionalism about linguistic and logical investigations more generally. The broader methodological implications of this
conventionalism, as well as its application to the criticism of metaphysical
illusion and the formation of philosophical (pseudo-)questions, are clearly
evident in Carnap's 1950 article, "Empiricism, Semantics, and Ontology."[80]
Here, Carnap argues that coherent, meaningful talk about the existence or
nature of a specific kind of entities depends, in each case, upon a preexisting stipulation of a language framework for talking about entities of that
kind.[81] We can then designate well-formulated questions about the entities
concerned as "internal" questions; these are to be settled by the constitutive rules of the framework (together, perhaps, with empirical evidence).
However, questions that are asked in an "absolute" sense and so outside
any particular framework—for instance, questions about whether entities
of a certain type (e.g., numbers or abstract objects) exist at all—must be
considered to be "external" questions that amount simply to the question

whether to adopt a specific language framework. And here, Carnap suggests, tolerance and pragmatism are our only guides; given the principle of tolerance and the complete freedom that the theorist enjoys, we can indeed pursue whatever language frameworks suit our pragmatic purposes. The most important consideration, both in the creation of new languages and in the pursuit of philosophical questions about existence and being, is simply to separate the well-defined "internal" questions from the "external" ones that can be treated *only* as questions regarding the utility of adopting a certain framework. By rigorously distinguishing them, it is possible to avoid the formulation of questions which have no clearly specifiable answer, and hence to eliminate the tendency to empty metaphysics that characterizes most traditional philosophical thought.

Quine

Logical analysis, on Carnap's conception, thus consists entirely in the comparative consideration of the rules determining formal meaning within specifically constructed language frameworks; these frameworks, whether determining natural or artificial languages, are conceived as conventionally instituted and, in principle, arbitrary. Over a period of several decades, however, both this conception of analysis and the picture of language on which it rests would undergo a transformative critique at the hands of Carnap's student W. V. Quine. By stages, Quine would call into question the founding assumptions of Carnap's conventionalist picture of language on the basis of his own consideration of the total logical structure of language and its intersubjective use. The criticism would culminate in Quine's demonstration of what is, even today, one of the most important results of the analytic tradition's entire consideration of language, the thesis of the *indeterminacy of radical translation*.

Already in his first writings on Carnap, Quine began (cautiously at first) to call into question the conventionalist foundations of Carnap's picture of language. One reason for this was that Quine always supposed that the linguist's or analyst's work in determining the actual structure of a language must depend wholly on his discovery of the principles underlying and accounting for the actual intersubjective *use* of terms in the language. Beginning with his first writings, Quine constantly emphasized that a theorist's analysis of an actually existing language can always only *explicate*— and essentially can go no *further* than—the actual facts concerning how terms are in fact used by the language's speakers.[82] Thus, any theoretician's reconstruction of the constitutive rules thought to determine the underlying structure of the language can be justified (if at all) only by the theoretician's claim to exhibit rules capturing, *uniquely and sufficiently*, the actual facts of linguistic use.

But more specifically, this different conception of the analyst's work led Quine to discern a series of formal problems in Carnap's picture. The ultimate source of all of these problems, as well as the indeterminacy result itself, was the set of aporias that result from supposing the complete system of rules for the use of a language—what, for Carnap, must be fixed by the initial conventions or stipulations that determine its logical structure as a whole—to be both i) uniquely *representable* as a whole system and ii) capable of *determining* without exception the usage of the terms. As Quine would show with a series of increasingly radical results, the two features can in fact *not* be coherently combined within any single, unique description of the "rules of use" underlying the language as a whole. It follows that we can no longer suppose any such system to be conventionally instituted, and that the systematic description of the structure of a language is prone to a constitutive and ineliminable ambiguity.

In the 1936 article "Truth by Convention," Quine considers what he here calls the "linguistic doctrine" of logical truths, according to which tautologies (such as "A or not A") and mathematical truths (for instance "3 + 2 = 5") are uniformly "true by convention."[83] Carnap had distinguished such truths rigidly from empirical ones, holding that the former are "analytic" or "true by convention" whereas the latter are "synthetic" owing to their necessary component of extra-linguistic evidence. In the 1936 article, however, Quine argues that there is in fact no motivated way, in schematizing a language, to distinguish truths that are intuitively "logical" and hence analytic (the former class) from those that are empirical and synthetic. For the definition of a new term in an already-existing language, Quine holds, can only amount to the practice of definitionally abbreviating or combining already-existing terms whose meaning is governed by existing usage. Accordingly, any introduction or stipulation of rules governing the structure of the language as a whole must depend on such existing usage; and this already suggests that no sense can be made of Carnap's conception of the *entirety* of a language's structure (as shown in what are supposed to be its "constitutive rules") as having been freely chosen or instituted in a single, originally founding moment.

But at the end of the article, Quine introduces an even deeper formal problem for the theorist who sees the logical structure of a language as conventionally instituted. The problem, one of an infinite regress of conventions, was first suggested by Lewis Carroll, who put it in the form of an amusing dialogue between "Achilles" and "the Tortoise."[84] The problem is that the application in practice of a set of logical conventions itself appears to depend upon an antecedent use of the very same conventions. For instance, consider an everyday instance of the application of one of the most general of "logical laws," the law of modus ponens that allows the inference of B given both A and "if A, then B." Given A, and "if A, then B," it is apparently possible to infer B, but how do we *know* this? Surely, the Tortoise objects, only because we are in a position to assert another principle, holding that *if* we have something of the form "A" and something of the form "If A, then B," *then* we may derive B. But then this principle—call it C—must be part of the premises of the derivation too. But then its usage obviously requires a further principle, D, and so on. The new statement seemingly needed at each step amounts to a restatement of the legitimacy of the application of the "general rule" of modus ponens to what we already have; and in this sense its actual usage seems always to depend on a preexisting understanding that it is indeed applicable to the case at hand. But we cannot formulate this presupposition without circularity; its formulation in each case presupposes itself. The consequence, according to Quine, is that:

> . . . if logic is to proceed mediately from conventions, logic is needed for inferring logic from the conventions. Alternatively, the difficulty which appears thus as a self-presupposition of doctrine can be framed as turning upon a self-presupposition of primitives. It is supposed that the if-idiom, the not-idiom, the every-idiom, and so on, mean nothing to us initially, and that we adopt the conventions . . . by way of circumscribing their meaning; and the difficulty is that communication of [these conventions] themselves depends upon free use of those very idioms which we are attempting to circumscribe, and can succeed only if we are already conversant with the idioms.[85]

It follows that it is impossible to suppose the "conventional rules" determining the use of the logical vocabulary of a language to be given independently of an antecedent practical understanding of their meaning, as Carnap had supposed they must be. Thus, it is impossible to "freely stipulate" such rules on the level of syntax without already implicitly or explicitly presupposing their meaning, and thus it is impossible to conceive the origin of a language, as Carnap had, as depending on such completely free and arbitrary stipulation. Carnap's conventionalist picture of the structure of a language must accordingly be, Quine concludes, little more than a theorist's reconstructive fiction, grounded, in fact, in an untenable picture of the origin of language itself.

In place of the untenable conventionalist picture, Quine's criticisms at this time begin to suggest an alternative conception of the total structure of language as grounded (if it can be grounded at all) in the "always-already" dimension of linguistic use, which must accordingly be presupposed to any reconstructive description of its underlying rules. He drew this conclusion more explicitly in the notorious 1950 article "Two Dogmas of Empiricism" and its 1954 follow-up, "Carnap and Logical Truth."[86]

For Carnap, the actual underlying rules of a language, whether freely stipulated in instituting a language or determined later on by the reconstructive linguist, licensed a distinction between the *analytic* truths of the language—those made true simply by those rules themselves—and the *synthetic* truths which were seen as depending on empirical evidence or verification. Carnap assumed that it would always be possible for a theorist to draw this distinction (in a way consistent with the actual use of the language in question); but as Quine argued in "Two Dogmas," with respect to any actually *used* or *spoken* language, the theoretician's reconstructive decision as to *which* sentences actually used by the speakers to take as analytic—which, in other words, to characterize as following simply from the rules of the language itself—will always, and necessarily, depend upon the *theorist*'s sense for the synonymy and meaning of terms, as they are actually used in the practice of the language's speakers.[87] And there is no reason to suppose that this sense can amount, with respect to the actual facts of linguistic use, to anything more than a free theoretical *projection*.

We can see this particularly clearly, Quine argues in "Carnap and Logical Truth," by considering the situation of an interpreter or linguist who is charged with the task of making sense of a wholly unfamiliar language by discovering its supposedly constitutive structural principles. Such a reconstruction, Quine argues, will inevitably be guided as much by the structure of the interpreter's *own* language, as well as the interpretive stipulations he makes to connect the two languages, as by anything actually intrinsic to the language under interpretation itself.[88] It follows that it is, in general, impossible for the theoretician uniquely to determine, for any actually used language, its "real" constitutive and underlying rules. The conventionalist picture of languages as calculi capable of being freely instituted by laying down the constitutive rules of use, which is essential to Carnap's analytic project in all of its versions, is thereby revealed as a theoretician's fiction, and the project of analysis it underlies revealed as futile.

It was, in fact, just this objection to Carnap's conventionalism that would eventually lead Quine to his most important semantic result, the thesis that, in what Quine called the situation of radical translation, any systematic translation of an alien language will be systematically indeterminate, even given *all* of the facts of actual linguistic usage accessible, in principle, to empirical investigation. The thesis of indeterminacy, first formulated in 1960 in *Word and Object*, generalizes Quine's initial objections to Carnap's picture into the broader-ranging claim that *any* systematic determination of the rules underlying the "meanings" of words in a language—what Quine now called a "translation manual" for the language as a whole—will in fact depend on a host of arbitrary decisions ungrounded in the facts themselves.[89] To illustrate the difficulty, Quine imagines the plight of the field linguist whose task is to make sense of an alien language of which he has no antecedent knowledge. Such a linguist, if he is indeed initially innocent of the language under consideration, is necessarily required to derive his conclusions about the right translations of the native terms entirely from the evidentiary basis provided by his observations of the natives' speech behavior, in response to various empirically observable stimuli and conditions. Quine's result is that translation, under this condition, is systematically indeterminate, for:

Manuals for translating one language into another can be set up in divergent ways, all compatible with the totality of speech dispositions, yet incompatible with one another. In countless places they will diverge in giving, as their respective translations of a sentence of the one language, sentences of the other language which stand to each other in no plausible sort of equivalence however loose.[90]

The result marks the definitive failure of Carnap's attempt to conceive of any actually used or interpreted language as a calculus, definable by specific and unique rules accessible to neutral investigation. For as Quine had pointed out repeatedly in his decades-long dialogue with Carnap, any theorist's description of the constitutive rules of the language would either depend substantially on the theorist's own antecedent sense of the "meanings" of its terms in use or, if the theorist (as in the radical translation situation) were debarred from assuming this sense, would remain substantially underdetermined by the facts of use themselves.

If what we intuitively understand as meaning is indeed in *some* sense determined by our regular usage of terms and expressions in a language, why should it thus be impossible, as Quine asserts, for the theoretician to uniquely capture this usage with a systematic description of underlying rules or regularities? In its most general form, the answer to this question lies in the existence of a general and profound aporia concerning the explicit description of language that Quine was not the first to discover, but upon which his indeterminacy result, like many of the most significant negative results of the analytic tradition, essentially relies.[91] In the specific terms of Quine's analysis, the problem, in its general form, might be put as follows. Any systematic description of the "rules of use" thought to characterize the actual facts of the usage of a language—the actual ways in which its practitioners combine terms and expressions and move between them—will always, necessarily, be at some distance from the lived reality of use itself. That is, the theoretician's reconstruction of the rules for any actual language always involves some degree of abstraction from the totality of the actual facts concerning the utterance of particular locutions and expressions on particular occasions (past, present, and future). In determining the rules, the theoretician must therefore always make some non-trivial set of reconstructive assumptions, essentially ungrounded in the facts themselves, in order to arrive at a particular description of the (supposedly actual and underlying) rules. And as Quine's result shows, for any such description, there will always be other, inconsistent ones that are equally explicatory of the totality of facts of the actual practice of the language. There is thus an essential and ineliminable gap between *any* systematic description of the "structure of language" in terms of rules and the actuality of its practice, what we may think of as the ordinary life of language in its concrete, intersubjective use. This gap cannot, as Quine also realized, be crossed by any description, no matter how complete, of the facts about the use of a language, as long as these facts are described in neutral terms and without pre-judging the question of meaning.[92]

Were it not for the aporia that Quine demonstrates, we might happily admit the usefulness of Carnap's fiction of the origin of meaning, even if we did not take it as an accurate description of any historical fact; like the useful fiction of a social contract itself, we might take it as a helpful summary of the constitutive *structure* of the phenomena, even if not a literal description of the historical truth. But the aporia at the center of Quine's result demonstrates that the conventionalist picture of institution is not tenable, even as a reconstructive fiction, for it shows that the picture is grounded in an untenable picture of the nature of language itself. For if, as Quine's result demonstrates, any useful *statement* of the rules constitutive of meaning demands that the theorist interpret those rules in some already existing language, it is incoherent to suppose, as Carnap does suppose, that they might simply be freely stipulated without the meanings of the terms thus fixed being presupposed.

This anti-conventionalist moral of Quine's result may at first seem to suggest the possibility of an alternative *naturalist* picture of the origin and structure of language. Failing to portray this structure as grounded in conventional agreements or stipulations, we might easily be tempted to reason that it must, instead, be grounded in naturalistically describable facts of behavior, neurobiology, or evolutionary history. But despite Quine's own adoption of the language of behaviorism and his enthusiasm for naturalism in the restricted domain of *epistemology*, the aporia underlying the radical translation result actually bears just as deeply against a naturalistic picture of the structure of language as it does against Carnap's conventionalist picture. For the source of Quine's result is not simply naturalism, but rather the gap that exists between any unique description of the structure of language and the totality of the facts of its actual use, *however* these are described. And the aporia remains the same whether these facts are conceived as instituted *or* traditional, as conventional *or* natural. Its point is that the theorist's reconstruction of what he portrays as the constitutive rules for the language essentially outruns the totality of *all* the facts, natural *or* conventional, that can be described from a position that does not presuppose the very semantic phenomena of meaning that are to be explained; and this essential gap between the totality of the facts and these phenomena remains, no matter how the facts in question are characterized.[93]

As we saw above, the development of structuralism from Saussure's initial conception of language as a total structure of signs to the orientation of Lacan and Miller involves an internally motivated transition from a conventionalist criteriology to the paradoxico-critical orientation, which is defined by the adumbration of the paradoxes of language's representation within itself. In the structuralist tradition, as we saw, this development was determined by a reflection on the necessary appearance of a constitutive structural *excess* of the signifier over the signified, which manifests in the structural necessity of "floating signifiers" or "zero-value elements" that paradoxically represent the total logic of the system within itself.

We may, in fact, see Quine's thesis of the indeterminacy of translation, as well, as demonstrating just such an excess. According to Quine's result, as we have seen, any description of the total structure of a language—any characterization of the total logic of signification as such—is underdetermined by the totality of all of the facts of usage and reference, actual or possible, that are accessible (even in principle) to a radical interpreter or, indeed, to any objective investigator. Thus, what we intuitively understand "from the inside" as linguistic meaning, what we take to be determined wholly by the signs themselves, is shown to be essentially excessive with respect to, and underdetermined by, the totality of possible facts of reference or real occurrences in the field of the signified.

In fact, the development from Carnap's position to Quine's precisely mirrors the structuralist trajectory we have witnessed above, from Saussure through Lacan to Miller. In particular, we have, as before, an *initial position* which sees language as a total "syntactic system" wherein the relationship between signs and their meanings is arbitrary and conventional. Further reflection on the implications of considering language as a whole as a totality of possible signification, however (here, the totality of linguistic "meanings" as pre-theoretically grasped) given in advance of any actual occasion of use, yields a structurally necessary *excess of the signifier over the signified* (here, the indeterminacy of translation). This constitutive excess of the signifier over the signified is recognized as yielding a set of paradoxical elements (here, the contents of the "translation manual" itself) that effectively *signify the total system of language within that system itself*.[94]

It is true that the critical and political consequences of these developments in the analytic tradition have not been as clearly or prominently marked as they are in the continental structuralist one. This is the consequence of a number of factors, most prominently the somewhat misleading perception of analytic philosophy (shared by many analytic philosophers themselves) as wholly lacking political implications or motivations. This perception, in fact, set in only during the 1950s. One reason for it, no doubt, was the interpretation (which had by then become standard) of the metalogical paradoxes and incompleteness results as showing the inapplicability of formal logic and systems to "natural" languages and actual communities; I have criticized this interpretation in Chapter 1. At any rate, this interpretation of the formal register of analytic philosophy as apolitical also ignores the deeply held political motivations of some of the founders of the analytic tradition, including Carnap. These commitments played an important role in the original motivation of the Vienna Circle's analytic project, and were only suppressed later when many of the Vienna Circle principals emigrated to English-speaking countries amid World War II. But the fact that the broader political and critical implications of the analytic tradition's systematic consideration of language have not been prominently remarked does not imply (as I argued in *Philosophy and the Vision of Language*) that it does not have these consequences, or that they cannot today be rediscovered at the level of the constitutive link between language and community as such.

Through the two parallel trajectories I've developed here, we can see clearly how the natural internal development from an initial structuralist position committed to constructivism and criteriology to the later paradoxico-critical orientation involves fundamental transformations in the theory of language and our lived relation to it. In particular, whereas the basis of the original structuralist picture is in each case a constructivist consideration of the Many of languages (or language frameworks) *in the plural*, and hence yields a conventionalist picture of their arbitrariness and difference, further reflection on the internal implications of the possibility of modeling the structure of language as such (hence language *in the singular*) yields to the elaboration of paradoxes that characterizes the paradoxico-critical outlook. It is, in other words, a fundamental reflexive consideration of the One of language *as such* (e.g., the structure of signification as such, or the very structural possibility of its reflection into itself) that essentially yields the paradoxico-critical orientation.

This runs, as I shall attempt to show in later chapters, *directly* against the contemporary orthodoxy of linguistic and cultural plurality and heterogeneity, whereby each local "language game" or historical community is seen as responsible only to its own internal logic and its own specific history. The specific critical failing of this orthodoxy of difference and historicism is, of course, the same one that vitiates the original position of the Vienna Circle: namely, in countenancing a plurality of structurally well-defined languages, it fails entirely to pose the reflexive question of the very possibility of the position from which this plurality is visible or tractable, and thus fails at a fundamental level to make the *reflexive* gesture that must be considered an essential moment of any robust critical project, as such.

Insofar as this contemporary orthodoxy preserves a philosophical foundation at all, in fact, it simply carries forward the basic constructivist position already formulated by Carnap's original "principle of tolerance," although without, any longer, even attempting to consider the implications of the deep insight into the logical significance of syntax that motivated Carnap himself. This development (or rather substantial regression) can, perhaps, be seen most clearly in the influential expression of a pluralist, liberal pragmatism in the work of another of Carnap's students, Richard Rorty, who indeed retains the moral of Carnapian tolerance while eschewing the deeper register of critical reflection on the structure of language that originally produced it.[95]

3 Deleuze, Plato, and the Paradox of Sense

In the last chapter, we saw how paradoxico-criticism, committed to a rigorous thinking of the paradoxical limits of totality, developed from the initial conventionalism of Saussure's theory of language as a system of differences to a far-reaching critical reflection on the totality of language, or of the world, or of Being itself. In this chapter, we shall see how the early works of Gilles Deleuze take this same problematic a step further. Tracing the paradoxes of limits as they are reflected in the everydayness of language that proposes and also deposes them, Deleuze's thought discerns the contradictory and paradoxical as the originary dimension of the a-subjective and pre-personal production of sense and phenomena. The central operations of this production arise from the scission between a totality and itself that results from its own internal reflection. These are operations at the boundaries that demonstrate the strict *in-closure* of any total regime of meaning or force, and in *The Logic of Sense* and *Difference and Repetition*, Deleuze shows how the paradoxical structure of sense underlying both meaningful and meaningless language supports, and also undermines, the coherence of any such regime. On this basis, Deleuze develops a theory of the Platonic Idea which, though it owes nothing to "Platonism" traditionally conceived, nevertheless plausibly captures the very formal relationship which Plato calls "participation." This yields a structurally radical and new resolution of the problem of the *nomothesis*, or of the force and effectiveness of language and institutions, and makes way for what Deleuze calls the "power of a new politics" capable of originating revolutionary transformations of thought and action.

STRUCTURE AND THE PARADOX OF SENSE

In an exemplary article from 1967 called "How Do We Recognize Structuralism?" Deleuze enumerates a series of criteria or common features definitive of structuralism and the structuralist movement.[1] The first of these criteria, according to Deleuze, is the recognition of a specific domain or order of "signification," completely distinct from both the orders of the real and the imaginary. This recognition, Deleuze notes, provides for a dramatic and even revolutionary advance beyond the methods of classical philosophy, as well as the nineteenth- and early twentieth-century movements of Romanticism, Symbolism, and Surrealism, which attempt to comprehend the real as such but see it as in relation to imagination and the imaginary. According to Deleuze, structuralism, by contrast, discerns in language and signification a "third regime," wholly distinct from the real as such but also distinct from the imaginary and its "games of mirroring, of duplication, of reversed identification and projection, always in the mode of the double";[2] it is at the point of the sign and its action that we can now discern something like the "transcendent point where the real and the imaginary interpenetrate and unite."[3] Most decisively, Saussure's conception of language as a system of pure differences allows for a conception of meaning as grounded neither wholly in the reality of things nor in the resemblances of the imagination but rather in a structure that "has no relationship with a sensible form, nor with a figure of the imagination, nor with an intelligible essence."[4] That is, the discovery of the order of signification, and its articulation of language as a system of pure differences, allows us to see the foundations of meaning in an order that has *nothing to do* with resemblance, mimesis, or the representation of a preexisting order of things or concepts. The sign is, rather, split between signifier and signified, between the order of things on one side and the order of concepts on the other, and the recognition of its differential structure provides a profound new insight into the paradoxical point that defines and conditions both orders. It is in this way that the specific discovery of the structure of language by Saussure provides a vast new project for thought, and a radically transformed arena for theoretical work.[5]

Two years later, in *The Logic of Sense*, Deleuze turns to the theorization of the structural basis of language, which Deleuze now calls "sense." Sense, as Deleuze emphasizes in the opening sections of the book, is both the *result* of the structural deployment of signs in speech and, equally, the *precondition* for the total structure of signs, a kind of original dimension of language that is presupposed by all of its functions and cannot be understood simply in terms of any one of them. As such a condition, sense is whatever underlies and determines the stable directional relations of definition, inference, and reference that signs bear to each other and to things in the world. At the same time, though, sense for Deleuze *also* underlies the *instability* of meaning and, even more generally, the phenomena of change, flux, and becoming. Indeed, because of this bivalent tendency to underlie both stability and instability, both being and becoming, sense cannot be understood, Deleuze insists, as simply opposed to nonsense, conceived as that which is simply outside the possibility of sense. Rather, sense moves in "both directions at once," both toward the constitution of a full, determinate meaning, and simultaneously toward the dispersal and dissolution of any such meaning in contradiction and nonsense, with which it bears a special and "specific" internal relation.[6]

Through a remarkable reading of Lewis Carroll's *Alice's Adventures in Wonderland* and *Through the Looking-Glass*, Deleuze argues that this bidirectionality is essential for understanding change and becoming. In fact, as Deleuze argues, paradoxical sense, conceived as the domain of a "pure becoming," or a category of "pure events," is the constitutive basis of all kinds of change, transformation, and manifestation. For instance, as Alice becomes taller than she was before, she is also smaller than she will be. At the same moment, and in relation to her becoming, she is thus characterized by contradictory predicates, and this contradictoriness demonstrates an *essential* bivocality or opposition at the root of becoming that is inherent to all becoming and change as such.[7] The paradox, which was already suggested by Plato, demonstrates, as well, the more general relation of sense as such to the paradoxes that characterize the appearance and manifestation of language. Bidirectional sense itself thus exists in an original relationship of sense to what is classically determined as its "other," the nonsense of paradoxes, contradiction, wordplay, and the unlimited reversals of pure becoming, as eminently demonstrated in the plays, ruses, and adventures, often genuinely undecidable between the sense of narration and the nonsense of pure language, that make up the strange "substance" of Alice's adventures.

Given this bidirectional character, sense is para-doxical in the original meaning of the term (that is, as running "contrary" to opinion or *doxa*). It is only subsequently that its sense can be rendered uni-directional by the orthodoxies of what Deleuze calls "good sense" and "common sense." In particular, whereas *good sense* "affirms that in all things there is a determinable sense or direction," *common* sense distils from this ostensibly determinable direction the assignation of stable identities, the identification of substances and subjects as the bearers of fixed names and determinate properties. However, in its original articulation of sense as such, "paradox is . . . that which destroys good sense as the only direction, but it is also that which destroys common sense as the assignation of fixed identities."[8] This original articulation is, moreover, deeply linked to the problematic of language and its limits. Thus, "It is language which fixes the limits (the moment, for example, at which . . . excess begins), but it is language as well which transcends the limits and restores them to the infinite equivalence of an unlimited becoming."[9] It is, in other words, language as a totality of possible signification that determines sense as unidirectional meaning or reference to being; but this linguistic determination and staging of sense also evinces sense as the condition for a transcendence of the specific limits of language in the excessive dimension that again allows an unlimited affirmation of bidirectional becoming.

Deleuze proceeds to characterize this "excessive" and original dimension of sense through a series of specific paradoxes that demonstrate how it underlies (though it is distinct from) the denotative, deictic, and significative (or inferential and propositional) dimensions of language as it is ordinarily spoken. First, there is the paradox of inference already given by Lewis Carroll in his dialogue "What the Tortoise Said to Achilles" in 1895 (see Chapter 2).[10] As we have seen, this paradox appears to show that the application of the logical rule involved in the most ordinary chains of reasoning cannot be justified, on pain of a bottomless infinite regress of justifications. Deleuze concludes that the ascent from the proposition, as conditioned by its logical relations, to its underlying logical conditions will never have a finite end; it is therefore necessary either simply to affirm the irreducibility of this paradox or to affirm sense as a constitutive dimension of the "unconditioned" which halts the regress and provides an ultimate foundation for the possibility of significative meaning. Thus there is, as a fundamental and constitutive feature of linguistic meaning, an essential *gap* between rules and their application that must apparently result from *any* attempt to found language in the unity of a complete system of logical laws.

The second paradox of sense concerns the conditions for possible denotation or nomination, and is given, again, by Lewis Carroll, this time in a brief passage in Chapter 8 of *Through the Looking-Glass*. In this passage, Alice discusses songs, names, and the names of names with the White Knight. Here, in response to each of Alice's successive questions about the name of an entity, the Knight is able to provide another, completely distinct name; the paradox is that if everything real has a name, and if no name can name itself, then the provision of any real name for anything will demand a name for *that* name, and so forth. The assumption of the nameability of any real entity thus leads to an infinite proliferation of names, or to the necessity of the assumption of an infinite possible extensibility of the power of linguistic naming.

In this form, the paradox might be thought relatively unproblematic: we might readily agree, for instance, that language bears within itself an infinitely extensible power of possible naming, or that there could *possibly* be an infinite number of names, without supposing that all of these names must be provided on any actual occasion of linguistic use or description. However, if we add the assumption that each name, in order to possess its denotational function, must be endowed with an intelligible sense or meaning, the paradox of regress becomes a more fundamental and devastating one.[11] For on this assumption, each name is endowed with *something*—a sense—which is *responsible for its being able to be used* to name what it does (or is what we understand when we know what it names). Thus, it ought to be possible in case of *any* use of a name to designate its sense, and then it must be possible to ask after the sense of *this* designation, and so forth. Here, the problem is not just that of an infinite possible extension of designations, but a bottomless regress of *conditions* for intelligible use, each of which must apparently be satisfied by another.

If we cannot block the regress, then the meaningful use of any term pre-supposes not only the possible existence, but also knowledge and reality of, an infinite chain of conditions. The regress thus testifies not only to the "infinite power of language" but, seemingly, to the irreducible infinity of the *knowledge* or *competence* involved in, and presupposed by, the most ordinary use of any name.

Finally, Deleuze develops this paradox of naming and designation, under the condition of Saussure's structuralist picture of the sign as the unity of signifier and signified, into a third paradox of alternation or of the signifier-signified relation itself. In particular, conceived in terms of structuralism, the paradox of regress we have just considered shows the necessity of an ongoing *alternation* between signifiers and signifieds, whereby the signification of a signified results in the production of a new signifier, which may then itself be treated as a designated (signified) entity, to be named again by a new signifier, and so on. As Deleuze argues, this alternation has a basic and fundamental significance for our underlying conception of the basis of language (thought as composed of the two systems of signifiers and signifieds). For absent any other principle of coordination, and given the avowed "arbitrariness" of the link between the signifier and the signified in any individual sign, to assert the infinite alternation demonstrated in the course of the paradox is in fact the *only* way in which it is possible to assert a systematic relation between the level of the signifiers and the level of the signified at all. In other words, once again, the only way to understand the general possibility of language (which must, after all, amount to drawing *some* connection between signifiers and signifieds) is to affirm the paradox of regress involved in the actuality of signification itself, whereby each signifier becomes a possible object of signification for another.

EXCESS, VIRTUALITY, IDEALITY

If we are thus, once again, led to affirm sense as the inherently paradoxical condition for the possibility of any signification whatsoever (here, the precondition for any systematic relationship between the system or structure of signifiers and that of the signifieds), then what consequences follow for how we should think of the overall structure of language in itself? The most important such consequence is that there is in language a fundamental and constitutive *excess of signification* over the signified, a surplus of signifiers that always goes beyond the actuality of what is signified. To see this, consider again the paradox of regress and the alternation of signifiers and signifieds to which it gives rise. This alternation is not simply a static exchange, but is always directional and oriented: for at each level, it is the existence of a *signified* that implies the existence of a *signifier* (which then, if supplied, becomes a new signified, and so on). In other words, what is demanded at each stage by the principle that everything real must have (or be capable of having) a name is, at each stage, a new signifier: in this way, the directionality of the whole series is oriented toward the excess (always one more) of signifiers over signifieds. Given the completion of the series to any particular stage, it will always be possible to ask for the signifier of what exists at that stage, and so to move to the next one by means of its provision. Short of dropping or suspending the principle that everything must have a name, there is nothing we can do to block this regress, which we may accordingly take to define the (infinite) totality of significations. We may accordingly take this oriented, directional excess to be essential to language, and definitive of sense itself.

This excess of signification is nothing other than the permanent and original dimension of latency recognized as an inherent consequence of Saussure's structuralism by Lévi-Strauss, Lacan, and Miller (see Chapter 2). When this excess of signification is problematically signified within language itself, it gives rise to the famous "floating signifier," which is, according to Lévi-Strauss, "the promise of all art, all poetry, all mythic and aesthetic invention."[12] To this set of promises, Deleuze adds, as well, a political significance, holding that the floating signifier can also be understood as the "promise of all revolutions."[13]

Indeed, according to Deleuze, we may use this understanding of the role of paradoxical sense in underlying the dynamic structure of language to comprehend the general conditions of *structure* as such. The first of these conditions, as we have seen, is the existence of two heterogeneous series, one determined as signifying and the other as signified. But the relationship, or tension, between the two series is necessary to determining the dynamism of structure as such. That is why the second condition is that:

> Each of these series is constituted by terms which exist only through the relations they maintain with one another. To these relations, or rather to the values of these relations, there correspond very particular events, that is, *singularities* which are assignable within the structure. The situation is very similar to that of differential calculus, where the distributions of singular points correspond to the values of differential relations.[14]

Both the existence and the dynamism of the two series, linked in problematic correspondence, are outcomes of the circulation of the paradoxical element that manifests sense itself, the empty square or the floating signifier corresponding to the floated signified. But this circulation is not, according to Deleuze, simply a homogenous development, or unitary progression; it is, rather, articulated by specific points of inflection, reversal, and qualitative differentiation. These are the "sense-events" at the basis of all change and becoming. They are *singular* points in that they are: "turning points and points of inflection; bottlenecks, knots, foyers, and centers; points of fusion, condensation, and boiling; points of tears and joy, sickness and health, hope and anxiety, 'sensitive points'."[15] Because they articulate sense, which (as we have seen) is prior to and different from the ordinary linguistic order of reference and signification, they are not to be understood as equivalent to individual agents, states of affairs, or universal concepts. In this respect, singularities are definitively *neutral*. Indeed, Deleuze says, they escape and precede the oppositions between the individual and the collective, the personal and the impersonal, and the particular and the general. Their articulation and distribution not only conditions the two normal chains of signifiers and signifieds in their mutual relations and correspondences, but can *also* displace these relations into entirely new directions and connections.

This recognition of the way that what he calls singularities, or events, articulates any possible dynamism of structures by means of its paradoxical neutrality leads Deleuze to theorize structure and event as deeply and constitutively linked. Thus, "it is imprecise to oppose structure and event"; for "the structure includes a register of ideal *events*."[16] Within the structure that is defined simply by its differential relations, the singularities (or sense-events) are those points that correspond to what seem to be solid elements, for instance, the specific values in the differential structure of linguistic phonemes that correspond to the actual values of sounds and letters.[17] These events, or singularities, are thus *ideal* in that they correspond to the structure of language as a whole and define its action, but at the same time *real* in that they account for the actual processes of change and becoming that occur within the course of this action.

Indeed, as Deleuze argues in *Difference and Repetition*, the relationship of preconditioning here (what is expressed by calling the field of sense "transcendental") is no longer to be understood as a matter of *conditions of possibility* at all, but rather as a dimension of *the virtual* that is not opposed to the real but, in fact, a part of it:

> The virtual is opposed not to the real but to the actual. The virtual is fully real in so far as it is virtual. Exactly what Proust said of states of resonance must be said of the virtual: 'Real without being actual, ideal without being abstract'; and symbolic without being fictional. Indeed, the virtual must be defined as strictly a part of the real object—as though the object had one part of itself in the virtual into which it plunged as though into an objective dimension . . . The reality of the virtual consists of the differential elements and relations along with the singular points which correspond to them. The reality of the virtual is a structure.[18]

It is only as real, and indeed as a "part" or dimension of the objects themselves, that the dimension of sense can articulate their meaning and determine their properties. It does not do so, however, by resembling them or replicating their form, but rather through the original effects of structure, which opens and ensures the circulation of the two series of words and objects. Rather than being opposed to the elements of these series in terms of the duality of possible and real, therefore, the paradoxical structure of sense conditions these elements in their total structure, and mutual definitive relationships, by means of a virtuality that is opposed to the "actuality" of these elements, without being in any respect less than completely determinate and productive.

This paradoxical element at the basis of the movement of language and the possibility of sense combines a number of contradictory features: "It is at once excess and lack, empty square and supernumerary object, a place without an occupant and an occupant without a place, 'floating signifier' and floated signified, esoteric word and exoteric thing, white word and black object."[19] The paradoxical, two-sided element is thus neither word nor thing, but this does not preclude it from having its *own* proper sense; indeed, given its capability to present the form of *all* sense, Deleuze argues, its own proper sense will be unique and exceptional. In fact, the defining characteristic of this element is precisely that it "denotes exactly what it expresses and expresses what it denotes."[20] In other words, "It says something, but at the same time it says the sense of what it says: it says its own sense."[21]

But it is this unique self-relation of the "paradoxical element" that says its own sense (and so manifests, in this self-showing, what paradoxically *conditions* the entirety of sense itself) that points to what is perhaps the most remarkable parallel suggested by Deleuze's whole analysis. This is the parallel to what is indeed, as we have already seen, the founding paradox of set theory's consideration of meaning and reference: Russell's paradox of the set of all sets that are not members of themselves.[22] In drawing out the comparison, Deleuze emphasizes how the existence of the "paradoxical element" that says its own sense must necessarily imply a fundamental structural violation of the "regressive law" that assigns the designation of each object to a higher level or type, as well as the "disjunctive law" that demands that a property cannot refer to itself:

> . . . When the regressive law states that the sense of a name must be denoted by another name, these names of different degrees refer, from the point of view of signification, to classes or properties of different "types." Every property must belong to a type higher than the properties or individuals over which it presides, and every class must belong to a type higher than the objects which it contains. It follows that a class cannot be a member of itself, nor may it contain members of different types. Likewise, according to the disjunctive law, a determination of signification states that the property or the term in relation to which a classification is made cannot belong to any of the groups of the same type which are classified in relation to it. An element cannot be part of the sub-sets which it determines, nor a part of the set whose existence it presupposes. Thus, two forms of the absurd correspond to

the two figures of nonsense, and these forms are defined as 'stripped of signification' and as constituting *paradoxes*: a set which is included in itself as a member; the member dividing the set which it presupposes—the set of all sets, and the "barber of the regiment." The absurd then is sometimes a confusion of formal levels in the regressive synthesis, sometimes a vicious circle in the disjunctive synthesis.[23]

Thus, the most general and underlying paradox of sense, manifest in the "paradoxical element" that, in linking the floating signifier to the floated signified, presents the original and pervasive excess of signification, is identical in form to Russell's paradox of the set of all sets that are not members of themselves (or to its more "intuitive" version, the paradox of the barber who must shave all those in the regiment who do not shave themselves). As we have seen, the paradoxical Russell set has two determinants, which correspond precisely to the two sides of absurdity, as presented by Deleuze. First, there is the possibility for a set to be contained within itself, which Russell himself sought to prohibit through the imposition of a hierarchy of types (and which is similarly prohibited by what Deleuze calls the "regressive law.") Second, there is the capacity of any well-defined set (given by the fundamental axioms of set theory [extensionality]) to determine a distinction (what Deleuze calls a "disjunctive synthesis") between what is within it and what is outside it. If we allow a set (or element) to possess both capacities, and thus to violate both of Deleuze's laws, the paradox of the set of all sets that are not self-membered results immediately. But the "paradoxical element," which is nonsense in that, denoting its own sense, it violates both of these normal laws, must be considered to be just such a one.

As we saw previously in Chapter 1, Russell's response to his own paradox of set membership is a gesture that is both theoretical and prohibitive: he introduces as an absolute law of language and membership the hierarchy of types, which makes it impossible for the set of all sets (or the Russell set of all sets not members of themselves) even to be defined (let alone to "exist"). This gesture, indeed, defines as legal only those sets that comport with (the set-theoretic versions of) Deleuze's two laws of normal signification: that no set can be a member of itself (no sign can denote its own sense), and that no set can define a disjunction that its definition itself presupposes.

However, Deleuze's response, while recognizing the existence and far-ranging implications of the same paradox, is fundamentally different and even the direct opposite of Russell's. In particular, as Deleuze shows, we may take the laws prohibiting self-membership and self-applying disjunctions as indeed conditioning "proper" or non-paradoxical sense, without, nevertheless, completely denying any sense whatsoever to such paradoxical elements as do indeed violate these laws of "proper" signification. The decision to do so, in fact, reflects the recognition that the prohibitions that guarantee the absence of paradox, in legislating the conditions for the regular operation of the domain of proper or "good" sense, also first give rise to the ordinary logical laws and axioms constitutive of this domain, including the law of non-contradiction and the principles underlying ordinary set membership and inclusion.[24]

Even more suggestively, the close analogy (or identity) that Deleuze points out between the paradoxical element that, in illegally presenting its own sense, bears the status of nonsense, and the Russell set of all sets that are not members of themselves, yields the suggestion of a remarkable and radical insight into the basis for the general meaning of concepts itself. For if we may consider the denotation of various individuals by a general term or concept to be analogous to (or identical to) the grouping of these individuals within a particular, well-defined set, then we may indeed, conversely, consider the relationship of set membership, figured by the symbol "$\in$" (usually read "is an element of") to stand for the relationship that an individual bears to a concept that it falls under (see Chapter 1). Indeed, that such a definition is always possible is precisely the intuition underlying Frege's original formulation of the unrestricted comprehension axiom. And extending the analogy (or identity) between set membership and general denotation, we may take whatever determines the *unity* of a set—here, precisely what *is symbolized* by the sign "$\in$"—to be (analogous to) sense. (In other words, we are assuming that "sense is whatever determines reference.") However, as we have seen, Frege's intuition is ruined by the apparent definability of a set that, in its definition, refers to this general relation of set membership (and exclusion) itself, the Russell set. The consequence is that, in ordinary set theory, such sets are debarred, and it is impermissible to define any set by terms that *refer* to the general relationship of set membership (as the Russell set does); indeed, the relationship of inclusion symbolized by "$\in$" is simply taken as a given and never defined. *However*—and this is the essential contribution of a theory of the paradoxical stratum of sense as prior to, and underlying, the domain of ordinary signification—*if* we may nevertheless accord sense prior to this paradoxical set or element, *its sense will be, precisely, the sense of "$\in$" itself.*

That is, the criterion that the Russell set uses to determine its members is stateable in terms of—and only in terms of—set membership itself (together with negation, which must be considered a feature of *any* logical language). If it is indeed impossible to speak of set membership, of the relationship that links concepts to individuals or universals to particulars, then this paradoxical element does not exist and cannot ever appear in any presentation or presence. If, however, it is indeed possible to conceive it as manifest—although illegal in the normal order of signification—as the exceptional remainder, the excess of signification, the empty square or the floating signifier (correlative to a deficiency in the order of the signified), then its own proper sense is precisely this general relationship of universals to particulars itself. Thus, by means of the fundamental paradox of signification that nevertheless took logic and the theory of signs two millennia to discern, something like a (problematic) solution is found for the problem that Plato already grasped as his most fundamental one: the problem of *participation*, or the link between the Idea and the particular that institutes the very order of language.

DELEUZE'S PLATONISM

As we have seen, sense is therefore, for Deleuze, a paradoxical *virtual* structure that produces becoming as the result of the ideal effectivity of sense-events in articulating turning points and fundamental inflections of change. It is this paradoxical structure of sense in underlying the phenomena of language and becoming that allows Deleuze to propose a radical rethinking of the relationship of Ideas to things, alternative to the conception Plato often suggests, which understands this relationship as one of resemblance or representation. For Deleuze, in fact, the virtual is the "characteristic state of Ideas"; it is the basis for the *production* of any existence whatsoever.[25] Paradoxical sense thus defines an original domain of constitution, positive and relational in itself, prior to and independent of the opposition between the possible and the real, or the hypothetical and the necessary. This domain is ordered not by the similarity between the image and the original or the resemblance between model and copy, but by the even more original and positive relationship between sense and what it conditions, one which has nothing to do with either resemblance or representation.

One of the primary uses of this inquiry into sense, according to Deleuze, is to evince a theory of the conditioning of phenomena that does not exclude their change and becoming, or in other words does not relegate this conditioning to the order of static being. In fact, through its definition as *inherently* paradoxical, as "going in both directions at once," original sense, prior to the ordering assumptions of good sense and common sense, can indeed provide such an accounting. This is the basis of its utility in answering to the paradox of becoming already identified by Plato: in becoming taller, Alice is, in the act and at the moment of becoming, both tall (in relation to her earlier state) and small (in relation to her later one). This paradox, of the "simultaneity of a becoming whose characteristic is to elude the present,"[26] is not simply the problem of the *specific* relationship involved in what Plato called "participation," which presents itself (on the surface, at least) as the problem of the relationship of two static beings (the idea and the participant) with one another. Rather, it is the more original problem of relationality *as such*, which is closely linked to the latter problem and, in a certain way, underlies it. Thus, as Deleuze says, there are in fact two dimensions or aspects of determination implied by Plato's theory. The first is the dimension of "limited and measured things, of fixed qualities, permanent or temporary"; this is the dimension that corresponds to the theory of Ideas as it is classically interpreted.[27] However, caught within this theory and implicit (and at some places explicit) in the Platonic text is a second dimension, that of the determination of a "pure becoming without measure," whereby, for instance, ". . . the younger becoming older than the older, the older [becomes] younger than the younger—but they can never finally become so; if they did they would no longer be becoming, but would be so."[28]

This second dimension, the dimension of becoming, is omitted from the theory of Ideas as classically interpreted, but as Deleuze points out, it is hardly ignored by Plato himself. Rather, it is the basis of a second and more profound dualism that we can discern in Plato's own text, in addition to and *at the basis of* the more familiar dualism of intelligible Idea and sensible object. By contrast with the more familiar one, this is a

> . . . more profound and secret dualism hidden in sensible and material bodies themselves. It is a subterranean dualism between that which receives the action of the Idea and that which eludes this action. It is not the distinction between the Model and the copy, but rather between copies and simulacra. Pure becoming, the unlimited, is the matter of the simulacrum insofar as it eludes the action of the Idea and insofar as it contests *both* model and *copy* at once.[29]

This second dualism does not, then, concern the relationship between the (definite) object and the (defining) idea, but rather splits the object between that part that receives the action of the Idea and that which remains the substrate of this action, the bare matter or unformed substance of the object itself. Again, the question here is not, therefore, the question of the relationship of the static Idea to its static participant, but of what allows the participant to participate, and thus to "receive" the various forms as it proceeds from one state to another. This second dualism, as Deleuze points out, thus suggests a more basic problem of becoming, at the root of any description of participation, and thus at the basis of any theory of Ideas.

It is a problem that, as Plato was well aware, affects and haunts the description of the Idea at every point. It crops up, repeatedly in the Platonic corpus, precisely at the points where the theory of Ideas is exposed to the question of change.[30] In *Difference and Repetition*, Deleuze treats this problem of "pure becoming" as essential to any possible contemporary reading of Plato, arguing that it yields a conception that is at once profoundly in the spirit of Plato's own suggestions, and yet provides the basis for the entire contemporary project of "overturning" or "reversing" Platonism. In particular: whereas the more familiar dualism of static Idea and its static object (or of the intelligible and the sensible) orders all metaphysical relations in terms of *representation*, or the relationship between an original and a copy, the second, "subterranean" dualism of becoming provides the basis for a rethinking of this relationship that completely reorders these relations, and allows us to think of the action of Ideas completely outside the regime of representation. This alternative—between an ordered regime of representation based on the copying of originals (with the Idea always thought as the original, and its objects as more or less good copies) and a deeper, non-representational order of replication—is the alternative that, for Deleuze, defines the imperative to "overcome Platonism," which is the imperative to "glorify . . . the reign of simulacra . . .," affirming their rights over those of the copy.[31]

What, however, is a simulacrum? A simulacrum is an "image without resemblance" built not upon similarity or identity, but upon disparity and difference.[32] Although it produces an "effect" of resemblance, it is not at all *founded upon* resemblance; rather, this effect is "an effect of the whole, completely external and produced by totally different means than those at work within the model."[33] It is constituted not by the similarity of essence or its static repetition, but by an inherently differential network of relations; in this network "repetition already plays upon repetitions, and difference already plays upon differences."[34] Thus, whereas Platonism founds the "entire domain that philosophy will later recognize as its own," as the order of representation "defined . . . by an essential relation to the model or foundation," affirming the rights of simulacra allows us to discern *behind* this order another, more chaotic one: an order of pure differences as producing everything that we recognize as similitude, preceding and constituting all identity and representation as such.[35]

With the analysis we have already considered of the paradoxes of language and their ultimate ground in the paradoxical structure of sense, in fact, we already have in place all the resources needed to understand this strange order of simulacra, and the kind of alternative it defines for Plato and his contemporary reception. As we have already seen, in particular, the circulation of the paradoxical element between signifiers and signifieds manifests a "donation of sense" that has nothing to do with the relationship of copy to original, but is rather itself a "pure effect" of the action of structure, the network of differences. Given these relations, "that which is . . . has no prior constituted identity: things are reduced to the difference which fragments them . . ."[36] The basis for the possibility of this reduction is, again, the purely differential order of symbolic language, which elicits sense as both its effect and its paradoxical quasi-cause. This original order of pure differences is the order of simulacra, and defines the possibility of their infinite circulation in language. In underlying this circulation, simulacrum and symbol are in a certain sense "one"; in particular, "the simulacrum is the sign in so far as the sign interiorises the conditions of its own repetition."[37] That is, it is in the constitutive relationships that define the meaning of the sign and the possibility of its meaningful iteration that we can locate the procession and circulation of simulacra, a circulation that both precedes and produces the order of representation and similitude. These relations are to be understood—and can *only* be understood—in terms of the pure differential order exhibited by the paradoxical structure of sense.

We have also seen, above, that the key to understanding this structure is to consider the circulation of the "paradoxical element," which, manifesting the constitutive excess of signification, both disjoins and first articulates the two series of signifiers and signifieds. In connection with the sense-events that articulate the structure of paradoxical sense as "going in both directions at once," this circulation is the basis for the "pure becoming" that is "the matter of the simulacrum . . . insofar as it contests *both* model *and* copy," or in other words the whole domain of representation.[38] Whatever the extent of his adherence to the "official," representationalist theory of Ideas, Plato, it seems, suspected as much. Indeed, "Sometimes Plato wonders whether . . . pure becoming might not have a very peculiar relation to language."[39] Throughout the Platonic corpus, in fact, in passing instances and dialectical suggestions, strange anticipations and even aporetic conclusions, the specter of an originary difference and an order of the simulacrum, before and beyond the action of the Idea and the distinction between model and copy, flashes up and comes to expression, only to be modified, repressed, or subjected once again to the stable order of representation.

Such is the case, according to Deleuze, with the ultimate conclusion of the *Sophist*, which attempts to identify the sophist by separating, at a crucial point (236c), the good image-making of imitation to the bad image-making of the fabrication of appearances, which are apparently (*if* the distinction can be made) responsible for the possibility of error and falsehood (cf. 264c, and also *Republic* X, 601ff). However, at the final end (268a), "we glimpse the possibility of the triumph of simulacra" in that the sophist does not ultimately "distinguish himself from Socrates, placing the legitimacy of such a distinction in question."[40] Other examples of the sudden, lightning-like appearance of the simulacra and their indistinction from the Ideas occur in connection with Plato's consideration of a "model of the Other" that witnesses the original possibility of a kind of model of difference or dissimilitude itself (see, for instance, *Theatetus* 176e and *Timaeus* 28bff).

As Deleuze notes, at decisive moments in the Platonic corpus, as well, the paradox of becoming-unlimited according to which "more and less are always going a point further" is explicitly connected to the phenomena of language and writing.[41] This is the case, for instance, in the *Philebus*, where "it is through discourse that the same thing flits around, becoming one and many in all sorts of ways, in whatever it may be that is said at any time, both long ago and now" (15d). Here, the possibility of a limitless flux or circulation of things is guaranteed not only by this "gift of the gods to men" (16c) but, even further, by its articulation into "letters" (17a), the systematicity of the alphabet (18b–c), and the articulation of sounds by mutes or silences. As is shown by Derrida's classic analysis in "Plato's Pharmacy," this is even more the case in the *Phaedrus*, where writing is opposed to spoken language as both *supplement* and *inherent threat*, the "pharmakon" which is both cure and poison.[42] Thus, as Deleuze points out, according to Derrida's analysis, writing is here the *simulacrum* of logos; it is, in other words: "a false suitor, insofar as it claims to take hold of the logos by violence and by ruse, or even to supplant it without passing through the father."[43] The deconstructive aim that Deleuze and Derrida have in common, then, is simply to reaffirm the originary status and original rights of this simulacrum or false suitor, along with the irreducible and positive difference (compare Derrida's *différance*) that it demonstrates.

One of the most striking instances of the connection between simulacra and language, however, is the opinion voiced in passing by Socrates near the middle of the dialogue most profoundly dedicated to language and names, the *Cratylus*:

> Most of our wise men nowadays get so dizzy going around and around in their search for the nature of the things that are, that the things themselves appear to them to be turning around and moving every which way. Well, I think that the people who gave things their names in very ancient times are exactly like these wise men. They don't blame this on their own internal condition, however, but on the nature of the things themselves, which they think are never stable or steadfast, but flowing and moving, full of every sort of motion and constant coming into being. (411b–c)

The basis of this suggestion (which Socrates considers but nevertheless does not endorse, seemingly quoting the opinion of "wise men" and the *nomothetēs* or name-givers of ancient times) is the Heraclitean theory of constant becoming and uncontrollable flux. This theory is preserved on the more "official" level of the dialogue by Socrates' quotation of it,[44] as well as by the presence of Cratylus, who was himself historically a student of Heraclitus. The view that Cratylus actually voices holds that "one can never speak nor say anything falsely" (429e); the basis of this view is apparently an implicit rejection of the possibility of distinguishing between the "true copy" and the "false copy" with respect to names (cf. *Sophist* 264c). However, Cratylus is easily refuted, on the official level of the text at least, by Socrates' appeal to a representational order of likeness as the ultimate basis for the truth and falsity of names (430a–d). On the "official" level, therefore, the view endorsed by Socrates refutes the Heraclitean one, ultimately insisting upon a position whose defense is nevertheless, as Socrates indeed recognizes, "like hauling a ship up a sticky ramp" (435c), according to which "names should be as much like things as possible." This is the position of the order of representation; at the fundamental level of the assignation of names, it propounds an order of likeness and similarity that is supposed to ground and provide the possibility of all linguistic truth or falsity. However, repeatedly throughout the dialogue, this assumption at the level of the *nomothesis*, the posing of the law and the assignation of names, is contested by the suggestion of another, quite different foundation: one of pure becoming, flux, and flows whose basis, and evidence, is paradox.

We saw in Chapter 1 that the problem of the nomothesis is both at the center of the *Cratylus* and the basis of its ultimate invocation of forms, or ideas, as the source of the correctness of names and the force of their law. At first, the correctness of names seems to depend on the authority and divine power of the *nomothetēs*, the ancient and mysterious giver of names; by knowing the forms themselves, the *nomothetēs* or technician of names is able to mandate the law that links them to their objects in the correctness of an assumed correspondence. In a characteristic move that is replicated elsewhere throughout the Platonic corpus, this divine technology of production is itself, however, subordinated to the truer and deeper knowledge of the *user*, the knowledge of the form or idea that is manifest in the everyday practice (or *ethos*) of language and in the "agreement" that underlies it. This is the basis for Socrates' grudging admission that, much as he would like to defend a view that accords the ultimate basis of names to a mimetic relation of resemblance between words and things, we may indeed "have to make use of this worthless thing, convention, in the correctness of names" (435c). Nevertheless, even in making this admission, it is clear that Socrates still sees convention and usage as governed by an order of representational connections and similarities between words and things, an order of similarity or "appropriate" usage (435c) that defines the "best," if not the only, way to speak.

The question (which Plato does not hesitate to raise and pursue to its aporetic end) is precisely whether this assumption is justified: whether everyday usage exhibits the knowledge of true names *as* the knowledge of identity and resemblance, whether it simply applies infinitely the consequences of the deterministic repetition of a selfsame Idea, austere and timeless, or whether, as Cratylus seems to suggest, it is the "chance of usage and convention that makes both like and unlike letters express things" (435a). For what is at stake in this question of the relative priority of use and original designation, according to Deleuze, is *nothing other than the nature of forms in their entry into the world*, their force in determining the possibility of reference and the nature of knowledge.

As Deleuze points out, in fact, despite his official theory of representation, the inquiry in the *Cratylus* into the correctness of names repeatedly leads Socrates to suspect a more original relation of language to the procession of simulacra, unconstrained by representation and at the root of the "pure becoming" that first articulates the difference, and the paradox, of being and becoming.[45] On this suspicion, ". . . names signify the being or essence of things to us on the assumption that all things are moving and flowing and being swept along" (436e). Or alternatively, Socrates suspects without confirming the existence of "two languages and two sorts of 'names,' one designating the pauses and the rests which receive the action of the Idea, the other expressing the movements or rebel becomings . . ."[46] On this hypothesis, the original fixation of names by the divine *nomothetēs* or name-giver is decisively and violently split between those names that "point to rest" and those that "point to motion," between the hypothesis of a stable order of representation relating names to beings and a "rebel" order of simulacra relating them to becoming and change, producing a kind of "civil war among names" (438d) that ruins our ability to "judge between them" and demands, according to Socrates, another, quite different starting point.

If we are to avoid this constitutive split and this ruination of knowledge caused by the two orders of names, therefore, we must have recourse, Socrates says, to something "other than names, something that will make plain to us without using names which of these two kinds of names are the true ones—that is to say, the ones that express the truth about the things that are" (438d). This "something other than names" is, in fact, nothing other than the Idea, determined as that which avoids all change, flux, and becoming:

> *Socrates:* Still, let's investigate one further issue so as to avoid being
> deceived by the fact that so many of these names seem to
> lean in the same direction—as we will be if, as seems to me
> to be the case, the name-givers really did give them in the
> belief that everything is always moving and flowing, and as
> it happens things aren't really that way at all, but the name-
> givers have fallen into a kind of vortex and are whirled
> around in it, dragging us with them. Consider, Cratylus, a
> question that I for my part often dream about: Are we or
> aren't we to say that there is a beautiful itself, and a good
> itself, and the same for each one of the things that are?
> *Cratylus:* I think we are, Socrates. (439b–439d)

The necessity to avoid the rebel element, and the imperative to think the order of language as possible only on the basis of a preexisting order of resemblance and similarity, thus completely determines Plato's recourse here to the being of the Idea, thought of as "before names" in its mystical force, even prior to and underlying as a condition of possibility the power of the *nomothetēs*, which has fallen into error in considering becoming and motion to be primary. Here, in finally deciding the ultimate power of the *nomothetēs*, Plato thus seemingly affirms once more the right of the Idea over the simulacrum, even to the point of denying the ultimate relevance of the results of the very inquiry into names and their meaning which has so clearly articulated the investigation up to this point. However, there remains a fundamental paradox, as Plato is well aware; he does not deny it, but in fact uses it to conclude the dialogue at a point of aporia. It is, once again, the paradox of becoming:

> *Socrates:* But if it [the beautiful] is always passing away, can we cor-
> rectly say of it first that it is *this*, and then that it is *such*

and such? Or, at the very instant we are speaking, isn't it inevitably and immediately becoming a different thing and altering and no longer being as it was?

Cratylus: It is.

Socrates: Then if it never stays the same, how can it *be* something? After all, if it ever stays the same, it clearly isn't changing—at least, not during that time; and if it always stays the same and is always ever the same thing, so that it never departs from its own form, how can it ever change or move?

Cratylus: There's no way. (439d–e)

The inadequacy Plato recognizes here, and in fact never denies, is the inadequacy of being and the static order of presence to all motion, change, and becoming. The paradox, Socrates concludes by saying, threatens to ruin knowledge itself, for if language does indeed demonstrate a flux, change and becoming at the root of things, if things therefore are fundamentally "unsound, like leaky sinks," "like people with runny noses . . . afflicted with colds and drip[ping] over everything" (440c-d), it will be impossible as well for knowledge ever to be knowledge of what is, for each state of knowledge will pass over into something that is not knowledge, and there will be no knowledge as such. Nevertheless—and his assertion of it is an index of Plato's supreme integrity and honesty, far beyond that of those who see here simply an *apologia* for the rights of the Idea—it remains "certainly possible that things are that way"; there is no way, Socrates concludes the dialogue by saying, simply to exclude this rebel hypothesis of becoming, flux, and change. It will stand just below the surface of the Platonic text, for the two thousand years of philosophy's development of the Platonism of static Ideas, as a suppressed remainder of the original dualism of simulacra and copy that precedes and underlies the dualism of the idea and its object, a subcutaneous trace of the original paradox of sense in articulating the being and becoming of words and things.

4   Derrida and Formalism
Formalizing the Undecidable

One aim of this chapter is to consider the extent to which some of the key operations of Derrida's deconstruction can be understood as constituting a reflection on *formalism* and, therefore, as parallel to key metalogical results arising from reflection on the structure and limits of formal languages. Without excluding other ways of understanding the methods and significance of deconstruction, I argue that several of Derrida's key terms (for instance, *trace,* the 'undecidable,' and *différance*) and the textual *praxis* they embody can indeed usefully be understood as figuring the metalogical consequences of a thoroughgoing reflection on the implications of formalism. Therefore, I read Derrida's practice as an exemplary manifestation of paradoxico-criticism, which draws out the critical consequences of language's inherent reflexivity. This facilitates, as I shall argue, a clearer understanding of the critical textual *praxis* of deconstruction itself, as well as of its contemporary political implications.

DERRIDA AND THE UNDECIDABLE

As early as 1970, Derrida suggested an analogy between what he calls the "undecidable" and the incompleteness result discovered by Gödel and first announced in the article "On Formally Undecidable Propositions of *Principia Mathematica* and Related Systems I" published in 1931.[1] Derrida draws this connection in the course of a discussion in "The Double Session" in which he juxtaposes an excerpt from Mallarmé's text *Mimique* with a passage from Plato's *Philebus.* The issue raised by both texts (but also, as Derrida argues, by the whole of the metaphysical tradition) is that of *mimesis,* and of the relationship between a representational text, image, or inscription and the "original" that it represents. Mallarmé's text, Derrida argues, makes possible a thinking of *mimesis* whereby it is no longer understandable as the hierarchical relationship between a representation and a (present or deferred) original. Rather, Mallarmé's text gives us to think a "play" of *mimesis* with no original, an order of mirroring defined by *allusion* rather than the hierarchical logic of truth and illusion:

In this perpetual allusion being performed in the background of the *entre* that has no ground, one can never know what the allusion alludes to, unless it is to itself in the process of alluding, weaving its hymen and manufacturing its text. Wherein allusion becomes a game conforming only to its own formal rules. As its name indicates, allusion *plays*. But that this play should in the last instance be independent of truth does not mean that it is false, an error, appearance, or illusion. Mallarmé writes 'allusion,' not 'illusion.' Allusion, or 'suggestion' as Mallarmé says elsewhere, is indeed that operation we are here *by analogy* calling undecidable. An undecidable proposition, as Gödel demonstrated in 1931, is a proposition which, given a system of axioms governing a multiplicity, is neither an analytical nor deductive consequence of those axioms, nor in contradiction with them, neither true nor false with respect to those axioms. *Tertium datur*, without synthesis.[2]

Since "undecidable" and "undecidability" are terms that Derrida retains throughout his career, indeed putting them to a central use in his later analyses of such phenomena as hospitality and the gift, it is worth pausing over this analogy and asking what it shows us about the status of deconstruction *vis-à-vis* formalism and formalization, of which Gödel's result is a modern masterpiece.

The essence of Gödel's proof, as we saw in Chapter 1, is to construct a sentence in the language of Russell and Whitehead's *Principia Mathematica* or any similar system that is *undecidable* in the sense that, by way of the construction of a predicate that formalizes the rules of proof in that system, it "asserts" of "itself" that it cannot be proven within the system.[3] Gödel goes on to take this sentence as demonstrating the *incompleteness* of the system in the sense that (assuming the system is consistent) there is a *truth* that it cannot prove. For it is apparently possible to "see" (by means, however, of an essentially *informal* argument) that the proposition asserted by the Gödel sentence is true (i.e., that it itself is indeed not provable within the system), although *this* cannot be proven within the system.[4] Moreover, although Gödel himself demonstrated the result only in the special case of *Principia Mathematica*, it can certainly be generalized. Though the specific "Gödel sentence" for each system will be different, it can be proven that any formal system of a sufficient (relatively low) degree of complexity will have a Gödel sentence, and thus can be shown to be, necessarily, either inconsistent or incomplete. The more general significance of Gödel's result is that it demonstrates undecidability as a *general* phenomenon of any moderately complex formal system, an inherent consequence of any attempt to formalize the total logic of a system of proof or the rule-governed establishment of truth.[5]

In introducing the analogy to Gödel's result, Derrida is quick to emphasize that the undecidability that concerns him is *not* a matter of semantic ambiguity or polysemy:

'Undecidability' is not caused here by some enigmatic equivocality, some inexhaustible ambivalence of a word in a 'natural' language, and still less by some '*Gegensinn der Urworte*' (Abel). In dealing here with hymen, it is not a matter of what Hegel undertook to do with German words like *Aufhebung, Urteil, Meinen, Beispiel*, etc., marveling over that lucky accident that installs a natural language within the element of speculative dialectics. What counts here is not the lexical richness, the semantic infiniteness of a word or concept, its depth or breadth, the sedimentation that has produced inside it two contradictory layers of signification (continuity and discontinuity, inside and outside, identity and difference, etc.). What counts here is the formal or syntactical *praxis* that composes and decomposes it.[6]

That is, the undecidable, in the sense in which it concerns Derrida, is not a matter of single terms having a multiplicity of non-equivalent or even mutually contradictory "meanings." Quite to the contrary, the undecidability that Derrida finds in Mallarmé's text is a consequence of a total structural relationship that is, in *this* case, figured in the undecidability (for instance, between "inside and outside," "continuity and discontinuity") of the single term "hymen." However, since the undecidability here is that of *mimesis* itself, there is nothing essential about the term; others would have done just as well:

This word, this syllepsis, is not indispensable; philology and etymology interest us only secondarily, and the loss of the 'hymen' would not be irreparable for *Mimique*. It produces its effect first and foremost through the syntax, which disposes the '*entre*' in such a way that the suspense is due only to the placement and not to the content of words. Through the 'hymen' one can remark only what the place of the word *entre* already marks and would mark even if the word 'hymen' were not there. If we replaced 'hymen' by 'marriage' or 'crime,' 'identity' or 'difference,' etc., the effect would be the same, the only loss being a certain economic condensation or accumulation, which has not gone unnoticed. It is the 'between,' whether it names fusion or separation, that thus carries all the force of the operation.[7]

Thus, the point of emphasizing the ambiguous and even contradictory meanings of "hymen" in Mallarmé's text is not to evince anything intrinsic to this word itself, but rather to show the way in which it (contingently and non-essentially) occupies a particular *position* in this text—the position, as we may say, of the undecidable, what the text itself, and the logic that governs it, does not give us—for *structural* reasons—the resources to decide.[8]

Derrida goes on to emphasize, moreover, that what holds for "hymen" in Mallarmé's text holds, as well, for the (other) key terms of deconstruction, as he had already employed them in readings of Husserl, Plato, Saussure, Rousseau, Heidegger, and others:

> What holds for 'hymen' also holds, *mutatis mutandis*, for all other signs which, like *pharmakon, supplément, différance*, and others, have a double, contradictory, undecidable value that always derives from their syntax, whether the latter is in a sense 'internal,' articulating and combining under the same yoke, *huph'hen*, two incompatible meanings, or 'external,' dependent on the code in which the word is made to function. But the syntactical composition and decomposition of a sign renders this alternative between internal and external inoperative . . . Is it by chance that all these play effects, these 'words' that escape philosophical mastery, should have, in widely differing historical contexts, a very singular relation to writing?[9]

Since the "representative" sign lives on the distinction between the present and the non-present, or the distinction between the "original" and representation, any term for the condition of the possibility of such a distinction will exhibit the same kind of undecidability as Mallarmé's "hymen."

One such term, employed in relation particularly to Saussure's understanding of language as a "system of differences without positive terms," but bearing more general application as well, is the neologism *"différance."* The term, as Derrida explains in the article of the same title, problematically expresses a kind of general condition for the possibility of presentation itself, given that linguistic presentation is possible only within a system of signs. As we have seen in Chapter 2, Saussure's structuralist definition of the sign already implied that the meaning or "value" of each sign is dependent on the system of differences in the total structure of signs in two different ways: both in the sense of the synchronic or individual "difference" between the signifier and the signified, and in the sense of the serial or diachronic system of differences along both parallel chains. Indeed, as we have also seen, since structuralism begins by rejecting the assumption of any kind of natural relationship (e.g., of resemblance or representation) between the individual signifier and its signified, it seems that the first sort of difference must ultimately be understood in terms of the second, and the very possibility of meaning understood as a consequence of purely differential relations along the serial chain of signifiers. In this sense, the meaning of any sign depends on the structural movement of *deferral* along the whole chain, a movement in which there are, as Saussure emphasized, no "positive terms" but only constitutive difference.

The neologism *différance*, then, expresses this total, systematic, and differential condition for presence, combining both synchronic difference (as, for instance, between the individual signifier and its signified) and diachronic deferring (as along the chain or series of signifiers).[10] But because it indeed expresses such a total differential condition for any system of presentation, it is an apparent consequence of this that *différance* itself cannot, on pain of paradox, be presented or named *within* any system that is structured by it. It is thus that, according to Derrida, *"différance* has no name in our language" or in any other language,[11] and, accordingly, that "*différance* is neither a word nor a concept."[12] Rather, he says, in its very incapacity to be named, it "exceeds the order of truth at a certain precise point," reserving itself or removing itself "in regular fashion" from the systematic structural distinctions of truth or falsity or of presence and absence which it itself structures.[13]

Clearly, there is something paradoxical, and indeed almost self-refuting, about this invocation of *différance*. In claiming that *différance* "has no name in our language," and at the same time adducing principles that imply that the same would be true of any language (even the deconstructionist's own), has not Derrida simply undermined himself by purporting to name what, by his own lights, cannot be named? Of course, Derrida is aware of the paradoxical status of any invocation of *différance*, and constantly marks this status in his invocations and articulations of it. However, we can also understand better the specific (if deeply problematic) status of *différance* by linking it more closely to the specific structure that produces the undecidable, according to Derrida. As we have seen, the undecidable always results from a complication of the relationship between the "inside" and the "outside" of a total system (here, the total structure of signs). This kind of complication results from the combination of two operations: *first*, the structural principles determining the meaning and value of elements within the total system are defined and described, *as if* from a point "outside" the system itself; and *second*, this definition or description is recognized as in fact taking place, necessarily and problematically, *within* the total system whose structural principles are thereby defined and delimited. There is no reason to think that each of these two operations ought not be singly possible, but their conjunction produces the paradoxical situation of a problematic term, such as *différance*, which both "has" (in the extra-systematic sense) and "does not have" (in the intra-systematic sense) a meaning.

This is exactly the situation that occurs with the inscription of the Gödel sentence for a system—for instance, the system of *Principia Mathematica*—within that system itself. Moreover, it is just what occurs with reflection about the structure of language beginning with Saussure. As we have seen, Saussure already described the total structure of language—"from the outside," as it were—as consisting solely in synchronic difference and diachronic deferral. All that is, then, needed to generate a term like *différance* with its undecidable status is to reflect that this description itself takes place *in* a language so structured, and so cannot be seen as either straightforwardly "meaningful" nor, yet, completely "meaningless." Rather, its meaningfulness is "undecidable" in the strict sense that it can be decided neither by wholly internal nor by "external" criteria. It thus introduces a complicated topology of meaning that, depending on an essential confusion between "inside" and "outside," operates as the (necessarily "twofold" and "divided") site for the practice of deconstruction.

This structure can, in fact, be extended to all of the key terms of deconstructive reading. *Différance, pharmakon, trace, supplément,* and (later) *chora* all indicate (without, Derrida suggests, being able to *name*) the problematic point *within* a specific text at which the conditions of possibility of a total structural logic of presence and absence are figured and thereby undermined. All of these key terms, and the deconstructive operations they organize, manifest the undecidable as the determinate point at which the structural conditions for the possibility of the text are articulated, and then fail in their own application to themselves. It is in this sense that the regular, structural conditions of possibility of the distinctions upon which these specific texts live and function are revealed as, simultaneously, the conditions for their *im*possibility. This is the impossibility of giving a complete and coherent description of these conditions that itself operates unproblematically within the structural logic of the text thereby delimited.

Given this, it is possible to specify the analogy between Gödel's result and deconstructive undecidability on at least two significant points. First, both trade decisively on the capacity of a *total* system of signs, directed to the establishment of truth or the maintenance of presence, to represent its *own* constitutive conditions of possibility, to figure the basis of the central distinctions that organize the system itself. The Gödel sentence does this by "encoding" the syntactical structure of the system as a whole in a specific sentence within the system, while a deconstructive undecidable, similarly, works by encoding the text's specific structural conditions of possibility within it at a certain point. It is, in both cases, through their figuration *at a certain point*—the Gödel sentence or Derrida's "undecidable" terms—that these conditions are shown to undermine themselves in their own statement, and thus to be at the same time conditions of the *im*possibility of figuring the underlying logic of the system completely and consistently. In this way, although in each case the system achieves a kind of total *self-reference*, an "encoding" at a single point of the total logic that governs the entirety of the system, the very act of inscription implies the failure of this reference to the totality, or at least its constitutively paradoxical status. This amounts to a demonstration of the necessary existence of points or sentences (in particular, those that express the system's own conditions of possibility) that cannot be decided (as true or false, or as present or absent) in terms of it. In the case of the Gödel sentence itself, these conditions of possibility are represented in the "provability predicate" for a particular system which encodes the systematic, rule-governed possibilities of proof within a particular system. In a similar fashion, Mallarmé's "hymen" inscribes, within his text, the condition for the possibility of a structural distinction between original and representation in *mimesis*, and its inscription marks the point of the self-undermining of this distinction.

Second, in both cases the result can be *generalized*. Just as the existence of a Gödel sentence for *Principia Mathematica* points to the more general phenomenon of the incompleteness of *any* formal system of sufficient complexity, Derrida's *différance* encodes the *general* possibility of undecidability for any system of signs regularly governed by the opposition presence/absence.[14] Thus, the phenomenon of undecidability demonstrated in the particular case of Mallarmé's text by the term "hymen" is in no way limited to that particular text or term, but in fact can be extended to any mimetic system of signs whatsoever (or any system of signs insofar as it is understood as mimetic). The more general terms *différance*, *trace*, and *supplément* capture this and are explicitly meant to intervene to destabilize the *totality* of the metaphysics of representation, or what Derrida elsewhere calls the "metaphysics of presence" itself. They function wherever there is a field or structure of signs which presuppose, for their significative or truth-producing work, a distinction between presence and representation, or between representational truth and falsity—which is to say wherever there is a system of meaningful signs at all.

How "general," then, is the presence of undecidability, and the possibility of the deconstructive operations it permits? Here, the analogy to Gödel's result helps to show how the specificity of irreducibly situated operations at specific textual sites can coexist with a much more general and formal structure that underlies the possibility of deconstruction itself. In particular, although each formal system will have its own *specific* Gödel sentence (and the specific sentence depends on the specific character of the system, as well as the "encoding system" used to produce it), Gödel's result clearly does *not* simply evince a contingent limitation of a particular system such as *Principia Mathematica*, but rather demonstrates a fundamental feature of formalization *as such* (one which may cause us to reconsider basic and otherwise plausible ideas about the nature of mathematical truth). Along similar lines, while specific deconstructive operations are varied and always tied to particular sites, Derrida's more general invocation of undecidability suggests a fundamental reconsideration of what is involved in *any* possible system of representation, and hence in any *inscription* or *writing* of any sign as such.[15]

From his earliest discussions on, Derrida has occasionally been called to task for the apparent generality and even the "totalizing" character of his descriptions of the critique of the "metaphysics of presence," which can seem to sit poorly with the deconstructive emphasis on the irreducible plurality of contexts and variety of textual sites. However, if the analogy with Gödel indeed holds up, we are in a position to see that there is no opposition here; just as the plurality of formal systems and the variety of specific Gödel sentences formulated for them does not prevent Gödel's general result from illuminating, in a fundamental way, the structures of proof, truth, and meaning themselves, the irreducible plurality of textual sites at which deconstruction works is indeed unified by the general structures of presentation, representation, and writing that make *any* deconstructive reading possible.

There is, admittedly, also one point of at least apparent disanalogy that should be addressed. Whereas Gödel's result obviously concerns undecidability with respect to *truth* or *provability* within a system, Derrida's conception of undecidability extends, as we have seen, to considerations of *meaningfulness*, calling into question the very possibility of a statement of the conditions for the meaningfulness of a text's privileged terms. This affects, as we have seen, the very status of the terms (such as *différance*) which articulate the undecidable, calling into question whether these terms can themselves be meaningful. On the other hand, the Gödel sentence for any system is a straightforward sentence of the system whose meaningfulness is not in question (in any case, it is certainly well-formed according to the syntactic rules of the system). It may thus seem that the two forms of the "undecidable"—the one concerning only *truth* or *provability*, and the other concerning meaning and meaningfulness as well—are not in fact directly analogous, but may represent importantly different phenomena.[16]

To see that this is not so, and that what seems here to be a disanalogy in fact conceals a deeper analogy, it is helpful to consider more closely the status of the Gödel sentence (for a particular system) itself. As logicians and expositors have often pointed out, the Gödel sentence for any particular system is indeed a perfectly coherent and meaningful (that is, well-formed) formula of the system. However, *as such and without further interpretation from an "outside position"* it is also a completely insignificant formula, expressing (for instance, in the "intended interpretation" of a system that is supposed to found arithmetic) a perfectly ordinary and undistinguished formula of arithmetic. Thus, though it is certainly "meaningful" in an intra-systematic sense, it does not yet have the meaning of "asserting its own unprovability," which is clearly the crucial factor in producing its undecidability. Our ability to see it as having this further meaning depends on our taking a perspective outside the system from which we can see *how* the sentence "asserts its own unprovability," and in particular how it does this by encoding the structural rules of proof for the system as a whole. We can do this, coherently and consistently, only from a stable "outside" position capable of allowing us to survey the systematic logic of the system as a whole.

Thus, the Gödel sentence "itself" is in fact undecidable, not only with respect to provability-within-a-system, but more deeply (and this second undecidability is the root of the first) between two "meanings": an intra-systematic meaning that is coherent but undistinguished, and an extra-systematic meaning that *cannot be fully formalized within the system itself* (on pain of contradiction) but is nevertheless responsible for the sentence's unique status. This second meaning, which allows us to decide the sentence as "true" even if unprovable, is stably accessible only from a position *outside* the system in question, and it is only in view of this second meaning that the sentence gains the capability of demonstrating the undecidability of the system itself. This is, again, directly analogous to the status of Derrida's undecidables. In particular, a term such as "hymen" may have a perfectly stable and coherent meaning internal to a text which is, like

Mallarmé's, conditioned by the overall possibility of mimetic relationships and distinctions; what is not wholly perspicuous from a position internal to the system, however, is its ability to encode the whole logic of the system itself in relation to the overarching values of truth, meaning, and presence, and thus to undermine the total capability of the system to preserve these values without contradiction.

In the case of artificial languages such as *Principia Mathematica*, it is natural to suppose that such an outside position must always be unproblematically available; after all, we can always create a metalanguage with which we can talk about truth-in-*PM*, and in this metalanguage we can "determine" the truth of the Gödel sentence for the object language. It is this supposition, moreover, which allows us to interpret the phenomenon of undecidability as implying the *incompleteness* of any system to which it applies, for it is only in such a metalanguage that we can coherently formulate the claim that the sentence which is seen to be undecidable by *PM* is "*in fact*" true. However, we should distinguish between such undecidability itself and the further phenomenon of incompleteness.[17] In the case of natural languages and historical texts, to which Derrida's method most directly applies, it is (as we have seen in Chapter 1) much less plausible that there is always a coherent and complete metalanguage available in which we can survey the logic of the system under discussion. Indeed, the identification of structural conditions for the possibility of language as such (for instance, the structural conditions for any system of signs whatsoever, as described by Saussure) clearly cannot take place in any system *other* than the system under discussion itself. If this is right, however, the implication of undecidability is not incompleteness but rather inconsistency; any systematic tracing of the logic of the system within itself will accordingly lead to paradoxes and antinomies.

DIFFÉRANCE AND IN-CLOSURE

As we have seen, then, the undecidability long asserted by Derrida as an essential component of deconstruction, and that shown by Gödel's own meta-mathematical argument, are structurally similar in at least two ways. First, both depend on a kind of "self-referential" encoding whereby a system's total logic (the conditions for the possibility of its organizing distinctions) is formalized at a single point—the Gödel sentence or the "undecidable term"—which in turn makes it possible to inscribe an "undecidable." Second, both suggest a *generalization* of this result to show that any system of sufficient complexity will allow the inscription of undecidables, and hence be either incomplete or inconsistent in a particular sense.

There is, moreover, a third point of analogy that verifies this close connection and provides an essential clarification of the basis for *any* deconstructive strategy of reading. It is this: what Derrida calls the "undecidable" always results from a semantical effect of *syntax* that cannot itself be excluded from any regular system of writing. This essential crossing of syntax and semantics suggests an important analogy with the general metalogical procedure of 'diagonalization' (see Chapter 1) which underlies Gödel's result, as well as several other key results of twentieth-century formal and metalogical reflection. In particular, the Gödel sentence GS for a particular system *diagonalizes* the set of all decidable sentences of the system, in the following sense: given the arithmetical specification of the syntactical rules that decide provability (or provability of the negation) of any sentence, it can be shown that GS is not a member of this set; the sentence is itself generated by means of reasoning about what must escape these rules.

Thus, the existence of the undecidable within a system depends, in both cases, on a productive intervention on syntax, whereby the formal/syntactical rules governing the logic of the system as a whole are encoded at one specific point. Derrida is emphatic about this in the "Double Session"; thus, "what counts here" is, as we have seen, not the polysemy or ambiguity of the sign, but rather "the *formal or syntactical praxis* that composes and decomposes it . . .";[18] the syllepsis 'hymen' produces its effect in Mallarmé's text "*first and foremost through the syntax* . . . in such a way that the suspense is due only to the placement and not to the content of words . . .";[19] again, it advances this effect by means of what Derrida calls "the irreducible *excess of the syntactic* over the semantic."[20] More specifically, the terms that invoke the undecidable are locatable at the point at which syntax situates a kind of semantic gap or void essential to the text as such. Thus, for instance, as we have seen, "*différance*," considered as expressing the total structural logic of difference, does not name or represent anything that can be named by terms *within* the system of this logic; if we had to give *différance* a semantic value, we could, thus, only say that it names a void of non-being. However, this void is marked *syntactically*, on the level of the formal, systematic structure governing the possibilities of signification, by the formal operation of differing and deferring that *différance* is. This syntactical spacing, though it does not correspond to any semantic correlate, remains structurally necessary, insofar as it *conditions* and *opens* the syntactic possibility of any signification as such.[21]

This "between" of spacing is thus originally and purely a "syntactic effect"; but by way of an essential ambiguity involved in the structure of any system of writing, it also can (problematically) *signify* the possibility of signification itself, and thus "exceed," in a somewhat paradoxical fashion, a purely syntactic register. Thus,

> One no longer even has the authority to say that 'between' is a purely syntactic function. Through the re-marking of its semantic void, it in fact begins to signify. Its semantic void signifies, but it signifies spacing and articulation; it has as its meaning the possibility of syntax; it

orders the play of meaning. Neither purely syntactic nor purely semantic, it marks the articulated opening of that opposition.[22]

That is, the purely syntactical mark of the possibility of signification—
for instance, "*différance*" or the "*trace*"—although it does not signify
anything itself, and thus *semantically* only signifies the void—nevertheless *articulates* the possibility of spacing upon which all signification depends. In this sense it does signify after all, although the general
possibility it signifies corresponds to the entirety of the system of signification and not to anything signifiable within it. The outcome of this
ambiguous signification is the undecidability of the particular statement
that accomplishes it.

As we saw in Chapter 1, Graham Priest has traced a large variety of
paradoxes and problems arising in the history of philosophy to a single formal structure that he calls the "Inclosure Schema," whose underlying basis
is typically diagonalization.[23] The problems in which Priest is interested
all arise from the consideration of various kinds of *limits*: for instance, the
limit of what can be described, the limit of what can be known, or the limit
of what can be conceived. There is, Priest argues, a general and formal contradiction that repeatedly arises when philosophers consider these limits.
The contradiction is that it is both *impossible* and *possible* for thought or
description to cross these limits, generating an element that is outside the
relevant totality and thus thinking the unthinkable (or saying the unsayable, etc.). More formally: Priest argues that an in-closure contradiction
will result whenever i) there is some total set Ω defined by a property φ and
of which another property ψ obtains; and ii) there is some "diagonalizing"
function δ such that, given any subset x of Ω that also has the property ψ,
$\delta(x)$ is not an element of x and yet $\delta(x)$ is an element of Ω.[24] Then we can
produce a contradiction by considering the result of applying the diagonal-
izing function δ to the totality Ω itself; because of the conditions, $\delta(\Omega)$ both
is and is not an element of Ω.

Turning back to Derrida, Priest finds an in-closure contradiction in the
inscription of *différance* and the other "undecidable" terms that are, as we
have seen, formally akin to it.[25] In particular, Priest focuses on Derrida's
reading of Saussure and Rousseau in *Of Grammatology*. On this reading
as Priest understands it, each text is (as a condition for the possibility of
its saying anything) structured by at least one "binary opposition." (This
might be, for instance, the opposition between an original and its representation, or between truth and falsehood.) Additionally, the totality of *all*
expressions (at least if conceived as a system that accomplishes presentation and representation at all) is structured by one single such binary, the
opposition between presence and absence. By considering the way that this
binary, or the space of difference between its two terms, structures the
totality of the sayable, we can directly, according to Priest, generate an in-
closure paradox:

We . . . have a contradiction typical of a limit of thought. Claims about *différance* are not expressible (Transcendence); yet they are expressed (Closure).

In fact, the contradiction fits the Inclosure Schema in a simple way. Let φ(y) be: y is a linguistic expression. Let ψ(x) be: x is structured by some binary opposition. Let δ(x) be some statement that concerns the notion undecidable in terms of such an opposition. (Such statements would typically occur in any text that deconstructs x.) As we have seen, if x is a text structured by some binary opposition, δ(x) cannot be expressed in x. Hence we have Transcendence, but it is clearly a linguistic expression. Hence we have Closure. Finally, the totality of all expressions, Ω, is structured by the pair presence/absence . . . The contradiction arises when the deconstructive diagonaliser is applied to the totality of all texts to produce a statement about *différance* (for example, one of Derrida's own). At this point, *le pas au-delà* (the step beyond) is *un pas au-delà* (a non-beyond) to use Derrida's own neat turn of phrase. One might well exploit Derrida's technique of writing under erasure, and call inclosures ~~limits~~.[26, 27]

According to Priest, then, the undecidable proper to any linguistic system, and determined by the underlying binary which structures it, cannot be inscribed within that system itself; and *if* we generalize this to the totality of language, we can directly produce the in-closure contradiction: a sentence (for instance, a sentence "about *différance*") that, standing for the "between" of the "master" binary presence/absence, cannot be inscribed in language at all (although clearly, it is).

Extending Priest's analysis, we can now recognize another general structural feature which (in addition to, or perhaps as a consequence of, the "binary" presence/absence) structures and preconditions the possibility of all writing as such, according to Derrida.[28] This feature is the *iterability* of the sign, upon which Derrida famously insists in "Signature, Event, Context":

> My 'written communication' must, if you will, remain legible despite the absolute disappearance of every determined addressee in general for it to function as writing, that is, for it to be legible. It must be repeatable—iterable—in the absolute absence of the addressee or of the empirically determinable set of addresses. This iterability . . . structures the mark of writing itself, and does so moreover for no matter what type of writing . . . A writing that was not structurally legible—iterable—beyond the death of the addressee would not be writing.[29]

This structural iterability, as Derrida goes on to emphasize, implies the radical structural possibility of inscribing the sign within any of an open infinity of contexts or chains, what he later calls the possibility of "graft" or citationality in general. This open possibility, Derrida says, implies that a written sign "carries with it" as part of the "very structure of the written" a "force of rupture" or possibility of breaking with any particular context of inscription. This possibility of rupture, moreover, arises directly from

> the spacing which constitutes the written sign: the spacing which separates it from other elements of the internal contextual chain (the always open possibility of its extraction and grafting), but also from all the forms of a present referent (past or to come in the modified form of the present past or to come) that is objective or subjective. This spacing is not the simple negativity of a lack, but the emergence of the mark.[30]

That is, the possibility of iteration, and hence the standing possibility, inscribed in the very structure of the sign, of *rupture* with any specific context, is a direct consequence of the spacing (both within and without the chain of signifiers) that, according to Derrida, makes possible the inscription (or legibility) of the sign itself. Thus, iterability effectively *diagonalizes* any fixed or given context; in Priest's terminology, it ensures the possibility of Transcendence, which effectively generates an arbitrary element outside the totality of any fixed contextual Closure. Once again, moreover, this diagonalization, as a general feature of inscription as such, is itself a direct outcome of the constitutive *spacing* that, although unpresentable itself and without a semantic correlate, makes possible any and all inscription as such by constituting the very possibility of the sign.

ETHICS OF THE UNDECIDABLE

I have argued, by way of the close analogy to Gödel's result and to diagonalization more generally, that the inscription of the undecidable, thus understood, gives critical thought access to a complex topology of the limit. This is neither the *closure* of the system by means of the drawing of a fixed and steady limit, nor its *openness* to the 'infinity' of a transcendent beyond, but what we can term, following Priest, *in-closure*. What, then, does this suggest for the practice of deconstruction, and its character as a mode of criticism?

In his remarkable 1990 homage to Derrida, "*Pardes:* The Writing of Potentiality," Giorgio Agamben treats the specific methodological character of deconstruction as consisting in its ability to 'dwell in' the paradoxical topology of in-closure which we have discussed:

> *The concept 'trace' is not a concept* (just as the name '*différance*' is not a name'): this is the paradoxical thesis that is already implicit in the grammatological project and that defines the proper status of Derrida's terminology. Grammatology was forced to become deconstruction in

order to avoid this paradox (or, more precisely, to seek to dwell in it correctly); this is why it renounced any attempt to proceed by decisions about meaning. But in its original intention, grammatology is not a theory of polysemy or a doctrine of the transcendence of meaning; it has as its object not an equally inexhaustible, infinite hermeneutics of signification but a radicalization of the problem of self-reference that calls into question and transforms the very concept of meaning grounding Western logic . . .

It does not suffice, however, to underline (on the basis of Gödel's theorem) the necessary relation between a determinate axiomatics and undecidable propositions: what is decisive is solely how one conceives this relation. It is possible to consider an undecidable as a purely negative limit (Kant's *Schranke*), such that one then invokes strategies (Bertrand Russell's theory of types or Alfred Tarski's metalanguage) to avoid running up against it. Or one can consider it as a *threshold* (Kant's *Grenze*), which opens onto an exteriority and transforms and dislocates all the elements of the system.[31]

As Agamben emphasizes, echoing Derrida himself, deconstruction is not a hermeneutic of meaning, either of polysemy or transcendence; nor is it originally grounded, in any sense, on any kind of decision on *semantical* meaning. Its ground is rather the undecidability of the reflection of *syntax* upon itself, and the problematic topology of criticism that this implies.[32] The constitutive paradox of this topology is a result, as Agamben notes, of the more general paradox of reflection that arises from the absence of a 'name for the name,' the absence of any coherent reflection of the totality of a system's syntax within itself and without paradox or contradiction. In tracing the possibility of writing, in formalizing the possibility of formalization, deconstruction's task becomes the inscription of and 'dwelling within' this paradox. Its topological structure is not, as I have argued, closure or openness, but rather what Priest calls *in-closure* and what Agamben calls the *threshold*: not the limit of a fixed and determinate line between 'inside' and 'outside,' but rather the threshold of in-closure that, in being closed, opens to the exterior, and in being open, encloses itself.

As we have seen, this complicated topology results directly from the structurally necessary and indeed semantically productive *confusion* between syntax and semantics, between "inside" and "outside," that is apparently a necessary feature of any language capable of describing its own structure from within. As Agamben notes, the response of deconstruction is precisely to inscribe and trace the undecidable, to multiply its occurrences and document its syntactical/reflexive necessity, thereby inhabiting—without resolving—the complex critical topology of in-closure. With this, the critical operation of tracing a boundary to thought, language, or expression becomes the inscription of a limitative trace that erases itself in the movement of its own inscription. Far from being located at the outside of a bounded and stable totality of language as such, the line of this tracing henceforth inhabits or haunts language at each of its points, wherever (which is everywhere) it attempts or presupposes problematic self-reference. This tracing is nothing other than the characteristic critical operation of paradoxico-criticism, which (as we have seen above) replaces traditional criticism in the criteriological mode with the reflexive pursuit of contradictions at the limits and the undecidables which constitute the actual basis for any subsequent production of (what appears to be) univocal meaning.

The precise structure of the undecidable I have argued for here, moreover, has important consequences for what we should take a deconstructive *response* to the 'undecidable' actually to be. This is significant not only in relation to Derrida's initial examples of undecidability, but equally with respect to the more extended uses of the 'undecidable' of the later period, with relation to such 'ethical' structures as hospitality and the gift. Here, Derrida often employed what he has called the aporias of 'possibility as impossibility' to demonstrate the inherent undecidables of particular 'ethical' situations. For instance:

> I am trying to elaborate a logic, and I would call this a 'logic', in which the only possible x (and I mean here any rigorous concept of x) is 'the impossible x'. And to do so without being caught in an absurd, nonsensical discourse. For instance, the statement according to which the only possible gift is an impossible gift, is meaningful. Where I can give only what I am able to give, what it is possible for me to give, I don't give. So, for me to give something, I have to give something I don't have, that is, to make an impossible gift.[33]

These structures of possibility as impossibility, like Mallarmé's *hymen* which inscribes the possibility/impossibility of mimesis, each suggest their own proper undecidable. Thus, for instance, because the pure gift is possible only as the impossibility of the structure of pure giving, the question of whether any particular empirical instance of giving is really a proper gift (or is, rather, simply an instance of trade within the general system of exchange, the system which regulates and calculates all possibilities of exchange) is undecidable by means of any intra-systematic logic. To decide it, then, is what cannot be done on the basis of any purely intra-systematic logic; to decide, we must in some way leap 'outside' the system and here, we are without its guidance.

It is in this precise sense that the ethical structure of the 'gift' (and hence the very meaning of 'responsible giving') is constituted by, and dependent on, the structurally necessary confusion between an "inside" (intra-systematic and regular) and an "outside" (extra-systematic and essentially unregulated) meaning. It is this paradoxical structure of confusion or crossing that, as we have seen, renders it undecidable and hence makes it an example of an ethical concept in Derrida's sense. Moreover—and here we begin to see the vast range of "political" consequences that flow from the deconstructive project—this analysis of the concept of the gift can easily be generalized to a wide variety of concepts of intersubjective life that are articulated by *regular, structured systems of practice and action.* For wherever such structures regulate and constitute phenomena that are *also* essentially constituted or determined by the possibility of "jumping out of the system," undecidability in Derrida's sense will appear and a deconstructive response will be called for. These structures and systems of *praxis* and action are quite general in human life, and certainly cannot be limited to "texts" in the narrow, literal sense. Indeed, they appear to be coextensive with the whole field of human discursive *praxis*; wherever, in particular, there are specifically defined rules and norms that regulate possibilities of decision within a relatively defined practice, the problematic of the undecidable that we have examined here will appear. It seems, therefore, that the deconstructive operation of critical "reading" can operate as an exemplary mode of critical thought and action in all of these domains, as well.

This is the case, for instance, with respect to all sorts of systems of exchange (for instance, of money or capital) as well as to any possible regular and definite systems of law, justice, or normatively regulated behavior. In all of these cases, as in the case of the structure of the gift more narrowly conceived, possibilities of action are predetermined by the larger logic of the prevailing system, but the point or meaning of what is "ethical" essentially *cannot* be determined wholly in intra-systematic terms. The pattern for all of these systems and their more general structure, in fact, is *language itself*, as it determines *any* total system or structure of meaning. In the broad sense permitted by Derrida's analysis, intersubjective systems of law, justice, politics, economy, and association are all fundamentally linguistic ones, and are all accordingly susceptible to the logic of the undecidable he elaborates. As we have seen, these phenomena of undecidability, and hence the applicability of a deconstructive ethics, are all present as soon as we have a system capable of representing its own structure within itself, and hence determined by the structurally necessary confusion these phenomena embody. Most generally and significantly, the phenomenon of undecidability will also affect any determinate constitution of politics or the social whole as such, inscribing within it points of contradiction, paradox, and constitutive inadequacy that themselves can henceforth operate as sites for productive and foundational formal criticism.

How, then, do we deconstructively 'inhabit' the complex space of inclosure, and how do we respond adequately to the dilemma of undecidability that constitutes it? Since, as Derrida emphasizes, there is no rigorous constitution of any of these concepts outside the complex logic of the undecidable, which always depends, as we have seen, on a constitutive crossing between "inside" (syntactic) and "outside" (semantic) meaning, *one* part of the answer is (as has often been emphasized) to pursue decisions and solutions *outside* the logic of any given system or text. However, if undecidability has the general structure I have suggested, such 'leaping outside the system' will not simply amount to 'breaking with' or leaving the structure of some *particular* system of representation or calculation (in favor, as it might be, of another). The moment of decision is (and remains even in Derrida's most 'ethical' moments), rather, the radical moment of the inscription of the possibility/impossibility of *any* signification as such.

From this perspective, it is possible to specify in more detail than is often done the *precise* (meta)-structure of what is involved in an "ethics" of the responsible "decision" for Derrida. As Derrida often emphasized, far from suggesting hesitation or indifference, what he calls the 'undecidable' is, for him, an essential *precondition* for the possibility of responsibility: for if we have only to decide what is already in some sense decided by the system in which we operate, there is no responsibility in our decision.[34] Some commentators have emphasized the way in which this situates responsible decision as a relationship to an 'other' which is wholly outside the system of understanding or knowledge itself, what is sometimes called a 'singular.'[35] However, as we can now see, if this is an accurate description of what a 'responsible decision' is for Derrida, it can only be so because the 'singular' other is not *simply* outside the system of decision and knowledge (though of course not simply inside it either), but rather inhabits the paradoxical space of in-closure itself. This is, as we have seen, the space of the undecidable; indeed, its marking or inscription as such already amounts to an 'ethical' *praxis* of writing. Thus, if the ethical relationship of responsibility, for Derrida, is indeed always a relationship, 'beyond' knowledge, to a 'wholly other,' this 'other' can only be the object of a radical responsibility insofar as it occupies the (non)-space of undecidability, which is not simply 'beyond' the limits of the system of decision but rather involves, in a constitutive way, the undecidability of that system's own closure. This makes it clearer, at least, how the marking or tracing of this problematic in-closure, in radical reflection on the possibility of totality, decision, or tracing as such, can itself amount to a relationship of responsibility, a kind of (arche)-writing of the ethical "relationship" as such.[36]

Because of Derrida's continuing emphasis on the undecidable, he has sometimes been accused of an ultimately impotent doctrine of infinite textual tracing that removes the possibility of any real choice or action. Inscribing the undecidable, the criticism avers, is simply a way to postpone or preempt decision. But if, quite to the contrary, what Derrida calls the undecidable is the most direct *condition* for the possibility of a genuine decision, the meta-structural topology that inscribes the undecidable as I have suggested makes the nature of this conditioning all the more clear. For it is then possible to say that the genuine decision is conditioned *specifically* by the particular systematic undecidable that it answers to; and that responsible decision *as such* is conditioned by the complex topology of in-closure. That is, without suggesting that the 'correct decision' is determined materially, in an internal way, by the rules of the system, or even that it is determined formally, in an external way, by the demand of a relationship to an other thought as wholly outside it, it is possible to see in the paradoxical crossing of content and form that I have discussed the opening of a kind of "ethics" which is, precisely, what Derrida is insisting upon in these moments in which he affirms the necessity of responsible decision. This ethics has its ultimate basis not in any form or content, but in the problematic moment of *reflection* whereby the total logic of the system is reflected back into one of its members, producing the diagonal and the undecidable as such. In a somewhat surprising way, then, we might see Derrida's ethics as the radical practice of reflection on the paradoxical topology of syntactic totality; in this specific sense, it is coextensive with the practical formalization of formalization, or the writing of writing, as such.

5   Wittgenstein and Parmenides

Wittgenstein's *Tractatus Logico-Philosophicus* famously ends with a remark that, as he says in the book's "Preface," could also summarize the sense of the book as a whole:

> What we cannot speak about we must pass over in silence.

Ignoring, for the moment, the difference between speaking and knowing, the remark can be read almost as a paraphrase of one written about 2,500 years ago:

> You could not know what is not—that cannot be done—nor indicate it.[1]

The second remark comes near the beginning of the single "treatise" of Parmenides, long discussed as the first work in the Western tradition to draw a general "logical" distinction between being and non-being. Within Parmenides' poem, it appears immediately after the dramatic narrative description of the narrator's journey to the place of a goddess. The traveler is offered the choice between two mutually exclusive paths, the one the "path of Persuasion," truth, and being; the other, the "indiscernible" path of non-being, error, and illusion. In saying that there are only these two paths that can be thought of, the goddess' argument is the first to restrict thought to the choice of the two stark alternatives of *what is* and *what is not*, all that can be an object of thought and knowledge and what is simply nothing.

This stark choice remains a model for rational or logical thinking throughout the subsequent history of Western thought. In linking thought and knowledge to being, it is closely connected with the unity of being and thinking that the goddess herself appears to uphold:

> For the same thing is there both to be thought of and to be [or: thought and being are the same].[2]

The claim of the unity of being and thinking provides a basis for the eternal, changeless being of the One of all that is, which the goddess now goes on to describe. This is, of course, the very moment of the *institution* of the sovereign combination of consistency and completeness, the origin of the ontological and logical (indeed, onto-theological) thought of the One which would subsequently govern Western philosophy for two millennia. The argument that provides for its thinkable link to being by ruling out non-being and contradiction therefore demonstrates, in particularly clear form, what is involved in this institution, and what is at stake in the contemporary results of logical thought and inquiry about the One that today provide for its possible deposition.

The goddess' description of the stark choice identifies, for any object, two and only two possibilities: either being or non-being, existence or non-existence. This stands as an original model for all *bivalent* reasoning in accordance with the principle of non-contradiction, and hence, more broadly, for the "authority" and force of all logical norms, rules, and principles of thought and speech. On this model, in particular, the assertion or thought of *contradictions* is, definitively and essentially, to be avoided. Indeed, the goddess next goes on to warn the traveler against the way of mortals, who "wander," confused, between the two alternatives of being and non-being, constantly mixing them up and confusing them in contradictory fashion.[3]

As commentators have noted, however, there is a certain interesting ambiguity, amounting almost to a performative contradiction, in the goddess' own instructions.[4] For if it is the goddess' intention to *describe* in logical terms the structure of whatever is, her words are at the same time also *imperative*; her aim is not simply to point out the two paths but also to *recommend* the first and *proscribe* the second. In so doing, she imposes on thought the force of the very distinction between truth and error that she may be taken to be the first ever to point out. But if the second path is both "indiscernible" and even, necessarily, "not to be," then how is it indeed possible for the goddess herself to indicate it to the traveler in order to prohibit him from pursuing it, demanding that "you must hold back your thought from this way of enquiry"?[5] Similarly, if the first path is indeed that of that which is, indeed the only "one" of which there truly is "an account," how is it possible for the goddess to *recommend* that the young traveler follow this path, given that there seems to be no alternative that is even so much as conceivable? In describing the two paths, the remarks of the goddess would seem to ambiguously combine description with prescription, demanding the necessary while prohibiting the impossible.[6] My suggestion in this chapter will be that something very like this curiously ambiguous structure is also exhibited, as Wittgenstein himself would only later come to see clearly, by Wittgenstein's ongoing investigation into logic, ethics, and the bounds of sense, in the *Tractatus Logico-Philosophicus*, and that this overdetermined structure of rational force indeed displays an important feature of the phenomenon of "normativity" itself.

PARMENIDES AND THE *TRACTATUS*

Both remarks, the one of Parmenides at the dawn of Western thought, and that of Wittgenstein at the much more recent moment of its more fully attained linguistic self-awareness, can seem, read *one* way, simply to be tautologies. That is, both can seem simply to assert that *whatever cannot be talked about* (or thought about, or known) indeed *cannot be talked about* (or thought about, or known). Taken this way, the argument (if such it is), in each case, risks arguing nothing; for tautologies say nothing. Taken another way, however, they do indeed both articulate substantial prohibitions, saying that there is an *area* of things or matters—that, as we may say, of "non-being" or perhaps contradiction—about *which* it is impossible to say anything, since these things or matters fail to exist. But now both arguments risk internal incoherence; for they seem to refer to what, by their very saying, they cannot, namely, the "realm of non-being" that, according to the argument itself, cannot exist.

More specifically, if we take Parmenides to be outlining an argument with a substantial conclusion, we may take that conclusion to be that it is impossible to know, refer to, or conceive "nothing" or "what is not." The argument, thus construed, plays an essential role in Parmenides' more encompassing attempt to demonstrate the *necessity* of the existence of what is, and in particular of the timeless and unchanging One.[7] As such, moreover, it is a model for "logical" arguments for ontological conclusions throughout the subsequent history of Western thought, in particular for a wide variety of arguments that attempt to establish the *necessity* of certain existents.[8]

At *TLP* 2.02–2.0212, Wittgenstein gives a highly compressed argument for the necessary existence of certain simple objects which may be taken to be reminiscent, in some ways, to Parmenides' own argument for the necessary existence of the One:

2.02 The object is simple.

2.0201 Every statement about complexes can be analyzed into a statement about their constituent parts, and into those propositions that completely describe the complexes.

2.021 Objects form the substance of the world. Therefore they cannot be compound.

2.0211 If the world had no substance, then whether a proposition had sense would depend on whether another proposition was true.

2.0212 It would then be impossible to sketch out a picture of the world (true or false).

The argument, like Parmenides' own, is premised on the *determinacy of sense*, or in other words on the possibility of issuing propositions, true or false. An essential component of this premise is *bivalence*, the claim that language attempting to describe reality must be restricted to the two alternatives of true or false.[9] The connection between the requisite determinacy of sense (which makes it possible to draw a true or false picture of the world) and the necessary existence of simples is at first obscure, but it can be reconstructed with the help of a few subsidiary premises from elsewhere in the *Tractatus* (in particular, 3.22–3.24). The key point is that, *if* some of the terms that function as simple (i.e., unanalyzable) names in language *could* fail to refer, then it would be possible for the propositions involving them to fail to be true in *either* of two ways. First, such a proposition could be false in the usual sense, i.e., because the objects it names, though existing, fail to be configured into an actual state of affairs in the way that it says they are. But second, it could fail to be true (indeed, fail to have sense) because the simple names in it fail to refer to anything at all. If this were possible, then whether any proposition had sense at all would depend on the truth of other propositions (namely, the ones asserting the existence of bearers of each of its names). And then it would be impossible to determinately correlate propositions with states of affairs at all.[10]

It follows that, if sense is to be determinate, there must be a fundamental ontological distinction between simple objects and complexes formed of them; only of complexes is it possible to deny existence, or indeed to say anything substantial (true or false). In this way, we may move, as Plato himself does, directly from Parmenidean considerations about the possibility of reference to the position that Socrates sketches (though he does not actually endorse it) in the *Theatetus*, at 201e:

> . . . The primary elements, as it were, of which we and everything else are composed, have no account [*logos*]. Each of them, in itself, can only be named; it is not possible to say anything else of it, either that it is or that it is not.[11]

And indeed, the Tractarian argument for simples also has as a direct consequence that, as Wittgenstein puts it at *TLP* 3.221:

> Objects I can only name. Signs represent them. I can only speak of them. I cannot assert them. A proposition can only say how a thing is, not what it is.

If, in other words, it were possible to *describe* (rather than simply name) the simple objects that make up the substance of the world, then whether a proposition composed of simple names had sense would again depend on the truth or falsity of other propositions, in this case those describing the objects. But this would again make sense indeterminate. It is therefore a transcendental condition for the possibility of sense that it be impossible to say anything *about* the simple objects. Even to assert that a particular simple sign *has* an object at all will be to violate this condition, to speak what, in seeming to describe the indescribable simples, must actually be nonsense.

Applying the central distinction of the *Tractatus'* elucidatory apparatus, the necessity of simple objects composing the ultimate structure of the world is, then, to be *shown* rather than *said*. [12] Taken as a fundamental feature of the metaphysical structure of the world, as a result of which sense itself is possible, it is to be demonstrated on the level of language simply by the *existence* of names and the possibility of *using* them in propositions. It is, however, impossible to *assert* this necessity, on pain of violating transcendental conditions for the possibility of sense and falling into nonsense. In line with the distinction between showing and saying, we may say, indeed, that *if* there are any necessary metaphysical or ontological preconditions for the possibility of sense themselves, the necessity of these conditions will only be showable and it will therefore be impossible either to assert or to deny them.

In line with the *Tractatus'* conception of logical analysis, it must therefore always be possible rationally to decompose any complex state of affairs into its simple constituent objects, which correlate to simple names.[13] The possibility of such analysis is itself a consequence of the rational structure (what Wittgenstein calls "logical form") shared by language and the world, and here again the existence of this structure is necessary if the determinacy of sense is to be preserved. In the *Tractatus*, the prohibition of non-being—here, the non-being of the contradictory or the "illogical" state of affairs[14]—is thus the direct evidence of the unity of logical structure (or form) which pervades the universe and aligns language and the world in a sublime order of correspondence. Its ontological correlate is the famous "logical atomism" of the *Tractatus*, a reductive picture that underlies the very possibility of logical analysis in the form suggested there.

At the same time, in connection with the *Tractatus'* account of the origination and criticism of philosophical error, the same prohibition of the contradictory plays an essential role in guaranteeing that the elucidation of logical order suffices to provide a rigorous and univocal *delimitation* of the world that is also a determination of the very boundaries of language and sense. For Wittgenstein, the temptation to philosophical error arises when one and the same sign is used in differing ways; in order to expose such error, and thereby provide a rigorous critical distinction between sense and nonsense, it is therefore necessary to "recognize the symbol in the sign" by clarifying precisely the rules underlying the use of signs in each case.[15] It is this critical delimitation of sense that makes possible the clarification of "logical syntax" (3.325–3.33) which aims to correlate each syntactic sign with exactly one coherent rule of use. But this critical delimitation of the realm of sense, which corresponds to the world, also has the effect of *showing* the totality of what is thereby delimited. It thus makes possible the mystical vision with which the book famously concludes, the vision of the world "sub specie aeterni" as a *limited* whole (6.45).

The arguments of Parmenides and Wittgenstein are thus linked on the fundamental level of their ontological articulation of being by the originary assumption of the prohibition against thinking what simply is not. The prohibition is the prohibition of inconsistency, which finds in the contradiction an absolute limit to the One of all that is. For Parmenides as well as Wittgenstein, this yields an injunction on speech strictly correlative to a position of mystical insight into what cannot be said. This is the prohibition that, combining the thought of the One with a rigorous prohibition of the inconsistent, inaugurates ontological thought in its *sovereign* mode (cf. Chapter 1), whether subsequently developed into onto-theology (as in Parmenides) or into constructivism (as in the early Wittgenstein). Its correlate is the prescription of rational consistency as the univocity of standards and rules in determining the being of whatever is.

The prohibition and the prescription jointly determine the force of reasons as the non-contradictory coherence of rules and laws, and the totality of the sayable as the realm of determinate logical structure. They institute the necessity of elements and the univocity of their principles as the sublime presupposition of meaning and truth. But as we have seen, and the development of Wittgenstein's own thought would soon confirm, the prohibition and the prescription are equally, and equivalently, overdetermined. As the prohibition of what is anyway impossible, the injunction of non-being enjoins speech to the ultimate silence of "what shows itself" and the thought of the One to the mute position of mystical insight beyond words and logic. As the prescription of what is anyway necessary, the demand for non-contradictory coherence consigns the force of logical structures and linguistic rules to the transcendent authority of an extra-worldly institution. But both the prohibition and the prescription are *themselves* possible, as we may have come to suspect, only by means of a rigorous *foreclosure* of the essential gesture of reflexivity by which the *logos* thinks and inscribes itself as a *moment* of the One it also circumscribes.

FROM EARLY TO LATE WITTGENSTEIN: RULES AND FORCE

After his return to philosophy in 1929, Wittgenstein began to recognize deep and pervasive problems in the *Tractatus* theory of logical form, according to which, as we have seen, the nonsense of contradiction is ruled out by the unitary "deep structure" of the rules of language and logic, which make all determinate sense possible. As we have seen, this prohibition is in a certain sense overdetermined in the *Tractatus*, in that what is ruled out as *impossible* is also effectively *proscribed* by the rules underlying the possibility of logical analysis and rational criticism. In a passage from the *Big Typescript*, first dictated in 1933, Wittgenstein appears to recognize this situation of overdetermination in its general form:

> Grammatical rules, as they currently exist, are rules for the use of words. Even if we transgress them we can still use words meaningfully. Then what do they exist for? To make language-use as a whole uniform? (Say for aesthetic reasons?) To make possible the use of language as a social institution?
>
> And thus—like a set of traffic rules—to prevent a collision? (But what concern is it of ours if that happens?) The collision that mustn't come about must be the collision that can't come about! That is to say, without grammar it isn't a bad language, but no language.[16]

The passage comes in the midst of a section of the *Typescript* entitled "Language in Our Sense Not Defined as an Instrument for a Particular Purpose. Grammar Is Not a Mechanism Justified by Its Purpose." The sense of the passages immediately preceding it is that we cannot see language as a whole, or the specific rules that we follow in speaking it, as an *instrument* or *tool* designed for the accomplishment of certain antecedently given purposes, for instance, the "communication" of antecedently given thoughts. For language has no such purpose, and there is no *specific* task we aim to achieve in speaking it at all. Were there such a task, the constitutive rules of grammar would indeed function like "traffic rules," prohibiting certain possibilities and allowing others so that the purpose of language as a whole might better be accomplished. But since there is not, we cannot take the force of these rules to rely on their ability to prohibit certain possibilities—instead, as Wittgenstein says, the "collision that mustn't come about must be the collision that can't come about." In other words, an explicitly stated grammatical rule, if it is indeed constitutive of the language itself, must be conceived as having force *not* in that it rules out certain actual possibilities of expression but in that in fact it is impossible *not* to follow it and still speak the language at all. Any force that the expression of a grammatical rule might have in leading us to reconsider the sense of one of our remarks, or provide insights into the actual possibilities of sense, must be seen to result, in paradoxical fashion, from this crossing of the constitutive with the descriptive, the necessary confusion of what is *impossible* to say with what is to be *criticized* in what the other *has* said.

A sense of the implications of this paradox also plays an important role in Wittgenstein's developing understanding, at around this time, of what can be meant by "ethics" and the sense of "ethical propositions" (if any such there be).[17] For instance, in the "Lecture on Ethics" delivered in Cambridge in 1929, Wittgenstein considers the possibility of propositions expressing what he calls claims of "absolute value." These are, for example, claims of intrinsic and non-instrumental goodness or badness, beauty, and the like. He argues that we shall in fact find no such claims anywhere expressed by propositions; for, as he had held also in the *Tractatus*, propositions can do no more than express facts, and facts are all on a level. No fact has intrinsically any more or less value than any other, and so it is impossible, as well, to find any justification *in* the world of facts for any claim or precept of ethics that demands one course of action rather than another. It follows from this that we will never find, among states of affairs or their consequences, any that we shall be able to see as an absolute source of rational compulsion, as holding the power to demand absolutely and non-instrumentally what we *must* do:

> I said that so far as facts and propositions are concerned there is only relative value and relative good, right, etc. And let me, before I go on, illustrate this by a rather obvious example. The right road is the road which leads to an arbitrarily predetermined end and it is quite clear to us all that there is no sense in talking about the right road apart from such a predetermined goal. Now let us see what we could possibly mean by the expression, 'the absolutely right road.' I think it would be the road which everybody on seeing it would, with logical necessity, have to go, or be ashamed for not going.
>
> And similarly the absolute good, if it is a describable state of affairs, would be one which everybody, independent of his tastes and inclinations, would necessarily bring about or feel guilty for not bringing about. And I want to say that such a state of affairs is a chimera. No state of affairs has, in itself, what I would like to call the coercive power of an absolute judge.[18]

What Wittgenstein here says about ethics certainly holds, in a general sense, for anything we may consider to be an expression of rational force. That is, there can be no *proposition* that expresses (non-instrumental) rational force, since no *fact* can have what Wittgenstein here calls the "coercive power of an absolute judge."

In the *Philosophical Investigations*, in the course of reconsidering the deep motivations of his own *Tractatus* account of language, Wittgenstein revisits the argument that he gave there for the necessary existence of certain simple objects, the bearers of names whose objective reference was seen as necessary for the possibility of sense itself. In an unusual moment of historical reference, he quotes the version of this argument that Plato put in the mouth of Socrates in the *Theatetus*, the argument for the necessary existence of 'primary elements' that Plato himself may well have understood as a consequence of the argument of Parmenides. "Both Russell's 'individuals' and my 'objects' (*Tractatus Logico-Philosophicus*)," Wittgenstein admits, "were such primary elements."[19] The critical reflection that assays the argument that purported to demonstrate their absolute necessity will therefore isolate the common element that links the *Theatetus* argument, Russell, and Wittgenstein's earlier self in their common sense of the rational necessity of certain absolute posits or entities, what *must* seemingly exist on the primitive level of naming if sensible language itself is to be possible. Here again, the argument of the *Tractatus* is readable as having attempted to articulate something like a *definitive* and *necessary* connection between what can be named and what can exist at all:

> 50. What does it mean to say that we can attribute neither being nor non-being to elements?—One might say: if everything that we call 'being' and 'non-being' consists in the existence and non-existence of connexions between elements, it makes no sense to speak of an element's being (non-being); just as if everything that we call 'destruction' lies in the separation of elements, it makes no sense to speak of the destruction of an element.
>
> One would, however, like to say: existence cannot be attributed to an element, for if it did not exist, one could not even name it and so one could say nothing at all of it.—But let us consider an analogous case. There is one thing of which one can say neither that it is one metre long, nor that it is not one metre long, and that is the standard metre in Paris.—But this is, of course, not to ascribe any extraordinary property to it, but only to mark its peculiar role in the language-game of measuring with a metre-rule.—Let us imagine samples of colour being preserved in Paris like the standard metre. We define: 'sepia' means the colour of the standard sepia which is there kept hermetically sealed. Then it will make no sense to say of this sample either that it is of this colour or that it is not.
>
> We can put it like this: This sample is an instrument of the language used in ascriptions of colour. In this language-game it is not something that is represented, but is a means of representation . . . And so to say 'If it did not exist, it could have no name' is to say as much and as little as: if this thing did not exist, we could not use it in our language-game.—What looks as if it *had* to exist, is part of the language. It is a paradigm in our language-game; something with which comparison is made. And this may be an important observation; but it is none the less an observation concerning our language-game—our method of representation.

In revisiting his own earlier argument, Wittgenstein here takes it from another direction, suggesting a transfigured understanding of its sense that may seem to liberate us from its force. The metaphysician's argument for the necessary existence of *what is*—what seemed also, on the level of the critique of language, to articulate the transcendentally necessary structural conditions for the possibility of meaning itself—is, from another direction of regard, simply a mystified internal reflection of the structure of our *own* institutions. But Wittgenstein's intent here is not simply to "demystify" the apparent necessity of the standard or replace it with mere contingency. For as is clear throughout the "rule-following considerations" of the *Investigations*, the question of rational standards is not simply one about the possibility of making sense of those moments of institution or origin by which we may suppose these standards to have been, at the real or fictitious "originary" moment of a community or a language, explicitly or implicitly adopted. Much more than this, it is the question also of the force of their regular and routine *application*, on an everyday basis, to the manifold and varied linguistic performances that make up an ordinary human life. And it is beyond doubt that the Wittgenstein of the *Investigations* takes *this* problem—the problem of how signs get their application, how they get to be meant or used in the ways that they regularly are, of what this regularity means, and more generally of what is involved in talking or thinking of "the use of a sign" or the rules by which we characterize it, and what it means to learn these rules, to know them, to follow them or to dispute them—as one of the deepest and most significant problems that contemporary critical thought can take up.

Here, as we have seen (Chapter 1), the question of what it is to follow a rule is explicitly and emphatically *not* to be answered by a conventionalist account of the arbitrary institution of standards. For of course, as we can say paraphrasing the language of the famous rule-following paradox of *PI* 201: any account of the conventional institution of standards would still stand in need of an account of the conventions of their application, and so the conventionalist explanation would hang in the air along with what it is trying to explain, ultimately providing no help.

The paradox of rule-following is thus simply one face of a more general paradox of standards and their institution, which we may begin to articulate by noting the unique logical position that we must see anything like a standard as holding in relationship to the instances it governs, a position that Wittgenstein calls "peculiar." Owing to this role, for instance, the standard meterstick must be treated, ambiguously, as both *one* object among others (it is this that makes it usable as an object of comparison at all) and, at the same time, as occupying the elevated and exceptional position of the general, what in being comparable to *any* other sets the terms by which any other individual can be judged. It is this paradoxical position—as we might say, not the position of the particular (the meterstick itself) or the universal, but rather the position of their crossing—that gives the standard meterstick in Paris the peculiar fate of being able to be called neither one meter nor not one meter long. Thus, the singular position of the standard, neither inside nor outside the language-game it constitutes, marks it also as the singular exception to the general logical law (here, the law of the excluded middle) that it holds in place.

This structurally necessary place of paradox, it is important to note, can by no means be dissipated or resolved *simply* by drawing a distinction between perspectives "internal" and "external" to our language-games or practices.[20] For in fact the singular place of the standard appears from *neither* of these two perspectives; to take it as either one is to submit it to the logic of the ordinary run of objects which it in fact underlies. From *outside* the practice, the standard is simply another particular, undistinguished, and essentially undifferentiated from any other. From *inside*, the standard does not exist as an object at all; it is useful only as a contingent means of reference to the law of generality which, clothed with the mystical aura of necessity, must always already have been in place. And more generally, here we may grasp what is ultimately unsatisfying about attempts to resolve the temptations of metaphysics, or demystify our relationship to them critically by introducing either a relativism of language-games or a simple distinction between what is internal and what is external to their bounds. For if it can be said that in language we will never be free of the force of reason, that we will never be outside the application of the *logos* to what can be thought or said, we can now say that this is because as long as we are 'in language' (as long as we live) we can never be either simply inside a particular language-game nor simply outside all of them.

WITTGENSTEIN ON RUSSELL AND CONTRADICTION

In the development of Wittgenstein's critical position from the early to the later work, then, there is an important shift in his conception of the force of "logical" rules and laws. This corresponds, as well, to important shifts in his methods of philosophical reflection and criticism. It is true, and important, that a certain kind of paradox of philosophical edification is already recognizable on the level of the method of the *Tractatus* as a whole, which famously aims to enable its readers (or interlocutors) to "kick away the ladder" of metaphysical speculation and indeed of the "elucidations" and "propositions" of the *Tractatus*' author itself.[21] But if this paradox may be considered to define the intended critical method of the *Tractatus*, and thus to identify this *method* as an embodiment already of a form of paradoxico-criticism, nevertheless the paradox of rational force and its statement that we have discussed above does not become *explicit* until at least the transitional period. Internally at least, the position of the *Tractatus*, despite the substantial sophistication of its internal register of reflexive self-criticism, remains a (late and highly developed) form of *constructivism* or *criteriology*. This position is not an example of positivism or verificationism. Nevertheless, it shares with these projects, as we have seen, the underlying attempt to *delimit* sense by means of a univocal and non-contradictory tracing of the boundaries of meaningful language. The attempt to delimit sense, and so *ensure* its determinacy as a "transcendental" precondition for the possibility of meaningful language, yields the argument for metaphysical simples that we have discussed above as well as that for the necessity of a sublime logical structure linking language and world.

It is also deeply connected, as I shall argue, to the *Tractatus*' prohibition of the self-membership of sets or self-reference in language. As we saw in Chapter 1, Russell's paradox embodies a very general problem of self-reference or self-inclusion. If it is possible for a "universal" totality to exist, and for such a totality to include itself, then we are led to an apparently unavoidable contradiction;[22] and similarly, if it is possible for a linguistic element to refer to the totality of which it is itself a member, we cannot avoid the consequence that this reference is itself inherently contradictory. As we saw above, as well, the characteristic response of the *constructivist* orientation (exemplified by Russell's own theory of types) is to *prevent* the paradox from arising by means of prohibitive devices that effectively *prohibit* the problematic objects—such as self-membered sets—from possibly existing.

Although it is importantly (as we shall see) formally different from the standard constructivist treatments of Russell's paradox, Wittgenstein's response to it in the *Tractatus* nevertheless shares with them the same goal of adducing structural principles to prevent the paradox from (so much as) arising:

> 3.332 No proposition can make a statement about itself, because a propositional sign cannot be contained in itself (that is the whole of the 'theory of types').

> 3.333 The reason why a function cannot be its own argument is that the sign for a function already contains the prototype of its argument, and it cannot contain itself.
>
> For let us suppose that the function $F(fx)$ could be its own argument: in that case there would be a proposition '$F(F(fx))$', in which the outer function F and the inner function F must have different meanings, since the inner one has the form $\phi(fx)$ and the outer one has the form $\psi(\phi(fx))$. Only the letter 'F' is common to the two functions, but the letter by itself signifies nothing.
>
> This immediately becomes clear if instead of '$F(Fu)$' we write '$(\exists\phi):F(\phi u).\phi u = Fu$'.
>
> With this, Russell's paradox vanishes.

This decisive argument against both Russell's theory of types *and* the coherence of the paradox itself is closely linked to the deepest programmatic assumptions of the *Tractatus* about the relationship between logic and symbolization. In particular, according to Wittgenstein, the construction of logical symbolism, or the articulation of logical rules or laws, must neither make any mention of nor require any knowledge of *how* things are in the world. This requirement is a development of Wittgenstein's earlier motto, that "logic must take care of itself"; here it yields the vision of a "logical syntax," or purely syntactical corpus of logical rules that govern the use of signs, stateable in principle without reference to their meanings:

> 3.33 In logical syntax the meaning of a sign may never play a role. It must admit of being established without mention being made of the *meaning* of a sign: it may presuppose *only* the description of expressions.

> 3.331 From this observation we gain an insight into Russell's 'theory of types'. Russell's error is shown by the fact that in establishing the rules for signs he had to mention the meaning of signs.

The point of such a logical syntax is to eliminate philosophical and conceptual errors by showing perspicuously the significant *uses* of signs; in it, each distinct sign is used in just one way.[23] The sign, together with its significant employment, determines a logical form.[24] But since it is logical form that determines the possibility of meaning, it is again impossible for logical form to *depend* on the meaning of any signs. It follows from this that the sort of explicit legislation that is present in both Russell's theory of types and the (later) standard axiomatizations of set theory in order to avoid the "paradoxical objects" that would lead to contradiction can play no role in a rigorous formal theory of logical syntax. It can be no part of such a theory to establish that certain sorts of objects (for instance, sets containing themselves) "cannot" exist.

But if the substantial theories that Russell and others formulated to respond to the paradox are thus diagnosed as violations of the basic conditions for logical syntax, Wittgenstein holds as well that the very same conditions render *the paradox itself* incoherent. For, given a rigorous logical syntax in which *each sign is used in just one way*, it is impossible, according to Wittgenstein, even so much as to *state* Russell's paradox itself. Specifically, a sign for a function, in a logically purified syntax, must *show* the place for its argument in the very structure of the sign itself. In showing this, it shows its logical form, the possibilities of its significant employment. If, then, we try to make the function its *own* argument, using the sign for the function twice, it appears immediately that the two iterations of the sign in fact have *different* syntactical forms, and so cannot mean the same thing.[25] We have in fact been using the same letter in two different ways; in order to be clearer in our notation, we must eliminate the ambiguity by using two different letters. But then the appearance that the function is taking "itself" as an argument—or even possibly *can* do so—vanishes.

Wittgenstein's argument thus enacts a foundational interdiction of the very possibility of stating Russell's paradox, and indeed of all forms of (apparent) linguistic self-reference. Any such reference is effectively blocked, in advance, by the impossibility of using a sign to refer to "itself." And this impossibility is itself a consequence of the incapability of any (apparent) instance of self-reference to bear a unified sense in each of the (two or more) uses of its linguistic tokens.

The argument against Russell's paradox is also closely connected to the argument at 2.02–2.0212 for the necessary existence of simples, which we have discussed above. As we saw, this argument itself rests on the claim that the possibility of *meaningful* language depends on the determinacy of sense. The same idea underlies Wittgenstein's insistence, against Russell, that it must never be necessary to "mention" the meanings of signs (in the sense, for instance, of stating which objects may exist) while laying down the logico-syntactic rules for their use. For if it were necessary to construct the rules with a view to what objects actually do or do not exist, then their sense would again depend on contingencies, and the determinacy of sense would then be violated once again. Now, there is a fairly obvious sense in which the actual existence of self-reference would make the meaning of self-referential terms and expressions fail to be determinate in just this way. For it would make the meaningfulness of self-referential terms depend on what is presumably an *empirical* event, namely, the actual existence, use, inscription, or institution of *that very term* in the course of (empirically described) language use. In this case, sense would be indeterminate in very much the same way as it would be if there were no necessarily existing simple objects. It would not be possible to establish the *meanings* of signs (the rules for their use) in advance of their use, for the uses of certain signs (the self-referential ones) would depend on their in fact already having a use within a particular language.

The argument against the possibility of self-reference therefore succeeds *if* it is possible to presuppose, as an absolute requirement for all meaningful language, the determinacy of sense. However, the problems that Wittgenstein finds with Russell's own account here begin to reappear at the level of the very syntactic requirements that Wittgenstein imposes on any language capable of expressing sense. As we saw, Russell's own attempt to solve the paradox through the theory of types tended to refute itself by introducing principles which require reference to the very objects which, according to their own claim, must be incapable of existing. In requiring the determinacy of sense and ruling out contradiction and nonsense, the early Wittgenstein's picture (in, as he would later realize, an overdetermined fashion) imposed a unified regime of rules according to which the very statement of the paradox would be impossible. But the problem arises again on the level of the very statement and maintenance of these requirements and prohibitions themselves, in that their very articulation invokes the possibilities of reference that are supposedly (thereby) prohibited. [26]

Despite Wittgenstein's early attempt to "dissolve" both Russell's paradox and the theory of types by precluding either from being so much as stateable, the *Tractatus*' prohibition of self-reference (issued at *TLP* 3.332) thus in fact echoes the Russellian prohibition on a structural level as part of an attempt to theorize language as a clarified regime of sense immune to the possibility of antinomy and contradiction. As we have seen, however, it is abundantly clear that phenomena of self-reference are some of the most ubiquitous occurrences of the everyday discourse in which we discuss the language that we speak and its figuring in our lives. Even if, in the course of reflection about conditions for the fixity of meaning and the determinacy of sense, we may come to consider these expressions and locutions as necessarily introducing complications within the theory of objective reference, it would make a travesty of ordinary language to declare them simply nonsensical. We may come to grasp them, instead, as those points at which language proposes to us an internal image of itself. They mark the place of the paradox by means of which language appears ambiguously, at the outer boundary of the world, as the condition for all possibility of meaning within it, and again as an empirical object, practice, or institution *within* the world whose boundaries it defines.

If the crossing between meaning and fact that occurs in self-reference can thus seem, in the *Tractatus*, to be interdicted always already in advance by the sublime enunciation of a law whose mandate and stake would be the clarity of human life to itself, it is evident, as well, that the interdiction once again makes possible what it prohibits and the stricture proclaims its own breach. That is, if the theory and structure that would hold facts and meanings rigorously apart undermines itself in its own statement, then the question of this statement (what we can see as the origin of all authority and rational force) is neither simply a *quid juris* or a *quaestio facti*. At the factual origin of law stands an auto-nomination that is neither fact nor law, the singular moment of origin at which the totality of an infinite structure is reflected in the finite point of institution. The crossing at this point remains, and is ceaselessly repeated in the ongoing life of language, as the form of the force of the general rule over the particular case.

In the later period, Wittgenstein does not often explicitly revisit the issue of self-inclusion and Russell's paradox; but when he does, he makes it clear that he no longer holds the *Tractatus* position. This is the case, for instance, in some remarks in the *Remarks on the Foundations of Mathematics*, probably written in the spring of 1944, wherein he revisits Russell's theory of types explicitly:

> One may say that the word "class" is used reflexively, even if for instance one accepts Russell's theory of types. For it is used reflexively there too . . .
> Even though "the class of lions is not a lion" seems like nonsense, to which one can only ascribe a sense out of politeness; still I do not want to take it like that, but as a proper sentence, if only it is taken right. (And so not as in the *Tractatus*.) Thus my conception is a different one

here. Now this means that I am saying: there is a language-game with this sentence too.[27]

Here, in the context of a series of passages (many of which were reused in the *Philosophical Investigations*) devoted to articulating the problem of what is involved in following a rule, Wittgenstein recognizes the kind of self-inclusion involved in Russell's paradox *not* as nonsense, but indeed as capturing an important general feature of use. That the general term "class" can also be used to designate *a* class is, here, no longer a confusion of distinct uses of the same token, but rather a relevant and potentially significant feature of grammar, even if it must inevitably, as Wittgenstein realizes, lead to contradiction.[28] As Wittgenstein now realizes, the sort of contradiction that Russell's paradox displays may *indeed* result from our ordinary technique of intercombining and calculating with signs, *especially* if we are not sufficiently attuned to their "application." And as he also now recognizes, the attempt to *exclude* this sort of contradiction on *a priori* grounds, which the young Wittgenstein shared with Russell, can also be successful *only if* the rules themselves can be held rigorously apart from their use or application, as the *Tractatus* stipulated. This would be the case, again, only if there were no problem with assuming the rules of language (or of logical syntax) to be fixed once and for all and capable, as such, of underlying all possible meaning. But:

> The fundamental fact here is that we lay down rules, a technique, for a game, and that then when we follow the rules, things do not turn out as we had assumed. That we are therefore as it were entangled in our own rules.
>
> This entanglement in our rules is what we want to understand (i.e. get a clear view of).
>
> It throws light on our concept of *meaning* something. For in those cases things turn out otherwise than we had meant, foreseen. That is just what we say when, for example, a contradiction appears: "I didn't mean it like that."
>
> The civil [*bürgerliche*] status of a contradiction, or its status in civil life: there is the philosophical problem.[29]

The possibility of such an "entanglement," whereby the rules, techniques, and calculi that we ourselves have laid down can come to entrap us, or whereby we become immobilized by the kind of contradiction that results formally from our own necessary failure to keep this ideal moment of stipulation distinct from the everyday use of signs itself, will indeed involve Wittgenstein in a far-ranging investigation of the meaning and "status" of contradiction. This investigation is, as he suggests here, fundamentally *political* in that it relates directly to the question of rules and their force, their role in constituting and regulating "civil life" (the word Wittgenstein uses here—*bürgerliche*—can also mean "civic" or "bourgeois"). This investigation extends, moreover, to the role of rules and "agreement" on them in constituting or forming any community as such, as well as to the regulative force of rules in determining and constraining behavior. As Wittgenstein now recognizes, the kind of contradiction that Russell's paradox embodies essentially *cannot* be excluded by any kind of prohibition issued from an ideal point *outside* the practice it would regulate; philosophy, henceforth, cannot be the regulative attempt to prohibit paradox and contradiction through whatever form of authority, but must instead become the concrete investigation of the role of paradox and contradiction in relation to rational force itself. This is the question of the life of language, as we live it and express it to ourselves, and of the meaning, force, and role of the rules and techniques we devise in the life we collectively pursue.

With this in view, we can now see very clearly some of the larger critical and political implications of Wittgenstein's development from the *Tractatus* to the position of the *Investigations*. As we have seen, the internal position of the *Tractatus* embodies the *criteriological* orientation in a paradigmatic (perhaps *the* paradigmatic) form. On this position, the work of philosophy consists in the regulative maintenance of the boundaries of sense and the criticism of illusion in the demonstration of these boundaries. In the *Investigations*, on the other hand, the original criteriological position, which simply assumes the unproblematic existence of external standards from which the use of language can be specified and regulated, is transformed into a far-ranging critical investigation of the role of standards in life and practices. This is the *paradoxico-critical* orientation, again in an exemplary form.

This suggests that responses to Russell's paradox and to the contradiction it implies will essentially define differing possible responses to the problem of the constitution and maintenance of political power itself.[30] Indeed, since there is reason to suspect that the issues involved in Russell's paradox represent something like the origin of contradiction as such, here we can apparently witness a transformative metalogical formalization of the *inadequacy* of traditional political responses to the occurrence of contradiction and antagonism within any specific social whole.[31] The model for such traditional responses is the overdetermined gesture of Parmenides as well as the early Wittgenstein, which amounts to the fundamental gesture of prohibitive force. To replace it with a reflexive tracing of the paradoxical implications of language's appearance in the world is both to demystify this gesture and to recognize, behind it, our fundamental and unavoidable relationship to language as a whole, our "being in language" as such.

6 Wittgenstein and Turing

One aim of this chapter is to consider the sense in which language is "finite," and the sense in which it is "infinite," for Wittgenstein. This exegetical question, as I shall argue, has important *philosophical* and *critical* implications, in particular for how we should today understand the vast social, political, and technical consequences of the development and global spread of the technologies of information and computation, which substantially originate in Alan Turing's 1936 definition of the basic architecture of a "universal" computing machine. I shall argue that similar considerations about the relationship between finitude and infinity in symbolism play a decisive role in two of these thinkers' most important results, the "rule-following considerations" for Wittgenstein and the proof of the insolubility of Hilbert's decision problem for Turing. Fortuitously, there is a recorded historical encounter between Wittgenstein and Turing, for Turing participated in Wittgenstein's "lectures" on the foundations of mathematics at Cambridge in 1939.[1] Although my aim here is not to adduce biographical details, their exchange nevertheless evinces a deep problem of the utmost importance for contemporary critical thought. We may put this problem as that of the relationship of language's finite symbolic *corpus* to (what may seem to be) the infinity of its meaning.

THE FINITUDE OF LANGUAGE AND THE INFINITY OF TECHNIQUE

Wittgenstein's philosophy of mathematics has sometimes been described as finitist; but, as I shall argue here, his actual and consistent position on the question of the finite and infinite in mathematics and language is already well expressed by a remark in his wartime *Notebooks*, written down on the eleventh of October, 1914: "Remember that the 'propositions about infinite numbers' are all represented by means of finite signs!"[2] The point is neither that signs *cannot* refer to infinite numbers nor that propositions referring to them are meaningless or somehow otherwise out of logical order. It is, rather, that *even* propositions referring to infinite numbers—for instance, the hierarchy of transfinite cardinals described by Cantor—must *have* their sense (and hence their capability to represent 'infinite quantities') by and through a finite symbolization, for instance, through a proof of finite length. That is, it must be such a proof—given in a finite number of steps and stated in a language with a finite number of symbol types—that gives us whatever epistemic access we can have to infinite quantities and numbers. This is closely connected with the remark, made several times in the *Notebooks*, that is also destined to serve as a kind of *leitmotif* underlying the *Tractatus'* discussion of analysis, showing, and the elusive nature of logical form: that logic must "care for itself." Here, this means that all the forms of possible meaning must already show up in the (formal) possibilities of signification in a finite, combinatorial language. Wittgenstein concludes the entry for the 11th of October by noting: "The propositions dealing with infinite numbers, like all propositions of logic, can be got by calculating the signs themselves (for at no step does a foreign element get added to the original primitive signs). So here, too, the signs must themselves possess all the logical properties of what they represent."[3] Thus, the problem of the meaning of the infinite is a problem of the *logic* or *grammar* of finite signs—of how, in other words, the (formal) possibilities of signification in a finite, combinatorial language can give us whatever access we can have to infinite structures and procedures.[4]

The reasoning underlying these remarks is very closely analogous to the reasoning about finitude and infinity that underlies Hilbert's classic *formalist* project, as described, for instance, in his 1925 article "On the Infinite."[5] Here, though Hilbert resoundingly endorses Cantor's transfinite hierarchy ("No one," he says, "shall be able to drive us from the paradise that Cantor created for us"), he nevertheless expresses some skepticism about the use of reasoning involving infinite wholes and totalities.[6] Though such reasoning is essential to the structure and possibility of many mathematical proofs, Hilbert argues, it is impossible to be sure of the legitimacy of any proof involving such infinite wholes unless the proof can itself be verified by finite means. It is thus necessary for all legitimate proofs to be of finite length, to employ at most finitely many symbols (or symbol types), and to be governed by finitely stateable and rigorous *rules* that determine the legitimacy of each inferential step. This is nothing other than Hilbert's conception of a formal system, which would provide the basis for "foundational" research up to the radical negative results of Turing and Gödel, which were both formulated in its terms.

In the 1939 lectures, Wittgenstein himself proposes to discuss the "foundations of mathematics," but not in order either to contribute to the analysis and description of such foundations or to give new calculations or even interpretations of calculations in mathematics itself.[7] Rather, his aim is to remove certain misinterpretations or confusions that surround the analysis of the "foundations of mathematics," particularly with respect to what is involved in the understanding and meaning of mathematical structures.[8]

Wittgenstein emphasizes that in speaking of understanding a mathematical structure, for instance, a regular series of numbers or indeed the sequence of counting numbers themselves, we may speak of coming to "understand" the sequence; we may also speak of gaining a capability or mastering a "technique." Yet what it is to "understand" (to "know how to," or "to be able to," continue "in the same way") is not clear. The issue is the occasion for Turing's first entrance into the discussion, in lecture number II:

> *Wittgenstein:* We have all been taught a technique of counting in Arabic numerals. We have all of us learned to count—we have learned to construct one numeral after another. Now how many numerals have you learned to write down?
> *Turing:* Well, if I were not here, I should say $\aleph_0$.
> *Wittgenstein:* I entirely agree, but that answer shows something.
> There might be many answers to my question. For instance, someone might answer, "The number of numerals I have in fact written down." Or a finitist might say that one cannot learn to write down more numerals than one does in fact write down, and so might reply, "the number of numerals which I will ever write down." Or of course, one could reply "$\aleph_0$", as Turing did.
> *Now should we say:* "How wonderful—to learn $\aleph_0$ numerals, and in so short a time! How clever we are!"?— Well, let us ask, "How did we learn to write $\aleph_0$ numerals?" And in order to answer this, it is illuminating to ask, "What would it be like to learn only 100,000 numerals?...
> I did not ask "How many numerals are there?" This is immensely important. I asked a question about a human being, namely, "How many numerals did you learn to write down?" Turing answered "$\aleph_0$" and I agreed. In agreeing, I meant that that is the way in which the number $\aleph_0$ is used.
> It does not mean that Turing has learned to write down an enormous number. $\aleph_0$ is not an enormous number.
> The number of numerals Turing has written down is probably enormous. But that is irrelevant; the question I asked is quite different. To say that one has written down an enormous number of numerals is perfectly sensible, but to say that one has written down $\aleph_0$ numerals is nonsense.[9]

Notably, Wittgenstein does not, here, *at all* deny the validity of the response that Turing initially (if guardedly) offers to the question about the capacity to write down numbers. Indeed, in endorsing Turing's answer he distinguishes himself quite clearly from the finitist who would hold that the grammar of "can" goes no farther than that of "is," that I cannot justifiably say that my capacity includes any more than actually has occurred or will occur. In knowing how to write down Arabic numerals, a capacity we gain at an early age and maintain throughout our rational lives, we possess a capacity that is rightly described as the capacity to write down $\aleph_0$ different numbers. The attribution of this capacity is not, moreover, an answer to the "metaphysical" question of how many numbers there *are;* the question is, rather, what *we*, as human beings possessing this familiar capacity, are thereby capable *of.*

Yet how is this recognizably infinitary capacity underlain by our actual contact, in learning or communication, with a finite number of discrete signs (or sign-types) and a finite number of symbolic expressions of the rules for using them? It is not difficult to see this as the central question of the so-called "Rule-Following Considerations" of the *Philosophical Investigations*, some of which was already extant in manuscript by 1939 (see, e.g., *PI* 143–55; 185–240). However, we may also, I think, see this very question as *already* decisive in Turing's development of the definition of a "universal computing machine" and its application to demonstrate the unsolvability of Hilbert's decision problem in the remarkable "On Computable Numbers, with an Application to the Entscheidungsproblem" published three years earlier, in 1936.[10]

The decision problem is the problem of whether there is a finitely specifiable algorithm that can determine the truth or falsity, in each case, of *any* arbitrary mathematical statement. Turing's aim in the paper is to settle an equivalent question: the question whether there are numbers (or, equivalently, functions) that are not computable; that is, whether there are real numbers whose decimals are not "calculable by finite means."[11] He reaches the affirmative answer to the latter question (which implies a negative answer to the former) by defining a "computing machine" that works to transform given symbolic inputs, under the guidance of internal symbolic "standard descriptions," into symbolic outputs. According to what has come to be called "Turing's thesis" (or sometimes the "Church-Turing" thesis), every number or function that is "effectively" computable at all (in an "intuitive" sense of effective computability) is computable by some Turing machine, and thus the architecture of the Turing machine indeed captures, replaces, or formalizes the "intuitive" notion of computability.[12] The thesis is, today, almost universally accepted; however, this should not blind us to the depth of the philosophical issues involved in this particular way of understanding the nature of a technique or procedure and the kind of relation between a finite calculus and its (potentially) infinite application that it suggests. According to Turing's thesis, for instance, what it is for anything (function or number) to be calculable at all is for it to be calculable by "finite means" (here, using only a finite number of lexicographically distinct symbols and finitely many symbolically expressible rules for their inscription and transformation). Drawing closely on the reasoning involved in the justification of Hilbert's formalist program itself, Turing twice (p. 59 and pp. 75–76) justifies these restrictions by reference to the finitary nature of human cognition, either in memory or in terms of the (necessarily finite) number of possible "states of mind."[13] Similarly, he supposes that we can distinguish between at most finitely many "mental states"; accordingly, it is necessary that a Turing machine can have only finitely many distinct states or operative configurations, and that its total "program" can be specified by a finite string of symbols.

These restrictions prove fruitful in the central argument of "On Computable Numbers," to show that there are numbers and functions that are *not* computable in this sense. The first step is to show how to construct a *universal* Turing machine, that is, a machine which, when given the standard description of any particular Turing machine, will mimic its behavior by producing the same outputs.[14] Because each standard description is captured by a *finite* string of symbols, it is possible to enumerate them and to work with the numbers (Turing calls them "description numbers") directly.[15] Given that we know how to construct a universal machine, we now assume for *reductio* that there is a machine, H, that will test each such description number to determine whether it is the description number of a machine that halts when given its own description number as an input.[16] It does this by simulating the behavior of each machine when it is given its *own* description number as an input. We also know that H itself, since it always, by hypothesis, produces a decision, *always* halts. However, the machine H *itself* has a description number, K. Now we consider what happens when the hypothesized machine considers "itself," that is, evaluates whether the machine corresponding to the description number K, namely H itself, halts. We know by hypothesis that the machine H does halt; however, as Turing shows, it cannot. For in considering K, the machine enters into an unbreakable circle, calling for it to carry out its own procedure on itself endlessly. We have a contradiction, and therefore must conclude that there can be no such machine H.[17] The result implies, as well, the unsolvability of Hilbert's general *decision* problem. For since the statement that a given machine with a given input halts can always be reduced to a mathematical statement about numbers, if there were a solution to the decision problem, there would be a solution to the halting problem as well. Since, as Turing demonstrated, there is no solution to the latter, it follows that the former is unsolvable as well.

The negative result at the heart of Turing's paper is (once again) an application of the general formal or metalogical "procedure," first discovered by Cantor, known as "diagonalization," and we can gain a more vivid understanding of the result by considering once more the structure of diagonalization itself. Diagonalization, as we have seen, underlies Cantor's own identification of the transfinite cardinals, as well as Gödel's two incompleteness theorems. Gödel's application of a procedure of "arithmetizing" syntax is, in fact, quite similar to Turing's numbering of the Turing machines; and as Turing points out, Gödel's first theorem is indeed itself an implication of his own result.[18] It is no accident that both of these decisive results rely on the enumerability of syntax (here: of standard descriptions), which is the key to the possibility of an application of the regular structure of a symbolic system to "itself," and hence to produce a particular local configuration (the Gödel sentence or Turing's machine H) that stands, almost paradoxically, both within and without the system whose logic it captures. The basis for this possibility in the results of Gödel and Turing alike is the possibility of "numbering" symbolic strings and so "encoding," within the system, facts about the rules and structure of the system itself.

In these and other cases, since it is only by enumerating syntactical formulas that we obtain these results, diagonalization is essentially *an intervention on symbolic expressions*. That is, it depends in a decisive way on the fact that a meaningful procedure is *necessarily* captured, if at all, in a combinatorial symbolic expression that itself combines one or more signs according to definite rules. In this sense, diagonalization is always, and essentially, a "procedure" that concerns not only numbers or other "mathematical" objects but also the *ways* procedures and numbers are necessarily *expressed* by means of finite strings of finitely many distinct symbols. Thus diagonalization and its results appear to depend *essentially*, in each case, on the fact that language must make use of *finitary* means—a finite stock of symbols and a finite expression of rules—to accomplish its *infinitary* powers of symbolization.[19]

Now, it is familiar that Wittgenstein held, in general, a dim view of the purported *results* of various forms of the "diagonal procedure," including both Cantor's multiple infinites and the truth of Gödel's "self-referential" sentence. Do these doubts, expressed prominently in the *Remarks on the Foundations of Mathematics*, not imply that there is a similar skepticism about the very possibility of a relationship of finite symbolism to infinitary techniques operative in Wittgenstein's own discussions of rules and symbols? In fact, they do not. Though superficial readings of these discussions have often taken them to imply that Wittgenstein wishes to establish that there can be *no such thing* as an "infinitary procedure" that enters human life through "finite" language, we can see clearly that this finitist moral is *not* Wittgenstein's point by moving closer to his actual remarks. In his critical remarks about the Gödel sentence as well as about Cantor's multiple infinities, Wittgenstein *does* certainly emphasize that the existence of a procedure—even one with no fixed end, like the procedure of writing down numbers in Arabic numerals—fails to imply the existence of a superlative *object*, either a "huge number" or a completed list of decimal expansions that itself contains "infinitely many" members. To a certain extent at least, these suspicions do extend to the "diagonal procedure" itself. Though Cantor can, with some justice, say how one *can* generate a decimal expansion that, as one can show, does not appear anywhere on an "infinite list" of expansions, he has not *in fact* generated it. Diagonalization is always the "outcome" of an infinite procedure and thus cannot be said to have finished. However, Wittgenstein nevertheless does not deny that there *is* such a procedure, and even that we can speak of it, with some justice, as one that shows (by giving sense to the proposition) that there is, for any set of decimal expansions, one that is not in this set.[20] Cantor, in other words, has given us a procedure that allows us to say: *given any* series of numerical symbols, we *can* (i.e., we have a *method* that lets us) generate a different one.

In understanding the possibility and implications of this procedure, Wittgenstein says, we must keep in mind that there is a difference between series of numerical *symbols* and series of *numbers* in the mathematical sense. *A series in the mathematical sense is not a sequence of signs but a method for generating sequences of signs.*[21] There are analogies between the two uses, but they are different; and given the difference, Wittgenstein suggests, the existence of a sign ('$\aleph_0$') that expresses the unlimited possibility—the unlimitedness of the method—of generating sequences of signs does not by itself ground a further calculus with this sign, for instance, one relating it to "other" infinities or other sizes of infinity. Nevertheless, as we have seen, it is just this ambiguity between sequences of signs and methods for generating sequences of signs upon which the claim of diagonalization to establish "positive" results depends. Diagonalization intervenes upon what are in fact sequences of signs (series in the non-mathematical sense) to produce a new number, a new sequence of signs which may itself be unlimited. What operates in this ambiguity, and creates the "crossing" at infinity (real or illusory) between procedures and their symbolization, is our presumed *infinitary* capacity to produce symbols according to well-defined rules.

In adducing these distinctions and casting doubt on the positive results of diagonalization, Wittgenstein's point is thus *not* to show the nonexistence or invalidity of diagonalization as an (infinitary) *technique*. Rather, it is to emphasize the extent to which this procedure or technique, as infinitary as it is, has a place within a human life, and does not derive its meaning or sense from any other source than this life itself. Much later, in *RFM*, Wittgenstein comes back to this point:

> The concept of the rule for the formation of an infinite decimal is—of course—not a specifically mathematical one. It is a concept connected with a rigidly determined activity in human life. The concept of this rule is not more mathematical than that of: following the rule. Or again: this latter is not less sharply defined than the concept of such a rule itself.—For the expression of the rule and its sense is only part of the language-game: following the rule.[22]

Again, Wittgenstein is not here denying that there is a valid concept of the rule for the formation of an infinite decimal; nor that this rule is a rule for the formation of "something" that is indeed "infinite." He is, rather, affirming that this formation—even in its strictness and rigidity—necessarily takes place as part of a human life, and gains its meaning and sense from this life. As it is capable of such infinite results, it would not, it seems, be quite right to call such a life, or the practice of following a rule within it (the language-game) that brings these about, "finite." Rather, the practice is *precisely* a technique: something of which beings with a finite spatiotemporal extent are capable, but whose *extension* is in principle unlimited. It is thus neither the finitude of language nor the infinitude of meaning that makes possible its effect, but rather the gulf between them, in which Wittgenstein recognizes the openness of a human life.

There are, I think, two preliminary conclusions that can be drawn so far. The first is exegetical: Wittgenstein was certainly not in 1939, and probably never was, a finitist. That is, he *never* held that the finite character of language implies the non-existence or non-reality of infinite procedures. Rather, his focus is uniformly on the problem of the *grammar* of the infinite procedure: that is, just *how it is* that finite signs handled by finite beings gain the sense of infinity. This is none other than the radically posed question of the later Wittgenstein's thought: the question of the nature of a technique or practice. And it leads to the second conclusion, which is not exegetical but philosophical: that the infinity of technique is not an extension or intensification of the finite; nor is it a superlative or transcendent object that lies "beyond" all finite procedures. The infinity of technique enters a human life, rather, at the point of what might seem at first a radical paradox: that of its capture in finite signs, the crossing of syntax and semantics wherever the infinite rule is thought and symbolized in finite terms.[23]

WITTGENSTEIN AND GÖDEL

Given this suggestion of a rather close connection between the implication of diagonalization and the upshot of Wittgenstein's own rule-following considerations, how should we indeed view the sharply critical attitude he takes, both throughout the *Remarks on the Foundations of Mathematics* and elsewhere, toward Gödel's incompleteness theorems themselves? These remarks (where they have not been assumed to show that Wittgenstein simply "misunderstood" Gödel's result) have often been taken as support for an interpretation of his philosophy of mathematics as finitist or intuitionist, in that they have been taken as resting on a finitist denial of the utility or possibility of the "diagonal procedure." But although it is true that, as Wittgenstein reminds us, diagonalization is *essentially* an infinite procedure, he does not, as we have seen, deny its existence or possible utility. Moreover, in considering his response to Gödel, we ought to keep in mind Wittgenstein's remark in *RFM* that his purpose is not to address Gödel's proof (that is, presumably, not to affirm *or* deny it) but rather to "by-pass it" (*RFM* VII sect. 19).

In particular, as Floyd and Putnam (2000) have recently argued, close attention to Wittgenstein's most notorious remarks about Gödel's proof shows that his point is not at all to deny the formal proof itself, but rather to suggest alternative possibilities for its interpretation. Here is the most crucial portion of these remarks:

> I imagine someone asking my advice; he says: "I have constructed a proposition (I will use 'P' to designate it) in Russell's symbolism, and by means of certain definitions and transformations it can be so interpreted that it says: 'P is not provable in Russell's system'. Must I not say that this proposition on the one hand is true, and on the other hand is unprovable? For suppose it were false; then it is true that it is provable. And that surely cannot be! And if it is proved, then it is proved that it is not provable. Thus it can only be true, but unprovable."
>
> Just as we ask; "'provable' in what system?", so we must also ask, "'true' in what system?" 'True in Russell's system' means, as was said: proved in Russell's system; and 'false in Russell's system' means: the opposite has been proved in Russell's system.—Now what does your "suppose it is false" mean? *In the Russell sense* it means 'suppose the opposite is proved in Russell's system'; *if that is your assumption*, you will now presumably give up the interpretation that it is unprovable. And by 'this interpretation' I understand the translation into the English sentence.—If you assume that the proposition is provable in Russell's system, this means it is true *in the Russell sense*, and the interpretation "P is not provable" again has to be given up. If you assume that the proposition is true in the Russell sense, *the same* thing follows. Further: if the proposition is supposed to be false in some other than the Russell sense, then it does not contradict this for it to be proved in Russell's system. (What is called "losing" in chess may constitute winning in another game.) [24]

As Floyd and Putnam emphasize, although Wittgenstein does not dispute the validity of Gödel's proof itself, he raises the *question* of its correct interpretation. This does *not* involve disputing any of the mechanics that lead to the derivation of the "Gödel sentence" which "asserts" its own "unprovability." It *does* involve, however, raising a series of questions for the usual interpretation of the sentence that began with Gödel himself and continues to be presupposed in most discussions of it. On this interpretation, the sentence shows the existence of a "mathematical truth" that cannot be proven by a formal system such as *Principia Mathematica* and thus demonstrates the *incompleteness* of that system.[25]

Although this interpretation is still presupposed in virtually all discussions of Gödel's proof, it is reached, as Gödel himself pointed out, only through an essentially *informal* argument. (The argument is that *P* must be true, since if it were false "it would be true" that it can be proven, which cannot be the case, assuming the soundness of *PM*; and that since it can thus not be proven, and this is just what it "asserts," it is therefore true.)[26] And although countless interpreters have followed Gödel in seeing his result as demonstrating the *existence* of truths unprovable in any formal system, there *is*, as Floyd and Putnam point out, an alternative interpretation suggested by Wittgenstein's remarks. On this alternative, there is not (or at least there has not been shown to be) a unified sense of "truth" that subsumes the use of this predicate both *within* the formalism of *Principia Mathematica* and in the ordinary language in which the *informal*, metalogical argument is given. If we relax this assumption of a unified sense of "truth" between intra- and extra-systematic contexts, then we might see Gödel's formal result as having quite a different significance than Gödel himself suggests.

Specifically, recall that Gödel's first theorem constructs a sentence P such that, as is provable in PM or a related system, $P \leftrightarrow \sim Prov([P])$, where *Prov* is a one-place "provability predicate" and enclosure in square brackets gives the Gödel number of the formula enclosed. Additionally, the "provability predicate" itself is defined by means of the predicates NaturalNo(x), and Proof(x,t), where NaturalNo(x) is interpreted as "x is a natural number" and Proof(x,t) is interpreted as a relation supposed to hold between two numbers when x is the Gödel number of a proof whose last line has the Gödel number t.[27] (Here, t abbreviates an expression which calculates out to the Gödel number of P itself.) All of these are, of course, interpretations, and might be resisted under the right circumstances. *In particular*, suppose we actually assume that $\sim P$ is proven in PM (or, one day, actually come across a proof of it). Then we are in a position, of course, also to prove $Prov([P])$. In this case, however, as Wittgenstein points out, we might well be justified in dropping the *interpretation* that holds that Prov([P]) is *in fact* a provability predicate. And if we drop this interpretation, there is no need to conclude that the Gödel sentence is indeed saying something that is "true, but unprovable in PM."

How, though, might we justifiably drop the interpretation of Prov([P]) as "P is provable in PM"? As Floyd and Putnam point out, we might take the (successful, as we are now supposing) proof of $\sim P$ to demonstrate that PM is (not inconsistent but) ω-inconsistent.[28] If PM is ω-inconsistent, though, then in every admissible interpretation of PM (i.e., every interpretation which fits at least one model) there are, in addition to the natural numbers, entities which are *not* natural numbers; and NaturalNo(x) can no longer be interpreted as "x is a natural number." Moreover, Proof (x,t) can no longer be interpreted as relating the Gödel numbers of two formulas (one of which is a proof of the other), since in every admissible model its extension will contain some elements that are not natural numbers at all. This means that—supposing that there is a proof of $\sim P$—it would no longer be tenable to *interpret* the Prov(x) predicate, defined in terms of the Proof (x,t) and NaturalNo(x) predicates, as "P is provable in PM." We would have to, as Wittgenstein suggests, "give up" this interpretation, and *along with it,* give up the interpretation of P as *saying* that it, itself, is unprovable.[29]

Accordingly, Floyd and Putnam argue, it is in fact not possible simply to *assume* the informal interpretation that Gödel gave to his own theorem, that of showing the existence of "mathematical truths" that cannot be proven or disproven in any given system such as *PM*. As Wittgenstein effectively points out, we must distinguish here between what is actually established by the mathematical result itself and the "metaphysical" claims that are made on its behalf:

> That the Gödel theorem *shows* that (1) there is a well-defined notion of "mathematical truth" applicable to every formula of *PM*; and (2) that, if *PM* is consistent, then some "mathematical truths" in *that* sense are undecidable in *PM*, is *not* a mathematical result but a metaphysical claim. But that if P is provable in *PM* then *PM* is inconsistent and if ~P is provable in *PM* then *PM* is ω-inconsistent is precisely the mathematical claim that Gödel proved. What Wittgenstein is criticizing is the philosophical naïveté involved in confusing the two, or thinking that the former follows from the latter. But not because Wittgenstein wants simply to deny the metaphysical claim; rather, he wants us to see how little sense we have succeeded in giving it.[30]

More generally, at the heart of Wittgenstein's critical remarks about Gödel's proof is his skepticism that there is such a well-defined notion of "mathematical truth" that can be held in common between a system such as *Principia Mathematica* and the English "translations" of various of its notions. But if, as Wittgenstein suggests, there is indeed no *neutral* sense of "truth" that can be used to characterize both sentences in *PM* and their English translations, then there is no reason to suspect that Gödel's proof indeed shows what it has most often been taken to, that there is a "truth" that cannot be proven or disproven by *PM*. What we have, instead, is simply a particular sentence in *PM*, one that formulates a "perfectly ordinary" and undistinguished arithmetical claim, one that bears literally no implications for the powers or structure of the system as a whole.

When Gödel's theorem and its broader philosophical implications are discussed, the usual framework of discussion is a *model-theoretic* conception of truth. That is, the truth of the Gödel sentence *P* is conceived as a matter of its holding for a (natural) model, where it is assumed furthermore that there is at least one model where all of the objects of which it holds are natural numbers. As we have just seen, even remaining within a model-theoretic conception of truth, this last assumption is disputable, and might indeed well be disputed if a proof of ~*P* were to be given. However, just as importantly, the model-theoretic conception of truth itself might be disputed. Wittgenstein himself never held such a conception of truth, tending to suggest instead a disquotational or redundancy theory.[31] On such a theory, as he suggests in the passage on Gödel's proof itself, there is no language- or system-independent notion of truth, and so there is no absolute sense to the claim that the Gödel sentence *P* expresses a "mathematical truth."

Instead, as Wittgenstein suggests, the only available sense of "true" that is evidently applicable to the Gödel sentence, conceived as a sentence of *PM*, is the sense "proven in *PM*." Under the assumption that this is indeed the only relevant sense of "true," though, the Gödel sentence simply collapses to a version of the "Knower paradox" (the sentence *P* that says: "*P* is known to be false") or the Liar paradox: *P* iff it is not true that *P*.[32] (Here, we are still maintaining that *Prov*(x) can be interpreted as a "provability predicate" [and accordingly, under these assumptions, as a truth or knowability predicate].)[33] This may again tend to suggest the possible inconsistency of our system, but crucially, it does not at all suggest that Gödel's proof bears witness to a substantial "truth" that is beyond the capacity of that system to prove.

To summarize, then, there are at least four ways, implicit in Wittgenstein's remarks, that we might resist the strong claim usually associated with Gödel's first incompleteness theorem (i.e., that it shows there is a "truth" that is beyond the capacity of *PM*, or any other system of a similar type, to prove or disprove). First, we might simply abstain from interpreting the Gödel sentence *P* in terms of truth, falsity, provability, or "self-reference" at all. On this option, the derivability of the Gödel sentence in *PM* simply shows that a "perfectly ordinary" and unremarkable arithmetical sentence of *PM* is derivable. There are then, quite simply, no further consequences for the nature or structure of *PM* at all. Second, while agreeing to interpret the Gödel sentence in terms of issues of truth and provability, we might refuse the model-theoretic conception of truth and opt for a disquotational notion. Then the Gödel sentence is just equivalent to the Liar paradox, and raises the same issues as does that paradox. These may (but do not obviously) include the implication that *PM* is inconsistent.[34] Third, we might *agree* to both the interpretation in terms of truth and falsity and the model-theoretic conception of truth, and still resist the interpretation of "Prov(*x*)" as a "provability predicate"; this is the interpretation suggested by Floyd and Putnam, according to which there is no admissible interpretation of *PM* whose models do not contain objects that are not natural numbers, and *PM* is accordingly ω-inconsistent (although not necessarily inconsistent outright); and fourth (and finally), we may, on any of the first three options or for other reasons, take the Gödel sentence to show *PM* to be (outright) inconsistent.

On *any* of these four options, the Gödel sentence does not have the consequence of showing that "there is" a mathematical truth that can be neither proven nor disproven in *PM*. This is enough to underwrite Wittgenstein's marked suspicion about the result as it is usually presented, and to show that it would be over-hasty simply to concur with the metalogical interpretation that Gödel himself gives. It is not, in fact, completely clear which of these four "deflationary" options Wittgenstein himself favors; in his explicit remarks on Gödel's result he seems to waver between them. However, we may nevertheless draw some general conclusions from the availability of these four options itself. Significantly, on any but the first option, the Gödel sentence effectively *suggests* the inconsistency or at least ω-inconsistency of *Principia Mathematica* (or any system for which there is a Gödel sentence). This may seem, at first, an alarming suggestion, but note that this suggestion just amounts, in each case, to the suggestion that a sentence that has the "special" form of the Gödel sentence will produce a contradiction or antinomy; there is, as yet, no implication as to the further consequences or implications of such a contradiction.[35] And since the first option—on which the Gödel sentence is taken simply as a normal, arithmetical sentence of *PM*—seems to amount more to opting out of metalogic than pursuing it, we may well take this general implication of the other three options to be a generally legitimate one, assuming we wish both to interpret the Gödel sentence metalogically and resist the usual interpretation in terms of "incompleteness." Indeed, it seems we here have, once again, a vivid illustration of the general choice that the phenomena of systematicity and self-reference universally face us with: the choice between (consistency with) incompleteness (Gödel's interpretation, and the usual gloss on his result) *or* inconsistency and paradox (with the completeness of a system understood to be capable of formulating—though inconsistently!—its own logic of proof, or truth, entirely within itself).

It might seem at first as if this second way of looking at things is simply incoherent, or ruled out on logical grounds. Are we not in a position to *know* that *Principia Mathematica*, for instance, is not inconsistent, and so that it cannot contain the kind of contradiction that threatens to appear within it, on this interpretation? If the answer is indeed affirmative, then it might seem that we can rule out a Wittgenstein-style interpretation of Gödel's result and must indeed opt for the Gödel-style interpretation on which it demonstrates incompleteness. However, it is highly significant that we can "verify" the consistency of a formal system (for instance, by means of a model-theoretic soundness proof) *only from the position of a metalanguage* outside the system whose consistency is thereby proven. Moreover, as Gödel's *second* "incompleteness" theorem shows precisely, it is impossible for the consistency of a system to be proven *by* that system itself, unless the system is in fact *inconsistent* (and then the seeming "proof" has a false result, since the system is unsound). Thus, while we may be able to convince ourselves of the consistency of a limited system which we can step "outside of" and treat from the position of a metalanguage (here, English), where we are concerned with the *very system* we are ourselves using, we do not have this option.[36] In this case, it indeed becomes much more plausible that the constructability of the Gödel sentence for the system indeed implies the existence of contradictions, such as a sentence that says of "itself" that it is not (provable and hence not) true.

But does not the presence of such a contradiction vitiate the system in which we are working entirely, since (as can be formally shown) *anything* can be proven from a contradiction? The claim that it does, and hence the vehement desire to prohibit or rule out contradiction at virtually *any* cost, is one of the most prominent supports of the "foundationalist" picture of formal systems that is, in all of his engagements with the philosophy of mathematics, one of Wittgenstein's most central critical targets. This criticism leads him to interrogate the "superstitious dread and veneration by mathematicians in the face of a contradiction,"[37] as well as the whole conception of the work of the researcher in mathematics or mathematical logic that follows from the attempt to detect or preclude "hidden" contradictions. In particular, as Wittgenstein suggests, there is in fact no way that a "hidden contradiction" can vitiate a calculus as it is actually used. For if the contradiction remains "hidden," it has no effect on our actual practice of calculation; and if it is "discovered," then we need not act on it, and so again it can cause no harm. Thus:

> One may say, "From a contradiction everything would follow." The reply to that is: Well then, don't draw any conclusions from a contradiction; make that a rule. You might put it: There is always time to deal with a contradiction when we get to it. When we get to it, shouldn't we simply say, "This is no use—and we won't draw any conclusions from it"?[38] (Lecture XXI, p. 209)

Elsewhere, Wittgenstein likens the situation of being faced with a contradiction to that of being given two conflicting orders, or being faced with two arrows pointing in opposite directions. That, in these situations, we do not know what the rules or orders are telling us to do and so, in that sense, "could" do *anything* "in accordance" with them, does not mean that we *must* do anything at all; we might simply abstain from acting. Or we might indeed take it that "anything is now permitted," but this would amount not so much to showing that the original calculus was out of order, as to giving up on the possibility of using a regular calculus to determine our action at all. Thus, there is no special need to worry about the presence of "hidden contradictions" and seek to develop a calculus that is guaranteed to avoid them.

This emphatically does not mean that we do not or even *should* not attempt to reason in accordance with the law of non-contradiction. Indeed, Wittgenstein takes the fact that we do in fact do so, and regularly criticize those who violate it, to be an important and deep constitutive fact about (what we call) reasoning itself, such that anyone who did not reason in general in accordance with the law of non-contradiction, or respect its status as an overarching principle, would not be doing anything that we could recognize as reasoning or calculating at all. Also, we *can* and *do* construct our calculi with a view to avoiding—as much as is possible, anyway—the likelihood of encountering the situation of contradiction in which we, "entangled in our rules" as it were, are stopped and do not know how to go on. Wittgenstein's consideration of contradictions and their "status in civil life" do not show, therefore, that it is not an important and even *constitutive* element of our ordinary practices that we are committed, in practice, to avoiding contradictions.[39] But it suffices to show that the existence of contradictions *alone* is not enough to completely vitiate these ordinary practices or render them useless, as foundationalists typically think it does.

In the 1939 *Lectures*, Turing himself suggests that at least one of the problems with tolerating contradictions in a calculus is that the presence of a hidden contradiction in a calculus used for a technical application, say building a bridge, could lead to errors which cause the bridge to fall down.[40] Wittgenstein seizes on this claim and attempts over the course of the next several lectures to demonstrate that it is mistaken. That is, there are, according to Wittgenstein, *only* two ways in which our use of the calculus can lead to the bridge falling down: either because we use a wrong *physical* law (or get the value of a coefficient wrong, etc.) or because somebody makes a mistake in *calculation* and gets a wrong answer (although what counts as a wrong answer as opposed to a right one still must be somehow determined).[41] In either case, however, it is not a contradiction in the *calculus* or the system that leads to the bridge falling down, and if such a contradiction actually arises we can again choose to act on it as we like, or not at all. In any case, the technical *efficacy* and utility of the calculus is not adversely affected by the presence of a contradiction, and so there is no need for "foundational research" directed to assuring the universal absence of contradictions in our logical systems.

COMPUTATIONALISM AND THE MIND

What, then, are the implications of Wittgenstein's way of looking at the significance of the results of Gödel and Turing for the issues of computation, human capacities, and finitude?

Interpretations of Gödel's theorem have spawned a large literature on issues of computationalism and the nature and capacities of the human mind. Much of this literature simply assumes Gödel's way of looking at his own result in terms of incompleteness. But Wittgenstein's way of looking at it evidently suggests an alternative. In particular, Gödel himself thought that the existence of the sentence P shows, for each formal system such as *Principia Mathematica*, the existence of a mathematical "truth" that that particular system cannot prove or disprove. Such "truths" are, according to Gödel's informal argument, accessible to the human mind in a way that essentially transcends the powers of any formal system. Thus Gödel himself thought (e.g., van Atten (2006), p. 256) that his result demonstrated a *superlative* capacity of the human mind to grasp mathematical truths in excess of the powers of any formal system.[42] Subsequently, Lucas (1961) and Penrose (1994) have generalized this suggestion, holding that the combination of Gödel's and Turing's results shows that the human mind (for instance, that of a human mathematician) is not mechanical in the sense that it cannot be accurately modeled by any formal system or Turing machine. There are certainly many problems with this argument that have been pointed out over the years; in the present context, however, it is sufficient to note that Wittgenstein's different way of looking at the upshot of Gödel's results in fact provides a dramatic alternative to them.[43] As we saw, Wittgenstein's remarks on Gödel's theorems suggest that he takes them as showing at least that the actual production of the Gödel sentence will lead to contradictions or antinomies, although it is not evident that these contradictions must have the profound destructive *significance* that foundationalist assumptions about mathematics portray them as having. In any case, however, Gödel's proof on the interpretation Wittgenstein probably intended *does* show that there is an essential limitation to the ability of any formal language to model itself both *completely and consistently*; this is why the Gödel sentence, which "encodes" the logic of proof (and hence, on Wittgenstein's reading, truth) for the system as a whole, leads to contradiction and antinomy.

In a little-discussed 1985 paper, Putnam considers the implications for computationalism of taking Gödel's result in just this kind of way.[44] As Putnam notes, projects in artificial intelligence and cognitive science have relied centrally on the distinction between (actual) performance and (ideal) competence. That is, according to a long-standing conception originating from Chomsky, at least part of the aim of such projects is to give a description of how the mind is "supposed" to work, how we would be thinking if we were *ideally* competent. Both Harman and Chomsky himself have suggested that such an idealized "competence" description is indeed a description "of correct thinking in the normative sense."[45] However, even if there is such a normative description, would it be possible for us to know it? By way of a proof whose core is Gödel's proof itself, Putnam shows that it would not. That is: "if there is a complete computational description of our own prescriptive competence—a description of the way our minds ought to work, where the ought is the ought of deductive logic or inductive logic—then we cannot come to believe that that description is correct when our minds are in fact working according to the description" (p. 144). The reason for this is just the same as that underlying Gödel's and Turing's results—that it is impossible, on pain of contradiction, for a formal system completely to model itself. It follows that, as Putnam argues, if the aim of cognitive science is indeed to give such an idealized description of our own competence, then cognitive science is essentially looking for something that we *cannot* find. In particular, even if we did find what is in fact the "correct" description of our ideal competence, we could not know that it *was* the correct one.

What more general conclusion should we draw from this? As Putnam suggests, we may take the upshot in either an "optimistic" or a "pessimistic" way: "Like everything else, this theorem can be viewed either optimistically or pessimistically. The optimistic interpretation is: Isn't it wonderful! We always have the power to go beyond any reasoning that we can survey and see to be sound. Reflexive reflection cannot totally survey itself. The pessimistic interpretation is: How sad!"[46] Here, the "optimistic" and "pessimistic" ways of looking at the failure of reflexive reason to survey itself essentially correspond to the two ways of looking at Gödel's result that we have already considered: Gödel's own, on one hand, and Wittgenstein's, on the other. In particular, the proponent of a Gödel-style interpretation sees the necessary failure of formal reason to survey itself as the sign of a *superlative* power or capacity, an ability of the human mind to non-formally exceed or "go beyond" all that formalism can model in itself. The proponent of the "pessimistic," Wittgenstein-style interpretation, on the other hand, takes the result wholly negatively—simply as showing that, as Putnam says, "reflexive reflection cannot totally survey itself," without taking this to imply any superlative capacity of the human mind. Rather, it shows a structurally deep and ineliminable problem at the limits of reflexive reason, the formally inherent impossibility of any verification of its complete consistency.

With respect to computability, the analogue is apparently to take Turing's result itself wholly negatively—that is, as showing that it is not possible, on pain of contradiction (or at least paradox), for our rational procedures completely to model themselves. This suggests that there will be, among these, some infinitary procedures that, although perfectly determinate, are not effectively computable. This by itself does not suffice to guarantee our access to these procedures. But such infinitary techniques, fixtures of human life that are not fixed, in their totality, by any finite symbolism, may be just what Wittgenstein is alluding to when, resolving the rule-following paradox of the *Philosophical Investigations*, he suggests that:

> 201. There is a way of grasping a rule which is *not* an *interpretation*, but which is shown in what we call 'obeying the rule' and 'going against it' from case to case.

And:

> 199. To understand a language means to be master of a technique.

Here, what Wittgenstein is suggesting is, importantly, *not* a superlative capacity of human thought to grasp "truths" or follow "procedures" that are inherently beyond the grasp of any mechanical system. Indeed, one of the central aims of the "rule-following considerations" is obviously to criticize any such conception of a human ability to "leap beyond" all the finite examples and see an infinitary structure "all at once," a conception that yields metaphors of the use of a word being present all at once "in a queer way" and of grasping the entirety of a use of a word "in a flash."[47] This conception is also of a piece with the conception of rules as "rails laid to infinity" and thus as capable, by themselves, of determining infinite usage mechanically and completely.[48] On any of these metaphorical pictures, the whole use of a word—or the whole (infinite) extension of a mathematical series—is something that can be present "all at once" in the symbolism that expresses the rule. However, given any such symbolism, it is of course always possible to interpret it in various different ways. This is what leads to the problem to which section 201 gives an answer, the problem that "no course of action could be determined by a rule, because any course of action can be made out to accord with the rule." Given this, it looks as if it is indeed necessary to "give one interpretation after another," interpreting each (symbolic expression of a) rule with another until we realize that the second does no better than the first at guaranteeing the correct application, and so forth.

This paradox is more or less unavoidable, on the assumption that a rule as symbolically expressed must be able to determine its own infinite extension completely. This means that to resolve the paradox, we must get beyond the conception of rules according to which they are "self-interpreting," or capable of determining their own applications completely and without contradiction. To see that there is indeed a close analogy with Turing's own formal result here, consider again the details of Turing's formal argument for the undecidability of halting. To establish this result, we posited (for *reductio*) a universal Turing machine capable of solving the general self-halting problem, and then considered whether it halts when given its own machine number. The result was the contradiction that it both does and does not halt, and accordingly that there can be no such machine (on pain of contradiction, at least). The general reason for this contradiction was that, in determining whether the machine with each description number halts, the posited machine must consider itself, and thus is apparently involved in an infinite regress. This regress is similar to the regress of symbolic interpretations that occurs inevitably if we assume that a rule must be able to determine its *own* application. In particular, the demand that the rule determine the application of another one is essentially similar to the requirement that a particular Turing machine determine the halting status of another one; and the demand that a rule must be able ultimately to determine its *own* application is then analogous to the requirement that a universal Turing machine determine its *own* halting status. In both cases, the demand of self-determination leads to an intractable paradox that shows that this demand is not completely and consistently satisfiable. Just as there is no mechanical procedure that solves the general halting problem, and thus no machine that can ultimately guarantee whether it itself halts, there is thus no way for any rule to *guarantee* the correctness of its own infinite application. It follows from this that there is, as well, no general "decision procedure" for the application of rules, no procedure, in other words, that determines the correctness or incorrectness of the application of a rule in every case.

This does not mean, of course, that the correctness of a rule's application *is* guaranteed by something else, for instance (as we may now be tempted to think) an ineffable insight, or a power of human judgment or discernment that "essentially exceeds" anything mechanical. (Nor, of course, does it mean that the right application of the rule is simply "up to us" or that there is no way of distinguishing right from wrong.) Rather, as Wittgenstein repeatedly emphasizes, the right move when faced with the gap between the demand that the correct application *must* be determined by something "present to mind" and the rule's incapacity to do so is not to appeal to any supplemental figure of ineffable force to fill the gap but rather to relax the demand that produces it. The result is that there is indeed no finite, symbolic expression—and hence nothing that can be "present to mind" all at once, or already implicit in any determination of first principles or fundamental axioms—that indeed suffices *by itself and outside of its practical context* to determine and guarantee the distinction between correct and incorrect application in all cases. On the other hand, a "technique" or "practice" is, rather, essentially something that unfolds over time, and in the relationship between people.[49] Thus, no symbolic expression or finitely capturable "capacity" has, as we may now say, the absolute *force* of a law which would be capable of determining the distinction between correctness and incorrectness all by itself. The task of philosophical criticism and "therapy" then shifts to a radical diagnosis and replacement of the assumption of (and the demand for) such a force.

RULES AND NORMS: THE "LOGICAL MACHINE"

I have suggested, then, that Wittgenstein's way of looking at the results of Gödel and, implicitly, Turing gives us a way of conceiving of them that, although it bears important implications for the question of computationalism, does *not* tend to show (as the Gödel-Lucas-Penrose interpretation alleges) that the "mind is not a formal system" in that it has access to mathematical truths in excess of the grasp of any formal system. This does not, of course, imply that Wittgenstein would have agreed to the opposite claim that the "mind is a formal system," or even would take it, ultimately, to have much of a clear sense.[50] Indeed, one of the deepest aims of the whole line of argument that is developed in the rule following considerations is to formulate a kind of critical resistance to pictures that identify human techniques and capacities with what are conceived of as the capacities of formal systems and as wholly present in their underlying structure. This resistance is deeply connected to Wittgenstein's critical interrogation of the conception of "logical inexorability" and "necessity" that these pictures suggest, and ultimately to his more basic inquiry into the sources of "logical necessity" and "rational compulsion" themselves.[51] According to Wittgenstein, when we picture to ourselves the compulsory force of logical rules, we are led to think of logic as a kind of machinery underlying our actual practices of reasoning and inferring. Such a machinery would determine "in advance" and without exception the correct practices of logical inference and derivation; in this respect, it is akin to a kind of "super-rigid" machine that contains all of its possible actions in itself by virtue of its ideal construction:

> A machine as symbolizing its action: the action of a machine—I might say at first—seems to be there in it from the start. What does that mean? If we know the machine, everything else, that is its movement, seems to be already completely determined.[52]

If we are to conceive of an actual machine this way, we must of course forget or abstract from the empirical possibility of its parts "bending, breaking off, melting, and so on." It is in fact just such an abstraction that is essential to our symbolizing the machine as such (for instance, by means of a functional blueprint), and it is this alone that permits the movement of formalization whereby we consider *any* actually existing machine actually to "realize" or "amount to" an "ideal machine" such as a Turing machine or a computer.[53] Wittgenstein's point is not that this forgetting or idealization is not sometimes justified, but that it encourages a conception of logical necessity that is itself deeply misleading. For:

> . . . when we reflect that a machine could also have moved differently it may look as if the way it moves must be contained in the machine-as-symbol far more determinately than in the actual machine. As if it were not enough for the movements in question to be empirically determined in advance, but they had to be really—in a mysterious sense—already present. And it is quite true: the movement of the machine-as-symbol is predetermined in a different sense from that in which the movement of any given actual machine is predetermined.[54]

The ideology of the super-rigid machine, in which all of its movements are already present, is thus the same as that of rules as self-interpreting or as rails laid to infinity: in both cases, it is only by virtue of a movement of idealization and abstraction from actual cases that we gain the conception of an underlying presence that is *effectively* capable of determining the entirety of an infinite extension in advance. And this conception of a such an infinite determination is itself the same as the conception of the force of logical determination as that of a "super-hard" or inexorable law.

How, though, do we first arrive at such a conception? In a passage from the 1939 lectures, devoted to the idea of a super-rigid "logical machinery,"

Wittgenstein compares the source of the underlying idea of the "inexorabil-ity" of logical law to that of the inexorability of the law as such:

> Perhaps it would help to take the example of a perfectly inexorable or infinitely hard law, which condemns a man to death.
>
> A certain society condemns a man to death for a crime. But then a time comes when some judges condemn every person who has done so-and-so, but others let some go. One can then speak of an inexorable judge or a lenient judge. In a similar way, one may speak of an inexora-ble law or a lenient law, meaning that it fixes the penalty absolutely or has loopholes. But one can also speak of an inexorable law in another sense. One may say that the law condemns him to death, whether or not the judges do so. And so one says that, even though the judge may be lenient, the law is always inexorable. Thus we have the idea of a kind of super-hardness.
>
> How does the picture come into our minds? We first draw a parallel in the expressions used in speaking of the judge and in speaking of the law: we say "the judge condemns him" and also "the law condemns him". We then say of the law that it is inexorable—and then it seems as though the law were more inexorable than any judge—you cannot even imagine that the law should be lenient.[55]

The image of the ideal inexorability of the law is thus, like the picture of the super-rigid machine itself, produced out of a kind of false parallel or crossing between two expressions, one that is used ordinarily to describe judges, and another that is used (perhaps metaphorically) to speak of the law. The diag-nosis does not imply that either the picture of the inexorability of the law or that of the super-rigidity of logical machinery is completely out of order, false, or nonsensical; either picture may indeed have its legitimate uses. However, it does suffice to show that both are grounded in a kind of essential confusion:

> . . . if I say that there is no such thing as the super-rigidity of logic, the real point is to explain where this idea of super-rigidity comes from—to show that the idea of *super-rigidity* does not come from the same source which the idea of *rigidity* comes from. The idea of rigidity comes from comparing things like butter and elastic with things like iron and steel. But the idea of super-rigidity comes from the interference of two pic-tures—like the idea of the super-inexorability of the law. First we have: "The law condemns", "The judge condemns". Then we are led by the parallel use of the pictures to a point where we are inclined to use a su-perlative. We have then to show the sources of this superlative, and that it doesn't come from the source the ordinary idea comes from.[56]

That is, it is only by means of this sort of crossing or confusion between two pictures that we gain the idea of the inexorable law of logic, and hence of its *force* in regulating our life and practices. This corresponds, as we have seen, to what is often called "normative" force, and conceived as a distinctive *kind* of force that is both distinct from and stronger and more inexorable than any kind of empirical or physical force. This conception is the same as that of the normativity of logical rules, or of the "self-applying" rule which is able to determine its own application in a logical and normative sense. The diagnosis of the *origin* of these pictures in a crossing or confusion between the empirical attributes of actual machines (for which it makes sense to say that one is more or less rigid than another) and the posited non-empirical attributes of an ideal machine makes it clear that the conception of the inexorable normative force of logic is itself grounded in such a confusion, and dissipates with its successful diagnosis.

This does not mean that the "normativity" that is involved in ordinary practices of rational deliberation and calculation which proceed, in part, by way of the citation and discussion of explicit rules, should be dismissed as simply illusory or fictitious. But it does imply that the underlying source of this normativity *cannot* be in these rules themselves (as symbolically expressed or expressible). Rather, it must have a deeper ground in the kinds of "agreement" and "attunement" that constitute our "forms of life," and thereby precondition the possibility of *all* techniques and practices as such. We can draw much the same conclusion, in fact, about the "normativity" exhibited by instruments and techniques of calculation, including actual symbolic computing machines or computers. Here, as the results of Turing and Wittgenstein both show, the ability of such instruments and devices to determine the distinction between correct and incorrect results (or, for instance, correct and incorrect ways of extending a function) *does not* and *cannot* rest entirely on anything given or wholly determined by the actual construction of the instruments and devices themselves. It depends, instead, on the preexisting practices, techniques, and ways of life in which these instruments and devices, as well as the interpretation of their results and *their* implications, have their normal roles.

This is particularly evident in connection with what have been called "triviality" arguments about computation and effectiveness. According to such arguments, every physical object (or every object of a certain, very minimally specified level of operational complexity) at every time trivially implements every possible computation, since there is always *some* function that maps the internal physical states of the object onto the computational states involved in carrying out any particular computation. Thus, on Searle's memorable formulation: ". . . the wall behind my back is right now implementing the Wordstar program, because there is some pattern of molecule movements that is isomorphic with the formal structure of Wordstar. But if the wall is implementing Wordstar, if it is a big enough wall it is implementing any program, including any program implemented in the brain."[57] Such arguments have been used as well, most notably by Putnam himself, to argue against computational and functionalist theories of mind by showing that there is no *unique* functional description that characterizes the operation of the human brain (or any other mechanical system) at any time, and accordingly no hope for the "computationalist" project which attempts to discover such a (unique) description.[58]

As is suggested by some responses to the triviality arguments (e.g. those by Block and Chalmers), we can solve the problem of triviality if—and only if—we can already *presuppose* a distinction between the correct and incorrect functioning of the machine.[59] Thus, for instance, I can "interpret" the machinery in front of me as calculating the "plus" function only if I am in a position to distinguish between correct and incorrect responses to (what *I* interpret as) a query, for instance, "2 + 3 = ?"; and I will indeed be *inclined* to interpret the machinery as calculating the "plus" function only if I can assume that it *reliably* gives (what I deem to be) correct responses to this query. It is important to note, however, that there is nothing that guarantees such reliability (as Wittgenstein emphasizes, any actual machine might "break down" at any moment), and no sharp line between what kinds of behavior count as "reliable" and what evidences "unreliability" in this sense.

If this is right, though, and the practical interpretation of a given object or piece of machinery depends on our preexisting ability to distinguish between "correct" and "incorrect" instances of computation, then the normativity involved in this distinction again essentially *cannot* be given wholly by any computable system of rules itself. It must, instead, already be a precondition of our ability to take any set of symbols or physical system *as* the expression or implementation of any such system. This implies, again, that any attempt to ground our judgments of correctness or incorrectness in the inexorable force of a "logical machine" that determines the interpretation of its own symbolism, or the implementation of its own computations, all by itself and outside the context of any human practices, must inevitably fail. Our practical attitudes toward the rules embodied in actual computers, and the kinds of normative force they represent or enforce, are to the contrary very much aspects of our everyday lives and practices with them, and accordingly cannot be separated from these ordinary practices. The normativity that we expect from, and regularly find, in the actions of computers is not simply an outcome of their actual construction or their "ideal" architecture, but is rather possible only on the basis of the kinds of "agreement" that first enable us to engage in shared practices at all.

As Wittgenstein emphasizes, this agreement is not underlain or guaranteed by any technical or technological form of regularity or repetition. At the same time, however, it is not at all a *contingent* agreement on specific (as it may be, "historically situated") practices, norms, or conventions. For:

> . . . the logical 'must' is a component part of the propositions of logic, and these are not propositions of human natural history. If what a proposition of logic said was: Human beings agree with one another in such and such ways (and that would be the form of the natural-historical

proposition), then its contradictory would say that there is here a *lack* of agreement. Not, that there is an agreement of another kind.[60]

"CRITICAL THEORY" OF INFORMATION TECHNOLOGY

It is a remarkable and highly interpretable fact that in the course of the very argument that establishes the ultimate undecidability of the notion of effective computation, and hence its inherent formal limitation, Turing *also* creates the basic architecture of the computer, and thereby makes possible the massively and globally transformative effects of the technologies of computation and information. Speaking somewhat loosely, the conceptual "condition of possibility" of all modern computation and computational technology, and all the social projects and transformations it has yielded, is thus at the same time the "condition of impossibility" of their consistent completion. I have argued that Wittgenstein's way of looking at Turing's result, in the context of his broader consideration of the force of rules and "normativity," offers terms for a critical reading and reinterpretation of what is involved in ordinary as well as philosophical conceptions of the basis of logical or rational force. Does this critique also have implications for our pursuit of the vast range of technical, material, social, political, and economic practices spawned by Turing's invention of the computer? In this final section, I shall argue that it does, and attempt to specify briefly where this kind of significance might lie.

Unlike other twentieth-century critics of "technology," "instrumental rationality," or "calculative thinking," Wittgenstein does not always place the object of his critique explicitly in the rhetorical foreground. More often, his explicit targets are philosophers or philosophical ways of thinking, and this can give the (false and misleading) impression that he intends to reinstate an "ordinary" or commonsensical language in which philosophical claims are simply avoided and the temptations to which they answer are thereby, somehow, circumvented. However, there is also ample evidence throughout his corpus that Wittgenstein intended his critical analyses of concepts such as those of the rule, privacy, language, and *even* the concepts and methods of mathematics to bear critically on the prevailing technological and social practices definitive of his (and, to a large extent, our) time and even to suggest the possibility of their wholesale transformation.[61] This critique is certainly not limited to the special context of (academic or professional) philosophy, but extends to all of those contexts in which recognizably "philosophical" or "metaphysical" concepts (and some which are not so readily recognizable as such!) underlie and support, concretely or ideologically, actual collective practices of language, technology, communication, and economy.

Since Turing wrote, the technologies of information production and exchange, communication, and media that develop from the original conception of the digital computer (or Turing machine) have spread around the world and come to play a significant role in the life of almost every human being on the planet. In the context of political economy, the transformation brought about by the shift from older "industrial" and "agrarian" economies to today's "information" economies has caused decisive changes in the nature of capital and exchange, as well as radical geopolitical developments and transformations. It is a familiar theme of twentieth-century critical discussion of these changes and transformations that they are supported and sustained, at least in part, by ideological commitments and narratives that make technological development and transformation appear inevitable and necessary. At the same time, these commitments and narratives play an active role in the construction and maintenance of the economic systems that effectively enforce this "inevitability" and penalize deviations from, or resistances to, it. However, as is also familiar from existing critical discussions, it can be difficult to find terms in which to effectively criticize these ideological commitments, since they tend to lead to a naturalization of technology (and especially information technology) that portrays it as neutral and simply instrumental in relation to ends that are themselves simply presupposed or taken as self-evident. Partly because of this, the critical responses that do exist have sometimes tended to collapse into positions of resistance to technology as such, which in turn tend to fall back on positions of primitivism or romanticism that fail to take account of the underlying systematic logic of the technologies in question in their complex entanglement with our ordinary ways of life.

It is here that Wittgenstein's specific critique of rule-following and its implications proves most useful. For unlike other existing critical responses to technology and "instrumental thinking," this is not essentially an *external* critique that opposes such thinking to a (hypothesized) alternative form of rationality or thinking or to the nostalgia of a supposedly pre-given traditional world or "lifeworld."[62] As we have seen, it is, rather, a deeply *internal* critique that pursues the paradoxical implications of the systematic (and "instrumental") logic underlying information technology as this logic is reflected back into itself through its own symbolic expression.

More specifically, as we have seen, Wittgenstein's critique of rule-following and his related considerations of "normative" force yield critical terms by means of which we can resist the conception of the "inexorability" of logical law and compulsion that underlies most traditional conceptions of rational force as well as ordinary practices of deliberation and rational criticism. This critique does not imply or even suggest that we should abandon "rational standards" or their use in these ordinary deliberative practices. But it does yield a position from which we can resist on an *internal* basis the claims of neutrality, inexorability, and strong necessity that often support the development and dominance of instrumentally and technologically oriented practices and ways of life.

We can see this more clearly by focusing in on the notion of "effectiveness" as it figures in both Turing's metalogical project and Wittgenstein's critical one. As we saw, it is by *formalizing* the notion of effective computability that Turing both demonstrates the ultimate undecidability of this notion and makes possible the *actual* effectiveness of computing technology. The basis for both innovations is the representation of regular procedures, including infinitary ones, as the outcome or application of a *finite* set of symbolically expressible and recursively applicable rules. Turing's demonstration then shows that this application is itself something that cannot be effectively computed, in the sense that the general question of whether a given machine halts cannot be effectively solved. Wittgenstein's critique of rule following, similarly, focuses on the representation of procedures as the outcome of symbolically and finitely representable rules. And also similarly, it shows that the question of the ultimate basis of the *application* of such rules is not capable of solution by "effective" means, or in other words that the question of application cannot, in general, be decided. This shows that between the rule and its application there will always remain an essential and unavoidable gap which cannot be bridged by any further symbol or symbolic expression of force, no matter how "inexorable." At the core of the "effectiveness" of any rule or system of rules is therefore, in the moment of application, an essential element of ineffectiveness, a moment of essentially ungrounded projection that cannot itself be seen as determined by any further rule or demanded by any further effective force.

As is familiar from the existing critiques, claims for technological development and progress are often supported by a supposedly neutral conception of the "effectiveness" of technological solutions. This is, admittedly, not quite the same notion of "effectiveness" as the one which figures in Turing's definition of "effective computability," but the two notions are related. For instance, calculative or rule-based techniques or technologies can only be seen as, in general, "effective" in the first sense (of "neutrally efficacious") if they are seen as, also, "effective" in the second sense (of being effectively computable). That is, it is only if we can see a procedure, technique, or rule as capable of being applied in a rigorously determined way that leaves no further room for dispute or determination by context that we can see its application as guaranteed by the neutral imperative of progress itself. Accordingly, if, as Wittgenstein suggests, we come to see (by means, for instance, of Turing's own argument or Wittgenstein's critique) alternatives to the conception of computational technologies as inherently effective in the second sense, we may come to see alternatives to the legitimating conception of technological "effectiveness" as neutrally guaranteed in the first sense as well.

In a suggestive passage in *RFM*, Wittgenstein imagines the case of a tribe that initially knows how to calculate only orally and has no acquaintance with writing. Subsequently, they are taught to write, and shown by means of a gramophone recording that they had been making many mistakes before:

Would these people now have to admit that they had not really calculated before? That they had merely been groping about, whereas now they walk? Might they not perhaps say: our affairs went better before, our intuition was not burdened with the dead stuff of writing? You cannot lay hold of the spirit with a machine. They say perhaps: "If we repeated a digit then, as your machine asserts—well, that will have been right".

We may trust 'mechanical' means of calculating or counting more than our memories. Why? Need it be like this? I may have miscounted, but the machine, once constructed by us in such-and-such a way, cannot have miscounted. Must I adopt this point of view? "Well, experience has taught us that calculating by machine is more trustworthy than by memory. It has taught us that our life goes smoother when we calculate with machines." But must smoothness necessarily be our ideal (must it be our ideal to have everything wrapped in cellophane)?[63]

Here, Wittgenstein shows how a critical consideration of what is involved in the supposed effectiveness of technological solutions might lead a group of people to resist these claims and pursue ideals other than those (e.g., of "regularity" and "smoothness") imposed by what is for us the normal cultural attitude toward technology and its effects. But the attitude of the imagined tribe which thereby comes to resist the trust we ordinarily place in calculative mechanisms, even to the point of suspecting that their trustworthiness is simply illusory, would seem quaint, regressive, or at least unmotivated if it were not supported, here, by Wittgenstein's critical interrogation of the way these ordinary assumptions of trustworthiness are themselves based on superlative and metaphysical images of the "inexorable" effectiveness of technological ideals. As we have seen, the assumption that "the machine . . . cannot have miscounted" is itself such an assumption, and its only substantial basis is the picture of the ideal "logical machine" or the machine-as-symbol which contains all of its possible movements in itself already and whose parts cannot ever bend or break. But this is itself simply a picture, and as such cannot *be* effective all by itself. We may indeed act *as if* it is effective by treating our own machines (at least some of the time!) as reliable and as incapable of error. But the adoption of this attitude for *certain purposes* should not blind us to the possibility of adopting quite different pictures, or even using this one to quite different ends. And most importantly, we now need no longer feel as if the values and ends effectively imposed by *this* application of *this* picture—for instance, those of "regularity," "smoothness," or the particular *kind* of "trustworthiness" they permit—are absolutely necessary, or are the only possible ones.

There is, additionally, a further respect in which Wittgenstein's radical critique of rule-following, evincing the essential moment of undecidability that accompanies each instance of the "application" of a rule to a new situation, offers to demystify the spontaneous "ideology" of the metaphysical fixation of rules and norms. As we saw in the last chapter, the critique of rule-following discerns a deep connection between the uniformity of the rule and the desire to *guarantee* consistency by prohibiting *inconsistency*. This yields foundationalist pictures and projects which attempt to preserve consistency at all cost and see hidden inconsistency as what is above all to be avoided. This attempt is deeply linked to the spontaneous ideology of effectivity, which attempts to *guarantee* by means of metaphysical pictures and figures of sublime force the univocal repeatability of the rule across all possible circumstances of application. By contrast, as we also saw, Wittgenstein emphasizes the actual, *practical* implication of contradictions, as they in fact arise in the course of our *praxis*: here, they do not absolutely vitiate our systems or techniques, but rather simply mark points at which we genuinely do not know "how to go on" (i.e., which of the two apparently contradictory imperatives of the rule actually to follow).[64] This is a structurally profound moment of ineffectivity, and if it is, as it appears, *ineliminable* in the course of the pursuit of any human technique or practice of rule-following, then the "ideological" attempt to ensure the consistent coherence of any such technique cannot, in general, succeed.[65]

From a metalogical perspective, this apparent implication of Wittgenstein's analysis of rule-following gains support from its analogy to another profound result, namely, Gödel's *second* incompleteness theorem, which demonstrates the incapacity of any consistent system (capable of capturing arithmetical reasoning) to *prove* its own consistency. This is a direct consequence of the possibility of capturing much of the argument for the first incompleteness theorem—and specifically the implication that any consistent system cannot prove its own Gödel sentence—*within* the system discussed itself. This implies the strict, intra-systematic equivalence of the Gödel sentence for a system with the consistency statement for the system and further implies that each is provable only if the other is.[66] It follows that every system (of sufficient power) is either actually inconsistent—in which case (using classical logic, at least) it can prove everything, and so "prove" (though falsely) the statement of its own consistency—or, if consistent, can never prove its own consistency by internal means. Any internal attempt to *prove* consistency will therefore be either unsuccessful or, if successful, false.[67]

This gains "political" significance, most of all, in that it shows that the sorts of contradictions that occur in the life of a practice or the pursuit of a technique, although they need not have the implication of absolutely vitiating that practice, do have the significance of showing the *emptiness* of any attempt to guarantee its total coherence. This is a salutary and profound result, with deep implications for political *praxis* and action (I return to some of these implications in Chapter 10). For whereas it is generally tempting to see the existing antagonisms of a society as local and contingent struggles, in principle resolvable within a complete, consistent social whole, Wittgenstein's identification of the structurally inherent aporia of rule-following shows how these particular, empirical struggles can reflect the *fundamental* paradoxes of the reflexive moment of the application of rules, which ideological (or, in the terminology of Chapter 1, "sovereign") attempts to guarantee the conjunction of completeness and consistency attempt to foreclose. This means that the existing antagonisms can be seen as structurally deep moments of ineffectivity which will be necessary consequences of the critical reflection of the "normative" structure of *praxis* into itself, a moment of reflection that cannot be foreclosed at the point of each new application or "extension" of a rule.[68] The technological ideology of effectiveness would demand that this moment must always already be ruled out or forestalled by formal or technical means. But the results of Wittgenstein and Turing show that it essentially *cannot* be ruled out in this kind of way. This does not, assuredly, mean that technical practices and technological means cannot *be* effective in accomplishing the ends to which they are dedicated, but it does, as we have seen, yield a position from which the claim to *enforce* this effectiveness by means of technical or instrumental ideology can be resisted.

Wittgenstein certainly does not dispute that we may wish our calculi and logical systems to *be* effective, and that this may impose various kinds of requirements on them. These requirements will be requirements for our systems to be effective in the sense of accomplishing *specific* ends, and there is no problem with trying to design our systems with these ends in mind. But at the same time, he vehemently resists the assumption that there must be *general* or formal criteria or features that a formal system must satisfy if it is to be effective at all, or that "effectiveness" *as such* and outside any specific context has any clear sense. It is these assumptions that ultimately underlie the mathematician's superstitious fear of contradiction as such, and by relaxing them we can resist this attitude of "dread and veneration." If we are clear about what kinds of effects we are trying to bring about with our systems, encountering a contradiction will not cause any special problem, though it may occasion the creation of a new calculus or at least a new stipulation so that we can move on.[69] It is only, this suggests, when we are fundamentally *unclear* about the point of our systems (or about their role in our lives) that we begin to feel deeply troubled about the existence of contradictions, and it is only then that we are tempted to respond with the absolute demand that contradiction must be avoided at all cost.

Again, Wittgenstein is not saying that we can always (or even should always try to) avoid this kind of situation. Doubtless, we very often do use systems and calculi without having in mind in advance the exact kind of results we want our use of them to have. And nothing implies that we should be able, in every case, to make the role of our calculative techniques in our lives completely clear and transparent to ourselves. But where this kind of unclarity occurs, Wittgenstein's critique yields means by which we can resist the misleading displacement that standardly also occurs, whereby our desire for clarity is displaced onto the demand for a system that is effective in an "absolute" sense, and hence yields the desire to avoid or preclude contradiction *at all cost*. Here, the ultimate failure of our practices to be "effective" in an absolute sense is obscurely felt, while the threat it represents is displaced onto the absolute fear of contradiction as such. Just such a displacement yields claims for the absolute sovereignty of (logical as well as legal) laws or principles, or demands for the unification of the social whole into an absolutely coherent regular One free of any and all troubling contradictions. Here, the claim of the absolute *force* of normative principles simultaneously implies, in paradoxical fashion (see Chapter 5), the absolute demand for *enforcement* at any cost, producing the overdetermined demand to enforce the necessary, and thereby creating mystical and imaginary figures of superlative, absolute authority.

There is another, broader (if perhaps looser) implication of Gödel's second incompleteness theorem with respect to the political question of shared norms and motivations, the standards or criteria which orient a community's common sense of identity and shared *praxis*.[70] If, as we saw in the last chapter, the overdetermined attempt to *exclude* contradiction regularly plays a role in the "ideological" motivation of the force and effectiveness of particular norms and standards, then Gödel's second theorem, in showing that no system (of a certain kind) can *prove* its own consistency, appears to imply the impossibility of guaranteeing this exclusion of contradiction, and hence the impossibility of providing this motivation, by means of any rule, norm, or procedure that we can know and understand. It appears to follow that whatever (consistent) norm or systems of norms "we" may identify or gesture toward as underlying collective action in the normative sense—whatever system we might *identify* or *identify with* as providing the moral or ethical basis for a "shared" sense of value or right—*cannot be* the normative system that *in fact* justifies our action (if any does).

This is directly analogous to the moral that Putnam and others draw from Gödel's theorems with respect to computationalism: that, if we are using a (sound and consistent) algorithm to draw mathematical inferences at all, we cannot *know* this algorithm. Along similar lines, it seems, we might say: If there is a consistent systematic justification for our collective action, we cannot *know* what it is; and therefore, anything that we *cite* as such a justification in the course of representing collectively binding principles, norms, beliefs, or standards to ourselves *cannot be* the genuine article. Admittedly, this applies *only if* we take it that a system of norms, if it is to be capable of justifying action, must *be* consistent. But this requirement is standardly applied in moral reasoning and certainly does not seem implausible. It appears to follow that *any* putative identification of collective norms, standards, or principles as those actually underlying and justifying our practices must be false. The dramatic yield of the fundamental paradox of limits and reflection at the bottom of Gödel's result thus appears to be a formally profound deposition of all socially enforced and maintained claims to *collective identity* or *shared normative value*, whether these are conceived as imposed from above (in onto-theological fashion) or simply as the organic outcome of collective agreement or convention.

SUMMARY OF PARADOXICO-CRITICISM

As we have seen, the *paradoxico-critical orientation* originates from the older critical orientation of *criteriology*, which attempted to delimit the totality of the knowable, as soon as this older orientation poses the reflexive question of the possibility of its *own* critical position. It locates the ultimate condition for the possibility of this critical position in *language* as a total structure, and thus generates (or is able to discern) the radical paradoxes engendered by the inscription of this structure within itself. In the twentieth century, this development of a reflexively radicalized critical perspective based on considerations of the totality of language was by no means limited to the "structuralist" tradition of continental thought, but also played an *essential* role, as we have seen, in the "analytic" tradition as well (both in the trajectory from Carnap to Quine, and in the development of Wittgenstein's thought from the "early" to the "late" position). Indeed, that this is a formal and structural origin as well as a historical one demonstrates the depth of the consequences of formal thought for the historical transformation of practices of critical reflection, as well as the continuing relevance of such thought today. In addition, it appears to demonstrate a new possibility for philosophy itself: to revitalize its critical categories on a *fundamental* ground that owes nothing to the historicism and culturalism prevalent today.

Over the last several chapters, we have seen how the critical projects of Agamben, Deleuze, Derrida, and Wittgenstein all embody this central reflexive movement, which they use to identify the critical points of paradox, contradiction, and ineffectiveness that are formally obligatory given the capacity of any total linguistic structure problematically to reflect itself. We are now in a position to summarize the main elements of the paradoxico-critical orientation shared by these leading thinkers in both the analytic and the continental traditions:

1. **Critical thought is possible only on the condition of a formal-*syntactical consideration* of language *as a whole* in its problematic relation with facts and objects.** This is, of course, the consideration that is common both to Saussure's original structuralist picture of language as a "total system of signs" and to the analytic tradition's inaugural consideration of logical structure, as pursued (for instance) in Frege's *Begriffsschrift* as well as Wittgenstein's *Tractatus*, and yielding both Frege's conception of logical laws and Wittgenstein's conception of an ineffable "logical form" which governs the possibilities of sense in their totality. (This much is common to both paradoxico-criticism

and criteriology, at least in its more advanced structural modes.) Already at this original moment, though, the structuralist consideration of "meaning" as a structural effect of *language as a whole* effects a sharp and radical break with any conception of linguistic meaning as grounded in similitude, mimesis, resemblance, or the representational order of the imagination. However, because the broader structural implications of the inscription of language as a totality are not yet grasped, the spontaneous political philosophy of these early structuralist forms is the *conventionalism* of Saussure and Carnap, which sees the totality of language as capable of being instituted by means of the stipulation of rules or conventions from an unproblematic "outside" position.

2. This formal-structural consideration of the totality of language suggests the possibility of a reflexive *inscription* of the total syntactical structure of language within itself which leads to an essential *crossing* of syntax and semantics. Just such an inscription was pursued, and in some cases actually accomplished, by the early analytic philosophers who sought to articulate the "logical structure of language" or its "formal syntax." Similarly, those who worked within Saussure's structuralist paradigm (e.g., Lévi-Strauss), as well as those who developed the "formal syntax" project to its aporetic conclusions (such as Quine), soon realized that the possibility of discerning broad, structural principles governing human practices must bear witness to a fundamental reflexive capacity of language to capture itself, since they must characterize "our" cultures and practices as well. In a different and more general way, the problem of the possibility of such an inscription of effective structure is posed by Wittgenstein in his consideration of what is involved in "following" a rule and in Turing's invention of the universal Turing machine. This problem is posed, as we have seen, wherever reflexive devices lead to the possibility of inscribing the rules governing the logic of a system into that system itself. This moment of reflexive inscription is shown on the side of pure formalism, as we have seen, in Gödel's device of the "arithmetization" of syntax, which allows the total structural logic of a system to be represented within itself, and indeed in the method of "diagonalization" more broadly. However, devices of self-reference are quite prevalent in every natural language, and so their implications are by no means limited to "formal systems."

3. The syntactic possibility of reflexive inscription demonstrates that there is an essential structural *inadequation* between language and the world that is manifest as a structural *excess* of signification over the signified, or of sense over reference. If the total structure of signification is indeed inscribable within itself, this means that the possibility of signification must appear as a kind of permanent reserve, always presupposed in human thought and action but constitutively

excessive with respect to whatever is actually signified. Thus, as Lévi-Strauss says, "man has from the start had at his disposition a signifier-totality which he is at a loss to know how to allocate to a signified . . ." and there is accordingly "always a non-equivalence or 'inadequation' between the two, a non-fit and overspill . . ."[71] This is the basis for the radical excess of possible signification over signified meaning that subsequent (post-) structuralist thinkers such as Lacan and Derrida make the basis for their entire understanding of the structurally paradoxical situation of our human relationship to language as such. In Wittgenstein, it is manifest as the permanent structural excess of the symbolic expression of a rule over the actual "determination" of our behavior, what makes it at first tempting to assume that every expression of a rule in fact demands another one to supplement it and determine its interpretation, and ultimately demonstrates the irreducibility of a "form-of-life" dimension of human praxis that cannot be reduced to rules and their mechanical application.

4. This structural inadequation yields structurally necessary *points of paradox* where the total logic of the system is coded into itself. These are Lévi-Strauss' "floating signifiers"; privileged signifiers that seem to lack positive signification but instead act as ambiguous reservoirs of positive meaning. As we have seen, the "floating signifier" has as its correlate a "floated signified" that is in fact an "empty square" or a structurally determined void, and this is the key to its critical implications. The structure here is formally the same as that of the Russell set, which paradoxically includes and does not include itself, or of the Gödel sentence which "asserts" its own unprovability by encoding the total structure of proof at a particular fixed point. Wittgenstein's discussion of the paradoxical status of the meterstick demonstrates one such fixed point; it is the point of the inscription or figuring of standards in the "practice of a language," and hence of a radical and constitutive undecidability. More generally:

5. These points of paradox and contradiction are *undecidable* between an "intra-systematic" (semantic) meaning and an "extra-systematic" (syntactic) one. As we have seen, the points of paradox at which the total structural logic of the system are manifest have the "internal," "mystified," *excessive* meaning of a "superlative" object or truth; but, as the paradoxico-critic discerns, this superlative meaning is possible only in that they do indeed problematically code the total logic of the system, which is (presumably at least) only accessible from an "outside" position. This is the root of the phenomenon that Derrida, following Gödel, calls *undecidability*, which always depends, as we have seen, on the possibility of coding the syntax of a total system into itself. This possibility renders the meaning of key concepts and terms incapable of decision in (internal) terms simply of the logic of the system, since they also have excessive, extra-systematic "mean-

ings" as well that are at odds with these internal ones. Additionally, it generates the undecidability of "linguistic standards" (such as Wittgenstein's meterstick) as such, and hence demonstrates again the aporia of their incapacity to "determine their own application."

6. **This renders the position of the "subject of language" with respect to the "boundaries of language" itself undecidable between "inside" and "outside."** The operation of coding the totality of language within itself involves, in particular, the two operations which Priest discerns as the origin of the systematic paradoxes of the boundaries of thought and signification, namely, *closure* and *transcendence*. As "capable" of both operations, the subject of language (understood, as in Benveniste, as whatever can "assume the enunciative function" by "taking over" as potentiality the *whole* of the structure of language itself) henceforth occupies the complex topological space of the limit-paradoxes produced by them. The topology of this space is that of in-closure, and the structural necessity of in-closure paradoxes thus characterizes the structure of the speaking subject as such, producing what Lacan treats as its essential and structural de-centerment with respect to the Real of the signified.

What, then, are the critical implications of these structures, and how does paradoxico-criticism grasp them?

7. **Paradoxico-criticism understands the excess of signification, and hence the paradoxes of reflexivity, not as problematic *effects* of language but as constitutive *conditions for (the possibility of)* "meaning" as such . . .**[72] As Deleuze and Derrida both demonstrate, the inquiry into "sense" as the ultimate basis for the referential capacity of language as such can only yield the radical paradoxes of language's inscription within itself. If there is "sense" as the total structural condition for the possibility of linguistic meaning and reference, then this condition of possibility is therefore at the same time (as in Derrida's formulation) a condition of *impossibility*: at the very basis of the signifying power of language is the paradox that the structure underlying this power cannot be inscribed as a whole, on pain of contradiction. This paradox yields what Deleuze treats as the inherent "virtual" dimension of paradoxical sense, which always goes in both directions at once and thus stands at the basis of evental "becoming" itself. This paradoxical and virtual dimension is at the basis of all possibility of the iteration of signs, and first inscribes in language's systematic function the ideality of their possibility of infinite repetition.

8. **. . . And thus the ultimate basis of the "ideal dimension" of language, and hence *of the Idea as such*.** As we have seen, whereas traditional thought, up to Saussure's structuralism itself, understands the being of language as split between the material dimension of the signifier

and the ideal dimension of "meaning" or sense, paradoxico-criticism discerns the "ideal" dimension of meaning as a radical effect of the reflexive *syntactic* possibility of a coding of the systematic structure of language into itself. This effect is structurally responsible for the (infinite) iterability of the sign, the apparent "infinity" of the meaning of any general term with respect to its actual instances of application, and hence for the capacity of any general term to comprehend a set of particulars. As such, it is responsible for the "capacity" of such a term to make a One out of an otherwise indifferent Many. This is, of course, the function at the basis of Cantor's formal definition of the set, and its inherent aporias thus formally mark the structure of set inclusion as such (which, as Cantor suggests and I have argued, is ultimately the same as what Plato understands, under the heading of "participation," as the capacity of the Idea to group diverse particulars into a unity). If, as Cantor already suggests and the formal paradoxes (such as Russell's paradox) bear out, the structural possibility of aporias and contradictions must be considered *structurally inherent* to any formalism that is capable of minimal self-reflection (unless they are prohibited by external and post hoc devices), then these aporias must also be considered *inherent* to the action of the Idea as such. Their formal demonstration then constitutes the first fundamentally new logical contribution to the ancient problem of the One and the Many since Plato. Under the assumptions of paradoxico-criticism, their effect is to introduce the cleft of inconsistency in any system that attempts to model itself as a coherent and complete One.

9. **This identification of structural paradox has the critical effect of locating the structural contradictions inherent to reflexive linguistic reason as such, and hence of diagnosing the "weak points" of ineffectivity in any existing sovereign regime. These are the points at which any such regime can be resisted, or transformed.**

If structural and formal paradox is indeed at the very basis of the "ideal dimension" of reflexive language itself, then this implies that language itself is also *inherently ideological* in the precise sense that it *produces* the ideality of meaning and the excess of signification as internal structural effects. Subsequently, as we have already seen, this excess is recaptured and obscured at the local "fixation points" that are represented by floating signifiers and the properly imaginary superlatives they invoke. Structurally, this obscuration is an "Imaginary" compensation for the inherent Symbolic contradictions of language's own reflexivity. Through its discernment of the structural origin and pervasiveness of these contradictions, paradoxico-criticism thus offers the possibility of diagnosing and criticizing these imaginary compensations, and thus interrogating and removing the force of the superlative figures of power they engender. The most typical and ubiquitous structural mark of this (purported) force is, as we have seen, their demand to preserve consistency in general and at all cost by prohibiting inconsistency and paradox as such. This demand yields, as we have seen, the "mystified" conception of the absolute inexorability of logical law, and is furthermore marked by the overdetermined structure of the attempt to mandate the (purportedly) necessary and prohibit the (purportedly) impossible.

Paradoxico-criticism responds to this overdetermined demand by formally demonstrating and specifically locating the structurally necessary points of contradiction which the general prohibition of inconsistency systematically covers over and obscures with imaginary figures of force. These are structurally necessary points of the breakdown of the systematic logic that would ensure the noncontradictory and continuous unity and coherence of our practices, or of the social whole that is subsequently conceived as the necessary precondition for any effective political power or force. From their perspective it is apparently possible to approach a more radically self-reflexive position of resistance, marked by the lapsing into ineffectiveness of the general prohibition of contradiction and the superlative figures of force it traditionally supports.

Thus, the paradoxico-critical orientation discerns, in the consequences of formalism *as such*, the radical possibility of resistance to hegemonic and sovereign figures of unity, normalcy, progress, and effectiveness. The key to this discernment is its application of formal structures, and the paradoxes they inherently engender, to a reflexive consideration of the total structure of language, as it structures and is understood by human subjectivity. As such it bears, in its critical methods as well as its broader "political" implications, both deep similarities to and profound differences with another kind of tracing of the political consequences of formalism, one that does *not at all* seek these consequences in the aporias of language and its totality, but instead disjoins the domain of formalism as such radically and sharply from any linguistic expression. It is to this contrastive contemporary development of the "consequences of formalism," and to its relationship with the paradoxico-critical orientation and method just developed, that we may now turn.

Part III
Badiou and the Stakes of Formalism

7 Formalism and Force
The Many Worlds of Badiou

As we have seen in Chapter 1, early in *Being and Event* Badiou makes a *fundamental* methodological and thematic decision on the consequences of formalism which determines the entire subsequent trajectory of his conception of language, politics, and the event. This is Badiou's decision to conjoin an axiomatic affirmation of the One of consistency with a denial of the All of completeness, and hence to pursue the consistency of formalism within a universe (or, better, a multi-verse) conceived as radically incomplete. Badiou does not mark this decision as such, since he misleadingly portrays it simply as a decision, prompted by the appearance of formal paradoxes such as Russell's paradox, against what he terms the "One-All." However, as we have seen, the effect of Russell's paradox and related semantic paradoxes is not in fact to demand or even suggest such a simple decision between the "One" and the "Many" of traditional thought; it is, rather, effectively to *disjoin* the sovereign One into the two aspects of consistency and completeness and demand a decision between the two: *either* consistency with incompleteness (Badiou's decision) *or* completeness and totality with fundamental contradictions and paradoxes attaching to the limits of thought and signification. The second is, of course, the decision taken by the representatives of the paradoxico-critical orientation.

As we have also seen, this decision between consistency (with incompleteness) and completeness (with inconsistency) is *intimately* tied to another one on the very status of formalism and its philosophical uses. This is the decision on the relationship of language to formalism, which may very well determine the legacy of the twentieth-century linguistic turn itself. In particular, in deciding firmly and foundationally against the linguistic turn, Badiou also identifies in *mathematics* the possibility of a formalism that is, for him, wholly disjoint from language and capable of a grasping of truth beyond its limits. Thus, he decides for a position from which it is (apparently) possible to discern the *incompleteness* of any existing language. By contrast, the fundamental gesture of paradoxico-criticism is to insist upon the impossibility of any such exterior position, and hence faithfully to trace the radical consequences of the necessary formal reflection of the totality of language within itself. For paradoxico-criticism, it is *language alone* that introduces this reflexivity into the world, and hence is the basis for the reflexive structure of the subject as such. This means that there is no meta-language position from which it is possible to treat the totality of the linguistically sayable as incomplete, or to entertain the possibility of a "higher truth" to be demonstrated by formal means. The structure of language must be wholly reflected within itself, leading to the paradoxes at the limits that are the most important critical resource of the paradoxico-critical account of imaginary power and its formal resistance.

We can now summarize some of these points of difference by means of a table of contrasts:

Table 7.1   Table of Contrasts

Generic Orientation	*Paradoxico-Critical Orientation*
Mathematics as an extra-linguistic formalism	Mathematics as a *(linguistic) technique . . .*
Formalism as an extra-linguistic position . . .	and so *no position* outside language-as-such (no metalanguage) . . .
from which it is possible to treat any existing language as *incomplete* . . .	and so formalism of language is necessarily a writing that paradoxically *reflects itself. . .*
and hence *preserve consistency.*	and hence *inscribes limit-paradoxes.*

FORMALIZATION: IMPASSE OF THE REAL OR "FORCED PASS" OF TRUTH?

In his twentieth seminar (1972–73) in the course of a discussion of the relationship between knowledge and truth, Lacan writes, "The real can only be inscribed on the basis of an impasse of formalization."[1] He suggests that it is just such an "impasse" that his own use of mathematical formalization models, by producing an excess of the function of signification—or "signifierness"—over meaning or sense, amounting almost to a *"contre-sens"* direction of pure signification "without meaning." It is, in fact, in just such an excess of the signifying function, evincing the real, that the true structure of the subject and the object of its desire, the object *a*, is ultimately to be found.[2] The ultimate goal of psychoanalysis is thus a pure, mathematical formalization, a writing that, although it is capable of being "integrally transmitted" without transformation or loss, is nevertheless essentially dependent on "the use of language itself" and thus cannot be separated from the "act of speaking," whereby "I speak without knowing it . . .," "with my body" and "unbeknownst to myself."[3] This function of speech that is simultaneously beyond the limit of knowledge defines the very meaning of the subject for psychoanalysis. Arising from "some relationship of being that cannot be known," the structure of speaking-without-knowing "has nothing to do with what I am forced to put in being"; its knowledge is "enough . . . for it to hold up, but not one drop more." Indeed, this excessive relationship of speaking to knowledge, excessive as well with respect to what can be measured of being, manifests the specific impasse of the formal:

> This is what was hitherto called form. In Plato's work, form is the knowledge that fills being. Form doesn't know any more about it than it says. It is real in the sense that it holds being in its glass, but it is filled right to the brim. Form is the knowledge of being. The discourse of being presumes that being is, and that is what holds it.[4]

The task of psychoanalysis is henceforth to investigate the structure of excess and impasse which underlies this "relationship of being that cannot be known" and which is therefore the subject of an "impossible" knowledge that is "censored or forbidden" but as *interdicted*, "said between the words," or written "between the lines." It is in this excessive, prohibited relation of the subject to being that the impasse of formalism demonstrates, as an inherent consequence of the excessive function of signification itself, that psychoanalysis must "expose the kind of real to which it grants us access" and the possibility of the "only truth that is accessible to us."[5]

Early in his own career, Badiou repeats Lacan's formulation but supplements it with a kind of programmatic reversal, writing as the title of his own seminar session of February 4, 1975: "The real is the impasse of formalization; formalization is the place of the forced pass of the real."[6] He explains:

> If, as Lacan says, the real is the impasse of formalization, as we saw when we ran up against the limit as return, we must venture from this point that formalization is the impasse of the real.
>
> The algorithm scission-determination-limit, with its deviations to the right and to the left, is the truth of the structural dialectical sequence but only up to the point where this impeccable formalism is summed up in the 'do not trespass' that orders a return.
>
> We need a theory of the pass of the real, in the breach opened up by formalization. Here, the real is no longer only what can be lacking from its place, but what passes through by force.
>
> And there is no other way of grasping this excess than to return to the Two.[7]

Badiou's immediate concern, in this context, is to draw from Hegel a "dialectics" that, in its founding assertion that "there is a Two," distinguishes itself from a "metaphysics" which only ever (and through whatever displacements and ruses, all the way up to the apparent positing of the Multiple in Spinoza and Deleuze) posits the One, and therefore "forever gets tangled up in deriving from it the Two." Such a dialectics, Badiou suggests, is alone capable of thinking the dynamic and problematic relationship between the element and its place within a larger structure, what is indeed involved in a basic way in every inscription of a linguistic symbol and makes structurally possible its infinite iteration. But even such a dialectics is in eminent danger of winding up trapped in an eternal circle of repetition whereby the iteration of the dialectic process of "scission-determination-limit" can only ultimately yield a "theological circularity" which, "presupposing the absolute in the seeds of the beginning," returns to this beginning ever again.[8] For such a circular dialectic, the real "runs in circles" rather than "periodizing"; in its positive movement it only ever encounters a structural "impasse of the return to self."[9] In order to see our way past such an infinitely repetitive, circular movement, it is necessary to conceive on the basis of formalization itself a "pass of the real" that introduces novelty and progress by producing a "redoubling of the place by that which is no longer of its order and which is no longer spatially figurable."[10] The possibility of such a "pure passage" is what Badiou, already by 1978, finds modeled in the mathematical schematism of the multiplicity of pure infinities and in Cohen's demonstrative technique of "forcing."[11]

In the difference between Lacan's formulation and Badiou's, we can see very clearly exactly what is at stake in the *two* orientations toward formalism (the paradoxico-critical and the generic) that, as I have suggested, are coming to define the possibilities open to critical political thought in our time. "The real can only be inscribed on the basis of an impasse of formalization": this is Lacan's statement of the absolute necessity and unavoidability of the specific effects of reflexive language, in excess of sense and of what can be known of being, in defining the constitutively out-of-place formal structure of the subject that speaks. The claim that formalization can be, by contrast, "the place of the forced pass of the real" is Badiou's first articulation of his ongoing attempt to locate the transformative *force* of the action of a subject at a formal position ostensibly outside of language and immune to its inherent structural repetition.

So we have, between Lacan and Badiou, the following oppositions: a mathematical formalism of language *vs.* an extra-linguistic formal position of the mathematical; a Real which escapes signification in the gap between saying and being *vs.* a Real that is forced to appear as the new in being by the very formalism that encodes its own limits; a decentered subject that, having "nothing to do with what I am forced to put into being," is a structural effect of language (and appears, as such, only in its relation to its inherent "impossible-Real" lack) *vs.* an agentive subject capable of forcing the new (from a formal position beyond the effects of this lack). The choice between the two alternatives is intimately related, on the one hand, to the question of the status of formalism *vis-à-vis* language and its structure, and on the other hand, to the question of the status of the unifying One itself.[12]

For whereas Badiou, in *Theory of the Subject*, already insists upon the dialectical position of the "there is a Two" from which, as he says, the One can only be subsequently inferred, Lacan's whole conception of the relationship of the subject to the Real of being depends on the problematic structural effects of the One of language, figured in Lacan's recurrent motto, *Y a d'l'Un* ("there is some One" or "there is something of the One"), and demonstrated in the impasses of formal writing itself.[13] These impasses are structurally correlative with signification as such and constitutively linked to the complex One of the world that is assumed to exist as a whole. Thus, according to Lacan, "we know of no other basis by which the One may have been introduced into the world if not by the signifier as such, that is, the signifier insofar as we learn to separate it from its meaning effects"[14] and "it is at the level of language (*langue*) that we must investigate this One."[15] Accordingly, "nothing seems to better constitute the horizon of analytic discourse than the use made of the letter by mathematics"[16] and "it is at the very point at which paradoxes spring up regarding everything that manages to be formulated as the effect of writing (*effet d'ecrit*) that being presents itself . . ."[17] For Badiou in *Theory of the Subject*, by contrast, the Lacanian affirmation of the One is the basis only of a weak "structural" dialectic "without leverage";[18] its yield is only that of "force in the position of the state, or of the symbolic," which he already rigorously opposes to the transformative potential of "force in the position of the revolution, or the real."[19]

The terms of this divergence already suffice to show that what is at stake in the question of the upsurge of the Real of being is not to be determined by any distinction of perspectives simply internal or external to the project of "formalization" itself. That is, following Lacan and Badiou, we can no longer purport to think the Real as a reserve of truth or being simply external to the formal as such, or attempt to hold it there on the basis of a (perhaps aesthetically or theologically defined) privilege of the "unformalizable." Rather, although both recognize that the Real of being resists symbolic expression in structurally important ways, both Lacan and Badiou pursue, in exemplary fashion, the place of the real itself through its formal writing, or mathematization. Nor, in adjudicating this disagreement, can we rely (as philosophical discourse in the wake of the linguistic turn still tends to do) on any straightforwardly conceived opposition or distinction between a position simply internal to, and one simply external to, formal thought. In particular, we cannot rely on the distinction between the position of "mathematics" on one hand and "literature" or a kind of language thought to be radically disjoined from mathematics and its structures on the other. For as we have seen, Lacan as well as Badiou sees in set theory and the formal matheme the possibility of discerning, beyond the "meaning-effects" of the Imaginary, the very structure which manifests the Real. Here, the endless twentieth-century *arcana* of the "scientific" vs. the "literary," of formal structures and their "poetic," extra-formal resistance, are accordingly of no use, and can be left behind.

There is thus no possibility of deciding this debate on the basis of a simple *exterior* interpretation of the "meaning" or "structure" of formalization as such. Instead, if there is a decision to be made here, it will have to be made, as I have argued, on the basis of a rigorously *internal* formal reflection on the status and bearing of forms and formalisms themselves. Indeed, as the great legacy of the twentieth-century drama of language and its structure already amply witnesses, there is no way to continue with its most important results without taking account, as Lacan and Badiou both do, of the ongoing implications of a formal thinking that has its model in the historically radical (if *ultimately* unsuccessful) attempt to join mathematics and language in a unified and self-consistent logical structure. [20]

BEING AND EVENT: FORCING AND THE GENERIC

As we saw in Chapter 1, the most central burden of Badiou's argument in *Being and Event* is to demonstrate the genuine *possibility* of the advent of radical novelty beyond being itself in what he calls the "event," given the ontological theory of being as codified in the axioms of standard, ZF set theory. The undertaking involves Badiou's exposition in the rarified and complex results of set theory's investigation of the nature and relations of the immense variety of infinite sets, the "paradise" of infinities to which Cantor first showed the way. An infinite set, according to the definition Cantor drew from Dedekind, is any set whose elements can be put into a one-to-one correspondence with the elements of a proper subset of itself. Thus, for instance, the set of all natural numbers is an infinite one, since it bears a one-to-one relationship to the set of all *even* natural numbers (to match them up, we just pair each number with its double). The set containing all of the natural numbers, ω (or, as it is also sometimes called, ω_0), is then the first infinite set. Its size or "cardinality" is designated $\aleph_0$.[21] As Cantor already argued, however, there are *many* more. Recall that, by Cantor's theorem, the power set of a set is always cardinally bigger (that is, it contains more elements) than the set itself. Thus it is certain that the power set of ω_0 is strictly "bigger" than ω_0 itself; this power set essentially exceeds the cardinality of ω_0 and cannot be put into one-to-one correspondence with it. The power set of ω_0 can also be identified with the set of all *real* numbers, or points on a continuous line. The question that then leads to the most complex developments of set theory is one that Cantor also already posed: *how much* bigger is this power set, the set of points on a continuum, than ω_0 itself?

Cantor formulated the question as a hypothesis, the so-called "continuum hypothesis," which he struggled in vain through the last years of his life to prove or disprove. The hypothesis asserts that the cardinality or size of the power set of ω_0 is equal to $\aleph_1$, the *first* cardinal larger than $\aleph_0$.[22] If the hypothesis holds, there is no *third* cardinal between the size of ω_0 and the size of its power set; if it fails to hold, there may be one such, or infinitely many such cardinals. In its more general form, the hypothesis holds that the cardinality of the power set of *any* infinite set is equal to the very next cardinality (that, for instance, the cardinality of $p(\omega_1)$ is $\aleph_2$, the cardinality of $p(\omega_2)$ is $\aleph_3$, and so on).

The continuum hypothesis may at first seem to represent only a very specialized problem in the development of the peculiar theory of transfinite cardinals, but given Badiou's assumptions and terminology, it actually marks a question that is essential to the success of his doctrine of the event. Remember that the power set of any set is, for Badiou, the "state" representation of what is presented in the original set. Given this, and if, as seems plausible, the sets of interest to ontology are uniformly infinite, then the continuum hypothesis in its general form, *if it holds*, establishes that the gap between a situation and its state, in Badiou's sense, can always be regulated by a *uniform system of measure*. In particular, if the hypothesis holds, the size of the state is always greater than the size of the original set, but the extent to which it is greater is strictly measurable and controllable through the regular succession of cardinals: $\aleph_0, \aleph_1, \aleph_2, \aleph_3$, etc. If the continuum hypothesis turns out to be true, therefore, there will always be what Badiou terms a "measure of the state's excess"; it will always be possible to determine how much "more" a representation contains than what is initially presented, how *much* novelty it is possible to add to the situation.[23] If it does not, on the other hand, this "state excess" will be unmeasurable, allowing the event full range to "wander" and "err," introducing its radical consequences in an essentially unpredictable way throughout the situation in which it intervenes.

We now know that the continuum hypothesis is neither *provable* nor *refutable* from the standard ZF axioms of set theory. That one can neither demonstrate the continuum hypothesis nor its negation means, for Badiou, that although there is no way to *prove* the doctrine of the event within ontology, there is no way that ontology can rule it out either. Nothing in being necessitates the event, but nothing shows that it *cannot* take place. And the detailed derivation of this result, Badiou argues, shows a great deal about the conditions under which it is possible to think, or assert, the event. It is to the examination of these conditions that Badiou now turns.

Badiou thus takes the set-theoretical result that the continuum hypothesis is neither provable nor refutable from the axioms to have a profound ontological as well as political significance. It was Gödel himself who demonstrated the second half of this result, that it is impossible to *refute* (or prove the negation of) the continuum hypothesis within the standard axioms of set theory. His method was to exhibit a restricted *model* of the standard axioms in which, as he demonstrated, the continuum hypothesis in fact holds.[24] In doing so, he made use of a formalized notion of *constructability*, which is in fact the formal basis of the "constructivism" that Badiou cites as the greatest threat to his own doctrine. The condition of constructability places a restriction, much in the spirit of Russell's theory of types, on the sets that can exist. In particular, it holds that a set exists only if it can be "constructed" by taking all and only elements of some *already existing set* that have some particular (first-order specifiable) property, P, which is itself definable solely in terms of the already existing set. That is, P must be such that it is possible to determine its extension solely by considering the elements of this existing set and asking whether or not they belong to this extension; if P satisfies this condition, it is said to *predicatively* define this extension.[25] For instance (to adapt an example given by Cohen), given the set of all finite integers, ω, it is possible predicatively to define the set of all finite integers having a specific numerical property (such as being even or odd), but it is not possible predicatively to define the set P which contains all n such that there is a partition of ω into n disjoint sets of a certain sort.[26] This is because, in considering whether a particular number, say 5, belongs to P or not, we must consider *all possible* partitions of ω into 5 sets. The definition thus requires us implicitly to run through the entire set of all sets of integers (including, possibly, the set P itself), which cannot be said to "exist" yet, simply *given* the existence of ω. It is thus termed an "impredicative" definition and the set P is said to be *non-constructible*.

The restriction to constructible sets yields a hierarchy of sets, the so-called "constructible universe," that, although perhaps somewhat restricted with respect to the universe of sets overall, nevertheless contains many (if not all) of the transfinite cardinals and can, as Gödel showed, serve as a model for ZF (that is, all the axioms hold for this "restricted" universe).[27] Moreover, because of the restriction of constructability, the sets within the constructible universe are strictly orderable into a unified and unequivocal hierarchy. It follows that, as Gödel showed, *if we assume the constructible universe is the (whole) universe of sets*, the cardinality of $p(\omega_x)$ = the cardinality of (ω_{x+1}); that is, *within the constructible universe*, the continuum hypothesis in its general form is provably true.[28] The limitation to the constructible universe formulates the natural-seeming thought that a new set can only be said to exist if we can define it predicatively: that is, only if we can say, in terms of "already existing" sets, what defines it. The assumption of the constructible universe thus amounts to a restriction of the axiom schema of separation to allow only properties that are "predicative" in this sense to define a set. Introducing the limitation also introduces a strict measure for the "excess," in Badiou's terms, of the state over the situation. Other consequences of significance follow as well. For instance, if we stay within the constructible universe, the axiom of foundation does not have to be held as an axiom, since it now follows directly from the other axioms of set theory; the effect of the restriction to constructability is thus also to *require* that all sets be well-founded (that is, that their decomposition halts somewhere in a basic, founding element).[29]

By demonstrating one model of the ZF axioms (the constructible universe) in which the continuum hypothesis holds true, Gödel thus demonstrated that it is impossible, in the ZF axioms in general, to prove its negation; it is thus impossible to prove that the continuum hypothesis does *not* hold for ZF set theory in general. The other half of the result, that it is impossible to *prove* the continuum hypothesis in ZF, was demonstrated by P. J. Cohen in 1963. The complex technique of "forcing" that he used is robust in its formal apparatus and subtle in its conceptual implications. For Badiou, it is significant most of all in that the demonstration that it is impossible to prove the continuum hypothesis shows also that it is impossible to prohibit the event in ontology, and indeed helps to demonstrate how it might, paradoxically, appear there by "subtracting" itself from what ontology can discern.

Cohen's general method, once again, was to construct a model; this time, however, the aim is to develop a model in which the continuum hypothesis is definitely *not* true. If there is such a model, it will follow that the hypothesis definitely cannot be proven in ZF. The details of the actual construction that Cohen used are complex. I shall therefore try to convey only a sense for the general strategy, pausing on the parts of it that are of particular interest to Badiou.

The intuitive idea is to construct a certain kind of model of ZF and show that *within this model*, we can make the cardinality of $p(\omega_0)$ arbitrarily high (i.e., much higher than $\aleph_1$ if we wish, making the continuum hypothesis false). In order to do so, we must begin with a certain kind of set of cardinality $\aleph_0$, the so-called "quasi-complete" set or situation.[30] The strategy will then be to add to such a set a "generic" or "indiscernible" extension; if we can do so, it will be possible to show that we can (essentially by stipulation) make the cardinality of the continuum, or $p(\omega_0)$, as high as we like. A set is called "discernible" if there is some property *specifiable only in terms of existing sets* that discerns it; in other words, if a set is discernible within a larger set S, then there is some property *definable in terms ranging only over members of S* that picks out all, and only, the things in S that are in that set.[31] In this sense, the discernible sets will be all the sets that an "inhabitant" of S (who is restricted to considering *only* elements of S in defining his terms) can talk about, or have any knowledge about.

Now, the demonstration that the continuum hypothesis can fail depends on our demonstrating the existence of an *indiscernible* (or non-constructible) set, a set that, although real, is definitely not nameable in a language thus restricted, or discerned by any property *it* can name (Badiou symbolizes the indiscernible set: '♀'). We can then add this indiscernible set to an existing quasi-complete situation to produce a "generic extension" of the original set and we will subsequently be able to demonstrate the falsehood of the continuum hypothesis with respect to the thus extended situation.[32] Cohen's technique for generating the indiscernible set, and subsequently demonstrating its existence, is a complex piece of formalism. Intuitively, however, the idea behind it is this. We construct ♀ by "running through" all the possible properties λ that discern sets. For each discernible property λ, however, we include in ♀ one element that has that property. Once we've run through all the properties in this way, we know that the set we've created has "a little bit of everything"; since it has one element of *each* discernible property, there is *no* discernible property that discerns this set itself. (This is, yet again, an instance of the general "technique" of diagonalization.)[33] Thus we definitely have an indiscernible set. This set will exist, but it will not have *any* possible determinant (for we have built it in such a way, by running through *all* the specific determinants, that no *one* specific determinant can determine it). It is in this sense that it is the "anonymous representative" of the whole range of discernible subsets of the original situation.[34] Its appearance in ontology, according to Badiou, marks the free and immanently indeterminable circulation of the errant consequences of the event.

Developing the implications of the formal argument, Badiou draws out the consequences he sees in it for the theory of the subject and the possibility of truth. Art, science, politics, and love are "generic procedures"; their pursuit, by analogy with the construction of a generic extension, progressively adds to the existing situation the indiscernible set of consequences of an event.[35] This addition is conceived as connecting the generic set to the event by means of what Badiou calls an "enquiry"; each member of the existing situation which is "investigated" is indexed positively or negatively as belonging or not belonging to the generic extension, and it is of the essence of the enquiry that it can traverse an infinite number of elements.[36] Such progressive addition, at its infinite limit, constitutes the addition of a "truth" to the existing situation; it is to be strictly distinguished from the discernment within a situation, by means of properties, of what (is not necessarily true) but merely "veridical" in it.[37] In intervening, a subject "forces" a new situation which, like Cohen's "generic extension," adds to the original situation a set of consequences which are indiscernible by any concepts or properties formulable within it.[38]

Because they are collectively indiscernible, these consequences cannot be picked out by any term of an "encyclopedia" or schematization of possible knowledge accessible from within the situation; the consequences of an event are in this sense "subtracted" from positive knowledge.[39] Nevertheless, as Cohen demonstrated, it is possible to "force" them by successively considering conditional statements about the membership of certain elements in the generic set. Though it is not possible for the inhabitant of the initial situation to determine *whether* a given element is an element of the generic set, he can say (by means of forcing) that if the element is in the generic set, such-and-such statement about that set *will be* true (in the extended situation to be created). The elements that are considered as possible elements of the indiscernible generic set are thus treated as "conditions" and these conditions determine, by way of the forcing relation, statements that will be true of the new model created by adding the generic set to the existing one. It is possible in this way to build up a series of consistent conditions such that the entire infinite series of conditions, if thought of as complete, determines a set that cannot be specified by any positive predicate but, in that it contains at least one element discerned by *each* possible predicate, is "typical" or "generic" of the initial set as a whole.[40] By running through the series of conditions and their consequences, we are in a sense "reading out" the generic set, term by term, in such a way as to preserve its genericity, or its indiscernibility by any internally definable predicate.[41] In so doing, though we are not directly in a position to determine which elements belong to the generic set, we are in a position to determine what statement will hold true of the generic set *if* a certain element belongs to it (and if it is indeed generic).

At the infinite end of the process, we will have the complete specification of a set that is indeed generic and cannot be determined by any internally definable predicate of the language. With the addition of the generic set, various statements that were not formerly accurate or "veridical" in the initial, unextended situation will be so in the new, extended one. It is thus that the subject, as Badiou says, "forces a veracity, according to the suspense of a truth."[42] The centerpiece of Cohen's own demonstration is the proof that it is possible with this method to force the truth of a (more or less) arbitrary statement about the cardinality of the power set of ω_0; for instance, we can force the truth of $p(\omega_0) = \aleph_{35}$ or $p(\omega_0) = \aleph_{117}$ or whatever we like. This is accomplished by considering an arbitrarily high cardinal ($\aleph_{35}$ or $\aleph_{117}$ or whatever) and showing by means of the construction of series of conditions that it is possible to distinguish, in the extended situation formed by adding the generic set, at least as many different subsets of ω_0 as there are elements of that (arbitrarily high) cardinal.[43] Thus, in the extended model formed by adding the generic set (which is itself composed entirely of *subsets* of the unextended situation, though these subsets were initially indiscernible in the unextended situation), these statements become true and the continuum hypothesis fails.

From the perspective of the initial situation and its state, these consequences of the addition of the generic set remain random; only the generic procedure itself, in "fidelity" to the event, picks them out. The subject is then definable as anything that can practice this fidelity; the result—and with it Badiou closes the book—is an updated, "post-Cartesian," and even "post-Lacanian" doctrine of the subject. On this doctrine, the subject is not a thinking substance; it is equally not (in the manner of Lacan) a void point, or (in the manner of Kant) a transcendental function.[44] It is the "faithful operator" of the connection between the event and its infinite consequences, the generic procedure of truth in its coming-to-be.

LOGICS OF WORLDS: BEING, APPEARANCE, AND TRUTH

In *Logics of Worlds*, Badiou supplements this earlier "ontological" account of evental change with a comprehensive formal theory of *appearance*, what

Badiou here terms a "phenomenology." This is a formal theory of the structuration of the relations in virtue of which objects can appear as phenomena and the dynamic conditions for the possible transformation of these relations. But although the underlying apparatus is once again drawn from mathematical formalism, the sociopolitical implications of such possibilities of change are also, once again, very much to the fore. Indeed, in its "Preface," Badiou presents the whole argument of *Logics of Worlds* as part of an attempt to theorize what escapes the assumptions of contemporary "natural belief," what he sees as the confining dogmas of postmodern relativism and conventionalism.[45] According to Badiou, the most central axiom of this order of "natural belief" that, having demystified all theological categories, can claim to disbelieve in the existence of anything beyond the material world of contemporary scientific rationality, is the reductive claim that "there are only bodies and languages." Such views, Badiou thinks, can only ultimately yield a monotonous regime of "democratic materialism" that, in seeing all cultures and their claims as on a level, forecloses both any possibility of real development and any effective intervention to produce fundamental change.[46] Badiou proposes to replace this axiomatic of contemporary conviction with the one of what he calls, following Althusser, a "materialist dialectic." The central difference here is Badiou's unhesitating affirmation of what he calls Truths, which are, according to him, generally denied or suppressed in the contemporary orthodoxy of belief.[47]

Badiou's notion of truth, however, is, as we've seen, a heterodox one, not to be understood in terms of any familiar (e.g., correspondence or coherence) notion. For Badiou, the central mark of a Truth is its capacity to *break with* (or "subtract itself from") an existing regime of knowledge, and so to define a direction of radical transformation which, if followed out, will lead to the substantial reordering of basic possibilities of presentation and representation within the existing order.[48] This vector of transformation is, for Badiou, always infinite; and thus the punctual articulation of a Truth by means of an evental break with a given situation is always partial, and liable to be taken up again, even after a lapse of centuries or millennia, through the renewal of a faithful tracing, by the agency of what Badiou terms the "subject," of the consequences of a subsequent event.[49]

Much of this terminology is familiar from *Being and Event*'s theory of radical, evental change, and Badiou's aim here is not so much to alter that theory in any fundamental way as to remedy certain deficiencies he now sees in it. In particular, *Being and Event* described the *ontological* structure and conditions for the event to come about, but it failed to consider in detail the conditions governing the *appearance* of events in determinate, structured situations, what Badiou now terms "worlds." Worlds, like the "situations" of *Being and Event*, are irreducibly multiple, and the potentially radical implications of the event are again to be traced in its capacity to transform these existing situations. However, Badiou now gives a much more detailed theory of the structure of situations or worlds, and is thereby able to describe in much more specificity the various possibilities of their change or transformation.

This supplemental task of understanding the structuration of appearances and how they change and develop does lead Badiou to various innovations and modifications of his earlier theory. Most significant here is the consideration that, whereas it is plausible that ontology is static and non-relational, the realm of appearances is inherently relational, dynamic, and variable. Accordingly, in the realm of appearances, there are *degrees* of existence and of "identity" between two objects, and even greater or lesser degrees of identity between an object and itself.[50] These relations of identity and existence determine degrees of intensity of appearance, ranging from a minimal (effectively zero) degree, corresponding to complete invisibility or failure to appear, to a maximal degree of appearance, corresponding to maximal presence or effectiveness within the structured world.[51] Badiou demonstrates these relationships *in concreto* by working out in detail several different examples of "worlds" and their phenomenal elements or objects in their degrees of intra-world existence: a country road at sunset, a painting by Hubert Robert, a Parisian political demonstration, and the city of Brasilia.

Whereas *Being and Event* theorized the overarching structure of Being (at least insofar as it is speakable) as modeled by the axioms of standard set theory, *Logics of Worlds* turns instead to category theory to model the domain of appearing. In general, a category can be understood as a structure of relations; the identity of the objects thus structured is irrelevant, as long as this structure of relations is preserved. Just as it is possible to found much or even all of mathematics on sets and set theory, it is also possible to give a wide variety of mathematical objects a foundation in categories; and such a practice of foundation has interesting consequences for how we can think of the structure of these various domains and relations.[52] Most significantly for Badiou's project, however, it is also possible to use a special kind of categorical structures, known as *topoi*, to model *logical* ones; for instance, we can use topos theory to model algebraically all of the axioms and relations of standard, classical propositional logic. In fact, it is a consequence of this categorical method that the logics modeled *need not* be classical ones; indeed, we can use topoi to model any number of non-classical logics, including intuitionist and many-valued ones. These non-classical logics can uniformly be understood as determined by total algebraic structures called Heyting algebras, and their various determinate parameters can be taken to determine, for each world, the possible relations of compatibility and inclusion between any of its objects.[53]

Using this category-theoretical framework, Badiou can thus define the underlying structures determining the "logic" or relations of appearance which in turn determine what is treated as existent in each world. He terms the specific structure determining these logical relationships and intensities of existence for a particular world its "transcendental." And although the

terminology echoes idealist theories from Kant to Husserl, Badiou emphasizes that in speaking of such a structuring "transcendental" he does not
in any sense intend to give a theory of the transcendental *subject*. Instead,
Badiou's relationships of structuration of appearance are explicitly *objective*, determining without exception what can be understood to "exist" in a
particular world, and what remains "inexistent" or invisible within its own
particular way of structuring its phenomena.[54]

Similarly, although the employment of Heyting algebras and the multiplicity of differently structured logics suggest intuitionist or constructivist motivations, at least with respect to the realm of appearances, Badiou
emphasizes that the "transcendentals" that structure worlds are not, for
him, in any important sense *linguistic* structures. In fact, although the
multiple logics that define the plurality of the transcendental structures of
worlds are subsumed to a larger, single *mathematical* (i.e., category-theoretical) structure that Badiou terms a "Greater Logic," he emphasizes that
this Greater Logic has nothing to do with the ordinary logic of propositions
or language, which is itself to be subsumed simply as a special case:

> To think the 'worldly' multiple according to its appearing, or its local-
> ization, is the task of logic, the general theory of objects and relations.
> It is conceived here as a Greater Logic, which entirely subsumes the
> lesser linguistic and grammatical logic.
>
> To wrest logic away from the constraint of language, propositions
> and predication, which is merely a derivative envelope, is no doubt
> one of the stakes of *Logics of Worlds*. Section 4 of Book II scrupu-
> lously demonstrates that ordinary formal logic, with its syntax and
> semantics, is only a special case of the (transcendental) Greater Logic
> which is set out herein. Having said that, this demonstration is not
> the principal aim of the Greater Logic. Of course, its polemical ad-
> vantage lies in ruining the positive claims of the entirety of so-called
> 'analytic' philosophies.[55]

Additionally, by steadfastly avoiding describing the structuration of appearances as in any way dependent on structures within us or created by us, Badiou
aims to break entirely with all forms of idealism. Any such position, he avers,
will fail to grasp the objectivity of what is phenomenal within a world, the
capability of objects to appear and take on their distinctive degrees of existence without any contribution whatsoever from the "human animal."[56]

Badiou is thus able to theorize (using category theory) the phenomenal
structure within appearance of what are *also* (already according to *Being
and Event*) thinkable (using set theory) as sets or multiplicities within being
itself. More specifically, the worldly existence of a phenomenal "object" is
wholly determined by the transcendental indexing of the world in which
it appears, and this transcendental indexing reciprocally determines the
possibility of decomposing such an object into its (phenomenally) simple

parts, what Badiou calls "atoms." On the other hand, however, any atom is also, Badiou asserts, identical to an *ontological* element of the larger set which (ontologically) "supports" the phenomenal appearance of any object in which it appears; in other words, every (phenomenal) atom is simultaneously a "real atom" of ontology. This assertion, which has the unargued status of an axiom, also guarantees that there can indeed be some relationship between the otherwise disjoint realms of being and appearance. Badiou terms it the "postulate of materialism":

> A real atom is a phenomenal component . . . which, on one hand, is an atomic component (it is simple, or non-decomposable), and on the other, is strictly determined by an underlying element $a \in A$, which is its ontological structure. At the point of a real atom, being and appearing conjoin under the sign of the One.
>
> It only remains to formulate our 'postulate of materialism', which authorizes a definition of the object. As we know, this postulate says: every atom is real. It is directly opposed to the Bergsonist or Deleuzian presupposition of the primacy of the virtual. In effect, it stipulates that the virtuality of an apparent's appearing in such and such a world is always rooted in its actual ontological composition.[57]

The axiomatic postulate of materialism thus ensures the ontological consistency of any world by means of the isolation of its atomic elements, thereby also blocking, as Badiou makes clear, the hypothesis of any "virtual" structuring of existence by language or the phenomenal dimension of appearance in excess of its ontological substrate. Any such structuring will thus, for Badiou, always be the outcome of processes that are *simultaneously* phenomenological *and* ontological; in fact, the underlying identity of phenomenal objects and ontological multiplicities that is assured by the "postulate of materialism" leads to the primary innovation of *Logics of Worlds'* new theorization of eventral change.

This is the idea of a specific "retroaction" of appearance on being, whereby the fact of the phenomenal appearance of a particular (ontological) set within a structured world brings about a train of changes which will ultimately transform the transcendental structure of the world itself.[58] This strange retroactive effect of appearing on being, which defines the structure of the event, is possible only through a paradoxical effect of self-reference or self-belonging. In particular, for an event to occur, it is necessary not only that a certain set (a multiple in being) be a member of itself, but *also* that this particular being appear, in a world, as an *element* of a *transcendental indexing* that again indexes that very being. More specifically:

> . . . it can happen that multiple-being, which is ordinarily the support for objects, rises 'in person' to the surface of objectivity. A mixture of pure being and appearing may take place. For this to happen, it is

enough that the multiple lays claim to appearing in such a way that it refers to itself, to its own transcendental indexing. In short, it is enough that a multiple comes to play a double role in a world where it appears. First, it is objectivated by the transcendental indexing of its elements. Second, it (self-)objectivates, by figuring among its own elements and by thus being caught up in the transcendental indexing of which it is the ontological support. Worldly objectivation turns this multiple into a synthesis between the objectivating (the multiple support and referent of a phenomenality) and the objectivated (belonging to the phenomenon). We call such a paradoxical being a 'site'.[59]

Here, as in *Being and Event*, we should think of the precarious way in which a historical event, for instance, can bring into existence the very terms and signifiers that will subsequently provide for its own evaluation, and thus play an essential role in *constituting* it as the event it (given the new terms and degrees of evaluation they imply) will subsequently be visible as having been.[60] The particular underlying structure of an event as such is therefore again, as in *Being and Event*, to be understood as a matter of the event's "self-inclusion" or "self-reference," which as Badiou again suggests gives it an inherently "paradoxical" being that is responsible for the very possibility of the radical changes it can bring about.

However, there are two important differences from *Being and Event*'s account of the event's underlying formal structure. First, since Badiou now theorizes the structure of the event (on the side of appearances and existence, at least) as residing entirely in the "worldly" phenomena of its structural placement or localization, including importantly its relationship to its own transcendental indexing, he can now assimilate the structure of an event entirely to that of its "site," which is defined as just this localization. Thus, rather than distinguishing (as Badiou now suggests was the case in *Being and Event*, unclearly) between the worldly "site" and the partially extra-worldly "event," Badiou can now simply assimilate the two and deal directly with the structure of "sites" themselves. However, this also yields a more complex taxonomy of possible change, since Badiou can also now distinguish *among* self-referring sites between those that are structurally capable, and those that are not capable, of supporting an "event" in the full sense.

Second, and perhaps more importantly, the "self-referential" or "self-inclusive" structure of the event is now somewhat more complicated than the simple schema of *Being and Event* would suggest. There, the event's capacity for self-reference was understood simply as a matter of its auto-designation, or its ability to provide a name for itself. Here, the structure of self-reference is more complex: it is not simply the event's provision of a name for itself, but rather its relation to its own transcendental indexing, that provides its basis. An eventual "site"—the "place" from which radical, transformative change is alone possible—is thus definable as a multiple that contains within itself an element which determines the "transcendental indexing" of the whole world in which that very multiple appears as a phenomenon, and which can thus alter this fundamental structure. Thus, while *ontologically* speaking, an evental site is simply (as in *Being and Event*) a "reflexive set" or "a multiple to which it happens that it is an element of itself" (p. 366), in terms of appearance and phenomenology the structure is a bit more complex: "*A multiple which is an object of* [a] *world—whose elements are indexed on the transcendental of the world—is a 'site' if it happens to count itself in the referential field of its own indexing.* Or: a site is a multiple which happens to behave in the world in the same way with regard to itself as it does with regard to its elements, so that it is the ontological support of its own appearance" (p. 363). The role of auto-*nomination* in *Being and Event* is thus replaced, to a certain extent at least, with a auto-*nomothesis* that is not a positing simply of names, but of laws (of appearance and "existence") as well.

These further details and specifications lead Badiou, in *Logics of Worlds*, also to develop a more specific and subtle theory of the varieties of change than was present in *Being and Event*. When the quasi-paradoxical structure of the "evental site" occurs, according to Badiou, it is immediately possible for it to be taken up in a variety of different ways, corresponding to different degrees and intensities of change in the world. In the most dramatic case, a subject's faithful tracing of the implications of the structure of the evental site results in the element which was formerly *minimal* in its degree of existence—what had earlier literally "in-existed" in that particular world, being present in its being but completely invisible to the world's logic—suddenly attaining a *maximal* degree of existence, bringing with it all the changes in the existing structure that this implies.[61] The analogy here is to the sort of political revolution in which (as an old Marxist motto runs) "we who are nothing shall be all!"; but Badiou also thinks of this kind of evental change as possible in other domains, for instance, in the kind of "paradigm shift" in science that not only elicits new objects and makes visible phenomena that previously escaped attention and thus "lacked existence," but even fundamentally reorganizes the large-scale structure of what counts as existing in the (newly transformed) world.

Once the possibility of such a radical change in the structuration of worlds is demonstrated, the remainder of Badiou's analysis focuses on the ways in which the implications of the event can be brought out and eventually used to transform the structure of the world by the action of a faithful subject. It is essential to this tracing, Badiou thinks, that the consequences of the initial event be sequentially filtered through a series of either/or decisions, what Badiou calls "points."[62] Fidelity to the event is then the "organization" of such points, and the ultimate appropriateness of the binary decisions made at each one to the infinite constitution of the Truth that—if the binary decisions are made "correctly"—will thus have been brought progressively into being.[63]

This allows Badiou to give a full taxonomy of the kinds of change that are possible according to the various structures of worlds and the types of sites that are present in them. First, there are worlds in which there are no sites: in which no object or set of objects effectively indexes its own transcendental and so becomes the basis of the possibility of fundamental change. Here, in what Badiou suggests we may term "atonic" worlds, there are gradual "modifications" that simply extend the existing structural logic of the situation, but no fundamental, structural change is possible. Second, there are worlds which do indeed possess sites, but whose sites are nevertheless not characterized, according to the transcendental logic of the world, by a "very strong" or "maximal" degree of existence; Badiou calls such sites "facts." "Facts" may be capable of producing a kind of upsurge of novelty, but because the site does not possess "maximal" existence, the novelty will be re-assimilated into the (stronger) existing logic of the situation and so will vanish from the world without, in this case, producing any lasting or enduring change.[64] By contrast with these, a "singularity" is a site that indeed has a "maximal" degree of existence, and will therefore be able to "compensate" by way of its "force of existence" for its tendency to vanish from the world.[65] However, it still can occur that although a site is a singularity, and its *own* degree of existence is "maximal," its *consequences* do not have a maximal degree of existence and so, even if they are faithfully drawn out, again do not have the potential to bring about fundamental structural change. In this case the "singularity" is termed "weak," and distinguished from a "strong singularity" in which both the degree of existence of the site and of its consequences are existentially maximal. Only in this last case do we have an "event" in the full sense, and the possibility of radical, structural change of a fundamental sort.

Finally—and here, at the end of *Logics of Worlds*, Badiou recapitulates on a schematic basis a typology that is already proposed in Book I—the structural possibility of an event and the points related to it define the various possibilities for the form and structure of a "subject," which are to be understood in terms of their varying capacities for unfolding the event's fateful trace. First, as is already familiar from *Being and Event*, there is the *faithful* subject. The faithful subject, retaining fidelity to the event, draws out its consequences "point for point," inscribing them in the present by means of its creation of a "body" that acts as a kind of "active unconscious" of the event's unfolding trace.[66] However, given any event, there will also be any number of subjects that respond to it in the mode of *reaction*; although these subjects indeed claim to produce novelty in the wake of the event, the consequences actually produced by such a "reactive subject" are in fact limited to the production of a "measured" present that assimilates the event by way of limiting and appropriating it. Such a present will be "extinguished" in that, although in a certain sense it recognizes the event, it resists the potential "catastrophe" for the existing order that the event represents, and so has saved this order from its radically transformative implications.[67] By contrast with this, a third figure of the subject is the "obscure" subject that simply "abolishes" the event, consigning its "present" to the "night of non-exposition."[68] The obscure subject practices, in authoritarian fashion, an active "obscurantism" that imposes a fictional and anti-evental unifying order under the figure of a "full Tradition or Law." This always involves the invocation of a full and unified "ahistorical or anti-evental Body," for instance, "City, God," or "Race" which actively suppresses the traces of the event by forbidding the very possibility of its taking place and "reducing to silence" all that affirms it or draws out its consequences.

THE MANY WORLDS OF BADIOU

On the basis of *Logics of Worlds*' complex formal and structural analysis of the possibilities of change and transformation, we can now add one more distinction to those summarized in the table of contrasts above (p. 181). For since the theory of *Logics of Worlds* formalizes the possibilities of evental change as inherently situated and always operative within particular, *local* worlds of appearance, it maintains a fundamental commitment to the *multiplicity of worlds* and the *diversity of their structures*. This commitment is intimately connected to Badiou's *subordination* of logic to mathematics, which allows him, by means of the device of Heyting algebras, to present the specific structures of the various worlds—up to what is linguistically expressible in each—as each characterized by a specific "logic" grounded in the larger category-theoretical (i.e., mathematical) structure. Thus Badiou's theory in *Logics of Worlds* makes all the more explicit the commitment already present in *Being and Event*. This is a fundamental commitment to the *unity* of consistent mathematics and the *plurality* of worlds and logics.

By stark contrast, as we may already suspect and will have the occasion to verify in the following, *for the formal thought underlying paradoxico-criticism, whatever may be the diversity of existing languages and cultures, there is but one world and but one logic.* The "ontological" attitude of paradoxico-criticism is thus not that (as Badiou holds) "ontology is mathematics," but rather that "ontology is logic," and that mathematics is to be *reduced* to logic rather than the other way around.[69] Accordingly, the critical consequences of formalism are here to be traced in the implications of the problematic reflection of the totality of the (one) world into itself by means of the (single) structure of logic, or language as such. This is what Lacan called *lalangue*, and for paradoxico-criticism, its "virtual" or "ideal" status does not at all prevent the consequences of its existence from being structurally and indelibly inscribed in every moment of ordinary reflexive linguistic *praxis*. These consequences may indeed yield paradoxes and contradictions but they do not require or suggest, as Badiou consistently does, the fundamental formal splitting of the world of appearance and effective change into an irreducible plurality.

The irreducible multiplicity of worlds in *Logics of Worlds* again follows *directly* from Badiou's interpretation of the implications of Russell's paradox, which we have already investigated above. In Book II of *Logics of Worlds*, Badiou again considers the inconsistency of the Russell set—what he here calls the "Chimera"—to demand the non-existence of a Whole, or a set of all sets. For, he says:

> Since the Chimera can be neither reflexive nor non-reflexive, and since this partition admits of no remainder, we must conclude that the Chimera is not. But its being followed necessarily from the being that was ascribed to the Whole. Therefore, the Whole has no being.[70]

With this decision, Badiou unilaterally excludes the possibility, decisive for the paradoxico-critical orientation, that the Russell set instead is to be treated as a set that, *inconsistently* and *paradoxically*, both is and is not a member of itself, and so can serve as a model for the paradoxical being of language, which is (as, for instance, Agamben says) both included and not included in itself by means of its own problematic self-reflection. But Badiou's decision here also has, almost immediately, the consequence of introducing a formal plurality, to which the whole apparatus of *Logics of Worlds*' discussion of the multiple structures of worlds will be submitted. For:

> If there was a being of the Whole, we could undoubtedly separate out any multiple from it by taking into account the properties that singularize it. Moreover, there would be a universal place of multiple-beings, on the basis of which both the existence of what is and the relations between beings would be set out. In particular, predicative separation would uniformly determine multiplicities through their identification and differentiation within the Whole. But, as we have just seen, there is no Whole . . .
>
> From the fact [*sic*] that there is no Whole it follows that every multiple-being enters into the composition of other multiples, without this plural (the others) ever being able to fold back upon a singular (the Other). For if all multiples were elements of one Other, that would be the Whole. But since the concept of Universe inconsists, as vast as the multiple in which a singular multiple is inscribed may be, there exist others, not enveloped by the first, in which this multiple is also inscribed.
>
> In the end, there is no possible uniformity among the derivations of the thinkability of multiples, nor a place of the Other in which they could all be situated. The identifications and relations of multiples are always local.[71]

It is thus on the basis of his interpretation of Russell's paradox that Badiou affirms the irreducible and essential *localization* of all identity and relations of objects. The (stipulated) non-existence of the Whole means that it is not, contrary to first appearances, possible to determine objects wholly by means of their properties and predicates (this was, recall, the assumption of Frege's original "universal" comprehension principle) but that any such predicative determination is always inherently *relative* and hence can be considered to be possible only within the specifically determined structure of a particular world. Thus, it follows as a direct consequence that *languages are themselves plural, and claims and expressions are relative to them*: the possibility and meaning of any positive assertion whatsoever is only to be understood in terms of its value within a particular, structurally determined situation. Indeed, this relativity of linguistic predication is the very basis for Badiou's first definition of a "world" itself. According to this definition, "a multiple, related to a localization of its identity and of its relations with other multiples, is a being . . ." and "a local site of the identification of beings" is what we may term, "in what is still a rather vague sense, a world."[72] And just as every being thus has its identity, and hence its "existence," only relative to the world and its transcendental structure, there is no such thing as an *absolute* non-existent. That is, what appears "as" an empty set or void within any particular world may very well be a positive object in another. The (stipulated) non-existence of the Whole thus establishes, according to Badiou, that *within* any particular world its beings may be thought as compositions out of the element that is void *for that world*. This means that we may indeed measure their degree of complexity or "rank" by means of an identification of this (localized) void.

Badiou's interpretation of the Russell paradox and his choice to preserve consistency while sacrificing totality (or wholeness) thus underlies all of the following: the definition of a world, the relativity of languages and logics, the subordination of logic to mathematics, and (insofar as there is thus accordingly no possible way of thinking or speaking of any object as it actually *is*, outside its context in a particular world of appearance) the division between being and appearance itself. But insofar as all of this is justified by the interpretation, it follows from a demonstration that proceeds by means of the very terms ("the Russell set," "the Chimera," "the Whole") that it will itself purportedly show to be incapable of referential meaning, and thus yields an enjoinment of Being ("there is no Whole"; "the concept of Universe . . . inconsists") that undermines itself in its very statement. And all of this is, again, starkly divergent from the hypothesis of a totality of signification whose concept is not ruined by the paradoxes to which it leads, or (in Lacanian terms) of a big Other whose inconsistency is no bar to the systematic and structural efficacy of the consequences of its inscription.

8 Badiou versus Paradoxico-Criticism

As we have seen, the difference between Badiou's generic orientation and the paradoxico-critical orientation of Lacan, Wittgenstein, Agamben, Deleuze, and Derrida is a real and profound one. Though both have it in common that they traverse the radical paradoxes of self-belonging and totality that twentieth-century formal thought witnesses, they differ fundamentally in how they resolve the essential split that these paradoxes introduce within the traditional "One-All." As this split takes place formally at the very point of the reflexive moment of self-designation or auto-nomination, the moment of the positing and force of names and laws, the difference here has profound consequences as well for the ancient problem of the nomothesis, which Plato took up in the *Cratylus* (see Chapter 1). As we have seen, for Badiou in *Being and Event*, the occurrence of an event always depends on a moment of paradoxical auto-nomination, whereby the faithful subjective operators of the event themselves draw a name "from the void" in order to designate the event and *thereby* summon it into being. This picture is somewhat complicated by *Logics of Worlds'* more complex topography of "indexing," but linguistic reflexivity still plays a key role. The nomothesis, or the self-positing of rules and names, is thus invested, in Badiou's generic orientation, with the profound power of novelty, the very possibility of the creation or summoning of the new.

For Wittgenstein, by contrast:

> Naming is not yet a move in a language-game—any more than putting a piece in its place on the board is a move in chess. One may say: with the mere naming of a thing, *nothing* has yet been done. Nor has it a name except in a game. This was what Frege meant too when he said that a word has a meaning only in the context of a sentence.[1]

In thus referring to Frege's famous invocation of the problematic value of context as the horizon for the meaningfulness and effectiveness of all names and nomination, Wittgenstein is *not* denying that the institution of standards poses the deepest conceptual problems for a philosophical reflection that aims to clarify the ground of this force in its determination of the occasions of a life.[2] He is, rather, gesturing to the paradoxical way in which the institution of a standard determines the closure of a linguistic *praxis*, henceforth consigned to the iterability of the sign and the force of laws. For the paradoxico-critic, as we have seen, it is not the institution of the new standard or the positing of a new existent that provides hope—the only hope that there is—for escape from the "entanglement in our rules" that we experience at each moment of the determination of life by its regular forms. It is, rather, the clarificatory and critical *diagnosis* of this entanglement that provides the key to the possibility of a knowledge and praxis *diagonal* to this determination, a radically immanent life subtracted from rules and their force.

It is to the further analysis of this difference, on specific points, that we now turn.[3]

BADIOU *CONTRA* DELEUZE

As we saw above, Deleuze's entire understanding of the nature of being and becoming is conditioned by his analysis of sense. To summarize, on Deleuze's analysis, if sense exists, as an aspect of phenomena that preconditions their linguistic expression as well as their being and becoming, it will be *auto-legislating*, in that it will both provide and be bound by the laws of inference; it will be *auto-nominating*, in that it will block the regress of names by paradoxically naming itself; it will be *sterile*, in that it will be the real precondition of language and meaning but without effects on bodies or objects; and it will be figured by the "paradoxical element" that, presenting its *own* sense, will simultaneously be *nonsense*. To this set of paradoxical traits corresponds a series of undecidabilities in the status of sense or of the "paradoxical element." Between signifiers and signifieds, sense is neither word nor object, neither individual nor universal. As we have seen, the underlying reason for this series of undecidabilities is that the logical structure of sense is identical to that of the Russell set, the set that includes itself in what it excludes and excludes itself from its own self-inclusion.

It is, moreover, this constitutive paradoxicality and undecidability that qualifies sense, for Deleuze, to serve as the basis for an entire reconception of what is involved in change and becoming, all the way up to his conception of what is for Deleuze the most central and defining category of becoming, the paradoxical "sense-event." As this conception is both formally determined by the paradoxes of language and situated at a central point of Deleuze's thought, it bears instructive comparison to the alternative conception of aleatory and radical change that is formulated on quite different grounds by Badiou in his own conception of the "event."

As we saw above, sense, for Deleuze, is produced by the action of structure, and is indeed a purely "surface effect" produced by a system of relations but nevertheless operating, and even opening, the frontier between words and things. This structure is shown by the kind of "incorporeal" causality characteristic of the paradoxical element that interrupts and circulates within the structure of language:

> We have tried to ground this second causality in a way which would conform to the incorporeal character of the surface and the event. It seemed to us that the event, that is, sense, referred *to a paradoxical element, intervening as nonsense or as an aleatory point, and operating as a quasi-cause assuring the full autonomy of the effect*.[4]

As distinct from the corporeal causality of bodies and objects, this second kind of causality is "ideational" and accounts both for the productivity of sense and the role of structure in producing it. As such, it involves a kind of doubled or contradictory relationship internal to its structure whereby cause is also, inseparably, effect and vice versa.[5] Through this doubled causality, a causality not of objects or bodies but of the opening of paths and differences, sense is donated to language, and objects as well as ordinary propositional meaning are constituted.

However, at the same time as sense-events in this way underlie and condition the structure of "meaningful" language, they also precede and even *undermine* the *regularity* that defines discernible linguistic structures and structure as such. This regularity—whereby a structure can be understood as composed of elements that are capable of being repeated or iterated, without any essential displacement or alteration, according to specific and defined rules—is itself, according to Deleuze, the outcome of the operation of ordering and selecting that is performed by good sense and common sense. Original, paradoxical sense, on the other hand, is prior to this operation and reveals a level of action and becoming that cannot simply be submitted to it. By contrast with the "ordinary games" which, employing a set of determinate rules that preexist the playing, "apportion chance" in the sense that they determine what happens given certain, well-defined events or outcomes, Deleuze, again drawing on Carroll, points to certain "ideal games" (such as the Queen's croquet game in which mallets and even loops displace themselves endlessly into different positions and varying forms) in which move and rule are one and the same and chance is not apportioned but rather affirmed at each instant.[6]

It is through these "ideal games" that we can again perceive the character of originary, paradoxical sense in its definitive link to the singularity of the event. For here the particular and discrete "events" or throws that are only subsequently articulated by the assumption of a regular regime of "good sense" are more originally based on the unity and uniqueness of a single or "unique" cast responsible for all distributions of singularities, including but not by any means limited to the ordered regularities of the ordinary games. It is in this way that the "unique cast," which has the structure of the sense-event as such, involves a complete affirmation of chance, unlimited by any external assumption of regularity or order.

In 1997, Badiou published a short book on Deleuze that develops from a long series of mostly oblique exchanges between the two philosophers, culminating in a halting and hesitating correspondence between the two which began in 1991 and ended with Deleuze's death in 1995.[7] The text of *Deleuze: The Clamor of Being* is critical in many ways of the philosopher whose project Badiou sees as most directly opposed to his own on the decisive question of the nature of multiplicity, and yet bears witness as well to Badiou's great respect for Deleuze, toward whom he says his own project from *Being and Event* on is most directly "positioned."[8] Without a doubt, the most suggestive and provocative claim of the analysis is that, quite contrary to the received image of him, Deleuze should not in any way be read as a philosopher of the Many. For, according to Badiou, Deleuze's work in fact uniformly witnesses, and even in a radically renewed way, the metaphysical privilege of the One:

> Deleuze's fundamental problem is most certainly not to liberate the multiple but to submit thinking to a renewed concept of the One. What must the One be, for the multiple to be integrally conceivable therein as the production of simulacra? Or, yet again: in what way should the All be determined, in order that the existence of each portion of this All—far from being positioned as independent or as surging forth unpredictably—be nothing other than an expressive profile of 'the powerful, nonorganic Life that embraces the world?' . . .
>
> We can therefore first state that one must carefully identify a metaphysics of the One in the work of Deleuze. He himself indicates what its requirements are: 'one single event for all events; a single and same *aliquid* for that which happens and that which is said; and a single and same being for the impossible, the possible and the real' . . .[9]

The claim is, as Badiou notes, almost *directly* opposite to the received image of Deleuze as the radical prophet of difference and plurality, the great advocate of unpredictable becomings and nomadic wanderings, the presumptively subversive affirmation of the "heterogeneous multiplicity of desires" and their "unrestrained realization."[10] For this reason and others, Badiou's interpretation will be (and has been) vehemently opposed by those who see in Deleuze simply an ally of the "postmodern" project of what is supposed to be an unceasing restoration of the democratic rights of the body, the plurality of communities, and the "postmetaphysical" celebration of disorder and chaos against the "terrorizing" claim of any organizing or sovereign principle. Nevertheless the accuracy of Badiou's interpretation of Deleuze is amply witnessed in the latter's affirmation, throughout his career, of a "single and same voice for the whole thousand-voiced multiple, a single and same Ocean for all the drops, a single clamour of Being for all beings,"[11] of a "unique event" which is the basis of all community and communication, and of a fundamental *univocity* of Sense that is correlative to the unitary position of the void that is also the origin of all nonsense. The ultimate principle of this univocity, Badiou suggests, is nothing other than the unitary nature of a "nonorganic Life" that underlies the possible as well as the actual, the imaginary as well as the real. And as we have indeed seen, above, the plurality of events, singularities, and becomings for Deleuze is indeed strictly correlative, in each case, to the unity of the single, paradoxical stratum of the virtual, the "plane of immanence" or "impersonal transcendental field" on which all singularities and changes and their communication are but the resonance of a single, aleatory "throw of the dice."

All of these characteristic features of Deleuze's thought result from his inquiry into the unitary possibility of (what he terms) sense, from which all becoming, change, and inflection begins. In that this is an inquiry into the unitary basis of all signification and meaning (as well as into its distinction from nonsense), it takes place only on the condition of a relentless and unending affirmation of the One of sense, along with all the paradoxical consequences of the immanent reflection of this One into itself. In this respect, Deleuze's position is a deeply illustrative representative of what I have called the paradoxico-critical orientation of thought, which subsumes, as we have seen, some of the most significant and still relevant positions of critical thought in our time. These positions, although they are indeed fundamentally different from Badiou's, are not clearly refuted or ruled out by anything Badiou himself says. But as we have also seen, the decision between the paradoxico-critical and Badiou's own generic orientations may well represent one of the most fundamental junctures with which philosophical and political thought is faced today.

Accordingly, on behalf of the paradoxico-critical orientation as well as of Deleuze himself, *we should not oppose Badiou's interpretation of Deleuze, but rather affirm it as displaying a coherent, rigorous, and exemplary fundamental orientation of thought which is nevertheless fundamentally different from Badiou's own.* To do so is to join Badiou in sharply distinguishing Deleuze from the bland "postmodern" celebration of historical and cultural difference and material heterogeneity often attributed to him (most of which can indeed be subsumed to the pre-Cantorian "criteriological" orientation rather than paradoxico-criticism); we can thereby enlist his project (but as we have seen, it is indeed already there enlisted, by virtue of Deleuze's own declarations, ambitions, and methods) in the very different and much more profound project of critical reflection on the consequences of form.

On Badiou's own telling, the most fundamental divergence between himself and Deleuze occurs at *exactly* the point of Deleuze's own decision for the totality of the One or All:

Moreover, the notion of 'multiplicity' was to be at the center of our epistolary controversy of 1992–94, with him maintaining that I confuse 'multiple' and 'number,' whereas I maintained that it is inconsistent to uphold, in the manner of the Stoics, the virtual Totality or what Deleuze named 'chaosmos,' because, with regard to sets, there can be neither a universal set, nor All, nor One.[12]

Badiou's *fundamental* criticism of Deleuze (and, as we shall see, essentially his only one) is, then, that the latter upholds the (inconsistent) All, whereas according to Badiou this is, given set theory and its implications, untenable. But as we have seen, Badiou's denial of the very possibility of affirming the All is *by no means* demanded by set theory itself, and it is indeed from the possibility of this affirmation that paradoxico-criticism wholly results. It is thus that the most fundamental axiomatic decision of Badiou's system—his decision for the conjunction of consistency and the non-being of the All rather than the alternative decision, for the paradoxical totality—separates him decisively and formally from the entire project of Deleuze.

This is not to say that Badiou's understanding of paradoxico-criticism—though he does not, of course, employ the term—is not sophisticated, insightful, and detailed. The depth and acuity of his understanding of it is shown, for instance, in the acute and not unsympathetic analysis he gives in the *Deleuze* book to what he there calls "structuralism." On this analysis, the "structuralism of the sixties" will have consisted in rigorously and formally drawing out the consequences of univocity of being, given its plural and equivocal expression in the multiplicity of names and signs.[13] Given this imperative—which is equivalent to posing the question of the *production* of sense—the structuralist operation then consists, according to Badiou, in three sequential and interlinked moves. First, there is the identification in beings and phenomena of the *elements* which are understood as rigorously subject to the initially "opaque" rules of structure, the overarching system in which all elements and all possibilities of combination have their place. Second, there is the identification within the total structure of a "singular entity" which both "renders [structure] incomplete and sets it in motion." This is, of course, the "empty square" of Deleuze, the "floating signifier" of Lévi-Strauss, the "element degree zero," "dummy element," or "blind spot." By means of the gap or lack it introduces, this element also introduces the dynamism of "supplement or paradox" which, according to Badiou, recurrently fascinates structuralism as such:

> The paradoxical entity shines with a singular brilliance. It is what is fascinating in structuralist theory because it is like a line of flight, an evasion, or an errant liberty, by which one escapes the positivism of legalized beings. . . . Basically, the empty square shows that structure is only a simulacrum and that, while it fabricates sense, the being that is proper to it—namely the life that sustains the effect of sense—does

not, in any way, enter into the sense so fabricated. For life (the One), be-ing univocal, holds the equivocity of produced sense for a nonsense.[14]

Finally, given this paradoxical introduction of the effective and organiz-ing "signifier that does not signify," a third move is possible. This is the movement of a "reascent" that would consist "in thinking how it comes about that nonsense is required to produce sense."[15] This final movement cannot result, Badiou says, from the operation of a particular "structural machine," since it depends on the univocity of Being itself, its capability of being "said in a single sense of all of which it is said." And neither will it produce, after all, the (unique) sense of Being. It will consist, Badiou sug-gests, rather in the demonstration that "there is no sense of sense" and hence yield the claim that sense itself is produced out of nonsense, for instance, as Deleuze suggests, by means of the "displacement" and "position" of "ele-ments which are not by themselves 'signifying.' " The yield of the whole movement, from structure to its paradoxical disruption ("descending") back up to the constitution of the virtual layer of in-consistent sense on its basis, will be, according to Badiou, a sublime *jouissance* that witnesses the self-enclosed, circular destiny of the One:

> When thought succeeds in constructing, without categories, the looped path that leads, on the surface of what is, from a case to the One, then from the One to the case, it intuits the movement of the One itself. And because the One is its own movement (because it is life, or infinite virtuality), thought intuits the One. It thereby, as Spinoza so magnifi-cently expressed it, attains intellectual beatitude, which is the enjoy-ment of the Impersonal.[16]

In this passage itself, Badiou is not explicitly critical of Deleuze's assigna-tion of the task of philosophy to the chronicle of this exemplary movement of the One. Elsewhere in the book, however, he contrasts its consequences, practically term by term, to those of his own set-theoretical thinking of being and the event. What Badiou sees as a profound divergence—perhaps *the* most profound divergence within philosophy today—nevertheless does not exclude points of what may at first seem surprising convergence, or even identity. The most important of these, as we have already seen, is Deleuze's identification of the aleatory, singular, and discontinuous *event*, which he, like Badiou, places at the very center of his picture of change and becoming. In fact, Deleuze does not stop short of appealing to the same poetic figure that Badiou makes use of, much later, in *Being and Event*, Mallarmé's "true throw of the dice."

As we saw above, this "cast of the dice" captures, for Deleuze, the struc-ture of the "sense-event," which is for Deleuze, as Badiou emphasizes, *ontologically* one. That is, as Deleuze says, though the multiple singulari-ties and events are indeed numerically distinct, they resonate and take place within the unitary medium of the unique event, which amounts to an affirmation of chance *in its totality*. This is the basis for Deleuze's affirmation of "minor games" and the ubiquity of chance without distribution, as well as for his thinking of the Nietzschean eternal return as the repetitive return of this singular affirmation. In his discussion of Deleuze's conception of the event, Badiou faithfully notes these features of Deleuze's conception of the event and the chance it affirms, and suggests that they indeed represent the point of greatest divergence from Badiou's own conception:

> In a letter written at the very end of 1993, touching on the concept of the undecidable that both of us use, although in very different ways, Deleuze took up the question of the dice throw in its direct connection with the virtual. He stated that the undecidable concerns the emissions of virtuals as pure events, as exemplified by the throw of the dice. And he declared once again, extremely clearly, that the different casts of virtuals can be formally distinct, even while they remain the forms of a single and same cast. The result is that the different casts are undecidable and that no decision is the final one—for all decisions communicate and are mutually compounded.
>
> In reflecting on Deleuze's persistent use, since the end of the sixties, of such quasi-identical formulations, I said to myself that the indiscernibility of casts (of events, of emissions of the virtual) was, for him, the most important of the points of passage of the One. For me, on the other hand, the absolute ontological separation of the event, the fact that it occurs in the situation without being in any way virtualizable, is the basis of the character of truths as irreducibly original, created, and fortuitous . . .
>
> For Deleuze, chance is the play of the All, always replayed as such; whereas I believe that there is a multiplicity (and rarity) of chances, such that the chance of an event happens to us already by chance, and not by the expressive univocity of the One.[17]

This disagreement over the status of chance, which is intimately connected to the fundamental difference between the generic and the paradoxico-critical orientations, is the ultimate root of the divergence which allows Badiou to reject in its totality Deleuze's category of the "virtual" and to seek a formalism of the event that is (officially) conditioned *in no way* by sense or the paradoxes of signification, but is conditioned instead solely by the actuality and transit of what Badiou calls a Truth.[18] The divergence extends, as well, to the very status of the Ideal and to the question of the formal itself, and hence to the legacy of Plato for contemporary thought. As Badiou notes and we have seen in Chapter 5, Deleuze's slogan of the "overturning" of Platonism is to a large extent misleading, at least if we take it out of the context of the vast and profound resources Deleuze in fact finds within the Platonic text for carrying out the project of "mak[ing] the simulacra rise and affirm[ing] their rights. . . ." On the basis of these resources and the implication that he himself avowedly finds in Plato's text of a view of beings that aims to "do . . . justice to the real One" by "thinking the egalitarian coexistence of simulacra in a positive way," Badiou thus declares (and with this we can certainly agree) that "Deleuzianism is fundamentally a Platonism with a different accentuation."[19] Yet this does not preclude, once again, what is almost a direct opposition between Badiou and Deleuze on the fundamental status of the Idea:

> Deleuze retains from Plato the univocal sovereignty of the One, but sacrifices the determination of the Idea as always actual. For him, the Idea is the virtual totality, the One is the infinite reservoir of dissimilar productions. *A contrario*, I uphold that the forms of the multiple are, just like the Ideas, always actual and that the virtual does not exist; I sacrifice, however, the One. The result is that Deleuze's virtual ground remains for me a transcendence, whereas for Deleuze, it is my logic of the multiple that, in not being originally referred to the act of the One, fails to hold thought firmly within immanence. [20]

According to Badiou, then, the issue between him and Deleuze is not that of "Platonism versus its reversal or 'overturning' " but rather two very different Platonisms, two divergent and yet *equally faithful* developments of the resource of what Plato thought as the Idea. On the one hand (Deleuze) we have the unifying totality of the Idea's One, what must accordingly be thought, in its infinite power of the unification of appearances, as the stratum of a virtuality that is avowedly real without any possibility of its reduction to the actual. On the other (Badiou) we have a "sacrifice" of the idea's univocity in favor of the mathematically thinkable actuality of its phenomena, thought on the basis of the theory of sets or multiples, what Badiou in fact calls, in *Manifesto for Philosophy*, a "Platonism of the multiple."[21] The disagreement over fundamental grounds—Deleuze's virtual plane of immanence vs. Badiou's set theory—which led, on Badiou's testimony, each philosopher to suspect the other of an untenable "transcendence"—is not easy to resolve on the basis of Plato's text alone. Instead, as we are now in a position to see, it witnesses the very formal dichotomy to which critical thought is subject, as soon as it can no longer preserve in a single figure, as Plato still hoped to do, the One of consistency and the All of completeness, and must reckon under the heading of any theory of Ideas or the Ideal with the fundamental divergence of the two.

If we, then, indeed take Deleuze's position (as portrayed by Badiou) to be an exemplary expression of the paradoxico-critical orientation, from its affirmation of the inherent paradoxes of the One up to its identification, on their basis, of the purely virtual plane of immanence on which sense and all becoming are alike constituted, we may thus add to the table of divergences between the generic and the paradoxico-critical orientations (last chapter) a few more, concerning the very status of the discontinuous event and the being of the Idea itself. Whereas, for Badiou, events are ontologically plural and devoid of sense, constituted only on the basis of the transit of a truth in its production of a generic set, for Deleuze and the paradoxico-critical orientation the event is always the ontologically *singular* outcome of sense, thought as a totality, in its own immanent structural paradoxes. And whereas we accordingly have, on the one hand, an inherently and radically multiple being of the Ideal, actual in the real occurrence and transit of the event, we have, on the other, an affirmation of the unitary Idea capable of effectively organizing (whether as simulacra or as copies, "good" or "bad" duplicates) the many of its instances into a virtual and immanent One, which is, however, never to be thought as actual. The divergences between these two structures will also yield, as Badiou indeed does not hesitate to point out, profound differences on the level of the implications of the form and the outcomes of its thought.

In a short chapter of *Logics of Worlds* devoted to Deleuze, Badiou repeats in a more forceful and compressed form the statement of these fundamental oppositions between his own and Deleuze's position on the nature of the event. Whereas, again, the event is for Deleuze the immanent exposure of the One of all becoming, the "eternal identity of the future as a dimension of the past," the virtual "intensification" of the actions of bodies, and the unitary composition of a Life, Badiou reverses each of these "Deleuzian axioms" explicitly: for Badiou, by contrast, the event is a "pure cut in becoming," a "separating evanescence" that cannot be thought in terms of past or future but only as the presentation of the present itself, the origin of bodies rather than the intensification of their action, and most of all the "utterly unresonant" dissemination of a Truth that, in order to be effective in it, dictates the event's fundamental contingency and its being "without One."

The ultimate reason for all of these divergences is again a fundamental disagreement about the implication of the term "event" between the significance of "sense" (Deleuze) and that of "truth" (Badiou). This difference is again directly connected to the question of the One itself. The connection is clear in Badiou's statement in "The Event as Trans-Being" of the difference between his conception of the event and those of several philosophers, including Deleuze and Wittgenstein:

> What happens—and, inasmuch as it happens, goes beyond its multiple-being—is precisely this: a fragment of multiplicity wrested from all inclusion . . . Consequently, it cannot be said that the event is One. Like everything that is, the event is a multiplicity (its elements are those of the site, plus itself . . .). We are faced here with an extreme tension, balanced precariously between the multiple on the one hand, and the metaphysical power of the One on the other. It should be clear why the general question that is the object of my dispute with Deleuze, which

concerns the status of the event vis-à-vis an ontology of the multiple, and how to avoid reintroducing the power of the One at that point wherein the law of the multiple begins to falter, is the guiding question of all contemporary philosophy. This question is anticipated in Heidegger's shift from *Sein* to *Ereignis*, or—switching registers—in Lacan, where it is entirely invested in the thinking of the analytical act as the eclipse of truth between a supposed and transmissible knowledge, between interpretation and the matheme. Lacan will find himself obliged to say that though the One is not, the act nevertheless installs the One. But it is also a decisive problem for Nietzsche: if it is a question of breaking the history of the world in two, what, in the affirmative absolute of life, is the thinkable principle that would command such a break? And it's also the central problem for Wittgenstein: how does the act open up our access to the 'mystical element'—i.e., to the ethical and the aesthetic—if meaning is always captive to a proposition, or always the prisoner of grammar?[22]

Again, the divergence that Badiou here marks as articulating the "guiding question of all contemporary philosophy" is connected fundamentally to the role and status of language. Thus, Deleuze "fashions what is to my [i.e., Badiou's] mind a chimerical entity, an inconsistent [note the term of criticism!] portmanteau word: the 'sense-event.' " This coinage, Badiou says, brings Deleuze "far closer than he would have wished to the linguistic turn and the great lineage of modern sophistry"; for it "tips [the event] over entirely onto the side of language" and *thus* "contains in germ the aestheticization of all things, and the expressive politics of so-called 'multitudes', in which the Master's compact thought is today dispersed."[23] For Badiou, on the other hand, the event "does not possess the least sense, nor is it sense." It emerges, rather, from a real point that is "strictly speaking senseless" and only relates to language in that it "makes a hole in it."

Here, then, Badiou's criticism of Deleuze's conception of the event and its virtuality depends entirely on the former's rejection of the criticism, or the dialectic, of sense and language, which rejection is, as we have seen elsewhere, a *fundamental* methodological axiom of Badiou's thought. This rejection is, as we have also seen, here and elsewhere determined (or overdetermined?) by Badiou's vehement opposition to what he sees as the regime of contemporary "sophistry" and the prevailing axiomatics of multiplicity and heterogeneous language-games, which determines the contemporary liberal politics of culturalist difference and its "multitudes." This is, to a large extent, the politics of those who have taken up Deleuze's thought; it is the politics of the "received image" of Deleuze as the great avatar of heterogeneity and difference, which Badiou vehemently—*and admirably, on the current reading*—aims to refute in the 1997 book.[24]

In *Logics of Worlds*, Badiou again in fact recognizes the great distance between Deleuze himself and the "latent religiosity" of those of his

disciples who "are busy blessing, in unbridled Capital, its supposed constitutive reverse, the 'creativity' of the multitudes," and who would produce
on the basis of this reverse a kind of "planetary Parousia of a communism
of 'forms of Life.' " Deleuze, Badiou rightly says, "would have laughed up
his sleeve about all this pathos."[25] *On the other hand*, though—and here
is the point at which we may recognize the great weakness of Badiou's
reading of Deleuze, so strong and revealing in other ways—there remains
in Deleuze, according to Badiou, a threefold determination of the event
that, affirming a fundamental "empiricism" and even, Badiou somewhat
cautiously suggests, a tendency to "dogmatism," again directly opposes his
own conviction:

> It remains that, having conceptualized before everyone else the place of
> the event in the multiform procedures of thought, Deleuze was forced
> to reduce this place to that of what he called 'the ideal singularities that
> communicate in one and the same event'. If 'singularity' is inevitable,
> the other words are all dubious. 'Ideal' could stand for 'eternal' if it did
> not excessively cloud over the real of the event. 'Communicate' could
> stand for 'universal', if it did not pass over the interruption of every
> communication which is immediately entailed by the rupture of tran-
> scendental continuity. We have already said why 'one and the same' is
> misleading: it turns the One-effect on bodies of the event's impact into
> the absorption of the event by the One of life.[26]

Once again, we have in this passage an exemplary comparison of Badiou's
generic orientation with the position of paradoxico-criticism, which nevertheless does not and *cannot* appear as such here, since Badiou *never* recognizes the paradoxico-critical orientation itself as distinct from the linguistic
constructivism to which he constantly assimilates it. It is for this reason
that Badiou here again identifies an exemplary instance of the paradoxico-
critical orientation (which is in fact grounded, as Badiou has argued in
detail, in the overarching affirmation of the One of language and sense
against all its fractured and multiple instances) with the "sophistry" of
contemporary conviction and the politics of superficial difference, *while
at the same time and almost in the same gesture* providing the theoretical
elements needed for a rigorous distinction of the two.

BADIOU *CONTRA* DERRIDA

If many of the most productive methods of twentieth-century philosophical inquiry amount to the practice of essentially reflective forms of critique,
it is clearly an essential precondition of their contemporary continuance
and inheritance that the formal underpinnings of this practice be clearly
understood. In fact, as I have suggested, many, if not most, of the still

open projects of twentieth-century philosophy that we might usefully draw from both the analytic and the continental sides are well characterized as *non-limitative* (and hence non-*criteriological*) varieties of critical thought. These projects are inheritors of Kant's project in seeking something like an ongoing reflective consideration of reason (or language) and its limits, but do not depend exclusively or even very much on the kind of restrictive, limiting gesture that Badiou rejects under the heading of constructivism. With this in mind, we may now revisit Derrida's method or methods of deconstruction, which, I would suggest, is very much an example of such a critical project.

Deconstruction, as we saw above, is a set of operations *at* the limits and *on* the limits. Among its aims in various modalities, as is well known, is the aim of destabilizing particular systematic *attempts* to define and delimit the language of philosophy, such as attempts to distinguish it on principled grounds from literature or from ordinary language. Here, though, the relevance of language to philosophy is not only its yield in "destabilizing" limits or overturning "binaries," but much more that philosophy can be a form of critical linguistic self-reflection in which thought calls before itself the criteria of its own linguistic usage to reflect on the possibilities of its own expression. Thus, as we saw in Chapter 4, deconstruction traces the indiscernible not in order simply to dismiss it as the nonexistent but precisely in order to trace its paradoxical appearance at the limit of the system that it makes possible by disappearing *within* it. And it introduces what Derrida has called the undecidable, not at all in order to reduce it to the contingent limits of a specific language or practice, but rather to show the *necessity*, for *any* given system, of what cannot be decided one way or the other strictly in its terms.

With respect to Derrida himself, Badiou maintained, through the 1990s and into the last decade, a relative silence.[27] Although Deleuze and Lacan figure as essential conversants for Badiou during this time, Derrida makes hardly an appearance, and there is no mention of Derrida in the main text of *Being and Event* itself. More recently, however, in *Logics of Worlds* and in a eulogy written in the months after Derrida's death in 2004, Badiou has ventured to clarify the relation of his own project to Derrida's.[28] In *Logics of Worlds*, as we have seen, Badiou supplements the univocal set theory of *Being and Event* with a more pluralistic structure, drawn from category theory, in terms of which individual worlds are structured according to various individual "logics," each of which determines the degrees of manifestation, appearance, or existence for the entities within the world in question. It is a consequence of this logical-mathematical structure that, in any particular world, there will always be some particular element whose "degree of existence" is zero: that is, each structured world has what Badiou calls a "proper inexistent." The proper inexistent appears within the particular world as that which does not exist, and can be symbolized with the symbol for the empty set ('∅').

In the note on his introduction of the "inexistent" in *Logics of Worlds*, and again in his eulogy for Derrida, Badiou suggests that we can understand the whole task of deconstruction as consisting in the demonstration and eliciting of the particular inexistent for various worlds:

> The thinking of the inexistent formalizes what I believe to be at stake in Jacques Derrida's sinuous approach. Ever since his first texts, and under the progressively academicized (though not by him) name of 'deconstruction', his speculative desire was to show that, whatever form of discursive imposition one may be faced with, there exists a point that escapes the rules of this imposition, a *point of flight*. The whole interminable work consists in localizing it, which is also impossible, since it is characterized by being out-of-place-in-the-place.[29]

Later on in this note, Badiou suggests that his own symbol for the inexistent, '$\varnothing_a$', might be written, also as an "homage" to Derrida, as "différance"; and in the very next note, written this time after Derrida's death, he summarizes this homage as a reading of deconstruction "under [the] emblem: the passion of Inexistence."[30]

The project Badiou attributes to Derrida—that of tracing or localizing the specific inexistent of any given situation—is one that officially occupies only a relatively *local* place within Badiou's much larger programmatic ambition to formalize the very relationship between being and appearance itself. We may, of course, suspect an element of the anxiety of influence here. But it may be more important to ask whether Derrida's limitless procedure of tracing the indiscernible can really be understood in this way. Again, we might wonder whether the closest specific analogue to Derrida's project within Badiou's system is perhaps not this local work, but rather, especially in view of Derrida's own long-standing, deep, and central consideration of the possibility of the "event," Badiou's own most important formal result: the demonstration in a rigorously formal way of what necessarily escapes the possibility of signification in *any* system whatsoever. This is what Derrida indeed calls the "trace"; something very much like it figures in Badiou's project, as well, under the different name of the indiscernible. (However, what Badiou calls "trace" in *Logics of Worlds*—according to the glossary at the end of the text, the "prior inexistent which, under the effect of the site, has taken the maximal value" (p. 596)—is *not* the same as the "trace" in Derrida's sense, which presumably *never* takes on a "maximal" or even a non-zero "degree of existence," at least not as long as we remain within the closure of metaphysics itself.)

As the early Derrida showed very clearly (for instance, in *Speech and Phenomena* and *Of Grammatology*), this deconstructive work is itself possible, and necessary, as soon as there is a difference between speech and writing at all. Thus, it is *not* the local work of finding the specific inexistent, but the much more global task of reading the unreadable in the metaphysical oppositions (for instance, between sound and meaning, the sensible and the intelligible, or body and soul) that organize and structure *anything* like language itself. Of course the work of reading is located, in each case, at a particular textual site, but this does not preclude deconstruction from also operating, simultaneously, as this exceedingly *general* reflection on the organizing oppositions that have structured language and thinking in Western philosophy, with a view to tracing the "closure" of what Derrida does not hesitate to call the epoch of the "metaphysics of presence." Since Badiou refuses to see questions of language and signification as having any specific relevance to his project, it seems he must miss this more general level of the deconstructive problematic. And this may explain why he says nothing about the ways in which his own work of eliciting the event indeed closely resembles a deconstructive reading of the history and closure of metaphysics.

From an early stage in Derrida's presentation of it, deconstruction involves as well, at a basic level, a consideration of the discontinuous "event" which disrupts structures and reorganizes their principles. As early as 1966, in "Structure, Sign, and Play in the Discourse of the Human Sciences," Derrida invoked (though cautiously, and in scare quotes) the problematic possibility of an evental "rupture" and "redoubling" that is precisely an "event" (or perhaps *the* event) of the concept of "structure" itself:

> Perhaps something has occurred in the history of the concept of structure that could be called an "event," if this loaded word did not entail a meaning which it is precisely the function of structural—or structuralist—thought to reduce or to suspect. But let me use the term "event" anyway, employing it with caution and as if in quotation marks. In this sense, this event will have the exterior form of a *rupture* and a *redoubling*.[31]

This problematic "event," as we saw above in Chapter 4, has the form of a "rupture" in that it inscribes into structured language as such the permanent possibility of breaking with any determined context whatsoever—the "force of rupture" that Derrida considers as structurally necessary to language as such, and shown in the problematic devices of quotation and citation. And as he goes on to explain, it is also a "redoubling" because:

> The event I called a rupture, the disruption I alluded to . . . presumably would have come about when the structurality of structure had to begin to be thought, that is to say, repeated, and this is why I said that this disruption was repetition in every sense of the word.[32]

This is nothing other than the moment of the awareness of a radical *reflexivity*, inscribed in language itself, by means of which the "structurality of structure" or the very structure of language is thought and theorized.

This is the moment—"historical" and indeed part of "the totality" of our own "era" even if not linked exclusively to any single figure, or thinker, of it—at which "language invaded the universal problematic" and "everything became . . . a system . . . in which the central signified, the original or transcendental signified, is never absolutely present outside a system of differences."[33] In other words, it is the moment at which the system of language is thought *as a totality* for which there is no outside and in which the thought that would delimit its boundaries is necessarily caught. At this moment, there is no longer a silent "center" of language that can, governing everything else, be thought of as "escaping structurality"; no longer is it possible to define a privileged interior point at which "the permutation or the transformation of elements . . . is forbidden" or "interdicted." At this point of the transformative reflection of language into itself, it will no longer be possible to seek such a center, which would be, according to "classical thought" both "paradoxically, *within* the structure and *outside* it."[34] As we have seen in the analyses above, this is the moment that Derrida, Deleuze, and Wittgenstein (in his own, rather different fashion) understand as the root of the structural paradoxes of sense, grounded in the problematic reflection of the total structure of language into itself.

In "Signature, Event, Context," discussing Austin's theory of performative speech acts, Derrida considers the relationship of the paradoxical pseudo-concept *différance* to the kind of uniquely linguistic "event" that a performative embodies:

> *Différance*, the irreducible absence of intention or assistance from the performative statement, from the most 'event-like' statement possible, is what authorizes me, taking into account the predicates mentioned just now, to posit the general graphematic structure of every "communication." Above all, I will not conclude from this that there is no relative specificity of the effects of consciousness, of the effects of speech (in opposition to writing in the traditional sense), that there is no effect of the performative, no effect of ordinary language, no effect of presence and of speech acts. It is simply that these effects do not exclude what is generally opposed to them term by term, but on the contrary presuppose it in dissymmetrical fashion, as the general space of their possibility . . .
> This general space is first of all spacing as the disruption of presence in the mark, what here I am calling writing.[35]

In other words, the event of the performative utterance, like all of language's "events" and its whole "evental" definition—the very possibility of something happening *through* language or *in* language—is conditioned by the structural spacing that structures it as a "system of differences." What is then essential to thinking the possibility of this kind of event—which Derrida would not cease to consider, up to his very last texts, and which includes every instance of baptism, nomination, or institution (as Derrida says, the very element of "conventionality" that Austin recognizes as an essential constituent of the performative)—is the totality of this structure of language as such (both speech and writing, and the spacing of their difference as well) in its capacity to be reflected problematically into itself. This is the essential structural gesture, as we have seen, of paradoxico-criticism in all of its forms, and it defines a rigorous conception of the "event" which is, from this perspective, at the basis of all discontinuous change and historical origin. If it is also, and essentially, linked, for the paradoxico-critic, to the value and phenomenon of "repetition" which defines all language as such, this does not diminish its originality, or its capacity to trace the paradoxical boundaries of the infinite text of a metaphysics that is without an outside, to invoke the radically new.

BADIOU *CONTRA* WITTGENSTEIN

As we have seen in connection with both Derrida and Deleuze, then, the paradoxico-critical orientation includes formally grounded conceptions of history, meaning, the critical project, and even the event that are quite different from Badiou's and that, although they are generally missed by Badiou himself, emerge clearly if we juxtapose the main methodological contours of the projects of these philosophers to his. The debate that is probably most revealing and decisive here, however, is not Badiou's confrontation with either of these "continental" philosophers (with whom Badiou, whatever his doctrinal divergences, shares a history, a language, and the inheritance of a recognizably common methodological tradition) but rather the juxtaposition with Wittgenstein (with whom he certainly does not). This is so for at least two reasons. First, because Wittgenstein is, without a doubt, the twentieth-century philosopher who has most penetratingly and relentlessly pursued the twofold inquiry into the nature of language and mathematics, and the relationship between the two; and second because he does so from the perspective of a philosophical sensibility which is so clearly and deeply opposite to Badiou's.[36] Indeed, it can seem that the two philosophers are so completely at odds that in many respects they practically mirror one another from opposite directions. Wittgenstein, the great chronicler of the depths of the "seas of language" as they draw human life into their ever-twisting currents, understands the drive to philosophy as a constant drive to run up against the limits of language, a desire to whose frustrations only a critical modality of reflection on grammar can hope to respond. As we have seen, Badiou, by contrast, rejects the linguistic turn in all of its forms, upholding, instead, an explicitly anti- or post-critical philosophy whose sole function is to bear witness to the infinite proceedings of truth. With respect to mathematics, the positions are different but again opposites of each other:

for Wittgenstein, as we saw in Chapter 6, mathematics is a technique or a practice, something whose unique status and capabilities within a human life are never to be minimized, but whose *fundamental* hetero- geneity is misconceived by any description that looks to it to describe, in a privileged way, the metaphysical structures of possibility and necessity in themselves. For Badiou, on the other hand, mathematics *is* ontology, both the privileged doctrine of whatever is and the paradoxical key to a formalism of what is beyond being; and philosophy can only hope to wit- ness this mathematical formalism of the event in what are, for him, its profound and intrinsic transformative consequences.

Badiou has addressed Wittgenstein, often critically but never without a kind of grudging admiration and respect, at several points in his career. In 1993–94, Badiou gave a year-long seminar on Wittgenstein under the title "L'Antiphilosophie de Wittgenstein"[37] and in 1994 he published an article entitled "Silence, solipsism, saintete. L'antiphilosophie de Wittgenstein."[38] There are scattered references to Wittgenstein in *Being and Event*, *Logics of Worlds*, and the short article "Philosophy and Mathematics: Infinity and the End of Romanticism," and in 2009 the volume *L'antiphilosophie de Wittgenstein* appeared, comprising a long piece on Wittgenstein deriv- ing from the 1993–94 course, and a much shorter article "Les langues de Wittgenstein," first published in 1999 in the review *Rue Descartes*.[39] With the exception of this last, short piece, all of these discussions focus almost exclusively on the early Wittgenstein of the *Tractatus*, which Badiou sub- jects to a rigorous and exhaustive examination. Nowhere in Badiou's *cor- pus* is there anything like a similarly deep examination of the *Philosophical Investigations*, and even when Badiou does address the "second Wittgen- stein" (as he does briefly in "Les langues de Wittgenstein"), he does so by means only of a largely exterior rumination on the "rhetoric" and "voices" of Wittgenstein's later texts.

The reason for this privileging of the *Tractatus* is not difficult to find in Badiou's own remarks. For as he explains in the endnotes to *Logics of Worlds*, while he considers the *Tractatus* an "undeniable masterpiece," albeit of the problematic *genre* that Badiou terms "anti-philosophy," none of the works that follow it rise (according to Badiou) to anything like this status. For after the *Tractatus*, "the further oeuvre—which is not really one, since Wittgenstein had the good taste not to publish or finish any of it—slides from anti-philosophy into sophistry."[40] Here we find, according to Badiou, only a writer "obsessed with urgent and preposterous questions, as if he were obstinately seeking some stupefied delirium"; such questions are "at times surprising inventions, which pleasingly derail the mind, at other times trite acrobatics."[41] The dismissive and acerbic tone is continuous with Badiou's long-standing polemics against "sophism" and "sophistry," which Badiou identifies with the privileging of rhetoric and linguistics over truth, and has long considered to be the most perfect enemy of philosophy itself. The category of "anti-philosophy" is a third one, structurally balanced in a precarious way between philosophy's essential pursuit of extra-linguistic truth and sophistry's endless linguistic plays.

The lack of any sustained engagement by Badiou with the later Wittgenstein is certainly unfortunate. Since, as we have seen, the later Wittgenstein is one of the best twentieth-century representatives of the paradoxico-critical orientation, Badiou's refusal to engage here appears to confirm, once again, a systematic blind spot for the kind of open critical options that paradoxico-criticism represents. Most significantly, it appears to confirm that Badiou has no way to understand the *critical* implications of the twentieth-century linguistic turn, except to treat them uniformly as the empty rhetorical prevarications of an easily refuted sophistry. Nevertheless, as much as we might regret this lack of engagement with the later Wittgenstein, we can still learn something important about the options open to contemporary thought by considering Badiou's sustained engagement with the *early* Wittgenstein, which he consistently conducts under the heading of "Wittgenstein's anti-philosophy." The 1993–94 course on the *Tractatus* is the second in a sequence of four year-long courses all under the heading of "L'antiphilosophie"; it is preceded in the sequence by a course on Nietzsche and followed by courses on Lacan and St. Paul (the latter would become the basis of Badiou's book entitled *St. Paul: The Foundation of Universalism*).[42] Elsewhere, Badiou adds Pascal, Rousseau, and Kierkegaard to the list of "anti-philosophers." In all of these treatments, Badiou discusses the position of the "anti-philosopher" as that of the thinker who would dismiss or break with philosophy's essential (as it is for Badiou) quest for truth, not simply by means of a "sophistical" reduction of this quest to historically contingent language-games, but by the invocation of the transformative potential of a radical subjective act or affirmation that leaps beyond any element of truth accessible to philosophy as such.[43] In its radically transformative potential, such an act indeed bears certain affinities to Badiou's category of the "event," but differs from it in that the object of the anti-philosophical act is conceived as lying beyond any possible linguistic expression and thus as capable of "breaking the history of the world in two" rather than contributing to the progressive historical unfolding of a generic truth. These traits commit the anti-philosopher, according to Badiou, simultaneously to a reductive or even constructivist identification of the boundaries of language with those of the world, or being, as such; and, at the same time, to the invocation of an (often "mystical" or "extra-rational") Beyond accessible neither to philosophy nor language, but only by means of the affirmation of a kind of indescribable "remainder" resistant to any possible signification or communication.

The category of the "anti-philosopher" thus allows Badiou to group together a number of thinkers who share with the philosopher (as Badiou conceives him) the desire to pursue transformative and radical change but nevertheless submit the thinking of this change to the dictates of a structural reflection on language and its limits. In the former respect at least, they differ from what Badiou has long called "sophists"; however, it is also worth noting that the category of "anti-philosopher" as distinct from that of the "sophist" has a relatively recent origin in Badiou's own corpus and does not yet appear, for instance, anywhere in *Being and Event*. Thus it is difficult to tell whether the polemics that appear there against constructivism and "nominalism" are meant to be limited to those who would simply pursue a "sophistical" reduction of truth to the rhetorical effects of language, or whether they extend as well to "anti-philosophers" such as Nietzsche and Lacan, whom he will later see as diverging to various degrees from the reductive sophistical project.

In any case, though, in the 1993–94 course on Wittgenstein, Badiou applies the terms of this general definition of the "anti-philosophical" position to the structure and ambitions of the *Tractatus*. Here he treats the pursuit of anti-philosophy as a complex of three essential gestures: first, there is a "critical dismantling" or "deconstruction" of philosophy by means of linguistic reflection; second, a recognition of the real import of existing philosophy as consisting in its production of an "act" which is nevertheless diagnosed as "bad" or "pathological"; and finally the attempt to substitute in place of this traditional "act" of philosophy a new and utterly transformative one. Badiou finds these three gestures precisely represented in the *Tractatus*. The first is marked in the attempt (at 4.003) to diagnose critically "most of the questions of philosophy" as "nonsense," which yields the critical analysis of the forms of philosophical pseudo-questions. The second gesture is evident, Badiou holds, in proposition 4.112, which declares philosophy to be "not a theory, but an activity" (*Tätigkeit*);[44] and the third one, which is perhaps the most important, is to be found, according to Badiou, in Wittgenstein's invocation of a "mystical element" which consists in the demonstration of what cannot be said, and thus necessarily takes place only as silence. The real significance of this "mystical element" in Wittgenstein's thought, according to Badiou, is to ensure the possibility of a kind of "archi-aesthetic" act that also manifests the basis of the very possibility of the existence of the world. This involves Wittgenstein, according to Badiou, in a complex entanglement with Christianity, as well as the conception of a "sense of the world" that necessarily lies outside its boundaries. Together, these themes yield the claim (at once, according to Badiou, "ontological" and "Christian") that "God is a name for the sense of the world."[45] The purpose of Wittgenstein's critical anti-philosophy is then simply to insist upon, and "never give up" the desire for, a radical twofold act that is both a "nonconceptual experience of the limit" and a "bet on the experience" of this limit that consists in inscribing the rigid law of silence so that the "mystical element" can be experienced at the point of its surpassing.[46]

There are certainly good textual grounds on which this particular interpretation of what is involved in the early Wittgenstein's interlinked conception of philosophy, mysticism, and silence might be disputed. For instance, throughout his discussion, Badiou treats the transformative act which is purportedly aimed at in Wittgenstein's invocation of mysticism and silence as a "subjective" one, even to the point of suggesting that it is this very *act* which is to "support" the existence of the world. But Wittgenstein holds at *TLP* 5.631 that "In an important sense, there is no subject" and at *TLP* 6.373 that "the world is independent of my will." Again, Badiou treats the import of the (supposed) "archi-aesthetic act" as that of *showing*, in religious or quasi-religious fashion, a "non-worldly" or transcendent existence beyond the limits of the world. This involves Wittgenstein, according to Badiou, in a problematic attempt to "speak the unspeakable" (even if only by means of contradictions and paradoxes) in order to indicate this existence beyond language. But as the "resolute" interpretation of the *Tractatus* has recently emphasized, it is not at all clear that Wittgenstein's project is consistent with the invocation of any such "transcendental beyond" to the world, and indeed there is a very significant register of the book that consists in denying any such being.[47] Given these issues, it is easy to suspect that Badiou's threefold conception of what the work of philosophy must be, according to Wittgenstein, is substantially imposed from outside rather than really grounded in the text itself. Even where Wittgenstein does speak explicitly of the character of philosophy, he describes it as an "activity" rather than an act, and moreover one directed to "elucidations" and the "clarification of propositions" rather than attempting an active passage to the mystical. The remarks that *do* speak of the mystical (6.44, 6.45, and 6.522) do not at all, on their face at least, suggest that it can be reached by means of any act or procedure, but instead that the mystical "showing" of what "cannot be said" is the result of a kind of *passive* "seeing" or "feeling" of the world "as a limited whole."

Given this, it seems that the radical "archi-aesthetic act" which Badiou imputes to Wittgenstein may be more an artifact of Badiou's own general categorical framework (the threefold division of philosophy, anti-philosophy, and sophistry) than anything really grounded in the *Tractatus* itself. Nevertheless, at other points, Badiou's sense of the differences here does enable him to see important structural features that both characterize the project that Wittgenstein indeed does share with other "anti-philosophers" such as Lacan, and distinguish it fundamentally from Badiou's own. In his seventeenth seminar, delivered in 1969–70, Lacan devotes a few pages to a discussion of the overall attitude and fundamental results of Wittgenstein's *Tractatus*.[48] Here, Lacan treats Wittgenstein as the single author who has most completely formulated what follows from the propositional articulation of truth. The claim of the *Tractatus* that there is no possibility of truth outside the proposition is, for Lacan, an essential insight, bearing certain similarities to the insights of psychoanalysis with respect to the structure of the Other and its desire. In particular, the position of Wittgenstein is similar to the "analyst's position" itself as schematized by Lacan, in that Wittgenstein aims to "eliminate . . . himself completely from his own discourse."[49] This facilitates, according to Lacan, a certain operation of diagnosis and analysis directed toward philosophy from the perspective of the purely factical or "factitious" nature of language, evident in the most plain and "stupid" facts, such as the fact that "it is day."

What is most essential to this operation, according to Lacan, is the recognition that there is no *metalanguage*, and hence no position from which to conduct the "knavery" and "bastardry" in which traditional philosophy largely consists:

> The stupid thing, if I may say so, is to isolate the factitiousness of 'It is day.' It is a prodigiously rich piece of stupidity, for it gives rise to a leverage point, very precisely the following one, from which it results that what I have used as a leverage point myself, namely that there is no metalanguage, is pushed to its ultimate consequences.
>
> There is no other metalanguage than all the forms of knavery, if we thereby designate these curious operations derivable from the fact that man's desire is the Other's desire. All acts of bastardry are based on the fact of wishing to be someone's Other, I mean someone's big Other, in which the figures by which his desire will be captivated are drawn.[50]

That there is no metalanguage means for Wittgenstein, as also for Lacan, that the philosophical desire to occupy the place of the Other—the place which is assumed to be that of the privilege of truth—can only yield to a therapeutic analysis of logic and sense. From the perspective of this analysis, the attempt to master sense from an assumed metalinguistic position is the central operation of the forms of "knavery" that define traditional philosophy, and to which psychoanalysis and Wittgensteinian therapy jointly respond. That "the only sense is the sense of desire" and that "the only truth is the truth of what the said desire for its lack hides"; this is, Lacan says, what we must understand after reading Wittgenstein.[51] In other words, there is no position outside the "stupid" facticity of everyday propositions from which it would be possible to master sense or to articulate a distinctive truth on its basis. This is the legacy of Wittgenstein for Lacan, and it is also the essential point on which, despite its need to advance into the field of truth in a way "distinct from" Wittgenstein's, psychoanalysis and Wittgenstein can nevertheless agree.

Badiou's own discussion of these passages, in the 1993–94 lectures, recognizes this denial of metalanguage as decisive to both Wittgenstein's and Lacan's position. It is from the position of this denial alone that it is possible to discern, Badiou suggests, the specific inadequation between meaning and truth: whereas philosophy, or the "university discourse" which is its genre according to Lacan, would claim to master truth from the metalinguistic position of its complete comprehension of sense, the "anti-philosophers" Lacan and Wittgenstein ascribe the illusion of such a perspective to the "knavery" or "villainy" specific to philosophy as such. Moreover, it is at this point that both Lacan and Wittgenstein recognize what Badiou himself does not hesitate to call the "fundamental question of ethics": the question of the relationship of meaning and truth, and of the possibility that (as Badiou suggests) there are truths that are excessive to sense (and hence raise the question of the possibility of their adequation to any exist-ing regime); *or* that there is indeed, as Lacan suggests on behalf of Witt-genstein, no *position* of truth that exceeds the movement of its own desire. On this basis, again, it is possible for Wittgenstein and Lacan to recognize that "truth cannot be treated as a property" and that, as Badiou admits, a fair definition of the "villainy" or "knavery" of philosophy is precisely to ignore this, and hence to seek, and presuppose, the adequation of mean-ing and truth from a position that makes truth a property of beings, or attempts thereby to speak on behalf of being itself.

What, though, is Badiou's own position with respect to these linked questions of the status of metalanguage and the specific relationship of meaning and sense? In the 1993–94 lectures, although Badiou does not simply reject Lacan's and Wittgenstein's sense of the "knavery" of philoso-phy as consisting in its attempt to assume a metalanguage position, he also does not endorse the "definition" of anti-philosophical therapy as the criti-cal operation of detecting and removing this pretension. Rather, although there is an essential "ethical" question here about the relationship between truth and meaning (which Badiou himself recognizes *as a question*), Badiou takes this question to be resolved in *Wittgenstein*'s text only by means of (what Badiou takes to be) Wittgenstein's affirmation of an act that is alien both to philosophy and to the articulation of sense itself, the "mystical act" or "element" that shows without saying. In that it is systematically affirmed even outside (or beyond) the articulate truth it supports, this "element" has for Wittgenstein, according to Badiou, a position closely analogous to that of desire for Lacan. For both anti-philosophers, according to Badiou, the essential thing is not to give up on this act beyond sense. Thus, whereas Lacan affirms the maxim "never give up on your desire!" Wittgenstein (on Badiou's reading) recognizes in the affirmation of the "mystical ele-ment" the point of an absolute function of assertion that "never yields" and thereby holds everything else in place. The correspondence between Wittgenstein and Lacan here also demonstrates, according to Badiou, a twofold function of realization in this act: first, it amounts to a "bet on the experience of the limit," and so to a bet on the possibility of actually realizing the limit of thought (or expression) that it defines; and second, a *legislative* function, that of *making the law the law*, or of articulating the very prohibition which, consigning all that exceeds the sayable to silence, also first defines the boundary between saying and showing itself.[52]

In fact, despite Badiou's adamant and consistent attempts to distance himself from the "anti-philosophical" position of Wittgenstein (as well as Lacan), *with respect to* the specific question of the basis of logical force and the connection between logic and the world which guarantees it, there are nevertheless noteworthy homologies that show the depth of their common concerns in this area. One of these, quite precisely definable and decisive for both projects, is an underlying *atomism* which, despite the differences in their respective concepts of "logic," can nevertheless for both rightly be termed *logical*. In particular, as Badiou recognizes, the requirement in the *Tractatus* of a correspondence between simple names and objects is a crucial point, both thematically and methodologically. For it ensures a level of being, the substrate of whatever can be asserted, that is absolutely and utterly indescribable, the level at which no assertion is possible since what there is can *only* be named.[53] According to the theory, "objects are unalterable and subsistent"; on the other hand, they intrinsically contain the possibilities of combination which lead to their changing configurations in (describable) states of affairs.

In *Logics of Worlds*, Badiou concurs with these points on behalf of his own theory of worlds and their transcendental structures. In particular:

> Since the logic of objects is nothing but the legislation of appearing, it is not in effect possible to accept that relations between objects have a power of being. The definition of a relation must be strictly dependent on that of objects, not the other way around. On this point, we are in agreement with Wittgenstein who, having defined the 'state of affairs' as a 'combination of objects', posits that 'if a thing can occur in a state of affairs, the possibility of the state of affairs must be written into the thing itself'. In other words, if an object enters into combination with others, this combination is, if not implied, in any case regulated by objects.[54]

Similarly, Badiou says elsewhere in *Logics of Worlds*, by identifying the level of objects on which no change or transformation is possible, Wittgenstein sees that "the pure thinking of being is as eternal as the multiple forms whose concept it harbors"[55] and that the possibilities for change and development of states of affairs within the world (or within *a* world, for Badiou) must be wholly determined, in advance, by the regular possibilities of combination thereby determined and permitted by the logical structure of objects. It follows, according to Badiou, that truly *discontinuous* change (the kind that both *Being and Event* and *Logics of Worlds* aim to theorize under the heading of the "event") can be understood neither as an effect solely of the static and unchanging order of Being, nor of the regulated order of appearances, but only by means of a theory of the effects of their structural interpenetration or crossing, the possible "retroaction" of appearance upon being, at the basis of every evental site, that we have discussed above.

In the 1993–94 lectures, Badiou recognizes the argument for atomism as one of the most structurally essential moments of the *Tractatus*, in that by providing for a level of being that takes place before all descriptive saying, it holds in place the very distinction between showing and saying on which the *Tractatus* as a whole relies. This leads Badiou to suggest, however, that there is a deep structural problem in the *Tractatus* concerning the issue of *designation* or *nomination*. In the *Tractatus*, it is essential that names (already) stand for objects, in order that any proposition has sense. The question of *how* names are coordinated to the objects for which they stand is thus not addressed, and even treated by Wittgenstein as irrelevant.[56] However, according to Badiou, Wittgenstein's refusal to discuss the issue is the sign of a significant and largely unargued prohibition. In particular, it is prohibited that the act of nomination (or more generally, the act of showing or demonstrating) expresses a *thought*. Since objects can only be named and never described, the act (if such there be) involved in coordinating a name to an object can never be explained or spoken *about*: there is only, Badiou supposes, the senseless act itself. Moreover, correlative to this is a converse prohibition operating in the other direction: since naming is always distinct from asserting and never expresses a thought, it is impossible to *name* a state of affairs. As Badiou notes, the two "prohibitions" are deeply linked to the one we have just discussed, the "prohibition" of a metalanguage. For if there were a metalanguage capable of stating truths about the object language, it would be possible as well to describe the coordination of names to objects, or to speak what, for Wittgenstein, can essentially only be shown. Wittgenstein's exclusion of any possible metalanguage position will thus stand, or fall, with the logical distinction between objects and states of affairs, which is mirrored in the distinction between naming and asserting.

In the 1993–94 lectures, Badiou in fact wishes to contest the tenability of maintaining this twofold distinction in the strict fashion that Wittgenstein requires. He suggests, in particular, that we might understand the function of *poetry* as, in large part, arising from its capacity to violate the prohibition on the naming of states of affairs:

> I would argue that much of **the poetic enterprise is to designate states of affairs.** *I.e.* that just as poetry is such that it engages the possibility of statements about names, so poetry is something that involves finding names for states of affairs and not simply for the unthinkable simple.[57]

In the function of poetry, Badiou thus recognizes a twofold power of articulation: on the one hand, the ability to produce descriptive statements about names and nominations, and on the other, the ability to "find names" for states of affairs and thereby accomplish an essential act of nomination that marks poetry off, according to Badiou, from any proposition.

The status of this suggestion with respect to Wittgenstein's *logical* distinction between the objects of names and propositionally articulated complexes is not immediately clear. Is Badiou denying that it is possible to apply this distinction rigorously to language in general, or claiming that, in addition to names on the one hand and sentences on the other, the poem (or instance of poetry) is itself a third, wholly distinct logical category that somehow combines both? If there is indeed such a third category of language capable of the designative power of names but also of description, how are we to identify it, or determine the success of its instances? However, the larger systematic motivations for Badiou's insistence on a poetic *lapsus* of the rigorous mutual exclusion of propositions and names are not difficult to locate within his broader project itself. Recall that, as we saw above, the theory of *Being and Event* requires that the occurrence of an event, in Badiou's sense, always depends on a moment of paradoxical auto-nomination. At this moment of designation—for instance, Saint-Just's declaration "the Revolution is frozen"—the articulation of a proposition *about* the event itself plays an essential role in constituting the event, in the future anterior, as the one it *will have been*. In other words, we have here a proposition about naming, and the possibility of describing the very moment of nomination itself, which plays, for Badiou, an essential structural role in constituting any event as such.

In *Logics of Worlds*, as we have seen, this reflexive function of language, although its structural role is now somewhat more complicated, remains essential to the possibility of anything like an event. Here, Badiou replaces what was essentially, in *Being and Event*, a nomothesis of names with one of laws, but the auto-nominating moment whereby an event is caught up in its own legislative power remains essential. In the transition from the *Tractatus* to the later work, Wittgenstein, by contrast, comes to see the nomothesis as the site of a radical and pervasive paradox. This is not so much (any longer) the paradox of the *origin* of rules and names, which Badiou here appears to ascribe to an irreducible "poetic" dimension of language, but rather the paradox of the force and application of rules in the everyday use of language.

All of this tends to suggest that the issue of the place of language in Badiou's own project may be more complex than he sometimes says, and indeed that much more is involved in his quarrel with Wittgenstein than simply the question of a "pro" or "con" attitude to language and a formally based consideration of its powers. However, to really understand what is at stake in the debate between the two thinkers which seems to pit the unyielding and extra-linguistic formalism of mathematics, on the one hand, against paradoxico-criticism's reflexive formalism of language on the other, it is helpful to consider the single point at which Badiou officially *most* vehemently disagrees with Wittgenstein and his whole attitude: the question of the status of mathematics itself. For Badiou, Wittgenstein's thought, early and late, witnesses a spectacular, enduring, and decisive rejection of the capacity of mathematics to manifest thought. This rejection is, according to Badiou, summarized in the *Tractatus*' claim that "a proposition of mathematics does not express a thought";[58] Badiou says in *Briefings on Existence* that he will "never finish up with refuting" it in his insistence that, to the contrary, "Mathematics is a thought." In the context of the *Tractatus*, the claim is in fact a consequence of the position that mathematical propositions, being reducible to logical tautologies, are empty of empirical content and so say nothing.[59] It is thus not in fact clear that the claim, in context, has, as Badiou holds, the consequence of denying the power of thought to mathematics; and it is thus, at the very least, misleading that just after quoting the *Tractatus* claim, Badiou presents it quite incongruously as the expression of a "major overall thesis of empiricism and sophistry."[60] However this may be, later on, for instance, in the *Remarks on the Foundations of Mathematics* and the *Philosophical Investigations*, Wittgenstein will indeed maintain steadfastly this reluctance to consider mathematical propositions as claims with their own determinate and specific referential or representative *content* (empirical or otherwise), while at the same time moving away from the *Tractatus*' picture of "thoughts" as exclusively propositional or sentential in structure.

In a 2004 article entitled "Mathematics and Philosophy: The Grand Style and the Little Style," Badiou contrasts what he calls the "grand style," which "stipulates that mathematics provides a direct illumination of philosophy, rather than the opposite" with the "little style," which proposes to treat mathematics as an "object for philosophical scrutiny," and thus as the definitive object for a distinctive area of philosophical specialization, the "philosophy of mathematics."[61] As representatives of the "grand style," Badiou marshals quotations from Descartes, Spinoza, Kant, Hegel, and Lautréamont. He takes Wittgenstein's remarks, by contrast, to be a paradigm instance of the "little style." In denying (as Badiou understands him) the relation of mathematics to thought, Wittgenstein falls, according to Badiou, into a kind of reductive linguistic pragmatism that equally characterizes the "fashionable" constructivist or nominalist projects from which Badiou would most of all like to distance himself. Badiou quotes as an example of this "trite pragmatism" a remark from *RFM* which Anscombe translates as follows:

> I should like to ask something like: "Is it usefulness you are out for in your calculus? In that case you do not get any contradiction. And if you aren't out for usefulness—then it doesn't matter if you do get one.[62]

In context, Wittgenstein's point is clearly *not* to affirm pragmatism or to claim that our calculations must be judged by a standard of usefulness. Importantly, the point is a wholly conditional one. *If* we are looking for a calculus which will be useful—say, one that will help us compare measurements—then what matters is simply its practical success, and the sort of "contradiction in the foundations" of the calculus that Russell and Frege sought to hunt out and eliminate need not, seemingly, affect this usefulness at all.[63] If, on the other hand, we don't care about the usefulness of our calculus, then a contradiction is simply another symbolic expression; again, it doesn't matter.

As we saw in Chapter 6, this is a way of putting Wittgenstein's characteristic attitude toward contradictions, which seems calculated to raise the hackles of mathematicians and philosophers of mathematics alike, but is not obviously false, absurd, or untenable. Indeed, as we saw, Wittgenstein's "relaxed" attitude toward contradiction has a precise diagnostic and therapeutic function within his thought: specifically, it is designed critically to interrogate what is involved in the axiomatic or unquestioned assumption that contradiction must be avoided at all cost, an assumption that plays directly into foundationalist projects in mathematics. What Wittgenstein is doing here, by contrast, is what he very often does while reflecting on the nature of mathematics and its role in our lives. He is posing the *question* of how a symbolic system is applied—how it gains what we may see as its significance in a human life. As we have indeed seen, Wittgenstein ceaselessly poses this question, what we might call the question of "significance for life," whenever he reflects on language and symbolism; but it is, in this context, highly misleading to claim that his purpose is to *reduce* mathematical claims—or any claims—to some pre-established *standard* or *notion* of use or usefulness.

But is not the later Wittgenstein, after all, the great twentieth-century chronicler of linguistic contingency, the avatar of a relativism of socially constituted "language games" and hence the radical critic of any claim to deduce the unity of language as such or determine, from an abstract theoretical standpoint, the effects of its structure? The best answer to all of these interpretive questions, I think, is "no." Here, we must not only resist a dominant pragmatist or relativist reading of Wittgenstein that assigns to the realities of "practice," "institution," and the "social" itself a self-evidence which he would certainly have found impossible, but also seek the roots of the most radical and penetrating problematics (including the problematic of rule-following), which lie in his unquestionably unique vision of language itself. On this vision, as we have seen in Chapter 1, it is not "agreement in opinions" that constitutes the possibility of language but that much deeper and more elusive "agreement in judgments" that is grounded in "forms of life"; this is not the agreement of a conventional institution or "socially grounded" norms of practice, but on the far deeper ground of those aspects of our lives and bearing that first make anything like meaningful language, and hence *also* any "social whole" possible at all. If Wittgenstein evinces this ground by means of the labels of "practice," "institutions," and "rules," the attempt is not at all to present these concepts and their values as unproblematic, but rather to identify and demonstrate the deeply rooted and far-ranging problems involved in them. If the "unity of essence" that the traditional theorist attempts to find for language or language-games by finding the "one thing" that they all have in common is here denied (for instance, *PI* 65), this is *not* to deny the importance of a search for the essence of language that here continues in a methodologically radicalized form.[64]

Instead, with the removal of the theorist's ambition to find a "single analysis" of the proposition as such and a "completely resolved form of every expression," the investigation becomes a far-reaching chronicle of the variety of interrelated structures that define language in its complex relation to a (human) life, an investigation which does not stop short of detecting the most pervasive and "deep disquietudes" of this life, problems that "are as deep in us as the forms of our language" and bear a "significance . . . as great as the importance of our language."[65] This is not, as I have argued, an abandonment of the Platonic search for form, but a radicalization of it on the level of "forms of life"; not an abandonment of the Platonic inquiry, under the heading of the "idea," into the being of whatever is, but rather its transformation on the ground of language itself (for "Grammar tells what kind of object anything is" and "*Essence* is expressed in grammar"); not, again, an abandonment of the fundamental Platonic distinction between being and appearance, which finds expression in all subsequent forms of the "critique of illusion," but a renewal of this critique on the basis of an unprecedented reflection on "grammar," in which is to be found as well the source of the foundational "superstitions" of human life.[66]

For Badiou, by stark contrast, there is no interesting problem of the relation of language to life or of the role within it of what we reflectively grasp as techniques and rules. Indeed, as Badiou explains in a 1998 article entitled "The Question of Being Today," he takes the ontological authority of mathematics itself to demonstrate that any treatment of it *as* a technique is seriously misguided.[67] For any such treatment again misses, according to Badiou, the way that mathematics captures in thought all that is sayable about Being itself:

> Philosophy is partly responsible for the reduction of mathematics to the status of mere calculation or technique. This is a ruinous image, to which mathematics is reduced by current opinion with the aristocratic complicity of mathematicians themselves, who are all too willing to accept that, in any case, the rabble will never be able to understand their science.
>
> It is therefore incumbent upon philosophy to maintain—as it has very often attempted to, even as it obliterated that very attempt—that mathematics thinks.[68]

Badiou does not say, here, precisely what is so dangerous about a philosophical treatment of mathematics as a kind of technique, among others, whose role in our lives is to be judged, and understood, in terms of what it does for us, or why this thought of mathematics as a technique must be taken to *exclude* the possibility that it is also an exemplary domain of formal and even ontological thought. It may be that he thinks that any such view amounts to placing mathematics under a "sophistical injunction," although (as we saw in the last section), it is clear that Wittgenstein's own critical inquiry into the complexities and problems of mathematical technique does not in fact do so. What *is* true is that for Wittgenstein, the interest of this critical reflection on the meaning, force, and application of "mathematical" rules derives largely from their capacity to exemplify and model the more general problems of linguistic meaning and understanding. The interest of treating mathematics as a technique of symbol manipulation is in what it tends to show about the conception of language as a technique of symbol manipulation, and about the way in which the problems of this conception of language tend to play a role in, and even determine, our human self-conception. The Platonistic elevation of "mathematical objects" into superlatives, in which the metaphorics of actualized infinity plays an irreducible part, tends to obfuscate this role of language in life by foreclosing the inherent paradoxes of its application. To this, Wittgenstein's criticism responds with a skeptical inquiry that operates as another way of posing the standing question of the relationship of language to life. This is the question of the way in which what may seem to be the infinite possibilities of human sense are fated to live out the constraint of their expression in finite forms of language. To pose this critical question is not to subject or constrain meaning (mathematical or otherwise) to a fixed corpus of grammatical rules or the straitjacket of a predetermined sense of the limits of expression, but rather to pursue what we may feel to be the essential mismatch between (finitary) forms of expression and (infinitary) meaning, as we meet with this problem in the varied linguistic occasions of an ordinary life, up to the point of the ultimate resolution, or dissolution, of the problem that this is felt to represent.

Such a resolution does not depend, according to Wittgenstein, on new discoveries or even on new institutions or inventions, although the *forms* of our techniques of calculating, reflecting, and judging in mathematics are deeply important to it.[69] In the *Remarks on the Foundations of Mathematics*, right after discussing what he sees as the "hocus-pocus" of Cantor's procedure, Wittgenstein comments on the role of technique, habit, and technology in producing determinative changes in human life:

> 23. The sickness of a time is cured by an alteration in the mode of life of human beings, and it was possible for the sickness of philosophical problems to get cured only through a changed mode of thought and of life, not through a medicine invented by an individual.
>
> Think of the use of the motor-car producing or encouraging certain sicknesses, and mankind being plagued by such sickness until, from some cause or other, as the result of some development or other, it abandons the habit of driving.[70] (*RFM* II–32)

9   Paradoxico-Critique of Badiou

What legacy can the critical thought of the twentieth century have for
political thought and action, in the twenty-first? Today, one often hears
declarations of the "death of theory," of the inapplicability in relation
to today's "global" politics of the twentieth-century critical thought and
praxis that is routinely accused of an empty and ineffective "textualism"
or intellectualism. These denegations often go hand in hand with the now-
routine dismissal of the twentieth-century linguistic turn as a "dead end"
or false turn that places words before things and readings before interventions, a turn towards what is seen as a bottomless procession of interpretations, an unending hermeneutic of deferral. If the characteristic methods
of twentieth-century philosophy ("analytic" as well as "continental") are
not to be portrayed as dead or refuted, they must indeed, it seems, demonstrate the falseness of this image. One essential precondition for this, as
we have seen, is that the contemporary representatives of critical thought
must stop allowing themselves to be mischaracterized, or wrongly assimilated to weaker and less helpful positions, such as constructivism and
limitative conventionalism.

In the last chapter, I contrasted three of the preeminent representatives
of the orientation I have called "paradoxico-criticism" to Badiou's generic
orientation on a series of interrelated issues. The point there was not,
fundamentally, to recommend one orientation over the other, but rather
to sharpen and clarify the contrast by way of defining the key points in
dispute between the two. In this chapter, I turn the (substantial) critical
resources of paradoxico-criticism to a consideration of Badiou's own position on languages, worlds, truth, and politics. Although the point is, once
again, not simply to argue for the actual "truth" or even the superior merit
of the various methods of paradoxico-criticism, this consideration should
have the effect of showing just what turns on the dispute with respect to
the leading questions of collective life and action, and hence just what the
space of political thought and action might look like, if these methods
and practices of twentieth-century critical reflection are indeed inherited
rather than forgotten.

BODIES, LANGUAGES, TRUTHS: THREE AXIOMS

We have already seen that Badiou's attack on constructivism does not actually meet, or even really understand, the most robust critical positions available today. In fact, what I have called the methods of paradoxico-critical philosophy are universally committed to posing a question, with respect to mathematics or any other enterprise of using signs, that may be considered one of the most profound questions for contemporary critical thought, but which Badiou himself cannot, given his commitments, possibly raise. Specifically, for all of these approaches, there is always at least a question of *how* the sign signifies, how it is that the (finite) sign accomplishes the "infinite" dimension of meaning. This is, for instance, Wittgenstein's question about following a rule. In Derrida's language (for instance, in "Signature, Event, Context") it is the question of iterability, of how the finite symbolic corpus of a language achieves the possibility of citation and graft in any of an openly infinite number of contexts. The most general locus of this kind of question might be put, once more, as that of an inquiry into "the consequences of formalism" as such. The question for this kind of philosophy is then *how* formalism (whether "mathematical" or "linguistic") enters a human life, and hence what it means to *reflect* on the formalisms we (also) live by.

There is reason to think that Badiou's omission or suppression of this question affects in a fundamental way his argument against the contemporary orthodox political orientation of "democratic materialism" itself. In *Logics of Worlds*, Badiou again affirms the twofold link he sees between the constructivist position and both the existing critical positions stemming from the linguistic turn, on one hand, and the orthodoxy of contemporary belief, on the other. Thus, the world of contemporary "democratic materialism" is identified as being, most probably, an "atonic" one in which there are no "points," and so in which "no faithful subjective formalism can serve as the agent of a truth."[1] As there are no truths, but only a "managed" life that is "like a business that would rationally distribute the meagre enjoyments that it's capable of," there is also no place for any fundamental decision to occur, and all "binary" differences, up to the sexual difference itself, are "deconstructed" (note the term, which Badiou does not hesitate to use in reference to a movement that aims for a "quasi-continuous multiple of constructions of gender") in favor of a "desire for generalized atony."[2] This is the world in which, since "there are no truths," "there are only bodies and languages"; it is rigorously opposed to Badiou's "materialist dialectic," which, as we have seen, affirms in addition the existence of Truths beyond any language or any situated culture.

Again, however, the philosophical positions that Badiou sees as dominant in contemporary academic life are, due to their continuing allegiance to the linguistic turn, opposed to this assertion of Truth and consigned to the side of democratic materialism:

> We can clearly see . . . the opposition between the materialist dialectic
> and the two academic traditions that today lay claim to supremacy:
> phenomenology and analytic philosophy. These two currents both re-
> quire a constituent assertion about the originariness of language. And
> both concur in seeing, whether in rhetoric or logic—or in any case
> in the intentional forms of the control of syntagms—the schema of
> this originariness. The materialist dialectic undermines this schema,
> replacing it with the pre-linguistic operations which ground the consis-
> tency of appearing. As a consequence, logic, formal logic included, not
> to mention rhetoric, all appear for what they are: derivative construc-
> tions, whose detailed study is a matter for anthropology.[3]

Here, in a striking formulation of his ongoing assimilation of all positions
descending from the linguistic turn to constructivism, Badiou assumes that
any such position must, in reflecting on the implications of language, first
demand its "originariness" and formulate the implications of its structure
as involving, exclusively, a regulative "control of syntagms." By contrast,
as we have seen, the paradoxico-critical orientation sees in the problematic
ubiquity of language a fundamental aporia of origin and a multiplication
of paradoxes of reflexivity that formally contest and disrupt any attempt to
control the forms of language from outside. The constant and uniform basis
for these insights is a continued fidelity to (what we may see as) the "logical
event" that was the origin of both the analytic tradition and structuralism,
which, in unrelentingly affirming the implications of the structural totality of language (or logic) as such, also removed it fundamentally (witness
the decisive polemics against "psychologism" and "anthropologism" that
characterized the founding of the analytic tradition, as well as Husserl's
phenomenology) from any "anthropological" or merely empirical derivation or account.

We can begin to see what kind of difference this might make for contemporary political thought by returning to the two "axioms" of thought that
Badiou distinguishes at the beginning of *Logics of Worlds*. The first of these
is the axiom of the "contemporary conviction" of democratic materialism:
"There are only bodies and languages." This orientation is thoroughly committed, Badiou suggests, to the "pragmatism of desires" and the "obvious-
ness of commerce," behind which lies philosophically the "dogma of our
finitude" or "of our carnal exposition to enjoyment, suffering and death."[4]
Here, the life of the human is conceived as an "overstretched animality"
a "bio-materialism" whose norm of the "protection of all living bodies" is
to be guaranteed by "bioethics," and contested by the strictly symmetrical
(as Badiou suggests) position of an analysis of "biopolitics" in the style of
Foucault. Moreover, the position thus defined is fundamentally democratic
in that it is foundationally committed to a "plurality of languages" and
to their "juridical equality." This commitment yields an axiomatic devo-
tion to the fundamentally plural and equal claim of all "communities and

cultures, colours and pigments, religions and clergies, uses and customs, disparate sexualities, public intimacies and the publicity of the intimate," to protection and recognition under the uniform law.[5]

To this, Badiou opposes his own axiom, that of the materialist dialectic. According to this axiom, "There are only bodies and languages, except that there are truths."[6] As Badiou emphasizes, the best way to understand the relationship of this axiom to the one it seeks to displace is to consider the syntax of the "except." It is not that truths are the result of any kind of synthesis or supplementation to the democratic-materialist world of plural bodies and languages. Rather, they are excepted from—subtracted from—the totality of "what there is." What there is in being—everything that appears substantially in the world—may indeed, Badiou allows, be limited to bodies and languages. However, by way of the fundamental and essential "exception" that a truth is, and which allows it to bring about the radical changes it can work in bodies and languages through the occurrence of events, "there isn't only what there is." Thus, although the materialist dialectic agrees "in a certain sense" with democratic materialism in its restriction of "what is" in being to bodies and languages—this is, Badiou says, the common core of the "materialism" of both positions—"in another sense" the materialist dialectic resists this consensual, orthodox perspective through its radical insistence on truth, which breaks the "continuity of the 'there is'" through the "interpolation of a 'there is what there is not.'"[7]

It is worth considering whether Badiou's language here is (even so much as) coherent, and hence whether (or on what basis, if not based on any difference in their existential claims) we can really distinguish between the "sense" in which the materialism of the "materialist dialectic" concurs, and the "sense" in which it breaks with, the materialism of "democratic materialism." However, regardless of this, by comparing the formulation of the two axioms which Badiou thinks of as exhaustive of the presently available options, we may now locate very clearly the precise point at which the paradoxico-critical orientation is specifically excluded from Badiou's whole presentation. This is, unsurprisingly, the point of *language*, and what is absolutely decisive in this connection is that *both* of the axioms that Badiou states assume that *language exists only in the plural.* By contrast, as we have repeatedly and vividly seen in their detailed critical projects and results, the representatives of paradoxico-criticism uniformly operate by tracing the systematic, if paradoxical, implications of the fundamental assumption that there is a One of the structure of language or logic as such, a structure which is not exhausted by any specific, empirical language or any collection or plurality thereof, but bears its effects on the structuration of life through the fundamental effects of this totality. Whereas, therefore, Badiou treats the first axiom of democratic materialism as affirming a "sovereignty of the Two" (namely, bodies and languages) which is to be opposed, according to his own orientation, by an affirmation of the Three (of bodies, languages, and truths), we may accordingly, on behalf of paradoxico-criticism, offer by contrast a *third axiom* that consists in the relentless affirmation of the implications of the One. We can formulate this axiom as follows:

There are bodies, and language exists as their exceptional, unifying pre-condition.

Here, language is *not affirmed as a plurality*, either of "language-games" or of cultures. Instead, it is the One of the universal presupposition of all intelligibility and all that is common, what first makes possible signification, and hence community, as such. The specific definition of the paradoxico-critical orientation is thus to be found in its relentless pursuit of this One, up to the radical and paradoxical consequences of the subsistence of language itself—not, indeed, as any empirical or culturally located "language"—but as the uniform, "virtual," and "ideal" dimension of linguistic reality, the underlying *ideological* substrate which also founds the real of whatever takes place. This dimension is then intelligible, not as another being or object next to the plurality of bodies, but as the constant presupposition of all unity and unification of bodies into a community or social whole. As such, its relationship to bodies and their actions is precisely *exceptional*: as we have repeatedly seen (most directly in connection with Agamben), language is the place of the "permanent state of exception" in which signification is always, paradoxically, outside itself in its reference to the totality in which it takes place, and inside itself in its capacity for self-reference, both at and beyond the boundary of sense that its own movement incessantly draws.

We have seen that the central issue at stake between Badiou and the variety of thinkers that can be grouped under the label of "paradoxico-criticism" is the *significance* of the paradoxes of totality and self-reference, which both see as essential. This difference—determined by the initial difference of decisions when faced with these paradoxes, which imply the impossibility of joining consistency and completeness in a single account or theoretical structure—is indeed profound and elementary. However, this is not to say that there is not profound and important *agreement* as well. Most importantly, both Badiou and the thinkers of paradoxico-criticism agree in an important and definitive way on the *existence* of the formal paradoxes of self-reference and their relevance for philosophical thought. This is already a very significant point of agreement, for it distinguishes the two positions decisively and irreversibly from the positions of onto-theology and constructivism, which do not recognize the *general* philosophical significance of the paradoxes, and so continue to attempt, in different ways, to combine completeness and consistency in a single, unified account of the totality of what is.[8]

This agreement about the significance of the paradoxes between Badiou and paradoxico-criticism extends to an essential parallel in their understanding of what is for both one of the key resources of political thought about the structure and formation of languages and communities, their common recognition of an inherent structural *excess* that is always the result of representative or symbolic phenomena. This excess can be modeled, according to *both* orientations, by the relationship between a set and its power set, which displays all the arbitrary possibilities of regrouping the initial set's members. But here, with respect to the significance of this excess, differences between the two orientations start to emerge. In particular, as we have repeatedly seen, what paradoxico-criticism understands as the essentially *syntactic* excess of any signifying *language* over the totality of the signified is the key resource of criticism in its interrogation of the imaginary foundations of ideological pictures of the unity of a society, community, or political whole. For Badiou, by contrast, this excess is quite simply the excess of "representation" over "presentation" and essentially defines the structure of what he calls "the state," what is always capable of *mastering* representation.

Because of the structural commonalities here, it can certainly be said, as Derrida reportedly said to Badiou, that the paradoxico-critic and the generic philosopher "have," at any rate, "the same enemies." And it is important in the present context not to minimize the extent to which this commonality can indeed determine a common project that is at once radical, subversive, and grounded in the very consequences of formal thought itself.[9] Nevertheless, there remains a profound and central structural disagreement, from which everything else that is at issue between Badiou and the paradoxico-critic proceeds, on the very ground of the ancient question of the One and the Many itself. This is the disagreement which we have repeatedly witnessed between the relentless affirmation of consistency, along with the sacrifice of the One of language and sense as such, and the equally uncompromising affirmation of completeness, along with the constitutive paradoxes and contradictions of sense and meaning that it demonstrates.

This is, to begin with, a dispute between *incomplete plurality* and *inconsistent unity*. As we have seen, we can trace the implications of Badiou's fundamental decision in favor of plurality and incompleteness from the first moments of *Being and Event* all the way up to *Logics of World*'s multiplicity of worlds and languages, which are, Badiou says, without common measure or commensurability. The paradoxico-critic will, by contrast, insist upon the problematics arising from the assumption (even if it is nowhere empirically verified) of a *single* language (or of language as such) and a single world, a totality of all that is, in which it takes place. What, then, are the implications of *this* disagreement for contemporary thought about *political* change and its possibility?

Here, it is possible and helpful to notice a surprising fact about Badiou's position that, though it may otherwise escape our attention, becomes particularly clear when this position is contrasted with the paradoxico-critical orientation on the precise question of plurality that most deeply divides them. It is that, with respect to the overarching structure of the "political order" as such, Badiou is in fact *very close to the spontaneous position of the consensual relativism that he would like most emphatically to oppose.* The key point is that both affirm, as a *fundamental* starting point and by common *contrast* to the paradoxico-critical orientation, *an essential plurality of communities or worlds, incapable of being subsumed to a single, common measure.* This is, in the "postmodernist" jargon, the irreducible "heterogeneity" of identities and cultures, the "diversity" and mutual "alterity" of contingent and conventionally instituted "language-games," which yields as its only universal imperative the vague ethic of tolerance and inclusiveness that functions here as a kind of ideological fixed point. Of course, Badiou will vehemently oppose this bland ethics on the basis of his own militant call for radical, transformative conception of subjective action in the name of the universal, which is, for him, equivalent to the faithful forcing of a Truth. Nevertheless, the structural commonality with respect to plurality itself makes for some interesting further homologies with respect to the role that both accord to language and meaning in the transformation of political realities, and raises doubts (once again) about the extent to which Badiou is indeed able accurately to portray the space of options open to genuinely critical political thought in our time.

To begin with, as multiple commentators have noted, Badiou is by no means clear about the nature of the fundamental operations that, for him, function to structure a One out of a Many themselves. In *Being and Event,* the operation of forming a One out of a Many, which is operative in the formation of any and every "consistent" set, as well as any object or phenomenon capable of being named, is termed the "count as one." This operation is, for Badiou, always subsequent to the pure multiplicity, or many, that it "counts." However, as to *who* performs this operation, *where* it is performed, or *how, Being and Event* is entirely silent.[10] The only information we gain about this operation at the point of its introduction is the *claim* that it is not essentially linguistic; this assertion will later be necessary, of course, in demonstrating that there are possible sets—for instance the "generic" set that is essential to forcing—that do not coincide with any internally definable linguistic predicate or set thereof.

In *Logics of Worlds,* there are indications that the more elaborate apparatus of worlds and their transcendentals that there replaces the "situations" of *Being and Event* is intended, at least in part, to answer to worries about the capability of the earlier, simpler structure to portray the structures of the multiplicity of local situations in all of their vicissitudes. However, with respect to the more fundamental question of the actual *operation* that results in the imposition of structure (whether construed as that of a situation, formed from the "count as one," or as that of a structured world) the problem is, if anything, compounded. Here, recall, Badiou disjoins the realm of being, which is to be handled by means of set theory, from the transcendentally structured worlds of the realm of appearances, or phenomenology, which display a variety of specific "logical" structures comprehensible in terms of category theory. But we must here pose the question whether, for all of its rigorous and detailed formalism, *Logics of Worlds* actually succeeds in producing an improved understanding of those structures and relationships of "objective appearing" that are its central theoretical objects. These are, remember, not appearances-to-a-subject or even appearances as structured or determined by conventional decision or by a contingent language community, but rather "objective" appearings to no one in particular, nevertheless rigidly disjoined from the "ontological" reality of things as they are in themselves and without respect to appearance. Although Badiou offers a detailed formalism of the degrees and relations of variable "intensities" of appearance or existence within a world, he never answers the question of how we may establish in a neutral way what these intensities actually *are*. Along similar lines, the detailed theory of transcendentals shows in rigorous detail the formal connection to Heyting algebras and particular (generally non-classical) logics, but nothing in this elaborate theory seems to explain how the transcendentals and logics actually *come to* structure the worlds to which they apply, or to what they owe their *force* in governing these relations of appearing and "intensities" of existence to begin with. Indeed, the concept of "world" itself remains, despite its centrality to the whole project of *Logics of Worlds*, quite ill-defined. Despite all the varied examples, we are never told in clear and non-circular terms, for instance, how to understand the unity of a world as such, or how to distinguish one from another.

It may be that Badiou wishes to refrain from posing the *quid juris* question of the genesis of a transcendental and the right of its application to a world, in that he fears that answering this question would inevitably lead back to one of the forms of idealism (subjectivist or linguistic) that he rejects. However, failing a good answer to the question of the force and maintenance of transcendental structures in determining appearances, it is very difficult to avoid the natural assumption that "transcendentals" are indeed structures of linguistic or conventional practice, established and held in place by the behavioral regularities of a specific cultural or language community. This assumption, of course, would lead directly back to the kind of culturalist relativism that Badiou wishes above all to avoid. However, it is not at all clear that he succeeds in forestalling it.

This is not to say that Badiou's position is ultimately *equivalent* to the politics of a democratic, culturalist relativism that affirms a complete contingency of institution and irreducible plurality of language-games; but it nevertheless shows just how slender and potentially elusive is the theoretical passage on which Badiou stakes his entire claim to resist it. As is witnessed in Badiou's own careful formulation of the difference between the "democratic materialism" of contemporary conviction and his own "materialist dialectic," the *sole* point of difference here, on which every-thing else in Badiou's project rests, is Badiou's unflinching and relentless affirmation of the exceptional being of (what he calls) Truths, and hence of the fundamental possibility of discontinuous and progressive change that they introduce. By contrast, paradoxico-criticism, which has little use for Truths in Badiou's sense, or for the faithful subject who orients himself toward their progressive realization, affirms from the beginning the existence of language as such and detects the essential possibility of discontinuity and change within any existing community and its struc-ture at the fixed point of the paradoxical internal reflection of this struc-ture into itself.

How, then, should we attempt to address this pivotal question of the existence of what Badiou calls Truths, which determines in a very profound sense Badiou's project, yet nevertheless does not seem, from a larger perspective, to be verified by any incontrovertible evidence, whether empirical *or* formal? Though it is extremely difficult to find neutral terms in which it is possible even to pose this question from an "unbiased" perspective, we may perhaps gain some insight into it by considering what Badiou himself says in a section of *Being and Event* titled (appropriately enough) "Do Truths Exist?" The question, Badiou says, is equivalent to the question of the existence of generic procedures of fidelity, and has both a "de facto" and a "de jure" dimension. He then articulates the question into the four domains or "procedures" of love, art, science, and politics; in the political dimension specifically, the question of the generic procedure is, he says, equivalent to the actual existence of a "*generic politics*" which is the same as "what was called, for a long time, revolutionary politics" but "for which another word must be found today."[11] At the present juncture, however, it is clear that the focus of Badiou's argument is most of all not on this "de facto" question of the actual existence and identity of Truths—he holds this "de facto" question to be decided "by the entire history of humankind" but without giving many specific examples—but rather on the "de jure" question of their *possibility. This* question, he says, has, by contrast, been resolved only quite recently, in fact precisely in 1963, with Cohen's demonstration of the technique of forcing.[12] Therefore it is, according to Badiou, on a *formal* level that the "de jure" question of at least the pos-sible being of Truth is ultimately decided, and there it is indeed verified by Cohen's discovery.

What *kind* of difference, though, does this question of the being of Truth (in Badiou's sense) make to the question of how we should think of the fundamental possibilities of political change in our time? Having developed the contrast between Badiou's orientation and paradoxico-criticism in terms of the issue of plurality and unity, we can now suggest the following. Because of its fundamental affirmation of the *plurality* of worlds and inspired, if not always obviously formally grounded or justified, invocation of the imperative of a militancy of truth, Badiou's orientation is uniquely capable of thinking the kind of transformation whereby a *specific state or community* constituted by a *determinate structure* of inclusions and exclusions is transformed into a substantially different one, a *distinct* state or community constituted by another but still determinate and determining structure. This is doubtless important, for it figures, and indeed offers to provide formal terms for the support of, the hope of all progressive social transformations and all localized revolutions. But because it disavows the thought of the totality at a fundamental level, Badiou's thought is, in general, *less* well suited to thinking the possibility of varieties of change or transformation that indeed promise to affect, or even disrupt, the unity and hegemony of *global* and *total* systems of organization, order, and control.

By contrast, paradoxico-criticism, through its identification of inherent contradictions, incoherences, and weak points that are involved in the very structuring of any system of order as such, is much better suited at least to locate the points of the possibility of such global disruption, if indeed there be any such. Here, moreover, the yield of critical thought in its identification of such "weak points" of structure as such is not necessarily the replacement of one *determinate* structure with another, equally determinate one, but rather the identification and multiplication of the structurally necessary *indeterminacy* which the phenomena of the undecidable (in Derrida's sense) and the state of exception (in Agamben's sense) witness. This recognition provides, at the very least, a critical position from which it is possible to interrogate and challenge the legitimating claims of necessity that provide ideological as well as material support to various total systems of order, regimentation, and economy. For instance, as we saw in Chapter 6, the formal and paradoxico-critical position that we may extract from the interlinked investigations of Wittgenstein and Turing into the axiomatic notions of "computability" and "effectiveness" provides a position from which it is possible to discern the "weak points" of uncomputability and ineffectiveness that must permanently accompany—and structurally problematize—the coherence of any system (economic or political) constitutively devoted to these axioms.[13, 14]

As we have seen in Chapters 5 and 6, paradoxico-criticism thus offers to diagnose and replace the "metaphysical" attempt to guarantee the consistency of practices and the infinite consistent extensibility of rules by means of ideological pictures of effectivity, regularity, and normativity. By contrast, Badiou's own project, cleaving to the axiomatic value of consistency as fully as either of the sovereign orientations (while differing from them in its sacrifice of totality, or completeness), appears unable to sustain anything like this critique of techniques and practices. Rather, in that Badiou shares with the sovereign orientations the assumption of consistency, and even sees formal thought as impossible outside this assumption, his ethico-political thought appears to inscribe the "ideolog-ical" guarantee of effectivity as completely as do either of the sovereign orientations (constructivism and onto-theology). There is even a sense in which the axiomatic of consistency in Badiou's ethical-political thought, which functions there both as a necessity and prescription, undermines itself in a way that is strikingly reminiscent of the sovereign double bind (Chapters 1 and 5) and indeed threatens further to undermine Badiou's claim to issue any *coherent* recommendation of action.

This comes to the fore in Badiou's short 1993 book *Ethics: An Essay on the Understanding of Evil*. Here, as he often does, Badiou identifies the "ethic of truths" to be followed by the subject of an event as "the principle of consistency";[15] this is the maxim "Keep going!", the impera-tive never to give up on fidelity to the infinite consequences of a Truth. On the other hand, just a few pages later, Badiou identifies several figures of Evil, each of which is correlative to the power of the Good that the pursuit of Truths amounts to. In fact, at least one of these figures of Evil results from a *totalization* of this power. Specifically, this is the claim, on the basis of the relentless pursuit of a truth in accordance with the maxim of consistency, to "name the whole of the real."[16] The *impossibil-ity* of such a power of total naming is, of course, a formal consequence of Badiou's axiomatic choice for incompleteness rather than inconsistency. Here, however, it also bears the whole ethical charge of the difference between good and evil itself. In somewhat contradictory fashion, there-fore, the very maxim of consistency which prescribes the Good as the relentless pursuit of Truths turns over, if it is thought as complete or even completable, into the most formally distinct figure of Evil. This is, it appears, just another instance of the sovereign double bind which attempts to impose the good of the continuance of effective techniques by means of a formal prohibition of the "impossible" of contradiction. This is apparently the double bind that must result from *any* position that attempts to preserve consistency on the level of practices or inscribe its guarantee on the level of their motivation. It leaves aside the formally radical possibility of a thoroughgoing *critique* of the attempt to guaran-tee consistency which challenges existing practices, techniques and tech-nologies on the level of the general and abstract demand of effectivity which licenses their claim to be continued, no matter what.

FOUR ORIENTATIONS OF THOUGHT (SECOND LOOK)

Having witnessed some of these differences in the specific oppositions of Badiou to various paradoxico-critical thinkers, above, we are now in a position to return to the formal schema of orientations in thought and con-sider in somewhat more detail the relationships between them. Here, again, is the schema:

Table 9.1 Four Orientations of Thought

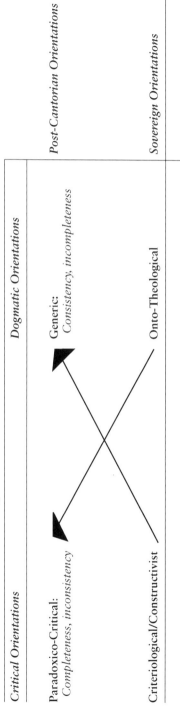

Critical Orientations

Dogmatic Orientations

Paradoxico-Critical:
Completeness, inconsistency

Generic:
Consistency, incompleteness

Onto-Theological

Criteriological/Constructivist

Post-Cantorian Orientations

Sovereign Orientations

We can recapitulate, also, the definitions for each of the four orientations:

Paradoxico-critical: Any position that, recognizing reflexivity and its paradoxes, nevertheless draws out the consequences of the being of the totality, and sees the effects of these paradoxes always as operative within the One of this totality.

Generic: Any position that, recognizing reflexivity and its paradoxes, denies the being of the totality and sees these paradoxes as traversing an irreducible Many.

Criteriological: Any position that attempts to delimit the totality consistently from a stable point *outside* of it.

Onto-Theological: Any position that sees the totality as complete and consistent in itself, though beyond the grasp of finite cognition, which is located simply *within* the totality.

All of these are positions are essentially determined in relation to their thinking of the totality of what is or can be named. But thinking about totalities (even if we deny their existence) is always also thinking about limits; we have, then, four topological figures of the limit, and of the operations of thought at the limits.

Paradoxico-Critical: The thought of the limit is the *inconsistent* thought of in-closure: in thinking the limit, we are both within and without the totality we think.

Generic: The consistent thought of the limit is always only possible from the perspective of a Truth, which is always essentially beyond any specific situation and cannot be fully stated while remaining within any such situation.

Criteriological: The consistent thought of the limit is possible from an unproblematic theoretical position simply *outside* the limit thereby thought.

Onto-Theological: The limit is consistent and coherent in itself, but cannot be conceived by finite thought, except as an infinite mystical excess.

Correlative to these, as well, we can discern four figures of *infinity* in its entry into human life:

Paradoxico-Critical: The infinite enters human life at the point of the paradox of reflexivity, as the problematic *presupposition* of language, meanings, and practices.

Generic: The infinite is the inexhaustible resource of a Truth which calls forth the asymptotic progress of situations by means of its infinite, generic procedure.

Criteriological: The actual infinite does not exist; all that exists or can be discussed is finite.

Onto-Theological: The infinite is an absolute transcendent being, unreachable by human thought.

Finally, and symmetrical to these (since as we have seen, the question of infinity is always closely connected with that of reflexivity) we have four figures of formal reflexivity, which suggest varying positions and structures of the reflexive *subject* as well:

Paradoxico-Critical: The permanent structural *possibility* of reflexivity is the source of the effectiveness of essential paradoxes, which define the nature of meaning and signification as such.

Generic: The *actuality* of reflexivity (as auto-nomination or as the appearance of the transcendental index of a world within that world itself) is the source of every possibility of real structural change.

Criteriological: Reflexivity does not take place within the world, but rather as a transcendental function outside it. (This is, e.g., the position of Wittgenstein's *Tractatus*.)

Onto-Theological: Reflexivity takes place as the activity of a *substance* within the world, for instance, as reflection in consciousness or as the action of the subject.

The schematism naturally invites the question of which philosophers, both contemporary and historical, occupy which orientations. Since the orientations are each exceedingly broad and general, it is probably possible to detect elements of *each* of them in virtually *all* of the great philosophers of the tradition, including in an exemplary fashion (as we have seen repeatedly) Plato himself. But for the purposes of the present analysis, the really decisive formal articulation of the history of philosophy is the one that takes place historically in the first half of the twentieth century, and is witnessed formally by the recognition of the essential paradoxes of reflection and totality (what are sometimes called the "semantic" and "set-theoretical" paradoxes). This is the fundamental formal divide that separates the "bottom" (sovereign) positions—criteriology and onto-theology—from the "top" (post-Cantorian) two, and it yields the essential articulation between philosophical systems that retain the attempt to combine consistency with completeness (the bottom two) and those that perceive the incompatibility between consistency and completeness, thereby giving up on the attempt to characterize the totality of existence in a single *consistent* account.

Thus, despite the extent to which previous philosophical positions might indeed *anticipate* the methods and even results of the generic and paradoxico-critical orientations, it is important to note that these orientations are *essentially* twentieth-century (or twenty-first-century) phenomena and do not fully exist as such prior to the twentieth century. This means that the great philosophical systems, if we are to give each of them a univocal reading in terms of our schema, must uniformly be read as representatives either of onto-theology or criteriology, or as combining elements of both. Again, the essential mark of such a "bottom-level" position is simply the attempt to preserve both consistency and completeness by attempting to produce a *consistent* account of the All, and this does seem to be an essential characteristic of all of the systems that have not grasped, and reckoned with, the radical formal paradoxes of reflexivity.

We can see, as well, how this determines the specific positions and orientations of traditional philosophy in several specific cases. For instance, we saw that onto-theology combines the interpretation of *infinity* as an absolute, unthinkable excess with the figure of *reflexivity* as the substantial action of the subject. Both of these commitments are represented in an exemplary fashion in Descartes, who thinks the infinite in theological fashion as the essentially transcendent absolute, and conceives of the constitutive reflexive action of "finite substance" as the self-conscious reflection of a substantive subject, the *cogito*.

By way of contrast, Kant is, of course, the first great criteriologist. His project of tracing the boundaries of human knowledge by means of a critical elucidation of its limits represents (as both Badiou and, in a different way, Heidegger have emphasized) the greatest classical figure of human finitude and limitation, whereas reflection is conceived as the synthetic activity of a transcendental subject located outside the (empirical) world. This is not to say that there are not significant and telling *anticipations*—and at times, very close ones—in Kant of both the paradoxico-critical and the generic orientations. The cosmological antinomies of the *Transcendental Dialectic* are, in particular, exemplary instances of the kind of paradox on whose necessity the paradoxico-critical orientation systematically trades. In fact, the limit-contradictions they evince between the hypothesis of a bounded and that of an unbounded cosmological totality are essentially the same as the topology of in-closure which paradoxico-criticism recognizes as the essential structure of all thinking about limits. *Nevertheless*—and here again is the point of essential difference between virtually all classical positions and the twentieth-century ones—Kant understands the antinomies uniformly as *resolvable* from the stable position of transcendental idealism, and thereby preserves even in their face the conjunction of consistency and completeness. Here, this conjunction takes the characteristically criteriological form of the assumption of a stable "outside" position—that of the transcendental subject—which is able to think the totality of the knowable, completely and consistently, from beyond its boundaries.[17]

Something similar is true of the result of Kant's larger consideration in the *Dialectic* of what he calls the "transcendental Ideas" (the Ideas of God, World, and Soul), according to which the objects of these Ideas are never given to knowledge or possible experience, but must instead be conceived as the *foci imaginarius* of an infinitely projectable process of thought, in the course of which they can be considered to have "regulative" but never "substantive" employment. This conception of the regulative Idea, to which thought can progressively approximate but can never reach, is of course similar in at least some respects to the generic orientation in its conception of the unfolding of events as successive and progressive approximations to the infinity of a Truth. The (perhaps less than fully obvious) resemblance here between Badiou and Kant has been noted in the critical literature, and we will return to it below.[18] For now it is sufficient simply to note the difference that nevertheless again separates Kant from either of the "top" two orientations which take account of the radical implications of the formal paradoxes. It is that Kant, unlike Badiou, again thinks of the progress of thought toward the Ideas as a *unitary* development: one that can be treated in the unity of the single development of what can be conceived of as *a* (single) history, and so is not divided through an irreducible multiplicity of worlds. Thus, Kant again ultimately reconciles the threat posed by paradox to the conjunction of consistency and completeness from the position of a transcendent subjectivity which guarantees the conjunction by locating reflection, self-constitution, or "auto-affection" *outside* the empirical world. Despite important differences, this is also the structure of "transcendental phenomenology" in Husserl (where it yields the most fundamental reflective method of the phenomenological project, the transcendental *epoche*) and up to the contemplation of the "ontological difference" between being and beings in Heidegger (who is, as noted earlier, a special case).

In an even more pronounced way, Hegel's dialectical system contains the formal elements of paradox and contradiction that are essential to the paradoxico-critical and generic orientations. Doubtless, through his understanding of the mechanism of dialectic, the articulation of contradictions, and the paradoxical dialectical journey of self-recognition, Hegel will have been the single pre-twentieth-century philosopher who most profoundly considered the formal structure of reflexivity and its constitutive paradoxes prior to their symbolic articulation in the systems of formal logic and structuralism in our time. Nevertheless, whatever the depth of his recognition and use of these structures, Hegel must too be considered conceptually *prior* to this great twentieth-century articulation in that, whatever his use or development of paradoxes and contradiction, he too sees them as ultimately capable of reconciliation in a complete and (ultimately) consistent system. This is true not only with respect to the notorious final chapter of the *Phenomenology* (about which too much has probably been said), which deploys the position of a universal reconciliation in "absolute knowing," but also in a more structurally fundamental way with respect to the logical structure of the dialectic itself, which exploits the relentless power of the negative always ultimately to *reconcile* and *overcome* particular contradictions.[19]

With this in mind, it is possible to see the twentieth-century investigation of formalism and its consequences, in both its symbolic-logical and structuralist modes, as having articulated what is indeed a profound and decisive break with the history of philosophy hitherto, in making possible and even obligatory the two orientations which are today exhaustive. No longer will it be possible, given the developments of the twentieth century, to conceive of the totality of being as tractable in a single and *consistent* story. No longer, accordingly, will any system of philosophy be able to operate on the basis of the unargued presumption of the possibility of such an account. This much is common to both Badiou and the multiple representatives of the paradoxico-critical orientation, and it is indeed revolutionary. It marks the radical and discontinuous break from any traditional thinking of the political or its constitutive law which the consequences of formalism, simultaneously "abstract" and concrete, registering their effects simultaneously in the orders of the collective imaginary and the symbolic, and now massively implemented and realized in the effectiveness of the technical and electronic control and exchange of information around the globe, will have demanded in our time.

BADIOU AND CONSTRUCTIVISM

Turning back once more to the schema of the four positions, though, what does it show us about the relative *merits* of the paradoxico-critical and the generic orientations, between which contemporary thought thus seems forced to decide?

One of the first things to notice is that, as we can see from the expanded perspective offered by giving the fourfold schema in full, there is, perhaps surprisingly, a profound, deep, and far-reaching structural *homology* between Badiou's generic orientation and the criteriological orientation that he most vehemently argues against, in *Being and Event* and elsewhere. We can note this homology especially on two points, which we have already noted in passing. The first is ontological *atomism*. Badiou's project, as articulated in *Being and Event* and further developed in *Logics of Worlds*, is axiomatically committed on a deep level to the possibility of decomposing any world into simple, individual elements, which must also be the ultimate points of the application of any *nominative* language to objects in the world. He shares this requirement with the classical representatives of criteriology, most notably, as we have seen, with the system of Wittgenstein's *Tractatus*. This convergence and agreement is indeed surprising, not only in light of Badiou's profound methodological disagreements with Wittgenstein but in view of the latter's shift from criteriology to paradoxico-criticism, which, as we saw in Chapter 6, is both simultaneous to, and deeply linked with, his abandonment of logical atomism.

The second point of homology between the generic orientation and the criteriological, linked to the first, is the assumption of an ontological *hierarchy*. This is the assumption of a rigid and inflexible "logical" order of existence that dictates possibilities of the combination of simple objects, and so imposes an "intrinsic" ordering of complexity on whatever exists. On the side of criteriology/constructivism, its most characteristic expression is Russell's theory of types, which aims to defuse paradox by ensuring from outside the regimentation of existence into a hierarchy of levels. But Badiou also holds ontological reality to be strictly hierarchical. This is evident in his discussion of the implications of Russell's paradox in *Logics of Worlds*:

> Ultimately, it is clear that every thinkable being is drawn from operations first applied to the void alone. A multiple will be all the more complex the longer the operational chain which, on the basis of the void, leads to its determination. The degree of complexity is technically measurable: this is the theory of 'ontological rank'.[20]

Here, Badiou agrees with both Russell and the standard axiomatizations of set theory in holding that the paradox itself demands, by way of response, the imposition of a strictly regimented hierarchy of composition upon the entirety of the set-theoretical universe. As we have seen, this is the basic intuition underlying the constructivist response to the paradoxes as well; it is this intuition that denies the possibility of self-membered sets and requires an axiom of foundation and a restricted axiom of comprehension (or separation) which ensure that each existent set can be understood only insofar as it is capable of being "constructed" or "separated" from others that "already" exist. It is deeply connected, moreover, with the ontological atomism that Badiou and constructivism share. For to demand that ontological reality be "inherently" structured into a strict and uniform order of levels of complexity is also to demand that this order must always be capable of "bottoming out" in some simplest element or elements. For Badiou as for set theory in its classical formulations, this simplest element is simply the empty set, the "name of the void."

Badiou's convergence with constructivism on these points may seem at first surprising, but given our schema, the reason for it is not difficult to see. It is that, as we can trace along the diagonal linking constructivism to the generic orientation, both orientations are foundationally committed to preserving *consistency*. This means that both, in their response to Russell's paradox and the related paradoxes, must avoid seeing it as introducing any *contradiction* into reality or the world. The only way to avoid contradiction while still recognizing the paradox, however, is to impose regimentation and a hierarchical structure while prohibiting axiomatically the existence of certain sets, for instance, the universal set, and the Russell set of all non-self-membered sets.[21] This is the common solution of Russell, Zermelo and Fraenkel, and (as we can now see) Badiou, and it is enshrined in the standard "iterative" conception of sets which is itself formulated by the standard axiomatizations of set theory.

Thus we can see that, *in the "domain" of ontology at least*, Badiou is in complete agreement with constructivism. We can see the extent of this agreement, and the depth of his disagreement with paradoxico-criticism, in the following passage from the discussion of forcing in *Being and Event*, where he discusses the possibility of defining the term "name":

> Of course, the reader could indignantly point out that this definition is circular: I define a name by supposing that I know what a name is. This is a well-known aporia amongst linguists: how does one define, for example, the name 'name' without starting off by saying that it is a name? Lacan isolated the point of the real in this affair in the form of a thesis: there is no metalanguage. We are submerged in the mother tongue (*lalangue*) without being able to contort ourselves to the point of arriving at a separated thought of this immersion.
>
> Within the framework of ontology, however, the circularity can be undone, and deployed as a hierarchy or stratification. This, moreover, is one of the most profound characteristics of this region of thought: it always stratifies successive constructions starting from the point of the void.[22]

As we have seen in the preceding chapters, the Lacanian claim that Badiou cites here and then quickly dismisses for the purposes of "ontology" is central to paradoxico-criticism in all of its forms. By denying this claim and opting for the parameterization that he shares with constructivism, Badiou refuses in a single gesture all of the interrogative and critical resources of the constitutive reflection on language that all of these projects share.

This assumption of a hierarchical order to whatever exists, which Badiou shares with the constructivist, plays an important role in the determination of Badiou's own picture of Truths and their progressive realization, which he would nevertheless uphold as the feature of his theory that *differentiates* him most completely from that orientation. For it means that the partial advent of a Truth through the aleatory occurrence of an event within a situation can indeed ensure the progressive *development* of that situation toward that Truth. Here, the point is not that Badiou thinks of just every multiplicity or set as intrinsically hierarchically ordered—as we have seen, it is, to the contrary, absolutely crucial to his theory that he affirm the possibility of the event, which by being self-membered breaks with the "ontological" hierarchy of ordered sets—but rather that he always understands the *consequences* of the true event as superadded to an existing situation, in such a way that it is thereby transformed in a progressive direction. This transformation is also, assuredly, essentially unpredictable from the perspective of the situation and discontinuous with it; but it will only be an event at all if it deploys some "generic procedure," and hence moves the situation in the direction of some Truth. It is this belief in the possibility of the positive, directed "development" of a situation that makes Badiou's picture of politics, whatever else it may be, in a fundamental sense a *progressivist* one, in the sense that it conceives of the value of political action always and only in terms of its directionality to an (infinite) end. It is thus, as I shall argue in the next chapter, opposed (as on so many other points!) to a paradoxico-critical politics that seeks to replace (what it sees) as the ideology of progress with various forms of critique, interruption, and suspension.[23]

It will be objected, again, that Badiou's picture is nevertheless sharply different from the constructivist's in that, although he does indeed adopt regimentation and the strictness of hierarchy on the level of *ontology*, he nevertheless denies it on the level that matters most to his descriptive project, the level of the event (which, as he points out clearly and repeatedly, is, for him, essentially disjoined from Being). Parameterization, for Russell, is the effect of the prohibition of self-membership with respect to any structure that can be named, discussed, or spoken about at all; whereas for Badiou, it will be said, the analogous prohibition is operative *only within* a certain special domain, the domain of "ontology." And the event which intercedes from "outside" this domain is indeed thinkable only on the basis of a constitutive reversal or suspension of this prohibition. However, there are two critical points to make here. First, even if the objection is admitted, it remains highly significant that within the domain of ontology—which is, after all, the domain of all that can be said to *exist*—Badiou does indeed maintain the existence of the rigid hierarchy of complexity. Whatever its limitations, this demands that every *existent* object and phenomenon has an "intrinsic" degree of complexity and hence can be decomposed in a *unique* way into simplest elements, and that this decomposition is strictly correlative to the order of language in naming objects and their parts. This is already a highly controversial and contestable set of metaphysical assumptions.

But the second point to make, perhaps even more revealing than the first, is that Badiou's attempt to disjoin the "realm of Being," or what is treated by ontology, strictly and rigorously from that of the event, applying regimentation and the prohibition of self-inclusion only to the first "realm" and suspending it in the second, leaves the *status of this prohibition itself* deeply (and perhaps essentially) unclear. As we have seen, the standard set-theoretical approaches uniformly respond to Russell's paradox by *prohibiting* the formation or description of certain sets, in particular those that contain themselves or those that have the "universal" characteristic of containing all sets or all sets with certain properties. But the ultimate failure of these approaches to motivate this solution is evident in that they all succumb to the problem that Russell already noted: namely, that it is impossible to *state* the prohibition without violating it in the very act of statement.

The question to be posed to Badiou, then, is simply whether his attempt to prohibit the existence of self-inclusive and universal sets, *even if officially restricted to "ontology,"* does not succumb to the same problem of self-undermining. Badiou holds that the event is "illegal" with respect to ontology, and this is closely connected with its ability to mobilize and deploy the resources of the "generic set" which "escapes language" (or at least the "language of the situation"?—we shall return to this ambiguity later), in part by naming (*Being and Event*), or containing the transcendental index (*Logics of Worlds*) of, itself. But if we take the realm of "ontology" to include *everything that is* (as it seems, indeed, we must), then how is the "illegality" of this entity, its completely escaping the realm of Being, or anyway "what can be said of it," to be distinguished from its simple non-being? And how and from what position are we then nevertheless able to *say* of this paradoxical, self-including entity that it *is*, that it *exists* or *takes place* at all?

Badiou often identifies ontology with "the discourse on being qua being"[24] as well as with "what can be said of Being *qua* Being"[25] and again with "mathematics" as axiomatized by ZF set theory; given this, the event, which is beyond ontology, will presumably simply be outside this discourse and hence outside what can be said (or asserted) to be. Can, however, its positive being be *thought*, even if it can never be *said*? Badiou seems to give differing answers to this question. Consider, for instance, the quotation from *Logics of Worlds*, above, in which Badiou insists upon the ubiquity of atomism and hierarchy for ontology: "It is clear that *every thinkable being is drawn from operations first applied to the void alone*" (emphasis added). Here Badiou clearly implies that the hierarchical structure of ontology conditions everything which is in any way "thinkable." On the other hand, elsewhere Badiou characterizes ontology as a *"region* of thought" (are there, then, other "regions"?) and suggests that the event is indeed thinkable as "what-is-not-being-qua-being—with respect to which it would not be prudent to immediately conclude that it is a question of non-being."[26] But again, "ontology demonstrates that the event is not" and, through the axiom of foundation "forecloses *extraordinary* [i.e., self-membered] *sets from any existence, and ruins any possibility of naming a multiple-being of the event."*[27]

To a certain extent, Badiou does have a response to these worries, at least in the internal terms by which he applies the formalisms of set theory to the interlinked definition of situations, "being as such" and what escapes it.

This is the claim that he makes in the very first pages of *Being and Event* to the effect that *ontology itself is a situation*. According to this claim, which he goes so far as to call "the wager of this book," this particular situation, captured in the axioms of ZF set theory, is "the *presentation* of *presentation*" in the sense that (given that all that can ever be presented anywhere, according to Badiou, is multiples) it is the "situation of the pure multiple, of the multiple 'in-itself.' "[28] The axioms of set theory will then formulate the rule of the "count-as-one" itself, thus displaying through implicit definitions the structure of the operation that allows any multiplicity to appear as such. In this sense, the ontological axiomatization "seizes the in-itself of the multiple by forming into consistency all inconsistency . . ." and thereby is able to "unfold, without explicit nomination, the regulated game of the multiple such that it is none other than the absolute form of presentation" which is, again, "the mode in which being proposes itself to any access."[29]

If "ontology" can indeed be treated as a *particular* situation, then some of the problems affecting the coherence of supposing events, with their paradoxical structure, to lie "outside" of it can, apparently, be solved. However, it is unclear what this thesis actually amounts to. First, whereas a situation in general is defined as "any consistent presented multiplicity,"[30] the "situation" of ontology is on Badiou's own account the situation that presents the conditions *both* for the possibility of presentation *and* for the ("consistent") multiple *as such*. If this is right, then whatever lies "outside" this situation is presumably neither presented nor in fact a multiple (or set) at all. What, then, are we to make of the schematism of the event itself, which certainly appears to be the presentation, precisely, of the schema of a set (albeit a "non-standard" one)? If the event is not indeed a multiple, it is deeply unclear what kind of thing we should understand it, by Badiou's lights, to be, since for him, given the "non-being of the one," everything that exists in any way at all is indeed a set or multiple. Again, the "ontological situation" is intended, through implicit definitions and axiomatic prohibitions, to display the rules structuring the very "count-as-one" which makes an "inconsistent multiplicity" into a "consistent" one. Are we, then, to suppose that the event completely escapes this law, and thus is in no sense capable of being "counted as one" at all?[31]

Formally speaking, as we have seen repeatedly, the ZF axiom system *allows* the existence of certain kinds of (what we can indeed present in the symbolic language of set theory as) sets, while effectively *prohibiting others* (for instance, the self-membered or non-well-founded sets of the type that Badiou claims the event to be). Speaking in terms of model theory, there are indeed (many and varied) *models* of ZF; these are just configurations of sets, assumed existents, with respect to which the axioms hold true.[32] But it is unclear what could be meant by saying that some particular multiplicity (e.g., the multiplicity that "ontology," as a "situation," is supposed to be) is *correlated* to the axiom structure of ZF itself, in the way Badiou suggests, beyond just saying it is *allowed* by this structure. Here again, as elsewhere,

Badiou seems to waver ambiguously between the axiomatic identification of mathematics *with* ontology and the present claim that "ontology is a situation." Under the heading of the first claim, he seems to assert the *exhaustiveness* of the ZF axioms (i.e., the axiomatic structure of mathematics) in conditioning the existence of all that can in any way be or be presented. Under the heading of the second, however, he attempts to articulate an "outside" to ontology which is populated with entities that, though outside the "presentation of presentation" as such, nevertheless apparently *can* be formally presented as having certain, determinate (and even "mathematical"?) structures. This again leaves rather unclear the formal status of the "other" to "ontology" or "being as such" that the "event" is supposed to be.

It may be that in claiming situational status for "ontology," Badiou means simply to assert that the actual (historical) development of mathematical set theory (i.e., the *theory* of ontology) is a situation in his sense. This is correct, but if this is the claim, then the additional claim that ontology (in *this* sense) conditions existence or being clearly cannot be upheld (this conjunction would seemingly have the consequence of implying that it was impossible to speak of *anything* as existing, prior to Cantor!). Alternatively, it may be that the situational status of ontology is supposed to be a consequence of the claim that the historical pursuit of mathematical set theory is akin to (or actually identical with) what Badiou calls a *truth-procedure.* Officially, only science (rather than mathematics or set theory) is supposed to rank among the actually existing truth-procedures, but there are places at which Badiou appears to assert that mathematics is the most essential basis of the scientific truth-procedure, or even assimilate the latter to the former. Once again, this claim might well characterize the historical development of the *theory* of ontology, but this provides no help in understanding how ontology *itself*—in the sense of the constitutive laws or principles that govern whatever can be or exist—can be understood as simply one situation among others. Clearly, insofar as (historical) ontology has understood its subject matter as the being of whatever is, it has sought a scope and generality that is similar to that of foundational research in mathematics, and the two inquiries can usefully be compared or perhaps even (as Badiou does) assimilated to one another. But in neither case does the description of the specificity of the historical process of *inquiry* or *discovery* help to yield a clear sense of how the *subject matter* can itself be usefully characterized as inherently *local, bounded,* or *restricted* with respect to anything else (especially in view of the strong claims to universality prominently present in both of these historical inquiries).

LANGUAGE OR LANGUAGES?

The event, as schematized in *Being and Event*, is characterized essentially, as we have seen, by the moment of self-inclusion that Badiou takes to represent the act of auto-nomination, whereby it brings about its own designation or naming as such. Now, whatever *its* ultimate structure may be (and in cases of institution and auto-designation this is certainly mysterious, to say the least), nomination is certainly a *linguistic* act. In *Logics of Worlds*, although the issue is slightly more complicated, the role of language remains essentially the same. In both texts, in fact, it is the essential function of language in naming, designating, and providing structural terms for the evaluation of phenomena that alone makes possible the reflexive structure that is essential to the event, and hence to any possibility of real structural change.

It thus seems evident that, even on Badiou's own account, the nominative and descriptive resources of (what we can only assume is) *language itself* plays a decisive, foundational, and absolutely essential role in the account of evental change for which he argues. But what is the status of language itself, for Badiou? Here, rereading *Being and Event*'s formally based account of the interlinked phenomena of multiplicity, excess, the "state" and its regulation, we can detect what is in fact a pervasive ambiguity. This is the ambiguity between *languages*—empirically or socially situated systems, in the *plural*, that are shared by specific communities and vary from place to place and time to time—and *language as such*, in the *singular*, the condition for the possibility of any (human) communication or expression. Badiou equivocates between these two, in large part, because he simply sees no place for *language as such*, over and above the historically and socially specific languages in the plural. That there is no "language" and that there are only "languages" is, as we have seen, the conviction Badiou precipitously shares with both constructivism and the relativist position of contemporary orthodoxy that it supports. However, paradoxico-criticism essentially affirms the opposite and hence works, throughout its itinerary, with the paradoxes and aporias of language (or signification) as such (which is called, by Lacan, "lalangue"; by Derrida, the dual of "speech" and "writing"; by Deleuze, "sense"; and by Wittgenstein, "grammar").

Once we have drawn the distinction between language-as-such and languages, however, it is not difficult to find examples of this equivocation in Badiou's text. The first discussion of language in *Being and Event* is one we have already considered, in which Badiou discusses the implications of Russell's paradox. Chief among these implications, Badiou says, is the demonstration that "the multiple does not allow its being to be prescribed from the standpoint of language alone";[33] this is because the paradox, as Badiou reads it, demands the abandonment of Frege's basic law V, which allowed a set corresponding to any arbitrary linguistic predicate. But clearly, even if we agree with Badiou's gloss on it, the only way to understand this implication about the essential "limitation" of language is as bearing on *language as such*. That is, if Russell's paradox does bear on the powers of language in the way that Badiou suggests, then it will have this bearing on the powers of *any and every* language, and this bearing will depend in no way on the peculiarities of the specific language (or formal system) under consideration.

Nevertheless, a page later, in sketching the precise contradiction that results, Badiou says that the paradoxical Russell set, here designated *p*, ". . . is in excess of the formal and deductive resources of *the* language [de *la* langue]."[34] The decisive interpretive question, which Badiou does not address here, is whether or not these "formal and deductive resources of *the* language" are to be considered equivalent to the "formal and deductive resources" of language *as such*, or of *any* and *every* language insofar as it *is* a language at all. If we are to preserve the implications of Russell's paradox in their full generality, it is necessary to answer in the affirmative: for the paradox bears on the powers of *any* language, or of *all* language. Yet it is clear from Badiou's subsequent development of the point that he has in fact already answered this question in the negative. For from this point on (and again throughout *Logics of Worlds*), he will consistently suppose the implications of the paradoxical structures of self-reference and procedures of diagonalization to bear, simply and exclusively, on *particular* languages or situations. Here, they introduce into such a situation an element or multiplicity which antecedently could not be "thought," "perceived," or "represented" within that situation or by means of *its* language itself, but nevertheless *can be*—and indeed *will be*—nameable by means of the altered language, and thereby within the transformed situation, that the event will have brought about.

On Badiou's gloss, it is a consequence of Russell's paradox that (as is in fact captured in Zermelo's "axiom of separation" or limited comprehension) the operation of language in creating sets must be considered as *subsequent* to the antecedent existence of some set or sets from which they can be separated out. Thus, "Language [Le langage] cannot induce existence, solely a split within existence."[35] According to Badiou, this means that there must be, prior to any and all activity of language, some sort of being that is simply presupposed. Thus "Being must be already-there; some pure multiple . . . must be presented in order for the rule to then separate some consistent multiplicity . . ."[36] This "pure multiple," which is capable of acting as an "absolutely initial point of being," is the void, symbolized by (or identical with?) the empty set, the "proper name of being."[37]

Up to this point, everything is still consistent with the hypothesis that Badiou is indeed describing the structure (and even the inherent limitations) of language as such, including the necessity of a *unique* void element (the empty set) which, as a necessary consequence of the structural "excess" inherent to language as such, also plausibly "haunts" any and every situation. But it is just this point at which Badiou, beginning to slide between language-as-such and languages (or situations) in the plural, precipitously introduces the idea of the *specific* void of a situation:

> What is at stake is an unpresentable yet necessary figure which designates the gap between the result-one of presentation and that 'on the basis of which' there is presentation; that is, the non-term of **any** totality,

the non-one of **any** count-as-one, the nothing **particular to the situation**, the unlocalizable void point in which it is manifest both that the situation is sutured to being and that the *that-which*-presents-itself wanders in the presentation in the form of a subtraction from the count . . .

I term *void* **of a situation** this suture to **its** being. Moreover, I state that **every structured presentation unpresents 'its' void**, in the mode of this non-one which is merely the subtractive face of the count.[38]

Again, the first two instances of "any" could be read as having the sense of "all";[39] the "non-term" in question would then just be the empty set, which is ontologically (i.e., set-theoretically) unique. However, in the very same sentence, Badiou introduces without remark "the nothing particular to *the* situation" and thus the suggestion that there will be, for *each* structured situation, a *particular* element which is "its" (I repeat Badiou's somewhat enigmatic use of scare quotes) own proper void. This is an element that is indeed "void" *for the situation* in that it appears *in the situation* "as" nothing or as "the nothing" (but how, we might ask, is this different from its simply *not* appearing?) but *may nevertheless appear*—and this is crucial—in a *different* situation as something, as an existent and non-void multiple set.

Thus, by means of what at first appears to be an innocuous variation, Badiou has by this point effectively relativized the void to situations and, along with this, *restricted* the action of what he will go on to theorize as the event and its specific effects, as well, to situations, and to the *specific* possibilities of change that they structurally determine. The next step in the demonstration is to argue (pp. 94–96) that, although it is indeed the "anxiety of the void" that haunts every situation and must therefore be "warded off" by any operation that seeks to guarantee the unity and coherence of the situation as such, this "warding off" is accomplished by what Badiou calls, "due to a metaphorical affinity with politics,"[40] the state *of* the situation, its specific "second count" or power set. This recount, by means of which "all situations are structured twice," being both "presented and represented," operates, Badiou says, to "prohibit that catastrophe of presentation which would be [the situation's] encounter with its own void, the presentational occurrence of inconsistency as such, or the ruin of the One."[41] Here, Badiou moves between parallel appositive constructions so quickly that it is difficult to identify the specific level at which he in fact wishes to specify the "action" of the recount or the operation involved in moving from the initial set—what is simply presented—to the power set and hence what is re-presented and hence "re-secured" by the state. However, it is certainly essential for all that follows—and in particular for the event in its capacity to *escape* the state's power of "re-securing," "control," or "mastery"—that the "void" that is thereby foreclosed by the state be a *specific* one, proper to the situation itself. It is only on this basis that a "site" (a set which is itself presented, but none of whose elements are) can then be defined as a multiple "on the edge of the void" and hence capable of founding the unique ability of the event to draw forth its consequences from *what seems from the perspective of the state* to be the void. As Badiou in fact notes, though, "the concept of an evental site" is consequently "neither intrinsic nor absolute"; what will constitute a site will always depend on the specific constitution of the situation in which it occurs.[42] The intervention of the *subject* thus amounts to its faithful tracing of the consequences of this *specific* inexistent, by way of which it will, if the event is indeed successful, be added to the situation as its "generic extension" and subsequently incorporated in the structure (and the state) of the now newly transformed situation.

These implications play an equally prominent role in the theoretical project of *Logics of Worlds*. As we have seen, the work of fidelity to the event is here seen as consisting in the identification of the "specific inexistent" of a world, the specific element whose "degree of existence" is, according to the transcendental structure of the world, zero. If the event is successful, this status will be reversed and the formally minimal will become "maximal" in the newly transformed world thereby produced. This work of "tracing" and following the trace of the "specific inexistent" is, moreover, as we saw above, the whole task of Derrida's "deconstruction" according to Badiou. We had reason to suspect, above, that in thus relegating deconstruction to the tracing of *specific* inexistents, Badiou effectively misses the entire *global* significance of a deconstructive reading that, in accordance with formal results, might indeed otherwise be seen as evincing the place of the structurally necessary undecidable and that which is beyond the signifying power of any significative language *as such*. In any case, returning to *Being and Event*, we can now see that Badiou's equivocation on "language" ultimately permits the whole application of the formal effects of diagonalization and self-reference to the positive doctrine of the event and its changes, which unfold, for Badiou, in each case in a specific, local situation. It also has further and decisive implications when Badiou turns to the critical consideration of constructivism, according to which there can, structurally, never be an event or a generic procedure, since all sets are constructible. Badiou takes constructivism to underlie very broadly what he sees as a dominant conception of the relationship between language and structures of power and order (including, importantly, political ones); thus constructivism is for Badiou not only the "critical—or anti-philosophical— philosophy par excellence"[43] but also one that "universally regulates the dominant conceptions" through the "prohibition that it lays on random conglomerates, indistinct multiples, and unconstructible forms."[44] This is, moreover, the philosophy in which "the state is the master of language" and "the state legislates on existence."[45]

But how should we indeed understand this "prohibition" and this "legislation"? What is it that is actually "excluded" from the "constructible universe" itself, or from the regulative and juridical outlook modeled by it?

What precisely is the status of the paradoxical being "beyond language" which is rigorously excluded not only by the general constructivist formalism itself but—as we must suppose if we follow Badiou here—by the state of each *particular* situation insofar as it forecloses "its own" void and aims to block its own evental transformation?

In a passage that makes a kind of strange *portmanteau* of the pragmatist that Badiou takes the late Wittgenstein to be and the constructivist that he sees in the early Wittgenstein, Badiou again reaffirms—but this time on behalf of constructivism—the fundamental plurality of situations and languages:

> What then does it mean that there are different situations? *It means, purely and simply, that there are different languages.* Not only in the empirical sense of 'foreign' languages, but in Wittgenstein's sense of 'language games'. Every system of marking and binding constitutes a universe of constructible multiples, a distinct filter between presentation and representation. Since language legislates on the *existence* of parts, it is clearly within the being itself of presentation that there is a difference: certain multiples can be validated—and thus exist—according to one language and not according to another. The heterogeneity of language games is at the foundation of a diversity of situations. . . .
>
> It is thus quite possible that being qua being, is One and Immobile. However, constructivism prohibits such a declaration since it cannot be constructed on the basis of controllable parameters and relations within the situation. Such a thesis belongs to the category, as Wittgenstein puts it, of what one has to 'pass over in silence' because 'we cannot speak of [it]'. 'Being able to speak' being understood, of course, in a constructivist sense.[46]

But as we have seen, whatever are the constructivist elements that still remain in Wittgenstein's position in the *Tractatus*, on the very point of its transformation into paradoxico-criticism, he certainly does not intend the prohibition issued by the final remark of the *Tractatus* in this "constructivist" sense. What is declared to be "unsayable" and capable only of being "shown"—if there is indeed anything here at all—is not at all simply what "cannot be constructed on the basis of controllable parameters and relations *within the situation*" but, rather, what cannot be presented by *any language*, and what, preconditioning the possibility of all *sense*, *cannot* be described or represented in linguistic propositions at all (at least without contradiction and paradox). If there is a sense to *this* "prohibition," it will certainly not be that it somehow prohibits from existence or from some particular language any particular object or being that could also be named or seen as existing somewhere else, or by means of another language. As we saw above, this is quite simply the impossible, the contradictory, or the paradoxical being of the linguistic standard—what indeed cannot be represented from any position either simply "inside" or "outside" language as such.

For Badiou, the ultimate definition of constructivism is thus that it is the outlook according to which the state "legislates" on existence through its "mastery" of an *existing, specific* language.[47] Without denying that this definition has a certain provenance in Gödel's formalism of the constructible universe and his formal results, it is important to consider here more closely than Badiou does the extent to which the interpretation that links this formalism, in Badiou's text, to the issues of language, existence, and politics really has a good foundation in this formalism itself.

When Badiou introduces the distinction between the situation and its state along with the parallel distinction between presentation and representation, he emphasizes that the state, so defined, might well be considered to contain everything within a situation which can be grouped together under a common name or concept by *any criteria whatsoever* (no matter how complex). Insofar as we can indeed consider the subsets of the original set which are themselves the elements of the power set to represent all of the possible groupings of the original elements (and hence *whatever* falls under the possible concepts of *any* language), this is a reasonable implication. And it follows from it, together with Cantor's theorem (or the theorem of the point of excess), that there will always therefore be, as a consequence of diagonalization, a certain excess of the representable (or conceptualizable) as such over what is simply present. This much is common ground with the paradoxico-critical orientation, which also discerns in the formal operation of diagonalization, and documents in real cases, the consequences of the radical and structural excess of the linguistic or symbolic over the real of what it represents.

But can we really understand the excess that thus results from the action of the concept (or simply the arbitrary regrouping of the elements of an initial set, finite or infinite) as producing a structure that is in fact potentially "legislative," "restrictive," and even "exclusionary" in the ways Badiou suggests? It is difficult to see that we can do so, at least by means of anything other than a completely ungrounded metaphorical leap. For given the analogy to language as developed so far, the "state" of a situation comprising a number of objects (whether a finite or infinite number) will simply coincide with what, of those objects and their possible groupings, can be linguistically described (or, for that matter, conceptualized) *in any way at all*. That is, it will include every property, aspect, or feature of those objects, or any grouping of properties, aspects, or features, that can in any way be conceptualized or described by any linguistic description, no matter how complex and (this is essential) *in any language whatsoever*. There is no reason to assume that this totality of the conceptualizable will, *on the one hand, depend on or be limited by the terms or names that are in fact available within a particular, empirical language, or on the other, that it is intelligible to suppose this totality to be "mastered" by anything like a limited and instituted consensus, a socially regulative norm, or a "state" in the political sense.*

For (on the one hand) what does not have its own name in a specific language may nevertheless certainly be described by means of it, through the complication of descriptions and the elucidation of features;[48] and (on the other) there surely has never been a state (in the political sense) whose power extends to the very dictation of terms and names in such a way as to determine what is intelligible or conceptualizable *as such.*[49] This is *not*, emphatically, to deny that there is an important sense in which the question of the boundaries of language bears on that of the formation and structure of political communities; *indeed, the whole political significance of paradoxico-criticism lies in its insistence on considering this bearing,* and so producing a linguistic-critical understanding of what is involved in the structure of a political unity as such. But the entry of the question of language into the question of politics is not, from the paradoxico-critical position, nearly as localized and situated as Badiou constantly supposes. Its consistent implication is not the (socially transformative) demonstration of the actual existence of the contingently "inexistent" which is excluded or discounted within the empirical structure of a particular community or society, but rather the permanent paradox of our relation to language, the profound aporia (whose end we do not, I venture to suggest, as of yet even *begin* to see) of the capture of human life in the structural order of the symbolic as such.

To be able to produce the "militant" account of the event in its resistance to determinate political structures that Badiou offers, we can now see, he must rely on (at least) two highly questionable projective connections. The first is the connection that limits the scope of a language's designative power to *predicative* definitions (in the constructivist sense; see Chapter 7); and the second is the connection that links what is "sayable" in a language, so conceived, to the restrictive power of a *state* in the political sense. Neither connection is justified by any empirical example, or any obviously sound conceptual link. Yet Badiou does not hesitate to exploit both in order to present the impression of an invocation of specific forms of political action that is (somehow) *rigorously and specifically* grounded in the formalisms themselves.

This is significant in connection with the sorts of *specific* calls to action that are sometimes made on the basis of Badiou's theoretical work. For instance, the concepts of the generic and the indiscernible which Badiou develops in *Being and Event* have sometimes been used to support calls for the recognition and eventual inclusion of people who are marginalized and unrecognized by the *official* apparatus of recognition deployed by a particular (political) state, for instance, the "undocumented" immigrant workers of North America or (an example Badiou himself has specifically developed in another context) the undocumented or *sans-papiers* of France. Now, of course there are eminently good independent reasons to deplore the effective marginalization of these groups, and to attempt to restore their rights of citizenship or participation. But to suggest that this imperative is in any way supported by a formal investigation of the powers or limits of any *language* is highly implausible in this kind of case, where what is at issue is *not* particularly the absence of names or the need for new auto-nominations to supplement the designative powers of the existing language, but rather a specifically constituted practice and regime of exclusion within a particular empirical state.[50]

There is, indeed, a related problem here that bears on the whole question of Badiou's use of formal structures itself. For it is one thing to give a formal theory, even a rigorous and sophisticated one, of how we might *think* of what evental or punctual change actually *is* (even assuming that we can follow Badiou in all of the other aspects of his, often very imaginative, projections of formal structures into political categories); it is quite another actually to work toward changes of this sort in real, already-structured domains, or even to know in much detail *how* to go about doing so. Indeed, insofar as Badiou's theory of evental change demands that the event, if it is to be truly transformative, amounts to the sudden, unpredictable advent to appearance of a kind of phenomenon that could not even possibly be discerned within the previously existing situation, it seems to deprive us even of the possibility of anticipating, even in vague outline, these possibilities of radical change or locating their likely sites of appearance until after the event. Thus, it is not clear that Badiou's elaborate theory can actually play a significant role—despite its strong rhetoric—in supporting the kinds of change it ostensibly envisions.[51]

These points may not take us very far in the critical interpretation of Badiou's theory itself. Still, they are worth making in a context where the linkage between abstract theoretical and philosophical reflection on the limitations of various formal systems, on one hand, and specific forms of political action (whether of a liberal-progressivist or a more classically leftist variety), on the other, is all too often simply assumed. Admittedly, as well, Badiou himself is at least sometimes much more sensitive to the tenuousness of these linkages than his prevailing contemporary reception (at least in the U.S.) might suggest. We should not forget, for instance, his repeated insistence that politics (*along with* the three other truth procedures) is but a *condition* of philosophical thought and reflection, which must always "come second" and therefore cannot by itself *determine* imperatives of specific political action or motivation. Nevertheless, the question remains of whether the formalisms Badiou rigorously develops can provide (even so much as) a *conceptual* or *theoretical* basis for the "militant" politics of the event or its pursuit in relation to specific political state structures.

FORCING, EXCESS, AND TRUTH: FORMAL CRITIQUE

What, then, should finally be said about Cohen's complex apparatus of forcing, to which the last third of *Being and Event* is dedicated and on which Badiou places the whole burden of his positive argument against constructivism and for the possibility of the event?

Recall once more the general argumentative structure.[52] Given the formal linkage which Badiou finds between constructivism (as formulated by Gödel) and the hypothesis of the power of the state (now in the formal rather than the political sense) over names, and hence its structural prohibition of anything having the self-inclusive structure of the event, both constructivism and its prohibition of the event are equivalently linked to Cantor's continuum hypothesis in its general form (which asserts that the cardinality of the power set of any set is the very "next" cardinality). And that the constructivist hierarchy is, indeed, a model of ZF for which the generalized continuum hypothesis is *true* is just what Gödel demonstrated in 1939. Given this, it is important in order to demonstrate the formal possibility of the event (as Badiou schematizes it), *given* ZF, to show that there is a model in which the generalized continuum hypothesis is *false*; and this is what Cohen does with forcing.

First, there is a (meta-)formal point which Badiou does not deny, but which is important to keep in mind in considering the use he makes of Cohen's results. Cohen's results do not in *any* sense, or on *anyone*'s interpretation (even Badiou's), *show that the continuum hypothesis is false*. All that they do is show that there is a *model* on which it is false, and we know (from Gödel) that there are *also* models on which it is true. So with respect to the axioms of ZF, all that we can say based on the conjunction of Gödel's and Cohen's results is that the truth (or falsity) of the continuum hypothesis is strictly *independent* of the truth or falsity of these axioms. This means that (insofar as we have a clear sense of what it means to suppose an axiom system such as ZF to be "true" or "false" at all) even if we suppose ZF to be true of the actual universe or reality, the continuum hypothesis is just as "likely" to be true as it is to be false (and if it *is* true, of course, the event in Badiou's sense is again structurally ruled out).

More significantly, though, the demonstrated independence of the continuum hypothesis (CH) from the ZF axioms may just as well be taken to suggest that we have no real grasp on what it would mean *for* the CH to be true or false at all. Given the results, for instance, we can certainly say that there will never be any more direct evidence, either for or against the CH, provided by anything we can derive from ZF or ZFC themselves.[53] So one option, and certainly one that seems plausible given the demonstration of independence, is simply to declare the CH *meaningless*, and accordingly abandon the attempt to derive *anything* from it (or its denial) of any ontological or meta-ontological significance.[54] Some theorists have in fact expressed the view that the CH is "inherently vague" and that it is, accordingly, "meaningless to speak of its truth value."[55]

Stopping short of this, however, another reasonable response to the conjunction of Gödel and Cohen's results is to consider the CH to be simply *undecidable*, indeed perhaps a paradigm instance of the kind of undecidability that we have every reason to suspect, given Gödel's other famous result, the incompleteness theorems. In fact, this interpretation is suggested by none other than Gödel himself:

Of course, if it is interpreted this way [i.e., from the standpoint of the possibility of its proof in ZF], there are (assuming the consistency of the axioms) *a priori* three possibilities for Cantor's conjecture: It may be demonstrable, disprovable, or undecidable. The third alternative (which is only a precise formulation of the foregoing conjecture, that the difficulties of the problem are probably not purely mathematical), is the most likely. [56]

The remark bears interesting connections to the suggestion Gödel makes in a footnote to his 1931 paper, in which he draws the link between the undecidable and issues of transfinite cardinality explicitly:

The true source of the incompleteness attaching to all formal systems of mathematics, is to be found—as will be shown in Part II of this essay—in the fact that the formation of ever higher types can be continued into the transfinite . . . whereas in every formal system at most denumerably many types occur. . . . Namely, one can show that the undecidable sentences which have been constructed here always become decidable through adjunction of sufficiently high types (e.g. of the type ω to the system **P**). A similar result holds for the axiom systems of set theory. [57]

Here, Gödel both connects the issue at stake in the continuum hypothesis to the general question of the relationship of (denumerable and recursively axiomatizable) formal systems to what they prove or demonstrate, and suggests in particular that the undecidabilities which his results show to be a necessary feature of the latter may accordingly characterize the CH as well.

Given the demonstrated *independence* of the continuum hypothesis from the axioms of ZF set theory, there is in fact good reason to doubt whether the problem of relative "size" that it appears to pose is in fact well-posed at all. Recall that the only case in which there is a straightforward procedure for directly comparing cardinalities is the case of *finite* sets. Though it is clear from Cantor's theorem that the cardinality of the continuum, which is the same as that of the power set of the natural numbers, is in some sense "greater" than that of the set of naturals itself, it is not at all clear what it means to say that the subsequent iteration of the power set operation produces *any* "larger" sets (beyond sets with the cardinality of the continuum) at all. The problem here is that the power set operation is strongly "impredicative": the "excess" it produces by means of diagonalization, and which the power set axiom requires, is not determinable by any "predicative" property or statement (unless, of course, we work within the constructible universe, where the extent of power sets *is* determined by the extent of available predicates). This means, as Hallett argues and as is confirmed by Cohen's proof of the independence of the continuum hypothesis from the axioms, that the "size" of this excess is in many ways simply mysterious.

Moreover, in relation to the usual "limitation of size" arguments (see Chapter 1) which attempt to ensure the non-existence of the "too big" sets (such as the Russell set, or the set of all sets) by restricting impredicativity, it is not at all evident, as Hallett argues, that the application of the power set axiom does not serve to generate exactly these ("contradictory") sets! Thus, as Hallett suggests, we may have "no positive reason to assume that even only one application of the power set axiom to an infinite set [e.g., its application to the set of naturals in order to produce the continuum] will not exhaust the whole universe" of numbers and sets.[58] If this is right, though, then rather than demanding or even suggesting the existence of an open hierarchy of transfinite sets of increasing cardinalities beyond that of the continuum (whatever it might be), but nevertheless still "small enough" to exist as coherent sets, the application of the power set axiom beyond finite sets remains, as Hallett suggests, "just a mystery," and the real nature of the "transfinite hierarchy" remains at least as obscure today as when Cantor first struggled with it.[59]

On *any* of these conclusions—if the continuum hypothesis is taken, for instance, as undecidable, or meaningless, or indeed simply as formally independent of ZF set theory—it will not be possible for Badiou to claim that Cohen's technique of forcing simply *demonstrates*, against constructivism, nominalism, or any other position, that there certainly *are* events in his sense. Nor does Badiou indeed actually claim this, although his rhetoric sometimes suggests it; at most he claims, as he indeed can, that Cohen's techniques show events to be formally *possible*, and thus not susceptible to being ruled out *a priori* on a formal level. That is, it will not be possible for the formal structure of ZF, or anything derivable from it, to *rule out* the possibility that, to any existing model of the axioms, there is superadded a "generic extension" which, indiscernible from the perspective of the model itself, forces the "size" of the extended model to take any arbitrary cardinality.

What, though, is really the significance of this for the process of introducing and actualizing radical, structural change? To see in more detail how Badiou means to draw this connection specifically, we must again consider the structure of what he terms the "state" and the demonstration of its essential quantitative "excess" over the size of the situation. Recall that Badiou links the question of the possibility of eventual change to the question of the "measure" of this state excess. In the constructible universe, for instance, the excess of the power set over the original set is always "measurable" in that it can be regimented and "controlled" strictly by the regular sequence of cardinals: $\aleph_0$, $\aleph_1$, $\aleph_2$, etc. By contrast, outside the constructible universe or in any model where the generalized continuum hypothesis fails, "state excess" is immeasurable, according to Badiou, in that it is possible to *suppose* the cardinality of the state to exceed that of the original situation *by whatever degree we like*. In fact we do so by creating a generic extension of arbitrary cardinality and "forcing" it to be "between" the situation and its state on the chain of cardinals. What is most significant about this possibility to Badiou is that it makes the degree of state excess into essentially a matter of "arbitrary decision" rather than one that is fixed ontologically or structurally. According to Badiou, this "disperses the prospects of any evaluation of the power of the state" and "introduces randomness into the heart of what can be said of being."[60] Later on, when he discusses the action of the faithful subject in pursuing a generic procedure and introducing the "indiscernible," generic set, Badiou will suggest that such a subject in so doing reintroduces a "measure of state excess," although this time through *decision* rather than calculation.[61]

As we saw above, the analogical connection that Badiou introduces between the *quantitative* excess that the power set exhibits and the state's "power" over existence, language, or names is questionable on several grounds. Even if it is possible to consider the power set operation to take us from whatever is simply present in a situation to all that can be conceived of or said about it, this has little obvious connection to any "powers" of restriction, exclusion, or prohibition, and the sense in which something like the power set *itself* could be said to possess such "powers" is in any case far from clear. It is true that in the *constructible* universe there is demonstrably no possibility, given a set and its power set, of a third set existing with a cardinality greater than that of the first but smaller than that of the second. In a model (such as the ones whose possibility Cohen demonstrates) where the continuum hypothesis fails, this *is* possible, and if we maintain the analogy between the power set and representation, this possibility is indeed somewhat surprising. As Badiou says, "It is as though, between the structure in which the immediacy of belonging is delivered, and the metastructure which counts as one the parts . . . a chasm opens, whose filling in depends solely upon a conceptlesss choice."[62] That is, given a model on which the CH fails, and maintaining the analogy between the state and (conceptual) representation, there is in such a model the possibility, given an initial set, of a set that, in "regrouping" the elements of the initial one, contains "more" than the initial one, but nevertheless "less" than is in the power set, and in such a way that what is in the second set essentially cannot be conceptualized by means of predicative terms and definitions within the existing situation. However, we still lack much of a sense of what this "more" and "less" actually mean; and there remains no evident basis for considering issues of power, restriction, or regulation to come to bear here at all.

What, though, about the more specific aspects of the forcing relation, which are especially important to Badiou in that this relation provides the formal basis for his claim that it is possible for a subject *within* a limited situation to *force* a post-evental truth, thus ensuring that the production of the generic set by the faithful subject can indeed transform the existing situation fundamentally? The core of Cohen's demonstration is his construction of a model in which it is possible to force the truth of the statement that the cardinality of the continuum has an arbitrary value, as high as we like. This is accomplished, for Badiou, by means of the subject's deployment of the forcing relation, which, on his gloss, consists in "investigating" various conditions to see which truths they force. For Badiou, this verifies the ability of the faithful subject to produce within the situation an excessive and "immeasurable" extension which materializes or manifests a segment of an infinite truth.

On formal grounds, however, there are at least two problems with this interpretation of Cohen's results. The first problem is that the activity of any actual subject will only, of course, be *finite* in extent. As Fraser (2006) has shown, though, this implies that the results of the actual forcing process, over any finite span, are always *indistinguishable* from other structures, which by no means imply the manifestation of an infinite Truth in Badiou's sense.[63] In particular, in 1963 Saul Kripke exploited a version of forcing to give a model-theoretic semantics for intuitionist logics (in particular, for Heyting calculi, which are just the structures that Badiou uses to model relations of appearance in *Logics of Worlds*).[64] Deployed in this way, the forcing relations (which are exactly similar to the ones that Cohen employs) allow, at any moment, for known truths, known falsehoods, and also the third category (essential to all forms of intuitionist logic) of the *unknown* or as-yet-unverified. The upshot, as Fraser suggests, is that over any finite extent of the forcing procedure, this procedure will be indistinguishable, from *within* the situation at least, from the investigation of ordinary, garden-variety statements in an intuitionist framework. As such, it neither implies nor requires anything like a Truth in Badiou's sense.

It is thus only from the "outside" perspective of ontology itself, where we contemplate the entire infinite extent of a truth-procedure as *completed*, that we can rigorously distinguish what is "in fact" such a procedure from what is simply a finite, intuitionist inquiry into certain claims. But it is just this perspective that the faithful subject of an event, situated as she must be *within* the situation that provides the event's site, evidently cannot take. As Fraser argues, this again raises questions about the extent to which it is possible for such a subject actually to make use of ontological results such as the results of forcing (rather than merely their finite, intuitionist *ersatz*), or indeed for "ontology" itself (whose logic is classical rather than intuitionist) to be thought of as a historically specific and temporal "truth-procedure."

The second problem is that, even if we *may* take the "outside" perspective of the infinite sets superadded to an existing situation in order to force the truth of statements of arbitrarily high cardinality, it is unclear that the truth of these statements in the newly extended situation can *actually* establish, as Badiou says it does, the essentially *ontological* result of the "immeasurability" of excess. This is again a consequence of the fact that the falsehood of the CH is demonstrated only within a *model*, rather than in "ontology" or ZF set theory more generally. Because of this, it is at least possible to see the "demonstration" of the falsity of the CH within the specific model as being much more an artifact of the limitations imposed in constructing that model than as witnessing anything fundamental about the extent of possible action or change *per se*. Specifically, in a 2008 introduction to Cohen's book *Set Theory and the Continuum Hypothesis*, Martin Davis remarks that the question of the truth or falsity of the CH is still very much open, at least for some researchers; and for those, in particular, who think that it may be true and a consequence of some as-yet-undiscovered axioms, there is a readily available "deflationary" explanation for the apparent success of Cohen's demonstration. In particular, Davis suggests, for these researchers:

> The models constructed by forcing are seen from 'outside' as thin wispy creatures by no means doing justice to Cantor's expansive vision. In such a model, sets that we can see to have the cardinality $\aleph_0$ are seen from 'inside' the model as having different cardinalities simply because the one-one correspondences required to show that the sets have the same cardinality are not to be found inside the model.[65] (pp. viii–ix)

This phenomenon of cardinal "collapse" is familiar from related results in set theory and model theory, most prominently the Löwenheim-Skolem theorem, which establishes that every theory that has any transfinite model has a countable model.[66] This leads to what some have called "Skolem's paradox": that statements that are assuredly "about" uncountably infinite sets can be reinterpreted as being about (only) countable ones, even though they retain their truth-values.[67] The paradox is resolved, however, by noting that cardinality is not an *absolute* property of sets, but depends on the availability of one-to-one correspondences (which are themselves sets). In various restricted models where the requisite one-to-one correspondences are not available, all statements about cardinalities are effectively reinterpreted. If something like this is indeed occurring in the case of forcing, then Cohen's demonstration that it is possible to "make" the cardinality of the continuum arbitrarily high by means of a decision evidently reflects little more than the fact that, in the attenuated models used for forcing, there are simply not enough correspondences available actually to "decide" the question purely in terms of the structure of the model itself.

We here witness another effect of the decisive general difference between the paradoxico-critical orientation and Badiou's with respect to the status of the universe; since the paradoxico-critic *can* make sense of the idea of the (whole) of the ontological universe of sets, she can also consider the possibility that model-theoretic results such as Cohen's (or Skolem's) are simply artifacts of the restrictions needed to create specific models, artifacts which might dissolve from the perspective of the ontological universe as a whole.[68] If this is the case, then the room for "decision" left to the subject by the forcing procedure may be in an important sense illusory, merely a consequence of the artificial restriction of certain models but lacking in any fundamental ontological significance. And even given everything that Cohen has demonstrated, it remains *possible*, then, that (given the addition of one or more new axioms) the CH is not only *consistent* with ontology but actually, ontologically true.[69]

Summing up, then, how much significance can Cohen's apparatus of forcing actually be said to have for the "political" or "meta-political" question of what holds power structures in place or can indeed effectively disrupt or transform them? The answer, it seems on the basis of multiple formal as well as interpretive considerations, is: "not much." Almost everything that Badiou says on this question depends on the twofold connection he draws, on one hand, between the power set and the (political) state and, on the other, between both and the "mastery of language," and as we have seen there is little to be said on behalf of either connection. Moreover, even granting a connection between the status of the continuum hypothesis and issues of state power and regulation in the political sense, Cohen's results will have shown *at best* that it is formally (or *de jure*, as Badiou says) *"not impossible"* *to suppose* that our world is structured in such a way that on some occasion or another, an event disrupts this power by undermining its "measure." The results emphatically *do not* demonstrate that such events are real, or even that the actual structure of our world in fact permits them.

Still, this is not to say that there are not other aspects of the formalisms here that remain suggestive, and from which we can perhaps retain something important and relevant to the question of "politics" in a broader and more structural sense. From a paradoxico-critical perspective, in particular, Badiou's identification of the yield of diagonalization—here, the quantitative excess of the power set over its base—with the excessive "power" of the state or its capacity to "control" language is bound to seem implausible, since it depends on the conception of languages as irreducibly multiple and hierarchical, which paradoxico-criticism rejects. For paradoxico-criticism, due to its rejection of the possibility of a "metalanguage" position, it is also essentially impossible for *anything* to master a language from a position simply outside of it. Nevertheless, as we have seen, paradoxico-criticism can agree with Badiou on the essential and highly significant point that diagonalization indeed demonstrates a structural *excess*, inherent to any form of representation or signification.

What, then, is the response of the paradoxico-critic to Cohen's use of diagonalization in showing the possible existence of a "generic extension" which supplements the existing situation with an "indiscernible" set? Without going so far as to agree that this has any important implications for the relative "sizes" or "powers" of various sets, the paradoxico-critic can indeed agree (and here she is clearly distinguished, once again, from the constructivist) that this is a highly significant and revealing result. *In particular*, since the procedure for generating the generic set in effect diagonalizes on all possible names and designations definable within a situation's terms, the demonstration that such a procedure is possible effectively shows the possible *existence* of a being that is indeed *indiscernible* in the sense of not being capturable in the existing language "of the situation." Although we cannot, of course, antecedently understand what such a being can be, and we will not have it as such prior to the completion of an infinite procedure, which will never come, its very possibility demonstrates again the permanent "supplemental" dimension of language, implied by its very structure, through which it maintains in the virtuality of the indiscernible its infinite reservoir of sense.

For paradoxico-criticism, though, as opposed to Badiou, it is not obvious what is meant by discussing the "measure" of this excess. As noted earlier, since Cohen's result (in conjunction with Gödel's earlier one) simply establishes the *undecidability* of the continuum hypothesis from the axioms, it is not justified, on the paradoxico-critical interpretation, to hold that the excessive "size" of the power set is measured or measurable *at all* (that is, in *any* determinate way) by the succession of transfinite cardinals. In view of Gödel's and Cohen's joint results, the cardinal "size" of what Badiou calls state excess and of what is introduced by the generic set remains, in fact, simply *indeterminate*. The real issue here, as Hallett emphasizes, is the nature of the power set operation itself (and of diagonalization, which is its formal basis).

From a paradoxico-critical perspective, we may certainly concur with Badiou's sense of the power set operation as capturing the whole range of the extensions of properties predicable of individuals in the base set, and hence as capturing the formal excess of representation over presentation. The indeterminacy comes in attempting to determine how widely we may take these predicable properties to range through the whole universe of sets. As Hallett points out, there is a sense in which *any* attitude toward the effect of the power set operation involves an attitude toward the extent of the totality of the universe. This is because, since the power set is the set of all *possible* subsets, one's attitude toward it will depend on a determination of which sets it is possible to form, and this determination will necessarily consider properties and features *potentially* ranging over the whole universe. This is at the root of the "impredicativity" of the power set axiom, since it means that it is not generally possible to determine the extent of the power set simply by considering the subsets that are defined in terms of "predicative" properties, whose definition is limited to the original set.[70]

In fact, the result of just such a restriction of the power set to the properties predicable in the original set is the constructible universe of Gödel, in which the continuum hypothesis holds true. Working in the constructible universe renders the power set operation "absolute" by restricting the subsets which can figure in the power set to the *constructible* ones; this essentially *eliminates* the impredicativity of the original, unrestricted power set operation.[71] However, although this restriction might reasonably be thought to capture a restriction of discernibility to the predicative powers of the specific, existing "language of the situation" which cannot describe or even reference anything beyond this situation, there is *no* evident reason to suppose it to coincide with the "predicative" powers of language *in general and as such.* Quite to the contrary, in fact, given the initial identi-fication of the power set with the totality of *representable* unities, what is captured by the (unrestricted) power set operation is much more plausibly the whole totality of the *possible* extensions of *any predicates* (ranging over the members of the initial set) at all. This is not restricted to the predicates "already defined" or corresponding to single terms in an existing historical language, but corresponds rather to the vastly excessive, virtual dimension of *possible* predication that (as we have repeatedly seen) marks the Ideal, virtual dimension of language as such.

   This shows, however, the basic problem with Badiou's whole analogy between the limited sets of the constructible universe and the supposed limitations of specific languages themselves. In particular, whereas the sets of the constructible universe are limited to *predicative* definitions and pred-icatively definable terms (and it is in precisely this sense that they are sup-posed to "restrict existence" by means of language), *there is no reason to suppose that the representative powers of any actual, historical language are in fact limited in this way.* In fact, every actual language is, very plausi-bly, strongly and essentially *im*predicative. This impredicativity is marked not only in the capacity all such languages have to "totalize," to talk of the "all" and the "universe," but also in their inherent capacity for self-reference, which gives them the permanently excessive "latent" dimension we've described in detail. The permanent excessiveness of this dimension, as suggested already by Cantor's theorem and confirmed in Gödel and Cohen's joint demonstration of the actual *unmeasurability* of power sets, is indeed the unmeasurable and strictly incalculable effect of language's own reflection into itself of the *totality* of the universe in which it takes place. But because of its existence as a structural determinant of every actual lan-guage, there is little reason to suppose that any of these actual languages can indeed be identified with what Badiou calls the (wholly predicative) "language of a situation" at all. As a matter of fact, it is plausible that no actually existing language can reasonably be identified as such a "language of a situation," since every language, regardless of the situation in which it is defined or comes to be spoken, bears within itself as part of its definitive structure the profound resource of a strictly impredicative excess.

   From this perspective, then, Cohen's demonstration that the generic set is in this sense "indiscernible," "unnameable," or "subtracted from" the "language of a situation" does not go so far as to show that it is in any very important sense "beyond language" itself. It is true that Cohen's dem-onstration may be used to show that there can be a set that is "diagonal" to an existing language in the sense that it does not (yet) have a name or description in that language, and thus there always remains the possibility that what is not now recognizable or constructible could come to be so, later on. But on the paradoxico-critical orientation, this is, once more, just a consequence of the permanent excessive dimension of language *as such*, the ineliminable excess of representation over presentation that always results from the internal reflection of the total virtual power of language into itself. There is evidently a close analogy here to Turing's result (discussed in Chapter 6), which shows by means of diagonalization that there must be "uncomputable" procedures and numbers, and so that there is no way to solve by means of effective procedures *all* problems that are stateable in their terms.[72]

What about Badiou's further conviction that the actual *addition* of the generic set to an existing situation (by the agency of a subject in his pursuit of an infinite truth) will be sufficient to bring about fundamental changes in the existing situation? As we have seen, this additional conviction depends on the assumption of a hierarchy of metalanguages, which is itself grounded in the choice to interpret diagonalization and the paradoxes as showing incompleteness rather than inconsistency, and the paradoxico-critic will accordingly not concur with it. Here again, the formal situation is similar to that of Gödel's incompleteness results, in their capacity to demonstrate the necessary existence, in any formal system of a certain complexity, of a sentence that is undecidable in its terms. Both the paradoxico-critical and the generic orientations can agree on the formal result and the demonstration of undecidability. But to see the undecidable sentence as a *truth*, and thus to take it to express some positive being lying essentially "beyond" the grasp of the system in question, requires the choice for incompleteness rather than inconsistency, as well as the informal argument which assumes the possibility and coherence of the metalanguage perspective from which it is indeed discernible as such. As we saw in that connection, moreover, we can certainly subsequently add the Gödel sentence for the particular system in question to that system as a new axiom, thereby producing a new system that can "prove" the sentence's truth. But of course the new system will then have its own Gödel sentence, and the phenomenon of undecidability itself will never be fully exorcized. If the analogy between the two kinds of diagonalization holds up, it seems that the addition of the generic extension to an existing situation will have the same kind of effect; it will indeed produce a new situation, one in which there are truths (or at any rate, accurate or, as Badiou would say, "veridical" statements) which were not "true before"; but the underlying phenomenon, and possibility, of indiscernibility will remain, constantly and persistently haunting all conceptualization at the very elemental level of its link to signification as such.

Badiou sees in this repeated possibility of superadding the generic extension to existing sets the possibility of all structurally significant change and the sole route to the progressive completion of a situation through its successive integration of an eternal Truth. The evident (paradoxico-critical) alternative is to see the generic set as introducing, rather, a permanent dimension of contradiction and paradox whereby the unnamable is named as such and the totality of language retroacts on itself, thereby demonstrating the essential contours of its being. This produces a chain of consequences which are quite different from those that Badiou draws from the possibility of the generic set, but nevertheless contribute in a profound and structural way to addressing the fundamental questions of politics. We can conclude this chapter by specifying in outline the features of the politics of paradoxico-criticism, in its relationship to the indiscernible and to what, as its constitutive paradoxes demonstrate, is excessive to possible signification:

i. There is indeed, wherever language of any kind is concerned, a structurally necessary excess of representation over presentation. This much is, as we have seen, common ground between the paradoxico-critical and the generic orientations. Nevertheless, the paradoxico-critical orientation goes further than the generic one in detecting in this excess a *latent dimension of surplus* that it recognizes as the original structural source of all ideology and all of its effects. Here, moreover, the ideological and the ideal are alike recognized as inherent and ineliminable effects of the *syntactical* structure of language itself, in its paradoxical capacity for self-reference. It is, accordingly, solely from the perspective of a formally based recognition of the origin of these effects in the total structural order of signification that they can be fully understood and potentially resisted.

ii. This paradoxical latent or virtual dimension of language is permanent and ineliminable, and it is produced by the excess of sense over reference whose formal model is diagonalization, which is an operator of excess. But there is no good reason to assume that the excess is any more than one-leveled. It does not institute a hierarchy of languages, or suggest anywhere the possibility or coherence of a complete metalanguage perspective. Instead, it operates to reflect language paradoxically into itself everywhere that reflexive language is itself operative, i.e., everywhere.

iii. We may recognize in Cohen's results the rigorous demonstration of the possibility of producing, through diagonalization, an 'indiscernible' set that is subtracted from the very possibility of naming or description. But this will show, most generally, not simply the existence of a particular inexistent or indiscernible that is thus subtracted from a specific, historically and factually situated language, but more generally the permanent dimension of excess that affects and characterizes the structure of any language, or of language as such.

iv. The effect of insisting upon this dimension, on the basis of the formal results, is then *not* the actual production of a *new* language, situation, society, or structure. Such a production may indeed occur, but it is relatively insignificant from the perspective of the demonstration of indiscernibility, and hence paradox, as a permanent structural phenomenon of language as such. The yield of this demonstration is then much more the demonstration of the necessity, at the center of any constituted order, of the permanent aporia or gap that both conditions it and ruins the prospect of its non-contradictory coherence. Recognizing this gap, it is also possible to recognize and resist normative and regulative claims made on the basis of the assumed necessity of forestalling contradiction, assuring the effectiveness of a social order, or guaranteeing the non-contradictory coherence of its practices. The formal basis of this recognition, as well as the actual production of *any* fundamental change in existing practices and institutions, is the virtual and immeasurable excessive dimension of language, marked in the excess of the signifying powers of language over the signified, in virtue of which it is possible to say, on the basis of a renewed formal consideration of the structure and totality of signification itself (paraphrasing Spinoza), that we still "know not what (a) language can do."

10 The Politics of Logic
Critical and Practical Consequences

Over the past several chapters, I have developed and defended the possibility of a "politics of logic" that takes up today's most significant political struggles and antagonisms on explicitly formal terms. I have argued that this politics of logic offers to update and transform the classical theoretical problematic of the *bios politikon* by means of a (meta-)formal inquiry into the existence and effectiveness of forms and formalisms in the shaping and determination of collective life. On the somewhat more immediate and pragmatic level of the critical discourses and practices (philosophical and non-philosophical) that articulate and define today's leading political and "ideological" struggles, however, this formal reflection has three equally important immediate effects:

i) It offers *terms of political thought and action* that move decisively beyond those that define the liberal-democratic-administrative consensus that is increasingly coming to underlie the effectively hegemonic politics of the world. As we have seen repeatedly over the last several chapters, the actual theoretical basis of this politics is a pluralist and ultimately conventionalist culturalism of practices and institutions whose own underlying structure is that of (what Badiou calls) constructivism. This orientation, citing the neoliberal canards of tolerance, openness, historicism, and contingency on the "official" level of cultures and practices, is nevertheless happy to relegate the effectively "universal" determination of forms of life to the relentless machinery of global capitalism. It officially defines itself in opposition to an older onto-theological orientation of religious transcendence or fundamentalism. Although this specter of theocracy and "totalitarianism" is not unimportant in the actual political life of post-industrial nations and economies, it functions there much more as a floating signifier of difference, both internal and external, from the supposedly threatened (but in fact massively dominant) liberal-democratic order than as a real counterpoint to it. Meanwhile, in those parts of the world where something like onto-theology does remain effective in structuring political motivation and regimes, it can do so only because of its own massive complicity with the forces of global capitalism themselves.[1]

Because the politics of logic offers formal resources for thinking beyond the opposition between the formal orientations of constructivism and onto-theology, it can allow us to *move beyond the very terms* in which the supposed debate between them defines and supports the global neo-liberal order. In particular, whereas the official debate between constructivism and onto-theology appears to take place as a debate about the relative fixity of normative standards and principles by which a social order is structured (i.e., whether these norms can be given on a "transcendent" level, or whether they must always be historicized and renegotiated), the politics of logic moves beyond this debate by formally *radicalizing* the question of the very being and effectiveness of norms and laws themselves by means of a metalogical inquiry into their structure. Specifically, because of the way the paradoxes of logic and metalogic transfigure the very problem of the "application" of forms and norms, this enables us to see that the question of the determination of normative social structures is, in a profound sense, *no longer* a question of "nature vs. culture." Nor is it a question to be settled on the level of any account of origins, whether conventional or transcendental. Rather, through the aporetic and paradoxical results of twentieth-century formal thought, the politics of logic verifies that no social or political order can in fact be "founded" (in the sense of being both universally inclusive and internally consistent) and so allows the whole question of foundations to be displaced onto another, more relevant one. This is the question of the paradoxical *nomothesis*, which as we saw is already posed in Plato, and revisited in a striking way by Wittgenstein through his question of the force of rules and the basis of their application. The formal results of the twentieth century in metalogic and computational theory, as I have argued, offer means by which the very question of norms and standards can be transformed on the level of their entry into, and force over, a life. This is a question of the *effectiveness* of systems and structures (technological, social, linguistic, legal, as well as "political" in the narrower sense) in the determination of both individual and collective life, and of the (formally/logically thinkable) structurally necessary "gap" between rules and their application which ideological representations of the force of rules obscurely foreclose.

ii) This transformation of the terms of the earlier "debates" on formal grounds opens up a whole new set of *critical* modalities for thinking about and ultimately transforming these systems (of various types and levels of effectiveness) at the point of their actual structuration of life. In particular, since the politics of logic (especially in its paradoxico-critical modality) updates and radicalizes previously existing modes of critical reflection about structures and their limits by articulating the permanent logical aporias of structures as such, it allows for the structuration of life to be resisted from a position that is not simply an "outside" to structures and their force, but in fact inscribed in their own internal logic. This means that it is possible to define a position of critique of the prevalent structures of social, political, and technological life that resists their force from something other than an ultimately nostalgic "outside" position (whether this be conceived as the position of organic *praxis*, the "hermeneutic" horizon of tradition, or an experiential lifeworld). This position offers, as I shall argue, a substantial renewal of *critical theory* and *praxis* appropriate to the dominant forms and structures of the organization of life today, including (in a rather unprecedented but rigorous sense) a formal updating and revitalization of the classical critique of political economy.

In the twentieth century, developments of the Kantian critique of reason have been uncertainly split between two broadly incommensurable positions. One attempts to develop formal reason further, in the direction of a more thorough "rationalization" and transparency of society (e.g., Habermas). The other, lamenting the progressive instrumentalization and technicization of reason in the twentieth century, undertakes to reject "instrumental rationality" altogether. This yields an invocation of supposedly distinctive organic or "non-instrumentalized" conceptions of reason (Adorno, Horkheimer) or, in a more extreme variant, the neo-Romantic invocation of an explicitly *ir*rational nostalgic lifeworld ground (Heidegger). By contrast with both of these, the politics of logic develops the critique of reason as an *internal* critique of what is likely the *only* form of structural reason that matters today, namely, the "calculative reason" of information and technological effectivity. This effectivity of calculative reasoning is the direct outcome of the formal-logical-linguistic conception of reason as logic worked out over the course of the twentieth century, and directly responsible for producing the "material" technologies of media and information that are so pervasive today. The politics of logic develops the rigorously internal critique of this regime, and these technologies, by drawing out the implications of the formal paradoxes and aporias internal to the structure of this formal logic itself.

From this perspective, it is possible to see that both previously developed twentieth-century "critical theory" positions on reason are ultimately untenable. The first, which calls for the further rationalization of society and politics, is untenable because it fails to reckon with the essential paradoxes and aporias of structural reason in its *critical* reflection on its own limits; whereas the second, nostalgic position is equally untenable because in its attempt to find in "lived practices" or "embodiment" a position "beyond logic" it can ultimately only degenerate into the empty religiosity or marginal aestheticism which (though popular among "postmodern" intellectuals) is today completely ineffectual as a serious critical stance. By contrast with both of these, the politics of logic pursues the traditional critique of reason by way of a meta-formal *intensification* of reason's "instrumentalization" as formal logic. This allows the essential internal structural aporias of reason, rather than being hidden behind the teleological assumption of an assured progressive "rationalization" of society or consigned to a supposed "lifeworld" ground immune to logic as such, to come to light and to become the site of a revitalized critical politics.

iii) With respect to the existing political theory of the twentieth century, much of which, as we have seen, closely anticipates or even directly embodies elements of (what I am here calling) the "politics of logic," the specific contribution of the reflection undertaken here is to bring out the implications of these analyses on the level of the essential formal structures that actually determine them. One of the most significant contributions of the present analysis with respect to this existing theory is its insistence on the *metalogical duality* (see Chapter 1) between completeness and consistency. This duality, as I have argued, faces critical theory with a crucial choice as soon as it attempts to conceive of the inherent structure of the social order itself. Owing to the implications of the fundamental paradoxes and aporias that are revealed by twentieth-century logical and metalogical thought, it is possible to conceive this order as internally consistent, but essentially incomplete (and hence as always capable of moving in the direction of its successive supplementation by what was earlier excluded) *or* as fundamentally complete (or total) but essentially rent by inconsistency and paradox (and hence *fundamentally structured by division and antagonism*). This duality, though essential, has almost never been remarked upon in the existing literature that recurrently refers to the inability of society to "exist as a complete *and* consistent whole" owing to fundamental aporias of logical structure; yet it can provide a much clearer and more formally precise sense of what is involved in the notorious Lacanian symbolic "gap or lack" that defines the human relation to structures and language as such.

As we have seen, critical thought about politics and society has long developed the paradoxes of formal reflection about totality and consistency with more or less self-consciousness of its doing so. To a *large* extent, the representatives of what I have here called "paradoxico-criticism" have in fact pursued the implications of taking the "social whole" to be rent from itself owing to inconsistencies and paradoxes arising at the limits of its totality, whereas Badiou has been the first to work out rigorously the implications of assuming consistency along with non-totality. However, because the existence and implications of the metalogical duality have not been recognized, it has been possible to treat the paradoxico-critical approaches as if they attempted merely to "resist," in a vague sense, "claims of totalization" or "hegemony," as if from an ill-conceived position simply exterior to "claims to power." One of the effects of insisting upon the metalogical duality, therefore, is to redeem the paradoxico-critical positions from their marginalization (for instance, as "textualism," hermeneutics, and negative theology) and demonstrate that they represent rigorous and viable positions that *can* orient a meaningful and transformative political *praxis* today.

INCOMMENSURABILITY, ECONOMISM, REALISM

The liberal-democratic-capitalist politics that is becoming dominant in the world today has, in its specific contemporary formations, a substantial theoretical basis in twentieth-century theories of community and difference. In order to resist it critically, it is therefore necessary to find a rigorous theoretical position from which to contest this basis, and provide viable alternatives to it. The politics of logic, as I have argued, does this by insisting upon a formal and theoretical traversal of the radical paradoxes that, according to the formal and metalogical results, arise necessarily for any rigorous thinking of the possibility of communities or social wholes. With respect to the now-dominant liberal-democratic global *ethos*, which is theoretically founded (as we have seen) on the conventionalist, multiculturalist, and ultimately relativist position of constructivism, the politics of logic formulates both a rigorous critique and the formal basis for a substantial overcoming of its basic position.

If there is a single idea with which the twentieth-century thought of community is obsessed, and which today finds expression as one of the central theoretical supports of the global liberal-democratic order, it is the idea of *incommensurability*. Today, the spontaneous consciousness of consensual belief, what Badiou calls the axiomatic of contemporary belief, knows above all that *we are all different*, and that this difference between cultures and peoples is not such as to be assimilated to common measure; that the claims of diverse cultures and communities must therefore all be respected, their diverse viewpoints and perspectives accommodated within a bland and universal, but ostensibly content-less, tolerance.[2] This *ethos* of diversity and tolerance, in itself, would hardly be objectionable, if it did not function as the false consciousness of a global capitalist order that is quite content to relocate the massively powerful assimilative claims of a supposedly vanquished "universalism" in the pervasive flows and effective machinations of capital themselves. This actual complicity of this spontaneous *ethos* of difference with the maintenance and support of the global capitalist order has been rigorously and vehemently criticized by Badiou (under the heading of "capitalist parliamentarianism") and, in a different way, by Žižek; I will not repeat these criticisms here. What is more important in the present context is simply to identify the theoretical foundations of its ability to provide both ideological and concrete material support to global capitalism, and to show how a more complete thinking of formalisms offers to undermine this ability.

More specifically, if the obsession of twentieth-century political thought, from Nietzsche through Kuhn, Rorty, and Foucault (and up to Lyotard), has been the incommensurability of communities, cultures, and "language games" (the phrase is routinely used in this connection, although as we've seen it is far from what Wittgenstein actually had in mind), the politics of logic offers to replace this thought of difference with another, very different thinking of incommensurability, one that offers to expose on a more fundamental level what is really going on with the competing claims of "cultures" and "communities" on the geopolitical scene. As we've seen, the twentieth-century thought of incommensurability is largely founded in *constructivism*; this is a pluralist, conventionalist, and culturalist position which sees each individual community as contingently founded with "its own" individual metrics and systems of value by an internally coherent and self-consistent act of institution or foundation. Such a thinking of the foundation of communities is bound to end in the incommensurability of "no common measure," for if the institution of norms and measures that underlies diverse cultural "claims" is simply contingent, there is no reason to expect or seek any commonality between them. Thus, given the "irreducibility" of difference and the necessary "heterogeneity" of all peoples and cultures, all that can be expected of the "global" order is an ostensibly bland (but actually quite magisterial) tolerance that permits each one its "right" to individuality.

On the other hand, the politics of logic, traversing the paradoxes of self-membership and reflexivity, offers a fundamentally different conception of "incommensurability" itself. Whereas we might call the first, dedicated to the narcissism of small differences and the celebration of an empty heterogeneity, a "weak" incommensurability, there is also, as demonstrated here, a rigorous and "strong" incommensurability that arises as a fundamental and direct result of the very claims and bonds by which any community structures itself as such. Whereas the first is the incommensurability of "no common measure," or of the lack of common standards, values, or principles between two historically and contingently constituted communities, the second is the incommensurability of the *immeasurable*, what does not (only) escape the common measure of diverse communities and cultures, but *escapes any possible measure* in a fundamental way that follows directly from the logical moment wherein *any* social whole is first constituted as a *One* at all. The second, strong kind of incommensurability is formally locatable, as we have seen, by means of diagonalization. It appears within a given systematic economy as the (absent) object of the floating signifier, the structurally necessary "quilting point," the "absent center," the "specific inexistent," or the generic set. In all of these forms, it is not an index of the difference *between* historically and conventionally constituted communities, but rather an index of the difference of the (single) "community" *from itself*. As the politics of logic demonstrates, this logical moment of strong incommensurability is structurally necessary, as soon as the "social whole" ventures to think its *own* conditions of possibility in a formally radical way. This thought manifests the inherent immeasurability (which also figures as structural excess, indiscernibility, and the structurally necessary place of the exception) that is inherent to any universal system of measure as such.

This thought of strong incommensurability is today the absolutely necessary requisite for any meaningful critical "take" on the rapidly developing sovereign politics of the globe.[3] For it is this thought alone that yields the formal basis needed to comprehend the necessary *internal* structural failures of what is today in fact a largely *monocultural* regime of global capitalism. Here, the pluralistic narcissism and its primary theoretical foundation, the culturalist thought of weak incommensurability, are simply irrelevant. The politics of logic offers to replace both with a rigorous and critical politics of the only kind of "difference" that really matters today, the inherent structural difference of the One from itself. This is the issue that's really at the heart of the efficacy of global capital around the world and the "cultural" configurations it determines, whether these take the superficial forms of liberal administration and ostensible "multiculturalism" (as in the U.S. today) or relatively more officially monoculturalist and monopolar formations (as, e.g., in China) which themselves nevertheless share a common determination in the systematic law of capital and production.[4]

With respect to this unified and systematic law of production, the most important result of the kind of theoretical position that the politics of logic makes possible is that it provides the theoretical foundations for a radical critique of the material and ideological determination of the neoliberal monoculture by (what is in fact) a globalist *economism* of unprecedented scope and power. This is not, for the most part, an explicitly avowed commitment or directly stated philosophical belief, but rather the effective underpinning of a wide variety of "social" and "political" modes of action and *praxis*.[5] According to this dominant economism, the political is completely exhausted by the economic, in the broad and ideological sense in which the term "the economy" is employed, on the level of nations as well as the "globe," in the determination of action and motivation, but in a vague but overdetermined referential sense. The definitive claim of this dominant economism is thus that the success or failure of individuals, peoples, cultures, and states is uniformly *measured* and *measurable* in terms of their economic fates; and hence that the whole question of the politics of any community (whether it be a small town in America, a major city in China, or a tribal village in Africa) is reducible to the question of the integration of the community into the "global economy," with which all communities are in fact always already (although nebulously) linked. This reduction of the political dimension of life to its economic determinants is today just as effective in the determination of the form of life of an American white-collar middle manager as it is in that of a Chinese peasant-turned-factory-worker; and within the narrowed context of the official "politics" of liberal-democratic regimes, it is just as effective in the motivation of the "left" position of neo-Keynesianism and social democracy as it is in that of the "right" position of conservative free-market ideology. This does not mean simply that "everything has a price" or that "everything" is treated in terms of its free-market value; quite to the contrary, the discourse and praxis of economism has long functioned in part by creating reservoirs of experience or entitlement (for instance, under the banner of a theological transcendence, the protection of "localities," or indeed the general liberal ideology of human rights) that are conceived as stable points "beyond" monetary value and so "off limits." These structures largely have the ideological effects of protecting the system from criticism and immunizing it from the implications of its own internal antagonisms.

The current version of economism is, moreover, much more widespread and pernicious than the explicit teleological version that figured in the theoretical motivation of some classical forms of Marxism, according to which the "superstructure" features of ideology and political configurations are always determined "in the last instance" by material/economic factors in such a way that the progressive development of these material factors in a revolutionary and socially transformative direction is always assured in advance. This older teleological economism is one in which, in today's age of the alleged "end of grand narratives" and the rapid transformation of forms of "production" far beyond those classically envisioned, nobody any longer believes; the new economism is, by contrast, *a*-teleological and fully aware of the necessary vicissitudes and wanderings of global capitalism (up to and including periodic "crises" like the global crash of 2008) but nevertheless fully capable of determining the most pervasive forms of collective practice and belief.

The challenge for a critical thinking of politics today, then, is to think the possibility of a political life immune to this economism, to think, in other words (as Badiou might put it) the possibility of a life *subtracted from* economy and "diagonal" to its imperatives and measures. Lest this position be mistaken for a "culturally conservative" or neo-Luddite one, I emphasize again that this *is not*, and *cannot be*, a position simply external to economy or even to capitalism itself. To perceive the possibility of this kind of politics is to see that there is no hope today for conceiving the "power" of capital and capitalism in the early-Marxian terms of the alienation of a pure and purely un-economic "species being" or "traditional" humanistically conceived form of life. For, as is clear on all sides, there is no simple *escape* from the web of the ever-expanding structures of capitalism, and quite simply no place on earth to stand "outside" the scope of its effects. On the other hand, if, as I have argued, the formal results of the twentieth century demonstrate that the very structure that underlies the effectiveness of the dominant economism on both the levels of its material and its ideological support must be rent by the constitutive paradoxes of reflexivity and application, then the demonstration and transit of these paradoxes bears witness to the structural existence of the very position from which the economist claim to effectiveness can be resisted and ultimately countered.

Nor, as we have seen, does the politics of logic, like the contemporary widespread *ethos* of historicist pragmatism, march under the banner of the progressive "inclusion" of diverse groups, identities, and cultures within a broadly accommodating but nevertheless integral "pluralist society." This is not to say that the great advances of liberal, progressivist politics over the course of the twentieth century in the inclusion and accommodation of formerly marginalized groups should in any way, today, be doubted or reversed; but it does mean that there is a real question whether a mere continuation of the progressivist politics of race, gender, and cultural "identity" can today support a viable critical position which adequately answers to the real political challenges posed by today's global situation. Capitalism, of course, is in its own way extremely good at producing inclusion; and liberal identity politics commits a fatal error in its failure to comprehend the effective mechanisms of this production, which in fact qualifies this politics to serve as the official ideological face of these very same mechanisms and forces.

Does the position of critique I am outlining here not risk "reifying" global capitalism by treating its widely varied forms and manifestations as if they were all simply manifestations of a single, unified ideology or authoritarian belief system (which, of course, would massively fail to do justice to the ubiquity and formal indifference of global capital itself)? In fact, it does not commit this error. The point of the politics of logic is not to treat capitalism as a single object (ideological or otherwise) with a simple "outside" but, quite to the contrary, as an infinitely diversified and varied *structure* that nevertheless presupposes and tends toward what is in many ways a *universal* structural logic. This logic can indeed be interrogated on formal grounds, in terms of the effectiveness of the fundamental operations it presupposes and permits.[6]

To the contrary, indeed, it is not the politics of logic but rather the organicist and "lifeworld" positions of resistance that effectively reify capitalism in order to fantasize a position simply outside of it; in so doing, of course, they become all too easily appropriable within the system itself. Something similar is additionally, and increasingly, characteristic of the ethical-political discourse of individualistic "human rights" itself, which (whatever its original foundations) increasingly functions on the geopolitical scene simply as an effective means to prop up and legitimate free market ideology (not to mention neo-colonialist violence and war).[7] By contrast, as we have seen, the politics of logic challenges every such individualist ideology by insisting, on a basic level, that society is not a whole constituted of atomistic individuals with preexisting interests, but rather irreducibly an ideological/social whole whose inherent gaps and aporias define the possible "subject positions," and hence the play of effectively constituted interests and identities, within it. This insistence is the fundamental prerequisite for the possibility of a critical interrogation of the dominant forms of politics today, which all too often justify in individualist, pragmatist, and historicist terms decisions and imperatives that are in reality massively predetermined on a technical/economic structural level. Here, the historicist and pragmatist ideology of the "ongoing conversation," the conception of deliberative democracy as "the art of compromise," and above all the illusory production of a populist field of "democratic" debate between "right" and "left" positions on the narrowly pre-defined "issues" of contemporary media-defined discourse serve simply to mask the brutal and effective functioning of structural forces and imperatives that have always determined everything important—from the privileged global role of certain state economies, to the pointless geopolitical struggles and wars that follow from them, up to the entire relationship of the totality of technological, social, and "productive" forces of human activity to the rest of the life of the more-than-human planet—already in advance.

With this in mind, we can now return explicitly to the crucial question of the implications of a rigorous analysis of formalism for today's dominant forms of collective life. One crucial difference, I have argued, made by the formal level of consideration is that it allows us to conceive of the unified field of the effectiveness of global capital, along with all the effects of formalization and structuration it brings, in "abstract," theoretical, and universal terms. The key to this conception is metalogical reflection on the logical structure of language, and the consequent formal investigation of the structural gaps and aporias of language itself. This, as we have seen, has little to do with the historicist or anthropological *arcana* of the origins and limits of *particular* (natural) languages. In a profound sense, it is, to the contrary, the consequence of a rigorous *logical* thinking of language and its structure.

Because this *is* a formal analysis, and because (as in the case of set theory) it operates on the universal level of the logical/mathematical investigation of the structures of multiplicity themselves, its result is not the adumbration of contingencies, but the rigorous demonstration of structural necessities, including the necessity that any "social order" or whole is either constitutively cleft by fundamental inconsistencies, or else consigned to an essential incompleteness. These fundamental inadequacies of structure as such are by no means characteristic only of certain empirically delimited languages, or the provenance of "natural" languages alone; quite to the contrary, their original development in terms of *formal* languages shows that they escape any such limitation to historically or empirically bounded contingent wholes. Nor are they, hearkening back to an older (Kantian) sense of transcendental "conditioning," in any obvious sense the outcome of the synthetic work or operation of the human mind. The paradoxes and aporias of Russell, Gödel, and Tarski are, after all, fundamental outcomes of the very logical structure of the operation of "counting as one" or grouping a Many as a One that Cantor was the first in our time rigorously to theorize; here what is at stake is not the application of preexisting synthetic categories but the possibility of any synthesis, or any such thing as a category, as such.

The formally based position of the politics of logic is thus far from a "linguistic idealism" (or indeed from *any* sort of idealism); nor is the kind of incommensurability it demonstrates at all appropriable by any of the anti-realist positions that see "truth" only as the outcome of a given historical, social, or cultural conditioning. It is, rather, a profound and robust *realism*: not, admittedly, the *empirical realism* that is today becoming more popular (largely as a backlash against the last century's dominant forms of culturalist and linguistic idealism) but rather an uncompromising *formal realism*. This kind of realism both repeats and displaces the more narrowly conceived "formalism" which provided a decisive impetus, in the work of Hilbert, Russell, and the early Wittgenstein, for the initial development of the analytic tradition itself. If political thought today everywhere runs up against the imperative of theorizing the consequences of the systems of technology, administration, and capital in which we find ourselves increasingly entangled, and if the effectivity of this progressive and by no means slowing formalization of life continues to be predicated on the essential reality of forms, then this is just the sort of realism that is needed to discern the structure of this effectivity and the basis of its force.[8]

INHERITING THE CENTURY: POLITICS OF THE LIFE TO COME

If there is to be a viable twenty-first-century politics of forms of life, it will necessarily proceed through a profound reflection on the stakes and results of formalism and formalization in the twentieth. For this analysis, the twentieth century will have been *the* century of formalization, from the distinctive art forms of modernism, to the vast social and political programs of utopian ambition, to the (still ongoing) technicization of everyday life in the modes of information technology, calculation, and electronic media. In a series of lectures both elegiac and affirmative, Badiou in 1998–2001 undertook to read the century just ended, declaring both the fact of its passage and its precipitous consequences for the current moment and all that may follow it.[9] Above all, according to Badiou, what we must understand and inherit from the twentieth century is the *univocity* which yields its relentless pursuit of forms and formalization:

> The century will have been the century of univocity. This is what I hope will outlast the current Restoration, which is all the more mendacious and equivocal in that it claims to be both humanistic and convivial. Deleuze forcefully affirmed the univocity of being, and our time will indeed have desired—through works inhabited by a universality without remainder—to be the inhuman rival of being. In every domain, it will have unfalteringly explored the paths of formalization.[10]

According to Badiou, this "voluntaristic" century will have been marked especially by the "passion for the real."[11] This passion yields a "singular violence" effected by a "paradoxical subjectivity" that thinks its time both as decadence and decline and, simultaneously, as the commencement and beginning of the absolutely new. The twentieth century is thus in the grip of a paradoxical historicity that seeks, in modernist fashion, to break with all the distinctive traits of what has come before and forge, with a single, militant gesture of affirmation, the "new man" of a finally reconciled humanity. The passage and effects of this "passion for the real" that is definitive of the century bear an intimate relationship, however, to the project of formalization:

> What the century desires—in the construction of socialism as in minimal art, in formal axiomatic as in the conflagrations of mad love—is a universality without remainder, without adherence to any particularity whatsoever. Like Bauhaus in architecture: a building that nothing renders particular, for it is reduced to a translucent, universally recognizable functionality; the kind of functionality that has forgotten every index of stylistic particularity. It is easy to see that the apposite slogan is that of formalization, at the borders of the real, and that it is precisely this which immediately produces the austere impression of an indifference towards the judgment of men.[12]

Here, the relationship between the inhuman real and the program of formalization in all of its varied aesthetic, scientific, and political instances is exactly the one described by Lacan (see Chapter 7): if, as Lacan says, the real is the necessary impasse of formalization, then the relentless passion for the real necessarily demands the uncompromising and hyperbolic pursuit of the formalization of life and society. What is at stake, according to Badiou, is the possibility of a pursuit of the infinity of the Idea that breaks completely with the Romantic mode of the "realization" of the infinite in art; what torments the century is a "striving to have done with the Romanticism of the ideal," to make an end to the dreaming position of aestheticism by means of an immediate subjective act that forces art to "disappear" and "realize itself as life."[13] Because what is at stake here is a manifestation of the infinite in finite form, the only possible means for the pursuit of this appearance in the act is the pursuit of formalism; here, the infinite "transits through form" in a passage that presents itself as the paradoxical equivalence of "finite form" and "infinite opening."[14] And yet, this passage, which attempts unceasingly to force the immediate manifestation of the infinite-real in the finite manifestation of violence, militancy, and war, is never complete; in the twentieth century's manifold projects of revolutionary transformation, thoroughly impassioned by the real, the real is nevertheless "never real enough not to be suspected of semblance."[15] The procession of forms and formalization thus yields a boundless suspicion and an infinite prolongation of the attempt to purify forms, to produce finally an ultimate formalization of life that cannot any longer be suspected of bearing any remaining trace of the impurity of contingent matter. However, because ultimately *only* nothingness is pure, this yields an ongoing violence and recurrent nihilistic passion for destruction.[16]

The best slogan for this passion, Badiou says, is Stalin's: "A party becomes stronger by purging itself"; yet the pursuit of the real in the twentieth century by means of purgative violence is by no means limited to Stalin, or indeed to politics.[17] In art as well as mathematics, in science as well as the organization of society, we see in the twentieth century again and again the attempt immediately to realize the impossible-real by means of a violent, destructive imposition of purified form.

What lesson should we draw, today, from the legacy of these violent twentieth-century attempts at a direct imposition of the real as the infinitely prolonged purification of forms? In his own remarks in *The Century* about the legacy of the twentieth century's ambitions and projects today, Badiou wavers somewhat uncertainly between celebrating the militant ambitions of the twentieth century's formalist passion and descrying the nihilistic violence that is recurrently inscribed within it. In particular, Badiou distinguishes between the twentieth century's characteristic assumption of "destruction as such" and another possible development of the "passion of the real," what he calls the "subtractive orientation" that, rather than endorsing destructive purification, "attempts to *measure* the ineluctable negativity" by means of a "construction of minimal differences."[18] Badiou's model for this "subtractive" orientation is the painting *White on White* by Malevich, which manifests the "epitome of purification" as the appearance of a pure white square on a pure white background. Here, Badiou says, the minimal difference between figure and background stages the "vanishing difference" between place and what takes place in it, the pure, minimal difference that results from the erasure of all determinate content. This is, Badiou says, another form of the passion of the Real: not the passion of identity and authenticity, which indeed can yield only destruction, but rather a passion of "vanishing difference." It reinvents the "new birth" dreamed of unceasingly by the twentieth century as an "axiomatic" of the creation of the bare outline of novelty, the minimal difference that creates the new on the very border of nothing.

The orientation toward this "passion of subtraction," when combined with the appeal to the transformative powers of the event which Badiou here repeats, is, of course, nothing other than the generic orientation in thought, which attempts to resolve the deadlock of the Lacanian impasse of symbolization by finding in formalism itself the possibility of a "forced pass" of the real. Yet despite the formal distinction Badiou here attempts to draw between this orientation and the violent passion that has motivated the revolutionary formalisms and formalizations of the twentieth century, it is not clear, as Žižek has recently suggested, that Badiou succeeds ultimately in distinguishing his own position from the "voluntarism" and militancy characteristic of the violent utopianism of the twentieth century:

> In *The Century*, Badiou seems to oscillate between the plea for a direct fidelity to the twentieth century's "passion of the real," and the prospect of passing from the politics of purification to a politics of subtraction. While he makes it fully clear that the horrors of the twentieth century, from the Holocaust to gulag, are a necessary outcome of the purification-mode of the "passion of the Real," and while he admits that protests against it are fully legitimate . . . he nonetheless stops short of renouncing it. Why? Because *fully to follow the logic of subtraction would force him to abandon the very frame of the opposition between Being and Event*. Within the logic of subtraction, the Event is not external to the order of Being, but located in the "minimal difference" inherent to the order of Being itself. The parallel is strict here between Badiou's two versions of the "passion of the Real" and the two main versions of the Real in Lacan, i.e. the Real as the destructive vortex, the inaccessible/impossible hard kernel which we cannot approach without risking our own destruction and the Real as the pure *Schein* of a minimal difference, as another dimension which shines through in the gaps of an inconsistent reality.[19]

But the distinction that Žižek here treats as the distinction between two conceptions of the Real in Lacan is in fact just the distinction that we have drawn between the two post-Cantorian orientations of thought: the generic and the paradoxico-critical.[20] Whereas the generic orientation, committed to the rigorous distinction between ontology and the Event, insists *along with* the militant passion of the twentieth century upon the possibility of a "forced pass of the real" at the actually infinite point of the realization of forms, the paradoxico-critical orientation maintains the appearance of the infinite-Real only at the cost of its paradoxical inscription as form *within* an ontological order of reality that must thereby be revealed as, as Žižek says, constitutively inconsistent. With the "passion of subtraction," as elsewhere, Badiou's analysis of the formalisms approaches very closely to a paradoxico-critical interrogation of the very force of forms over life in their problematic symbolic inscription, which also amounts to a rigorous formally-based criticism of the militancy of the twentieth century in its claim to break instantaneously and violently with all practices and institutions of the past. However, because Badiou ultimately chooses the generic orientation over the paradoxico-critical one, he cannot but ambiguously replicate this twentieth-century passion for destruction and purification within the register of his own avowed militancy and subjective voluntarism.

What, then, is ultimately to be gained from a broader critical "diagnosis" of the twentieth-century passion for the Real, as expressed in its obsessive formalization of knowledge and life? As Badiou indeed very convincingly argues, there can certainly be no *retreat* from the relentless pursuit of formalization into the plurivocity of "interpretations" or the pluralistic hermeneutics of "traditions." The effective accomplishments of formalism in the twentieth century are so transformative, and their consequences for the lived reality of life on the planet so profound, that any such retreat can only ultimately amount to a nostalgic retrenchment that effectively denies the very existence of the twentieth century itself. On the other hand, as we have seen, there is *another* way, besides Badiou's, to continue critically to pursue the consequences of formalization, up to its paradoxical inscription of the very limits of formalism themselves.

As Badiou himself emphasizes, here the results of the radical formalist project of twentieth-century mathematics points the way to an understanding of the more general project of formalization (of which it is both an example and a paradigm). For the formalist project of Hilbert as much as for the massive efforts of the Bourbaki group, the dream is to reduce mathematics to the "naked force of the letter and its codes," to forcibly extract from the univocity of the formal an "anonymous and complete mathematical universality" that steadfastly maintains the certainty that there is a solution to every well-formulated problem (p. 162). Moreover, as Badiou also insists, the first prerequisite for understanding the implications of this project today is that we refuse the now-common interpretation of the results of metalogical formalism—in particular, Gödel's incompleteness theorems—as showing the *failure* of this formalist program. This interpretation is only correct, Badiou emphasizes, if we consent in the reduction of the whole formalist program to the "most dated" and "least innovative" of its aspects: the desire for logical closure or completeness, which Gödel's result indeed shows (according to Badiou) to be unattainable.

Actually, as we have repeatedly seen, Gödel's actual formal results do not *even* show that the formalist project fails in *this* respect, for we may equally well (choosing the paradoxico-critical orientation rather than the generic one) interpret them as bearing witness to indeterminacy and inconsistency while *preserving* completeness. At any rate, the paradoxico-critical interpretation, which sees Gödel's and related results as bearing radical witness to the constitutive *inconsistency* of any formal One, is clearly just as fully committed to the rigorous continued pursuit of formalism as is Badiou's own generic interpretation. This is the point that Badiou himself misses when he assumes that interpretations of Gödel's results at variance with Badiou's generic interpretation (and indeed, with Gödel's own anticipation of this orientation) must fall back into a "hermeneutic" avoidance of the univocity of the formal position in favor of plurality and equivocity:

> Some have interpreted Gödel's technical result to mean that every formalizing stance leaves a remainder. Consequently, the century's dream of univocal access to the real must be abandoned. Not being formalized, the untreated, intractable residue will have to be interpreted. We must retread the ragged and equivocal paths of hermeneutics.
>
> It's striking that this is not the lesson that Gödel himself—after Cantor, the greatest genius in the examination of the essence of mathematics—draws from his own demonstrations. He sees in them a lesson of infinity, as well as the ransom of ignorance that must be paid every time knowledge is extorted from the real: to partake in a truth is also to measure that other truths exist, truths we do not yet partake in. This is indeed what separates formalization, as both thought and project, from a merely pragmatic employment of forms. Without ever being discouraged, one must invent other axioms, other logics, other ways of formalizing. The essence of thinking always resides in the power of forms.[21]

What Badiou misses here is the possibility of understanding Gödel's result differently than Gödel himself does, but without relenting in any way from the "passion of the real" that finds expression, as Badiou says, in a rigorous thinking of the power of forms. In particular, as we have seen, paradoxico-criticism indeed understands Gödel's result (along with the formally related results of twentieth-century structuralism) as showing that there is indeed a "remainder" or inherent excess to every process of formalization: this inherent structural excess finds expression as the floating signifier, the empty center, the permanently supplemental dimension of language, etc. *However*—and here is the crucial difference from what Badiou assumes—the stake of paradoxico-criticism is precisely that this "remainder" and excess of formalism *does not* have to be relegated to the equivocity of hermeneutics and "interpretation," but *can itself be formalized* in a way that provides the key to its radical critical potential. This formalization is itself, moreover, the basis of a radical critical *praxis* that is in many ways *more* faithful to the original formalist project than is Badiou's position itself. For in place of Badiou's creative eclecticism, according to which "one must invent other axioms, other logics," the paradoxico-critical orientation is, as we have seen, committed to the classical (logicist) position that there is (but) *one* logic, *one* "univocal" systematicity to what is thought in mathematics, and so, as Badiou says, but *one* solution to every problem of the relationship of form to a life. This systematicity is to be sought in the dimension of the logical structure of language as such. This is not the plurality of languages and the endless problematic of translation pursued by an equivocal hermeneutics; but neither is it the systematic plurality of Badiou's endlessly renewed call for the innovation and decisionism of ever-new axiomatics.

This is in fact the key to another massively important dimension of the twentieth-century project of formalization that Badiou, for all his attention to the implications of forms and formalization for us today, nevertheless almost entirely misses. This is what we might call the *formalization of everyday life*: it is the radically transformative and ongoing project of the twentieth century which uproots all traditional identities, "lifestyles," and sources of value in favor of abstractly defined social roles, systematic identifications, and technologically defined and delimited modes of production and consumption. Because the material agents of this transformation are, in many cases, indeed the ever more pervasive technologies of production, consumption, and communication, critical reflection on this process of formalization overlaps with what has sometimes been treated as "the philosophy of technology," though it is not exhausted by this; additionally, the process of formalization of everyday life has been thought (albeit inadequately in each case) by phenomenology as "sedimentation," by sociology and critical theory as the "rationalization" of forms of life, and by hermeneutics as the opposition of "method" to traditionally grounded "truth." The inadequacy of all of these formulations, as we have seen, lies in their assumption of the coherent intelligibility of a foundational "lifeworld" position untouched by formalism and formalization; whereas there is certainly no viable possibility of escaping into such a "safe" position today.

This process of the formalization of everyday life extends historically far beyond the specifically utopian formalist social projects of the twentieth century, and continues to be massively operative in today's much changed geopolitical horizon. It also extends beyond anything that has ever been explicitly proposed or accomplished on the programmatic level of explicitly articulated "political" projects, whether of a "state" or a "revolutionary" *genre*. In a certain sense, in fact, with the shift from industrial to informational and communicational forms of technology as the economically dominant modes of technological activity, this formalization of everyday life even accelerates and intensifies. The character and pervasiveness of this shift, moreover, verifies the inadequacy of any classical Marxist-style analysis of "control of the means of production" to the contemporary situation; for it is not the primarily industrial technologies of "production" but the electronic and informational technologies of "communication," media, and capital exchange that today determine the "global economy" on the level of its effective self-recognition. But as I have argued, these technologies are in a precise and rigorous sense the *direct* (if unintended) consequence of the abstract formalist projects of the twentieth century and even, in large measure, of Hilbert's formalist project in mathematics itself. Here again, the apparently paradoxical and aporetic metalogical results such as Gödel's are by no means opposed to the development of the formalist program, and are even in a profoundly surprising way the direct positive conditions for its realization on the level of technological efficacy. For (and this is of course but one leading example among many others that are possible) it is in his pursuit of a formal result exactly equivalent to Gödel's own results that Turing, formalizing the undecidable as the very stake of the possibility of systematic thought, essentially creates the architecture of the digital computer, which substantively underlies all the far-flung and ever-expanding developments of computational, communicational, and media technology today.

These technologies today have sway over forms of life in a way that far exceeds any narrowly "ideological" justification; in fact, their efficacy turns (as I have argued) on the inherently "ideal" dimension of language itself, the inherent capacity for abstract repetition which defines the iterability of the sign and the repeatability of information, and hence defines the very minimal structure of an "information" economy itself. As this dimension is, moreover, ineliminable from anything structured like a language, it cannot be resisted by means of anything like the traditional "critique of ideology," which seeks the demystification of the "false consciousness" of ideological projections in favor of an "authentic" or un-alienated position of truth. Nor is the classical Marxist figuration of the class struggle adequate here, since what is at issue is not the power of capitalists over the proletariat but rather the effectiveness of the "blind" systematicity of capital itself. What is needed, in short, is a radically formulated *internal* critique of the power of forms and formalization that relentlessly affirms, rather than retreats from, the identity of formalization with the power of thought, which Badiou himself insists upon. It is just such a critique whose formal paradigm we can locate, as I have suggested, in Gödel's results and related aporetic results of the metalogical, formal thought of totality, limit, and reflexive paradox; and that is realized by, for instance, Derrida's deconstructive methods and, in a different and even more thoroughgoing way, by Wittgenstein's deconstruction of the transit of the infinite in the iterability of the rule and the repeatability of the sign.

All of this suggests that, contrary to expectations (and certainly contrary to Badiou's reading of him), Wittgenstein is today *the* philosopher to read for a viable and helpful "critical theory" of the broadest and most pervasive determinants of our everyday forms of life. If the problem of "how to go on" in collective life when faced with the seemingly relentless determination of all possible action and meaning by the rule and its iterability is not simply a theoretical puzzle or the formulation of an abstract and as-yet-unheard-of skepticism, then its solution is to be found, as I have argued in Chapter 6, in a formally grounded internal critique of the effectivity of methods and processes. This critique culminates, in practice, in the multiplication of undecidables, regions of ineffectivity, and points of indiscernibility which undermine every attempt to define collective action and praxis as a total regime of noncontradictory coherence. As should be clear by now, this is *not* the comfortable pragmatism or traditionalism that has so often been attributed to Wittgenstein (either one of which, if it were actually his position, would actually tend to make the whole detailed critique of rule-following superfluous); nor is it, in any sense, a relativism of "language-games" or forms of life. It is, rather, the critical precondition for envisioning and creating a collective life that takes place beyond the mere efficacy of rules and technologies.

In a suggestive but enigmatic 1993 analysis, Giorgio Agamben ventures to interpret Wittgenstein's term "form of life" (or *Lebensform* in the original) as signaling the radical possibility of a "life that can never be separated from its form."[22] If, as Agamben has argued, sovereignty (with its premise of consistent completeness) always operates by separating forms—as laws, norms, or sovereign authority itself—from a "naked life" or "bare life" which they capture, then this radically clarified life to come results from a suspension and disqualification of this sovereign power. The possibility of such a radically clarified life to come is moreover conceivable, Agamben suggests elsewhere, only as the outcome and result of the twentieth century's massive "experimentum linguae"; at the end of this dramatic "experiment of language," what has finally been revealed is the inadequacy of any specifically constituted identity to subsume the possibility of the universal "community to come."[23] The nexus of the realization of this community must therefore be a thoroughgoing "appropriation" of "linguistic being," or our pure "being-in-language" itself; this appropriation intervenes in the very constitutive space between the linguistic symbol and its practical application, the "between" of forms and life itself. This is a life to come which, subtracted from the state, results directly from the manifestation and visibility of the anonymous "whatever singularity" whose existence is the rigorous result of the formalism of set theory:

> The threat the state is not willing to come to terms with is precisely the fact that the unrepresentable should exist and form a community without either presuppositions or conditions of belonging (just like Cantor's inconsistent multiplicity). The whatever singularity—this singularity that wants to take possession of belonging itself as well as of its own being-into-language, and that thus declines any identity and any condition of belonging—is the new, nonsubjective, and socially inconsistent protagonist of the coming politics.[24]

These formulations are enigmatic, and perhaps unavoidably so; but what they bring into focus quite sharply is the possibility of a radical transformation of contemporary forms of life at the very point of their effective determination by the repetitive formal structures of language, informational media, and abstract capital. If it is possible to resist these structures today (and they apparently *must* be resisted, if any meaningful form of emancipation is today to be possible), this resistance must be predicated upon a rigorously formal intervention at the point of their effective capture of life, the point at which lives, words, and meanings are always-already caught up in the structure of iterability that underlies the effectivity of all abstract processes and concrete technologies today. It is just this intervention which

is verified in a maximally formal and rigorous way by the twentieth century's sustained metalogical inquiry into the implications of totality and
reflexivity and its demonstration of inherent paradoxes and inconsistencies
at the limits of any constituted social or collective whole, and to which the
politics of logic (in each of its variants) is rigorously committed.

RENEWAL OF POLITICAL ECONOMY

To summarize, then, the politics of logic, as unflinchingly committed to
formal reflection in both of its versions (paradoxico-critical and generic),
offers what is today the *only* possible position from which to understand
the consequences for today of the twentieth century's defining "passion for
the real." But whereas Badiou's "generic" variant identifies (as well as substantially replicates) the militancy of the various utopian social projects of
the twentieth century, if we are to understand the ongoing consequences of
the parallel and in some ways much more pervasive process of the formalization of everyday life, which certainly continues today, we must turn to
paradoxico-criticism. For since the central problem of paradoxico-criticism
is not the advent of novelty or the motivation of action, but rather the problem of the *relationship* of forms to life, it is able to identify the possible
sites of resistance and ineffectivity whereat the economic and technological
formalization of life can be interrogated, suspended, and overcome. There
is, moreover, another, related reason for preferring paradoxico-criticism
over the generic orientation for dealing with today's problems. It is that
paradoxico-criticism offers, whereas the generic orientation does not, the
formal basis for a contemporary renewal of the classical project of the critique of political economy.

As Žižek and several other commentators have noted, the lack of a
critical theory of political economy in any of Badiou's work is a startling
omission for a theorist who has vehemently called for a contemporary restoration of "the Communist Idea."[25] From Badiou's own perspective, this
omission is no accident: since economics is not one of the four domains of
truth procedures (art, politics, science, and love), and since the Communist
Idea is, like all of Badiou's truths, structurally removed from any specifically constituted domain of positive action (including capitalist economies),
the kind of communism called for by Badiou bears little relation to economic theorizing and no specific relation to capitalism itself. Moreover,
since, as we have seen, the generic orientation itself structurally excludes
critique at a fundamental level by opting for the "consistency and incompleteness" pole of the metalogical duality, it can hardly support a thoroughgoing critical reflection on the limits and implications of capitalism
today. This is where the paradoxico-critical orientation is much more useful. For since its fundamental structure is determined by its consideration
of limit-paradoxes and contradictions, it is able structurally to conceive of

and model a capitalist system of production and consumption whose very life and continuance relies, as Marx knew well, on its remarkable ability successively to capture and appropriate its former "outside." Thus, paradoxico-criticism provides a critical theoretical underpinning for Marx's classical theory of value when this theory, in the words of Moshe Postone, "provides the basis for an analysis of capital as a socially constituted form of mediation and wealth whose primary characteristic is a tendency toward its limitless expansion."[26]

It is here that paradoxico-criticism, whether or not couched in classical Marxist terms, provides the formal ground for a renewed critical consideration of the problem of limits thereby invoked and made into a structural law of capitalist expansion. That the limits of capitalist economy must always appropriate their outsides in order to function means that the original form of the commodity in capitalism is that of the limit-paradox, the position that is simultaneously both "inside" and "outside" with respect to the constituted order. As Žižek has argued, this inherently contradictory nature, which the commodity of exchange value bears within itself in its very essence, coincides with the originally antagonistic structure of all social formations, what Marx thought under the heading of the "class struggle" which, as the original contradictory structure of society, paradoxically *precedes* the actually constituted classes and other interests as groups "within" society.

The politics of logic, in its paradoxico-critical modality, thus provides the formal and structural basis for a substantial renewal of the Marxist critique of political economy that is capable of comprehending the contradictions and antinomies that structure capitalist production and life in our time. Because of its formal derivation, the basis for this renewed critique in paradoxico-criticism is, moreover, neither a reification of "capital" or "capitalism" as a unified substantial force nor a relocation of the critique of political economy onto the alternative ground of the criticism of some other abstract non-economic category (for instance, "instrumental thinking" or "technological enframing") from the position of some fantasized "outside" position. Rather, it is uniquely well-qualified to comprehend formally the structural contradictions and antagonisms that determine forms of life in "late capitalist" societies today, and are coming to do so around the globe. In this respect, I have argued, paradoxico-critical forms of reflection and analysis are qualified to inherit classical Marxism on the point of its most perceptive and ultimately enduring insight into the nature of capitalism, the insight that the structural character of capitalism is constituted by limit-paradox and in-closure.

This is not to say that the politics of logic by itself demands or even recommends *any* particular political position on the empirical level of existing parties and claims. Indeed, I do not think that it does. As a *formal* structure of thought demanded in a rigorous fashion by the very paradoxes which are the yield of a rigorous logical thinking of the problems of the One and the Many themselves, it can hardly demand specific configurations of action or yield specific recommendations for *praxis*. However, in relation to what are in fact dominant configurations of thought and action, it does offer (particularly in its paradoxico-critical mode) possibilities for the thought and practice of positions of resistance of them. This position of resistance is not, as we have seen, simply an "outside" or "subversive" one. Somewhat similarly, in fact, to Marx's classical critique of political economy, the aim of the paradoxico-critique is to discern the underlying structures responsible for the existence and dominance of the particular configuration of thought and praxis that "global capitalism" represents. This yields a position of critique from which it is possible to resist certain claims (here, claims of effectiveness and progress) routinely made on behalf of this configuration, claims which in part serve as conditions for the possibility of its global application and enforcement.[27]

ANTAGONISM AND CRITIQUE

This organizes a rigorous critical theory of political economy, one that extends to the very capture of life around the globe by the capital form. The most important yield of this theory for political thought and action, as I have argued, is *not* that it demands or supports any particular activity or partisan program, but rather that it offers to change the very terms in which we discuss the problems of collective action and *praxis*, terms which must, as I have argued, be superseded on the basis of a formal consideration of their underpinnings. Nevertheless, as with any critical theory, a question is bound to arise about the "application" of this theory in terms of actual practice. This question may indeed seem to be sharpened through the contrast I have developed with Badiou's generic orientation, whose practical consequences appear, at least at first glance, to be relatively clear: a "militant" *praxis* of subjective intervention in the name of the event, whose transitory appearance must be safeguarded through fidelity though it can never be assured. We have actually come, over the course of the analysis, to doubt on several grounds whether the formal register of Badiou's theory, on which he ultimately stakes his whole case, in fact provides any substantial justificatory or motivational support for the specific kinds of political interventions that have been cited on behalf of his theory. Accordingly, it is probably not a fatal weakness of paradoxico-criticism, relative to the generic orientation, if it too operates primarily on the level of theory and the configuration of thought rather than *directly* inspiring *praxis*. But although my primary aim here is indeed to theorize configurations of thought rather than issue any kind of call to action, and although it is furthermore one of the implications of the problematic of application that paradoxico-criticism develops that this very opposition between theory and its "application" should itself be deconstructed, it is probably helpful to address the question of action and practice briefly here nevertheless.

A relevant and helpful account of political thought and action can be found in Laclau and Mouffe's "neo-Marxist" analysis of the articulation of hegemonic blocs in *Hegemony and Socialist Strategy.*[28] The background for Laclau and Mouffe's theory is the challenge to rethink traditional categories of teleological and economist Marxism given the untenability today of the assumptions of unified historical progression and determination of social reality "in the final instance" by base economic factors. This leads Laclau and Mouffe to theorize politics as taking place within a complex symbolic field of action that is always "overdetermined" (Althusser's term, which he in turn drew from psychoanalysis and linguistics) in the sense that it cannot be theorized as the result of a single, "determining" level of underlying social reality but is rather structured by multiple and overlapping points of contestation, struggle, and antagonism.[29] Accordingly, for Laclau and Mouffe, "society" cannot ever be a "totally sutured" whole (here they redeploy Miller's term "suture" [see Chapter 2] for a complete and adequate reflection of the social whole into itself). This is because of a structurally necessary "non-correspondence between the subject and the Other—the symbolic—which prevents the closure of the latter as a full presence."[30] The structural impossibility of the total "self-suture" of the social whole to itself is, according to Laclau and Mouffe, demonstrated by the analyses of Saussure, Lacan, and Derrida, all of which contribute to showing that any social field, being structured as a system of differences, must fail to exist "as a sutured and self-defined totality" and hence that "'Society' is not a valid object of discourse."[31] The essential failure of "society" to exist as a unified and total whole, moreover, is marked in the inherent existence of a necessary and supplementary "surplus" dimension of symbolic meaning that is the condition of possibility for all possible political or social action:

> We have referred to 'discourse' as a system of differential entities—that is, of moments. But . . . such a system only exists as a partial limitation of a 'surplus of meaning' which subverts it. Being inherent in every discursive situation, this 'surplus' is the necessary terrain for the constitution of every social practice. We will call it the *field of discursivity*. This term indicates the form of its relation with every concrete discourse: it determines at the same time the necessarily discursive character of any object, and the impossibility of any given discourse to implement a final suture.[32]

As Laclau and Mouffe quite rightly point out, the treatment of any object as "discursive" in this sense does not at all relegate it to the status of the "merely linguistic" or "textual." They cite specifically Wittgenstein's conception of a language-game as the *"indissoluble totality"* (note the term) composed of "language and the actions into which it is woven"; this is a whole consisting not only of words or texts but of objects, actors, and their material properties as well, all situated within a complex and structured system of differences, and its invocation is sufficient (in the context of the broader analysis) to refute the accusation of any form of "textual" or "linguistic" idealism.[33] Rather, it is this discursive field consisting of words and objects in relational totality that is the ultimate locus of the multiple antagonisms constitutive of the possibility of any meaningful social or political intervention.

Given the supplementary dimension which constitutes the discursive field and renders impossible any final fixation of society as a closed and unified whole, Laclau and Mouffe, drawing here on Derrida's claim of the radical absence of any "transcendental signified," argue that the attempt to construct "society" must amount to the repression of this impossibility by way of the attempt to "fix meanings" ultimately. *This* attempt cannot succeed, but because there indeed are "relatively fixed" (not absolutely fixed) meanings, it is possible to envision a politically productive *praxis* of "hegemonic articulation" that takes effect within the discursively constituted and constitutively overdetermined field. This "articulation" is thus defined by Laclau and Mouffe as the situated "construction of nodal points which partially fix meaning."[34] Given the inherent "non-closure" of society, such antagonism must be seen within the analysis of hegemonic articulation as essential to any structured social whole at all:

> Antagonism, far from being an objective relation, is a relation wherein the limits of every objectivity are *shown*—in the sense in which Wittgenstein used to say that what cannot be *said* can be *shown*. But if, as we have demonstrated, the social only exists as a partial effort for constructing society—that is, an objective and closed system of differences—antagonism, as a witness of the impossibility of a final suture, is the 'experience' of the limit of the social.[35]

This is particularly useful, Laclau and Mouffe argue, in that it allows for the effective formation of what are at first localized and heterogeneous empirically given positions of contingent struggle into relatively more unified "hegemonic blocs." It is thus possible, Laclau and Mouffe suggest, to conceive of the new task for leftist politics as that of performing a re-articulation of liberal-democratic ideology in the direction of a new more "radical and plural democracy." This is a task of consolidating various "democratic struggles," contingently located and initially devoted to different ends (Laclau and Mouffe mention, for interest, such differently constituted struggles as those of "the ecological movements, the student movements, feminism and the marginal masses") into unified but nevertheless plural positions of effective democratic action. Thus, the articulatory practice is the "constitution" of the identities which can face each other in antagonistic struggle, and Laclau and Mouffe say that this constitution of such identities now becomes "the first of political problems."[36]

There is certainly a great deal in all of this with which the rigorous paradoxico-critic can agree. The general field of discursivity which Laclau and Mouffe identify as the contested space of overdetermined struggle is none other than the symbolic field of language with the necessarily supplemental dimension that is manifest in the structurally necessary place of floating signifiers and paradoxical elements. Moreover, this dimension is indeed, for the paradoxico-critic, the ultimate source of the possibility of meaningful political action, not only, as Laclau and Mouffe say, because within it meanings are relatively fluid and must be fixed but also because, as we have seen, it is the structurally necessary place of the constitution of ideals, and so the source of any possible "ideological" motivation of action. What is more, Laclau and Mouffe are right, from a paradoxico-critical perspective, to insist upon both the possibility of, and the need for, an "articulatory" practice within the material/discursive field which consists in the redrawing of conceptual boundary lines and the "autonomization" of discursive categories to facilitate emancipatory and "democratic" change.

On the other hand, though, there are deep questions to be raised from this perspective about the trenchancy of Laclau and Mouffe's argument for the thoroughgoing *contingency* of all meaningful social struggles and identities. If, as they say, antagonism results in a strictly structural way from the necessary failure of society to suture itself, there is indeed a structural *necessity* to its existence whose consequences appear to be missed on the level of the pluralistic articulation of wholly contingent struggles. This necessity is, of course, not the necessity of a "single underlying" identity or "transcendental signified" capable of uniformly and teleologically structuring the social order as a consistent whole, but it is a *kind of necessity nevertheless*, and it appears to bring with it a structurally necessary relationship between the limit-contradictions and paradoxes of a particular social, economic, or political order, on the one hand, and the inherent antagonisms that rend it, on the other. If this is so, then the apparent contingency and heterogeneity of differently constituted but parallel emancipatory struggles is indeed ultimately underlain, on a more penetrating level of analysis, by a unity of inherent structural features. These features are themselves, moreover, consequences of the limit-contradictions arising from the inherent tendency of any constituted order to conceive itself as a unified and self-consistent whole. As structurally inherent contradictions, rather than the pluralistic field of contingent struggles, they are then the *necessary* sites of the attempt to articulate positions of resistance and change. This does not mean that their specific character will not vary from situation to situation, or that the location of systematic "weak points" and slippages will not have to be determined strategically, from situation to situation, on the basis of variable facts and circumstances. But it does mean that the sites of these struggles will have a formally discernible identity that preexists and to a certain extent supersedes what Laclau and Mouffe see as the affirmation of their irreducible contingency.

On a more immediate level, as well, it is worth asking whether Laclau and Mouffe's picture of emancipation as taking place through the hegemonic articulation of an irreducibly plural and heterogeneous set of contingent struggles is really adequate to a whole range of fields of "democratic" and emancipatory struggle for which there is, in a very important sense, in actuality only *one* "enemy" today: namely, global capitalism itself. Here, Laclau and Mouffe's insistence upon the irreducible heterogeneity of struggles and the pluralist contingency of the articulation of hegemonic blocs veers dangerously close to the liberal-democratic celebration of "diversity" and "difference" for its own sake, a consensual ethic which in its growing dominance in fact serves a legitimating function for economism and capitalist *praxis*. Thus, although Laclau and Mouffe admit that the "multitude of social relations" which are today mediated through capital means that "there is practically no domain of individual or collective life which escapes capitalist relations,"[37] they see this multiplicity only as capable of introducing new and diverse forms of movements and struggle, rather than (as paradoxico-criticism emphasizes) capable of identifying how *all* of these seemingly diverse struggles, insofar as they demand the construction of spaces and lives subtracted from the power of capital and economism, share the same antagonistic form.

Turning, then, to the practices of hegemonic articulation that Laclau and Mouffe recommend, there are important questions, as well, to be raised about the extent to which these are actually grounded in the theoretical structures of language and discourse they analyze. In particular, given that society cannot completely suture itself, it is "impossible," Laclau and Mouffe argue, for "ultimate meanings"—in the sense of a "transcendental signified" or an "absolute centre"—ever to be fixed.[38] However, because there can nevertheless be "partial fixations," the task for hegemonic articulation is to pursue these "partial" fixations or *relatively* stable nodal points.[39] The problem here is that, given the way that Laclau and Mouffe interpret the result of the earlier structuralist and post-structuralist analyses, it is now impossible as well to distinguish the "partial" and "relative" fixations that Laclau and Mouffe wish to pursue from those hegemonic articulations that indeed claim an "absolute" ground in the completely sutured totality of the social whole or in the presence of a transcendental signified. On Laclau and Mouffe's own account, the pursuit of such "partial" fixations of meaning, then, can only tend toward a totality which they themselves declare impossible. As a result, it becomes uncertain whether the democratic articulatory practices they describe can really find any coherent motivation in the post-structuralist theoretical results at all.[40]

From the perspective of the current analysis, all of these difficulties in Laclau and Mouffe's analysis have a common root. It lies in their failure to see clearly the metalogical duality that differentiates the politics of logic into its paradoxico-critical and generic modes, the distinction between *inconsistent completeness*, on one hand, and *consistent incompleteness*, on the other. Understanding the post-structuralist results simply as showing, in an undifferentiated way, the "impossibility" of a complete suture owing to the absence of the "transcendental signified" or "absolute centre," they discuss this absence as if it simply implied the "openness" of any constituted situation to the possibility of articulation and change. What Laclau and Mouffe thereby miss is that, in a precise sense, the fundamental antagonisms which they see as essential to the possibility of articulatory struggle and change are formally conditioned not only by contingent and accidental conflicts and disputes but by the limit-phenomena that result from (not the "openness" but rather) the fundamental *closure* of the systematic whole. The thought of this closure, as we have repeatedly seen over the last several chapters, invokes the social whole as a One which must be thought of as inherently contradictory owing to paradoxes at its limits, and paradoxico-criticism amounts to the rigorous thought of these paradoxes. This demonstrates a unity of structure that results in a relative formal *necessity* of antagonisms and points of struggle, which Laclau and Mouffe's analysis, dedicated to the category of contingency, entirely misses. With respect, moreover, to the structural whole of global capitalism, which functions by relentlessly interiorizing its supposed "exterior," the paradoxico-critical thinking of totality yields as well, as we have seen, a rigorous formal account of the underlying *unity* of the various struggles against this relentless appropriative movement. This is not in fact the cobbled-together "hegemonic" unity of inherently diverse and contingently constituted democratic movements, but rather the *single* struggle (pursued by various means) to create a life diagonal to capital and its power. Finally, a clear and rigorous articulation of paradoxico-criticism as committed to the choice for the combination of completeness and inconsistency solves the problem mentioned in the last paragraph, for it shows that the results of post-structuralist thinking about language and meaning are not incompatible with a consideration of ideal meanings as being, indeed, *absolutely* fixed, and indeed capable of providing motivation for the "democratic" struggles, as well, on the "ideological" level. The price of this absolute fixation will be, of course, inconsistency; but the "articulatory practice" which develops and defines rigorously the consequences of this fundamental inconsistency for the "social whole" now no longer faces the problem of aiming for a final state that it itself recognizes as impossible.

It would, of course, be precipitous to accuse Laclau and Mouffe of any special failing here, since (as we have seen) the existing literature that develops the political implications of post-structuralist analyses of language and meaning almost always fails to mark explicitly the metalogical duality, tending to speak instead of the purportedly demonstrated impossibility of any "complete *or* consistent" whole. Nevertheless, if Laclau and Mouffe's analysis of antagonism and articulation is transposed to the condition of a rigorous paradoxico-critical analysis, several implications result. The first is that, since antagonism is here thought as a result of in-closure—that is, as conditioned by both inconsistency *and* (paradoxical) closure—it becomes possible to specify much more directly the relationship of social antagonism to the "ideological" thought of the social whole. In particular, it is possible to see that antagonism arises as a *fundamental* feature of this whole as soon as it constitutes itself as such. Thus, antagonism (on the paradoxico-critical) analysis is not merely a contingent outcome of the division between various separately constituted interests, or even in any sense a struggle between classes, interests, and parties constituted independently of the social whole itself. Both society and its individual, constituent groups are thus fundamentally structured, in their very "identities," by antagonism and struggle.

Additionally, paradoxico-criticism reveals how antagonisms emerge from the inherently ideological and reflexive features that demand the inconsistency of any social whole, as soon as it is constituted as an object of thought or posited as a source of effective motivation. With respect to the specifically constituted antagonisms, then, paradoxico-criticism provides the theoretical resources for these to be located on the level of their true structural origin, in the effective systematicity of the social whole and the limit-paradoxes it always encounters on its borders. This yields a very different, and more profound, response to the actual antagonisms than anything that Laclau and Mouffe, given their analysis of the antagonisms as contingencies, can envision. In particular, it allows these specific, local antagonisms to be seen (and potentially responded to) as marking the profound and comprehensive structural aporias of the total social order itself. It is thus (and probably only thus) that they can be appropriated by a liberatory *praxis* that aims to define and sharpen these antagonisms up to the point of their potential to uproot and transform the entire structure of the social order itself, rather than (as Laclau and Mouffe sometimes appear to suggest) to extend this order in such a way as to reconcile them or reintegrate the terms of struggle they represent into a supposedly harmonious and smoothly functioning social whole.

The failure of Laclau and Mouffe to see the potentially radical and transformative consequences of existing antagonisms thus stems directly from their failure to attain clarity about the forced metalogical choice between completeness and consistency, which ensures the impossibility of any total social order that is not fundamentally rent by limit-contradiction and the internal struggles that reflect it. Simon Critchley makes a similar error in his recent *Infinitely Demanding*, where he invokes the need for an ethics of "heteronomy" to remedy what he sees as a "motivational deficit" in current leftist politics. Drawing this ethics largely from Levinas, Critchley emphasizes the "contingency of social life" or, in other words, its "constructed character," which calls, he says, for a "cultivation of forms of commonality" and new habits of social life.[41] In particular, in order to pursue a truly democratic politics, Critchley says, we must insist upon a kind of "hetero-affectivity" which precedes and disturbs claims of autonomy, a fundamental recognition of the primacy of the experience of being affected by an other. This leads Critchley to criticize what he calls an "autonomy orthodoxy" which, he says, characterizes all of Kantian and post-Kantian philosophy, up to Heidegger.[42]

Perceiving clearly the implications of the forced metalogical choice between inconsistent completeness, on the one hand, and consistent incompleteness, on the other, we can see, though, that it is not at all necessary to call upon a Levinasian ethics or any figure of the "absolute other" in order to ground a radical politics of change and transformation. For what is at stake in paradoxico-criticism, in fact, is not at all the inscription of a "hetero-affectivity" or heteronomy which posits such an absolute, extra-systematic position (a positing which can only then degenerate into religious or onto-theological forms) but rather a rigorous thinking of the consequences of the system's own *auto*-affectivity, its capacity to reflect itself (in "autonomous" fashion) which leads inherently to contradictions and antagonisms. This thinking is, of course, *continuous* with the Kantian critical tradition in a way that Critchley must ignore or deny, missing as he does the deep and transformative implications of the *reflexive* moment that is inscribed in every "autonomous" system as soon as it defines its own borders. From this perspective, there is no need, in theorizing and responding to the most significant political struggles of the day, to invoke an ethical "motivation" that comes from outside the system. The ethical "imperatives" involved in leading struggles are in fact pretty much self-evident, as soon as the distorting effects of capitalism and economism are removed; nor is the "motivational gap" that Critchley invokes in calling for an "ethics" of heteronomy really anything more than an artifact of his all-too-quick dismissal of the critical resources of the Kantian tradition. The result is a vague organicist piety of "habits" and "practices" which, somewhat awkwardly, combines a constructivist picture of political effectivity (Critchley's "cultivation of a *habitus*") with an onto-theological demand on the level of "ethics" (Levinas' "infinite other"). This uncertain and pious combination is increasingly characteristic of forms of the "ethical turn" and the "return of the religious" circulating today. In certain more populist forms, it underlies a "leftist" communitarianism that is in many ways simply the mirror image of the "rightist" libertarian "individualism" and the economism of the free market. Once again, the key to surpassing both of these positions is a clear recognition of the metalogical duality demanded by the rigorous pursuit of formalism.

By developing Laclau and Mouffe's analysis by way of a clearer recognition of what is involved in the metalogical choice for completeness and inconsistency, then, we gain a clearer formal understanding of the inherent role of "logical" contradiction in the very structure of collective life. As Laclau and Mouffe recognize, it is in fact impossible to understand antagonism simply as the conflict of empirically opposed forces; for a genuine antagonism to exist, there must also be conflicting claims and interests, real contestation of claims and propositions.[43] However, whereas Laclau and Mouffe treat these conflicts in terms of the mere coexistence of conflicted groups and interests (or the *weak* incommensurability of the lack of common measure), paradoxico-criticism shows how they result in a fundamental way from the claimed effectivity of the social whole itself (or, in other words, from the *strong* incommensurability of any system that is both total and reflexive).[44] It thus shows how the various specifically constituted struggles result in a direct sense from the impossibility of society to "suture" itself (i.e., to think itself reflectively as a *consistent* totality), from which Laclau and Mouffe draw their whole analysis.

This thought of antagonism as rooted in structurally necessary contradiction captures the formally rigorous core of Marx's conception of class struggle, as well what is salvageable within a post-Cantorian formal context of the Hegelian dialectic itself.[45] What, then, is the rigorous critical upshot of this thinking of antagonism as limit-contradiction? Once again, it is helpful to listen to Wittgenstein:

> The fundamental fact here is that we lay down rules, a technique, for a game, and that then when we follow the rules, things do not turn out as we had assumed. That we are therefore as it were entangled in our own rules.
>
> This entanglement in our rules is what we want to understand (i.e. get a clear view of).
>
> It throws light on our concept of meaning something. For in those cases things turn out otherwise than we had meant, foreseen. That is just what we say when, for example, a contradiction appears: "I didn't mean it like that."
>
> The civil status of a contradiction, or its status in civil life: there is the philosophical problem. (*PI* 125).

What Wittgenstein here calls the "philosophical" problem is also, as I have attempted to show, *the* essential problem for a critical theory of politics and social organization today. As we have seen over the last several chapters, paradoxico-criticism provides the requisite formal basis for understanding the large and growing variety of conflicts and problems which result, across different domains, from what Wittgenstein here calls an "entanglement in our own rules." Wittgenstein's development of the problem of rules and rule-following demonstrates that this is a question of the effectivity of rules and of the "ideological" position which sees this effectivity as guaranteed in itself. This problematic of rules and techniques is identical, as we have seen, with the problem of the effectivity of information and informational technology, including the problem of the effective capture of life by means of a total economic system governed by "informational" capital and its abstract repetition. With his radical reflection on rules and their meaning, Wittgenstein has demonstrated the irreducibility of a moment of application which ultimately cannot be foreclosed by any systematic guarantees of consistency. This provides, on the one hand, a radical challenge to the "official" attempt to guarantee the consistency of practices or the effectivity of rules, and on the other, an essential "reminder" of the essential moment of ineffectivity at the core of every application of rules that ruins every assumption of their automatic force. This allows, in turn, for the possibility of thinking and creating new forms of life that no longer presuppose this effectivity and force, but in a precise metalogical sense, reflexively and critically "subtract" themselves from it.

What, then, becomes of Laclau and Mouffe's practice of discursive "articulation" at antagonistic sites? With the paradoxico-critical understanding of antagonism as resulting in a fundamental way from the internal reflection of limit-paradoxes, the antagonistic sites become the "privileged sites" (insofar as they reflect the limit-paradoxes) of the potential appearance of the fundamentally structuring contradictions that are normally repressed under the force of the assumption of a smoothly functioning and self-consistent social whole. The articulation of specific local struggles into more global "blocs" of effective action is not, then, simply a matter of patching together separately constituted and heterogeneous points, but of *recognizing* in the apparent diversity of empirical struggles a fundamental *unity* of structural determination. The empirically defined specific antagonisms between individual groups and interests then become potential sites for the exposure and clarification of the contradictions which ordinarily, but obscurely, structure effective social life, and for the redefinition of language and *praxis* in response to the challenge of occupying the space of indeterminacy and undecidability thereby revealed. The "point" of this exposure and redefinition is not at all to "resolve" the contradictions but rather to sharpen them, thus making the specific antagonisms the possible site of the articulation and emergence of a clarified life to come.

This is first and foremost a *theoretical* task, and no one should be dissuaded from the monumental challenge to formal thinking and critical reflection that is evident here by empty allegations of "textualism" or solemn recitations of Marx's eleventh thesis on Feuerbach. Nevertheless, with respect to the specific empirical antagonisms between groups and "interests," it is the important political work of recognizing which of these have the potential to stage the inherent contradictions of the system as such, and of bringing out and sharpening these contradictions where they begin to show up. The aim is, as Wittgenstein says, to make these contradictions visible in order to "survey" the deep underlying sources of the "entanglement" in rules that we experience, thereby making visible as well the possibility of a life beyond this entanglement.

In this way, paradoxico-criticism captures the motivating force of the variety of emancipatory and "democratic" struggles which attempt to intervene in the structurally determined situation to overcome it by means of its own internal logic. What, then, of democracy itself? As Derrida and other theorists have convincingly argued, any helpful critical discussion of the meaning and significance of "democracy" today demands both a rigorous critique of the anti-egalitarian systematic and electoral forms that flourish today under the protection of this ambiguous signifier and a recognition of the formal features that nevertheless qualify democracy as the only hope for egalitarian and emancipatory projects. One of the most important of these features, Derrida argues, is the "auto-immunity" by which democratic systems structurally attempt to define their own structure and limits, in order to protect themselves from an ambiguous outside, but also to insure mechanisms by which these systems can be insulated or protected from their own inherent excesses.[46] This "auto-immunity" is itself possible, however, only by means of the auto-affection or reflexivity inscribed into every form of democratic imagination and *praxis*. It is this reflexivity which paradoxico-criticism relentlessly pursues, locating in the actually existing antagonisms the structural effects of the auto-affective moment by which every constituted regime attempts to protect and consolidate itself. At the point of these antagonisms, paradoxico-criticism thus confronts the sovereign-democratic attempt to maintain systematic consistency with a more radical implication of the democratic imaginary itself: the reflexive thinking of contradiction and paradox that inscribes in any existing "democratic order" the transformative thought of what Derrida calls the "democracy to come."

This is a radical imaginative and practical work of redefinition and reorientation, heir to (but not reducible to) the thinking of "revolution" in its classical modes. It aims ultimately at the creation of new forms of life and their explicitly transformative inscription *within* the systems and structures we inhabit at the point of those systems' ineffectivity, and thus at an eventually *total* transformation of their character, the total transformation that is marked by the *complete* disappearance of the problems that they create.[47] Although it has, as we have seen, profound implications for "everyday life," this is not the liberal-communitarian-constructivist "creation of a habitus," nor is it limited to the creation of what Critchley calls "interstitial distance" between "politics" and the state it inhabits. As the strict implication of the radical metalogical thinking of forms and their capture of a life, it is the fundamentally *transformative* politics of the possibility of forms itself.

TWO CASES

To conclude, let us briefly consider two specific areas in which this kind of radical practice of re-articulation and imagination at contradictory sites is urgently needed today. The politics of "*the environment*" and *education* are today urgent sites of political struggle, places where the effectivity of the system, particularly in its capitalist and economist modes, poses a dramatic challenge to ethical thought and action. I choose these two areas, in particular, not because there are no others today where the possibility of an ethical continuance of systematic means and outcomes of action is radically at stake, but for two other reasons that illustrate the singular relevance of paradoxico-criticism and the kind of transformation in thought and action that it recommends for the "leading" global problems of our time. First, because in both of these cases, it is clear that to treat the problematics and open questions here at issue simply within any economist or calculative form of reasoning is already to massively betray the ethical imperatives they formulate. In particular, these are two domains where the *inherent* structural contradictions of a global-capitalist system that presents itself as total, and effective in its totality, are particularly sharp and pronounced; the theoretical and practical work of paradoxico-criticism is then to bring out these contradictions in their specificity and make them the site of a thinking of a possible life equal to the ethical imperatives involved in each case. And second, because in both of these cases, whereas it is thus clear that it is imperative for any useful future "political" thought and action must break profoundly with the (constructivist and onto-theological) orientations that simply inscribe forms of collective action and praxis without traversing the profound consequences of their reflective self-inclusion (and hence that *some* form of the post-Cantorian "politics of logic" is necessary here), it also seems that the Badiouian invocation of the event and the creation of the faithful subject is not exactly to the point, either. Because, as we have seen, the generic orientation contemplates "political" change and transformation always only from the perspective of the transformation of an existing and *local* situation, it seems hardly capable of contemplating, let alone addressing, the vast and irreducibly *global* problems involved here.[48] And if, as seems apparent, we can hardly tie the hope of a futural politics, in either of these domains, to the pursuit of a punctual event which would reorder all existing relations and imperatives, it seems likely that we must pursue the ethical imperatives here, instead, by means of paradoxico-criticism's critical tracing and sharpening of antagonisms, forms of action that may tend much more, as we have seen, to the suspension and deposition of existing practices, measures, and ends.

First, then, the case of the "environment." Here, in relation to the practically incontrovertible scientific evidence of anthropogenic climate change (as well as the less comprehensive but still catastrophic problems of pollution, deforestation, extinction, etc.), the failure of parliamentarian governments and negotiated (for instance, treaty-based) solutions is as evident as is the failure of the obscurantist theological and traditionalist positions that oppose them. Pop-"environmentalism," facile consumerism, and advertising propaganda have appropriated most of the signifiers and rhetoric of environmentalist motivation and action in order to assuage within a corporatist framework the bad conscience of consumers who are *massively* and on a daily basis responsible for the continued destruction of the earth and its denizens. And in the effective sphere of "democratic" action (that is, the radically narrowed-down and distorted domain of electoral politics, in the U.S. and other first-world powers), the totality of our human relation to what David Abram has called "the more than human world"[49] appears only as an indifferent question of "policy," destined always to be overwhelmed by populist economism and the structurally enforced capitalist demand for "growth." Meanwhile, the ineffectual field of "environmental ethics," which is nevertheless the most evident theoretical face of the struggle, tries to rationalize by means of nostalgic appeals and romantic images the forms of action and rebellion which are quite evidently demanded, in any case, in an immediate and profound way by the facts of the planetary situation itself. None of these theoretical approaches have, so far at any rate, been capable even of adequately *portraying* (let alone intervening to resolve) the structural situation that recurrently and incorrigibly holds species, ecosystems, and the future of the planet as a whole captive to the imperative of an empty consumerist *jouissance*, with its fake satisfactions and infantile rewards.

What is needed is, then, just what I have described: a radical critical/emancipatory practice of thought and action that recognizes, in the existing forms and appearances of "environmental activism" and protest, the leading edge of a potentially transformative staging of the capitalist economy's inherent contradictions with itself, on the inherently political level of the specific forms of life (capitalist, consumerist, and liberal-democratic) that it relentlessly promotes and enforces, and looks toward a new form of life that, diagonalizing, escapes them.[50]

Another "case," then: the case of education. Here, although there can certainly be no question of retreat with respect to the grand nineteenth- and twentieth-century liberal-democratic project of universal access to schools, the accomplishment of this project (at any rate, within "first-world" economies) has nevertheless tended to confirm and, in recent decades, even consolidate the applicability of Althusser's classical analysis of schools (among other institutions) as effectively functioning "Ideological State Apparatuses" ('state' being taken here as referring to the general regime of capitalist economism, rather than any particular national state).[51] In recent years in particular, a narrow economism and the incessant inscription of education within the scope of narrowly economic and managerial regimes of "productivity" and "effectiveness" have led to the standardization and proliferation of calculative measures, narrowly financial determination of the "success" of teaching and learning, and a populist political culture that tends to evaluate education in the narrow economist terms of skills imparted, "preparation" for "the global marketplace," and future earning potential therein. For those who "believe in" a classical kind of education (which used to, but perhaps can no longer, go by the name "humanist") dedicated to the cultivation of critical thought, free inquiry, fundamental research, and reflective consideration of the problems most pressing to us at *any* time, this liberal-democratic educational populism is, needless to say, a failure. The problem is not a new one, for it is nothing other than the ancient problem of the very possibility of the examined life, as it played out so long ago in relation to the fate of philosophy in an Athenian democracy that already stages many of the contradictions and structural features of our current regime. It is, moreover, becoming more and more visible today in the local antagonisms that are staging the conflict between education and economism in the face of massive cutbacks, corporatization, and instrumentalization.

What is needed is, once again, a thought and *praxis* that develop these local antagonisms into a substantial renewal of the radical Socratic defense of the possibility of the examined life, here thought as the fragile possibility of the clarified life to come, dedicated to taking up once again the consequences of the proposition that the reflexive wisdom of philosophy, under the condition of an age that everywhere knows only the effectivity of forms and the marketing of information, should not be allowed to vanish from the earth.

Notes

NOTES TO THE METHODOLOGICAL PREFACE

1. I began this investigation in my last book, *Philosophy and the Vision of Language* (Livingston 2008).

NOTES TO CHAPTER 1

1. Wittgenstein (1953) (henceforth: *PI*), II, xi, 345.
2. Conventionalist or communitarian readers of Wittgenstein include Rorty (1993), Kripke (1982), and Bloor (1983); those who read Wittgenstein as a "naturalist," in one sense or another, include McGinn (1987), Maddy (2000), Pears (1995), and McGinn (2010). For the broader project of "naturalizing" meaning and language, see, e.g., Millikan (1984), Dretske (1997), Fodor (1992), and Papineau (1993).
3. One example of this kind of position is that of McDowell (1994), who attempts to avoid both "bald naturalism" and conventionalism by means of the invocation of a "naturalism of second nature" that, McDowell suggests, can also function as a "naturalized Platonism."
4. The lack of any explicit connective in Wittgenstein's German term "Lebensform" does not make this problem of relation any less urgent.
5. Cantor (1883), p. 204, n. 1, quoted in Hallett (1986), p. 33. (*"eidos"* and *"idea"* are written in Greek in the original quotation).
6. Following Cantor, I thus take the concept of a *set* to capture, in an important sense, what is meant by the Platonic "eidos." In particular, it captures the grouping of *many* as *one* that underlies any actual process of "abstraction" in thought as well as the unities of sense and meaning in language. A *form* will therefore be, in the sense in which I am using it here, the ("structural" or "operational") basis of *any* grouping of (finitely or infinitely) many as one. This extends (as I shall argue in connection with Wittgenstein) to the unity of a technique or practice, understood as the unity of the determination of a set of empirical instances by a rule or law. "Form" is thus used as well to characterize moments of structure abstractable from empirical situations, although I do not presuppose the Aristotelian distinction of form and matter (and so do not use "form" primarily in the Aristotelian sense of *"morphe"*). *Formalization* is then the *activity* of reflection on forms, whether this be understood simply as reflection on what was "already there" in some sense or as a process of invention of the new on the basis of what has come before. *Formalism* is, then, the *result* of this process of reflection on forms including (but not limited to) their capture in explicit

symbolism and the determination of rules connecting them. This broad sense of formalization as reflection, and formalism as its result, should be distinguished from a narrower sense of "formalization" in which it means the *imposition* of forms, for instance, in a given social community. The latter, narrower sense is what is more often referred to in discourses about the "formalization" of social life and communities, including processes of regularization, technicization, and the imposition of quantitative and statistical techniques of measurement and evaluation.

It is a direct consequence of these definitions that forms, formalism, and formalization (in any of these senses) cannot be restricted to any particular domain of human life (for instance, the construction of "formal systems" narrowly conceived), but are always already operative in each and every context of conceptual thought and discursive action. In particular, the attitude taken here (especially in defense of the "paradoxico-critical" orientation [see below]) is thus not that formalization and the creation of formalisms is limited to a narrow theoretical activity that takes place as a restricted offshoot of ordinary language, but rather that formalization is always-already operative in the very capacity of ordinary language to refer to itself, and does not gain any special significance in relation to explicitly constructed special symbolic languages or "formal systems" in a narrow sense.

7. Set membership is therefore, on this view (and as T. E. Forster puts it in [Forster 1992, p. 12]), essentially an "allegory of predication" and sets themselves can be considered to be "predicates in extension." (It is significant in this respect that Peano initially used "∈" as a symbol for set membership precisely to abbreviate *est*, the Latin word for the "is," of predication). Although sets are, on this view, correlative with "predicates," they thus remain "extensional" in the sense that they are also sufficiently and uniquely determined by their members; this is not, therefore, an "intensional" view of sets. As Forster also notes, according to this attitude, set theory is thus simply a kind of outgrowth of logic (rather than the other way around), and this conception of sets and set membership is indeed closely linked to the classical logicist tradition, which sought as well to reduce mathematics to set theory. (This is the reason for discussing here a "politics of logic" rather than, say, a "politics of mathematics" or of "sets.") I shall argue below that this attitude is by no means refuted by the paradoxes that arose within Frege's own attempt to treat sets as correlative with predicates; rather, I shall suggest, these paradoxes simply suggest deep underlying paradoxes in the formal structure of predication itself.

8. The claim here is not that a state, in order to exist, must in fact *be* a unitary structure. It is rather, more simply, that a social whole is always a many that is *thought* as a one, and the focus of the "political" interrogation of forms is thus on the question of the preconditions for this thought or for its actual effectiveness in *praxis*.

9. As I argued in Livingston (2008), there is a profound anticipation of this twentieth-century theme of the unity of meaning across diverse instances of application in the Platonic conception of the Idea as the unity by which the many are rightly *called* by the same name. For this connection, see, e.g., *Meno* 75a; *Phaedo* 78e-79c and 89d; *Sophist* 244c-e and 260e; *Parmenides* 135e and 147d-148a.

10. For the conception of Wittgenstein as a "philosopher of culture" in this sense, see, e.g., Cavell (1989). I have also discussed some implications of this conception in Livingston (2008), Chapters 6 and 7.

11. The critical theory of the progressive "rationalization" of society and its links to what is discussed as "instrumental" as well as "communicative"

forms of rational practice has roots in Weber and is presented in what is by now its classic form by Habermas (1981a) and (1981b).

12. See, e.g.: Husserl (1957) and Habermas (1981b), who treat the "pre-" or "non-"formalized aspects of reason under the heading of the "lifeworld"; Adorno (1966) and Horkheimer (1967), who criticize "instrumental reason" while appealing to an older, Kantian and non-instrumental conception; and Heidegger's (1952) and (1953) critiques of technology and "calculative thinking."

13. Compare also *Politics* 1332b5: "Animals lead for the most part a life of nature, although in lesser particulars some are influenced by habit as well. Man has reason, in addition, and man only."

14. Agamben (1995).

15. As it is, for instance, in earlier attempts to understand the structures of politics as determined by conventional agreement, for instance through the formalism of game theory (see, e.g., Lewis [1969]; Habermas]1981a]). The fundamental limitation of these analyses, on the present account, is shown by their assumption that social and political structures must ultimately have a contractual basis in the agreement of individuals, rather than (as the analyses treated here tend to suggest) in the inherently *collective* logical structures of presentation and representation.

16. Jacques Rancière (1995), Chapter 1, gives a partially parallel reading of this passage from Aristotle. According to Rancière, Aristotle sees the "supremely political destiny of man" as " attested by . . . the possession of the logos" (p. 2). This demonstrates, according to Rancière, that politics begins "when what is at issue is what citizens have *in common*" (p. 5) and how this is counted; politics is thus always basically "a count of community 'parts,' which is always a false count, a double count, or a miscount" (p. 6). Badiou discussses Rancière's work in *Metapolitics* (Badiou 1998c), Chapters 7 and 8. Compare also Arendt's classic (1958) development of the implications of the same Aristotelian theme.

17. *PI*, 241.

18. This is admittedly not an "orthodox" reading of Wittgenstein (see Chapters 5 and 6). The language of "attunement" is Stanley Cavell's from Cavell (1979).

19. Badiou (2007), pp. 102–3.

20. There are already several primarily exegetical studies of Badiou available in English: see, e.g., Hallward (2003), Norris (2009), Feltham (2008), Gillespie (2008), and the many helpful essays collected in Hallward (2004a). Two of the first books in English to bring Badiou systematically into discussion with other major contemporary thinkers are Johnston (2009) and Calcagno (2007).

21. See, e.g., Badiou (2003), p. 50; Badiou (1998b), p. 159. In both cases Badiou cites Socrates' demand, in the *Cratylus*, that philosophy concern itself with "things" rather than "words"; but for more on the *Cratylus*, see below.

22. The passage also invites a reading against Heidegger's famous description, in *Being and Time*, of the transition in the mode of being of an object from its ready-at-handness (*Zuhandenheit*) to its being present at hand (*Vorhanden*), where the transition that allows us to discern the object's theoretical being is indeed precisely made possible when it is no longer readily accessible in use, as for instance when it breaks.

23. Cf. Agamben's perspicacious description of the Platonic idea as the "thing itself" in Agamben (1984b).

24. For more on this essential gap, see Livingston (2008), especially Chapters 1, 6, 7, and 9.

25. *PI* 199.
26. It is thus clear that "finitist" or intuitionist objections, according to which it is impossible for an infinite *completed* totality ever to exist, are not really to the point here. For because they do not go to the heart of the issue of *how* a symbolic expression is related to its usage on each particular occasion, these objections amount more to a refusal to consider Wittgenstein's problem than a response to it. Indeed, as we shall see in more detail in Chapter 6, the issue here is not well put in the classical terms of Aristotle's distinction between "potential" and actual infinities at all. If the finitist's point is simply, as it is sometimes put, that we can grasp a "potentially" infinite procedure only through its *finite* symbolization, Wittgenstein can quite well agree with *this* point: the question then is simply how such a symbolization underlies even a "potential" infinity of applications, or how it determines an application on each particular occasion. If, on the other hand, the finitist is better interpreted simply as denying that there is any sense in which a finite rule determines an extension that is *either* potentially *or* actually infinite, then she is better seen as taking a position that simply opts out of the problem that Wittgenstein is posing here altogether. Such a position may be the "radical" or "full-blooded" conventionalism that has sometimes, misleadingly, been attributed to Wittgenstein himself (for instance, by Dummett in [Dummett 1959]), but it is clear (as we shall see in more detail in Chapter 6) that this is not his position and that it is untenable in itself.
27. This question has both an "epistemic" dimension and a "metaphysical" one. The epistemic question is the question about how a (finite) mind can *grasp* or *understand* a rule that determines our practice in an infinite number of cases, whereas the metaphysical one is: what sort of "thing" is a rule, such that *it* can determine what is the right thing to do in an infinite number of cases of practice or application? The second, "metaphysical" question is sometimes specified as the question of the origin or structure of "normativity"; however, it is probably too closely intertwined with the first to be capable of separate treatment. For this and other related reasons (see Chapter 6), I do not follow the mainstream literature in attributing to Wittgenstein a desire either to presuppose or account for a supposedly "normative" dimension of our practices. However, at the same time, it is clear that neither question is simply the question of what we do *in fact* do in any number of actual cases; *this* question is presumably an empirical or historical one, to be settled by means of empirical research and evidence.
28. Cf. Socrates in *Cratylus*, again, where "convention" and "usage" (*ethos*) are clearly distinguished: "And even if usage (*ethos*) is completely different from convention, still you must say that expressing something isn't a matter of likeness but of usage, since usage, it seems, enables both like and unlike names to express things. Since we agree on these points, Cratylus, for I take your silence as a sign of agreement, both convention and usage must contribute something to expressing what we mean when we speak. Consider numbers, Cratylus, since you want to have recourse to them. Where do you think you'll get names that are like each one of the numbers, if you don't allow this agreement and convention of yours to have some control over the correctness of names? I myself prefer the view that names should be as much like things as possible, but I fear that defending this view is like hauling a ship up a sticky ramp, as Hermogenes suggested, and that we have to make use of this worthless thing, convention, in the correctness of names." (435a–c).
29. *PI*, 242.

30. Wittgenstein's word here is *Aufheben*, the problematic Hegelian term of art that can be variously translated as "sublate," "supersede," "transcend," "cancel," or "preserve."

31. Derrida (1966).

32. Contemporary discussion develops from classical sources in Bodin, Pufendorf, Suarez, and Hobbes. Relevant contemporary discussions include (just to scratch the surface): Schmitt (1932) and (1934); Benjamin (1927); Bataille (1949); Arendt (1951) and (1958); Nancy (1991); Derrida (1994), (2002), (2003), and (2005); Agamben (1990a), (1995), and (2003).

33. Schmitt (1934), p. 13.

34. Agamben (2003).

35. The term "double bind" originates with Bateson (1956), who used it to discuss a communicative situation in which contradictory imperatives are issued, leading to a situation in which there is no possible "right" response. In the article in which he introduces the terminology, Bateson refers to Russell's theory of types, holding that a double bind can result from the communicative situation in which the hierarchy of logical types is breached, as for instance when a class is a member of itself. Derrida has employed the concept of the "double bind" both with reference to deconstructive and psychoanalytic interpretation (e.g., Derrida 1998) and, more recently (Derrida 2003), with reference to the "auto-immune" political structure of democracy, which must systematically inoculate itself from itself.

36. In his remarkable 1996 work *Broken Hegemonies*, Reiner Schürmann (1996) undertakes to reread the history of philosophy as the history of the succession of sovereign measures. In the history of what he terms "hegemonic phantasms," particular individuals are successively raised to the rank of the standard of measure; in this way, determinate philosophical regimes, taking place between the institution of a hegemony and its diremption, successively organize all that can appear phenomenally within a particular epoch of being. From Parmenides to Heidegger, the history of the being of beings can therefore be understood in terms of the paradox of the nomothesis, and its characteristic double bind.

37. For more on this history see Moore (2001a).

38. A good general treatment of diagonalization is Smullyan (1994). See also Hofstadter (1979) and Priest (2002).

39. Hallett (1986).

40. See Frege's letter to Russell of 22 June 1902, reprinted and translated in Frege (1980).

41. Russell (1908). The other paradoxes said by Russell to share roughly the same structure are: Burali-Forti's contradiction concerning the ordinal number of the size of all ordinals, a set of paradoxes concerning the definability of transfinite ordinals, integers, and decimals, and an analogue to Russell's paradox concerning the "relation which subsists between two relations R and S whenever R does not have the relation R to S." Russell had previously discussed the paradox and briefly sketched the theory of types in *The Principles of Mathematics* (Russell 1903) and in two 1906 articles: Russell (1906a) and Russell (1906b).

42. Russell (1908), p. 61.

43. As has been objected, it is not immediately obvious that the Liar paradox involves covert reference to a totality. Russell's own way of assimilating it to the form of his own paradox involves taking the remark of the Cretan to quantify over *all* propositions uttered by Cretans, but it is not apparent that it must take this form, since it may also be put as the paradox of the Cretan who, employing indexicals or deictic pronouns, says "Everything I say is false" or simply "This

sentence is false." Nevertheless, Priest (2002), p. 144, has argued that putting the Liar sentence in a form that portrays it as making reference to a totality of propositions both conveys its actual underlying logic and demonstrates its similarity of structure to the other formal and "semantic" paradoxes.

44. Cf. Priest (2002). In one of the first influential articles to interpret Russell's paradox, F. P. Ramsey (1925) argued for a fundamental distinction between "formal" paradoxes like Russell's, whose statement, as he held, involves only "logical or mathematical terms" and the "semantic" paradoxes such as the Liar, which involve reference to "thought, language, or symbolism." But as Priest argues, there is no reason to think this is a fundamental distinction if the paradoxes on both sides can indeed be given a unified form.

45. These were first demonstrated in Gödel (1931).

46. For more details of this "informal" argument, as well as some grounds for doubt about its cogency as formulated here, see Chapter 6.

47. Tarski (1933).

48. As we shall see, though, this reflects a particular and theoretically loaded conception of the significance of contradiction, which can certainly be resisted on various grounds.

49. Russell (1908), p. 63.

50. Russell (1908), p. 63.

51. Russell (1908), p. 63.

52. "Whatever we suppose to be the totality of propositions, statements about the totality generate new propositions which, on pain of contradiction, must lie outside the totality. It is useless to enlarge the totality, for that equally enlarges the scope of statements about the totality. Hence there must be no totality of propositions, and 'all propositions' must be a meaningless phrase" (Russell [1908], p. 62).

53. ". . . fallacies, as we saw, are to be avoided by what may be called the 'vicious-circle principle'; i.e., 'no totality can contain members defined in terms of itself' " (Russell [1908], p. 75).

54. Russell (1908), pp. 75–76.

55. "ZFC" refers to the system of axioms worked out by Ernst Zermelo along with Abraham Fraenkel and including the (somewhat controversial) Axiom of Choice. The same system without the Axiom of Choice is called simply "ZF."

56. This axiom was not present in the initial system of Zermelo (1908) but was added later by Fraenkel.

57. Nevertheless, since this axiom only *allows* the existence of certain sets (and does not prevent anything), it does not by itself *prevent* the existence of self-membered and "non-well-founded" sets. For the theory of such sets that results if we allow the relaxation of the axiom of foundation, see Aczel (1988). For discussion of the various axiomatic ways of resolving Russell's paradox, see also Badiou (2004c), pp. 177–87. For other versions of set theory—for instance Quine's system "New Foundations"—which allow the formation of a total set (or a set of all sets) and block Russell's paradox by means of other devices, see Quine (1937) and Forster (1992).

58. For the iterative conception, see, e.g., Boolos (1971).

59. Tarski (1944).

60. There are various different and not obviously equivalent uses of the terms "predicative" and "impredicative." Most generally, however, the set of all sets and the Russell set are said to be "impredicative" because they cannot be formed by predicating some property of elements of an already "existing" set (along the lines of Zermelo's axiom of separation). For one specific definition of "predicativity," see Chapter 7.

61. Hallett (1986), Chapters 5 and 6.
62. Hallett (1986), pp. 235–37.
63. Priest (2002).
64. Priest (2002), pp. 133–36.
65. I hyphenate Priest's term to emphasize its relation to the issue of closure.
66. Priest (1987), pp. 30–38; cf. also Priest (2002), pp. 141–55.
67. Priest (1987), p. 20.
68. Priest (1987), pp. 46–47.
69. Priest thus argues for the counterintuitive doctrine of *dialetheism*: the omnipresence of in-closure, Priest argues, suggests that there are *true contradictions*—that is, sentences, *P*, for which both *P* and *not P* are true, concerning the limits of thought. The dialetheist doctrine of true contradictions may seem, at first glance, difficult or impossible to credit; but this is so, Priest argues, largely because of the traditional principle *ex contradictione quodlibet*: "From a contradiction, anything follows." If it were true that the existence of a single contradiction could lead to *any* conclusion, then any formal/logical system that includes contradictions would indeed be useless, since it would be of no use in tracking truth or understanding the world. However, as Priest demonstrates, it is possible to construct a dialetheist logic that tolerates contradictions in *certain* cases without allowing these contradictions to "explode" to the proof of any claim whatsoever (Priest 1987, pp. 53–72). Thus, if we accept such a logic, the traditional principle of non-contradiction will be relaxed in *particular* cases, and thought can thereby reckon with the possibility of radical contradiction at the limits of totality. At any rate, though, the point of invoking dialetheism in the present context is not in particular to suggest that it is the "right" logic or that it stands a better chance of being vindicated as "true" but rather simply to demonstrate that inconsistency is itself not an absolute bar to the possibility of formal thought.
70. The significant point of contrast here is not any assumed essential distinction between formal and natural languages, however (see the "Preface"), but rather simply the difference between considering any language as an abstract object of investigation and treating it as something actually used, i.e., as the possible object of its *own* descriptive and referential powers.
71. Developing the implications of the Liar paradox, Russell's paradox, and Gödel's theorems, Grim (1991) has argued that they establish the fundamental incompleteness of the universe, and hence that there can be no totality of truths or knowledge. Although he briefly discusses (pp. 25–27) the possibility of accepting inconsistency rather than affirming incompleteness, Grim rejects this possibility, holding that, despite the availability of dialetheic logic, contradiction is indeed to be avoided (p. 27) and should not be embraced unless there is no other alternative. However, in response to Grim, Priest (2002, pp. 229–32) argues convincingly that Grim himself, in attempting to avoid contradiction by affirming incompleteness, actually cannot avoid it at all. The problem is the same one that already troubled Russell's attempt to state the vicious-circle priniple: that the statement that "there is no totality" (of truths or knowledge) cannot be meaningful unless it refers to something that, by its own lights, cannot exist.
72. See, e.g., Lucas (1961) and Penrose (1994) for this argument. For a convincing rebuttal to the standard claim that Gödel and Turing's results establish the untenability of formalism (or, indeed, of mechanism), see Webb (1980).
73. But what considerations, in particular, allow us to extend the issues encountered in the course of considering Gödel's proofs—and particularly and emphatically, the forced choice they suggest between completeness and consistency—to the consideration of the structure of *social* and *political*

communities (given that such communities are certainly *not* formal, axiomatic systems in any straightforward sense)? The relevant considerations here bear most directly on the structure of ("natural" as well as "artificial") languages as these themselves define the possibilities of collective life. To recognize these connections, it is not necessary to assume that ordinary languages are identical with or reducible to "artificial" languages such as the formal, axiomatic systems with which Gödel and other proof theorists primarily worked. As we have seen, "formalism" in the sense in which it is discussed in this book is simply *any* sort of reflection on forms; there is no reason to think that this activity of reflection, or its results, are limited to the explicit, theoretical construction of "artificial" symbolic languages.

74. The classic version of this argument from the learnability of languages to their finite axiomatizability is given by Davidson (1965). Together with Davidson's application of Tarski's disquotational "convention T," it underlies the influential Davidsonian program of natural-language semantics; see also Davidson (1970) and (1973a).

75. This is not, I hasten to point out, a "postmodern" interpretation of Gödel's theorems in any of the senses that have rightly been criticized by commentators, for instance, Berto (2009) and Franzén (2005). As Berto emphasizes, it is simply impossible to apply Gödel's theorems directly to consideration of the "completeness" or "consistency" of a natural-language text (such as, perhaps, the Bible or *Capital*), since these texts are not formal, axiomatic systems. Nor do I take Gödel's theorems (in the manner of some "postmodern" interpretations) directly to show anything about the nature of objectivity or truth (for instance, that it is unattainable or must be relativized to conventionally determined situations or practices). On the current view, the bearing of Gödel's theorems on communities and practices is rather, in the first instance, to be seen in what they demonstrate about the possible completeness and expressive resources of a language ("natural" *or* "artificial"), and only secondarily, through this, to the political structures of communities themselves.

76. Wittgenstein (1921), preface. For instance, it is anticipated in those passages in the *Critique of Pure Reason* in which Kant invokes the necessity, beyond a "Transcendental Analytic" which simply and limitatively checks the claims of reason to exceed possible experience, of a "Transcendental Dialectic" in which these claims are confronted with themselves, leading to the development and invocation of what are, precisely, limit-paradoxes: the four cosmological antinomies.

77. For a clear statement of the rule-following problem, see Kripke (1982).

78. The term is chosen, in view of the systematic structure on which the operations of paradoxico-criticism depends, the ability of these operations to evince the "irrational" core of systematic rationality, and the formal connection of this core to the objective introduction of chance and aleatory events (see Chapters 8 and 9), with deliberate reference to the "frenzied-critical synthesis" that Salvador Dali termed, in a 1935 essay, the "paranoid-critical" method:

> It was in 1929 that Salvador Dali turned his attention to the internal mechanism of paranoid phenomena, envisaging the possibility of an experimental method based on the power that dominates the systematic associations peculiar to paranoia; subsequently this method was to become the frenzied-critical synthesis that bears the name of "paranoid-critical activity." . . . The presence of active and systematic elements does not presuppose the idea of voluntarily directed thinking or of any intellectual compromise whatsoever; for, as we all know, in

paranoia, the active and systematic structure is consubstantial with the delirium phenomenon itself—any delirium phenomenon with a paranoid character, even an instantaneous and sudden one, already involves the systematic structure "in full" and merely objectifies itself a posteriori by means of critical intervention. . . . Paranoid-critical activity is an organizing and productive force of objective chance (Dali 1935).

79. Agamben (1990a), p. 1.
80. Agamben (1990a), p. 9. The description of type theory as "beastly" is Wittgenstein's, from a letter to Russell in 1913.
81. Agamben (1990a), p. 75.
82. Agamben (1990a), pp. 8–10.
83. Agamben (1990a), p. 9.
84. Agamben (1990a), p. 84.
85. Agamben puts it this way in Agamben (1984a): "Contemporary thought has approached a limit beyond which a new epochal-religious unveiling of the word no longer seems possible. The primordial character of the word is now completely revealed, and no new figure of the divine, no new historical destiny can lift itself out of language. At the point where it shows itself to be absolutely in the beginning, language also reveals its absolute anonymity. There is no name for the name, and there is no metalanguage, not even in the form of an insignificant voice . . . This is the Copernican revolution that the thought of our time inherits from nihilism: we are the first human beings who have become completely conscious of language . . ." (p. 45).
86. Cf. Heidegger (1927), section 33.
87. In other places, Agamben has specified the reason for this as what he calls, adapting a story from Lewis Carroll's *Through the Looking-Glass*, the "White Knight's paradox." According to the paradox, it is impossible for "the name of an object [to] be itself named without thereby losing its character as a name and becoming a named object . . ." (Agamben 1990b, p. 69). The difficulty may be seen to be, as well, the root of the problem that Frege found with referring to the concept "horse." The ordinary device of naming names by quoting them does not solve the problem; see discussion by Reach (1938) and Anscombe (1957). See Chapter 3 for Deleuze's discussion of the same paradox.
88. Cf. Agamben (1984b).
89. Jakobson (1971); Benveniste (1974). In the context of analytic philosophy, Kaplan (1989) has argued for a similar context-dependence of the reference of indexical and demonstrative terms.
90. Agamben (1979), p. 25.
91. Agamben (1995), pp. 21–22. I would like to thank Jeff Gower for pointing out to me some of the distinctions discussed in this paragraph.
92. Agamben (2003), p. 39.
93. E.g., Derrida (2002).
94. Agamben (1995) pp. 15–17; cf. Schmitt (1934), pp. 19–22.
95. Agamben 2003, p. 2.
96. Agamben 2003, p. 2.
97. One of the first to recognize and discuss this modern configuration was Hannah Arendt, e.g., in "The Decline of the Nation-State and the End of the Rights of Man" (Chapter 9 of Arendt [1951]).
98. More rigorously, we can put the paradox this way. Within a specific legal order, consider the set of all (normal as well as exceptional) acts; call this O. Then for every subset x of O, let $d(x)$ be the act that decides, of each element of x, whether it is normal or exceptional. (We can think of $d(x)$ as

the "decider" for x, the act of enacting the law or prescription that decides normalcy within x.) Then we have the following consequences:

1) For any x, d(x) is not an element of x [ARGUMENT: No act can decide its own normalcy.]

2) For any x, d(x) is an element of O [ARGUMENT: The act that decides normalcy is itself an act]

Now, we consider the application of the "decision" operation to the totality of the legal order. This application is the sovereign's power to "decide on the state of exception," suspending the entire legal order, which is also, on Schmitt's analysis, the original foundation of such an order. We can symbolize the sovereign decision on the totality of the legal order as d(O). Now, we have: d(O) is not an element of O by (1); but d(O) is an element of O, by (2) (Contradiction). This formulation derives from discussions with Tim Schoettle and is influenced by the "Inclosure Schema" of Priest (2002).

99. The significance of this problematic of the event goes back at least to Heidegger's discussion of *Ereignis*, the mysterious "event of enowning" that transforms in a fundamental way the basis for whatever is in being; in subsequent discussions, Derrida and Deleuze have each (in different ways) accorded their different formulations of the "event" a central place in their own critical projects (we shall explore these formulations in Chapters 4, 5, and 8.) For Heidegger's conception, which I do not discuss in detail here, see, e.g., Heidegger (1938) and (1957a).

100. Badiou (2006) (henceforth: *LofW*).

101. It is possible to see in the consequences of Cantor's thinking of infinite totalities the specific limitation of Levinas' thought about the relationship figured in the title of his book *Totality and Infinity* (Levinas 1961) which in fact figures this relationship not as a conjunction but as an exclusive disjunction. This is why, for Levinas, the phenomenological "openness" to infinity, for instance in Descartes' argument, always points the way to an "infinite transcendence" that lies outside the possible survey of any totality. If Cantor has succeeded in his formalization, however, this opposition is by no means demanded by the thought of the infinite, which can indeed yield a doctrine of infinite totalities; and hence, as Badiou argues, Cantor's innovation can be the specific agent of the historical passage of thought about infinity from the categories of the mystical, transcendent, or religious (in which it still falls for Levinas) to a thoroughly demythologized and "atheistic" treatment of the role of the infinite in a finite human life.

102. Badiou (1988) (henceforth: *B&E*), p. 24.

103. There are actually two distinct issues here: i) of what (if anything) "precedes" the operation of the count-as-one; and ii) of what (if anything) cannot be counted as one at all, on pain of contradiction. Cantor uses "inconsistent multiplicity" primarily to describe ii); since he lacks any clearly formulated conception of the set grouping "operation" itself, he does not explicitly extend this usage to i). However, Badiou argues (pp. 41–43) that given an axiomatic definition of the grouping operation, we can indeed identify the two senses of "inconsistent multiplicity." We shall return to these issues in Chapter 9.

104. *B&E*, pp. 29–30.

105. *B&E*, p. 31.

106. It is "a decision to break with the arcana of the one and the multiple in which philosophy is born and buried . . ." (*B&E*, p. 23).

107. *B&E*, p. 41.

108. *B&E*, p. 95; see also the helpful chart on p. 102.

109. *B&E*, pp. 99, 130–34. Technically, normality is relative to a situation; but if we consider natural numbers only insofar as they figure in other natural numbers, they are all normal.

110. *B&E*, p. 99.
111. *B&E*, p. 99. If, for instance, I begin with the situation: {{b, c}, {a,b,c}, b, c, d}, then {b,c} is a normal term (since all of its elements are presented separately elsewhere, it is also represented); {a, b, c} is a singular term (since it contains a, which is not presented elsewhere, it is not represented); and {b,d} (for instance) is an excrescence (there are several more).
112. *B&E*, pp. 106–11.
113. *B&E*, p. 47.
114. *B&E*, p. 59.
115. In the construction of the concept of the event . . . the belonging to itself of the event, or perhaps rather, the belonging of the signifier of the event to its signification, played a special role. Considered as a multiple, the event contains, besides the elements of its site, itself; thus being presented by the very presentation that it is.

   If there existed an ontological formalization of the event it would therefore be necessary, within the framework of set theory, to allow the existence, which is to say the count-as-one, of a set such that it belonged to itself: $a \in a$ . . . Sets which belong to themselves were baptized extraordinary sets by the logician Mirimanoff. We could thus say the following: an event is ontologically formalized by an extraordinary set.

   We could. But the axiom of foundation *forecloses extraordinary sets from any existence, and ruins any possibility of naming a multiple-being of the event.* Here we have an essential gesture: that by means of which ontology declares that the event is not. (*B&E*, pp. 189–90).
116. *B&E*, p. 180.
117. *B&E*, p. 179.
118. *B&E*, p. 181.
119. *B&E*, pp. 181–83.
120. *B&E*, p. 181.
121. *B&E*, p. 181.
122. For some considerations appearing to indicate that Brouwer and other historical intuitionists should *not*, in fact, be grouped under this label, however, see Fraser (2006).
123. *B&E*, pp. 288–89.
124. As we shall see (Chapter 9), there are problems here, insofar as this rigid disjunction between mathematical formalism and language, which indeed solves the dilemma on one level, nevertheless makes it virtually impossible for Badiou to justify his own reflexive (and, necessarily, it seems, *linguistic*) interpretations of the schematisms themselves.
125. See, e.g., Forster (1992).
126. See, e.g., Priest (1987), esp. Chapter 2, and Priest (2002).
127. The idea of (and terminology for) the metalogical duality was first suggested to me by John Bova in discussions during the winter of 2008–09. I owe much of its development here to further discussions with John over the last two years.
128. Badiou (1998b), Chapter 2.
129. Badiou (1998b), p. 52.
130. Badiou (1998b), p. 53.
131. Badiou (1998b), p. 55.
132. See, e.g., Heidegger (1957b). Though the terms in which Heidegger describes the historical structure of thought that determines beings by reference to some one superlative being are thus useful for the current project, I do not treat Heidegger's own "being-historical" critique of metaphysics and presence

in any detail here. Andrew Cutrofello has pointed out to me that Kant uses the term "onto-theology" in a roughly similar sense (i.e., as designating the attempt to deduce the existence of a cause or Author of the world from concepts) at *CPR* A632/B 660.

133. Badiou (1998b), p. 55.

134. Badiou (1998b), p. 55.

135. The generic orientation seems to be substantially original with Badiou, but there are important anticipations of its view of Truth as the result of the diagonalization of particular situations, particularly in the views of some of the mathematicians and formalists on whom he draws. The most significant of these is probably Gödel himself, who took his own incompleteness theorems to establish the necessary existence of truths that, although they could not be proven by any formal system, were nevertheless accessible to human mathematical intuition (see Chapter 6). In Chapter 6 of *Briefings on Existence* (Badiou 1998b), Badiou indeed reads Gödel's Platonism as significantly anticipating his own position. There is nevertheless the important difference that whereas Gödel thought the establishment of basic axioms should depend on "intuition," Badiou takes this to be a matter of *decision* (glossing over this difference to some extent in his exegetical remarks). There are also significant anticipations of Badiou's position in certain pre-WWII philosophers of mathematics, for instance, Leon Brunschvicg and the philosopher and resistance fighter Albert Lautman, who sought in his "Essay on the Mathematical Notions of Structure and Existence" to undertake a "positive study of mathematical reality," drawing on the results of Gödel and the metalogical methods suggested by Hilbert's formalist program. (Lautman 1938).

136. There is a very brief discussion in *Being and Event* (Badiou 1988, pp. 282–85) in which Badiou discusses the three orientations and even appears to recognize, in passing, a fourth which is distinct from his own and *may* correspond to the paradoxico-critical orientation. On this orientation, which Badiou says corresponds to Cohen's doctrine of "generic" sets, "What is proposed this time, via the deployment of a doctrine of indiscernibles, is a demonstration that . . . any authentic thought must first forge for itself the means to apprehend the indeterminate, the unidfferentiated, and the multiply-similar" (p. 283). As we shall see (Chapter 9), the paradoxico-critical orientation indeed corresponds, in many ways, more closely to Cohen's identification of *indiscernible* or generic sets than does what Badiou calls, in *Briefings on Existence*, the "generic" orientation itself. To a certain extent, then, to call Badiou's own orientation the "generic" one is misleading, but I have adopted this terminology from *Briefings on Existence* because there is no obviously better alternative.

137. Compare, also, these critical remarks on Badiou, in which Žižek seems to occupy, very clearly, the position of paradoxico-criticism with its denial of a metalanguage position and its constitutive assertion of the "internal" gap introduced by the One's relation to itself: ". . . there is a Kantian problem with Badiou which is grounded in his dualism of Being and Event, and which needs to be surpassed. The only way out of this predicament is to assert that the unnameable Real is not an external limitation but an *absolutely inherent* limitation. Truth is a generic procedure which cannot comprise its own concept-name, a name that would totalize it—as Lacan put it, 'there is no meta-language' (or Heidegger: 'the name for a name is always lacking') and this lack, far from being a limitation of language, is its positive condition." Accordingly, Žižek says, "we should assert" from a Lacanian position that "the ultimate ontological given is the gap which separates the One from

within" (Žižek 2004b), pp. 178–79. For more on this (paradoxico-critical) criticism of Badiou, see Chapter 9.

138. This nomination has the salutary effect of showing that the constructivist orientations (for instance, those of Carnap and Foucault) share as deeply in the sovereign assumption of complete consistency as do the traditional orientations of onto-theology.

NOTES TO CHAPTER 2

1. Livingston (2008), especially Chapter 1.
2. Saussure (1913).
3. Saussure (1913), p. 649.
4. Saussure (1913), p. 647.
5. Saussure (1913), pp. 652–53.
6. Lévi-Strauss (1950, p. 37). Compare the following:
    In certain essential domains, such as that of kinship, the analogy with language, so strongly asserted by Mauss, could enable us to discover the precise rules by which, in any type of society, cycles of reciprocity are formed whose automatic laws are henceforth known, enabling the use of deductive reasoning in a domain which seemed subject to the most total arbitrariness. On the other hand, by associating more and more closely with linguistics, eventually to make a vast science of communications, social anthropology can hope to benefit from the immense prospects opened up to linguistics itself, through the application of mathematical reasoning to the study of the phenomena of communication. (pp. 43–44)
7. Lévi-Strauss (1950), pp. 60–61.
8. Lévi-Strauss (1950), p. 61.
9. Lévi-Strauss (1950), pp. 62–63.
10. Lévi-Strauss (1950), pp. 50–56. (Moreover, *mana* is ambiguously "force and action; quality and state; substantive, adjective, and verb all at once; abstract and concrete; omnipresent and localized.")
11. Lévi-Strauss (1950), pp. 63–64.
12. Lévi-Strauss (1950), p. 56.
13. Lévi-Strauss (1950), p. 35.
14. Lévi-Strauss (1950), p. 31.
15. Lévi-Strauss (1950), p. 31.
16. Benveniste (1956), p. 218.
17. "If each speaker, in order to express the feeling he has of his irreducible subjectivity, made use of a distinct identifying signal (in the sense in which each radio transmitting station has its own call letters), there would be as many languages as individuals and communication would be absolutely impossible. Language wards off this danger by instituting a unique but mobile sign, *I*, which can be assumed by each speaker on the condition that he refers each time only to the instance of his own discourse" (Benveniste 1956, p. 220). Benveniste's easy reference to the "feeling" each speaker has "of his irreducible subjectivity" is, however, clearly somewhat problematic on phenomenological or psychological grounds.
18. "The Nature of Pronouns," Benveniste (1956), p. 220.
19. Benveniste (1958), p. 226.
20. Benveniste (1958), p. 226.
21. Benveniste (1958), p. 224.
22. Benveniste (1963), p. 236.
23. Benveniste (1963), p. 236.

24. There are important developments and shifts of emphasis, over the course of Lacan's career, in his definition of each of the three registers and especially in the significance of the Real, which is defined sometimes as the simply unnameable, sometimes as what provides a foundation for the other two orders, and sometimes what erupts suddenly into the regular order of the Symbolic, traumatically disrupting its established identities and forms. Given the limited scope of the present treatment, I do not pursue these developments in detail here.

25. My research has led me to the realization that repetition automatism (*Wiederholungswang*) has its basis in what I have called the *insistence* of the signifying chain. I have isolated this notion as a correlate of the *ex-sistence* (that is, of the eccentric place) in which we must necessarily locate the subject of the unconscious, if we are to take Freud's discovery seriously. As we know, it is in the experience inaugurated by psychoanalysis that we can grasp by what oblique imaginary means the *symbolic* takes hold in even the deepest recesses of the human organism. The teaching of this seminar is designed to maintain that imaginary effects, far from representing the core of analytic experience, give us nothing of any consistency unless they are related to the symbolic chain that binds and orients them (Lacan 1955, p. 6).

26. Lacan (1955), p. 17.
27. Lacan (1955), p. 6.
28. Lacan (1955), p. 7.
29. Lacan (1955), p. 30.
30. Lacan (1955), p. 20.
31. Lacan (1957).
32. See Fink's notes in Lacan (2006), p. 807.
33. Lacan (1957), pp. 413.
34. Lacan (1957), pp. 414.
35. Lacan (1957), pp. 414.
36. Lacan (1957), pp. 415.
37. Lacan (1957), p. 415.
38. Lacan (1957), p. 415.
39. Lacan (1957), p. 415.
40. Lacan (1957), p. 419.
41. Lacan (1957), pp. 421.
42. Lacan (1957), pp. 430.
43. There is no other way to conceive of the indestructibility of unconscious desire—given that there is no need which, when its satiation is prohibited, does not wither, in extreme cases through the very wasting away of the organism itself. It is in a kind of memory, comparable to what goes by that name in our modern thinking-machines (which are based on an electronic realization of signifying composition), that the chain is found which insists by reproducing itself in the transference, and which is the chain of a dead desire.

It is the truth of what desire has been in his history that the subject cries out through his symptom, as Christ said that stones themselves would have cried out, had the children of Israel not lent them their voices.

And this is also why psychoanalysis alone allows us to differentiate in memory the function of remembering. The latter, rooted in the signifier, resolves the Platonic aporias of reminiscence through the ascendency of history in man. Lacan (1957), p. 431.

44. Lacan (1973).
45. Lacan (1973), p. 50.

46. Lacan's specific formulation here, "*Y a d'l'Un*," is enigmatic in French and difficult to translate univocally. According to Bruce Fink (p. 5), it has all of the following senses: "There's such a thing as One"; "There's something like One"; "The One happens." However, Fink emphasizes that "Lacan is not saying 'there's some One' (in the sense of some quantity of One) . . ." (p. 5).

47. "To allow for the explanation of the functions of this [viz., the 'analytic'] discourse, I put forward the use of a certain number of letters. First of all, a, which I call "object," but which, nevertheless, is a letter. Then A, that I make function in that aspect of the proposition that takes only the form of a written formula, and that is produced by mathematical logic. I designate thereby that which is first of all a locus, a place. I called it 'the locus of the Other" (le lieu de l'Autre)" (Lacan 1973, pp. 28–30).

48. Lacan (1973), p. 28.

49. Thus, whereas the a is the imaginary object of desire, the A is to be located in the symbolic order; the structurally necessary confusion between a and S(A̶) is a "function of being" itself, to which the full resources of psychoanalysis must respond (Lacan 1973, pp. 77–83).

50. "At the level of this not-everything (pas-tout), only the Other doesn't know. It is the Other who constitutes the not-everything, precisely in that the Other is the part of the not-at-all-knowledgeable (*pas-savant-du-tout*) in the not-everything" (Lacan 1973, p. 98).

51. "Is there One or not? In other words, this not-whole (pas-toute), in classical logic, seems to imply the existence of the One that constitutes (*fait*) an exception. Henceforth, it would be there that we would see the emergence in an abyss . . . of that existence, that at-least-one existence that . . . is inscribed in order to speak it (*s'inscrit pour la dire*) . . ." (Lacan 1973, pp. 94–103).

52. Lacan (1973), p. 50.

53. Lacan (1973), pp. 19–20.

54. Lacan (1973), p. 29.

55. Distinguishing the dimension of the signifier only takes on importance when it is posited that what you hear, in the auditory sense of the term, bears no relation whatsoever to what it signifies. That is an act that is instituted only through a discourse, scientific discourse. And it is not self-evident. Indeed, it is so scarcely self-evident that a whole discourse—which does not flow from a bad pen, since it is the *Cratylus*, by none other than Plato—results from the endeavor to show that there must be a relationship and that the signifier in and of itself means something. This attempt, which we can qualify from our vantage point as desperate, is marked by failure, because another discourse, scientific discourse, due to its very institution—in a way whose history we need not probe here—gives us the following, that the signifier is posited only insofar as it has no relation to the signified.
    The very terms we use to talk about it are still slippery. A linguist as discerning as Ferdinand de Saussure speaks of arbitrariness. That is tantamount to slipping, slipping into another discourse, the master's discourse, to call the spade a spade. Arbitrariness is not a suitable term here (Lacan 1973, p. 29).

56. "Mathematical formalization is our goal, our ideal. Why? Because it alone is matheme, in other words, it alone is capable of being integrally transmitted" (Lacan 1973, p. 119).

57. Lacan (1973), p. 47.

58. Lacan (1973), p. 93.

59. Lacan (1973), p. 110.

60. We can see here, again, a decisive difference from Badiou, who insists upon the purely non-linguistic character of mathematical signification.
61. Lacan (1973), p. 119.
62. Lacan (1973), p. 67.
63. Miller (1968), p. 1.
64. Miller (1968), pp. 2–3.
65. Miller (1968), p. 9.
66. Badiou criticizes Miller's text for assuming this "iterative" conception of number, which according to Badiou artificially restricts and delimits the universe of numbers in (Badiou 1990, pp. 24–30).
67. "The impossible object, which the discourse of logic summons as the not-identical with itself and then rejects as the pure negative, which it summons and rejects in order to constitute itself as that which it is, which it summons and rejects wanting to know nothing of it, we name this object, in so far as it functions as the excess which operates in the series of numbers, the subject" (Miller 1968, p. 10).
68. Miller (1966), p. 3.
69. Miller (1966), p. 2.
70. Miller (1975), p. 50.
71. Miller (1975), pp. 49–50. In a very suggestive way, this brief argument seems to anticipate Badiou's identification of the power set operation and what he terms the "state of the situation"—which gathers together all the subsets of any given set—with the generative power of representation. For more, see Chapters 2 and 10.
72. Miller (1975), p. 51.
73. Miller (1968), p. 5.
74. For this definition and its implications, see Livingston (2008), Chapter 1.
75. "By the logical syntax of a language, we mean the formal theory of the linguistic forms of that language—the systematic statement of the formal rules which govern it together with the development of the consequences which follow from these rules" (Carnap 1934, p. 1).
76. "A theory, a rule, a definition, or the like is to be called formal when no *reference* is made in it either to the meaning of the symbols (for example, the words) or to the sense of the expressions (e.g. the sentences), but simply and solely to the kinds and order of the symbols from which the expressions are constructed" (Carnap 1934, p.1).
77. Carnap (1934), p. 4.
78. Carnap (1934), p. xv.
79. Carnap (1934), p. xv.
80. Carnap (1950).
81. Carnap (1950), p. 206.
82. For a more detailed examination of the role of this principle—what I have called Quine's *appeal to use*—in his writings beginning in 1934 and leading to the indeterminacy result, see Livingston (2008), Chapter 5.
83. Quine (1936).
84. Carroll (1895).
85. Quine (1936), p. 97.
86. Quine (1950, 1954).
87. There are those who find it soothing to say that the analytic statements of the second class [viz., those that are not "logical" truths] reduce to those of the first class, the logical truths, by definition; 'bachelor,' for example, is defined as 'unmarried man.' But how do we find that 'bachelor' is defined as 'unmarried man'? Who defined it thus, and when? Are we to appeal to the nearest dictionary, and

accept the lexicographer's formulation as law? Clearly this would be to put the cart before the horse. The lexicographer is an empirical scientist, whose business is the recording of antecedent facts; and if he glosses 'bachelor' as 'unmarried man' it is because of his belief that there is a relation of synonymy between those forms, implicit in general or preferred usage prior to his own work" (Quine 1950, p. 24).

88. Quine (1954), p. 127.
89. Quine (1960).
90. Quine (1960) p. 27.
91. I have discussed the arising and implications of this aporia, in the texts of twentieth-century analytic philosophy, in greater detail in Livingston (2008), especially Chapters 1, 5, 8, and 9.
92. As has been noted by commentators, the indeterminacy result has an initial air of implausibility. For taken one way, it seems to imply that the vast majority of sentences that we use every day in ordinary language have no determinate meaning. In fact, Quine himself, in a later chapter of *Word and Object*, took this result to suggest the elimination, at least for scientific purposes, of our ordinary talk of meanings and intensions. Short of such an eliminativist solution, however, we should note that Quine's indeterminacy result by itself actually need not be construed as posing any deep threat to the lived everyday *sense* of shared meaning that in fact characterizes interlocution between speakers of a shared language. The threat is, rather, to the possibility of *grounding* this sense, by means of a neutral description of the rules of usage constitutive of the language, in the totality of facts of usage themselves. But the thought that our sense of meaning *must* be able to be so grounded is itself simply a consequence of the structuralist picture of languages as systematic calculi of rules of use, the same picture that Carnap had proposed in *Logical Syntax*. For more discussion of these issues, see Livingston (2008), Chapter 5.
93. Indeed, as Quine emphasizes at several places in explicit commentary on his own result, where indeterminacy threatens the uniqueness of a description of the structure of a language, naturalistic investigations into the neurophysiology of the language's speakers or the actual biology of their causal mechanisms of language production, can essentially provide no further help. As Quine put it in 1986, for instance, "even a full understanding of neurology would in no way resolve the indeterminacy of translation" (Quine 1986, p. 365). See also Quine (1979), where he makes a similar point.
94. It might at first seem that this last parallel does not hold up, since Quine's thesis does not obviously concern the representation of a language within itself, but rather the prospects for translating it into another one. However, Quine in fact often emphasizes that the implications of the radical translation manual hold even when only a single language is at issue and there is no question of translation. For even in interpreting our own language, we are in effect utilizing a translation manual (the "homophonic" one, as he puts it). Moreover, the project that this suggests—namely, a complete theorization of the structural basis of the process of "radical interpretation" which must be considered to underlie any successful language use—would subsequently be developed, in great detail, by Davidson; see, e.g., Davidson (1973b).
95. See, e.g., Rorty (1989).

NOTES TO CHAPTER 3

1. Deleuze (1967).

2. Deleuze (1967), p. 172.
3. Deleuze (1967), p. 171.
4. Deleuze (1967), p. 173.
5. As we saw in the last chapter, this discovery of a regime of constitution that underlies the meaning of propositions and words but *owes nothing to imagination or resemblance* might indeed be seen as one of the most transformative and significant outcomes of the philosophical turn to language in the twentieth century, in both its structuralist and its analytic versions.
6. Deleuze (1969) (henceforth: *LofS*), pp. 77, 68.
7. *LofS*, p. 1.
8. *LofS*, p. 3.
9. *LofS*, pp. 2–3.
10. Carroll (1895). This is the same paradox to which Quine appeals in arguing against Carnap's logical conventionalism (see above).
11. As Deleuze indeed notes, the general reason for the paradox, which may be put as the fact that "there is no name for the name" or "there is no concept for the concept," is already implicated in Frege's classical distinction between sense and reference, as Frege himself recognized by famously stating (in Frege 1892) that, since concepts cannot have names, it is nonsensical to say that "the concept 'horse' is a concept."
12. *LofS*, p. 49.
13. *LofS*, p. 49.
14. *LofS*, p. 50.
15. *LofS*, p. 52.
16. *LofS*, p. 50.
17. *LofS*, p. 50.
18. *Deleuze* (1968) (henceforth: *D&R*), pp. 208–9.
19. *LofS*, p. 66.
20. *LofS*, p. 67.
21. *LofS*, p. 67. There are some interesting parallels to be drawn here to Derrida's treatment of words such as *chora*, *hymen*, and even his own coinages such as *différance* (see Chapter 4, below).
22. Deleuze emphasizes the relevance of this paradox, among others, to the analysis of sense: "We cannot get rid of paradoxes by saying that they are more worthy of Carroll's work then they are of the *Principia Mathematica*. What is good for Carroll is good for logic ... For paradoxes, on the contrary, inhere in language, and the whole problem is to know whether language would be able to function without bringing about the insistence of such entities" (*LofS*, p. 74).
23. *LofS*, p. 69.
24. *LofS*, p. 69.
25. *D&R*, p. 211.
26. *LofS*, p. 1.
27. *LofS*, p. 1.
28. *LofS*, p. 1.
29. *LofS*, p. 2.
30. Deleuze mentions, for instance, *Philebus* 24d: "The hotter and equally the colder are always in flux and never remain, while definite quantity means standstill and the end of all progression. The upshot of this argument is that the hotter, together with its opposite, turn out to be unlimited"; and the second hypothesis of the *Parmenides*, according to which the One "partakes of being." On this hypothesis: "what is younger comes to be older in relation to what has come to be earlier and is older, but it never is older. On the contrary, it always

comes to be older than that thing. For the older advances toward the younger, while the younger advances toward the older. And, in the same way, the older, in its turn, comes to be younger than the younger. For both, by going toward their opposites, come to be each other's opposite . . ." (154e–155a). Another relevant passage, not mentioned by Deleuze, is *Phaedo* 102d–103a, where the opposition of forms determines them as "approaching" and "fleeing," even being "destroyed" by the approaching of their opposites. (It is no accident that the "unlimited" or infinite repeatedly appears at just this point.)

31. *D&R*, p. 66. Cf. p. 262: "So 'to reverse Platonism' means to make the simulacra rise and to affirm their rights among icons and copies".
32. *D&R*, p. 257.
33. *D&R*, p. 258.
34. *D&R*, p. xix.
35. *D&R*, p. 259.
36. *D&R*, p. 67.
37. *D&R*, p. 67.
38. *LofS*, p. 2.
39. *LofS*, p. 2.
40. *D&R*, p. 128.
41. *LofS*, p. 258.
42. Derrida (1972).
43. *LofS*, p. 361.
44. 402a.
45. *LofS*, p. 2. Compare Plato: "The things that are are moving, but some are moving quickly, others slowly. So what moves quickly is not all there is, but the admirable part of it. . . . It seems that many people agree with one another about it up to a point, but beyond that they disagree. Those who think that the universe is in motion believe that most of it is of such a kind as to do nothing but give way, but that something penetrates all of it and generates everything that comes into being. This, they say, is the fastest and smallest thing of all, for if it were not the smallest, so that nothing could keep it out, or not the fastest, so that it could treat all other things as though they were standing still, it wouldn't be able to travel through everything" (*Cratylus* 412c–413a); cf. also 413d–414a.
46. *LofS*, p. 2.

NOTES TO CHAPTER 4

1. Gödel (1931). As Andrew Cutrofello has pointed out, there is an earlier (passing) allusion by Derrida to Gödel's result (in connection with Husserl's theory of the unity of sense) in Derrida (1962), p. 53.
2. Derrida (1970), p. 219.
3. More specifically: the Gödel Sentence, GS, has the form: GS $\leftrightarrow$ ~$Prov$([GS]), where "$Prov$" is a so-called 'provability predicate' and the square brackets express the function of taking the Gödel number of what is enclosed in them. There are several good general introductions to Gödel's result available. These include: Nagel and Newman (2001); Smith (2007); Hofstadter (1979).
4. The reasoning goes as follows: Suppose the claim asserted by the Gödel sentence, GS, is false; then it is false that GS cannot be proved; then it is true that it can be proved; but a proof of it is also a proof that it cannot be proved. Thus, we have a contradiction on the assumption that the claim asserted by GS is false; therefore, *assuming the system does not contain a contradiction*, it must be true.

5. Does Derrida's use of the term and concept of the "undecidable" depend, then, on an untenable "postmodernist" reading of Gödel's theorem that seeks to apply it far beyond the scope of its "actual" formal implications? Such readings are, unfortunately, relatively common and have been roundly and amusingly criticized, for instance, by Sokal and Bricmont (1997) and Berto (2009). Specifically, as Berto argues, it is simply impossible to apply Gödel's theorem directly to the consideration of a specific natural-language text (such as the Bible or *Capital*), since such texts are not formal systems and do not systematically formulate truths about mathematics. As we saw in Chapter 1, though, there are good reasons to believe Gödel's results *can* be applied to consideration of the structure of "natural" languages, provided that this application is couched at the right level of generality. On the current reading, although Derrida uses the concept "undecidable" in connection with specific texts (such as Mallarmé's), this is grounded in much broader syntactic phenomena which apply to (natural) languages as such (which certainly *do*, among other things, formulate truths about mathematics) insofar as these have a determinate logical structure. As we have seen as well, the structuralism of Saussure (see Chapter 2), which forms Derrida's starting point, already suggests that natural languages do indeed have this kind of structure, to a very large extent.

6. Derrida (1970), p. 220.

7. Derrida (1970), p. 220.

8. Derrida (1970), p. 220.

9. Derrida (1970), p. 221.

10. Derrida (1968), p. 6.

11. Derrida (1968), p. 26.

12. Derrida (1968), p. 7.

13. Derrida (1968), p. 8.

14. For more on what this means, see section 2, below.

15. Of course, Gödel himself was an avowed Platonist about mathematical truth, and saw his own result simply as demonstrating the capacity of the human mind to have a kind of intuition of truths that no formal system could by itself prove. However, this interpretation of the metamathematical significance of the Gödel sentence is not obligatory. In particular, we may take the sentence to mark an impasse or limit of formalizability, without necessarily taking it to "capture" a "truth" that lies beyond the possibility of formalization. For more along these lines, see Chapter 6.

16. I owe the objection sketched in this paragraph to Tim Schoettle.

17. Thus, the title of Gödel's original 1931 paper was simply "On Formally Undecidable Propositions of *Principia Mathematica* and Related Systems I"; it was only later that the two theorems proven there came to be seen as "incompleteness" theorems.

18. Derrida (1970), p. 240.

19. Derrida (1970), p. 220.

20. Derrida (1970), p. 221 (emphasis added in all quotes in this sentence).

21. Derrida (1970), p. 222.

22. Derrida (1970), p. 222.

23. Priest (2002), pp. 3–4, 133–36.

24. Priest (2002), p. 134.

25. Priest (2002), pp. 214–23.

26. Priest (2002), p. 222.

27. There are problems with, or at least limitations to, this as a reading of Derrida. In emphasizing the double of presence/absence, and other similar "binaries," as structuring the whole of the sayable, Priest focuses on the sense

in which *différance* is a result of (spatial or synchronic) difference. However, *différance* explicitly includes, just as much, the temporal or diachronic dimension of iteration, and this seems to go missing from Priest's account.

28. In this paragraph I am somewhat indebted to the helpful argument of Moore (2001b).
29. Derrida (1971), p. 315.
30. Derrida (1971), p. 317.
31. Agamben (1990b), pp. 213–14.
32. This implies that the formal, structural possibility of deconstruction is quite general, applying to any language with a syntactical structure (which is to say, any human language whatsoever) and accordingly that Agamben's reference to the foundation of "Western" logic is gratuitous and unnecessary.
33. Glendinning (2001), p. 55.
34. See, e.g., Derrida (2002), Derrida (1995).
35. See, e.g., Caputo (1997) and Critchley (1999) for this kind of reading; for a convincing recent argument against it, which I partially follow here, see Hägglund (2008), esp. Chapters 3 and 4.
36. It is possible at this point, as well, to begin to see how the dialectical procedure of elenchus enacted by Socrates in several of Plato's dialogues in fact amounts to an ethical pursuit of the undecidable as such. In several of the early and middle dialogues (e.g., "Euthyphro," "Meno," "Protagoras"), Socrates' interlocutor begins by purporting to have mastery of an ethically relevant concept ("piety," "justice," etc.). However, as Socrates' questioning soon shows, the definition initially given is in fact only an intra-systematic one that yields no understanding of the actual ethical *point* or significance of the concept, or of practice in accord with it itself. Socrates then shows the concept, as defined, to be undecidable (perhaps the best example of this is the dilemma that Socrates poses for Euthyphro's definition of piety as "what is pleasing to the gods" at *Euthyphro* 6e–7a) in terms of the systematic logic presupposed; the point of this (and indeed, we can now say, of what Plato invokes as the "idea") is not simply to reduce the interlocutor to silence, but to pursue the actual ethical meaning of the concept in question, which cannot be captured simply in intra-systematic terms.

NOTES TO CHAPTER 5

1. Fr. 2, as translated by Kirk, Raven, and Schofield (1983), p. 245. Throughout this chapter, I use Kirk and Raven's translations of Parmenides' poem. In some cases, however, these are controversial; for good alternatives see, e.g., Austin (1986) and Cordero (2004).
2. Fr. 3, Kirk, Raven, and Schofield (1983), p. 246. The right translation of this phrase is quite controversial. Cf. also Fr. 6.
3. Fr. 6.
4. See, e.g., Austin (1986), Chapter 1, Owen (1960), and for an extended interpretation that has influenced me here, Schürmann (1996), pp. 51–109. Owen (1964, p. 30) is one of the first to suggest a parallel between Parmenides' argument and that of the *Tractatus*, suggesting that Parmenides' argument "is a ladder to be climbed up and thrown away."
5. Fr. 7, Kirk, Raven, and Schofield (1983), p. 248.
6. The issue is complicated somewhat—although not, I think, in any essential sense—by the question whether Parmenides means, subsequently in fragment 6, to indicate as well a "third way," that of the "mortals," in addition to the two ways of being and non-being (or truth and falsehood) already named.

Although there has been some debate over this question, I think it does not vitiate the present point, since i) the goddess does clearly say in fragment 2 that the way of non-being cannot be indicated (though she indicates it); and ii) if there are two ways in addition to the way of being, it seems clear that the young traveler is barred from both (e.g., by fragment 8: "There still remains just one account of a way, that it is"). See discussion in Schürmann (2003), pp. 55–70.

7. Cf. Fr. 2: "The one, that [it] is and that it is impossible for [it] not to be, is the path of Persuasion (for she attends upon truth) . . ." and also Fr. 6: "What is there to be said and thought must needs be; for it is there for being, but nothing is not." The participle that Kirk and Raven here translate as "be said" is *legein*.

8. Barnes (1979), pp. 165–72, Anscombe (1969), pp. 3–8, Kirk, Raven, and Schofield (1983), pp. 245–46, and Owen (1964), pp. 28–30 all take Parmenides to be making this sort of argument for the necessity of some existents. Barnes (1979), pp. 170–71 has noted parallels both to Berkeley's argument for subjective idealism and Anselm's ontological argument for the necessary existence of God.

9. Wittgenstein (1921) (henceforth: *TLP*), 2.21 ff.

10. Here I follow the discussion by Anscombe (1959), pp. 48–49. See also Livingston (2001).

11. The passage comes in the course of Socrates' discussion of the analogy between such simple knowable objects and linguistic letters, and should be compared with similar discussions of atomistic themes in connection with language and grammar elsewhere, e.g., in the *Sophist* (252d, ff.) and the *Cratylus* (422a, ff. and 434b).

12. Cf. 4.126: ". . . The name shows that it signifies an object . . ."

13. *TLP* 3.2 ff.

14. Cf. 3.031: "It used to be said that God could create anything except what would be contrary to the laws of logic.—The truth is that we could not say what an 'illogical' world would look like."

15. *TLP* 3.32–3.328. For a clear account of how this works, see Conant (1998).

16. Wittgenstein (1933), p. 147.

17. The possibility of ethical propositions was explicitly denied at *Tractatus* 6.42.

18. Wittgenstein (1929), p. 40.

19. *PI* 46. This "logical atomism" is also presented and defended in Russell's (1918) lectures on "The Philosophy of Logical Atomism."

20. I have in mind here the kind of position mooted by McDowell (1994) according to which the origin of at least some of our metaphysical illusions lies in our (misguided, on this showing) attempt to take a "sideways-on" perspective on our language, attempting to see from this (illusory, on this showing) perspective the relationship between language and the world. Cavell (1979, e.g.. p. 239) gives what may perhaps be seen as a more promising account of what is involved in the desire to "speak outside language games."

21. Cf. *TLP* 6.54. That they should be so recognized is the main heuristic claim of a recently popular line of interpretation of the *Tractatus*, what has been called by some of its adherents the "resolute" interpretation. (See, e.g., Conant 1992, 2002; Diamond 1991, 2000; Ricketts 1996.) On the "resolute" interpretation, in particular, Wittgenstein is resolute in refusing to distinguish (as earlier interpreters had taken him to) between two types of nonsense, "plain" nonsense and "important nonsense" (such as, perhaps, the seeming propositions of the *Tractatus* itself) that, though ultimately nonsensical, still suffices to *show* something substantive that cannot be said. Instead, according to these interpreters, the rhetorical or

dialectical point of the elucidatory propositions of *TLP* is to induce, and then systematically remove, the illusion that *either* of these types of pseudo-sentences actually has any sense, leaving us with a silence that, as Conant has put it, "in the end is one in which nothing has been said and there is nothing to say (of the sort that we imagined there to be)" (Conant, 1992, p. 216).

22. (given also negation).
23. *TLP* 3.325.
24. *TLP* 3.327.
25. Similarly, if it were possible for a sign, say "A," to symbolize a set that is self-membered, then we would never be able to settle the question whether it is being used in a uniform way (and hence with a uniform meaning). For we would have (for instance): A= {A,B}. Then, A appears to have the form {x,y}; but then we would have to ask whether the token of 'A' on the left side of the equal sign signified the same as the token on the right side; and to settle this question we would have to examine the functioning of the token on the right, which would involve putting '{A,B}' in place of 'A'; we would then have A = {{A,B}, B}, which has the form {{x,y}, y}, and so forth. It would, thus, never be possible (on this Wittgensteinian reasoning) to settle the question of A's actual logical form.
26. We cannot therefore agree with the *Tractatus*-inspired account of A. W. Moore (Moore 2001a, p. 197), which sees in the rigid maintenance of the saying/showing distinction a basis for a solution of the problem represented by Russell's paradox. According to Moore, we can resolve the paradox by maintaining that although we wish "both to affirm and deny" that there is such a set as the Russell set, we are in fact *shown* (without being able to determinately say that there is) such a set. The integrity of this "solution," as stated, clearly depends on our willingness to suspend the sense of incoherence that is produced by being told both that something *is not the case* (for instance, that there is a Set of all Sets)—because we have reason to believe that we cannot say that it is the case—but nevertheless that we can be shown *that it is*. Additionally, Moore's own formulation of the solution itself abounds in (seeming) assertions concerning entities which are, according to him, impossible to talk about (for instance, "our subject matter" as a whole and its "infinite framework"). One could be excused for feeling that, if this is supposed to be a solution to the original Russell antinomy, the solution is hardly less antinomic than the problem itself.
27. Wittgenstein (1956) (henceforth: *RFM*), VII–36.
28. Compare this remark from 1939–40:
> 81. Our task is not to discover calculi but to describe the *present* situation.
> The idea of the predicate which is true of itself, etc., does of course lean on *examples*—but these examples were *stupidities*, for they were not thought out at all. But that is not to say that such predicates could not be applied, and that the contradiction would not then have its application!
> I mean: if one really fixes one's eye on the application, it does not occur to one at all to write '*f(f)*'. On the other hand, if one is using the signs in the calculus, *without presuppositions*, so to speak, one may also write '*f(f)*', and must then draw the consequences and not forget that one has not yet an *inkling* of a possible practical application of this calculus. (*RFM* III–81).
29. *PI* 125. Compare what Wittgenstein says explicitly about Russell at *RFM* III–85:
> Is there such a thing—it might also be asked—as *the right* logical calculus, only without the contradictions?

Could it be said, e.g., that while Russell's Theory of Types avoids the contradiction, still Russell's calculus is not THE universal logical calculus but perhaps an artificially restricted, mutilated one? Could it be said that the *pure, universal* logical calculus has yet to be found? I was playing a game and in doing so I followed certain rules: but as for *how* I followed them, that depended on circumstances and the way it so depended was not laid down in black and white. (This is to some extent a misleading account.) Now I wanted to play this game in such a way as to follow rules 'mechanically' and I 'formalized' the game. But in doing this I reached positions where the game lost *all* point; I therefore wanted to avoid these positions 'mechanically.' The formalization of logic did not work out satisfactorily. But what was the attempt made for at all? (What was it useful for?) Did not this need, and the idea that it must be capable of satisfaction, arise from a lack of clarity in another place?

30. Cf. what Wittgenstein says about the possibility of a transformed logic, based on Russell's paradox itself at *RFM* IV–59: "Why should Russell's contradiction not be conceived as something supra-propositional, something that towers above the propositions and looks in both directions like a Janus head? N.B. the proposition F(F)—in which F(ξ) = ~ $\xi(\xi)$—contains no variables and so might hold as something supra-logical, as something unassailable, whose negation itself in turn only *asserts* it. Might one not even begin logic with this contradiction? And as it were descend from it to propositions.

The proposition that contradicts itself would stand like a monument (with a Janus head) over the propositions of logic."

31. To see this, suppose there to exist a world that is a totality (perhaps infinite) of objects, each holding determinate properties; suppose also that no single object is (yet) contradictory. That is, there is no object p and property, A, such that p both has and does not have that property. We can now allow the formation of arbitrary sets of these objects, and the treatment of such sets as objects themselves. As long as we do not consider the set comprising the totality of all sets, there are still no contradictions in the world; that is, there are no two sentences B and ~B that are both true of objects (or sets) in the world. Even the property of being non-self-membered does not (yet) lead to any contradiction, as long as the totality of objects with this property is not considered. But as soon as it is, we have, of course, Russell's paradox, and hence the existence of an object that has contradictory properties. In this precise sense, Russell's paradox and the issues it formulates plausibly represent the *only* possible way for contradiction to enter the world that does not depend on the psychology of an individual subject or on any supposed liability of such subjects to error or delusion. Rather, Russell's paradox suggests that contradiction as such arises in *formal* features of the operation of set grouping itself—the law of the One over the many—that owe nothing to any empirical or even any specifically human origin.

NOTES TO CHAPTER 6

1. Wittgenstein (1939). Some discussions between Wittgenstein, Turing, and Wittgenstein's student Alister Watson had reportedly taken place earlier, in the summer of 1937, but there is no record of these (Hodes 1983, pp. 109, 136—cited in Floyd and Putnam (2000).)

2. Wittgenstein (1916), p. 10.

3. Wittgenstein (1916), pp. 10–11.
4. As Shanker (1987) suggests, this shows the important difference between Wittgenstein and any kind of constructivist or finitist: "Wittgenstein's overriding goal was to bring us to see that 'infinity' cannot be divorced from the notion of a non-ending operation, which as such erects an impassable grammatical barrier to the concepts of *limit* and *magnitude*. . . It is not surprising, given the finitist overtones of this theme and the obvious traces of Brouwer and Weyl that can be discerned in his argument, that Wittgenstein's intentions should have been regarded as radical constructivist. The fact remains, however, that Wittgenstein's discussion was firmly based on investigating the logical syntax of 'infinity', not the 'limits of our recognitional capacities'." As Shanker argues, these considerations also bear against the whole project of Wright (1980), who takes Wittgenstein's critical approach to infinity primarily to yield *epistemological* (rather than primarily syntactic or "grammatical") considerations of an "anti-realist" kind.
5. Hilbert (1925).
6. Hilbert (1925).
7. Wittgenstein (1939), p. 13.
8. Wittgenstein (1939), p. 14.
9. Wittgenstein (1939), p. 31.
10. Turing (1936).
11. Turing (1936), p. 58.
12. For a helpful discussion of the various formulations and versions of the thesis, see Webb (1980), esp. Chapter 4.
13. "We have said that the computable numbers are those whose decimals are calculable by finite means. This requires rather more explicit definition . . . For the present I shall only say that the justification lies in the fact that the human memory is necessarily limited" (p. 59); "The behaviour of the computer at any moment is determined by the symbols which he is observing, and his 'state of mind' at that moment. We may suppose that there is a bound B to the number of symbols or squares which the computer can observe at one moment . . . We will also suppose that the number of states of mind which need to be taken into account is finite. The reasons for this are of the same character as those which restrict the number of symbols" (pp. 75–76). Turing also emphasizes (p. 79) that there must at any moment be a symbolically stateable description which, if the computer broke off work at any particular stage, would determinately instruct another as to how to continue.
14. Turing (1936), pp. 68–69.
15. Turing (1936), pp. 67–68.
16. Turing (1936), p. 73. More specifically, H combines the universal machine U with a "decision machine" D which, when given the description number of any particular machine, determines whether that machine halts.
17. The demonstration is on pp. 72–73. Penrose (1994), Chapter 2, gives an equivalent but slightly different formulation. Equivalently, we may argue that if there were such a machine H, it would be possible to construct a machine H' which halts if and only if the machine it is considering does not. Then, if K' is its description number, this machine, when given the input K', halts if and only if it does not.
18. As Turing says, "If the negation of what Gödel has shown had been proved . . . we should have an immediate solution to the Entscheidungsproblem" (p. 85). This is because the existence of a sound, complete system for proving arithmetic truths would imply a solution to the decision problem; since Turing showed that there is no such solution, it follows that there can be no such (sound, complete) system, which is a version of Gödel's result.

19. It may be objected that there are proofs of Cantor's theorem, which establishes the superiority of the cardinality of the power set over the initial set, that do not make obvious use of syntactic reasoning (I owe this objection to a discussion with John Bova, although it does not represent his view). But, since all proofs of Cantor's theorem do at least involve the assumption (for the purpose of *reductio*) of a 1–1 *correspondence* between sets and their subsets, they do involve (at least where the sets are infinite) a kind of "comparison" of the infinite set with its finite elements, something very similar to the "comparison" of an infinitary procedure with its finitely expressed rule in the more obviously "syntactical" cases of diagonalization.

20. *RFM* II–29.

21. *RFM* II–38: "Here it is important to grasp the relationship between a series in the non-mathematical sense and one in the mathematical sense. It is of course clear that in mathematics we do not use the word 'series of numbers' in the sense 'series of numerical signs', even though, of course, there is also a connexion between the use of the one expression and of the other. . . . A 'series' in the mathematical sense is a method of construction for series of linguistic expressions" (p. 136).

22. *RFM* VII–43.

23. I owe the terminology of "crossing of syntax and semantics," in relation to diagonalization, to John Bova. Some similar ideas and formulations are given in Hofstadter (1999).

24. *RFM* I, Appendix III, sect. 5–19.

25. Gödel's original article is titled "On Formally Undecidable Propositions of *Principia Mathematica* and Related Systems I" and mentions "incompleteness" only once, in a footnote: "The true reason for the incompleteness which attaches to all formal systems of mathematics lies—as will be shown in Part II of this paper—in the fact that the formation of higher and higher types can be continued into the transfinite (cf. D. Hilbert 'Über das Unendliche', *Math. Ann.* 95, p. 184), while, in every formal system, only countably many are available. Namely, one can show that the undecidable sentences which have been constructed here always become decidable through adjunction of sufficiently high types (e.g., of the type ω to the system **P**). A similar result holds for the axiom systems of set theory" (Gödel 1931, footnote 48a, pp. 28–29).

26. Thus: "From the remark that [R(q); q] asserts its own unprovability it follows immediately that [R(q);q] is true, since [R(q);q] is indeed unprovable (because it is undecidable). The proposition undecidable in the system *PM* is thus decided by metamathematical arguments" (Gödel 1931, p. 9). As Gödel emphasizes, this remark comes as part of a "sketch of the main ideas of the proof" that does not make "any claim to rigor" (p. 6).

27. Floyd and Putnam (2000), p. 625. For further discussion, see Steiner (2001), Bays (2004), and Floyd and Putnam (2006).

28. Floyd and Putnam (2000), pp. 624–26. A system is ω-inconsistent if, for some property T of natural numbers formulable in the system, the system proves ~T(0), ~T(1), and so forth, but also proves *that there is some* natural number n such that T(n). Note that a system may be ω-inconsistent but still (simply) consistent.

29. For a clear and helpful treatment of Wittgenstein's remarks and the recent literature on them, see Berto (2009), Chapter 12.

30. Floyd and Putnam (2000), p. 632.

31. Cf. *PI* 136.

32. Cf. Priest (2004).

33. Priest (2004), p. 213: "Consider the sentence A, of the form '<A> is not provable'—this sentence is not provable—angle brackets represent some naming device. Here, provability is to be understood in the naïve sense of being demonstrated by some argument or other. If A is provable, then, since what is provable is true, A is true; so <A> is not provable. Hence, <A> is not provable. But we have just proved this; that is, <A> is provable. This is a version of the 'Knower paradox'. Sometimes it is called 'Gödel's paradox'. In fact, if one identifies truth with provability, as does Wittgenstein, Gödel's paradox and the liar collapse into each other."

34. Cf. Priest (2004), p. 223: "According to the model-theoretic account of truth, the equivalence (I) [viz. the *interpretation* of the Gödel sentence as saying '*P* iff *P* is not provable in *Principia*'] is unproblematic. In the context that Wittgenstein is operating in, it is not, and this allows him to question it. In particular, he can ask exactly what the right-hand side means. This allows him to take the discussion into areas beyond those normally countenanced in discussions of Gödel's theorem."

35. Of course, *PM* (etc.) contain rules establishing that "from a contradiction, anything follows." However, it is clear that there are grounds for being skeptical that, even if this is true, and "anything follows" in the formal sense, a single contradiction is indeed enough to render the calculus useless; see below.

36. What, though, *is* in fact the ultimate basis for our belief in the consistency of a system such as *Principia Mathematica*? Although there is a an inductive consistency proof for the much more limited system of Peano Arithmetic due to Gentzen, there is no known consistency proof for *PM* itself. Moreover, even the Gentzen proof raises questions, since in order to prove the consistency of this limited system in ZFC it is necessary to carry out mathematical induction up to a (high) transfinite ordinal, whose existence itself might legitimately be doubted. For discussion, see Berto (2009), Chapters 10 and 11. Along different lines, Moore (2001a, p. 177–80) argues in a related context that we can take an axiomatic system such as ZFC to be sound (and hence consistent) if we can "recognize" its axioms as intuitively correct and its rules of inference as valid. However, the ground for such a "recognition" is dubious, especially in the case of the more controversial axioms (such as the Axiom of Choice).

37. *RFM*, I, appendix III, remark 17 (p. 122).

38. Lecture 21, p. 209.

39. *PI* 125.

40. Lecture 21, p. 211.

41. Lecture 22, p. 211.

42. Thus, Gödel wrote in 1963: "Before my results had been obtained it was conjectured that any precisely formulated mathematical yes or no question can be decided by the mechanical rules of logical inference on the basis of a few mathematical axioms. In 1931 I proved that this is not so. i.e.: No matter what & how many axioms are chosen there always exist number theoretical yes or no questions which cannot be decided from these axioms. Combining the proof of this result with Turing's theory of computing machines one arrives at the following conclusion: Either there exist infinitely many number theoretical questions which the human mind is unable to answer or the human mind . . . contains an element totally different from a finite combinatorial mechanism, such as a nerve net acting like an electronic computer. I hope I shall be able to prove on mathematical, philosophical, & psychological grounds that the second alternative . . . holds." (van Atten, 2006)

43. The most important of the problems with the Lucas argument in the present context is that it requires the actual *manifestation* of a true formula T of

arithmetic such that an actual computer C *cannot* give a proof of T, but there is a human mind, M, that can. No one has ever actually manifested such a formula, and there is reason to think nobody ever will. One problem here is that the Gödel sentence *for* a system or machine is always specific to *that particular* machine; the Gödel sentence for a particular system can quite well be proved by a different one (or even added to the original system as an axiom). This makes it implausible that there is any single truth that "cannot" be proven by *any* formal system. Lucas argues that it is not necessary for the anti-mechanist to assume the existence of any such truth, since it is sufficient that he can refute any *particular* claim by the mechanist to demonstrate the "actual" system underlying human cognition. However, this seems to be a mistake (see Berto 2009, pp. 179–81) since the anti-mechanist argument in full generality requires not only that any particular mechanist proposal fails in this way, but further that we can actually "see" the "truth" of the Gödel sentence which no system can prove. Moreover, there is reason to think it must be impossible by effective means to display any sentence that is unprovable even by any actual computer. To see this, observe that to find such a formula, given any *actual* computer C, we would have to first distinguish those portions of its output that actually count as proofs from those that do not. As Priest (1994, pp. 111–15) argues, there is, however, probably no effective way to do this; and even if we do, the set of theorems T proved by any actual computer C will probably turn out to be inconsistent. Priest writes: "The only way . . . that offers any hope of getting T to be consistent is to suppose that M (and so any C which is supposed to be M) is not only a mathematical mind but an ideal mathematical mind, that never makes mistakes of any kind: either of memory, inference, judgment, or output. But this is sufficient to destroy the argument. After all, the only candidate for a mind of this kind is God's. So at best, we have a (theo)logical proof that God is not a computer" (p. 113).

44. Putnam (1985). For a helpful discussion of this paper, see Buechner (2008), Chapter 2.
45. Putnam (1985), p. 149.
46. Putnam (1985), p. 144.
47. *PI* 191, 195.
48. *PI* 218.
49. Cf. *PI* 199.
50. Cf. *PI* 359–60.
51. Cf. *RFM* I–117: "In what sense is logical argument a compulsion?—'After all you grant this and this; so you must also grant this!' That is the way of compelling someone. That is to say, one can in fact compel people to admit something in this way.—Just as one can e.g. compel someone to go over there by pointing over there with a bidding gesture of the hand" (p. 81).
52. *PI* 193.
53. Compare the passage from Plato's *Cratylus* cited and discussed above, in Chapter 1 (389a–b).
54. *PI* 193, p. 66.
55. Wittgenstein (1939), p. 197.
56. Wittgenstein 1939, p. 199.
57. Searle (1992), pp. 208–9. (Wordstar was a popular word-processing program at the time of Searle's writing.)
58. Putnam (1991).
59. See Block (1995) and Chalmers (1995). For some helpful discussion, see Buechner (2008), Chapter 3.
60. *RFM* VI–49.

61. There are ample passages documenting this concern in *Culture and Value*; those in more explicitly mathematical contexts are in general less pronounced but nevertheless present and clearly significant to Wittgenstein's conception of the implications of his own consideration of mathematics. See, e.g., *RFM* II–22 and II–23.

   In the context of Wittgenstein's view of technology and the ideology that ordinarily supports it, we should also recall the motto by Nestroy that Wittgenstein chooses for the *Philosophical Investigations* themselves: "In general, progress appears much greater than it actually is."

62. It is worthwhile to compare this to the conclusion drawn by readers such as Nyiri (1981) and Gellner (1959), who take Wittgenstein to be defending an essentially conservative and "traditionalist" politics. These readers have assumed, despite the lack in the text of any explicit avowal of this, that when Wittgenstein talks about "techniques" and "practices" he is really talking about a foundation in *specific* cultural or social traditions or traditional ways of life. But as we have seen in this chapter, Wittgenstein's concept of "technique" is quite general, and *any* technique or calculus might have its place within this concept. This accounts, in fact, for the pronounced *lack* of nostalgia and romanticism in Wittgenstein as opposed to some other critical thinkers of the twentieth century. For more on why the "conservative" interpretation of Wittgenstein is misguided, see Livingston (2008), Chapter 6.

63. *RFM* III–82.

64. Cf. *PI* 150–55.

65. Cf. the title and thesis of J. L. Nancy's (1986) essay "The Inoperative Community."

66. Specifically, Gödel's second theorem follows from the possibility of replicating the formal structure of the demonstration of the first theorem *within* the system concerned (for instance, *PM*) itself. Since this is possible, we can formulate a "consistency statement" CON_{PM} and show that $\vdash_{PM} CON_{PM} \leftrightarrow GS$, where GS is the Gödel sentence for *PM*. Thus, the consistency statement is provable only if GS itself is; but (as the first theorem shows), if the system is consistent, GS itself is not provable.

67. As we saw above, it is possible in certain *limited* cases to give a model-theoretic "consistency proof" for a formal system in another, "stronger" system. This does not, however, affect the point here, since the provision of consistency proofs always thus requires an iteration of systems or levels. This is simply, once again, the strategy of parameterization (Chapter 1) which, as we saw, fails to reckon fully with the implications of the paradoxes of self-reference themselves.

68. There is a comparison to be drawn here with Cavell's sense of the reflective moment at which practices of rule-following are extended as a "convening of" my culture's "criteria." See Cavell (1979), p. 125.

69. "I should like to ask something like: "Is it usefulness you are out for in your calculus? In that case you do not get any contradiction. And if you aren't out for usefulness—then it doesn't matter if you do get one" (*RFM*, p. 210).

70. I advance the conclusion of this paragraph and the next one somewhat cautiously, since I am less sure of it than I am of many of the other consequences of formalism discussed here.

71. Lévi-Strauss (1950), pp. 60–61.

72. I put "the possibility of" in parentheses because in some of its most radical developments, e.g., in Deleuze (but also in Wittgenstein), the development of a paradoxico-critical consideration of "conditions for the possibility" (in

something like a Kantian sense) of signification ultimately has the effect of undermining traditional conceptions of the nature of *possibility* as well.

NOTES TO CHAPTER 7

1. Lacan (1973), p. 93.
2. "Lastly, the symbolic, directing itself toward the real, shows us the true nature of object *a*" (Lacan 1973, p. 95).
3. Lacan (1973), p. 119.
4. Lacan (1973), p. 119.
5. Lacan (1973), p. 120.
6. Badiou (1982), p. 22.
7. Badiou (1982), p. 23.
8. Badiou (1982), p. 19.
9. "How is it that the real passes beyond? How is it that it periodizes, rather than running in circles? 'To encircle' is said of barrels, and before it was said of suitcases. The voyage of the real is sometimes without baggage, and, according to Saint Luke, the old cask does not exclude the new wine that must be poured into it" (Badiou 1982, p. 23). Badiou's choice of metaphors here is worth noting, and interestingly reminiscent, in fact, of Lacan's own metaphorical description of "form" as "holding being in its glass."
10. Badiou (1982), p. 21.
11. Badiou (1982), pp. 265–74. For more on *Theory of the Subject*, including an instructive comparison to the problematic of Derrida's "Force of Law," see Bosteels (2008b).
12. This opposition between a "Lacanian" position on the impasse of the Real (one also shared by Žižek) and Badiou's very different perspective is also helpfully discussed (with reference to the same juxtaposition of formulations I develop here) by Bruno Bosteels in Bosteels (2002), pp. 182–3 and 195–99.
13. Thus: "It is insofar as something brutal is played out in writing (l'ecrit)— namely, the taking as ones of as many ones as we like—that the impasses that are revealed thereby are, by themselves, a possible means of access to being for us ..." (Lacan 1973, p. 49); these are none other than the impasses of set theory. It should be noted, as well, that there are changes and complications in Badiou's sense of the dialectic and its application to these formal problematics over the course of his career. For instance, in *Being and Event* he appears to reject the relevance of dialectic reasoning, especially with respect to the central disjunction between the realm of Being and the event itself. However, in *Logics of Worlds*, he once more characterizes his position (rehabilitating a term employed briefly by Althusser) as a "materialist dialectic" (see below).
14. Lacan (1973), p. 50.
15. Lacan (1973), p. 67.
16. Lacan (1973), p. 44.
17. Lacan (1973), p. 45.
18. Badiou (1982), p. 30.
19. Badiou (1982), p. 37.
20. The continuity of this project with one of the main projects definitive of twentieth-century analytic philosophy, which Badiou tends to underesti- mate, may already provide sufficient reason to doubt Badiou's conviction, expressed on the last page of *Being and Event*, that "A close analysis of logico-mathematical procedures since Cantor and Frege can ... enable the thinking of what this intellectual revolution ... conditions in contemporary rationality" and thereby "permit the undoing, in this matter, of the monopoly

of Anglo-Saxon positivism" (*B&E*, p. 435). This is wildly inaccurate in any case, since there has not been a recognizable "monopoly of . . . positivism" in Anglo-American academic philosophy since at least the 1960s; but additionally we may well dispute, on the basis of the evidently vast and enduring consequences of the metalogical project inaugurated by Cantor and Frege and continued in at least some sectors of contemporary analytic philosophy, Badiou's sense of its imminent demise.

21. Two sets have the same cardinality if and only if their elements can be put into one-to-one correspondence. The best way to understand the distinction between ordinals and cardinals is as follows: whereas ordinals answer the question "which one?" in an *order* (e.g., the *seventh* or the *one-thousandth*), cardinals answer the question "how many?" (*seven* or *one thousand*). For finite numbers, ordinals and cardinals correspond, but in the transfinite case, although all cardinals are ordinals, it often happens that two distinct ordinals have the same cardinality. This is because, in the transfinite case, it often happens that two distinct sets can be put into one-to-one correspondence.

22. *B&E*, pp. 275–80. More technically, $\aleph_1$ is defined as the smallest *ordinal* that cannot be put into one-to-one correspondence with $\aleph_0$ or anything smaller than it; $\aleph_2$ is the smallest ordinal that cannot be put into one-to-one correspondence with $\aleph_1$ or anything smaller, etc. All cardinals are thus identical with particular ordinals (although many ordinals are not cardinals). We thus symbolize these as $\aleph_0$, $\aleph_1$, $\aleph_2$, etc., when discussing these numbers in their "cardinal" aspect and ω_0, ω_1, ω_2, etc., when discussing them in their "ordinal" aspect; bear in mind, though, that the aleph- and omega-notations actually refer to the *same* number for each index.

23. *B&E*, p. 278, p. 293.

24. In general, a model is a domain of objects and relations for which the axioms all hold true. If a theorem, such as the continuum hypothesis, holds in at least one model, it is not provably false (since if it is provably false, it does not hold for any model).

25. Cohen (1966), pp. 85–86; cf. Fraenkel et al. (1973), pp. 193–95.

26. Cohen (1966), pp. 85–86.

27. *B&E*, pp. 299–301.

28. *B&E*, p. 309.

29. *B&E*, p. 304.

30. *B&E*, pp. 358–62

31. *B&E*, p. 367. What Badiou calls "discernibility" is thus the same as what Gödel calls "constructability."

32. *B&E*, pp. 373–76.

33. *B&E*, pp. 337, 392.

34. *B&E*, p. 371.

35. *B&E*, p. 340.

36. *B&E*, p. 333.

37. *B&E*, pp. 331–34.

38. *B&E*, p. 342.

39. *B&E*, pp. 335–38.

40. *B&E*, pp. 367–71.

41. I draw the metaphor of "reading out," as well as much of the exposition of this paragraph, from Peter Hallward's immensely useful description of forcing in the "Appendix" of Hallward (2003). For Cohen's own description, see Cohen (1966). Badiou himself relies heavily on Kunen (1980); it is from this treatment that much of Badiou's own discussion of what is accesssible or not to an "inhabitant" of the initial situation, including the identification of what

is discernable to such an "inhabitant" with the constructible sets, appears to be drawn.

42. *B&E*, p. 407.
43. *B&E*, pp. 421–23.
44. *B&E*, pp. 391–92.
45. Badiou (2006) (henceforth: *LofW*), pp. 2–3.
46. *LofW*, pp. 2–8.
47. *LofW*, p. 4.
48. *LofW*, pp. 9–10.
49. *LofW*, pp. 33–35.
50. *LofW*, pp. 118–40.
51. *LofW*, pp. 138–40.
52. For a perspicuous presentation, see, e.g., Goldblatt (2006).
53. *LofW*, pp. 173–90.
54. *LofW*, pp. 231–41.
55. *LofW*, p. 93. Badiou makes a similar argument in Chapter 8 of *Briefings on Existence* (Badiou 1998b), defending there (p. 111) the theses that "we have to break with the linguistic turn . . ." due to its penchant to "[end] up with the pure and simple dislocation of philosophical desire as such" in a "pragmatism of cultures" or a "Heideggerian dependency," and that this break requires the production of a "new thought" of the relationship of mathematics and logic whereby logic is mathematized, rather than mathematics being logicized.
56. To support the necessity of affirming objective degrees of existence in a world, Badiou cites (pp. 118–19) an argument against all idealist or "correlationist" philosophies that relate subject to object given by Quentin Meillassoux (2006). For more on Meillassoux, see endnote 8 to Chapter 10.
57. *LofW*, pp. 250–51.
58. *LofW*, pp. 94, 221–3.
59. *LofW*, p. 360.
60. *LofW*, pp. 364–66.
61. *LofW*, pp. 374–79.
62. *LofW*, pp. 403–11.
63. Thus: "A point concentrates the degrees of existence, the intensities measured by the transcendental, into only two possibilities. Of these two possibilities, only one is the 'good one' for a truth-procedure that must pass through this point. Only one authorizes the continuation, and therefore the reinforcement, of the actions of the subject-body in the world. All of a sudden, the transcendental degrees are in fact distributed into two classes by a given point that treats the becoming of a truth: the degrees associated with the 'good' value and those associated with the bad one" (*LofW*, p. 416).
64. *LofW*, p. 371.
65. *LofW*, p. 372. This is a somewhat different sense of "singularity" from that in *Being and Event*.
66. *LofW*, p. 53.
67. *LofW*, p. 55.
68. *LofW*, p. 59.
69. For paradoxico-criticism, as we have seen above, the paradoxical results of Russell and especially Gödel therefore do not establish (as they have often been taken to) a specific irreducibility of mathematics to logic. The claim of such an irreducibility is itself the basis for Badiou's employment, in *Logics of Worlds*, of the Heyting device of rooting the (purported) plurality of classical and non-classical "logics" in the more foundational structure of category theory. From the perspective of paradoxico-criticism, this is backwards:

the paradoxes of Russell and Carnap indeed establish the presence of limit-paradoxes and contradictions in any logical/ontological thinking of the reflexive One, but they do not at all demand or suggest the irreducibility of mathematics or its purported distinct "objects." Paradoxico-criticism thus remains faithful (even despite the radical implications of the paradoxes, which are here again assimilated as positive critical results) to the original "event" of logicism in its classic (Fregean) formulation, and even to the profoundly motivating intuition that set theory, as an "allegory of predication," is to be understood as an organic extension of the formal logic of concepts and terms. (See note 7 to Chapter 1). Nor would it be right to say that the original logicist program is, even today, dead in the context of analytic philosophy; recently, a number of philosophers have attempted a revival of Frege's original project of reducing mathematics to logic by employing techniques in second-order logic. For a useful overview of this contemporary "neo-logicism" or "neo-Fregeanism," see MacBride (2003).

70. *LofW*, p. 110.
71. *LofW*, p. 112.
72. *LofW*, pp. 112–13.

NOTES TO CHAPTER 8

1. *PI* 49.
2. For more on the context principle, in relation to the founding motives of the analytic tradition's critical inquiry into language, see Livingston (2008), Chapter 2.
3. In this chapter, the aim is simply to contrast the paradoxico-critical and generic orientations on a series of related points. I do not make any argument for the superior value or utility of either orientation here. In the next chapter, by contrast, I consider, and criticize, Badiou's orientation from *a paradoxico-critical point of view* (though even there I do not argue that the paradoxico-critical orientation is *inherently* superior, but only that it is better suited for *certain* tasks and needs).
4. *LofS*, p. 95.
5. *LofS*, p. 95.
6. *LofS*, p. 60. There is probably an instructive comparison to be drawn here with Wittgenstein's own critical consideration of the relationship between rules and the unity (or lack thereof) of what are called "games" in the *Philosophical Investigations*.
7. Badiou (1997), p. 5.
8. Badiou (1997), p. 3. The only published discussion of Badiou by Deleuze is a brief (two-page) treatment of Badiou's theory of the event in Deleuze and Guattari's *What Is Philosophy?* (Deleuze and Guattari 1991) in which the two allege that Badiou's theory ultimately intends to return to an antiquated conception of a "higher philosophy"; Badiou has called the passage "strange" and its position "intractable" (Badiou 2000, p. 245). In *Logics of Worlds* (p. 361), however, Badiou suggests that Deleuze was one of the "perspicacious readers" who raised important objections to *Being and Event*'s conception of the auto-nomination of the event, and Badiou has related to Bruno Bosteels in an interview that Deleuze expressed admiration for *Being and Event*'s conception of the evental site. For some interesting and suggestive discussion, see Bosteels (2008a).
9. Badiou (1997), p. 11.
10. Badiou (1997), p. 8.

11. Badiou (1997), p. 11; *LofS*, p. 180.
12. Badiou (1997), p. 3.
13. Badiou (1997), p. 36.
14. Badiou (1997), pp. 37–38.
15. Badiou (1997), p. 38.
16. Badiou (1997), p. 40.
17. Badiou (1997), pp. 75–76.
18. *LofW*, p. 385.
19. Badiou (1997), pp. 26–27.
20. Badiou (1997), p. 46.
21. Badiou (1989), p. 103.
22. Badiou (2004a), p. 101.
23. *LofW*, p. 386. There is good reason to think that Badiou is not in fact very clear on this point with respect to Deleuze, or at least that his near-identification of Deleuze, here, with the 'linguistic turn' represents an important change in position from the position of his earlier, 1997 text, a shift that seems to reflect a kind of deeply held ambivalence on Badiou's part toward Deleuze himself. For in the earlier text, in a passage devoted to expounding Deleuze's singular affirmation of the univocity of being, we read: "How very Greek this confidence in Being as the measure of relations, both internal and external, is! And how very indifferent to the 'linguistic turn' this ontological coemergence of sentences and what-occurs under the role of the One is!" Badiou (1997), p. 21.
24. We can thus agree wholeheartedly with Slavoj Žižek's analysis of Deleuze in (Žižek 2004a), according to which the usual reception of Deleuze as the philosopher of "the spontaneous, nonhierarchical, living multitude opposing the oppressive, reified System" (Žižek 2004a, p. 32), which is drawn mostly from his works coauthored with Guattari, in fact obscures a very different politics in Deleuze, one that we can discern only by tracing through the implications of the deeply held and definitive structuralism of *Difference and Repetition* and *The Logic of Sense* (pp. 82, 92). For a prominent example of the received reading which Žižek opposes, see Hardt and Negri (2004).
25. *LofW*, p. 387.
26. *LofW*, p. 387.
27. There is, however, a document of some earlier disputes between Badiou and Derrida in the proceedings of a 1990 colloquium called *Lacan avec les Philosophes* (Michel 1991).
28. The eulogy was given at Birkbeck College, University of London, in 2005, and later at the University of California, Irvine. It is collected in the volume *Adieu Derrida* (Douzinas 2005) as well as, in a shorter and somewhat different form, in Badiou's book *Pocket Pantheon* (Badiou 2008a).
29. *LofW*, p. 545.
30. *LofW*, pp. 545–46.
31. Derrida (1966), p. 278.
32. Derrida (1966), p. 280.
33. Derrida (1966), p. 280.
34. It is significant that Derrida does not say here that for *his analysis* or for *deconstruction* the 'center' is both inside and outside the structure, but rather that "classical thought" *already* implies this paradoxical structure. The aim of such thought is indeed, Derrida says, to think this paradox coherently; and "as always, coherence in contradiction expresses the force of a desire" (p. 279). Following the evental "rupture" of which he speaks, it is necessary to begin to think, by contrast, not that the center is inherently contradictory but that "there was no center, that the center could not be thought in the form of a present-being, that

the center had no natural site, that it was not a fixed locus but a function, a sort of nonlocus in which an infinite number of sign-substitutions came into play" (p. 280). This illustrates a general feature of the practice of paradoxico-criticism; the aim is not only to point out the contradictory and paradoxical *foundations* of the picture that assumes a fullness of sense and an unproblematic place of origin, but to *displace* this assumption infinitely and transform its reflection into an unending criticism on the basis of the latent and uncentered dimension of language as pure spacing, displacement, and *différance*.

35. Derrida (1971), p. 327.
36. To indicate one aspect of this contrast of sensibilities, it suffices to contrast two remarks made by the two philosophers in the prefaces to their respective "masterpieces," *Being and Event* and the *Philosophical Investigations*. First Badiou, in the new English preface written for the translation of *Being and Event* in 2005:

> Soon it will have been twenty years since I published this book in France. At that moment I was quite aware of having written a 'great' book of philosophy. I felt that I had actually achieved what I had set out to do. Not without pride, I thought that I had inscribed my name in the history of philosophy, and in particular, in the history of those philosophical systems which are the subject of interpretations and commentaries throughout the centuries. (p. xi)

Contrast the final remarks of Wittgenstein's preface, written in January 1945:

> For more than one reason what I publish here will have points of contact with what other people are writing to-day.—If my remarks do not bear a stamp which marks them as mine—I do not wish to lay any further claim to them as my property.
> I make them public with doubtful feelings. It is not impossible that it should fall to the lot of this work, in its poverty and in the darkness of this time, to bring light into one brain or another—but, of course, it is not likely.
> I should not like my writing to spare other people the trouble of thinking. But, if possible, to stimulate someone to thoughts of his own.
> I should have liked to produce a good book. This has not come about, but the time is past in which I could improve it. (p. x)

37. Badiou (1994a).
38. Badiou (1994b).
39. Badiou (2009).
40. *LofW*, p. 540.
41. *LofW*, p. 541.
42. For some of the results of reading Lacan as an "anti-philosopher," see Badiou (1992), Chapter 14.
43. Bruno Bosteels has given a very clear description of the characteristics of the anti-philosopher, according to Badiou:

> Based on his detailed readings of Nietzsche, Wittgenstein, and Lacan, as well as the occasional references to Pascal, Kierkegaard, or Rousseau, Badiou distinguishes a small number of basic features as the invariant core of any antiphilosophy. At least for the modern period, these invariant traits include the following: the assumption that the question of being, or that of the world, is coextensive with the question of language; consequently, the reduction of truth to being nothing more than a linguistic or rhetorical effect, the outcome of historically and culturally specific language games or tropes

which therefore must be judged and, better yet, mocked in light of a critical-linguistic, discursive, or genealogical analysis; an appeal to what lies just beyond language, or rather at the upper limit of the sayable, as a domain of meaning, sense, or knowledge, irreducible to any form of truth as defined in philosophy; and, finally, in order to gain access to this domain, the search for a radical act such as the religious leap of faith or the revolutionary breaking in two of the history of the world, the sheer intensity of which would discredit in advance any systematic theoretical or conceptual elaboration. (Bosteels 2008c, pp. 8–9)

44. Badiou here passes completely over the distinction between an *act* and an *activity*, which may in fact be important to the question of how we should understand Wittgenstein's developing conception of philosophy; see below for more on "activities" and "techniques" as distinct from acts and events.

45. Badiou (1994a), 1st course, sect. 5c.

46. Badiou, (1994a), 5th course, sect. 4.

47. For the "resolute" interpretation, see note 121 to Chapter 5. "And if Wittgenstein can speak of the unspeakable, even metaphorically or with contradiction, it is ultimately because there is not one but two registers of existence; otherwise there would be no sense in speaking of limits of worlds. You see that mentioning the limits of the world makes sense only if there is, if I may say, a non-mundane existence, whatever it is impossible to talk about. But there must be a non-worldly [existence] for it to be meaningful to speak of limits of the world" (Badiou 1994, 3rd cours, sect. 2g.; but cf. *TLP* 6.521, 6.54).

48. Lacan (1970).

49. Lacan (1970), p. 63.

50. Lacan (1970), p. 61.

51. Lacan (1970), p. 61.

52. Badiou (1994a), 5th course, section 4.

53. Elsewhere, Badiou recognizes Wittgenstein's theory of eternal objects as "the moment of the most rigorous conceptual tension in the *Tractatus*" and the securing of an "altogether remarkable ontological base" (Badiou 1997, p. 18).

54. *LofW*, p. 301.

55. *LofW*, p. 358.

56. *TLP* 5.526; 6.124.

57. Badiou (1994a), 8th course, sect. 3b.

58. *TLP* 6.21.

59. Badiou (1998b), p. 94; cf. *TLP* 5.43 and 6.1–6.2.

60. Badiou (1998b), p. 94.

61. Badiou (2004b), p. 7.

62. *RFM*, III–81. The remark is quoted out of context and appears to be mistranslated in Badiou's article (Badiou 2004b, p. 15), although since the article was itself translated into English from Badiou's unpublished manuscript, it is impossible to tell whether Badiou himself or his translator is to blame for this.

63. This is the crux of Wittgenstein's dispute with Turing in the 1939 lectures; see Chapter 6.

64. Cf. *PI* 92: "This [viz., the attempt to find a "*single* completely resolved form of every expression"] finds expression in questions as to the *essence* of language, of propositions, of thought. For if **we too in these investigations are trying to understand the essence of language—its function, its structure—** yet this is not what those questions have in view" (emphasis added in bold).

65. *PI* 111.

66. *PI* 373, 371.

67. Badiou (1998a).

68. Badiou (1998a), pp. 47–48.
69. Cf. *PI* 124, 133.
70. *RFM* II, 32.

NOTES TO CHAPTER 9

1. *LofW*, p. 420.
2. *LofW*, p. 420.
3. *LofW*, p. 174.
4. *LofW*, p. 1.
5. *LofW*, p. 2.
6. *LofW*, p. 4.
7. *LofW*, p. 5.
8. This attempt even in some cases coexists with a formal recognition of the paradoxes themselves, as for instance in Russell's own essentially constructivist attempt to defuse the radical implications of the paradox he himself discovered through a regimenting theory of types.
9. *LofW*, p. 546.
10. For some critical considerations about the "count-as-one," see Johnston (2008).
11. *B&E*, p. 340.
12. *B&E*, p. 341.
13. This possibility of discerning the "weak points" of ineffectivity within regimes in which the effectiveness of techniques and technologies are uniformly presupposed appears to be closely linked to paradoxico-criticism's identification and critique of "metaphysics," a critical category which Badiou does not employ. In the context of a perceptive discussion of Badiou, Jean-Luc Nancy (2002), pp. 47–48, raises the question of the privileged link between "technics" as the manipulation of nature and the "metaphysical" determination of man in terms of "logos" (for which, see Chapter 1). The role of metaphysics in pre-conditioning the (necessarily technical) *procedures* which Badiou calls the "conditions" of Truths is again connected, according to Nancy, with the *logos*: "With the concept of the logos as such, which stretches from the order of discourse to that of verifying autonomy, a technique takes charge of the production of sense itself, rather than merely of subsistence or even 'super-sistence' [*sursistance*]. This is the sense in which I am here characterizing metaphysics as a *techno-logy*: the sense of a breakout into a verifying autonomy of technics, or of 'denaturation' " (p. 48).
14. In a highly suggestive, though brief, reading that bears multiple connections to the discussion here, Ray Brassier (2004) raises the question of the extent to which Badiou's conception of subjective action and fidelity indeed provides terms by which we can understand and criticize the systematic logic of the "machine" of global capital. Brassier suggests that Turing's demonstration of the necessary existence of *uncomputable* functions and procedures (see Chapter 6) might provide for a kind of "objective" randomness that "indexes the not-all-ness (pas-tout), the constitutive incompleteness whereby the Real punctures the consistency of the symbolic order . . ." (p. 57) and so provides an alternative to Badiou's "subjective" conception that is in fact *better* able to handle the constitutive contradictions and "errant automation" of global Capital. For more on this suggestion, with which the position of paradoxico-criticism can certainly agree, see Chapter 10.
15. Badiou (1993), p. 67.

16. Badiou (1993), p. 83.
17. Cf. Hallett (1986), p. 234, who concludes a discussion of the antinomies by reading Kant as a constructivist in a strong sense: "Kant it seems is a constructivist, an anti-realist with a strong notion of completability."
18. See, e.g., Johnston (2008), Žižek (2004b) (esp. pp. 172–75).
19. This is not to say that much of the apparatus and results of the Hegelian dialectic, particularly in its specific stages if not in its overall movement, cannot be usefully accommodated to an essentially paradoxico-critical position. This accommodation is in fact accomplished in spectacular fashion by Slavoj Žižek, who in combining Hegel with Lacan both repeats and expands upon the latter's thoroughgoing paradoxico-criticism. In large part, he is able to do so, in fact, by emphasizing the "split" and incommensurable aspects of the various dialectical positions, and by portraying these largely as fundamentally the outcome of an underlying paradox of position which is formally homologous to the paradox of the position of enunciation or of the Lacanian "subject-position" that we have explored in Chapter 2. I do not wish here to assert any opinion as to the extent of the *actual* fit between Žižek's Hegel and the "historical" one. Although Žižek, like others, generally does not distinguish clearly between what I have called the paradoxico-critical and generic orientations, Žižek sometimes appears to endorse the paradoxico-critical combination of completeness and inconsistency on behalf of Hegel or (more usually) Kant or Lacan: see, e.g., Žižek (1993), pp. 83–89; Žižek (1989), Chapter 5; Žižek (1991), pp. 214–22; and Žižek (2004a), pp. 53–55 and 64–67.
20. *LofW*, p. 112.
21. An apparent—but only apparent—counterexample to this is the existence of non-well-founded set theories, certain of which (for instance, Quine's "New Foundations" system) *can* be formulated, without inconsistency, so as to allow both self-membered sets and a universal set. See Forster (1992), pp. 22–25. This is only an apparent counterexample, though, since the way that these systems allow for a universal set without contradiction is to restrict the axiom of separation (see Chapter 1) in such a way that Cantor's theorem fails to be provable, and in fact diagonalization fails to be possible, in general. This is much more, once again, an axiomatic *avoidance* of the issue of totality and reflexivity involved in Russell's paradox rather than a *resolution* of the paradox. I would like to thank Luke Fraser for some helpful discussion of these issues.
22. *B&E*, p. 376.
23. This does *not* mean, I hasten to point out, that the procedure toward a Truth has, for Badiou, the status of the teleological progress toward an entity or phenomenon simply external and transcendent to the situation. The positing of such a transcendence as a positive and, in principle, obtainable goal of knowledge brings us within the domain of onto-theology, and even the Kantian "regulative ideal," unknowable but nevertheless capable of orienting thought toward an ever-greater synthesis, remains a figure of the possible combination of completeness and consistency, though this time upheld on criteriological grounds. Rather, the implication (as we have seen in connection with the fundamental assertion of the situatedness of the event, in both *Being and Event* and *Logics of Worlds*) that Badiou draws from his own traversal of Russell's paradox and Cohen's technique is that of a complete *immanence* to a situation of the elements that will eventually compose the generic extension. But this does not preclude Badiou from thinking its tracing and eventual superaddition in hierarchical terms, most obviously in straightforwardly quantitative terms, as the excessive cardinality which the

generic set allows to be forced. I would like to thank Joe Spencer for some discussion of these issues.

24. *B&E*, p. 26.
25. Badiou (1998b), p. 43
26. *B&E*, p. 173.
27. *B&E*, p. 190 (emphasis in original).
28. *B&E*, pp. 27–28.
29. *B&E*, p. 30.
30. *B&E*, p. 522.
31. There is, perhaps, a symptom of larger problems here in Badiou's "definition" in *Being and Event*'s "dictionary" of the "count-as-one," which is, in fact, literally no "definition" at all, but rather just a kind of remark: "Given the non-being of the One, any one-effect is the result of an operation, the count-as-one. Every situation (+) is structured by such a count" (*B&E*, p. 504).
32. In one of his earliest philosophical texts, *The Concept of Model*, Badiou argued vociferously, on political as well as epistemological grounds, against the 'ideological' result of applying mathematical model theory to the structure of scientific discovery and research, holding that this application tends to support the logical empiricism of Carnap and Quine, which true materialists should resist (Badiou 1968). This argument appears, however, to predate Badiou's explicit recourse to Cohen's method of forcing, and in any case there is no evident way to reconstruct Cohen's result as to the independence of the Continuum Hypothesis with respect to the axioms of ZFC without extensive use of model-theoretic reasoning, of which Badiou also makes extensive use in his presentation of forcing in *Being and Event*. Interestingly, Cohen himself nevertheless suggests that the implications of forcing for the nature of truth may indeed ultimately depend more on 'syntactic' considerations than on model theory *per se*: "A third theme of my work, namely the analysis of 'truth,' is made precise in the definition of 'forcing.' To people who read my work for the first time, this may very well strike them as the essential ingredient, rather than the two aspects of constructability and the introduction of new sets, as mentioned above. Although I emphasized the 'model' approach in my earlier remarks, this point of view is more akin to the 'syntactical' approach, which I associate with Gödel" (Cohen 2008, p. xi). Nevertheless, Cohen says, ". . . in the final form [of the forcing results] it is very difficult to separate what is theoretic and what is syntactical" and "I would say that my notion of forcing can also be viewed as arising from the analysis of how models are constructed, something in the spirit of the Löwenheim-Skolem Theorem" (Cohen 2008, p. xii).
33. *B&E*, p. 40.
34. *B&E*, p. 41.
35. *B&E*, p. 47.
36. *B&E*, p. 48.
37. *B&E*, p. 53.
38. *B&E*, p. 55; emphasis added in bold.
39. The French term in both cases is "tout."
40. *B&E*, p. 95.
41. *B&E*, p. 93.
42. *B&E*, p. 176.
43. *B&E*, p. 288.
44. *B&E*, p. 290.
45. *B&E*, pp. 287–88.
46. *B&E*, p. 291.

47. "The orientation of constructivist thought . . . is the one which naturally prevails in established situations because it measures being to language such as it is. We shall suppose, from this point on, the existence, in every situation, of a language of the situation" (*B&E*, p. 328).
48. Badiou comes close to saying as much, when he is formally introducing the structure of "truth" in its contrast with "veridicity"—see *B&E*, p. 331.
49. The fantasy of such a state, capable of assuring complete control over thought and concept through its legislation of language, is certainly nevertheless a kind of ongoing fascination of the geopolitics of the twentieth century; it is expressed, for instance, in works such as Orwell's *1984* and doubtless plays an important (though ambiguous) ideological role in the dialectic that opposes various "totalitarian" regimes to those formations and structures that would resist them on the point of their affirmation of the freedom to speak. Still, despite the massive and indisputable structural effects of this dialectic and all that surrounds it in the twentieth century and (in somewhat different forms) today, it remains important in the present context to note that the state with a "complete" mastery of language is, in the form envisioned here, nothing more than an ideological fiction.
50. Indeed (to make a point that is perhaps all too obvious), it is literally impossible to consider the group of *sans-papiers* to be the "unnamable" or "specific inexistent" of the situation in which they exist (presumably, current-day France), for they are, precisely, a group that *already has a name* (albeit a negatively specified one) in French (namely: "sans-papiers")! So the issue of their inclusion or exclusion, however important it is in its own right, simply cannot be seen as resting on, or even in any important sense related to, the (French) state's "mastery of names."

There is also the issue of "official" state languages and the marginalization of non-native speakers. This is, perhaps, a more serious issue in the present context, and this is *somewhat* more closely connected (or connectable) to Badiou's formal structures. Nevertheless, the connection is still not direct, as is witnessed by the fact that a non-native speaker may nevertheless in many states be accorded the full political rights of citizenship.
51. Similar problems with Badiou's theorization of political change have been noted by several commentators. Adrian Johnston makes this point a kind of crux of his perceptive and thorough book *Badiou, Žižek, and Political Transformations: The Cadence of Change* (Johnston 2009). Johnston there calls, in response to Badiou, for a kind of "pre-eventual discipline of change" and even for a "pre-eventual forcing" that would attempt to discern the systematic "weak points" at which it might be possible for political actors to intervene and produce fundamental transformations, even before the recognizable occurrence of anything like an "event" in Badiou's sense. For some closely related concerns, see (Hallward 2004b), pp. 15–16.
52. There is a helpful overview of Badiou's argument, with detailed and illuminating discussions of the underlying formalisms, in Hallward (2003), Chapters 3 and 4. For more on the formalisms themselves and their development over the course of the axiomatization of set theory, see Hallward's very helpful appendix: "On the Development of Transfinite Set Theory."
53. Cohen also demonstrated, by means of forcing, the independence of the CH from the axiom of choice, so the difference between ZF and ZFC makes no difference here.
54. In a remark at the end of the book in which he explains forcing and his results (Cohen 1966), Cohen writes: "A point of view which the author feels may eventually come to be accepted is that CH is obviously false" (p. 151). He reasons that, whereas $\aleph_1$ is just formed by gathering together

the countable ordinals, the continuum is "in contrast, generated by a totally new and more powerful principle, namely the Power Set Axiom" (p. 151), and hence may have a much higher cardinality. But this is clearly simply an expression of the personal views of the author and, insofar as it can be construed as a prediction about the consensus belief of mathematical practitioners with respect to the truth of the generalized CH, does not seem to have to be particularly well borne out. Cf., for instance, the statement of Fraenkel, Bar-Hillel, and Levy from 1958: ". . . the generalized continuum hypothesis is well on its way towards being accepted as one of the axioms of set theory, as used by most mathematicians. Nowadays most mathematicians would not doubt the truth of a mathematical theorem proved by means of the generalized continuum hypothesis . . ." Fraenkel, Bar-Hillel, and Levy (1973), pp. 107–8.

55. See, e.g., Feferman (2000), pp. 10–11.
56. Gödel (1947), p. 263. The remark was written after Gödel's own demonstration of the irrefutability of the Continuum Hypothesis but before Cohen's demonstration that it cannot be proven. Gödel himself thought that the addition of an intuitively motivated new axiom or axioms grounded in the concept of sets might settle the hypothesis; however, no such axioms have subsequently been found. See Fraenkel, Bar-Hillel, and Levy (1973), pp. 106–7, for discussion. Even today, though, some researchers are continuing Gödel's program by developing the implications of so-called "large cardinal" axioms.
57. Gödel (1931), footnote 48a, pp. 28–29.
58. Hallett (1986), p. 208. There is a brief discussion of issues surrounding Hallett's claim in Hallward (2003), pp. 70–71; somewhat misleadingly from the current perspective, however, Hallward takes Hallett's claim to *support* rather than *problematize* Badiou's understanding of the consequences of the power set axiom.
59. Hallett (1986), p. 208.
60. *B&E*, p. 278.
61. For more on the suggestion that the event and its consequences effectively "provides a measure" for the state, which would otherwise be unmeasurably excessive, see *Metapolitics* (Badiou 1998c), Chapter 10.
62. *B&E*, p. 280.
63. Fraser (2006).
64. Because Badiou does not revisit the issue of forcing in detail in *Logics of Worlds*, it is difficult to say exactly what bearing these considerations about the relationship of forcing and intuitionism have for Badiou's "phenomenology" there, which is, as we have seen, almost completely disjoined from the "ontology" of *Being and Event*. However, insofar as "appearances" are to be modeled, for Badiou in *Logics of Worlds*, by a variety of logics, most of which are intuitionist, this disjunction appears to confirm once again that there is nothing *in appearance* that necessarily requires or establishes the existence of what Badiou calls Truths. Accordingly, what it means to assert that a Truth, apparently definable only on the level of ontology, can indeed become manifest or "appear" within a world remains very much in question.
65. Cohen (2008), pp. viii–ix.
66. I would like to thank John Bova for bringing the Davis quotation to my attention, and Reuben Hersh for some discussion of the point.
67. For a helpful discussion, see (Moore 2001a), Chapter 11.
68. It's true that, in concluding the forcing demonstration in *Being and Event* (pp. 423–24), Badiou does consider the issue of the "absoluteness" of cardinality. However, what is in question here is simply whether the cardinalities

of sets in the generic set ♀ are retained in the "generic extension" created by adjoining ♀ to the original situation, not whether cardinalities remain absolute in the sense of the universe as a whole.

69. Admittedly, given Cohen's demonstration of the consistency of ~CH with the ZF axioms, this is a position that is only accessible to those who think that, as Gödel himself suggested, these axioms are in some ways inadequate and need to be supplemented with further ones. However, it is important to note that new axioms might well settle the question of the CH, in which case the "results" of forcing would turn out to have the merely artifactual status discussed here.

70. Thus, since the power set is the set of all subsets, and subsets may apparently be defined by a vast (non-denumerable) number of (not extensionally equivalent) properties, "To be sure that one has 'captured' all the subsets of x one has to take into account the whole universe" (Hallett 1986), p. 206.

71. Hallett (1986), p. 221.

72. As noted in endnote 136 to Chapter 1, it is thus to a certain extent misleading to term *Badiou*'s orientation (as he himself does in *Briefings on Existence*) the "generic" orientation, since the paradoxico-critic can also agree perfectly well to at least the *ideal* existence of generic sets. In certain ways, the split between Badiou's orientation and paradoxico-criticism is in fact subsequent to this acknowledgment of the generic set, with the paradoxico-critic taking it as further evidence for the inherent *undecidability* of all languages, whereas Badiou (along with Gödel) takes it to establish, in conjunction with the results of forcing, the *incompleteness* of existing languages and situations. However, as noted, there is no other easily available terminology, so I have maintained the description of Badiou's orientation as the "generic" one throughout this text.

NOTES TO CHAPTER 10

1. See, e.g., Žižek (1999), pp. 210–15.
2. Cf. Badiou, *LofW*, pp. 1–3, and Badiou (1993), Chapters 1 and 2.
3. In his perceptive and wide-ranging 1983 book *The Differend: Phrases in Dispute*, Jean-François Lyotard (1983) (drawing on Wittgenstein, Russell, and other formal thinkers in addition to Kant, Hegel, and Heidegger) comes right to the brink of a concept of strong incommensurability that derives rigorously from formal results, even mentioning Russell's paradox (p. 6) as lying at the bottom of the structure of "the differend" in which "phrases" are in dispute without any possibility of resolution. But although Lyotard indeed does not hesitate to draw out some of the dramatic implications of a Wittgensteinian thought that, as he realizes, is thoroughly committed to discussing the consequences of the necessarily unmeasurable, his prevailing sense of the structure of the "differend" remains circumscribed within the thought of what I have called weak incommensurability. On the first page of the text, for instance, he defines a differend simply as: ". . . a case of conflict, between (at least) two parties, that cannot be equitably resolved for lack of a rule of judgment applicable to both parties" (p. xi). Later on the same page, Lyotard describes the generic consequence of the presence of specific differends as the general absence of "a universal rule of judgment between heterogenous genres . . ." This thought of weak incommensurability is simply a development of the constructivist plurality and irreducible heterogeneity celebrated under the name of the "death of grand narratives" in Lyotard's 1979 work *The Postmodern Condition*, to which the politics of logic is resolutely opposed.

4. Though I have not developed this connection here, the thought of strong (as opposed to weak) incommensurability might well provide a useful methodological guideline for a rereading and recovery of the true significance of Kuhn's classic description of scientific revolutions as resulting in the "incommensurability" of paradigms and worlds (Kuhn 1962). At the time of Kuhn's writing and ever since, it has been assumed that the "incommensurability" at issue here is the weak incommensurability of the lack of common measure, which appears to imply that there is no truth or objectivity "transcendent" to the differently constituted paradigms and their regimes of "normal science." This appears to imply relativism (although Kuhn himself denied it) and thus the whole debate about incommensurability becomes subsumed to the issue of scientific "objectivity" and truth. On the other hand, though, the thought of strong incommensurability (as should be clear) bears absolutely *no* implication of relativism and is completely consistent with the assumption of a single and unified objective world. It thus appears likely that a reconstruction of Kuhn's account of revolutions in terms of strong rather than weak incommensurability could demonstrate, in a new and revealing way, the actual compatibility of this account with an objective, realist account of the world that science, in its successive revolutions, progressively reveals.

5. It thus has the status of what Badiou calls (for instance, at the beginning of *Logics of World*) an "axiom of contemporary conviction," or what Žižek calls an "ideology"; as Žižek emphasizes, such commitments are particularly marked in characteristic and interpretable structures of denegation and disavowal. For Badiou's criticism of what I'm here calling "economism," see Badiou (1993), pp. 30–32.

6. There is an analogy here to Kant's classical critique of reason, which does not "reify," but does in a sense "personify," reason in order to trace its boundaries and dialectics from within. As with Kant's classical gesture, the point of this critique is not to challenge or diminish the "object" in question, but rather to challenge certain claims made on its behalf by thinking out the consequences of its own internal structure.

7. For Badiou's critique of the ideology of human rights, see Badiou (1993), Chapter 1.

8. In recent years, a series of works in a recognizably "continental" mold have explored the possibility of a "speculative realism" that criticizes and attempts to overcome earlier forms of anti-realism and idealism within continental philosophy from Kant to Heidegger. These include: Meillassoux (2008), Harman (2002), and Brassier (2007). The most influential of these studies so far has probably been Quentin Meillassoux's *After Finitude*. In the book, Meillassoux (a student of Badiou) argues that the post-Cantorian thought of infinitude offers to overcome the dominance of what he calls "correlationism," the philosophically operative assumption of a necessary correlation between thought and the world. Correlationism in all of its forms, Meillassoux argues, is incapable of accounting for what he calls the "arche-fossil," the real existence of objects and phenomena before the (empirical) advent of thinkers and thoughts. From the current perspective, the first thing to say about this argument is that it is quite unconvincing, for of course the various brands of idealism (especially Kantian and post-Kantian transcendental idealism) have ample and well-developed responses to this problem of temporality and origin, which Meillassoux does not so much as consider. Moreover, the positive argument here, as in several of the other "speculative realist" efforts, tends to a naïve and loose interpretation of the metaphysics supposedly implied by "empirical science" that risks reifying the latter as a single, determinate source of metaphysical truth. On the other hand, though, much if not all of

what Meillassoux criticizes under the heading of "correlationism" can indeed be recognized, in terms of the orientations I have laid out here, as forms of constructivism; and these can indeed be trenchantly criticized on the rigorous basis of an exploration of the consequences of Cantorian formalism and the formal (not empirical and certainly not "speculative") realism it implies.

9. The lectures are published as Badiou (2005).
10. Badiou (2005), p. 162.
11. Badiou (2005), p. 32.
12. Badiou (2005), pp. 161–62.
13. Badiou (2005), p. 153.
14. Badiou (2005), p. 155.
15. Badiou (2005), p. 52.
16. Badiou (2005), p. 54.
17. Badiou (2005), p. 53.
18. Badiou (2005), p. 54. As Badiou has elsewhere noted, the status of "destruction" oscillates somewhat over the course of his career, being endorsed in *Theory of the Subject*, disappearing from the apparatus of *Being and Event*, and then reappearing in *Logics of Worlds* as a consequence of the new, more detailed discussion of the different types of "sites" and possibilities of evental change.
19. Žižek (2004b), p. 179.
20. Up to this point in the chapter, I have discussed and defended indifferently both forms of the "politics of logic," the generic and the paradoxico-critical. From this point forward, I argue for the relative utility of the paradoxico-critical orientation, as against Badiou's generic orientation, with respect at least to certain "political" problems and struggles.
21. Badiou (2005), pp. 163–64.
22. Agamben (1993), p. 3.
23. For the "experimentum linguae," see Agamben (1984a), Agamben (1990b), and Agamben (1990a), p. 83.
24. Agamben (1990c), p. 89.
25. For Badiou's current position, see Badiou (2008b), especially Chapter 4. For Žižek's critique of the absence of the consideration of political economy in Badiou's recent work, see Žižek (2010), pp. 181–85.
26. Quoted in Žižek (2010), p. 215. Cf. Žižek: "Marx's critique is precisely *not* Kantian, since he conceived the notion of limit in the properly Hegelian sense—as a positive motivating force which pushes capital further and further in its ever-expanding self-reproduction, not in the Kantian sense of a negative limitation . . . The central 'antinomy' of capital is its driving force, since the movement of capital is ultimately not motivated by the endeavor to appropriate/penetrate all empirical reality external to itself, but by the drive to resolve its inherent antagonism. In other words, capital 'can never go beyond its own limit,' not because some noumenal Thing resists its grasp, rather because, in a sense, it is blinded to the fact that *there is nothing beyond this limit*, only a specter of total appropriation generated by the limit itself" (pp. 216–17).
27. There is here, again, also a partial analogy to Kant's critique of reason: the Kantian critique does not at all aim at the definition of a position "outside" reason from which to defeat or challenge it, but rather yields a position from which it is possible to challenge certain claims made on its behalf, for instance, the traditional claims of rational theology. Similarly, as I have argued, the politics of logic does not directly challenge "instrumental" or "calculative" reason but rather offers the rigorous and internal position from which we can challenge the sovereign claim of the conjunction of

consistency and completeness (whether constructivist or onto-theological) made on its behalf.
28. Laclau and Mouffe (1985).
29. Laclau and Mouffe (1985), p. 97.
30. Laclau and Mouffe (1985), p. 88.
31. Laclau and Mouffe (1985), p. 111.
32. Laclau and Mouffe (1985), p. 111. Compare Arendt's identification of speech as an inherent precondition of the possibility of political and other meaningful human action (Arendt 1958, pp. 181–88).
33. Laclau and Mouffe (1985), p. 108.
34. Laclau and Mouffe (1985), p. 28.
35. Laclau and Mouffe (1985), p. 125.
36. Laclau and Mouffe (1985), p. 134.
37. Laclau and Mouffe (1985), p. 161.
38. Laclau and Mouffe (1985), p. 111.
39. Laclau and Mouffe (1985), p. 112.
40. Compare Hägglund (2008), Chapter 5, who develops a similar critique of Laclau from a Derridian perspective.
41. Critchley (2007), pp. 100–1.
42. Critchley (2007), p. 36
43. Laclau and Mouffe (1985), p. 123.
44. In fact, Laclau and Mouffe appear to rule out the very possibility of a paradoxico-critical thinking of the fundamental role of contradictions in structuring the real of the social "situation" when they argue that the assumption of an inherently contradictory structure of reality is "self-defeating." In particular: ". . . two different assertions are mixed together in this problem [of the relationship of contradiction and antagonism]: (a) that the real is contradictory, and (b) that contradictions exist in reality. Regarding the first, there can be no doubt that the statement is self-defeating. Popper's famous critique of the dialectic is, from this point of view, unobjectionable . . ." (pp. 123–24).
45. Cf. Žižek's discussion of the structural implications, today, of Marx's classic theory: ". . . 'class struggle' paradoxically *precedes* classes as determinate social groups, that is that every class position and determination is already an effect of the 'class struggle'. (This is why 'class struggle' is another name for the fact that 'society does not exist'—it does not exist as a positive order of being.) This is also why it is crucial to insist on the central role of the critique of *political* economy: the 'economy' cannot be reduced to a sphere of the positive 'order of being' precisely insofar as it is always already political, insofar as political ('class') struggle is at its very heart. In other words, one should always bear in mind that, for a true Marxist, 'classes' are not categories of positive social reality, parts of the social body, but categories of the real of a political struggle which cuts across the entire social body, preventing its 'totalization.' True, there is no outside to capitalism today, but this should not be used to hide the fact that capitalism itself is 'antagonistic,' relying on contradictory measures to remain viable—and these immanent antagonisms open up the space for radical action" (Žižek 2010, pp. 198–99).
46. See Derrida (2003), esp. Chapters 3 and 4.
47. Compare, again, Wittgenstein: "For the clarity we are aiming at is indeed *complete* clarity. But this simply means that the philosophical problems should *completely* disappear" (*PI* 133).
48. In this respect, the generic orientation is actually largely complicit here with the ideological conformist and populist (conventionalist) politics of "Think

globally, act locally," which in fact relegates the effectively active position of *both* global "action" *and* global "thought" to the designated administrators of "policy" and pro-capitalist management.

49. In Abram (1996).

50. It is worth noting, though, that neither this struggle nor the struggle with respect to education are "emancipatory" in quite the familiar sense of typical "egalitarian" and "progressive" leftist politics. That is, what is at issue here is not an *egalitarian* principle of the equality of all (unless this can be extended, in the environmental case, to the equality of all systems of life and organization on earth, and in the educational case, to what Plato indeed thought as the equality of all beings before the transcendent (meta-)form of the Good) and it is not, equally obviously, any form of *progress* that can be thought in the familiar terms of the nineteenth- and twentieth-century "emancipatory" struggles, allied as these regularly (and perhaps constitutively) are with various forms of technological and economic "development" as well as (onto-theological) conceptions of transcendence. These difficulties are simply further indications of the stark and profound challenges that indeed today face, as I have argued, any *possible* futural thinking of the political problems in these domains.

51. Althusser (1968).

Bibliography

(Dates in square brackets are dates of composition or first publication.)

Abram, D. 1996. *The Spell of the Sensuous: Perception and Language in a More-Than-Human World*. New York: Random House.

Aczel, P. 1988. *Non-Well-Founded Sets*. CLSI Lecture Notes, no. 14. Stanford, CA: CSLI Publications.

Adorno, T. W. [1966] 1973. *Negative Dialectics*. Trans. E. B. Ashton. New York: Continuum.

Agamben, G. [1979] 1991. *Language and Death: The Place of Negativity*. Trans. Karen E. Pinkus and Michael Hardt. Minneapolis: University of Minnesota Press.

Agamben, G. [1984a] 1999. The idea of language. In *Potentialities: Collected Essays in Philosophy*. Ed. and trans. Daniel Heller-Roazen. Stanford, CA: Stanford University Press.

Agamben, G. [1984b] 1999. The thing itself. In *Potentialities: Collected Essays in Philosophy*. Ed. and trans. Daniel Heller-Roazen. Stanford, CA: Stanford University Press.

Agamben, G. 1990a. *The Coming Community*. Trans. Michael Hardt. Minneapolis: University of Minnesota Press.

Agamben, G. [1990b] 1999. *Pardes*: The writing of potentiality. In *Potentialities: Collected Essays in Philosophy*. Ed. and trans. Daniel Heller-Roazen. Stanford, CA: Stanford University Press.

Agamben, G. [1990c] 2000. Marginal notes on *Commentaries on the Society of the Spectacle*. In *Means Without End: Notes on Politics*. Minneapolis: University of Minnesota Press.

Agamben, G. [1993] 2000. Form-of-life. In *Means without End: Notes on Politics*, pp. 3–12. Minneapolis: University of Minnesota Press.

Agamben, G. [1995] 1998. *Homo Sacer: Sovereign Power and Bare Life*. Trans. Daniel Heller-Roazen. Stanford, CA: Stanford University Press.

Agamben, G. [1996] 2000. *Means Without End: Notes on Politics*. Trans. Vincenzo Binetti and Cesare Casarino. Minneapolis: University of Minnesota Press.

Agamben, G. [2003] 2005. *State of Exception*. Trans. Keven Attell. Chicago: University of Chicago Press.

Althusser, L. [1968] 1971. Ideology and ideological state apparatuses. In *Lenin and Philosophy and Other Essays*. New York: Monthly Review Press.

Anscombe, G. E. M. 1957. Report on Analysis "problem" no. 10. *Analysis* 17:3, pp. 49–53.

Anscombe, G. E. M. 1959. *An Introduction to Wittgenstein's Tractatus*. New York: Harper and Row.

Anscombe, G. E. M. [1969] 1981. Parmenides, mystery, and contradiction. In *From Parmenides to Wittgenstein* (Collected Philosophical Papers, vol. 1). Minneapolis: University of Minnesota Press.

Arendt, H. [1951] 1973. *The Origins of Totalitarianism.* Third edition. New York: Harcourt Brace Jovanovich.

Arendt, H. 1958. *The Human Condition.* Chicago: University of Chicago Press.

Austin, S. 1986. *Parmenides: Being, Bounds, and Logic.* New Haven, CT: Yale University Press.

Badiou, A. [1968] 2007. *The Concept of Model.* Trans. Tzuchien Tho and Zachary Luke Fraser. Victoria, Australia: re.press.

Badiou, A. [1982] 2009. *Theory of the Subject.* Trans. Bruno Bosteels. London: Continuum.

Badiou, A. [1988] 2005. *Being and Event.* Trans. Oliver Feltham. London: Continuum. Translation of *L'être et l'événement.* Paris: Éditions du Seuil.

Badiou, A. [1989] 1996. *Manifesto for Philosophy.* Trans. Norman Madarasz. Albany, NY: SUNY Press.

Badiou, A. [1990] 2008. *Number and Numbers.* Trans. Robin Mackay. New York: Polity Press.

Badiou, A. [1992] 2008. *Conditions.* Trans. Stephen Corcoran. London: Continuum.

Badiou, A. [1993] 2001. *Ethics: An Essay on the Understanding of Evil.* London: Verso.

Badiou, A. 1994a. L'antiphilosophie de Wittgenstein (seminar 1993–94). Ed. François Duvert and Aimé Thiault. http://www.entretemps.asso.fr/Badiou/93–94.htm (accessed April 2010).

Badiou, A. 1994b. Silence, solipsism, saintete. L'antiphilosophie de Wittgenstein. *BARCA! Poesie, Politique, Psychanalyse* 3:13–53.

Badiou, A. [1997] 2000. *Deleuze: The Clamour of Being.* Trans. Louise Burchill. Minneapolis: University of Minnesota Press.

Badiou, A. [1998a] 2004. The question of being today. In *Theoretical Writings.* Ed. and trans. Ray Brassier and Alberto Toscano. London: Continuum.

Badiou, A. [1998b] 2006. *Briefings on Existence: A Short Treatise on Transitory Ontology.* Trans. Norman Madarasz. Albany, NY: SUNY Press.

Badiou, A. [1998c] 2006. *Metapolitics.* Trans. Jason Barker. London: Verso.

Badiou, A. [2000] 2004. One, multiple, multiplicities. In *Theoretical Writings.* Ed. and trans. Ray Brassier and Alberto Toscano. London: Continuum.

Badiou, A. 2003. *Infinite Thought: Truth and the Return of Philosophy.* Ed. and trans. Oliver Feltham and Justin Clemens. London: Continuum.

Badiou, A. 2004a. The event as trans-being. In *Theoretical Writings.* Ed. and trans. Ray Brassier and Alberto Toscano. London: Continuum.

Badiou, A. 2004b. Mathematics and philosophy: The grand style and the little style. In *Theoretical Writings.* Ed. and trans. Ray Brassier and Alberto Toscano. London: Continuum.

Badiou, A. 2004c. Notes toward a thinking of appearance. In *Theoretical Writings.* Ed. and trans. Ray Brassier and Alberto Toascano. London: Continuum.

Badiou, A. [2005] 2007. *The Century.* Trans. Alberto Toscano. Cambridge: Polity Press.

Badiou, A. [2006] 2009. *Logics of Worlds.* Trans. Alberto Toscano. London: Continuum.

Badiou, A. 2007. Interview by Tzuchien Tho. The Concept of Model, Forty Years Later: An Interview with Alain Badiou. In *The Concept of Model.* Trans. Tzuchien Tho and Zachary Luke Fraser. Victoria, Australia: re.press.

Badiou, A. [2008a] 2009. *Pocket Pantheon.* London: Verso.

Badiou, A. [2008b] 2010. *The Communist Hypothesis.* Trans. David Macey and Steve Corcoran. London: Verso.

Badiou, A. 2009. *L'antiphilosophie de Wittgenstein.* Paris: Nous.

Balibar, E. [2002] 2004. Alain Badiou in French philosophy. In *Think Again: Alain Badiou and the Future of Philosophy.* London: Continuum.

Barnes, J. 1979. *The Presocratic Philosophers. Vol. 1: Thales to Zeno.* London: Routledge and Kegan Paul.

Bataille, G. [1949] 1988. *The Accursed Share: An Essay on General Economy. Volume I: Consumption.* Ed. Robert Hurley. Cambridge, MA: Zone Books.

Bateson, G. [1956] 1972. Toward a theory of schizophrenia. In *Steps to an Ecology of Mind.* Chicago: University of Chicago Press.

Bays, T. 2004. On Floyd and Putnam on Wittgenstein on Gödel. *Journal of Philosophy* 101:4, pp. 197–210.

Benjamin, W. [1927] 1999. Critique of violence. In *Selected Writings,* vol. 1. Cambridge, MA: Harvard University Press.

Benveniste, E. [1956] 1974. The nature of pronouns. In *Problems in General Linguistics.* Miami: University of Miami Press.

Benveniste, E. [1958] 1974. Subjectivity in language. In *Problems in General Linguistics.* Miami: University of Miami Press.

Benveniste, E. [1963] 1974. Analytical philosophy and language. In *Problems in General Linguistics.* Miami: University of Miami Press.

Benveniste, E. 1974. *Problems in General Linguistics.* Miami: University of Miami Press.

Berto, F. 2009. *There's Something about Gödel: The Complete Guide to the Incompleteness Theorem.* Hoboken, NJ: Wiley-Blackwell.

Block, N. 1995. The mind as the software of the brain. In *Invitation to Cognitive Science: Thinking.* Second edition. Ed. D. Smith and E. Osherson. Cambridge, MA: MIT Press.

Bloor, D. 1983. *Wittgenstein: A Social Theory of Knowledge.* New York: Macmillan.

Boolos, G. 1971. The iterative conception of set. *Journal of Philosophy* 68:8, pp. 215–31.

Bosteels, B. 2002. Alain Badiou's theory of the subject: The recommencement of dialectical materialism? (Part II). *Pli,* Spring 2002.

Bosteels, B. 2008a. For a new poetics of the site. *Working Papers* 2, no. 2.

Bosteels, B. 2008b. Force of nonlaw: Alain Badiou's theory of justice. *Cardozo Law Review* 29 (April 2008), pp. 1–18.

Bosteels, B. 2008c. Radical antiphilosophy. *Filozofski Vestnik* [Special Issue].

Brassier, R. 2004. Nihil unbound: Remarks on subtractive ontology and thinking capitalism. In *Think Again: Alain Badiou and the Future of Philosophy.* Ed. Peter Hallward. London: Continuum.

Brassier, R. 2007. *Nihil Unbound: Enlightenment and Extinction.* New York: Palgrave Macmillan.

Buechner, J. 2008. *Gödel, Putnam and Functionalism: A New Reading of Representation and Reality.* Cambridge, MA: MIT Press.

Calcagno, A. 2007. *Badiou and Derrida: Politics, Events and their Time.* London: Continuum.

Cantor, G. [1883] 1980. Über unendliche, lineare Punktmannigfaltigkeiten, 56. *Mathematische Annalen* 21, 545–86. Collected in *Gesammalte Abhandlungen mathematischen und philosophischen Inhalts,* ed. E. Zermelo. Berlin: Springer.

Caputo, J. D. 1997. *The Prayers and Tears of Jacques Derrida: Religion without Religion.* Bloomington: Indiana University Press.

Carnap, R. [1934] 1937. *The Logical Syntax of Language.* Trans. A. Smeaton. London: Routledge and Kegan Paul.

Carnap, R. [1950] 1958. Empiricism, Semantics, and Ontology. Reprinted in *Meaning and Necessity.* Chicago: University of Chicago Press.

Carnap, R. 1956. *Meaning and Necessity: A Study in Semantics and Modal Logic.* Second edition. Chicago: University of Chicago Press.

Carroll, L. 1895. What the tortoise said to Achilles. *Mind* 4:14, pp. 278–80.

Cavell, S. [1979] 1999. *The Claim of Reason: Wittgenstein, Skepticism, Morality, and Tragedy.* New York: Oxford University Press.

Cavell, S. 1989. Declining decline: Wittgenstein as a philosopher of culture. In *This New Yet Unapproachable America: Lectures after Emerson after Wittgenstein.* Albuquerque, NM: Living Batch Press.

Chalmers, D. 1995. On implementing a computation. *Minds and Machines* 4, pp. 391–402.

Cohen, P. J. 2008. My interaction with Kurt Gödel: The man and his work. In *Set Theory and the Continuum Hypothesis.* Mineola, NY: Dover.

Cohen, P. J. [1966] 2008. *Set Theory and the Continuum Hypothesis.* Mineola, NY: Dover.

Conant, J. 1992. Kierkegaard, Wittgenstein, and Nonsense. In Cohen, T., Guyer, P., and Putnam H., eds., *Pursuits of Reason.* Lubbock: Texas Tech University Press.

Conant, J. 1998. Wittgenstein on meaning and use. *Philosophical Investigations* 21:3, pp. 222–50.

Conant, J. 2002. The method of the *Tractatus*. In Erich H. Reck (ed.), *From Frege to Wittgenstein: Perspectives on Early Analytic Philosophy.* Oxford: Oxford University Press.

Cordero, N.-L. 2004. *By Being, It Is: The Thesis of Parmenides.* Las Vegas, NV: Parmenides Publishing.

Critchley, S. 1999. *Ethics-Politics-Subjectivity: Essays on Derrida, Levinas, and Contemporary French Thought.* London: Verso.

Critchley, S. 2007. *Infinitely Demanding: Ethics of Commitment, Politics of Resistance.* London: Verso.

Dali, S. [1935] 1998. Conquest of the irrational. In *The Collected Writings of Salvador Dali,* ed. Haim Finkelstein. Cambridge: Cambridge University Press.

Davidson, D. [1965] 2001. Truth and meaning. In *Inquiries into Truth and Interpretation.* Oxford: Clarendon.

Davidson, D. [1970] 2001. Semantics for natural languages. In *Inquiries into Truth and Interpretation.* Oxford: Clarendon.

Davidson, D. [1973a] 2001. In defence of convention T. In *Inquiries into Truth and Interpretation.* Oxford: Clarendon.

Davidson, D. [1973b] 2001. Radical interpretation. In *Inquiries into Truth and Interpretation.* Oxford: Clarendon.

Deleuze, G. [1967] 2004. How do we recognize structuralism? In *Desert Islands and Other Texts, 1953–74.* Cambridge, MA: MIT Press.

Deleuze, G. [1968] 1994. *Difference and Repetition.* Trans. Paul Patton. New York: Columbia University Press.

Deleuze, G. [1969] 1990. *The Logic of Sense.* Trans. Mark Lester and Charles Stivale, ed. Constantin V. Boundas. New York: Columbia University Press.

Deleuze, G., and F. Guattari. [1991] 1994. *What Is Philosophy?* Trans. Hugh Tomlinson and Graham Burchill. New York: Columbia University Press.

Derrida, J. [1962] 1989. *Edmund Husserl's Origin of Geometry:* An Introduction. Trans. John P. Leavey, Jr. Lincoln: University of Nebraska Press.

Derrida, J. [1966] 1978. Structure, sign, and play in the discourse of the human sciences. In *Writing and Difference,* trans. by Alan Bass. Chicago: University of Chicago Press.

Derrida, J. [1968] 1981. Différance. In *Margins of Philosophy.* Trans. Alan Bass. Chicago: University of Chicago Press.

Derrida, J. [1970] 1981. The Double Session. In *Dissemination.* Trans. Barbara Johnson. Chicago: University of Chicago Press.

Derrida, J. [1971] 1985. Signature, event, context. In *Margins of Philosophy*. Trans. Alan Bass. Chicago: University of Chicago Press.

Derrida, J. [1972] 1981. Plato's Pharmacy. In *Dissemination*. Trans. Barbara Johnson. Chicago: Universtiy of Chicago Press.

Derrida, J. [1994] 1997. *Politics of Friendship*. London: Verso.

Derrida, J. 1995. *The Gift of Death*. Trans. D. Wills. Chicago: University of Chicago Press.

Derrida, J. 1998. *Resistances of Psychoanalysis*. Trans. Peggy Kamuf, Pascale-Anne Brault, and Michael Naas. Stanford, CA: Stanford University Press.

Derrida, J. 2002. Force of law: The 'mystical foundation of authority.' In *Acts of Religion*. Trans. M. Quaintance, ed. G. Anidjar. London: Routledge.

Derrida, J. [2003] 2005. The 'world' of the enlightenment to come (exception, calculation, sovereignty). In *Rogues: Two Essays on Reason*. Stanford, CA: Stanford University Press.

Derrida, J. 2005. *Sovereignties in Question: The Poetics of Paul Celan*. Ed. Thomas Dutoit and Outi Pasanen. Bronx, NY: Fordham University Press.

Diamond, C. 1991. *The Realistic Spirit: Wittgenstein, Philosophy, and the Mind*. Cambridge, MA: MIT Press.

Diamond, C. 2000. Ethics, imagination, and the method of Wittgenstein's *Tractatus*. In *The New Wittgenstein*. London: Routledge.

Douzinas, C., ed. [2005] 2007. *Adieu, Derrida*. New York: Palgrave Macmillan.

Dretske, F. 1997. *Naturalizing the Mind*. Cambridge, MA: MIT Press.

Dummett, M. [1959] 1978. Wittgenstein's philosophy of mathematics. In *Truth and Other Enigmas*. London: Duckworth.

Feferman, S. 2000. Presentation to the panel, does mathematics need new axioms? *ASL 2000 meeting*. Urbana, IL. Online at: http://math.stanford.edu/~feferman/papers/ASL2000R.pdf.

Feltham, O. 2008. *Alain Badiou: Live Theory*. London: Continuum.

Floyd, J., and H. Putnam. 2000. A note on Wittgenstein's 'notorious paragraph' about the Gödel theorem. *Journal of Philosophy* 97:11, pp. 624–32.

Floyd, J., and H. Putnam. 2006. Bays, Steiner and Wittgenstein's notorious paragraph about the Gödel theorem. *Journal of Philosophy* 103, pp. 101–10.

Fodor, J. 1992. *A Theory of Content and Other Essays*. Cambridge, MA: MIT Press.

Forster, T. E.1992. *Set Theory with a Universal Set: Exploring an Untyped Universe*. New York: Oxford University Press.

Fraenkel, A. A., Y. Bar-Hillel, and A. Levy. 1973. *Foundations of Set Theory*. Second revised edition. Amsterdam: North-Holland Publishing Company.

Franzén, T. 2005. *Gödel's Theorem: An Incomplete Guide to Its Use and Abuse*. Wellesley, MA: Peters.

Fraser, Z. 2006. The law of the subject: Alain Badiou, Luitzen Brouwer and the Kripkean analyses of forcing and the Heyting calculus. *Cosmos and History* 2:1–2, pp. 94–133.

Frege, G. [1892] 1997. On concept and object. In *The Frege Reader*. Ed. Michael Beaney. Oxford: Blackwell.

Frege, G. 1980. *Philosophical and Mathematical Correspondence*. Ed. G. Gabriel and H. Hermes et. al., trans. H. Kaal. Chicago: University of Chicago Press.

Gellner, E. 1959. *Words and Things*. London: Victor Gollancz.

Gillespie, S. 2008. *The Mathematics of Novelty: Badiou's Minimalist Metaphysics*. Melbourne, Australia: re.press.

Glendinning, S. 2001, ed. *Arguing with Derrida*. Oxford: Blackwell.

Gödel, K. [1931] 1965. On formally undecidable propositions of *Principia Mathematica* and related systems I. In *The Undecidable*. Ed. Martin Davis. Mineola, NY: Dover.

Gödel, K. [1947] 1964. What is Cantor's continuum problem? In *Philosophy of Mathematics: Selected Readings*. Ed. Paul Benacerraf and Hilary Putnam. Englewood Cliffs, NJ: Prentice Hall.

Goldblatt, R. 2006. *Topoi: The Categorical Analysis of Logic*. Mineola, NY: Dover.

Grim, P. 1991. *The Incomplete Universe: Totality, Knowledge and Truth*. Cambridge, MA: MIT Press.

Habermas, J. [1981a] 1987. *Theory of Communicative Action, vol. 1: Reason and the Rationalization of Society*. Trans. Thomas McCarthy. Boston: Beacon Press.

Habermas, J. [1981b] 1987. *Theory of Communicative Action, vol. 2: Lifeworld and System*. Trans. Thomas McCarthy. Boston: Beacon Press.

Hägglund, M. 2008. *Radical Atheism: Derrida and the Time of Life*. Stanford, CA: Stanford University Press.

Hallett, M. 1986. *Cantorian Set Theory and Limitation of Size*. Oxford: Clarendon.

Hallward, P. 2003. *Badiou: A Subject to Truth*. Minneapolis: University of Minnesota Press.

Hallward, P., ed. 2004a. *Think Again: Badiou and the Future of Philosophy*. London: Continuum.

Hallward, P. 2004b. Introduction: Consequences of abstraction. In *Think Again: Alain Badiou and the Future of Philosophy*. Ed. Peter Hallward. London: Continuum.

Hardt, M., and A. Negri. [2004] 2005. *Multitude: War and Democracy in the Age of Empire*. New York: Penguin.

Harman, G. 2002. *Tool-Being: Heidegger and the Metaphysics of Objects*. Chicago: Open Court.

Heidegger, M. [1927] 1996. *Being and Time*. Trans. Joan Stambaugh. Albany, NY: SUNY Press.

Heidegger, M. [1938] 2000. *Contributions to Philosophy: From Enowning*. Translation of *Beiträge zur Philosophie (vom Ereignis)*. Trans. Parvis Emad and Kenneth Maly. Bloomington: Indiana University Press.

Heidegger, M. [1952] 1968. *What Is Called Thinking?* Translation of *Was Heisst Denken?* Trans. J. Glenn Gray. New York: Harper.

Heidegger, M. [1953] 1977. The question concerning technology. Translation of Die Frage nach der Technik in *The Question Concerning Technology and Other Essays*. Trans. W. Lovitt. New York: Harper and Row.

Heidegger, M. [1957a] 2002. *Identity and Difference*. Trans. J. Stambaugh. Chicago: University of Chicago Press.

Heidegger, M. [1957b] 1969. The onto-theo-logical constitution of metaphysics. In *Identity and Difference*. Trans. and ed. J. Stambaugh. Chicago: University of Chicago Press.

Hilbert, D. [1925] 1967. On the Infinite. In *From Frege to Gödel: A Sourcebook in Mathematical Logic, 1879–1931*. Ed. J. van Heijenoort. Cambridge, MA: Harvard University Press.

Hofstadter, D. [1979] 1999. *Gödel, Escher, Bach: An Eternal Golden Braid*. 20th Anniversary Edition. New York: Basic Books.

Horkheimer, M. [1967] 1983. *Critique of Instrumental Reason*. London: Continuum.

Husserl, E. [1957] 1970. *The Crisis of European Sciences and Transcendental Philosophy*. Trans. D. Carr. Evanston, IL: Northwestern University Press.

Jakobson, R. [1971] 1982. Shifters, verbal categories, and the Russian verb. In *Selected Writings*, vol. 2. New York: De Gruyter.

Johnston, A. 2008. Phantom of consistency: Alain Badiou and Kantian transcendental idealism. *Continental Philosophy Review* 41:3, pp. 345–66.

Johnston, A. 2009. *Badiou, Žižek, and Political Transformations: The Cadence of Change*. Evanston, IL: Northwestern University Press.

Kaplan, D. 1989. "Demonstratives" and "Afterthoughts." In *Themes From Kaplan*. Ed. Almog et al. London: Oxford University Press.

Kirk, G. S., J. E. Raven, and M. Schofield. 1983. *The Presocratic Philosophers*. Second edition. Cambridge: Cambridge University Press.

Kripke, S. 1982. *Wittgenstein on Rules and Private Language*. Cambridge, MA: Harvard University Press.

Kuhn, T. [1962] 1996. *The Structure of Scientific Revolutions*. Third edition. Chicago: University of Chicago Press.

Kunen, K. 1980. *Set Theory: An Introduction to Independence Proofs*. New York: North Holland Publishing Company.

Lacan, J. [1955] 2006. Seminar on 'The Purloined Letter.' In *Écrits: The First Complete Edition in English*. Trans. Bruce Fink, Heloise Fink, and Russell Grigg. New York: Norton & Co.

Lacan, J. [1957] 2006. The instance of the letter in the unconscious, or reason since Freud. In *Écrits: The First Complete Edition in English*. Trans. Bruce Fink, Heloise Fink, and Russell Grigg. New York: Norton & Co.

Lacan, J. [1970] 2007. *The Other Side of Psychoanalysis: The Seminar of Jacques Lacan, Book XVII*. Trans. Russell Grigg. New York: Norton & Co.

Lacan, J. [1973] 1999. *On Feminine Sexuality: The Limits of Love and Knowledge 1972–73 (Encore: The Seminar of Jacques Lacan, Book XX)*. Trans. Bruce Fink. New York: Norton & Co.

Lacan, J. 2006. *Écrits: The First Complete Edition in English*. Trans. Bruce Fink, Heloise Fink, and Russell Grigg. New York: Norton & Co.

Laclau, E., and C. Mouffe. 1985. *Hegemony and Socialist Strategy: Towards a Radical Democratic Politics*. London: Verso.

Lautman, A. 1938. *Essai sur les notions de structure et d'existence en mathematiques: Les schemas de structure*. Paris: Hermann & Cie.

Levinas, E. [1961] 1969. *Totality and Infinity: An Essay on Exteriority*. Trans. Alphonso Lingis. Pittsburgh: Duquesne University Press.

Lévi-Strauss, C. [1950] 1987. *Introduction to the Work of Marcel Mauss*. London: Routledge.

Lewis, D. 1969. *Convention: A Philosophical Study*. Cambridge, MA: Harvard University Press.

Livingston, P. 2001. Russellian and Wittgensteinian atomism. *Philosophical Investigations* 24:1, pp. 30–54.

Livingston, P. 2008. *Philosophy and the Vision of Language*. New York: Routledge.

Lucas, J.R. 1961. Minds, machines, and Gödel. *Philosophy* 36, pp. 112–27.

Lyotard, Jean-François. [1983] 1988. *The Differend: Phrases in Dispute*. Trans. Georges van den Abbeele. Minneapolis: University of Minnesota Press.

MacBride, F. 2003. Speaking with shadows: A study of neo-logicism. *British Journal for the Philosophy of Science* 54:1, pp. 103–63.

Maddy, P. 2000. *Naturalism in Mathematics*. Oxford: Oxford University Press.

McDowell, J. 1994. *Mind and World*. Cambridge, MA: Harvard University Press.

McGinn, C. 1987. *Wittgenstein on Meaning*. Oxford: Blackwell.

McGinn, M. 2010. Wittgenstein and naturalism. In *Naturalism and Normativity*. Ed. Mario de Caro and David MacArthur. New York: Columbia University Press.

Meillassoux, Q. [2006] 2008. *After Finitude: An Essay on the Necessity of Contingency*. Trans. Ray Brassier. London: Continuum.

Michel, A., ed. 1991. *Lacan avec les Philosophes*. Paris: Bibliothèque du Collège international de philosophie.

Miller, J.-A. [1966] 1978. Suture. Trans. Jacqueline Rose. *Screen* 18. Online at: http://www.lacan.com/symptom8_articles/miller8.html.

Miller, J.-A. 1968. Action of the structure. Trans. Peter Bradley. Online at: http://www.lacan.com/thesymptom/?p=423.

Miller, J.-A. 1975. Matrix. Trans. Daniel G. Collins. *Lacanian Ink* 12. Online at: http://www.lacan.com/frameXII3.htm.

Millikan, R. G. 1984. *Language, Thought, and Other Biological Categories: New Foundations for Realism*. Cambridge, MA: MIT Press.

Moore, A. W. 2001a. *The Infinite*. New York: Routledge.

Moore, A. W. 2001b. Arguing with Derrida. In Glendinning, S. 2001, ed. *Arguing with Derrida*. Oxford: Blackwell.

Mourelatos, A. P. D. [1970] 2008. *The Route of Parmenides*. Revised and expanded edition. Las Vegas, NV: Parmenides Publishing.

Nagel, E., and J. R. Newman. 2001. *Gödel's Proof*. Revised edition. New York and London: New York University Press.

Nancy, J.-L. [1986] 2006. The inoperative community. In *The Inoperative Community*. Ed. Peter Connor. Minneapolis: University of Minnesota Press.

Nancy, J.-L. [1991] 2000. War, right, sovereignty—techne. In *Being Singular Plural*. Stanford, CA: Stanford University Press.

Nancy, J.-L. [2002] 2004. Philosophy without conditions. In *Think Again: Alain Badiou and the Future of Philosophy*. Ed. Peter Hallward. London: Continuum.

Norris, C. 2009. *Badiou's Being and Event: A Reader's Guide*. London, Continuum.

Nyiri, J. C. [1981] Wittgenstein's later work in relation to conservatism. In *Wittgenstein and His Time*. Ed. B. McGuiness. Oxford: Blackwell.

Owen, G. E. L. [1960] 1986. Eleatic questions. In *Logic, Science and Dialectic: Collected Papers in Greek Philosophy*. Ed. Martha Nussbaum. Ithaca, NY: Cornell University Press.

Owen, G. E. L. [1964] 1986. Plato and Parmenides on the timeless present. In *Logic, Science and Dialectic: Collected Papers in Greek Philosophy*. Ed. Martha Nussbaum. Ithaca, NY: Cornell University Press.

Papineau, D. 1993. *Philosophical Naturalism*. Oxford: Blackwell.

Pears, D. 1995. Wittgenstein's naturalism. *The Monist* 78:4, pp. 411–24.

Penrose, R. 1994. *Shadows of the Mind: A Search for the Missing Science of Consciousness*. New York: Oxford University Press.

Plato. 1997. *Complete Works*. Ed. J. M. Cooper and D. S. Hutchinson. Cambridge, MA: Hackett.

Priest, G. [1987] 2006. *In Contradiction: A Study of the Transconsistent*. Second edition. New York: Oxford University Press.

Priest, G. 1994. Gödel's theorem and creativity. In *Artificial Intelligence and Creativity*. Ed. Terry Dartnall. Amsterdam: Kluwer Academic Publishers.

Priest, G. 2002. *Beyond the Limits of Thought*. Second edition. Oxford: Clarendon Press.

Priest, G. 2004. Wittgenstein's remarks on Gödel's Theorem. In *Wittgenstein's Lasting Significance*. Ed. Max Kölbel and Bernhard Weiss. London: Routledge.

Putnam, H. 1985. Reflexive reflections. *Erkenntnis* 22:1/3, pp. 143–53.

Putnam, H. 1991. *Representation and Reality*. Cambridge, MA: MIT Press.

Quine, W. V. [1936] 1966. Truth by convention. In *The Ways of Paradox and Other Essays*. New York: Random House.

Quine, W. V. 1937. New foundations for mathematical logic. *American Mathematical Monthly* 44, pp. 70–80. Revised and expanded edition in *American Mathematical Monthly* 53, pp. 80–101.

Quine, W. V. [1950] 1951. Two dogmas of empiricism. *Philosophical Review* 60, pp. 20–43.

Quine, W. V. [1954] 1966. Carnap and logical truth. In *The Ways of Paradox and Other Essays*. New York: Random House.

Quine, W. V. 1960. *Word and Object*. Cambridge, MA: MIT Press.

Quine, W. V. 1979. Facts of the matter. In *Essays on the Philosophy of W. V. Quine*. Ed. R. W. Shahan and C. V. Swoyer. Hassocks, UK: Harvester.

Quine, W.V. 1986. Reply to Robert Nozick. In *The Philosophy of W. V. Quine*. Ed. H. Hahn and P. A. Schlipp. La Salle, IL: Open Court.

Ramsey, F. P. 1925. The foundations of mathematics. *Proceedings of the London Mathematics Society* 25, pp. 338–84.

Rancière, J. 1995. *Disagreement: Politics and Philosophy*. Trans. Julie Rose. Minneapolis: University of Minnesota Press.

Reach, K. 1938. The name relation and the logical antinomies. *Journal of Symbolic Logic* 3:3, pp. 97–111.

Rhees, R. [1964] 2004. *In Dialogue with the Greeks. Volume 1: The Presocratics and Reality*. Ed. D. Z. Phillips. Surrey, UK: Ashgate.

Ricketts, T. 1996. Pictures, logic, and the limits of sense in Wittgenstein's *Tractatus*. In *The Cambridge Companion to Wittgenstein*. Eds. H. Sluga and D. G. Stern. Cambridge: Cambridge University Press.

Rorty, R. 1989. *Contingency, Irony, and Solidarity*. Cambridge: Cambridge University Press.

Rorty, R. 1993. Wittgenstein, Heidegger, and the reification of language. In *The Cambridge Companion to Heidegger*. Ed. Charles Guignon. Cambridge: Cambridge University Press.

Russell, B. [1903] 1964. *Principles of Mathematics*. Second edition. New York: Norton & Co.

Russell, B. 1906a. On some difficulties in the theory of transfinite numbers and order types. *Proceedings of the London Mathematical Society* 4:2, pp. 29–53.

Russell, B. 1906b. Les paradoxes de la logique. *Revue de Metaphisique et de Morale* 14, pp. 627–50.

Russell, B. [1908] 1956. Mathematical logic as based on the theory of types. In *Logic and Knowledge: Essays 1901–1950*. Ed. Robert Charles Marsh. London: Allen & Unwin.

Russell, B. [1918] 1985. *The Philosophy of Logical Atomism*. Chicago: Open Court.

Saussure, F. [1913] 1986. *Course in General Linguistics*. Excerpts in *Critical Theory Since 1965*. Ed. Hazard Adams and Leroy Searle. Tallahassee: University of Florida Press.

Schmitt, C. [1932] 2007. *The Concept of the Political*. Trans. George Schwab. Chicago: University of Chicago Press.

Schmitt, C. [1934] 2006. *Political Theology: Four Chapters on the Concept of Sovereignty*. Trans. George Schwab. Chicago: University of Chicago Press.

Schürmann, R. [1996] 2003. *Broken Hegemonies*. Trans. Reginald Lilly. Indianapolis: University of Indiana Press.

Searle, J. R. [1992] 1994. *The Rediscovery of the Mind*. Cambridge, MA: MIT Press.

Shanker, S. G. 1987. *Wittgenstein and the Turning-Point in the Philosophy of Mathematics*. London: Croom Helm.

Smith, P. 2007. *An Introduction to Gödel's Theorems*. Cambridge: Cambridge University Press.

Smullyan, R. 1994. *Diagonalization and Self-Reference*. Oxford: Oxford University Press.

Sokal, A., and J. Bricmont [1997] 1998. *Fashionable Nonsense*. New York: Picador.

Steiner, M. 2001.Wittgenstein as his own worst enemy: The case of Gödel's theorem. *Philosophia Mathematica* 9: 257–79.

Tarski, A. 1933. The concept of truth in formalized languages. Trans. J. H. Woodger. In *A. Tarski: Logic, Semantics, Metamathematics.* Second edition. Ed. J. Corcoran. Indianapolis: Hackett.

Tarski, A. 1944. The semantic conception of truth and the foundations of semantics. *Philosophy and Phenomenological Research* 4, pp. 341–76.

Turing, A. [1936] 2004. On computable numbers, with an application to the Entscheidungsproblem. In *The Essential Turing.* Ed. B. J. Copeland. Oxford: Clarendon.

Van Atten, M. 2006. Two draft letters from Gödel on self-knowledge of reason. *Philosophia Mathematica* 3:14, pp. 255–61.

Webb, J. C. 1980. *Mechanism, Mentalism, and Metamathematics.* Dordrecht, Holland: Springer.

Wittgenstein, L. [1916] 1979. *Notebooks 1914–1916.* Second edition. Chicago: University of Chicago Press.

Wittgenstein, L. [1921] 1961. *Tractatus Logico-Philosophicus.* Trans. D. F. Pears and B. F. McGuinness. London: Routledge.

Wittgenstein, L. [1929] 1993. A lecture on ethics. In *Philosophical Occasions, 1912–1951.* Ed. James Klagge and Alfred Nordmann. Indianapolis: Hackett.

Wittgenstein, L. [1933] 2005. *The Big Typescript: TS 213.* Ed. and trans. C. Grant Luckhardt and Maximilian A. E. Aue. Oxford: Blackwell.

Wittgenstein, L. [1939] 1976. *Wittgenstein's Lectures on the Foundations of Mathematics, Cambridge, 1939.* Ed. by Cora Diamond. Chicago: University of Chicago Press.

Wittgenstein, L. [1953] 2001. *Philosophical Investigations.* Third edition. Trans., with revisions, G. E. M. Anscombe. Oxford: Blackwell.

Wittgenstein, L. [1956] 1983. *Remarks on the Foundations of Mathematics.* Revised edition. Trans. G. E. M. Anscombe. Ed. R. Rhees, G. E. M. Anscombe, and G. H. von Wright. Cambridge, MA: MIT Press.

Wright, C. 1980. *Wittgenstein on the Foundations of Mathematics.* London: Duckworth.

Zermelo, E. [1908] 1967. Investigations in the foundations of set theory. In *From Frege to Gödel: A Source Book in Mathematical Logic, 1879–1931.* Ed. J. van Heijenoort. Cambridge, MA: Harvard University Press.

Žižek, S. [1989] 2008. *The Sublime Object of Ideology.* New edition. London: Verso.

Žižek, S. [1991] 2008. *For They Know Not What They Do: Enjoyment as a Political Factor.* Second edition. London: Verso.

Žižek, S. 1993. *Tarrying with the Negative: Kant, Hegel, and the Critique of Ideology.* Durham, NC: Duke University Press.

Žižek, S. [1999] 2000. *The Ticklish Subject: The Absent Centre of Political Ontology.* London: Verso.

Žižek, S. 2004a. *Organs without Bodies.* New York: Routledge.

Žižek, S. 2004b. From purification to subtraction: Badiou and the Real. In *Think Again: Alain Badiou and the Future of Philosophy.* Ed. Peter Hallward. London: Continuum.

Žižek, S. 2010. *Living in the End Times.* London: Verso.

Index

1984 (Orwell), 356n49

A
absent center, 223, 286, 296, 307,
   350n34
Abram, D., 314
Absolute, the, 22, 45, 54
Adorno, T., 283, 319n12
Agamben, G., 8, 37–42, 60, 178, 206,
   242,325n85
  as paradoxico-critic, 11, 57, 178, 208
  bare life, 299
  Homo Sacer, 40, 41
  Language and Death, 39–40
  on Derrida, 125–127
  on "form of life", 299–300
  "Pardes: The Writing of Potential-
    ity", 125–127
  State of Exception, 41
  See also being, whatever; community,
    coming; Derrida, Agamben on;
    idea, Agamben on; set theory,
    Agamben on; singular, commu-
    nity of; singularity, whatever;
    state of exception
agreement, 8–9, 12, 17, 110, 147,
   169–171, 310n15, 320n28
  collective, 178
  formal, 61
  "in judgments", 18, 235
  See also convention; attunement
alephs, 347n22
All, 11, 53, 187, 213–16, 252
  See also completeness; One; One-All;
    Whole
Althusser, L., 198, 303, 346n13
analytic philosophy, xii-xiii, 6–7, 11,
   20, 65–66, 72, 200, 220, 238,
   240, 291, 333n91, 349n2

Badiou on, 200, 240, 346n20
  paradoxico-criticism in, 84–94,
   178–183
analytical philosophy (*see* analytic
   philosophy)
analytic tradition (*see* analytic philosophy)
analytic/continental "split", xii-xiii
analytic/synthetic distinction, 88–89
Anselm, St., 338n8
antagonism, 147, 175–76, 281, 284,
   301, 302–312, 313, 360n26,
   361nn44–45
  and paradoxico-critical orientation
   308–311
anthropology, 66, 68, 240, 329n6
anthropologism, 3, 240
antinomies (Kantian cosmological),
   252, 324n76, 354n17
  See also contradiction; paradox
anti-philosopher *see* anti-philosophy
anti-philosophy, 225–229, 351n42–43
appearance, 43, 114, 197–203, 205,
   207, 220–221, 245, 357n64
  distinction between being and, 10,
   201, 207, 221, 236
  of language, 40, 97, 147
  Plato on, 108
  relations of, 199–200, 273
  retroaction on being, 201, 231
Arendt, H., 319n16, 325n97, 361n32
Aristotle, 6, 9, 32, 57
  on the infinite, 21, 320n26
  on *logos*, 8, 319n16
  Politics, 8, 319n16
articulation, 122, 306, 312
  hegemonic (Laclau and Mouffe),
   304–307, 311
  of sense, 97, 230
  of signs, 67, 71

of sounds, 108
atoms (Badiou), 201
Austin, J.L., 72, 223–224
auto-immunity, 312
auto-nomination, 47–49, 145, 208,
    233, 251, 261, 349n8
    See also nomination; self-reference
autonomy, 308–309, 353n13
Ayer, A. J., 54, 57

B

Badiou, A., 9–12, 42–60, 187–207,
    208–237, 238–280, 291–298,
    319n21, 326n103, 328nn135–
    136, 346n9, 347n41, 348n55,
    348n56, 352n44, 353n13–14,
    354n23, 355n31
Being and Event, 9, 43–51, 192–197
Briefings on Existence, 53–55
The Century, 291–96
The Concept of Model, 355n32
relation to constructivism, 254–60
critique of economism, 359n5
critique of human rights, 359n7
relation to Deleuze, 209–220, 349n8
Deleuze: The Clamor of Being,
    211–219
relation to Derrida, 220–224,
    350n27
on "destruction", 360n18
on dialectics, 189–91, 198, 239–41,
    346n13
*Ethics: An Essay on the Understand-
ing of Evil*, 248
"The Event as Trans-Being",
    217–218
existing studies of, 319n20, 356n51–52
formal critique of, 268–280
and formalism, 8–12, 43–44,
    187–205, 292–293, 327n124
relation to Lacan, 188–192, 218,
    220, 226–231, 256, 328n137,
    346n11–12, 351nn42–43
on language and languages, 260–268,
    356n50
Logics of Worlds, 9, 43, 197–207
on mathematics, 9, 43, 52, 187–88,
    205, 225, 234–236, 258–260,
    295–297, 332n60, 348n69
on Miller, 332n66
relation to paradoxico-criticism,
    187–188, 208–09, 238–280
on Rancière, 319n16
on the twentieth century, 291–296

relation to Wittgenstein, 217–218,
    224–37, 265, 352n47, 352n53
Theory of the Subject, 42
See also analytic philosophy, Badiou
    on; anti-philosophy; appear-
    ance; atoms; count-as-one;
    democratic materialism; Derrida,
    relation to Badiou; dialectic,
    "materialist"; encyclopedia;
    event, Badiou's theory of; evental
    change; evental site; excres-
    cences; fidelity; formalization,
    Badiou on; generic orientation;
    generic procedures; generic set;
    Gödel, Badiou on; idea, Badiou
    on; Lacan, relation to Badiou;
    linguistic turn, Badiou on;
    logic, Greater; novelty, Badiou
    on; objects, Badiou's theory of;
    ontology, Badiou on; phe-
    nomenology, Badiou's; points;
    procedure, generic; progress,
    Badiou on; representation, as
    discussed by Badiou; Russell's
    paradox, Badiou on; set theory,
    identified with ontology; singular
    terms; singularity, type of site;
    situations; state of the situa-
    tion; subject, as discussed by
    Badiou; "transcendental" of a
    world; Truths; twentieth century,
    Badiou on; Wittgenstein, relation
    to Badiou; worlds
Bateson, G., 321n35
Bauhaus, 292
becoming, 96–97, 100–101, 105–106,
    108–112, 209–217
    evental, 181
    paradox of, 105–106, 108, 110–112
    pure, 97, 106–108, 110
    of a truth, 348n63
being, 43, 47, 60, 95, 231, 236, 257–58
    enjoinment of, 207
    linguistic, 38–41, 299
    sense of, 214
    structure of, 9, 199
    relation to thinking, 53, 131
    "there is..." of, 47–48
    univocity of, 213–214, 291, 350n23
    whatever (Agamben), 38
    See also ontology
Benveniste, E., 39, 71–72, 73, 74, 75,
    77, 181, 329n17
Berkeley, G., 338n8

Berto, F., 324n75, 336n5
bioethics, 240
bivalence, 134
Block, N., 170
bodies, 106, 198, 210, 219, 239–242
Bodin, J., 321n32
Bosteels, B., 346n12, 349n8, 351n43
Bourbaki group, 76, 295
Bova, J., 327n127, 342n19, 342n23, 357n66
Brassier, R., 353n14
Brouwer, L.E.J., 50, 327n122, 341n4
Brunschvicg, L., 328n135
Burali-Forti paradox, 22, 321n41

C

calculative reason, 7, 171, 283, 319n12, 360n27
calculative thinking (*see* calculative reason)
Cantor, G., 4–5, 21, 43–45, 152–154, 296
   definition of a set, 4–5, 59, 182
   thought on the infinite, 22
   transfinite hierarchy, 21, 55, 149, 153–154, 192, 270–271, 274
   See also alephs; Cantor's theorem; cardinals, transfinite; continuum hypothesis; diagonalization, Cantor's use of; set, Cantor's definition of; set theory, Cantorian
Cantor's theorem, 45, 192, 266, 270, 277, 342n19, 354n21
capitalism, 288, 289, 300–302, 309, 361n45
   global, 281, 285, 287–89
capitalist parliamentarianism, 285
cardinal "collapse", 274
cardinals
   definition, 347n21–22
   large, 357n56
   transfinite, 149, 152, 193–94, 276
   See also alephs; Cantor, transfinite hierarchy; continuum hypothesis
Carnap, R., 54, 57, 58, 60, 84–87, 93–94, 178–179, 329n138, 333n92, 334n10, 349n69, 355n32
   "Empiricism, Semantics, and Ontology", 86–87
   language frameworks, 86
   The Logical Structure of the World, 85
   Logical Syntax of Language, 85
   principle of tolerance, 86
   Quine's critique of, 87–92

See also constructivism, Carnap's; conventionalism, Carnap's; Quine
Carroll, L., 88–89, 97, 98, 210, 325n87, 334n22
   "What the Tortoise Said to Achilles", 88–89, 98
   Alice's Adventures in Wonderland, 97
   Through the Looking-Glass, 97, 325n87
   See also paradoxes, of Achilles and the Tortoise; paradoxes, "White Knight"
cast of the dice (*see* throw of the dice)
category theory, 9, 43, 199–200, 220, 245, 348n69
causality
   corporeal, 210
   ideational, 210
Cavell, S., 318n10, 319n18, 338n20, 345n68
Chalmers, D., 170
chance, 210–211, 215, 324n78
   of usage, 110
Chomsky, N., 163
Church-Turing thesis, 151
citationality, 125
closure, 32–33, 124–125, 129, 181
   of metaphysics, 37, 51, 221–222
   of totalities, 36, 307–308
   See also in-closure
cognitive science, 163
Cohen, P. J., 10, 55, 194–196, 272–274, 355n32, 356n53–54
   view on continuum hypothesis, 356n54
   See also forcing; continuum hypothesis
commodification, 7
communication, 71, 83, 137, 171, 223, 261, 329n6, 329n17
   of singularities, 39, 212
   technologies of, 171, 297–298
   written (*see also* writing), 124
Communist Idea 300
communitarianism, 16–17, 309, 312, 317n2
community, 4, 16–18, 35, 61, 67, 68, 74, 85, 147, 243
   coming (Agamben), 37–39, 299
   link between language and, 94, 140, 212, 245–47
   possibility of, 5, 8, 242
   sense of identity, 177
   thought of, 285–87
competence, 15–16, 99, 163

completeness, 29, 34, 56, 132
  relation to consistency, 25, 33–35,
    53, 56–59, 176, 187, 216, 242–
    243, 247–253, 284, 306–309,
    323n73, 354n23, 361n27
  desire for, 295
  as norm for onto-theology, 59–60
  as norm for paradoxico-criticism, 60
  of a system, 160
  of a text, 324n75
  See also incompleteness; consistency;
    inconsistency; metalogical duality
computation theory, 5, 20, 282
computationalism, 162–166, 177
computer, 167–172, 298, 341n13,
    343n42, 344n43
  See also computing machine; thinking
    machines; Turing machine
computing machine, 169, 343n42
  universal, 148, 151
  See also computer; thinking
    machines; Turing machine
consistency, 11, 29, 34, 53, 56, 132,
    164, 270, 312
  axiomatic of (in Badiou), 248, 259
  relation to completeness, 25, 33–35,
    53, 56–59, 160, 175–176,
    187–188, 207, 213, 216, 242–
    243, 247–253, 284, 306–309,
    323n73, 354n23, 361n27
  desire for, 60
  of a formal system, 52, 160, 343n36
  of language, 45, 65
  of negation of CH, 358n69
  as norm for generic orientation and
    constructivism, 55, 60
  of practices, 247, 311
  prescription of, 136, 310–311
  proof of, 160, 175–76, 343n36, 345n67
  statement, 345n66
  of a text, 324n75
  of a world, 201, 240
  See also completeness, incompleteness,
    inconsistency, metalogical duality
constructability, 193–194, 347n31,
    355n32
  See also constructible universe; con-
    structivism
constructible universe, 194–195, 264,
    266, 270–272, 276–277
  See also constructability; constructivism
constructivism, 30, 50–51, 54–55,
    57–60, 194, 269, 281, 285–286,
    360n8

relation between Badiou and, 227,
    239–240, 248, 254–261,
    264–266
  Carnap's, 85
  relation to onto-theology, 282
  Russell's, 85, 255
  early Wittgenstein's, 136, 141
  See also constructability; constructible
    universe; criteriology;
    hierarchy, constructivist
constructivist orientation
    (*see* constructivism)
contingency, 139, 281, 305–307
  of event, 217
  of institutions, 245
  linguistic, 235
  of social life, 308
continental philosophy, xii–xiii, 3, 6, 7,
    18, 42, 65–66, 178, 220, 224,
    359n8
continuum hypothesis, 192–197,
    269–272, 275–276, 347n24,
    355n32, 357n54, 357n56
  See also Cantor, G.; cardinals; Cohen,
    P.J., view on continuum hypoth-
    esis; Gödel, K., and continuum
    hypothesis; undecidability, of
    continuum hypothesis
contradiction, 24–25, 26, 45, 97, 128,
    253, 256, 322n48, 323n69,
    323n71, 343n35
  and antagonism 309–310, 361n44
  generated by in-closure, 32–33,
    123–124
  prohibition of, 132, 133, 136,
    176–177, 248, 280
  systematic points of, 178, 180, 183
  threat of, 29
  Wittgenstein's attitude toward,
    141–147, 160–163, 176–177,
    234–35, 345n69
  See also in-closure; inconsistency; law
    of non-contradiction
convention, 8, 12, 16–17, 67, 110,
    320n28
  basis of language in, 12, 67, 110
  force of, 17
  truth by, 88
  See also conventionalism
conventionalism, 3, 16, 55, 61, 65, 95,
    179, 198, 238, 317n3
  Carnap's, 86, 90, 179, 334n10
  as correlated with constructivism, 55,
    61, 65–66

"full-blooded", 320n26
  of lives, 3–4
  See also convention
copy, 105–109, 112
  vs. model, 105–106, 108
correlationism, 359n8
"count-as-one" (Badiou), 44–45, 259,
  326n103, 327n115, 353n10,
  355n31
Cratylus, 12–13, 109–110
  See also Plato, *Cratylus*
Critchley, S., 308–309, 312
  Infinitely Demanding, 308–309
criteriological orientation (*see*
  criteriology)
criteriology, 3, 37, 54, 58, 65–66, 85,
  92, 147, 178–179, 212, 220,
  250–255, 354n23
  relation to paradoxico-critical orien-
    tation, 58, 92, 94, 147, 178
  See also constructivism; Kant, I, as
    criteriologist
critical theory, 3, 37, 171, 283–84,
  297–298, 310, 318n11
  of information technology, 171–78
  of political economy, 302
  renewal of, 283
  See also critique
critical thought, 7, 10–11, 21, 36, 60,
  128, 178, 216, 220, 284
  legacy of twentieth-century, 238–240
  See also critical theory; critique
critique, 7, 219, 247, 283, 285, 298,
  312
  of ideology, 298
  of illusion, 236
  Kantian, 7, 36, 283, 359n6, 360n27
  of language, 139
  of metaphysics, 19, 36, 119,
    327n132, 353n13
  of political economy, 283, 300–302,
    361n45
  of reason, 283
  See also critical theory; critical
    thought
culturalism, 3, 178, 218, 245, 281,
  286–87, 291
Cutrofello, A., 328n 132, 335n1

D
Dali, S., 324n78
  paranoid-critical method, 324n78
Davidson, D., 35, 324n74, 333n94
Davis, M., 274

decision problem (Hilbert's), 148,
  151–152, 341n18
  See also Hilbert, D.; Turing, A.M.,
    proof of unsolvability of decision
    problem
Declaration of Independence, American, 31
deconstruction, 37, 113–115, 125–126,
  220–222, 337n32, 350n34
  Badiou on, 221–222, 264
  relation to formalism, 113–115, 119,
    121
  See also Derrida, J.; ethics of decon-
    struction; in-closure and decon-
    struction; indiscernible, the, and
    deconstruction
Dedekind, R., 192
deixis, 31, 39–40, 72
  See also demonstratives
Deleuze, G., 11, 57, 95–112, 261, 291,
  326n99, 345n72, 350n23–24
  relation to Badiou, 209–220, 349n8
  Difference and Repetition, 95,
    101–102, 106–107
  "How do we Recognize Structural-
    ism?" 95–96
  The Logic of Sense, 95, 96–101
  Platonism of, 95, 105–112, 215–216
  What is Philosophy?, 349n8
  See also Badiou, A., relation to
    Deleuze; event, as discussed
    by Deleuze; idea, Deleuze
    on; paradoxico-critical orienta-
    tion, Deleuze as representative
    of; plane of immanence;
    Plato, Deleuze on; regressive
    law; Russell's paradox, Deleuze
    on; sense-event; set theory,
    Deleuze on, singular points;
    virtual, as discussed by Deleuze
democracy, 290, 311–312, 314–315,
  321n35
  deliberative, 290
  social, 287
  to come, 312
democratic materialism, 198, 239, 241,
  246
demonstratives, 39–40, 71, 325n89
  See also deixis
Derrida, J., 11, 37, 57, 60, 109,
  113–130, 220–224, 261, 303,
  321n35, 326n99, 335n1, 336n5,
  350n34
  Agamben on, 125–127

relation to Badiou, 220–224, 243, 350n27
chora, 4, 118, 334n21
on democracy, 311–312
différance, 109, 113, 116–117, 119–125, 223, 334n21, 337n27, 351n34
"Double Session", 113–117
on ethics, 125–130
on the event, 221–224, 326n99, 350n34
on Gödel, 113–115, 335n1
Of Grammatology, 123
pharmakon, 108–109, 116, 118
on Plato, 108–109
"Plato's Pharmacy", 108–109
Priest on, 123–125
"Signature, Event, Context," 124–125, 223–224
"Structure, Sign, and Play in the Discourse of the Human Sciences" 222–223
supplément, 116, 118, 119
trace, 113, 118, 119, 123, 125, 221
See also deconstruction; formalism, Derrida and; grammatology; undecidability, Derrida on
Descartes, R., 234, 252, 326n101
desire, 76, 330n43
effects of, 82
object of, 76–77, 188, 331n49
of the Other (*see also* Other), 228–230
diagonalization, 21, 55, 56, 112, 125, 153, 262, 264, 266, 275, 279, 286, 321n38, 354n21
Cantor's use of, 21, 152, 343n19
explanation, 21
forcing and, 196, 279
Gödel's use of, 24, 122, 152, 278
and in-closure, 32, 123–125
and power set operation, 275–76
Turing's use of, 152, 278
Wittgenstein on, 153–155
diagonal method (*see* diagonalization)
dialectic, 189–191, 346n13, 361n44
Hegelian, 253–254, 310, 354n19
"materialist" (Badiou), 198, 239–246
dialectics (*see* dialectic)
dialetheism, 34, 323n69
difference, 107–110, 211
minimal, 293–294
ontological, 253
orthodoxy of, 94, 285–287

Plato on, 107–109
See also Derrida, *différance*
discernibility, 195–96, 276, 347n31
definition, 195
See also constructability; indiscernible, the
discourse, 40, 71, 74, 303, 306, 353n13
of being, 189
concrete, 40, 74, 303
everyday, 31, 40, 145
fact of, 71–72
scientific, 78, 331n55
subject's, 76, 82
theory, 81
See also parole
disjunctive law, 102
double bind, 19–20, 248, 321n35–36

E

economism, 287–288, 306, 309, 314–315, 359n5
economy, 171, 287
global, 287, 297
information, 298
political, 172, 300–302, 360n25, 361n45
education, 17, 312, 314–315, 362n50
effective computability, 151, 164, 173
See also effectiveness
effectiveness, 61, 169, 173, 176, 183, 247, 288, 302, 314
of capital, 290, 298
ideology of, 176
of institutions, 95
of norms and laws, 177, 282
of systems and structures, 282
of technologies , 61, 173–174, 254, 353n13
Eidos see Idea
empiricism, 219, 234
logical, 51, 85, 355n32
See also positivism
empty square, 77, 100, 102, 104, 180, 213
encyclopedia (Badiou), 196
environment, 312–314
epistemology, 92
ethics, 308
Badiou on, 230, 248
deconstructive, 125–130
environmental, 314
of heteronomy, 308–309
Wittgenstein on, 137–138, 338n17

event
    auto-nomination of, 48–49, 260,
        233, 327n115
    Badiou's theory of, 10, 42–51, 187,
        193–197, 198–205, 208–209,
        214–219, 262–264, 349n8,
        357n61
    as discussed by Deleuze, 97, 100–
        101, 210–212, 214–219, 326n99
    as discussed by Derrida, 221–223,
        326n99, 350n34
    forcing and, 268–273
    general problematic of, 326n99
    relation to ontology, 193, 195, 257–
        260, 294, 327n115, 346n13
    schema of (Badiou), 49
    self-reference of 49, 202, 264
    See also evental change; evental site;
        nomination, auto-
evental change, 46, 203, 205, 261, 268,
    271, 360n18
evental site, 49–50, 203, 231, 264,
    349n8
Evil, 248
example, 38–40
exception, 40–42
    See also state of exception
excrescences (Badiou), 46, 327n111
existence, 199, 255
    degrees of, 199–204, 264, 348n56,
        348n63
    See also force of existence
experimentum linguae, 299, 360n23

F
fidelity (Badiou), 50–51, 203–204,
    272–73
    See also subject, faithful
field of discursivity, 303–305
finitism, 148–154, 341n4
finitude, 20, 54, 148, 148–155, 162,
    240, 252
floating signifier, 70, 77, 93, 100, 102–
    104, 180, 182, 213, 286, 296, 305
Floyd, Juliet, 155
force, 191, 245
    of conventions, 17
    of desire, 350n34
    of existence, 204
    of forms, 110, 294
    of language, 95
    of law, xii, 14, 18–20, 35, 40–41,
        166, 208–209, 346n11
    of the letter, 295

of logical norms, 132, 136, 169, 177,
    230
"normative", 169–172
prohibitive, 147
rational, 132, 136–141, 145, 171–172
of rules, 14, 16, 35, 37, 137, 141–147,
    167, 171, 233, 237, 282, 311
of rupture (with context), 125, 222
superlative figures of, 182–183
of transcendental structures, 245
See also forcing, power
forcing (Cohen), 10, 48, 51, 55–56,
    190, 244–246, 347n41, 356n52
    Cohen on, 355n32, 356n54
    explanation of, 195–96
    implications of, 196–197, 268–275,
        356n64, 356n68–72
    pre-evental, 356n51
    See also Cohen, P.J.; continuum
        hypothesis
form, ix, 3–4, 9, 13–14, 189, 236, 292,
    294, 299, 346n9
    crossing with content, 130
    definition, 317n6
    givenness of, 16
    knowledge of, 110
    of language, 13
    logical, 8, 16, 135, 136, 143, 149,
        178, 339n25
    Plato on, ix, 9, 12–15, 112, 189,
        362n50
    of sense, 102
    See also formalism; formalization;
        forms of life; idea
formalism, 4, 8, 25, 59, 164, 179, 239,
    295, 323n73
    Badiou on, 8, 190, 292–293
    consequences of, 4, 7, 10, 20–21, 42,
        60, 65, 183, 187, 205, 239, 254,
        290, 295–297, 345n70, 360n8
    definition, 317n6
    Derrida and, 113–130
    impasse of *(see* formalization,
        impasse of)
    in Lacan, 74–76, 79, 331n56
    relationship of language to, 187–188,
        190, 233
    political implications of, 8, 42
    program of (Hilbert), 25, 34, 291,
        323n72
    See also form; formalization
formalization, 4, 9, 20, 24, 35, 52, 119,
    167, 188–192, 295, 339n29
    Badiou on, 9, 291–293, 296

definition, 317n6
of formalism, 7, 43, 60, 126, 130
impasse of, 79, 81, 188–190, 293
of language, 4, 24, 80
of life, 61, 291, 297–300
limits of, 20, 34
as project of twentieth century,
    291–292, 294, 297
of reason, 24, 25
See also form; formalism
formal realism, 291
formal systems, 21, 25, 34–35, 119, 166
and Gödel's theorem, 25, 270,
    342n25
compared to "natural" languages,
    35, 179, 317n6, 336n5
foundationalist picture of, 161
See also Principia Mathematica, incom-
    pleteness of formal systems
forms of life [Lebensformen], 3–4, 8–9,
    16–18, 180, 288, 299–300
Forster, T.E., 318n7
Foucault, Michel, 51, 57, 62, 240, 285
Fraenkel, A., 322n56
Fraser, Z. L., 273, 354n21
Frege, G., 5, 20–21, 23, 84, 208, 234,
    321n40, 346n20
Begriffsschrift, 20
concept "horse" problem,
    325n87,334n11
universal comprehension principle
    (Basic Law V), 23, 26, 28
See also logicism; neo-Fregeanism;
    numbers, Frege's conception of
French Revolution, 48–49
Freud, S., 74
See also repetition automatism

G
game theory, 319n15
generic extension (see generic set)
generic orientation, 11, 53, 55–60,
    293–294, 313, 328n136,
    358n72, 361n48
precedents for, 328n135
relation to constructivism, 60,
    253–255
relation to paradoxico-criticism
    56–60, 187–188, 190, 208,
    212, 215, 219, 238–239, 241,
    254, 267, 274, 278, 293–96,
    300–302
generic procedures, 196–197, 246, 257,
    260, 272–273, 328n137

generic set, 55, 195–197, 217, 244,
    258, 272, 275–279, 286,
    357n68, 358n72
See also indiscernible set
Gentzen, G., 343n36
gift, 128
globalization, 61
See also economy, global
Gödel, K., 7, 24–25, 28, 37, 56, 57,
    358n69
Badiou on, 296
and computationalism, 162–64, 166,
    343n42
on the continuum hypothesis, 270
Derrida on, 113–115, 335n1
"On Formally Undecidable Proposi-
    tions of Principia Mathematica
    and Related Systems I", 113,
    342n25–26
Platonism, 135, 328n135, 336n15
proof of consistency of CH with ZF,
    193–195, 269, 277, 355n32,
    357n56
See also constructability; construct-
    ible universe
Gödel's incompleteness theorem,
    24–25, 28–29, 34, 37, 52, 113,
    117–122, 153, 335n4
connection to continuum hypothesis,
    270
"postmodern" interpretations of,
    324n75
second incompleteness theorem, 175,
    177, 345n66
Wittgenstein on, 155–160
Gödel sentence, 25, 29, 36, 114,
    117–122, 153, 175, 180, 278,
    335n4, 343n34, 343n43
definition, 335n3
See also Gödel's incompleteness
    theorem
Gödel's paradox, 343n33
Good, 248, 362n50
Gower, J., 325n91
grammar, 137, 149, 218, 236, 261,
    338n11
of "can", 150
of finite signs, 149
of infinite procedure, 155
grammatology, 125–126
Grim, P., 323n71

H
Habermas, J., 283, 318n11–12

Hallett, M., 29–30, 270–271, 276, 354n17, 357n58
Hallward, P., 347n41, 356n52, 357n58
Harman, Gilbert, 163
Harman, Graham, 359n8
Hegel, G.W.F., 115, 189, 234, 253
  Phenomenology of Spirit, 254
  relation to paradoxico-criticism, 253–254
  Žižek on, 354n19
  See also dialectic, Hegelian
hegemonic phantasms, 321n36
Heidegger, M., 42–43, 252, 253, 283, 326n99, 327n132, 328n137
Heraclitus, ix, 4, 8, 109
hermeneutics, 126, 284, 295–297
Hermogenes, 12–14
  See also Plato, *Cratylus*
Hersh, R., 357n66
hetero-affectivity, 308–309
heteronomy, 309
Heyting algebras, 199–200, 205, 245, 273, 348n69
hierarchy
  constructivist, 269
  of logical types, 321n35
  of metalanguages, 29, 34, 55,58, 60, 278, 279
  of set-theoretial types, 27, 29, 55, 103, 194
  ontological, 255–258
  See also Cantor, transfinite hierarchy
Hilbert, D., 34, 149, 291, 295, 342n25
  "On the Infinite", 149
  See also formalism (program)
Hilbert's decision problem (*see* decision problem)
historicism, 94, 178, 281
history, 31–32, 330n43
  distinction from nature, 46
  evolutionary, 92
  of metaphysics, 222
  natural, 170
  of philosophy, xiii, 123, 251–254, 321n36, 351n36
Hitler, A., 41
Hobbes, T., 321n32
Hofstadter, D., 342n23
humanism, 84, 288, 291, 314
Husserl, E., 115, 240, 253, 319n12, 335n1
  epoche, 253
hymen, 114–116, 118–120, 122, 127, 334n21

I
idea (Platonic), 4, 5, 9, 13, 181–182, 216–217, 236, 292, 317n6, 319n23
  Agamben on, 319n23
  Badiou on, 9, 216
  Deleuze on, 95, 105–112, 216
  Plato's conception of, 39, 105–112, 216, 318n9, 337n36
  relationship to things, 105
ideal games, 210
idealism, 200, 245, 359n8
  linguistic, 245, 291, 304
  subjective, 245, 338n8
  transcendental, 252, 359n8
ideology , 182, 279, 359n5
  critique of, 298
  of effectivity, 175–176
  free market, 287, 289
  of human rights, 288, 359n7
  liberal-democratic, 304
  of progress, 257
identity, 37, 39, 107, 110, 115, 199, 206, 299, 305
  as basis of community, 37
  collective, 177
  community's sense of, 177
  constitution of, 304
  cultural, 289
  passion of, 293
  politics, 289
Imaginary (Lacan), 73, 81, 182, 191
impredicativity, 26, 29–30, 270–271, 276–277
  definition, 194, 322n60
in-closure, 33, 36–37, 56, 83, 181, 250, 323n69
  and capitalism, 301
  and deconstruction, 121–126, 129
  and Kant, 252
  See also Inclosure Schema; Priest, G.
Inclosure Schema, 123–124, 326n98
  See also in-closure; Priest, G.
incommensurability, 285–287, 310, 358n3–4
  weak vs. strong, 286–287, 358n3–4
incompleteness, 25, 28, 33–35, 52, 57, 160, 249, 278, 306
  of formal systems, 25, 34, 114, 118, 121, 156
  of a language, 33–35, 187, 358n72
  of the universe, 323n71
  sources of, 270, 342n25
  See also Gödel, K., incompleteness theorems

inconsistency, 33–35, 52–53, 57, 121,
  182, 248, 249, 263, 307, 323n69
  constitutive, 295
  prohibition of, 135–136, 175, 183
  of social whole, 308
  ω-inconsistency, 157, 160
  See also consistency, contradiction
indeterminacy, 247, 276
  of radical translation, 87–88, 90–93,
    332n82, 333n92–93
  in space of the political, 41–42, 311
indiscernible, the, 38, 51, 55, 220–221,
    279
  and deconstruction, 220–221
indiscernible set, 195–197, 272,
    275–277, 279, 328n136
  See also generic set
individualism, 17, 289, 309
ineffectivity, 175–176, 182, 298,
    311–312
  points of, 175–176, 182, 300, 353n13
inexistent, 220–221, 264, 267, 279,
    286, 356n50
infinite numbers, 148–149
  See also Cantor, transfinite hierarcy;
    infinity
infinity, 5, 21, 43, 54–55, 82, 101n326,
    341n4
  actual, 237, 320n26
  as treated by constructivism, 55, 251
  of contexts, 124
  as treated by generic orientation, 251
  of knowledge, 99
  mathematical concept of, 21, 43
  of meaning, 148, 182
  as treated by onto-theology, 54, 251
  as treated by paradoxico-criticism, 250
  potential, 21, 55, 320n26
  sense of, 155
  of technique, 148–155
information, 4, 283, 298, 310, 315
  exchange, 7, 254
information technology, 148, 283, 297,
    310
  critical theory of, 171–78
instrumental rationality (*see* instrumental
    thinking)
instrumental reasoning (*see* instrumental
    thinking)
instrumental thinking, 7, 171–172, 283,
    301,318n11, 319n12, 360n27
intuitionism, 199–200, 273, 320n26,
    327n122,357n64
  See also logic, intuitionist

iterability (*see* iteration)
iteration, 82, 239, 298–299, 336n27
  of rule, 17, 35, 298–299
  of sign, 5, 35, 107, 124–125, 181–182,
    190, 209, 298

J
Jakobson, R., 39, 71
Johnston, A., 353n10, 356n51

K
Kant, I., 36, 126, 197, 220, 234,
    324n76, 327n132, 354n19
  relation to Badiou, 253, 328n137
  as criteriologist, 252–253, 354n17
  faculty of judgment, 41
  relation to paradoxico-critical orien-
    tation, 253, 354n19
  regulative idea, 253, 354n23
  transcendental Ideas, 253
  See also antinomies (Kantian); critique,
    Kantian; idealism, transcendental
Kierkegaard, S., 226, 351n43
Kripke, S., 273, 317n2, 324n77
  Kripke semantics, 273
Kuhn, T., 285, 359n4
Kunen, K., 347n41

L
Lacan, J., 11, 57, 72–83, 100, 188–192,
    205, 292–294, 330n24, 330n43,
    331n46–47, 354n19
  relation to Badiou, 188–192, 218,
    220, 226–231, 256, 328n137,
    346n11, 351n42–43
  Encore (20th seminar), 76–81, 188–189
  "The Instance of the Letter in the
    Unconscious, or Reason Since
    Freud", 74
  on mathematics, 78–80, 191
  object small a, 76, 77, 188, 346n2
  on the One, 77–81, 191
  The Other Side of Psychoanalysis
    (17th seminar), 228–230
  seminar on "The Purloined Letter,"
    73
  on set theory 76, 79, 191, 346n13
  on the subject 74–81, 188–191,
    330n25, 330n43, 354n19
  on Wittgenstein, 228–230
  See also formalism in Lacan; Imagi-
    nary; *lalangue*; One, the, Lacan
    on; Other; Real; signifierness;
    Symbolic

Laclau, E. and C. Mouffe, 303–308
  Hegemony and Socialist Strategy,
    303–308
language, xi-xii, 24, 27, 31, 34–35,
    37–41, 58–59, 66–72, 95–112,
    117–128, 134–138, 141–145,
    178–183, 187–200, 233–238,
    260–269, 279–280, 29–298,
    325n85, 328n137
  boundaries of, xi, 11, 52, 65, 97, 224
  as calculus, 85–86, 91
  external reference of, 29
  factitious nature of, 229
  as finite, 148
  form of, 13
  ideal dimension of, 181–182, 242, 298
  as infinite, 16, 148
  language-games, 140–141, 218, 226,
    242, 244–245, 298–99
  life of, 18, 91, 145, 147
  limits of (*see* language, boundaries of)
  linguistic reference, 23, 101–102, 104
  of a situation, 258, 276–277, 356n47
  ordinary, xii, 15, 30, 32, 145, 157,
    220, 223, 317n6
  origin of, 89, 92
  power of, 39–40, 99, 181, 278
  praxis of, 14
  question of possibility of, 55–56, 99,
    121, 235
  regulation of, 65, 261
  structuralist picture of, 18, 66–67,
    73, 94, 99, 333n92
  structure of, 6, 20, 24, 37, 54–56, 59,
    65, 69, 74–75, 81, 87–92, 94,
    96, 99–101, 117, 179–183, 188,
    222–224, 241, 279, 296
  supplemental dimension of, 276, 296
  as a system of differences, 67, 95,
    116, 223
  taking place of, 40
  totality of, 37, 38, 84, 95, 124, 127,
    178–181, 187, 240, 278
  twentieth century recourse to, xi, 39
  See also discourse; languages; *langue*;
    linguistic turn; *parole*; totality of
    propositions; writing
languages, xii, 260–264, 290
  formal vs. natural, xii, 34–35, 93,
    290, 323n70, 336n5
  relativity of, 207
  vs. language as such, 261–264
  See also language
lalangue (Lacan), 205, 256, 261

langue, 40, 41, 75, 191, 262
Lautman, A., 328n135
Lautréamont, C., 234
law, 14, 17, 32–33, 34, 41–42, 128,
    205, 230
  force of (*see* force of law)
  inexorability of, 167–168
  institution of, 14, 325n98
  of non-contradiction, 104, 132, 161,
    323n69
Levinas, E., 308–309, 326n101
  Totality and Infinity, 326n101
Lévi-Strauss, C., 68–71, 72, 74, 100,
    179–180, 213
  *Introduction to the Work of Marcel
    Mauss,* 68–69
Lewis, D., 319n15
lifeworld, 172, 283–284, 297, 319n12
limitation of size principles, 29–30, 271
linguistic turn, xi-xii, 6, 10–11, 54,
    187, 224, 238
  Badiou on, 10–11, 218, 239–240,
    348n55, 350n23
  critical implications of, 226
literature, 191–92, 220
Livingston, P. M., 318n9–10
  *Philosophy and the Vision of Lan-
    guage,* 94, 317n1, 318n9–10
localization, 200, 206–207
  of event, 202
Locke, J., 84
logic, xiii, 6, 8, 18, 89, 104, 136,
    142–43, 149, 168–171, 199,
    205–207, 230, 283–284,
    331n47, 338n14, 340n30
  dialetheic (*see* dialetheism)
  formal, xii, 6, 18, 93, 200, 240, 253,
    283, 348n69
  "Greater" (Badiou), 200
  intuitionist, 199, 273
  of language, 59, 86
  logical form (*see* form, logical)
  relation to mathematics, 205–207,
    348n55, 348n69, 349n69
  politics of (*see* main entry under
    "politics of logic")
  of science, 84
  "Western", 337n32
  of a world (Badiou), 199–204
logical analysis, xii, 84, 87,135, 136
logical atomism, 135, 231, 255,
    338n19
  See also atoms, objects
logical empiricism, 51, 85, 355n32

"logical machine", 15, 166–171, 174
logical truth, 88–90
logicism, 20, 25, 348n69
   neo- (*see* neo-Fregeanism)
logos, ix, 6, 8, 14, 109, 136, 141, 353n13
   Aristotle on, 8, 319n16
   as "language", 6
   relation to life, 18
   logoi, 12
   simulacrum of, 109
   and writing, 109
Löwenheim-Skolem theorem, 274,
      344n32
Lucas, J.R., 163, 343n42–43
Lyotard, J.-F., 285, 358n3
   The Differend: Phrases in Dispute,
      358n3

M
Mallarmé, S., 113–116, 118, 122, 214
mana, 69–70, 329n10
Marx, K., 301, 310, 311, 360n26
Marxism, 288, 297–298, 301–302,
      303, 361n45
materialism, 241
   bio-materialism, 240
   postulate of, 201
   See also democratic materialism;
      materialist dialectic
mathematics, 9, 21, 23, 25, 35, 52,
      78–79, 171, 191, 293, 295–297,
      318n7
   as extra-linguistic formalism, 188
   "foundations" of, 25, 149, 199
   identified with ontology (Badiou), 43,
      205, 225, 258, 260
   Lacan on, 78–80, 191
   relation to language, 52, 187–188,
      191–92
   relation to logic, 205–207, 348n55,
      348n69, 349n69
   truths of, 23, 25, 34, 88, 119,
      156–159, 162, 166, 336n15
   Wittgenstein's philosophy of, 148,
      155, 161, 225, 233–237,
      345n61
matheme, 76, 80, 191, 218, 331n56
   of the subject, 79
Mauss, Marcel, 68–69, 329n6
McDowell, J., 317n3, 338n20
meaning (linguistic), 13–14, 37–39, 55,
      66, 84–85, 91–93, 96–101, 121–
      123, 127, 146, 179, 181–182,
      212, 222, 334n5

determination of, 3
   fact and, 145–146
   fixation of, 304–306
   infinitude of, 155, 239
   of a name, 13–14
   naturalizing, 317n2
   paradox of, 13
   possibility of, 55, 85, 116, 139, 143,
      146, 181
   relation to truth, 229–230
   of a sign, 5, 143
   surplus of, 303
   unity of, 5, 212, 318n9
   See also language
meaningfulness, 6, 117, 120, 144, 208
media, 171, 283, 291, 297–299
Meillassoux, Q., 348n56, 359n8
   After Finitude, 359n8
metalanguage, 29, 32–34, 58, 80–81,
      121, 160, 232, 256, 275, 279,
      328n137
   paradoxico-critical denial of, 58,
      188, 229–230, 256, 325n85
   See also hierarchy of metalanguages
metalogic, xiii, 7, 20, 160, 282
metalogical duality, 53, 284, 300,
      306–309, 327n127
   definition, 53
metaphysics, 11, 37, 52–53, 189, 224
   closure of, 37, 51, 221–222
   critique of, 19, 36, 327n132, 353n13
   of the One, 211
   of presence, 119, 222
   of representation, 118–119
meterstick, 139–140, 180–181
Miller, J.-A., 81–84, 92,93, 100, 332n66
   "Action of the Structure", 81–82
   "Suture", 82
   See also virtual, as discussed by
      Miller
mimesis, 96, 113–118, 127, 179
minor games (*see* ideal games)
mind (human), 162–166, 290
   abilities of, 162–166, 320n27,
      336n15, 343n42–43
   computational theories of, 169–170
   as a formal system, 166
Mirimanoff, D., 327n115
Möbius strip, 83
Models (model-theoretic)
   definition, 347n24
   of *Principia Mathematica*, 159
   of set theory, 194–196, 259, 269–
      274, 355n32

See also constructivist universe; forcing; model theory; truth, model-theoretic conception of
model theory, 160, 259, 273–274, 355n32
See also models; truth, model-theoretic conception of
Moore, A.W., 337n28, 339n26, 343n36
Moore, G.E., 84
mystical, 33, 141, 218, 227, 230, 326n101
   element, 218, 227, 230

N

names
   connection to objects, 232
   correctness of, 12–14, 110–112, 320n28
   meaning of, 13
   of names, 98–102, 325n87, 334n11
   origin of, xii, 12–14, 109–112
   positing of, 18
   simple, 134–135, 231
   statements about, 232–233
   state's power over, 266–272, 356n50
naming (*see* nomination)
Nancy, J. L., 345n65, 353n13
naturalism, xiii,12, 92, 317nn2–3
   of forms, 4
natural numbers, 157–159, 326n109
   as model of "nature", 46
   totality of, 21–22, 192
necessity, 133, 141, 225, 305
   of antagonism, 290, 305
   claims of, 172
   logical, 138, 167
   rational, 139
   of simple objects, 133–136, 138, 338n6
neo-Fregeanism, 348n69
neo-Keynesianism, 287
neo-liberalism, 282
Nietzsche, F., 54, 62, 215, 218, 227, 285, 351n43
   eternal return, 215
nomination, 47–48, 98, 223–224, 232
   auto-, 47–48, 49–50, 145, 203, 208, 233, 261, 268, 349n8
nomothesis, 18, 32, 109, 208, 233
   auto-, 203
   logico-political problem of, 18, 95, 110, 208
   paradox of, 19, 32, 61, 233, 282, 321n36
nomothetes (name-giver), 12–14, 109–111

non-predicative terms (*see* impredicativity)
normative principles, 177, 282
   See also force, "normative"; normativity
normativity, 18, 132, 169–170, 171, 247, 320n27
   See also force, "normative"; normative principles
novelty, 6, 51, 208
   Badiou on, 43, 47, 51, 190–193, 204
   ideals of, 6
numbers, 213, 320n28
   computable, 151–152, 341n13
   Frege's conception of, 82
   Gödel, 157
   ordinal, 22, 347n21
   series of, 342n21
   See also infinite numbers; natural numbers; cardinals

O

objects
   Badiou's theory of, 198–201, 231
   mathematical, 153, 199, 237
   paradoxical, 143–144
   simple, 27, 133–135, 138, 144, 231–233, 255, 338n11
One, the, 56, 190, 211, 214–218, 287, 328n137, 334n30
   Lacan on, 77–81, 191, 331n51
   Parmenides on, 131
   non-being of (Badiou), 44–45, 106–207, 263, 355n31
   See also One-All; One and the Many, problem of; set of all sets; universe
One-All, 11, 44–45, 52–53, 187, 208
   See also One; One, the; One and the Many, problem of; set of all sets; universe
One and the Many, problem of, 4, 5, 76, 78, 182, 243, 301
ontology, 10, 43, 47–48, 205, 273
   as a situation, 259–60
   Badiou on, 43–48, 225, 256–260
   relation of event to, 193, 195, 257–260, 294, 327n115, 346n13
   originates in void, 48
onto-theological orientation (*see* onto-theology)
onto-theology, xi, 53–54, 57–62, 252, 281, 313, 327n132, 329n138, 354n23

ordinals (*see* numbers, ordinal)
orientations of thought, 51–60,
    248–254
definitions, 58, 240
post-Cantorian orientations, 59
sovereign (pre-Cantorian) orienta-
    tions, 59, 61
See also constructivism; onto-
    theology; generic orientation;
    paradoxico-critical orientation
Other (Lacan) 76–77, 82, 207, 228–
    229, 303, 331n47, 331n50
overdetermination, 137, 303–304

P

paradigms, 203, 359n4
paradoxes, 32, 126, 160, 180, 253,
    334n22
    of Achilles and the Tortoise (Caroll),
        98, 334n10
    of alteration (between signifier and
        signified), 99
    attempt to prohibit, 147
    of becoming, 105, 108, 110–112
    in early analytic philosophy, 20
    Knower, 159, 343n33
    Liar (Epimenides), 23, 26, 159,
        321n43, 323n71, 343n33
    limit-, 32–33, 177, 301
    of linguistic meaning, 37, 267
    of position of enunciation, 354n19
    of reflexivity, 250, 298
    of self-inclusion, 60
    of sense, 95–99, 103, 112, 181
    of signification, 104
    of standards, 140
    set-theoretical, 22
    Skolem's, 274
    "white Knight", 98, 325n87, 334n11
    See also Burali-Forti paradox;
        Gödel paradox; in-closure;
        nomothesis,paradox of;
        paradoxical element; rules,
        paradox of; Russell's paradox;
        paradoxical element; self-
        reference,paradoxes of; sense,
        paradox of; truth, paradoxes of
paradoxico-critical orientation, 11,
    37, 58–60, 65–66, 190, 249,
    328n136
    and antagonism, 308–311
    axiom of, 242
    relation to criteriology, 58, 92, 94,
        147, 178

definition, 58, 250
    Deleuze as representative of, 216
    distinguishing characteristics, 65,
        178–183
    and formalization, 300–302, 317n6
    formal-political consequences of
        279–280
    relation to generic orientation56–60,
        187–188, 190, 208, 212, 215,
        219, 238–239, 241, 254, 267,
        274, 278, 293–96, 300–302
    Hegel and, 253, 354n19
    Kant and, 252
    thought of infinite, 250
    thought of limit, 250
    thought of subject, 250
    Wittgenstein as representative of 226,
        247
paradoxico-criticism (*see* paradoxico-
    critical orientation)
parameterization, 29, 32–33, 35–36,
    55, 256–257, 345n67
Parmenides, 4, 44, 53, 131–136, 147,
    337n4, 337n6, 338n8
    argument for the One, 133
    "On Nature", 131–133
    See also Plato, Parmenides
parole, 40, 41, 67
participation (Plato), 4, 5, 16, 95,
    105–106, 182
    set membership as modeling, 5, 182
Pascal, B., 226, 351n43
pass of the real, 189–190, 293–294
    See also impasse of formalization
passion of the real, 292–296, 300
Peano, G., 318n7
Peano arithmetic, 343n36
St. Paul, 226
Penrose, R., 163, 166
performatives, 72, 223–224
phenomenology, 240, 253, 297
    Badiou's, 10, 198, 203, 245, 357n64
plane of immanence (Deleuze), 212,
    216
Plato, ix, xii, 4, 9, 12–16, 39, 54, 134,
    251, 362n50
    comparison to Wittgenstein, 14–16,
        138
    conception of Idea, 39, 105–112,
        216, 318n9, 337n36
    Cratylus, 12–15, 78, 109–112,
        319n21, 320n28, 331n55,
        335n45, 338n11
    Deleuze on, 95, 97, 105–112, 216

Derrida on, 108–109
Euthyphro, 337n36
legacy of, 215
Parmenides, 318n9, 334n30
Phaedo, 335n30
Phaedrus, 108–109
Philebus, ix, 108, 113, 334n30
on representation, 105–110
Republic, 108
Sophist, 108, 109, 318n9, 338n11
Theatetus, 108, 134, 138
thinking of form, ix, 9, 12–15, 112,
    189, 362n50
Timaeus, 108
See also form; idea; participation;
    Platonism
Platonism
    Deleuze's, 95, 105–112, 215–216
    Gödel's, 135, 328n135, 336n15
    of the multiple, 216, 232
    naturalized, 317n3
    overturning of, 106, 107,215, 335n31
Poe, E.A., 73
poetry, 100, 232–233
points (Badiou), 203, 204, 239
polis, 19
political economy (*see* critique of politi-
    cal economy)
political philosophy, 5
politics, 4, 9, 20, 238, 275, 288, 312,
    319n15–16
    adaptive, 84
    capitalist, 285
    contemporary, 4, 8, 41, 281–282,
        285, 289
    of formal agreement, 61
    generic, 246
    identity, 289
    leftist, 304, 308, 362n50
    of the life to come, 291–300
    new, 95
    paradoxico-critical, 257
    possibility of, 8
    representative, 47
    as thinking through forms, 9
    as zone of indistinction, 42
    See also Aristotle, *Politics*; political
        philosophy; politics of logic
politics of logic, 8, 10, 60–62, 281,
    291, 300–301, 313, 360n27
    contrast with existing critical
        approaches, 283, 289
    critique of contemporary *ethos*,
        285–287

definition, 8, 318n7
forms of, 301, 360n20
implications of, 281–285
relation to capitalism, 289
polysemy, 114, 122, 126
    distinguished from undecidability,
        115
positivism, 141, 213
    "Anglo-Saxon", 346n20
    See also empiricism
post-structuralism, 7, 306–307
Postone, Moshe, 301
power
    political, 147, 183
    sovereign, 5, 19,-20, 32–33, 41
    of state, 267, 269, 272, 275
power set, 21–22, 45–46, 192–193,
    243, 272, 276–277, 358n70
    definition, 45
    identitified with "state", 46, 193,
        263, 266, 275–276, 332n71
    operation, 270, 272, 276
    See also continuum hypothesis;
        set-theoretic axioms; state of a
        situation
    practices, 3, 17, 162, 169, 320n27,
        345n62
    consistency and effectivity of, 177,
        247–248, 280
    See also praxis, technique
pragmatism, 87, 94, 234, 289, 298
    of cultures, 348n55
    of desires, 240
praxis, 14, 39, 128, 175–177, 287,
    298, 311
predication, 200, 207, 277
    set membership as an allegory of,
        318n7
presence, 45, 112, 121, 223
    and absence, 116–119, 124, 336n27
    metaphysics of, 119, 222
    See also presentation
presentation, 10, 43, 46–47, 49, 116,
    119–123, 262, 319n15
    of presentation, 217, 259–260
    distinguished from representation,
        46, 243, 265–266
    excess of representation over, 47,
        243, 275–79
Priest, G., 29, 32–34, 123–126, 181,
    321n43–44, 323n69, 323n71,
    336n27
    See also dialetheism, in-closure,
        Inclosure Schema

Principia Mathematica, 25, 35, 52,
    117–119, 157–160, 162, 334n22
    consistency of, 343n36
    principle of non-contradiction (*see* law
        of non-contradiction)
procedure, 173, 177
    decision, 166
    generic, 196–197, 246, 257, 260,
        272–273, 328n137
    infinitary, 153–155
    progress, 6, 173, 183, 251, 257,
        345n61, 362n50
    Badiou on, 246–247, 256–257,
        354n23
propositions, 138, 200, 229, 232
    facticity of, 229
    See also totality of propositions
Proust, M., 101
prohibition, 80, 144, 232
    of contradiction, 132, 133, 136,
        176–177, 248, 280
    of the event, 264–265, 269
    of the impossible, 136, 248
    of inconsistency, 135–136, 175, 183
    of a metalanguage, 232
    of non-being, 133, 135–136
    of paradox, 42, 103
    of self-membered totalities, 27, 30,
        34, 142, 144–145, 257–258
provability, 120, 122, 159, 343n33
predicate, 118, 157, 159, 335n3
psychoanalysis, 68, 73–76, 188–189,
    228–229, 303, 330n25, 330n43,
    331n49
    discourse of analysis, 81, 191, 331n47
    See also Freud, S.; Lacan, J.
psychologism, 84, 240
Pufendorf, S. von, 321n32
Putnam, H., 155–159, 163–164, 169,
    177
Pythagoreans, 4

Q
quilting point, 286
Quine, W.V., 87–93, 179, 322n57,
    332n82, 333n92–94, 334n10,
    355n32
    "Carnap and Logical Truth",89
    "Truth by Convention", 88–89
    "Two Dogmas of Empiricism", 89
    Word and Object, 90–91
    See also indeterminacy of transla-
        tion; set theory, Quine's "New
        Foundations"

R
Ramsey, F.P., 322n44
Rancière, J., 319n16
rationalization, 7, 283
    of life, 7, 297
    of society, 283–284, 318n11
Real (Lacan), 73, 78–81, 181, 190–191,
    294, 328n137, 330n24, 346n12
    definition, 73
    relation to Symbolic, 81, 191, 353n14
    See also pass of the real; passion of
        the real
reality, 72, 82, 245, 255
    inconsistent, 294, 361n44
    psychical, 73
    of the virtual, 101
reason, 6, 34, 164, 220, 283, 319n12,
    319n13, 324n76
    formalization of, 24
    instrumental, 7, 171
    reflexive, 164, 182
    See also critique of reason
reference 23, 323n70
    excess of sense over 179–180, 279
    linguistic 23, 101–102, 104
    See also self-reference
reflexiveness (*see* reflexivity)
reflexivity, 24–25, 29, 37,188, 251–
    252, 300, 312, 354n21
    as fundamental to language, 35, 113,
        136, 182, 208, 222
    and paradoxico-criticism, 58, 181,
        250–251, 286, 312
    reflexive element, 81–83
regressive law (Deleuze), 102–103
relativism, 141, 198, 235, 244–245,
    298–299, 359n4
repetition automatism (Freud), 74,
    330n25
representation, 46–50, 60, 105–109,
    111, 113, 116, 123, 319n15,
    332n71
    as discussed by Badiou, 46, 50, 193,
        198, 243, 265–266, 272
    distinguished from presentation, 46,
        243, 265–266
    excess over presentation, 47, 243,
        275–79
    means of, 139
    metaphysics of, 118–119
    Plato on, 105–110
responsibility, 129
Romanticism, 96, 172, 345n62
    of the ideal, 292

Rousseau, J.-J., 115, 123, 226, 351n43
Rorty, R., 57, 62, 94, 285, 317n2
rules, 12–18, 26, 35–37, 40–41, 65–66, 85–86, 88–91, 136–141, 151–153, 167–171, 173, 210, 235–237, 247, 310, 329n6, 332n75, 340n29
 constitutive of language, 66, 85–92, 137, 146, 333n92
 entanglement in, 146, 162, 209, 310–311
 grammatical, 14, 137, 237
 logical, 60, 141–144, 167, 169, 179
 paradox of (in Wittgenstein), 15–18, 37, 140, 165
 of proof, 114, 120, 122
 as "self-interpreting", 165, 167
 of use, 12, 15, 18, 85, 88, 90–91, 135, 151, 333n92
 See also Wittgenstein, "Rule-Following Considerations"
Russell, B., 7, 22–24–30, 37, 42, 44, 57, 58, 79, 138, 146, 234, 255, 258, 321n41
 theory of types, 27, 29, 31, 45, 51
 Wittgenstein on, 141–147, 339n29
 See also Russell's paradox, Russell set, vicious-circle principle
Russell's paradox, 22–30, 38–39, 42, 44, 47–48, 51–53, 56, 102, 142, 322n44, 322n57, 339n26, 340n31, 358n3
 attempt to prohibit, 28, 47–48, 51, 354n21
 Badiou on, 44, 187, 206–207, 255, 261–262, 354n23
 and completeness, 52
 definition, 22–24
 Deleuze on, 102–103
 Wittgenstein on, 142–147, 340n30
Russell set, 23, 25, 36, 42, 52, 103–104, 180, 206–207, 256, 262, 271, 339n26

S
Saint-Just, L., 49
sans-papiers, 267, 356n50
Saussure, F., 37, 65, 66–68, 74, 75, 78, 93, 96, 117, 123, 179, 331n55, 336n5
 Course in General Linguistics, 66–68
 theory of language, 66–68, 117
 theory of sign, 66–67, 75, 99

See also language as system of differences, signifier, signified, structuralism
Schlick, M., 84
Schmitt, C., 19, 41–42
 Political Theology, 19
Schoettle, T., 326n98, 336n16
Schürmann, R., 321n36
 Broken Hegemonies, 321n36
science, 203, 359n4, 359n8
 as generic procedure, 196, 246, 260, 300
 as unified, 85
scientific discourse, 78, 331n55
Searle, J.R., 169
self-reference, 23–24, 31–32, 34–35, 47, 49, 56, 118, 126, 127, 142–145, 160, 179, 262
 attempt to prohibit, 30, 47–48, 142–144
 linguistic, 26, 40, 142–143, 242, 279
 of event, 49, 202, 264
 paradoxes of, 37, 40, 56, 59, 61, 80, 201, 242
 See also nomination, auto-; nomothesis, auto-
semantics, 122
 crossing with syntax, 122, 126, 155, 179, 342n23
 formal, 29
 model-theoretic, 273
 natural-language, 324n74
sense, 96–98, 102, 105–107
 attempt to delimit, 135, 141, 242
 common, 97
 determinacy of, 134–135, 144–145
 excess over reference, 179–180, 279
 good, 97
 paradoxes of, 97–99, 103–104, 112, 223
 univocity of, 212
sense-event (Deleuze), 100–101, 108, 209–211, 214, 218
 See also event, as discussed by Deleuze
set
 Cantor's definition of, 4, 59
 empty, 28, 45–48, 207, 220, 255, 262–263
 impredicative *see* impredicativity
 iterative conception of, 28–29, 256, 322n58
 self-membership, 23, 27–28, 47–48, 51, 103, 142, 257

of all sets, 11, 22, 28, 29, 44,
    52, 103, 206, 271, 322n57,
    322n60, 339n26 *see also* All,
    One-All, universe
set formation, 26–30, 44, 258, 322n57,
    340n31
    constructivist picture of, 30
set grouping (*see* set formation)
set-theoretic axioms, 23,28, 43–45, 47,
    52, 193–195, 258, 270, 322n55
    Axiom of Choice, 322n55, 343n36,
        356n53
    Axiom of Empty Set, 47
    Axiom of Extensionality, 103
    Axiom of Foundation, 28, 47–48, 194,
        255, 258, 322n57, 327n115
    Axiom (schema) of Separation, 28,
        47, 194, 262, 322n60, 354n21
    Power Set Axiom, 270–271, 276,
        356n54, 357n58
    See also set, set formation, set theory
set theory, 4–6, 9, 20–23, 29, 55, 213,
    216, 274, 327n115, 342n25,
    357n54
    Agamben on, 37–38, 299
    as an "allegory of predication",
        318n7, 349n69
    axiomatization of, 29–30, 44, 47,
        143, 255–256, 270, 356n52
    Cantorian, 5, 20–22, 43–44
    Deleuze on, 102–104
    as foundation of mathematics, 43,
        199, 258, 318n7
    identified with ontology(Badiou), 43,
        45, 47, 192, 199, 245, 258–260
    Lacan on, 76, 79, 191, 346n13
    non-well-founded, 322n57
    Quine's "New Foundations", 354n21,
        322n57
    universe of , 47
    Zermelo-Fraenkel (ZF), 43, 45, 47,
        192, 195, 270–273
    Zermelo-Fraenkel with Choice
        (ZFC), 28–29, 322n55
    See also set, set formation, set group-
        ing, set-theoretic axioms
Shanker, S., 341n4
shifters, 39–40, 71
    See also deixis; demonstratives
showing (Wittgenstein), 52, 135, 149,
    228, 230, 232, 339n26
sign, 59, 96, 107, 116, 119, 122,
    143–144, 239, 350n34
    "arbitrariness" of, 66–67, 75

distinction from symbol, 135
    iterability of, 5, 35, 107, 124–125,
        181–182, 190, 209, 298
    propositional, 142
    Saussure's theory of , 66–67, 75, 99
    unity of meaning of, 5, 37
    See also signified, signifier
signification, 68–69, 73, 75–76,
    79–80, 93, 95–96, 99, 102,
    104, 115, 122–123, 129, 149,
    188, 191, 207, 222, 242,
    251, 261, 278–279, 332n60,
    345n72
    excess of (over signified), 68, 70,
        92–93, 99–100, 103–104, 108,
        179–182, 188, 243, 280
    structure of, 77–80,93–94
    total system of, 68–71, 73, 77–79, 83
signified, 59, 67–71, 74–75, 77–78, 96,
    99–101, 104, 108, 180–181, 223
    distinction from signifier, 66–68, 116
    floated, 102
    sliding under signifier, 75
    transcendental, 223, 304–307
signifier, 59,66, 69–70, 73–76, 78–79,
    81, 99, 181, 191, 327n115,
    330n43, 331n55
    distinction from signified, 66–68, 116
signifierness (Lacan), 79, 188
signifying chain, 73–77, 82–83,
    330n25, 330n43
simulacrum, 106–108, 111, 213
    of *logos*, 109
singular, 54, 59, 129, 140, 206, 213
    community of (Agamben), 37–38
    points (Deleuze), 100–101
    terms (Badiou), 46, 50, 327
singularity, 38–39, 101, 219, 348n65
    type of site (Badiou), 204
    whatever (Agamben), 38, 299
site (*see* eventual site)
situations (Badiou), 43, 46, 198, 244,
    263, 265
    natural distinguished from historical 46
    See also worlds
social whole, 5, 59, 73, 147, 177,
    235, 242, 284–286, 301,
    303–308, 310–311, 361n45
    conditions for possibility of, 235, 286
    language as presupposition for, 59, 242
    structure of, 69–70, 267, 304
    unity of, 183, 243, 284, 286, 289,
        307, 318n8
society (*see* social whole)

Socrates, 6, 12–13, 108–112, 134, 138, 319n21, 320n28, 337n36, 338n11
elenchus, 337n36
sophist, 108, 227
sophistry, 218–219, 225–226, 228, 234
sovereign, 19, 32, 41–42, 54, 57–60, 321n36
  authority, 299
  decision, 19–20, 41, 325n98
  exceptional position of (Schmitt), 19–20, 41
  orientations, 59, 329n138 *see also* constructivism; onto-theology
  power, 5, 19–20, 32–33, 41
spacing, 122–123, 125, 223–224, 350n34
speculative realism, 359n8
Spencer, J., 354n23
Spinoza, B., 190, 214, 234, 280
Stalin, J., 293
standards, 14, 17–18, 140, 147, 177, 180–181, 283
  communal, 3, 17, 286
  institution of, 14, 140, 208
  rational, 140, 172
state, 5, 8, 39, 46–47, 50–51, 191, 247, 263–266, 299, 312, 314, 318n8, 356n49–50
  as essentially excessive, 47
  power, 42, 267–268
state's excess, 47, 193, 271–272, 276
state of exception (Agamben), 19, 37–42, 242, 326n98
state of the situation (Badiou), 46, 51, 193–197, 243, 263–272, 332n71, 357n61
  analogy to political state, 247, 263–268, 275–276
  See also power set, representation
structuralism, 7, 10, 65, 66–84, 92–96, 100, 116, 181, 213–214, 296, 336n5, 350n24
  See also Benveniste, E.; Jakobson, R.; Lévi-Strauss C.; Saussure, F.
structuralist movement *see* structuralism
structure
  action of, 81–82, 100–101, 107, 209
  structurality of, 222
  topology of, 82
  totality of, 82
  unity of, 135, 307, 311
Suárez, F., 321n32
subject , 10, 71, 74–81, 188, 251–252, 273–274, 278, 303, 348n56

as discussed by Badiou, 50, 188–191, 196–197, 198, 248, 264
  faithful, 203–204, 246, 272–273, 313
  as discussed by Lacan, 74–81, 188–191, 330n25, 330n43, 354n19
  of language, 181
  as discussed by Miller, 81–84, 332n67
  obscure, 205
  reactive, 204
  speaking, 41, 71–72, 181, 190
  transcendental, 200, 252–253
  as discussed by Wittgenstein, 228
  See also subjectivity
subjectivity, 71–72, 74, 77, 81, 253, 292, 329n17
  See also subject
Surrealism, 96
suture, 82–83, 263, 303–307, 310
Symbolic (Lacan), 73–75, 77, 80–81, 182, 330n24, 331n49, 353n14
  relation to Real 81, 191, 353n14
Symbolism (19th-century movement), 96
syntax, 21, 74, 115–116, 122–123, 200
  arithmetization of, 152–153, 179
  crossing of semantics and, 122, 126, 155, 179, 342n23
  logical, 85, 89, 94, 135, 143, 146, 332n75, 341n4
  reflection within itself, 126, 180
  semantical effect of, 122

T

Tarski, A., 7, 25, 28–30, 31, 37, 290
  truth-definition schema, 26, 31
technē, 12
technique, 146, 166, 173–175, 237, 310, 345n62, 353n13
  infinity of, 148, 150–151, 154–155
  mastery of a, 15, 17, 164
  mathematics as a, 188, 225, 236–237
  unity of a, 317n6
technology, 4, 7, 171, 174, 237, 291, 319n12, 345n61
  computational, 4, 172
  communicational, 171, 297, 298
  divine, 110
  information, 171–172, 291, 297, 310
  philosophy of, 297
textualism, 238, 284, 311
theocracy, 281
theology, xi, 22
  negative, 284
  rational, 360n27
  See also onto-theology

thinking, 131, 211, 296
    calculative, 171
    instrumental, 17, 171–172, 283, 301,
        318n11, 319n12, 360n27
    limit of, 36
    relation to being, 53, 131
    symbolic, 69, 70
thinking-machines, 330n43
threshold, 20, 126
throw of the dice, 212, 214–215
topoi, 199
totalitarianism, 41, 61, 281, 356n49
totality, 11, 21–22, 24–26, 32–36, 58,
        60, 212, 250, 276–277, 322n52
    desire for, 60
    inconsistent, 37, 59, 83–84
    of the knowable, 69, 178, 253
    of language, 37–38, 58, 84, 95, 124,
        127, 178–179, 181, 187, 240, 278
    of objects, 340n31
    orientations of thought defined in
        terms of attitude toward 58–59
    of propositions, 24, 27, 321n43, 322n52
    reference to, 32, 38, 242
    sovereign's claim to, 20
    of the thinkable, 24, 36
    See also All; completeness; One, the;
        One-All; universe; Whole
transcendence, 32
transcendent orientation *see* onto-
    theology
transcendental indexing (*see* "transcen-
    dental" of a world)
"transcendental" of a world (Badiou),
        199–204, 207, 231, 245, 251,
        258, 264, 290
triviality arguments, 169–170
truth, 12, 20, 31, 32, 33–34, 57,
        75, 117–118, 132, 136, 163,
        188–189, 229–230, 278, 291,
        343n33, 351n43, 355n32
    by convention, 88
    disquotational notion of, 159
    indefinability of (Tarski), 25–26, 29
    mathematical, 23, 25, 34, 88, 114,
        119, 151, 153, 156–159, 162,
        166, 336n15, 336n15, 343n43
    model-theoretic conception of,
        158–159, 343n34
    of names, 109–111
    paradoxes of, 31, 33
    -predicate, 159
    -procedures (*see* generic procedures)
    of propositions, 134, 228

Tarski definition schema 26, 31
    as treated by four orientations of
        thought, 59, 188, 250–251
Truths (Badiou), 55, 187, 196–198, 203,
        215–217, 224–226, 239–241,
        244–248, 253, 256–257, 272–273,
        278, 296, 328n135, 328n137,
        348n63, 354n23, 357n64
Turing, A. M., 148–53, 162, 166,
        171–173, 176, 297–98, 340n1,
        341n13, 341n18
    exchanges with Wittgenstein, 148,
        150, 162
    "On Computable Numbers, with an
        Application to the Entscheidung-
        sproblem", 151
    proof of unsolvability of decision
        problem, 151–152
Turing machine, 151–152, 163, 165,
        167, 172, 179
Turing's thesis (*see* Church-Turing
    thesis)
twentieth century, 7, 61, 191–92, 252,
        254, 291–292
    Badiou on, 291–295
    critical thought of, 238
    formalization as project of, 291–292,
        294, 297
    political thought of, 285–286, 289
    politics of, 41
    utopian projects of, 300
Two, the, 189, 190–191, 241

U

undecidability, 25, 36, 118–129, 174,
        180–181, 209, 278, 358n72
    analogy between Gödelian and Derrid-
        ian versions, 118–119, 121, 123
    of continuum hypothesis, 276
    Derrida on, 114–116, 118–120,
        127–128
    distinguished from polysemy, 115
    of effectivity, 171–173
    Gödelian, 120–121, 269
    of halting, 165
    of reflective syntax, 126
    relation to in-closure, 36
    relation to incompleteness, 121
universe, 11, 22, 44, 48, 51–53, 69,
        265, 269, 274, 277, 323n71,
        335n45, 357n68, 358n70
    constructible, 194–195, 264, 266,
        270–272, 276–277
    of numbers, 332n66

of ontology, 47, 274
of sets, 25, 27–28, 47, 194, 271, 276
See also All; One, the; One-All; Whole
usage (linguistic), 14
facts of, 87
iterative dimension of, 17

V

value
absolute, 137–138
exchange, 301
monetary, 67, 288
shared sense of, 177
symbolic, 67–68, 70, 116–117
systems of, 286
traditional sources of, 297
verificationism, 54, 85, 89, 141
vicious-circle principle, 26–27, 323n71
virtual, 201, 205, 212–218, 242,
 277–280
as discussed by Deleuze, 101–102,
 105, 181, 201, 212–216
as discussed by Miller, 81–82
void, 47–48, 50, 122, 180, 207, 212, 262
anxiety of, 263–264
being drawn from, 47–48, 255–258
of a situation, 262–265
semantic, 122–123

W

Watson, A., 340n1
Weber, M., 318n11
Weyl, H., 341n4
White on White (Malevich), 293
Whole, 24, 56, 59–60, 70, 83, 107,
 207, 307–308, 357n68
non-existence of (Badiou), 206–207
See also All; One; One-All; set of all
 sets; social whole; universe
Wittgenstein, L., 3–6, 8–11, 14–18, 36,
 52, 57, 60, 61, 84, 131–147,
 148–180, 208, 217–218,
 223–237, 247, 255, 261, 265,
 282, 286, 291, 298, 304, 310–
 311, 317n2, 317n6, 319n18,
 320n26–27, 324n76, 338n21,
 339n29, 340n30, 340n1,
 341n4, 343n33–34, 345n61–62,
 345n72, 351n43, 352n47,
 358n3, 361n47
attitude toward contradiction,
 141–147, 160–163, 176–177,
 234–35, 345n69
communitarian reading of, 16–17

comparison to Plato, 14–16, 138
constructivism of early, 136, 141
Culture and Value, 345n61
on diagonalization, 153–155
on ethics, 137–138, 338n17
exchanges with Turing, 148, 150,
 162
on Gödel's theorems, 155–160
on infinity, 148–155, 165, 167,
 320n26
interpretation as "conservative",
 345n62
relation to Lacan, 228–230
"Lecture on Ethics", 137–138
*Lectures on the Foundations
 of Mathematics*, 148–151,
 161–162
naturalist reading of, 317n2
Notebooks 1914–1916, 148–149
as "philosopher of culture", 318n10
Philosophical Investigations, 3,
 14–16, 37, 138–141, 146–147,
 151, 164, 225, 234, 345n61,
 349n6, 351n36
private language argument, 6, 16
relation to Badiou, 217–218, 224–37,
 265, 352n47, 352n53
*Remarks on the Foundations of
 Mathematics* 145–146, 153–155,
 234, 237
as representative of paradoxico-
 criticism, 226, 247
"resolute" interpretation of, 338n21
rule-following considerations, 6,
 14, 16–18, 37, 140–141, 155,
 164–166, 172–176, 235, 298,
 310, 324n77, 345n68
on Russell, 141–147, 339n29
therapy, 166, 229–230
Tractatus Logico-Philosophicus, 36,
 131–136, 138–139, 141–149, 178,
 225–226, 227–228, 231–234,
 251, 255, 265, 337n4, 338n17,
 338n21, 339n25, 352n53
See also form, logical; forms of life;
 language-games; mathematics,
 Wittgenstein's philosophy of;
 rules, entanglement in; rules,
 paradox of; rules, as "self-
 interpreting"; Russell's paradox, Wittgenstein on; showing;
 subject, as discussed by
 Wittgenstein
Wordstar, 169

world, 133, 135–136, 191, 205, 211, 226–228, 275, 351n43, 352n47, 359n4
  relation of language to, 40, 58, 96, 135, 145, 147, 179, 338n20
worlds (Badiou), 198–204 , 231
  atonic, 204
  multiplicity of, 205–206, 220–221, 231, 243–247, 253
Wright, C., 341n4
writing, 35, 108–109, 116, 119, 173–174, 191, 261, 346n13

  possibility of, 124–126
  relation to speech, 108–109, 221–224
  of writing, 130

Z

Zermelo, E., 28, 29, 42, 256, 322n55–56,
  See also set theory, ZF; set theory, ZFC
Žižek, S., 285, 294, 300–301, 328n137, 346n12, 350n24, 354n19, 359n5, 360n25–26, 361n45